Population Growth and Reproduction
in Sub-Saharan Africa

D1727580

A World Bank Symposium

Population Growth and Reproduction in Sub-Saharan Africa

Technical Analyses of Fertility and Its Consequences

edited by
George T. F. Acsadi
Gwendolyn Johnson-Acsadi
Rodolfo A. Bulatao

The World Bank
Washington, D.C.

© 1990
The International Bank for Reconstruction
and Development / THE WORLD BANK
1818 H Street, N.W., Washington, D.C. 20433, U.S.A.

Library of Congress Cataloging-in-Publication Data

Population growth and reproduction in sub-Saharan Africa / edited by
George T.F. Acsadi, Gwendolyn Johnson-Acsadi, and Rodolfo A.
Bulatao.
p.   cm. — (WORLD BANK symposium)
Includes bibliographical references.
ISBN 0-8213-1397-5
1. Fertility, Human—Africa, Sub-Saharan—Congresses. 2. Birth
control—Africa, Sub-Saharan—Congresses. 3. Africa, Sub-Saharan—
Population—Economic aspects—Congresses. I. Acsádi, György.
II. Johnson-Acsadi, Gwendolyn. III. Bulatao, Rodolfo A., 1944–
IV. Series.
HB1071.A3P66   1990
304.6′32′0967—dc20   89-21470
                                                           CIP

Contents

v

Preface

Population growth rates in Sub-Saharan Africa are the highest of any region in the world. From 1980 to 1985, its growth rate was 3.2 percent a year, whereas the growth rate in Latin America—the next highest—was 2.3 percent and that in Europe 0.3 percent. Moreover, the uniformly high and stable or rising levels of fertility and declining mortality portend even more rapid population growth for the future: the population will possibly double in little more than two decades. The question for policymakers is whether alternative growth rates are desirable and, if so, what policies and what interventions are appropriate. Delay is not advantageous, for it will cause populations to build up more momentum for further growth. Population growth may of course be interrupted by mortality crises, such as war or famine. Whatever the disastrous social effects of such events, their impact on growth tends to be transient. Even the AIDS crisis, from current projections, is unlikely to reverse the pattern of rapid growth.

In its task of development, Sub-Saharan Africa has had the assistance and cooperation of the international community. The World Bank, which shares the widespread and growing concern of international, governmental, and nongovernmental organizations regarding the region's serious problems related to population growth and development, has greatly increased its financial commitment to their solution. The Bank's concern has also been expressed in reports and policy studies; these include *Accelerated Development in Sub-Saharan Africa: An Agenda for Action* (1981), *Sub-Saharan Africa: Progress Report on Development Prospects and Programs* (1983), *Toward Sustained Development in Sub-Saharan Africa: A Joint Program of Action* (1984), and *Sub-Saharan Africa: From Crisis to Sustainable Growth* (1989). In 1983, the World Bank commissioned several scholars of African population and development problems to prepare background papers for a report on population strategies for Sub-Saharan Africa. These papers formed the basis for a World Bank Policy Study, *Population Growth and Policies in Sub-Saharan Africa* (1986).

In view of the dearth of reliable, up-to-date studies and analyses of demographic and socioeconomic conditions in Sub-Saharan Africa, and because the summary policy study used only a fragment of the valuable material from the commissioned papers—on the consequences of population growth, the underlying high fertility patterns, and the intricate cultural environment regulating reproduction in the region—a selection of these papers is collected in the present volume. The papers chosen for this publication have been edited, revised, updated, and in most cases severely condensed to expose the core of their arguments. The papers utilize the best information available, including reports or data tapes from the World Fertility Survey and worldwide surveys of the prevalence of contraception. The papers, selected to appeal to a broad audience, address not only government planners and policymakers but also community leaders and professionals responsible for public opinion, managers of family planning programs, economists, demographers, anthropologists and other academics, and students of the peoples of Sub-Saharan Africa.

The volume begins with information on demographic conditions in the region (part I). In part II, the economic consequences of population growth are viewed from the perspectives of agriculture, household energy, resources, and employment. The urban component of population growth and strategies for dealing with it are also discussed. Part III contains analyses of the impact of reproductive patterns upon the health of women and young children and of the region's high fertility upon the family and its resources. Part IV deals with the main component of rapid population growth, very high fertility, which is still rising in some areas. This part includes analyses of the proximate determinants of fertility, how they operate within Sub-Saharan African cultures, the constraints enforced by culture and tradition, and the causes and consequences of the high demand for children and low demand for contraception. Part V traces the changes during the past decade in the way Sub-Saharan government leaders and scholars view population policy and development, and specifically the control of population growth and organized family planning. It also discusses the various strategies for delivering family planning services that have been tried in the region.

A note on references in the text to the regions of Africa: East Africa includes the countries (listed in table 1-1 below) that comprise the Horn of Africa and East and Central Africa. (Central Africa is sometimes treated separately.) West Africa includes the Sahel, the coastal strip, and West-Central Africa. References to Southern Africa include the Zambezi countries.

We thank the contributors for their cooperation in producing this volume. We hope that their work will not only illuminate the relation of population growth to reproductive patterns, socioeconomic development, culture, health, environment, and resources but also

contribute to the discovery of solutions for the country-specific and regional problems of development in Sub-Saharan Africa.

We also thank several people who at different times coordinated the work on the policy study for which these papers were originally prepared: Nancy Birdsall, who encouraged and supported this compilation; Susan H. Cochrane, who, besides collaborating on two papers, assisted in this compilation at critical points; Ronald G. Ridker and Barbara K. Herz, the other two coordinators; and Susan Stout, who assisted them. Pat Donovan provided editorial assistance. Ella Hornsby, Amelia Menciano, and Suchila Burns typed, corrected, and assembled the final manuscript with accuracy and patience.

George T. F. Acsadi
Gwendolyn Johnson-Acsadi
Rodolfo A. Bulatao

Part I

The Demographic Situation

The 450 million people in mainland Sub-Saharan Africa in mid-1985 were distributed among forty-nine countries, many of them small and heavily rural, most of them showing dramatic declines in mortality coupled with high, stable fertility. The single chapter in part I, by Hill, reviews the demographic data for this region; describes the settlement pattern, urbanization, and migration; documents the fall in childhood mortality and the less certain trend in adult mortality and shows how trends vary across countries; and discusses the universally high fertility levels.

Demographic data are sparser for Africa than for other world regions, but most Sub-Saharan countries have nevertheless had at least two censuses and various national surveys. The completeness and accuracy of demographic information are improving over time, but various sophisticated estimation techniques are still necessary to obtain estimates of vital rates from available data.

Population densities, extremely variable across countries, range from 1 to more than 200 persons per square kilometer. Similar variation can be found within individual countries, as in the West African coastal strip, where dense coastal settlements subside into much lower densities inland. Overall, urbanization is lower than in other developing regions, averaging only 25 percent.

Mortality levels have declined dramatically since the 1950s. The decline in child mortality is well docu-

mented: in the 1950s, 30 to 40 percent of children commonly died before age five, but by the mid-1970s, losses of 20 percent or so were more common. Adult mortality may also have declined, but the data to illustrate this drop are much more limited. Considerable variation across countries does exist: West African mortality, in particular, generally exceeds East African mortality. The West African nations with lower mortality—Cameroon, the Congo, and Ghana—are countries that experienced rapid economic and educational development between the 1950s and the 1960s.

African fertility levels are high, with total fertility rates around 6 or 7. Except in a few pockets of higher socioeconomic status groups, fertility has proved resistant to change. Low fertility occurs in a few zones as a consequence of venereal disease and subfecundity rather than choice. Contraceptive use seldom involves more than a small percentage of eligible couples, usually a few of the more educated urban residents. Fertility differentials within countries are often related to customs of breastfeeding and postpartum abstinence. As these customs lose their hold, fertility may actually rise in some countries.

International migration is unlikely to ease the pressures from high rates of natural increase significantly. Substantial movements, for both economic and political reasons, have taken place in the past but offer no permanent solutions to problems of population pressure.

Population Conditions in Mainland Sub-Saharan Africa

Althea Hill

African demographic data are limited. Modern population censuses have been conducted only since World War II and rarely at regular intervals. No country possesses a complete and reliable vital registration system or collects complete or reliable migration statistics.[1] Information on mortality, fertility, and migration must therefore be collected in special demographic sample surveys or as part of census operations.

Sources of Demographic Data

Table 1-1 shows the dates of all censuses and major demographic surveys carried out in Sub-Saharan Africa since 1945, together with their availability. The situation looks superficially not unsatisfactory: only one country (Chad) has never had a census, and most have held at least two. A majority have taken censuses within the last ten years or have conducted at least one major demographic survey. Surveys within the World Fertility Survey framework have been carried out in ten Sub-Saharan African countries since 1977 and within the Contraceptive Prevalence Survey framework in another three. Results are now beginning to emerge from the new Demographic and Health Survey series but were not available in time for inclusion in this review.

Yet there remain important gaps. Several countries that carried out their first censuses in recent years have still not finished processing and analyzing the full census results (Benin, 1979; Equatorial Guinea, 1983; Guinea, 1983; Zaire, 1984; and Ethiopia, 1984). Several others are in a similar position with respect to their

This paper was written with the assistance of Edward K. Brown, Uche Isiugo-Abanihe, and Patience W. Stephens.

most recent census (Ghana, 1970; Kenya, 1979; Guinea-Bissau, 1979; Namibia, 1980; Sudan, 1983; Burkina Faso, 1985). The results of three more will never be released because of inflation of census figures (Nigeria, 1973) or because of alleged gross undercount (Gabon, 1981) or theft of questionnaires (Uganda, 1980). Delays of several years between fieldwork and full publication and gaps of more than the normal ten years between censuses are the norm.

Long lags between fieldwork and full publication have also been the rule for major demographic surveys. The results of some will never be released (the Swaziland multiround survey of 1975–76; the Liberia national demographic survey of 1978) or will be released in only the most summary, abbreviated fashion (Lesotho, 1973; Senegal, 1970–71).

To summarize the situation: for four of the largest countries in Sub-Saharan Africa, excluding South Africa (Nigeria, Ethiopia, Zaire, and Sudan) no published final census results less than fifteen years old exist, and the majority of countries possess no more than one fully published source of demographic data to cover the past twenty years.

Quality of Demographic Data

Demographic data for countries of Sub-Saharan Africa are generally of low quality by world standards, though they are comparable to data in certain other parts of the developing world, such as the Indian subcontinent, Indonesia, and parts of the Middle East and of Central and Andean Latin America. African data display uniformly, across countries and with only moderate improvements over time, all of the typical characteristics listed below.

Table 1-1. Censuses and Major Demographic Surveys, Mainland Sub-Saharan Africa, 1945–87

Region and country	1945-49	1950-54	1955-59	1960-64	1965-69	1970-74	1975-79	1980-84	1985-89
Horn of Africa									
Sudan			1955-57c**			1973C**	1979s**	1983C	
Ethiopia				1963——		70S**		1981S* 1984C*	
Djibouti									
Somalia				1960-61C			1975C**	1980S**	1986C
East and Central Africa									
Kenya	1948C**			1962C**	1969C**	1973s**	1977-78S** 1979C*	1982S 1984S**	1988-89S
Uganda	1948C**		1959C		1969C**			1980C	
Rwanda		1952——	57S**			1970S**	1978C**	1983S**	
Burundi		1952——	57S**		1965S**	1970-71S**	1979C**		1987S**
Zaire			1955-58S**			1974s*		1984C*	
Tanzania	1948C**		1957C**		1967C**	1973S**	1978C**		1988C
Zambezi countries									
Malawi					1966C	1970-71S**	1977C**	1984S**	1987C
Zambia		1950S**		1963C	1969C**	1974c		1980C**	
Mozambique		1950C**		1960C		1970C		1980C**	
Zimbabwe	1948S**			1962C	1969C**			1984S**	1987S 1988S
Southern Africa									
Botswana				1964C		1971C**	1977C**	1981C** 1984S**	1987S 1988S
Namibia								1980C	
Swaziland				1960S	1966C**	1970C	1975-76S 1976C**		1986C
Lesotho			1956CS**		1966C	1973S*	1976C*** 1977S***		1986C
South Africa		1950C		1960C		1970C	1980C		

4

Table of census and survey years by country (text rotated on page).

Region / Country	Census and survey years
Sahel	
Mauritania	1963–65S** 1976–77C** 1981S** 1987C
Mali	1961S** 1976C 1987C
Niger	1959–60S** 1977C 1988C
Chad	1964S** 1970–71S 1978S** 1988C
Senegal	1960S** 1975C* 1985C
Burkina Faso	1959–61S**
Coastal strip	
Gambia	1963C 1973C** 1983C
Guinea Bissau	1950C** 1960C 1970C 1979C
Guinea	1953–55S** 1983C
Sierra Leone	1963C 1974C** 1985C
Liberia	1962C 1970–71S** 1974C** 1978S 1984C 1986S**
Côte d'Ivoire	1975C 1978–79S** 1980–81S** 1988C
Ghana	1948C** 1960C** 1967–69S** 1979–80S** 1984C
Togo	1961CS** 1970C 1971S** 1981C
Benin	1961S** 1979C 1980–81S**
West-Central Africa	
Nigeria	1952–53C 1962C 1963C 1965–66S** 1973C 1980S
Cameroon	1960———65S** 1971–73S** 1976C 1978S** 1987C
Central African Republic	1959–61s** 1960C 1975C** 1981–82S**
Equatorial Guinea	1960C 1966C 1983C
Gabon	1960C 1969–70C 1981C 1988C
Congo	1961S** 1974C** 1984C
Angola	1950C** 1960C 1970C

C = population census
c = sample census
S = national demographic survey
s = large-scale but non-national demographic survey
* = only unpublished analyses available
** = mortality and fertility data collected and published
— = census or survey covered specified years
Source: Author's compilation.

Uncertain Completeness of Census and Survey Enumeration

Completeness of enumeration is generally thought to have improved over time, in the wake of improvements in census methods and procedures, accumulated experience in data collection, and general progress in communications and educational levels. The modern censuses in the early postwar period often returned population totals considerably higher than previous estimates from administrative records or prewar censuses; notable examples are Nigeria (1952–53) and Zambia (1963), with excesses over expected totals of more than one-quarter. Many of these early censuses, however, to judge from the evidence of later censuses, still undercounted populations by 10 percent or more (for example, Lesotho, 1956 and Uganda, 1959).

In the 1960s and 1970s, undercounts are mostly reckoned to have involved no more than a few percentage points, but fluctuations and exceptions are common. Undercounts of more than 10 percent were announced for Sierra Leone in 1974, Liberia in 1974, and the Central African Republic in 1975, and of nearly 8 percent in Cameroon in 1976. In other countries there are anomalous series of intercensal growth rates—for example, in Zimbabwe, with recorded annual growth of 4 percent between 1962 and 1969 and 2.9 percent between 1969 and 1980—which raise suspicions of substantial fluctuation in completeness of enumeration. Well-designed postenumeration surveys (PES) are seldom carried out and usually produce unhelpful results; evaluation of completeness must thus usually rely on comparisons of intercensal growth with independent estimates of natural increase and net migration.[2] As a practical consequence, intercensal growth rates do not reliably indicate true population growth and must be evaluated before acceptance.

Distorted and Inaccurate Age Distributions

In Sub-Saharan Africa, which has historically high levels of illiteracy and little indigenous tradition of exactly marking either ages or years, few persons know their exact age or year of birth. Thus in most cases the ages given are guesses by the respondents or estimates by the interviewer. Respondents tend to select desirable ages, while interviewers may be misled by erroneous ideas regarding physical development in children (for example, the notion that children begin to walk at one year) or by simplistic formulas (for example, the rule that women marry at fifteen years and bear a child every two years). The use of historical calendars has become widespread in an attempt to improve the accuracy of age estimation, but there is little evidence that it has succeeded.[3]

Such conditions produce characteristic distortions in age distributions. Recorded ages are heaped on digits 0 and 5. Women are pushed into the reproductive age range (15–49 years) both from below (if they are married or are evidently pubescent) and above (because of a decline in social prestige for women past childbearing or because of the presence of young grandchildren thought to be their own). Within the reproductive period, they are often concentrated in the 20–29 age group. Men, in contrast, are pushed out of the prime adult age groups, both to younger ages (because male puberty is later than female or because of fear of taxation or conscription) and to older ages (because old age in men carries added prestige).

Another source of distortion is selective underenumeration, particularly of infants, young men, and elderly women. Infants may be omitted from a belief that it is unlucky to mention them or because they are not yet considered full family members. Young men are particularly likely to be migrant, floating members of a household or solitary, single-person households (and hence may be forgotten or difficult to find); young men are also apt to be keen on avoiding taxation or conscription. Elderly women are often "marginal" household members with little social status. In addition, girls and adult women may be in purdah in Muslim areas, and the male household head may not report them accurately. One often overlooked practical implication of these age distortions is their effect on determination of fertility, mortality, and growth rates. The age distribution is often used directly to estimate fertility and enters indirectly into many methods of fertility and mortality estimation (see below). Moreover, crude birth and death rates, and hence growth rates, will be distorted if the age structure of the base population is incorrect. If males, babies, and elderly women are disproportionately omitted, for example, the crude birth rate will be inflated. Omission of the very young and very old, for whom mortality is highest, will deflate the crude death rate. Distorted crude birth and death rates in turn distort growth rates. This problem has too often been ignored in analyses of African data.

Poor-Quality Fertility and Mortality Data

In the absence of complete and accurate vital registration, data on mortality and fertility for Sub-Saharan African countries are collected through one-shot retrospective inquiries in censuses and surveys about vital events in the past or the survival of children and parents or from multiround longitudinal surveys in which households are visited repeatedly to ascertain vital events between visits.

In Sub-Saharan Africa, as in much of the developing world, such data can never be accepted at face value.

Births and deaths are seldom reported completely in retrospect, whatever the quality of interviewing. The reasons for omissions are many. They include the natural reluctance to speak of deaths; confusion of infant deaths soon after birth with stillbirths; misunderstanding of the questions (for example, a question about a woman's total number of births may be misinterpreted as referring only to children still alive or still living with her); errors with respect to the reference period of the question (when, for example, births or deaths during the twelve months prior to interview have been asked for); and poor memory. Events far in the past are particularly liable to omission. Occasionally, too, births and deaths may be inflated, for example, by errors over the reference period in the opposite direction or because women have included adopted or foster children with their own. Data from multiround surveys are also subject to some of these sources of error and, in addition, reflect the problem of maintaining interviewer quality over a long period.

To combat such inadequacies in the data, a body of techniques for evaluating and adjusting mortality and fertility data (usually called "indirect methods") has been developed over the past thirty years. These techniques rely heavily on consistency checks within and between data sets and between data sets and various demographic model systems (model life tables, stable population models, model fertility schedules, and so forth). They are subject to wide margins of error under the best conditions, and when the data are really poor, or when the methods are mechanically or mistakenly applied, they may be little better than guesses. Demographers nevertheless accept estimates based on such techniques as likely to be considerably closer to the truth than measures taken directly from the recorded data.

Population Size, Distribution, and Density

Table 1-2 shows total population size and national density in mid-1985 in each of the countries of mainland Sub-Saharan Africa. Two striking features are apparent. First, Sub-Saharan Africa is a region of small countries. Of about forty countries on the mainland, only Nigeria has more than 50 million in population, and only four (Ethiopia, Nigeria, South Africa, and Zaire) have more than 25 million. Indeed, only a dozen of all Sub-Saharan African countries have more than 10 million inhabitants, and nearly half are under or just 5 million. Moreover, ten countries are also geographically tiny (Burundi, Djibouti, Equatorial Guinea, the Gambia, Guinea-Bissau, Lesotho, Rwanda, Sierra Leone, Swaziland, and Togo). No other world region contains such a plethora of little countries or is so lacking in large national units.

Second, there is also great variation in density. National population densities vary from 1 to more than 100 inhabitants per square kilometer. Countries are distributed rather evenly across this range, with three in the range 100–200, seven in the range 50–100, one just below 50, thirteen in the range 20–40, four between 10 and 20, and thirteen below 10 inhabitants per square kilometer. No other world region is quite so heterogeneous. Two main zones of heavy settlement can be distinguished, the first running east-west along the West African coast and the second running north-south down the line of the East African Great Rift System and its accompanying highlands. Three major empty areas are found: the East-West Sahel zone, the west-central forest of Gabon and Congo, and the desert or semidesert western half of South Africa (figure 1-1).

The picture becomes more complex at a more disaggregated level. In only a few countries is the situation adequately represented by the national average: these are mostly the small, heavy-density "enclaves" (Burundi, Gambia, Lesotho, Rwanda, Swaziland) and a couple of the emptiest (Gabon, Mauritania). Elsewhere extreme variability is the rule. Kenya, for example, has three patches of heavy settlement (peak densities of more than 200) around Lake Victoria, in the central highlands, and along the Indian Ocean coast; elsewhere settlement is sparse, with large, almost uninhabited tracts (densities generally below 10). Cameroon has three small cores of high densities (50–200+) in the western highlands bordering Nigeria, the northern "peninsula," and around Yaoundé in the south; densities in the rest of the country are mostly under 15. The West African coastal countries are characterized by settlement that is heavy on the coast and becomes progressively sparser northward to the Sahel: in Benin, Ghana, and Côte d'Ivoire, for example, densities reach 200 at the coast and fall to under 20 in the extreme north. Generally speaking, populations cluster along coasts, lakes, and rivers and in highlands.

The settlement patterns developed in response to a variety of determining factors. These include ecological factors (soils, climate, rainfall, and groundwater availability); disease patterns (such as onchocerciasis, sleeping sickness, malaria, and venereal diseases); and historical and developmental factors (such as patterns of trade, warfare or slaving, communications, industry, mines, and agricultural development).

Urbanization and Patterns of Rural Settlement

Table 1-3 provides basic information on urbanization in Africa, including the percentages that are urban, the percentage share of the largest urban center, and intercensal urban growth rates. In examining these data,

Table 1-2. *Population Size and Density, Mid-1985*

Region and Country	Population (millions)	Area (thousands of square kilometers)	Density (persons per square kilometer)
Horn of Africa			
Sudan	21.9	2,506	9
Ethiopia	42.3	1,222	35
Djibouti	0.4	22	18
Somalia	5.4	638	8
East and Central Africa			
Kenya	20.4	569	36
Uganda	14.7	236	62
Rwanda	6.0	26	23
Burundi	4.7	28	168
Zaire	30.6	2,346	13
Tanzania	22.2	945	23
Zambezi countries			
Malawi	7.0	94	74
Zambia	6.7	753	9
Mozambique	13.8	802	17
Zimbabwe	8.4	381	21
Southern Africa			
Botswana	1.1	225	5
Namibia	1.2	824	1
Swaziland	0.8	17	47
Lesotho	1.5	30	50
South Africa	32.4	1,221	27
Sahel			
Mauritania	1.7	1,031	2
Mali	7.5	1,240	6
Niger	6.4	1,267	5
Chad	5.0	1,284	4
Senegal	6.6	196	34
Burkina Faso	7.9	274	29
Coastal strip			
Gambia	0.7	11	68
Guinea-Bissau	0.9	36	25
Guinea	6.2	246	25
Sierra Leone	3.7	72	51
Liberia	2.2	111	20
Côte d'Ivoire	10.1	322	31
Ghana	12.7	239	53
Togo	3.0	57	53
Benin	4.0	113	35
West-Central Africa			
Nigeria	99.7	924	107
Cameroon	10.2	475	21
Central African Republic	2.6	623	4
Equatorial Guinea	0.4	28	14
Gabon	1.0	267	4
Congo	1.9	342	6
Angola	8.8	1,247	7

Source: World Bank 1987.

Figure 1-1. *Population Density, 1980*

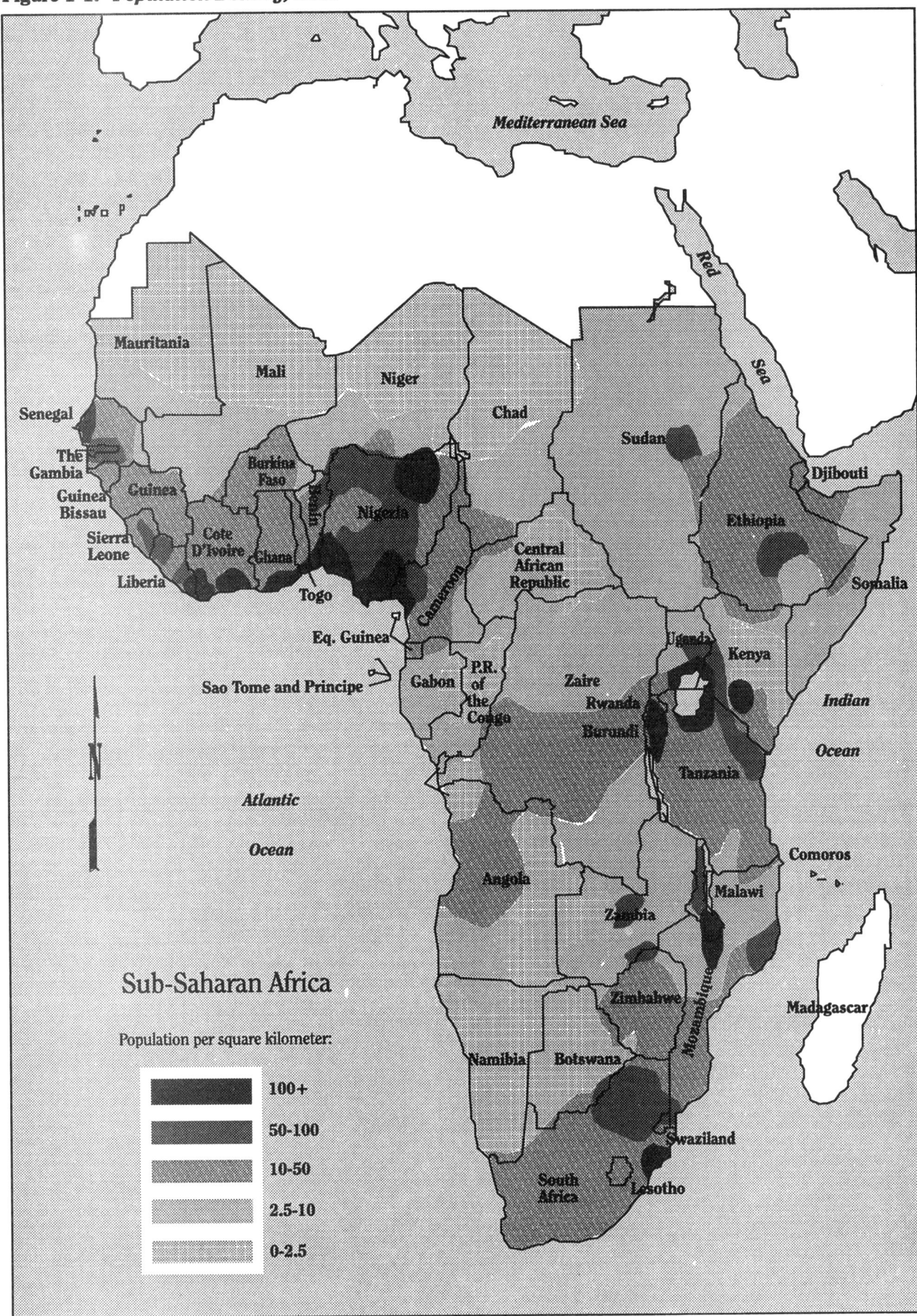

Sub-Saharan Africa

Population per square kilometer:

100+

50-100

10-50

2.5-10

0-2.5

Table 1-3. *Percentage Urban and in Largest City, and Rural and Urban Growth Rates, Specified Years*

Region and country	Year	Urban percentage	Percentage of urban population in largest city	Average annual intercensal population growth rate		
				Rural	Urban	Total
Horn of Africa						
Sudan	1956[a]	8.3	28.8	—	—	—
	1973	17.6	30.1	1.5	6.6	2.2
Ethiopia	1968	8.6	31.5	—	—	—
	1975[b]	11.2	—	1.8	6.7	2.4
Somalia	1975	35.0	33.0	—	—	—
East and Central Africa						
Kenya	1962	7.8	46.9	—	—	—
	1969	9.9	44.3	3.1	4.8	3.4
	1969	13.0	—	3.0	6.1	3.4
Uganda	1959	5.5	37.8	—	—	—
	1969	7.7	45.3	3.5	8.1	3.7
Rwanda	1970[c]	3.2	—	—	—	—
	1978	4.5	—	—	—	—
Burundi	1970[d]	3.3	—	—	—	—
	1979	4.5	33.3	2.9	4.8	3.1
Zaire	1958[e]	22.5	13.9	—	—	—
	1980	34.2	30.0	2.5	5.2	3.3
Tanzania	1957	4.9	29.1	—	—	—
	1967	5.5	40.2	2.5	4.3	3.0
	1978	13.8	31.2	2.3	11.6	3.2
Zambezi countries						
Malawi	1966	5.3	54.2	—	—	—
	1977	9.3	47.2	2.5	7.7	2.9
Zambia	1963	20.0	17.9	—	—	—
Mozambique	1969	29.4	22.0	0.5	—	2.5
	1970	5.7	82.4	—	—	—
	1980	43.3	22.1	2.1	6.5	3.1
	1981	9.0	83.0	—	8.5	3.9
Zimbabwe	1962[f]	18.1	32.9	—	—	—
	1969	20.0	37.9	6.3	0.2	4.9
Southern Africa						
Botswana	1964	3.3	24.3	—	—	—
	1971	9.6	32.0	0.6	17.5	1.6
	1981	16.1	39.6	3.5	9.4	4.3
Namibia	1951	15.2	—	—	—	—
	1960	23.5	29.2	1.0	6.9	2.1
	1970	24.9	32.6	3.5	4.3	3.7
Swaziland	1956	2.6	—	—	—	—
	1966	12.8	51.7	4.0	14.8	4.6
	1976	15.2	30.7	2.0	10.4	2.8
Lesotho	1966[g]	5.0	43.8	—	—	—
	1976	11.2	40.4	2.8	11.6	3.5

—Data not available.

a. Based on results of sample survey of population comprising 10 percent of rural and nomadic population and 10 percent of sixty-eight towns (urban).

b. Derived from the National Sample Survey 1968, first round; 1975 data are based on second round of the National Sample Survey.

c. Estimate based on results of sample survey of population covering 100,000 persons.

d. Report of the 1970–71 demographic survey in Burundi.

e. Data for 1958 based on results of sample survey excluding adjustment for certain areas not covered by survey.

f. European census taken September 1961.

g. The 1966 census excluded absentee workers, amounting to 12 percent of the total population.

h. Calculated from 1964–65 survey report.

i. Estimate based on results of sample survey; probably includes estimates of 209,000 nomads.

Region and country	Year	Urban percentage	Percentage of urban population in largest city	Average annual intercensal population growth rate		
				Rural	Urban	Total
South Africa	1951	42.6	17.0	—	—	—
	1960	46.7	15.4	1.8	3.3	2.3
	1970	47.8	13.8	2.8	3.3	3.1
	1980	53.4	—	1.9	4.1	3.0
Sahel						
Mauritania	1965[h]	6.7	21.4	—	—	—
	1977	21.6	42.2	1.5	9.8	3.4
Mali	1960[i]	10.0	31.6	—	—	—
	1976	17.2	37.5	2.4	5.1	2.9
Niger	1977	12.0	21.7	—	—	—
Chad	1963–64[j]	7.5	37.7	—	—	—
Senegal	1960–61[k]	22.7	53.1	—	—	—
	1976	34.9	46.6	1.7	5.9	3.0
Gambia	1963	8.8	100.0	—	—	—
	1973	16.0	100.0	—	5.4	4.5
Burkina Faso	1960[l]	—	—	—	—	—
	1975	19.2	33.7	—	—	—
Coastal strip						
Guinea-Bissau	1950	10.0	—	—	—	—
Guinea	1955[m]	10.9	27.9	—	—	—
	1977	21.8	66.6	2.6	6.6	3.3
Sierra Leone	1963	18.9	30.3	—	—	—
	1974	21.0	48.3	1.1	6.7	2.3
Liberia	1962	19.8	40.3	—	—	—
	1974	28.5	38.8	2.2	6.5	3.3
Côte d'Ivoire	1965	23.7	35.9	4.0	8.2	5.2
	1975	34.5	29.5	—	—	—
Ghana	1960	23.1	21.8	—	—	—
	1970	28.9	29.9	1.6	4.7	2.4
Togo	1960	10.4	57.6	—	—	—
	1970	13.0	56.9	2.8	6.3	3.2
Benin	1961[n]	9.4	55.3	—	—	—
	1979	16.0	—	2.2	5.5	2.6
West-Central Africa						
Nigeria	1953	10.2	8.6	—	—	—
	1963	16.1	7.3	5.3	0.6	6.4
Cameroon	1976	28.3	19.7	—	—	—
Central African Republic	1959–60[o]	22.3	56.0	—	—	—
	1975	34.5	42.5	3.6	7.6	4.7
Equatorial Guinea	1960[p]	26.0	—	—	—	2.1
Gabon	1961	18.0	38.8	—	—	—
Congo	1960–61[q]	24.5	69.7	—	—	—
	1974	47.6	48.2	1.0	7.3	3.8
Angola	1960	10.6	43.9	—	—	—
	1970	15.0	56.1	1.1	5.0	1.6

j. Estimate for de jure African population, based on results of sample survey.
k. Estimate of de jure population based on results of sample survey.
l. Sample survey, demographic sample survey in Upper Volta, 1960–61.
m. 1954–55 survey (France, 1959).
n. Data based on 1961 demographic survey in Dahomey.
o. Sample survey, 1959–60.
p. Based on unadjusted 1960 census total and the 1960 census population of Malabo and Bata.
q. Sample survey, de jure population, demographic survey in Congo.

the great variability of definitions of the urban population must be borne in mind. Sometimes the criterion is minimum population size of a locality; this can range from 100 (Uganda 1969) to 20,000 (Nigeria 1963). Alternatively, the criterion may be legal or functional (all localities registered as townships or all administrative centers of a certain level of administrative subdivision). A mixture of the two types is occasionally employed. All definitions may vary from one census to the next. Official urban boundaries may also change. Uncertainty regarding these points complicates evaluation of levels and trends of urbanization. Nonetheless, four broad features of African urbanization can be distinguished.

Low Level of Urbanization

Sub-Saharan Africa is not highly urbanized in comparison with either the developed world or the developing world. The urban percentage is nowhere higher than about 50 percent; it is less than one-third in about three-quarters of African countries and less than 15 percent in several (table 1-3). In contrast, the range for developed countries (where definitions of "urban" are similarly variable) runs roughly from 30 to 90 percent, with the majority above 60 percent and few below 50 percent. The contrast with other developing countries (again with a similar variety of definitions) is not so extreme; for example, only 20–25 percent of the populations of China, India, and Indonesia are urban, a level easily surpassed in much of West and Central Africa. Sub-Saharan Africa has two features, however, that set it apart from other developing-world regions. The first is the clusters of lightly urbanized countries in East and South Africa and in the Sahel, whose urbanization levels (below 20 and sometimes 15 percent) are found only as rare, isolated cases elsewhere. The second is its unique lack of urbanization levels above 50 percent.

Wide Interregional Variation

Within the continent there are wide geographical variations in levels of urbanization. As previously noted, a zone of light urbanization runs down East Africa, including Burundi, Ethiopia, Kenya, Lesotho, Malawi, Mozambique, Rwanda, Swaziland, Tanzania, and Uganda, with most of these countries less than 15 percent urban. These are regions of little or no indigenous urban foundation, apart from the Arab-influenced coastal areas, and urbanization was largely colonial and administrative in origin.

West Africa is more heavily urbanized as a result of a long tradition of mostly indigenous urbanization (comprising both the line of coastal ports and trading centers along the Atlantic and the interior network of strong, city-based empires in the Sahel and Sudan sa-

vanna) reinforced in modern times by colonization, economic development, and the offshore oil industry. In many of the coastal countries, one-quarter to more than one-third of the population is urban; in the less-developed Sahel countries, the proportions are lower, usually less than one-quarter.

Central and south-central Africa form a third category, with relatively high rates of urbanization (mostly 25–50 percent) that are not, however, due to any strong urban tradition but rather developed in response to the needs of colonial administrations and economic exploitation. Towns in Cameroon, Central African Republic, Congo, Gabon, South Africa, Zaire, Zambia, and Zimbabwe were established as colonial administrative headquarters to command sea, river, and railway communications and to serve mining, manufacturing, and agroindustries. General economic development and the rise of the oil industry have reinforced this urban growth since independence.

Dominance of the Primate City

The "primate city" may be defined as the largest city in size of population and is usually also the national capital. The share of primate cities in the total urban population in Sub-Saharan Africa usually ranges from 30 to 50 percent, with few countries below this range and several surpassing it. In contrast, most developed countries have less than 30 percent of their urban population living in the primate city. Much the same is true of Asia and the Middle East. Only in Latin America and North America is the primate city share rather similar in range to that in Sub-Saharan Africa.

The importance of large-town urbanization in Africa can be even better appreciated from the overall size distribution of urban centers. In most countries at least half of all urban dwellers live in towns with at least 50,000 inhabitants; in several the proportion is more than 60 percent. Another 10–30 percent live in towns of 10,000–50,000 inhabitants; where the proportion in the 50,000-and-over category is low or zero, this category will contain 40–80 percent of urban dwellers. Thus the typical urban dweller in Africa is the inhabitant of a respectably large town.

Rapid Pace of Urbanization

In those Sub-Saharan African countries with more than one set of census data available from which urban growth can be measured, urban growth over the past few decades has generally been two to three times faster than overall population growth (table 1-3). Interestingly, the pace of urbanization in much of the developed world, particularly Europe, has been comparable, if not faster. In the other developing regions, however, the pace of urbanization has been markedly slower than in Africa. Recent censuses offer some evidence that the rate of urban growth may now be slowing in Africa, but too few series of more than two censuses are yet available for any conclusions to be reached.

Patterns of Rural Settlement

Rural settlement patterns also vary markedly across Sub-Saharan Africa. Throughout much of East and South Africa, and in parts of Central and West Africa also, dispersed settlement is the norm. Families live in individual homesteads scattered throughout the countryside, without nucleation into hamlets or villages. In colonial times, the British in Kenya and the Portuguese in their colonies forcibly attempted to impose village settlement in order to prevent guerrilla activity. Since independence, Tanzania has pursued a similar policy in order to improve the efficiency of agricultural cooperatives and the delivery of social services, and some of the francophone countries have drafted similar plans. In general, such efforts have met with only limited success.

In most of West Africa, in contrast, villages and hamlets are the normal mode of settlement. Such groupings have been extremely mobile, however, with a continual tendency to change location, split up, or regroup. (The same is true, on a smaller scale, of the homestead pattern of settlement.) The lack of permanent buildings or infrastructure around which villages could crystallize (as happened in Europe) may have facilitated this mobility in the traditional system. The increasing establishment of roads, schools, health facilities, and so forth now may create the nuclei of more permanent settlements.

Migration

Migration may be international or internal, and both forms may include unforced migration undertaken for economic motives and forced migration caused by natural disasters or political upheaval. Of course, to the migrants themselves these distinctions may be blurred, and motivation may evolve over time as circumstances change.

Economic Migration

The populations of Sub-Saharan Africa are extremely mobile. All over the continent, large spontaneous streams of migrants travel long distances—often across national frontiers—for lengthy periods of employment. It is a particular characteristic of Sub-Saharan Africa's economic migration, however, that migrants maintain strong links with their home communities. One contributing factor to this pattern of migration is the heavy involvement of women in agriculture in many parts of Sub-Saharan Africa (the exceptions being areas of particularly strong Islamic influence or traditional dominance of women in commerce). Men are thus able to migrate in search of cash employment and leave wives and female relations to farm the land with only occasional assistance from male labor. Another contributory factor is the single short agricultural season in some regions of Africa, particularly the Sahel, which leaves men with many idle months that they can spend in migratory cash employment. Typically, such movements flow from poorer, less developed, and often densely settled rural areas into well-defined magnet areas of commercial agriculture or expanding industry and manufacture.

In West Africa, the principal attraction for migrants has historically been cash-crop agriculture, notably cocoa plantations, together with the towns and industries that developed from its profits. Migrants moved predominantly from the interior to the coast, from the Sahel and Sudan savanna to the richer forest.

Ghana was the first major West African magnet and, until 1960, the most important. Its plantation-based prosperity and developing economy pulled in a growing influx of migration from the 1920s up to the 1960s. At the peak of the influx in about 1960, 12 percent of Ghana's population (more than 800,000 people) were foreign nationals; of these one-third came from adjacent Togo, one-quarter from Burkina Faso, and a fifth from Nigeria. During the 1960s, however, Ghana's economy began to decline and immigration fell, trends that culminated in the mass expulsion of aliens in 1970. In the continuing economic deterioration of the 1970s, Ghana actually suffered a net loss of migrants, as former immigrants left and Ghanaians themselves were attracted to the newer magnets of Côte d'Ivoire and Nigeria. At the time of Nigeria's own expulsion of illegal immigrants in the mid-1980s, there may have been as many as three-quarters of a million Ghanaians in Nigeria.

Côte d'Ivoire replaced Ghana as principal magnet economy in the 1960s and 1970s, again on the basis of successful agriculture coupled with rapid urban growth. The 1975 census counted 1.4 million foreign nationals in Côte d'Ivoire, or 21 percent of the population. Of these, one-half came from Burkina Faso, one-quarter from Mali, and 10 percent from Guinea and Ghana. With the economic crisis of the early 1980s, however, the influx is thought to have diminished drastically.

The island of Fernando Po (now Bioko) provides an even more vivid small-scale illustration of the pattern. There a magnet economy based on cocoa plantations flourished in the 1950s and 1960s; at independence from Spain in 1968, the island was said to have the highest standard of living in contemporary West Africa. Plantation labor was supplied almost entirely by migrants from southeastern Nigeria and southwestern Cameroon, who, at the peak of the influx, made up two-thirds of the island's population. These migrants were driven out during the ensuing period of dictatorship, however, and the economy was consequently ruined.

Another more modest but long-standing West African migration magnet is the groundnut basin of Senegal and the Gambia, active for over a century. Seasonal migrants from Mali, Guinea, and Guinea-Bissau come in annually for groundnut cultivation, with additional seasonal movements between Senegal and the Gambia, according to growing conditions. Senegal's 1976 census counted more than 350,000 foreign nationals, nearly half of whom came from Guinea and Guinea-Bissau (and were also, at least in part, political refugees).

In recent years, oil and oil-based development has also become an important magnet, chiefly in Nigeria though with some limited movements also into Cameroon, the Congo, and Gabon. The influx into Nigeria, beginning in the early 1970s, is badly documented but had clearly assumed huge proportions by the early 1980s. According to government statements, 1.2 million West Africans left the country under the 1983 illegal alien expulsion order; of these 700,000 were Ghanaian, 180,000 were from Niger, 150,000 from Chad, and 120,000 from Cameroon. Migrants found employment opportunities less in the oil industry itself than in oil-financed investments in infrastructure, construction, public services, and expansion of government itself. Recent economic difficulties and the downturn in oil revenues have probably reduced these migrant streams considerably.

The demographic impact of this type of migration on West African countries varies. Among the receiving countries, the populations of Ghana, Côte d'Ivoire, and probably Gabon (whose own population is tiny) were significantly increased; Nigeria, however, has too large a population to be more than minimally affected even by an inflow of 1 million or 2 million immigrants. Among the sending countries, those most affected have been Burkina Faso, Togo, and Mali. In 1975, Burkina Faso had lost about 1 million nationals, or almost a fifth of its remaining population. In 1960, about 280,000 Togo nationals were in Ghana, almost a fifth of the population still in Togo. Mali nationals abroad in 1975 numbered about 420,000, or about 7 percent of the country's population. The special case of Ghana also deserves mention: by 1983 it had lost not only the 12 percent of the population gained through former immigration but also another 6 percent of its own population.

It must be remembered that crude percentages of total populations understate the demographic impact of economic migration, which is generally concentrated in the male adult age groups and hence may affect the sex ratio, the age structure of the population, and fertility and mortality levels quite considerably.

During the postwar West African economic boom based on cash-crop agriculture, Uganda and Tanzania were acting as magnets in East Africa. Sugar, sisal, tea, and coffee cultivation, together with accompanying urban and industrial development in Uganda, attracted steady streams of migrants from Burundi, Kenya, Rwanda, and eastern Zaire. These inflows had begun in the 1930s and 1940s and peaked in the 1950s and 1960s. The number of foreigners counted in the censuses of Uganda rose from 414,000 in 1948 to 682,000 in 1959 to more than 1 million in 1969, or from 8 to 12 percent of the total population.[4] The most important sending country was always Rwanda. Immigration into Tanzania was always less important; the 1967 census counted 443,000 foreigners, or 4 percent of the total population. The economic collapse of Uganda and deterioration of Tanzania in the 1970s halted these immigrant flows, although refugee inflows continued.

The demographic impact of this economic migration in East Africa has been less than in West Africa but is still significant for Burundi, Rwanda, some regions of Tanzania, and Uganda. By 1969, at least a quarter of a million Rwandese were abroad, of whom one-half or more, or about 7 percent of the population in Rwanda, were economic rather than refugee migrants. Figures for Burundi were similar, without any refugee element at that time.

For most of this century, economic migration flows, relating primarily to mining and only secondarily to commercial agriculture, have been an important phenomenon in southern Africa. South Africa has always been the principal magnet economy, though other countries, such as Zambia and Zimbabwe (and even the mines of southernmost Zaire), have acted as secondary magnets during periods of prosperity. The principal sending countries have invariably been Botswana, Lesotho, Malawi, Mozambique, and Swaziland, which are much less developed and have fewer mineral and agricultural resources.

The influx into South Africa, important since the late nineteenth century, reached a peak in the early 1970s. African immigrants then numbered about half a million, of whom more than 325,000 were mine workers. About 40 percent of the miners came from Malawi, a quarter each from Lesotho and Mozambique, and the remaining 10 percent or so from Botswana, Swaziland, Zimbabwe, and Zambia. The distribution of farm workers was probably similar.

During the 1970s, the influx into South Africa began a continued decline. The several causes include increasing employment of the rapidly growing domestic black labor force and the withdrawal of Malawian labor following the deaths of a Malawian group in a plane crash in 1974. The distribution of mine workers has also changed over time, according to political and economic trends in the neighboring countries.

The mining towns of Zambia became a temporary magnet during the boom years of the 1950s and 1960s, before copper collapsed in the 1970s. The 1969 census counted nearly 200,000 foreign-born Africans, or 5 percent of the total population. Of these, nearly one-third came from Zimbabwe, one-quarter from Malawi, and the rest mainly from Angola, Tanzania, and Zaire (including some refugee elements).

Zimbabwe attracted an important inflow between the mid-1940s and mid-1970s as a result of a strong commercial agricultural sector and accompanying industrial and urban growth. The 1969 census counted 338,000 foreign-born Africans, or about 7 percent of the total African population, of whom nearly half came from Malawi, one-third from Mozambique, and most of the remainder from Zambia. (Again, some refugee element was present).

Earlier in the century, Malawi was also a temporary magnet, mainly for Mozambique; the attractions were some commercial agriculture, availability of good land, and better living conditions than under Portuguese rule. Numbers peaked at about half a million in the 1940s; in the censuses of 1966 and 1977, these had fallen to about 300,000 foreign born, most of whom came from Mozambique.

The demographic impact of migration in southern Africa has been negligible for the receiving countries, even for South Africa (because of its large population size). Among some of the principal sending countries, on the other hand, the impact has been considerable. Zimbabwe and Zambia were little affected, being both sending and receiving countries with small net flows relative to population size; so also was Mozambique because of its relatively large population. According to the respective censuses of Botswana, Lesotho, and Swaziland in 1971, 1977, and 1976, however, emigrants to South Africa amounted to 8, 15, and 5 percent, respectively, of the population still in the countries, whereas Malawi lost about one-quarter of a million by the 1960s and 1970s, of whom more than half were in Zimbabwe and one-quarter in South Africa. Moreover, because economic migration in southern Africa, being strictly controlled in South Africa at least, has always been concentrated to an extreme degree in the adult male prime working age group, the demographic impact is much greater than the overall percentages would suggest. In Botswana, Swaziland, and Lesotho, one-quarter, one-fifth, and almost one-half, respectively, of the male work force is absent at any one time.

Finally, it should be noted that parallel migration streams to the international flows just described often exist within countries also; for example, movements from the northern savanna to the southern forest in West African countries and throughout Sub-Saharan Africa from poor rural regions to areas of commercial agriculture as well as to urban centers. The predominance of young adult males, however, is generally less marked in such internal flows.

Refugee Migration

Refugee movements can be generated by either natural disasters or political upheavals. The first type is less important because it is usually temporary and quickly reversed when normal conditions return. The biggest flows of this kind in recent years were during the Sahel drought of the early 1970s and the widespread drought of the mid-1980s, which was particularly severe in Ethiopia, Mozambique, and Sudan. The short-term demographic impact of these flows has been generally transitory, although one significant long-term outcome has been the acceleration of an already existing tendency to sedentarization among nomad groups.

More important are the flows of political refugees generated by war or political oppression. These began at the time of decolonization in the late 1950s and have remained a constant feature in the region. Most such movements have been of necessity across national frontiers but only into neighboring countries (except for elite groups that could find refuge throughout Africa and the Western world) and then mainly along the borders. The reason is partly that ethnic affinities often straddle national boundaries and partly that many refugees lack the resources for long-distance travel. Sometimes, however, the major towns of the host country are also important destinations because of their superior economic opportunities or public services.

Table 1-4 presents refugee numbers by country of refuge from 1970 to 1986, as taken from the U.N. High Commissioner for Refugees (UNHCR) reports.[5] During the 1960s, there were four principal sources of refugee outflows, almost all confined to central, eastern, and southern Africa:

- The struggle for independence in the Portuguese colonies of Angola, Guinea-Bissau, and Mozambique, beginning in the 1950s and intensifying throughout the 1960s
- The civil war in Sudan, beginning in the late 1950s and growing steadily in scale through the 1960s
- The ethnic conflict in Rwanda at the beginning of the 1960s
- The internal convulsions in Zaire from 1960 onward, which waxed and waned throughout the decade.

By 1968 the UNHCR registered more than half a million

Table 1-4. *Refugees by Country of Residence, Selected Years, 1970–86*

Region and country	1970	1972	1973	1975	1978	1980	1981	1986
Horn of Africa								
Sudan	61,000	57,000	51,000	90,000	270,000	480,000	550,000	974,000
Ethiopia	21,000	16,000	5,000		10,900	11,000	11,000	132,336
Djibouti					20,000	25,000	31,600	16,715
Somalia					500,000	200,000	700,000	840,000
East and Central Africa								
Kenya	1,000	2,500	2,400	2,450	6,500	3,500	3,400	8,046
Uganda	180,000	166,600	114,000	112,500	112,400	113,000	113,000	144,000
Rwanda		4,000	8,000	7,400	7,500	10,000	18,000	19,380
Burundi	38,800	42,000	49,000	49,500	50,000	50,000	234,600	267,477
Zaire		494,000	460,000	510,000	633,000	350,000	364,000	301,000
Tanzania	71,500	98,000	167,000	171,000	160,000	156,000	164,000	220,000
Zambezi countries								
Malawi								70,000
Zambia	16,000	25,000	37,000	36,000	80,000	36,000	40,500	138,300
Mozambique				14,500	100,000	100	100	662
Zimbabwe							111	65,215
Southern Africa								
Botswana	4,000			2,500	18,600	1,300	1,300	4,569
Swaziland					700	5,214	5,600	12,127
Lesotho					187	11,000	11,500	11,500
Sahel								
Senegal	67,000	82,000	84,000	46,000	5,000	5,000	4,000	5,513
West-Central Africa								
Nigeria					60,000	105,000	105,000	4,749
Cameroon					141,000	110,000	25,000	53,500
Central African Republic	27,200	22,000	5,000	5,000		7,000	4,000	12,951
Gabon						30,000		
Angola							93,000	92,207

Note: Small refugee populations were recorded in West African countries in 1987 as follows: Benin (3,742), Burkina Faso (218), Côte d'Ivoire (882), Ghana (156), Liberia (244), Sierra Leone (183), Togo (2,605). Data are for December 31 of the year specified.

Source: Annual Reports of the U.N. High Commissioner for Refugees.

refugees from the Portuguese colonies, more than 160,000 refugees from southern Sudan, more than 150,000 Rwandese Batutsi, and nearly 70,000 Zairians despite various repatriation efforts. The principal host countries were Burundi, the Central African Republic, Senegal, Sudan, Tanzania, Uganda, Zaire, and Zambia, some of which were both senders and receivers of refugee streams. Zaire, Uganda, and Burundi were particularly burdened, with total refugee loads of 470,000, 170,000, and 70,000, respectively.

A number of radical changes occurred in the 1970s in refugee flow patterns. Most established outflows diminished or were reversed. The Sudan stream increased until settlement of the civil war in 1973, when almost all refugees returned home. Portuguese colony outflows increased until independence in 1975, after which most Mozambicans then returned home. A large proportion of Guineans chose to stay in Senegal, however, whereas Angola never recovered enough stability to attract back more than half of its refugees. No further Rwandese outflows occurred, but most refugees abroad settled

down permanently. Outflows from Zaire continued sporadically, following fresh outbreaks of violence, so that refugee numbers at first more than doubled and then dropped to the 1960s level.

Seven major new outflows began in the 1970s as a consequence of wars of independence, internal ethnic conflict, or destabilization following abrupt changes of government. In addition, a new type of migration emerged: flights from oppressive dictatorships. West Africa was largely spared, with movements confined mainly to the center, east, and south of the continent, as follows:

• Outflows from Zimbabwe and Namibia during struggles for independence. The exodus from Zimbabwe was massive (one-quarter of a million) but brief (covering only 1976–78) and was almost entirely reversed following independence. The Namibian outflow was smaller and slower, reaching only about 80,000 by the end of the decade.

• Outflows from Chad and Burundi following ethnic

conflict. Refugees from Chad's continuing civil war numbered nearly 150,000 by 1981. The 1972 massacre of Bahutu by Batutsi in Burundi provoked an exodus of nearly 200,000 Bahutu over the next few years.

- Outflows from Ethiopia of Ethiopians, Eritreans, and ethnic Somalis following the revolutionary overthrow of the monarchy, the civil war with Eritrea, and the war with Somalia, reaching about 1.6 million refugees by 1981.
- Outflows from Uganda and Equatorial Guinea following the installation of an oppressive dictatorship and, in Uganda, its subsequent overthrow. By 1981 nearly one-quarter of Equatorial Guinea's population, and more than 130,000 Ugandans, had fled.

The principal host countries in the 1970s continued to include Sudan, Tanzania, Uganda, Zaire, and Zambia with the new additions of Angola, Botswana, Cameroon, Djibouti, Gabon, Mozambique, Nigeria, and Somalia. Again, many countries both sent and received refugee flows, either simultaneously (as with Angola, sending refugees to Zaire, Zambia, and Botswana and receiving them from Zaire and Namibia) or in rotation (as with Mozambique, which until 1975 sent refugees to Tanzania and Zambia and after 1975 received them from Zimbabwe). Tanzania and Zambia stand out as countries that have been continuing hosts for refugees without any important outflows of their own.

The 1980s saw the beginning of several new, massive movements, and many established refugee flow patterns of the 1970s ceased or were reversed by the end of the decade. Old refugee flow patterns that continued into the 1980s with varying and fluctuating intensity included:

- Outflows into western Sudan of Chadians fleeing ethnic rivalry
- Outflow of Ethiopians into Sudan, Somalia, and Djibouti, with 677,000, 840,000, and 16,000 Ethiopians estimated to be in the three countries, respectively, at the end of December 1986
- The flow of Ugandans into Sudan and Kenya.

Many new refugee movements in the 1980s were reversals of flows that had occurred either in the 1970s or in the early 1980s. There were four principal streams: (1) a large-scale repatriation of Zimbabwean refugees from Botswana, Mozambique, and Zambia following the independence of Zimbabwe in 1979; (2) return of some 150,000 Chadian refugees from Cameroon and the Central African Republic in 1981, following the cessation of hostilities; (3) another flow resulting from the organized repatriation of more than 40,000 Ugandan refugees from Zaire between July 1983 and February 1987;

and (4) repatriation of many Ethiopian refugees from Djibouti and Sudan. A total of some 160,000 Ethiopians spontaneously returned home between 1985 and 1986.

Apart from these reversals of earlier refugee movements, several new flows during the 1980s were spurred by war, political instability, or natural disasters. More than 65,000 Mozambicans fleeing fighting and insecurity went to Zimbabwe. Zambia also received a stream of Mozambicans estimated at about 23,000 by December 1986. Flowing into Somalia from 1984 to 1986 were more than 60,000 Ethiopian refugees, with an estimated rate of flow of 700 persons per day during one period of 1985–86. There was also a combined influx of more than 100,000 Sudanese refugees into Ethiopia in 1985–86.

As in the 1970s, Djibouti, Somalia, Sudan, Uganda, and Zambia continued to be principal host countries of refugees in the 1980s. New additions included Zimbabwe, which was a sending country in the 1970s, and Ethiopia, which, although experiencing a net loss of persons during the 1980s, received a large influx of Sudanese totaling more than 178,000 by June 1987.

The demographic impact of these refugee movements varies by country according to the size, length, and performance of outflows, factors that have been highly variable in Sub-Saharan Africa. Such flows are not nearly as age and sex selective, however, as economic migration flows, and their impact may thus be more limited even where their size is comparable to that of economic migrant streams.

Mortality

The most reliable mortality data for Sub-Saharan Africa—child survival reported retrospectively by mothers—concern only mortality in childhood. Data on adult mortality are scarcer, of worse quality, and more difficult to interpret. I will therefore present and discuss in detail estimates of childhood mortality (Hill 1987) and will provide only brief descriptions of adult patterns and the corresponding overall life expectancies.

Childhood Mortality

Table 1-5 gives estimates of childhood mortality, namely the proportion of children dying between birth and the fifth birthday, between 1930 and 1980.[6] (More recent data were not available in time for analysis in this review.) Trends in childhood mortality between 1930 and 1980 are also shown in figures 1-2 and 1-3.

Four striking general features of childhood mortality in Sub-Saharan Africa are apparent. First, declines have occurred in childhood mortality since World War II in most countries where data are available. Second, there

Table 1-5. *Childhood Mortality Estimates, Two Periods*

Region and country	Coale-Demeny model life table	Earlier period Reference year	Mortality	Later period Reference year	Mortality
Horn of Africa					
Sudan	north	1959	20.1	1965	19.3
Ethiopia	north	1958	23.6	1975	22.3
Somalia	north	1967	24.1	1974	21.4
East and Central Africa					
Kenya	north	1947	26.2	1975	14.9
Uganda	north	1957	24.5	1964	20.2
Rwanda	south	1956	26.8	1979	21.7
Burundi	north	1959	26.1	1976	22.4
Zaire	south	1944	30.5	1951	26.8
Tanzania	north	1953	26.2	1973	21.9
Zambezi countries					
Malawi	south	1958	36.7	1972	33.4
Zambia	north	1956	22.3	1970	17.2
Zimbabwe	north	1957	16.2	1978	13.7
Mozambique	south	1936	26.1	1974	28.2
Southern Africa					
Botswana	south	1959	17.7	1977	11.6
Swaziland	south	1951	24.1	1969	21.5
Lesotho	west	1956	20.7	1973	18.3
Sahel					
Mali	south	1947	37.5	1955	36.9
Niger	south	1945	29.7	1954	30.5
Chad	south	1950	34.2	1958	31.3
Senegal	south	1946	37.3	1971	27.6
Burkina Faso	south	1948	42.1	1971	27.5
Coastal strip					
Gambia	south	1960	34.9	1968	34.3
Guinea-Bissau	south	1941	30.1	1943	29.8
Guinea	south	1942	38.4	1949	37.6
Sierra Leone	south	1962	39.4	1969	37.8
Liberia	south	1957	32.1	1965	28.1
Côte d'Ivoire	south	1966	26.7	1974	20.7
Ghana	south	1935	37.1	1967	19.9
Togo	south	1949	34.7	1968	22.7
Benin	south	1948	36.3	1977	22.4
West and Central Africa					
Nigeria	south	1967	19.6	1978	16.9
Cameroon	south	1955	29.1	1973	18.9
Central Africa Republic	south	1948	36.0	1970	23.9
Gabon	south	1946	34.6	1956	24.9
Congo	south	1948	28.9	1969	14.5
Angola	south	1926	35.6	1934	36.2

Note: The childhood mortality estimates give the percentage of children dying between birth and fifth birthday. For description of the method used and sources of data, see Hill 1987.

is much variation among countries in the type of decline. Third, levels of childhood mortality themselves vary greatly across the continent. Fourth, there is a very marked overall difference in mortality levels between East and West Africa.

There are three interesting exceptions to these general patterns. First, a few countries have static or rising mortality (notably Angola, Ethiopia, Niger, Nigeria, Mozambique, and Rwanda). Second, mortality in a few West African countries (Cameroon, the Congo, Ghana) has fallen to East African levels. Third, one East African country (Malawi) has a childhood mortality level comparable to those in West Africa; indeed, the level is high even by West African standards.

Figure 1-2. *Summarized Trends in Child Survival in Eastern Africa, 1926–80*

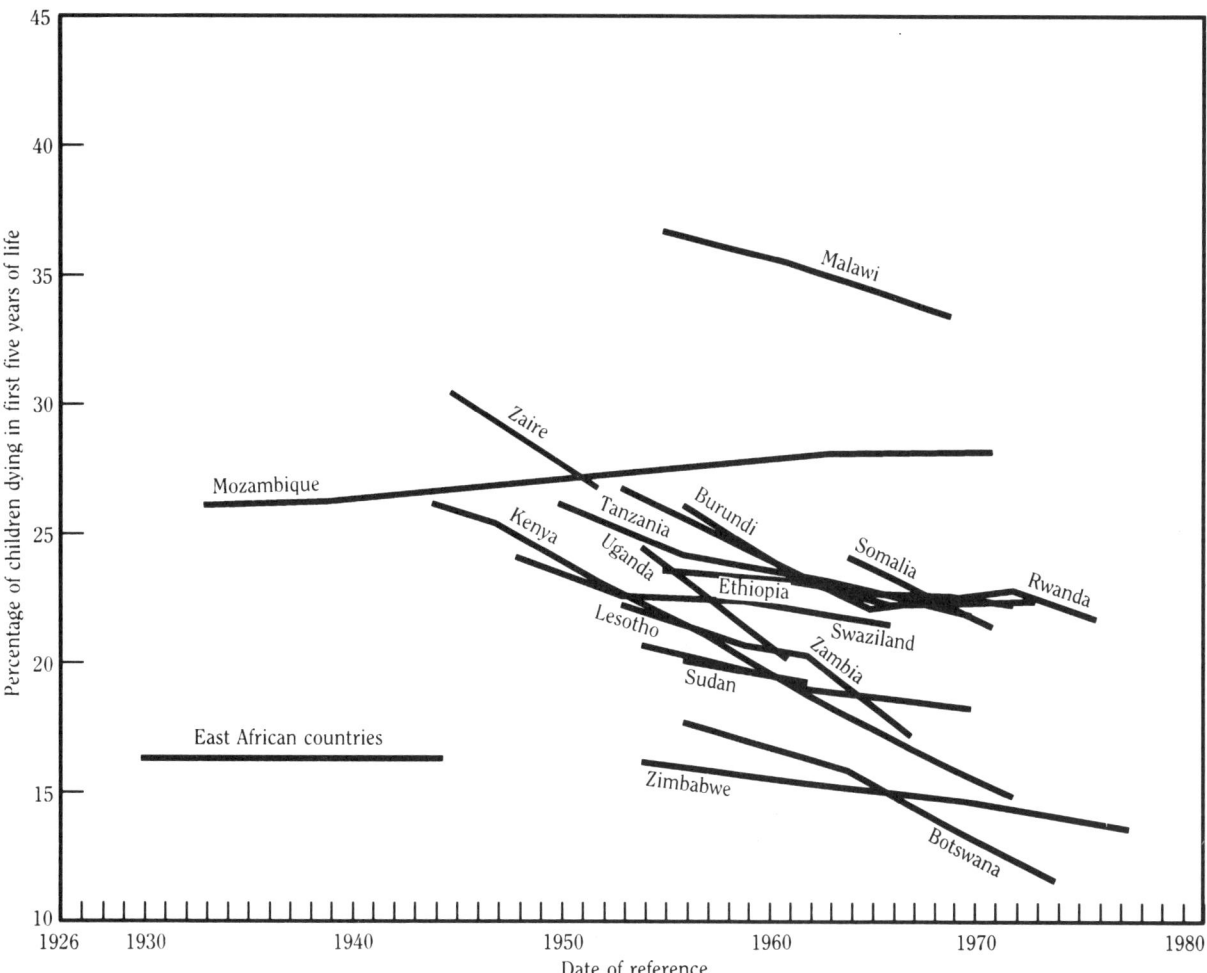

There appears to have been some decline in childhood mortality between the end of World War II and 1980 in the vast majority of Sub-Saharan African countries for which postwar data exist. The overall magnitude of the fall can be summarized by noting that, in the 1950s, countries commonly lost 30 to 40 percent of children before they reached the age of five; it was very rare to find countries that lost less than 22 percent. By the mid-1970s, however, very few countries of the region documented losses of more than 27 percent of children before age five, and losses of less than 22 percent were common. The drop represents a major postwar achievement in Sub-Saharan African development.

The observed declines vary greatly in size, timing, and pace, however, even when we take into account the methodological difficulties of dating retrospective child survival data. In some countries, declines in mortality have been dramatic. The percentage of children dying before their fifth birthday was cut almost in half in Ghana over the thirty years between the late 1930s and

late 1960s (from 37 to 20 percent); in the Congo over twenty years between the late 1940s and late 1960s (from 29 to 15 percent); and in Kenya over twenty-five years between the late 1940s and early 1970s (from 26 to 15 percent). In other countries, observed declines have been much more gradual. In Swaziland, for example, the percentage of children dying by age five fell only from 24 to 21.5 percent between 1950 and 1970; in Lesotho from 21 to 18 percent between the mid-1950s and mid-1970s; and in Sierra Leone from 39.4 to 38 percent over the decade of the 1960s. Indeed, in a few countries, such as Guinea and Mali (all with data available for only one early period), the observed decline was even smaller. In most countries, however, the changes were somewhere between these two extremes.

The variations in childhood mortality levels in Sub-Saharan Africa are truly impressive in all periods for which data exist, even though there has been some narrowing of the range over the post–World War II period. In the late 1950s, for example, the proportion

Figure 1-3. *Summarized Trends in Child Survival in Western Africa, 1926–80*

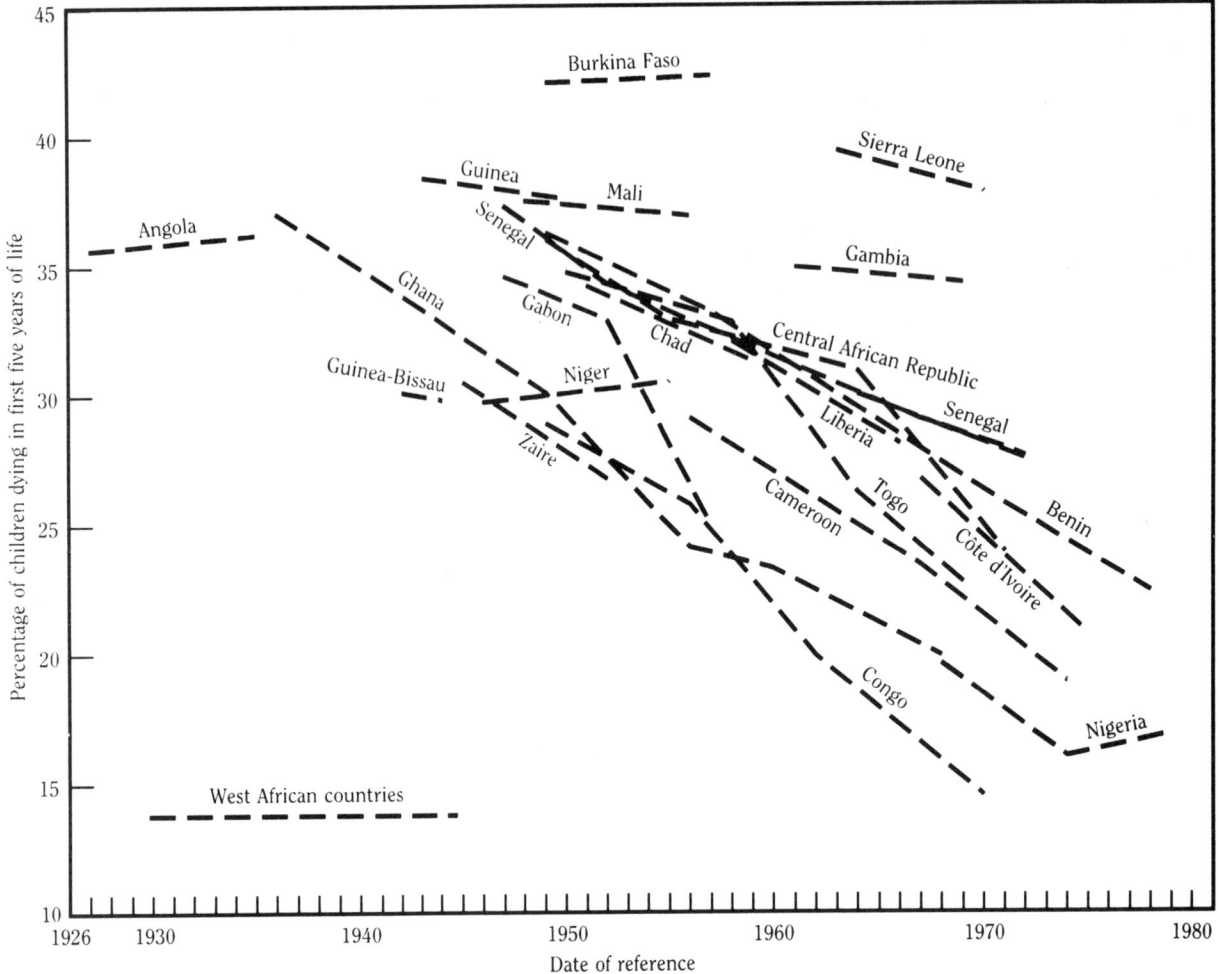

of children dying before age five ranged rather evenly from 16 to more than 40 percent, corresponding roughly to a difference of 20 to 25 years in life expectancy (30–35 years versus 50–55 years). Even by the late 1970s, the range was still 12–23 percent, though most countries fell below an upper limit of 27 percent.

There is, beyond doubt, a marked and consistent difference between childhood mortality levels in East and West Africa. This appears throughout the postwar period but has narrowed in more recent times. Childhood mortality has been generally much severer in West Africa than in East Africa, with a rough gradient across the continent from northwest to southeast. The highest levels of childhood mortality are recorded in West Africa and the Sahel, the next highest in Central Africa, lower levels in East Africa, and lowest of all in South Africa. Thus, in the 1950s, between 30 and 40 percent of children died before age five in most of West and Sahelian Africa, between 25 and 30 percent in Central and East

Africa, and between 15 and 25 percent in South Africa.[7] By the 1970s, much of West and Sahel Africa was experiencing losses of 22 to 30 percent, compared with 20 to 22 percent in Central and East Africa and 12 to 20 percent in South Africa.

There are some exceptions to the general patterns outlined above. Six cases of persistent stagnation or rises in mortality exist, namely Angola, Ethiopia, Mozambique, Niger, Nigeria, and Rwanda. To these may be added Sudan, on the basis of data for northern Sudan. Leaving aside Angola and Niger, for which only one data set for an early period is available, and the observed rise is slight, these countries have all suffered from civil wars or political upheavals, accompanied by stagnation in development during the period in question. Although the data sets are all individually subject to doubts or reservations, taken together they suggest (not surprisingly) that the evolution of childhood mortality may be very sensitive to such factors. Data are lacking for most

Sub-Saharan African countries in periods of such up-heavals over recent decades, but it may be wisest to assume that the almost universal postwar declines observed in countries at peace are absent in times of severe instability.

Figures 1-2 and 1-3 show, against the general background of higher mortality in West Africa and lower mortality in East Africa, three West African countries whose rapid mortality declines have brought them down from initial West African levels to a position unequivocally within the East African group. These countries are Cameroon, Congo, and Ghana. Nigeria is not included here because the data are of uncertain quality; in any case, it would require separate classification as a West African country in which childhood mortality has always been within the East African range if the directly reported child survival data were to be accepted.

The data from Ghana and Congo pose some difficulties of reconciliation and interpretation. According to the most plausible interpretation, however, these two countries began the post–World War II period already boasting the lowest childhood mortality in West Africa and then experienced (or continued to experience) dramatic declines throughout the 1950s and 1960s. By 1970, both had plunged well inside the east African range; Ghanaian childhood mortality was comparable to the level in contemporary Uganda and Zambia, whereas Congolese childhood mortality had actually reached the low level of contemporary Botswana and Zimbabwe. Trends since 1970 cannot be measured for Congo until the 1984 census results become available; for Ghana the picture is unclear, but there was probably some leveling off in mortality, though it was still within the east African range.

The interesting question is whether these two countries had always been unusual in their childhood mortality levels or whether they had simply experienced an earlier and steeper decline than the rest of West Africa. Very early data are not available for Congo, but 1930s data for Ghana do indicate mortality levels that somewhat resemble the severe mortality characteristic of West Africa in the late 1940s. Perhaps, therefore, the Congo and Ghana were exceptional, not in enjoying any natural initial advantage in health conditions, but in making an early start on their modern mortality decline. This early start could be explained in the case of Ghana by unusually early modern economic and social services development and in the case of Congo by the unusually high degree of urbanization long imposed by colonial development of the Congo railway.

Cameroon is a more recent and less spectacular case. In the mid-1950s, childhood mortality was at a comparatively low level for a West African country. By the mid-1970s it had rapidly fallen to within the East African range. The same factors were operating in Cameroon as in Ghana and Congo, namely, rapid economic and educational development and rather heavy urbanization. These factors may again have been responsible for the crossover.

Several other West African countries (Benin, the Central African Republic, Côte d'Ivoire, Gabon, Togo) were seemingly heading for a crossover at the last observed point in time. Indeed, Côte d'Ivoire had actually just passed the eastern countries with highest mortality by 1975; no doubt its comparatively rapid economic development and rapid urbanization were again important factors.

In East and Southern Africa, Malawi stands out as an exception to the general rule of relatively low childhood mortality. The proportions of children dying before age five in the late 1950s and early 1970s (37 and 33 percent, respectively) are not only far above contemporary ranges in East Africa but among the highest even in contemporary West Africa. There is no single obvious characteristic of Malawi that could be advanced to explain this anomaly.[8] The country has experienced political stability and good GNP growth over the past few decades and appears broadly similar to the rest of East and South Africa in climate, culture, and epidemiology.

How does Sub-Saharan Africa compare with the rest of the developing world in childhood mortality? It is often taken for granted that Sub-Saharan Africa is a region of uniquely severe mortality. The evidence presented above unequivocally indicates that this assumption is generally true. Two special features are responsible. First, Sub-Saharan Africa contains several countries, notably the Gambia, Malawi, and Sierra Leone, that experience the severest peacetime childhood mortality currently to be found in the world. Only Afghanistan (at the national level and in peacetime) has approached these levels in recent decades (World Bank 1986; UNICEF 1987). Second, only a few countries in Sub-Saharan Africa have attained the moderately low mortality common in much of East and Southeast Asia, Central and South America, and the Middle East. (Moreover, in South Africa, the low national level is partly the result of the European level of childhood mortality enjoyed by the large nonblack minorities).

It is equally important, however, to emphasize that many African countries are not exceptionally disadvantaged in childhood mortality. Much of East and Southern Africa, as well as a few West African countries, compares well with many parts of the Indian subcontinent, Indonesia, and several countries in Latin America, North Africa, and the Middle East. It is misleading, therefore, to portray Sub-Saharan Africa as a homogeneous region uniformly trailing the rest of the world in childhood mortality or to conclude that improvements in health conditions are necessarily more difficult to achieve there than elsewhere.

Adult Mortality and Life Expectancy

Levels and patterns of adult mortality in Sub-Saharan Africa have been little investigated, though it is estimated that the probability of dying between ages 15 and 60 in Sub-Saharan Africa is broadly similar to the probability of dying in childhood (Timaeus 1987). One reason is that, because adult deaths are much less frequent than child deaths, the surveys required to obtain reliable adult mortality estimates must use much larger samples than those for childhood mortality. Consequently, the collection of data in this area has lagged behind that for childhood mortality. Where data exist, indications are that adult mortality in Sub-Saharan Africa is high though variable and that the balance between childhood and adult mortality also varies across countries. In some countries, adult mortality appears to be low relative to childhood levels; in others, the reverse is true. Generally speaking, however, variations among countries in adult

mortality levels are less extreme than in childhood mortality.

For most estimates of life expectancy at birth, the absence or inadequacy of adult data have necessitated recourse to model life tables chosen on the basis of childhood mortality levels. The pattern of life expectancy is therefore similar to that already described for childhood mortality. In Africa in the 1950s, life expectancies of more than 50 years were rare. Surveys in Guinea during the mid-1950s and in Chad for 1963–64 suggest that life expectancy at age 15 years was about 30 years. By the 1970s, life expectancy at birth was below 45 years in very few countries, and major improvements had been made in life expectancy at age 15 years. Estimates of life expectancy at age 15 during the 1970s appear in table 1-6. These data indicate a wide range in life expectancy, with particularly low levels again in West African countries. West Africa's high adult (and childhood) mortality, relative to the rest of the continent, is not readily explained. It may be related to climatic and sociocultural factors that make normally mild diseases severe or fatal.

Table 1-6. *Estimates of Life Expectancy at Age Fifteen, by Sex, Selected Countries and Years*

Region and country	Year	Males	Females	Both sexes
Horn of Africa				
Sudan	1975	55.9	55.6	55.7
East and Central Africa				
Kenya	1974	49.5	55.9	52.7
Uganda	1965	53.4	53.8	53.6
Burundi	1970–71	43.1	46.2	44.6
Zaire	1964	—	—	42.8
Tanzania	1965	52.8	54.4	53.6
Zambezi countries				
Malawi	1974	48.4	45.4	46.9
Zimbabwe	1975	52.3	57.0	54.6
Southern Africa				
Botswana	1965	50.3	54.6	52.5
Swaziland	1972	41.8	49.3	45.6
Lesotho	1976	42.3	52.4	47.4
Sahel				
Mauritania	1975	49.6	53.3	51.5
Senegal	1978	48.9	51.5	50.0
Coastal strip				
Gambia	1978	42.7	45.0	43.9
Sierra Leone	1975	—	—	46.6
Liberia	1971	44.3	46.9	45.6
Côte d'Ivoire	1978–79	46.8	46.5	46.7
Ghana	1968–69	45.5	47.5	46.5
Benin	1970	46.2	48.3	47.3
West-Central Africa				
Cameroon	1975	50.5	54.2	52.4
Congo	1967	52.4	55.6	54.0

— Data not available in source.
Source: Timaeus 1987.

As with childhood mortality, variations in adult mortality in Sub-Saharan Africa appear to be fairly consistently related to region, with West Africa experiencing higher levels than East Africa.

Particular Features of African Mortality

Two features of the age-sex structure of African mortality merit particular notice. The first is the importance of "child" mortality, that is, the mortality of children between their first and fifth birthdays. Unlike the European pattern, in which childhood mortality risks concentrate in the first year of life, many small-scale African studies have shown very high risks also in the second and third years of life. On occasion, the risk of dying between the first and fifth birthdays has been found to be equal to, or greater than, the risk of dying in infancy. Similar patterns have since been identified in other parts of the developing world but are rarely as extreme as in Africa. It is still not clear how much variation in this pattern occurs across Africa, though there are some grounds for suspecting that it is weaker in East Africa than in West Africa.

The second feature is the lack of any systematic, marked female disadvantage in mortality, such as is found throughout the Indian subcontinent and, to a lesser extent, in parts of the Middle East and North Africa. Data from high-mortality African countries, mainly at earlier periods, show a modest female advantage or no systematic sex difference, as is usual at high mortality levels. Data from lower-mortality countries, including most of East Africa, show a somewhat greater female advantage; in a few southern countries, where mining is important, the male disadvantage in adulthood is exceptionally marked.

Determinants of Mortality

Information on the determinants of mortality in Sub-Saharan Africa is limited. At the individual level, patterns of variation are similar to those elsewhere. Childhood mortality is lower for urban residents, educated mothers, educated fathers, and families of higher income and higher status. Mortality is higher for children born to teenage or high-parity mothers and for those born preceding or following a short birth interval (chapter 6 in this volume). Various epidemiological, ecological, and cultural factors have also been identified as important, such as infant and child feeding practices, severe seasonal food shortages, and the burden of diseases such as malaria, measles, tetanus, and gastrointestinal infections.

Much of the variation between regions, countries, and subdivisions of countries, however, has not yet been explained or indeed much studied. The basic west-east gradient, for example, cannot be explained by standard economic or social factors such as per capita GNP or levels of education. Various other factors have been proposed as important, for example climate, altitude, ecology, epidemiology, basic diets, and patterns of population settlement as well as other cultural, social, political, and historical factors. Few systematic studies even of regional differences within countries have yet been carried out, however, let alone of differences between countries or cultural and ecological groups across country boundaries. As a result, much of the mortality variation in Africa remains a mystery.

One final note must be added on the emergence and importance of AIDS in Sub-Saharan African. This lethal disease, for which neither cure nor vaccine is yet in sight, is already spreading rapidly through several countries in Central, East, and Southern Africa. It has the potential to eliminate gains in infant and adult mortality from other causes and even to outweigh them to the point where mortality will rise overall. Too few data are yet available from the most severely affected countries, however, to judge its impact.

Fertility

Available estimates of national total fertility rates (TFR) for Sub-Saharan African countries over the past three decades appear in table 1-7. Two points should be noted. First, only estimates based on specific fertility data have been used. Fertility can be estimated from any age distribution, given some indication of mortality or growth rates, but this method of estimation is sensitive to the quality of the age distribution used as well as to the choice of mortality or growth levels. Such estimates have therefore not been included here. Second, because indirect techniques of estimation (as mentioned above) have wide margins of error, too much confidence should not be placed in slight differences between countries or over time. I have given an exact figure for the TFR for convenience, but often a range such as 6.0 to 6.5, or 6.75 to 7.25, would more honestly represent the results of the analysis.

Four very striking features emerge from these results. First, fertility in Sub-Saharan Africa is almost universally high by world standards. In most countries the TFR is more than 6, and in several it is more than 7. Similar levels can still be found in other developing continents—for example, in most of the Muslim world and in a few Latin American countries—but Africa is exceptional nowadays in the uniformity of high to very high fertility in country after country.

Second, fertility is distinctly higher in East Africa than in West Africa despite considerable variation within each region. The range of estimated TFRs in East African

Table 1-7. *Total Fertility Rate Estimates, 1955–85*

Region and country	1955–59	1960–64	1965–69	1970–74	1975–79	1980–84
Horn of Africa						
Sudan	—	—	—	6.6	—	—
Ethiopia	—	—	6.4	—	—	—
Somalia	—	—	—	—	7.1	7.4
East and Central Africa						
Kenya	—	6.8	7.6	—	8.1	—
Uganda	6.0	—	7.1	—	—	—
Rwanda	7.0	—	7.7	—	8.0	8.4
Burundi	6.4	—	6.2	—	6.5	—
Zaire	5.9	—	—	—	—	—
Tanzania	6.4	—	6.6	6.3	—	—
Zambezi countries						
Malawi	—	—	7.8	—	7.8	—
Zambia	—	—	7.0	7.0	6.8	—
Mozambique	—	—	6.5	—	—	—
Zimbabwe	—	—	8.0	—	7.1	6.4
Southern Africa						
Botswana	—	—	—	6.5	7.0	6.5
Namibia	—	—	—	—	—	—
Swaziland	—	6.9	—	6.9	—	—
Lesotho	—	—	—	—	5.2	—
South Africa	—	—	—	—	—	—
Sahel						
Mauritania	—	5.5	—	—	—	—
Mali	—	—	—	—	—	—
Niger	6.8	—	—	—	—	—
Chad	—	5.1	—	—	—	5.9
Senegal	—	5.4	—	6.4	7.1	—
Burkina Faso	6.1	—	—	6.6	—	6.5
Coastal strip						
Gambia	—	—	—	6.4	—	—
Guinea-Bissau	—	—	—	—	—	—
Guinea	5.8	—	—	—	—	—
Sierra Leone	—	—	—	6.4	—	—
Liberia	—	—	—	6.0	—	—
Côte d'Ivoire	—	—	—	—	7.0	7.0
Ghana	7.2	—	7.1	—	—	6.4
Togo	6.5	—	6.6	—	—	—
Benin	6.4	—	—	—	—	—
West and Central Africa						
Nigeria	—	—	—	—	—	—
Cameroon	—	4.9	—	—	6.5	6.5
Central African Republic	4.0	—	—	5.0	—	—
Equatorial Guinea	—	—	—	—	—	—
Gabon	3.5	—	—	—	—	—
Congo	5.3	—	—	6.0	—	—
Angola	—	—	—	—	—	—

—Not available in source.
Source: Author's compilation.

countries runs from 5.8 to 8.0, compared with a West African range of 3.5 to 7.1. All but one of the East and Southern African countries show recent TFRs of over 6.0, and four at some point reached 7.5 to 8.5. In contrast, only three West and Central African countries have reached a TFR as high as 7, and several fall, or formerly fell, below 6.

Third, there is a marked area of low fertility in Central Africa, where TFRs have generally risen in recent years to more typical levels. This area includes all or parts of

Angola, Cameroon, the Central African Republic, Chad, Congo, Gabon, Sudan, Zaire, and Zambia and accounts for most of the east-west difference at the lower end of the range. Other pockets of low fertility occur along the East African coast, around the south and east of Lake Victoria, in southern and central Uganda, and in western Burkina Faso.

Fourth, in almost all Sub-Saharan African countries, there has been no documented fertility decline since World War II. In some countries, generally those of low fertility, fertility has risen, and in the rest there has been no change. The only documented exceptions are Botswana and Zimbabwe, though in others (notably Kenya) evidence is accumulating (from contraceptive prevalence surveys) that changes are under way. Even in Botswana and Zimbabwe, declines have so far been modest and fertility is still high. Although other developing continents all have pockets where fertility has not fallen, none have been so massively resistant to change as Sub-Saharan Africa.

These four features occur against a background of general variability in fertility that is even more marked at subnational levels. Total fertility rates may vary as much as from 5 to 8 within a single country by geographical region or ethnic grouping. Remarkably little is known about the factors underlying these patterns and differentials. There is much variation in Africa, as elsewhere, in marriage patterns (such as age at marriage, polygamy, and marital stability) and in customs of breastfeeding, postpartum abstinence, female circumcision, and so on, and probably much of the observed pattern of differences could be explained by these factors.

Two additional factors peculiar to Sub-Saharan Africa, however, are thought to account for the areas of low fertility and the general failure of African fertility to decline. The first is widespread venereal disease, which was probably the cause of the abnormally low fertility, with accompanying high levels of sterility, found in much of Central Africa (as well as in pockets elsewhere). It is thought to have been introduced by European and Arab colonizers and traders earlier in the century, and its effects had reached their peak by the 1950s and 1960s. In some of these areas as many as 40 percent of all women had been unable to give birth to even one live child during the whole course of their reproductive years. Since the 1960s, however, fertility has been rising in all the afflicted areas for which later data exist. This general rise can most plausibly be attributed to the increasing use of antibiotics, either through specific public health campaigns of antibiotic therapy directed against yaws or against venereal disease itself or through the general diffusion of modern medicines through both public and private channels.

The second special feature is the relative absence of

modern birth control methods in most Sub-Saharan populations, which is why the region has as yet experienced no widespread fertility decline. The only exceptions, Botswana and Zimbabwe, are also almost alone in possessing strong and effective family planning programs that have produced relatively high levels of modern contraceptive use (16 percent in Botswana and 27 percent in Zimbabwe by 1984). Kenya also has a growing program and a nonnegligible level of contraceptive use (15 percent in 1984), but recent fertility estimates are not yet available.

Elsewhere only a few countries have contraceptive prevalence rates of more than a few percentage points. Use is heavily concentrated among urban and better-educated women, and there has been little sign of strong demand among the rural majority or of significant impact of minority use upon national fertility levels. There are signs, however, that this situation is beginning to change.

Conventional socioeconomic differentials in Africa also exist. Variations by female education are usually quite marked. Women with some primary education typically report slightly higher fertility than those with no education at all, whereas women with secondary or higher education report substantially reduced fertility. There is some indication that this "primary-school bulge" may diminish or disappear as education becomes widespread. Variations between urban and rural residents are usually also found, generally with reduced fertility among urban women. Contraceptive prevalence is probably an important factor here. Differences by employment status of women are found but are generally ambiguous and not marked. The single safe generalization is that the educated, urbanized, westernized elite has reduced its fertility almost everywhere in Africa.

Age and Sex Structure

The age and sex structure of a population is the joint product of the forces of fertility, mortality, and migration. At the national level, fertility is usually the most powerful determinant of age structure, followed by the weaker influence of mortality. Only rarely is migration large and selective enough to make a significant impact on population structures.

Sex Ratios

Reported overall sex ratios (number of males per 100 females) present a very puzzling picture in much of Sub-Saharan Africa. They are generally below any reasonable value, given any likely range of values for the sex ratio at birth, sex differences in mortality, and known migration patterns.[9] They also fluctuate in unlikely ways between counts, particularly in census-survey or survey-census series. This phenomenon has so far escaped general notice or detailed study but probably results chiefly from sex-selective undercounting. Within the overall low range of sex ratios, however, the effects of migration are as expected, with magnet countries recording relatively high sex ratios (more than 100) during their periods of attraction and sending countries reporting low ratios during their periods of outflow.

Age Distributions

Owing to past high levels of fertility, Sub-Saharan African populations are extremely youthful. In most countries, children aged 0–15 years make up at least 45 percent of the total population; 15–20 percent are children under age five years. The exceptions are almost all countries where fertility is still below normal Sub-Saharan African levels, and even there the proportion of children is rarely less than 40 percent. This youthfulness has been increasing over time. In almost every census series, the proportion of children has risen monotonically over time; the few exceptions are from pairs of censuses of questionable comparability (such as those of Kenya between 1969 and 1979 or Botswana between 1964 and 1971) plus one case of recent fertility decline (Zimbabwe between 1969 and 1982). Part of this general "rejuvenation" may be due to improvements in the coverage of children, particularly infants, but much undoubtedly results from the general postwar mortality decline (normally greater in childhood than in adulthood at such mortality levels), coupled occasionally with a rise in fertility.

Natural Increase and Population Growth

The estimation of rates of natural increase and population growth is even more subject to doubt than estimation of fertility and mortality, being the combination of fertility and mortality estimates with recorded or smoothed age/sex data and migration estimates. Since all these components are uncertain, their products—the crude birth rate, the crude death rate, the crude migration rate, the rate of natural increase (CBR − CDR) and population growth rate (CBR − CDR plus or minus CMR)—are ever more unreliable.

Some broad generalizations are possible, however, on the basis of models. Countries of very high fertility (for example, Kenya, Malawi, and Rwanda) will normally have crude birth rates of about 50 or more; provided that life expectancy is more than 40 years, their natural increase will be more than 3 percent. A rate of less than 2.5 percent would be possible only with a life expectancy of less than 35 years. But a country of only moderate

fertility, such as Chad or Zaire, will normally have a crude birth rate of less than 45; then the rate of natural increase would reach 3 percent only if life expectancy were 50 years or more. Some West African countries that have either relatively low fertility or high mortality, or both, probably still have not yet attained a natural increase as high as 3 percent, whereas many East African countries must already have achieved rates well over 3 percent. Strong migration flows may introduce variations of (typically) as much as one point from these natural increase rates. Population growth rates for all of these countries are high by current world standards, however, and even those of the deveoping world, because the unique persistence of high fertility in Sub-Saharan Africa outweighs even the frequently high mortality.

Growth Prospects for the Future

In the near future, rates of natural increase are likely to rise still higher in much of West and Central Africa, as fertility rises and mortality falls further. Voluntary fertility control through modern family planning is unlikely to become a significant factor in such countries until populations are assured of normal fertility and childhood mortality has declined substantially. Some Central African countries, however, may be sufficiently affected by the AIDS epidemic to experience stagnation or even rises in mortality and hence no further increase or even a drop in natural increase rates. The trend in East Africa and the more advanced parts of West Africa is more difficult to forecast. Fertility declines through family planning in the near future are a real possibility in those countries where, as in Zimbabwe, mortality is already very low; there may thus be little further rise in rates of natural increases. In other countries, the effects of AIDS may nullify or reverse mortality declines, and stagnation or drops in natural increase may follow. In many nations, however, the beginning of fertility decline will be outweighed by continuing mortality declines, so that some further minor rises in natural increase occur.

These general trends may easily be slowed, interrupted, or even reversed by political upheavals, economic recessions, or natural disasters and will certainly be affected by changing patterns of migration. Overall, however, most of Sub-Saharan Africa will probably continue to experience high and increasing rates of population growth for some time to come.

Notes

1. The nearest approach to a complete vital registration system was in Zaire in the 1950s, with an estimated 80 percent

coverage of births and 50 percent of deaths (Brass and others 1968). The system lapsed after independence.

2. Examples are: Ghana (1960), where the PES returned a population total 10 percent lower than the census total; Nigeria (1962), where the PES enumerators often merely copied down the census figures; Malawi (1966), where the same teams of enumerators in the same areas were used for both census and PES. As a result of these bad experiences, many census organizers in Sub-Saharan Africa have not considered it worthwhile even to hold a PES.

3. Historical calendars are lists of notable local or national events over the past century, against which the respondent's birth or approximate age at the time can be checked.

4. Some of the immigration in the 1960s was undoubtedly refugee movement from Rwanda, Sudan, and Zaire but probably often for mixed motives, because economic migration had been habitual even in normal times.

5. The reports of the United Nations High Commissioner for Refugees are the only available statistical source for refugee flows but are not always accurate. They are incomplete and liable both to underestimate (because they are mostly based on counts at refugee camps, which may not contain all or even most of the refugees) and to overestimate (because host countries may inflate numbers for political reasons or to attract more funding).

6. This proportion was recently termed by UNICEF the "under-fives mortality rate."

7. South Africa and Namibia are not included in this analysis because of a lack of child survival data—indeed of any available large-scale survey or census demographic data. Evidence from other sources, however, indicates that the mortality of the black population of South Africa conforms to this general gradient and is rather similar to that of its neighbors, Lesotho and Swaziland. The national level is, of course, the lowest in Africa because of the European levels of childhood mortality enjoyed by the large white, Asian, and colored minorities.

8. Moreover, it is interesting to note indications of excep-

tionally high childhood mortality also in neighboring areas of Mozambique, Tanzania, and Zambia. In the ethnically and culturally similar Eastern Province of Zambia, for example, nearly 30 percent of children died before age five in the mid-1960s, compared with 20 percent for Zambia as a whole (Hill 1985 and 1986).

9. Burkina Faso is a striking exception to this pattern but presents an equally implausible tendency in the opposite direction. Despite known heavy, male-dominated emigration, the de facto population had a sex ratio of 100.6 in 1975.

References

Brass, William, and others, eds. 1968. *The Demography of Tropical Africa.* Princeton, N.J.: Princeton University Press.

Hill, Althea. 1985. "Demography of Malawi." PHN Technical Note 85-19. Population, Health, and Nutrition Department, World Bank, Washington, D.C.; processed.

———. 1986. "The Demography of Zambia." PHN Technical Note 86-20. Population, Health, and Nutrition Department, World Bank, Washington, D.C.; processed.

———. 1987. "Trends in Childhood Mortality in Sub-Saharan Mainland Africa." Paper presented to the Seminar on Mortality and Society, Yaoundé, October 19–23; processed.

Timaeus, Ian. 1987. "Adult Mortality in Sub-Saharan Africa." Paper prepared for "Disease and Mortality in Sub-Saharan Africa," a World Bank conference held at Tunbridge Wells, October 30 to November 3; processed.

United Nations Children's Fund (UNICEF). 1987. *The State of the World's Children, 1987.* New York.

World Bank. 1986. *World Development Report 1986.* New York: Oxford University Press.

———. 1987. *World Development Report 1987.* New York: Oxford University Press.

Part II

Economic Consequences of Rapid Population Growth

Focusing on critical linkages between population growth and the economy, the four chapters in part II support two key propositions.

- Sub-Saharan African countries face diverse situations. Some of them are already struggling with a considerable population burden; others could support larger populations than they now have.
- Regardless of their resource situations, these countries need time to introduce necessary institutional and technological changes—time denied to them, at present, by rapid population growth.

Whether the focus is on agriculture or energy, the labor force or the cities, these two propositions still apply.

Agriculture presents a dilemma, as Ho (chapter 2) argues: estimates of potential suggest that, in this relatively low-density area of the world, substantially larger populations could readily be supported in several countries; nevertheless some evidence exists that agricultural productivity is already declining because of population pressure. Declining yields suggest that adequate technological change has not been taking place in agriculture. Fundamental changes in economic organization—for example, in the markets for land and labor—must also occur. To keep pace with rapid population growth, these changes must also be rapid. Ho estimates that they must occur six times as fast as they have historically in other areas of the world. Increased pop-

ulation density may confer such benefits as opportunities for trade and specialization and economies of scale in infrastructure development, but the speed with which increased densities are being approached makes such apparent gains difficult to achieve.

Household energy means essentially wood fuels, the production of which must surmount obstacles somewhat more severe than those in agriculture, as Barnes (chapter 3) notes. Growing populations in urban areas require intensification of tree production, but this lags behind agricultural intensification. The complex reasons include low prices for wood fuels relative to those of agricultural products, inadequate institutional definitions of property rights in bushland and tropical forests, and lack of incentives to manage tree production. As a consequence, rings surrounding growing cities expand outward as available trees are harvested and are not replaced. Deforestation leads to significant problems, which, like soil erosion, may not attain significance for some time. The situation is far from uniform across the region, however: dense savanna areas may be affected, and arid areas are affected even more and are unlikely to recover in the short term, whereas some relatively unpopulated tropical forests are affected least. At the same time that they impose problems, high population densities could lead to efficiencies in the production of wood fuels: better land use practices, improved technologies, reformed land tenure systems, more efficient markets. Such changes take time, however, and rapid population growth severely limits the time available.

Given the uncertain outlook for agricultural growth, the prospects for absorbing the growing labor force in Sub-Saharan Africa are not bright. Agriculture still involves seven out of ten workers and will have to absorb the major proportion of new entrants into the labor force. Hansen (chapter 4) therefore also focuses on agriculture in considering labor force prospects. Among various steps that can promote agricultural employment are land redistribution, small-scale irrigation schemes and drainage of land, and more intensive farming that requires more labor inputs. Nevertheless, Hansen estimates that only one in four Sub-Saharan countries has the potential to absorb rural labor force increases in the next dozen years without significant changes in labor market policy. The industrial sector is not a realistic alternative because it is typically only 5 to 10 percent of the labor force and has shown a disturbing decline in its employment absorption capability. Much surplus labor will by default enter the informal sector, but this sector is already producing at subsistence levels. Hansen concludes that even the best policies leave prospects for labor absorption everywhere bleak twenty years or so down the road if population growth does not rapidly moderate.

The cities, presumably the most dynamic sections of African societies, bear a disproportionate share of the burdens of rapid population growth, as Montgomery and Brown (chapter 5) show. Where populations are growing by 3 percent or so a year, cities are growing at close to 5 percent, in part because rural areas lack economic opportunities. A range of cities of varying sizes are all growing, but primate cities are especially important and the source of the most concern. What

is to be done? Urban growth is not unrelievedly negative in its consequences: many economic benefits result from the clustering in cities of various firms, and individuals also benefit personally from urban residence. Nor have other countries had much success in limiting migration to urban areas. Therefore, accommodation to urban growth is necessary, in the form of policies that eliminate distortions, favor rational locational decisions, rely to an appropriate extent on private firms to provide important services, and provide public services in both efficient and equitable ways. An accommodationist policy at least has a better chance of success than attempts to close the cities, but it is difficult to implement, given weaknesses in urban public administration. One important complementary policy, therefore, is emphasis on reducing natural increase in urban areas. Because natural increase accounts for about as much urban growth in the region as migration, substantial benefits could flow from reduction in urban fertility—in Sub-Saharan Africa, unlike other regions, urban fertility is not substantially below rural fertility.

Other linkages between rapid population growth and economic development will not be considered in any detail here. The impact of population growth on savings, for instance, is a complex issue to which full justice cannot be done in this volume. It is difficult to demonstrate that there is a link, but it is clearly unlikely that population growth would facilitate savings. Similarly, the impact of population growth on social services is difficult to explore because of limited data and complicated relationships; service institutions tend to adapt to increasing clientele, and individuals tend to seek alternative private services. Nevertheless, rapid growth does seem to impair the ability of institutions to respond adequately to human resource needs.

2

Population Growth and Agricultural Productivity

Teresa J. Ho

The relationship between population growth and agricultural growth is well recognized. In developing countries where population is growing at high rates, agriculture is under pressure to expand more quickly in order to feed the growing population or to generate the income to buy food necessary to feed the growing population. This statement is especially true for many countries of Sub-Saharan Africa, where population is growing at unprecedented rates and where large proportions of the population depend on agriculture for their income. Unfortunately, agricultural growth in this region has been exceptionally slow, so that increasing numbers of people remain in poverty and in fact suffer from deteriorating living conditions.

Population growth can also have a more direct influence on agriculture through its effect on the productivity of labor in agriculture, the result either of economies of scale at the earlier stages of population growth or of diminishing marginal returns to labor at the later stages as the population's size starts to exert undue pressure on fixed land resources. Because of low population densities, it is commonly believed that only economies of scale are currently operating in Sub-Saharan Africa; diseconomies are not anticipated until much later. This assumption seems especially reasonable because only a very small proportion of potentially arable land is under cultivation in the region, and except in extreme cases such as Burundi, the Kenyan highlands, and Rwanda, agriculture is under little pressure to move to marginally productive lands.

This chapter explores the hypothesis that population growth is causing declines in agricultural productivity in Sub-Saharan Africa despite the presence of large, untapped land resources and offers two explanations. First, the distribution of population is not congruent with the distribution of natural resources; hence, large differences exist in the population-resource balance across the region, with a few countries already at critical stages. Second, agriculture in much of the region has not progressed to higher levels of technology, and thus the onset of diminishing returns may have occurred earlier than would otherwise be expected.

Population Growth, Carrying Capacity, and Agricultural Growth

Between 1970 and 1982, agricultural production in Sub-Saharan Africa grew at an average of 1.5 percent per year, a much lower rate than the average of 2.5 percent for all low-income countries combined and lower than that for Bangladesh (2.3 percent) and India (1.8 percent). During the same period, the region's population grew at 2.9 percent per year, almost twice as fast as agricultural production. As a consequence, per capita food production for 1980–82 was only 92 percent of the 1969–71 level, reflecting a deterioration in agricultural performance over the decade of the 1970s. The low-income countries fared especially badly, as food production per capita in 1980–82 was only 87 percent of the 1969–71 level. In Bangladesh, the lowest-income non-African country, the per capita production index was 94 percent (table 2-1).

Much of the failure of agriculture in Africa has been blamed on a public policy structure that fails to provide the right incentives for growth. In particular, tariff and exchange rate policies that discourage agricultural exports and encourage food imports have been cited (World Bank 1981). Beyond the effects of price and incentives policies, however, are other factors that would make growth in agriculture difficult even if countries "got the prices right." One such factor is the effect of population pressure on limited land resources and hence on agricultural productivity.

Table 2-1. *Basic Population and Agricultural Data*

| Area | Population mid-1982 (millions) | Population density per square kilometer, 1982 | Annual growth rates | | Ratio of agricultural to population growth, 1970–82 | Index of per capita food production 1970–82 (1969–71 = 100) |
			Population, 1970–82	Agricultural production, 1970–82		
Sub-Saharan Africa	375.9	17.6	2.9	1.5	0.5	92.2
Low income	212.7	16.4	2.9	1.4	0.5	87.4
Middle income	163.2	19.6	3.0	1.5	0.5	93.0
South Asia						
Bangladesh	92.9	645.1	2.6	2.3	0.9	94.0
India	717.0	218.1	2.3	1.8	0.8	101.0
All developing countries	3,425.5	47.5	2.2	2.9	1.3	113.4
Low income	2,267.2	78.3	2.0	2.5	1.3	113.2
Middle income	1,158.3	26.9	2.5	3.2	1.3	113.6

Source: World Bank 1984a.

Table 2-1 shows that Sub-Saharan Africa differs from other developing regions in both population and agriculture. Demographically, it is less dense and is growing faster than other regions; agriculturally, it is growing more slowly than other regions. As I will note later, its agricultural technology is far more primitive than that of most other regions. These factors suggest that development in Sub-Saharan Africa may not necessarily follow a course similar to that experienced by other regions that are now further along in the agricultural transition.

Over the last decade, agricultural productivity in Sub-Saharan Africa contrasted sharply with what might be expected of a region with large tracts of unused land and much potential. Recent Food and Agriculture Organization (FAO) estimates (Higgins and others 1982) of agricultural potential in different regions of the world give the best estimates to date of the magnitude of Africa's potential. The estimates were computed on the basis of expected production levels, given local soil and climatic conditions, and were made for three different levels of technology—low, intermediate, and high. These input levels were defined on the basis of eight attributes relating to production system, technology employed, power sources, labor intensity, and landholdings.[1]

According to the FAO's estimates, Africa is at or almost at the low level of technology. It is far behind other developing regions that have covered roughly one-third to one-half the distance to the intermediate level. In contrast, Western Europe is at the high input level.

Potential population-supporting capacities were estimated for 1975 and 2000, with differences between the two years reflecting expected increases in irrigation production from planned irrigation programs and decreases in agricultural land from expansion in nonagricultural use of land due to population growth. The calculations for Africa as a whole confirm the conventional wisdom: even at low input levels, enough land is available to allow food self-sufficiency for a population 2.7 times larger than the actual population in 1975. This multiple rises to 10.8 at intermediate input levels and to 31.6 at high levels (Higgins and others 1982).

Despite such large potential for the region as a whole, important intercountry differences exist in the population-resource balance. Figure 2-1 shows the potential population-supporting capacities for various countries. The largest agricultural potential is concentrated in the humid tropical countries of Central Africa, where population densities of 100 persons per square kilometer or more can be supported at low levels of input. Carrying capacities decline with distance from this area, though fairly high potential (50 to 100 persons per square kilometer) still exists in semihumid coastal West Africa and Central Africa. The countries with lowest potential are those in the Sahel, much of East Africa, and the dry zones in Southern Africa. The greatest anomaly in population distribution relative to potential is in the high potential areas of Central Africa, where the lowest population densities (fewer than ten persons per square kilometer) are found. In contrast, higher population concentrations are found in coastal West Africa, especially Nigeria, in the highlands of East Africa, and to a somewhat lesser extent in Ethiopia and Kenya.

The result of this disparity in population and resource distribution is wide variation among countries in population-resource balances. Table 2-2 classifies forty countries in the region into three groups according to present and projected population-resource balance at low input levels, which most closely approximate present input levels in Sub-Saharan Africa. Potential population-supporting capacities in 1982 were estimated by linear interpolation from the 1975 and 2000 FAO estimates. All countries in each group were then ranked according to severity of the population-resource balance, using the ratio of potential capacity to actual population in 1982 and 2000 for Groups 1 and 2, re-

Figure 2-1. *Potential Population-Supporting Capacity, 1982*

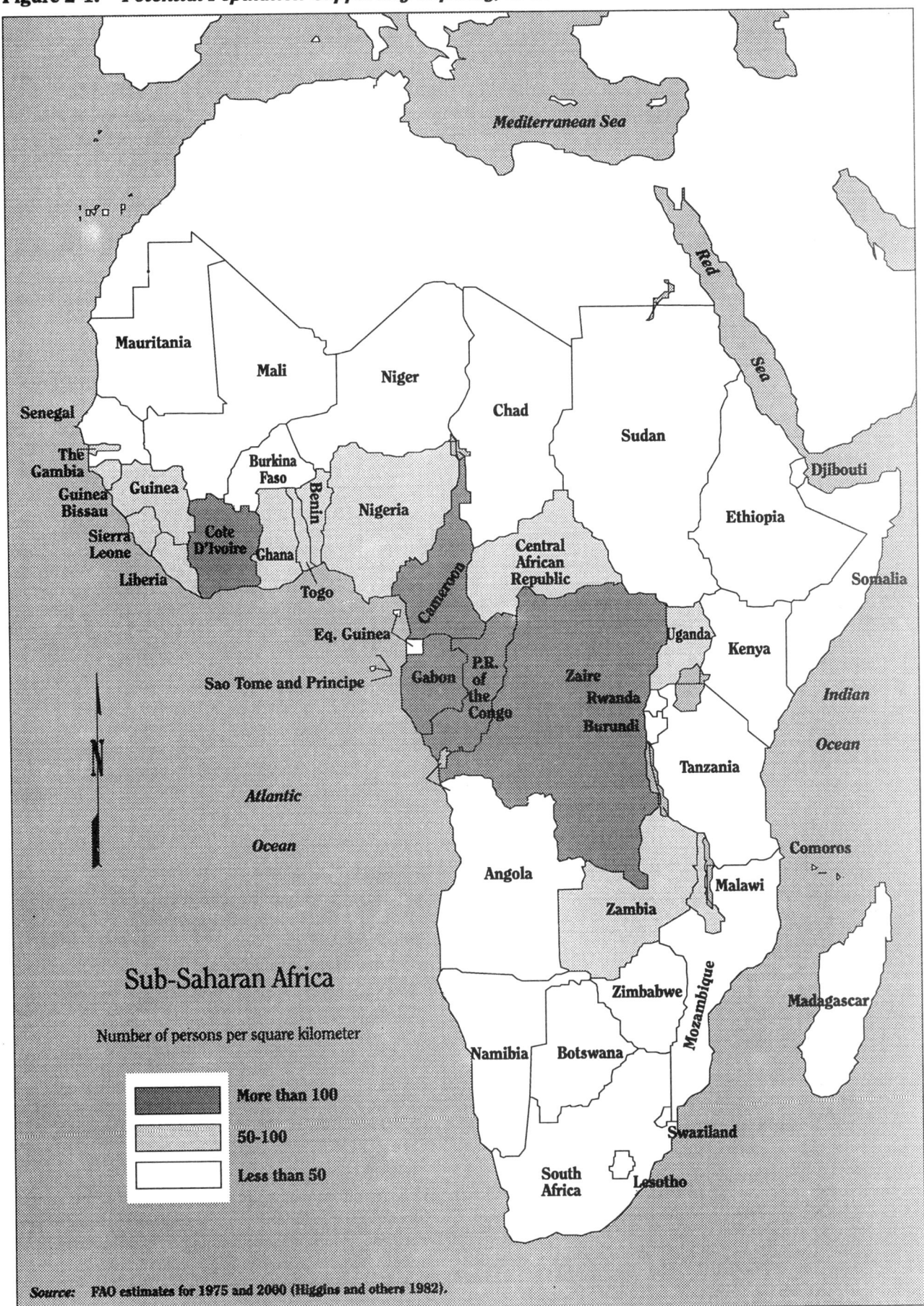

Sub-Saharan Africa

Number of persons per square kilometer

More than 100

50-100

Less than 50

Source: FAO estimates for 1975 and 2000 (Higgins and others 1982).

Table 2-2. *Sub-Saharan African Countries Ranked by Severity of Population-Resource Balance at Low Input Levels*

Group 1[a]		Group 2[b]		Group 3[c]	
Country	Ratio of potential to actual, 1982	Country	Ratio of potential to projected, 2000	Country	Year when capacity will be reached
Rwanda	0.1	Malawi	0.6	Tanzania	2003
Burundi	0.2	Swaziland	0.6	Sierra Leone	2005
Niger	0.2	Togo	0.8	Gambia	2008
Kenya	0.3	Zimbabwe	0.8	Mozambique	2011
Somalia	0.3	Benin	0.9	Côte d'Ivoire	2021
Lesotho	0.4	Ghana	0.9	Liberia	2025
Ethiopia	0.5	Mali	0.9	Guinea	2027
Mauritania	0.5			Sudan	2027
Namibia	0.6			Guinea-Bissau	2028
Nigeria	0.6			Chad	2035
Uganda	0.8			Madagascar	2048
Botswana	0.9			Zambia	2048
Senegal	0.9			Cameroon	2050
Burkina Faso	0.9			Zaire	2055
				Angola	2056
				Congo	2087
				Equatorial Guinea	2114
				Central African Republic	2115
				Gabon	2202

a. Actual 1982 population exceeded potential population-supporting capacity.
b. Projected 2000 population will exceed potential population supporting-capacity.
c. Potential population-supporting capacity will be reached after 2000 (assuming 1982 population growth rates and 2000 potential capacity).
Source: Author's estimates. Calculated from data in FAO (1982b) and World Bank (1984a).

spectively, and using the year in which capacity will be reached, given 1982 population growth rates and 2000 potential capacity, for Group 3.

Table 2-2 shows wide differences among the countries in population-resource balances. At one extreme are such countries as Burundi, Niger, and Rwanda, with potential population-supporting capacities only one- or two-tenths the actual size of their populations in 1982. At the other extreme are countries such as the Central African Republic, Equatorial Guinea, and Gabon, which will not reach potential even at low inputs for another one or two centuries.

Fourteen of the forty countries had populations that exceeded supporting capacity at low input levels in 1982; another seven will exceed supporting capacity by 2000. Hence, about one-half of all the countries can be said to have a precarious or critical population-resource balance. A surprising number of these countries (including Burundi, Kenya, Lesotho, Niger, Rwanda, and Somalia) have exceedingly low population-resource balance ratios of less than 0.5, which imply that they could support less than half their present populations, at internationally accepted levels of nutrition, on a continuing basis. Some of these countries have adjusted better than others to this intense pressure on the land. Kenya and Lesotho,

in particular, have progressed to more advanced levels of technology through increased use of fertilizers and increased mechanization (that is, tractor use) among other things. Somalia has also shifted to relatively more mechanized farming methods. Burundi, Rwanda, and Niger have been less able to purchase additional inputs, although the first two countries compensate to some extent by very extensive land use and cultivate the fertile but difficult to work marshes as well as steep slopes. In addition, labor-intensive soil conservation measures (mulching, contour ditching, and so forth) were prevalent in Burundi and Rwanda in the past and are still important factors, although they are becoming less so at present (Jones and Egli 1984). To the extent that their foreign exchange positions permit, these countries rely on food imports to fill the remaining gap. Lesotho and Somalia, for example, are highly dependent on food imports (seventy-nine and ninety metric tons per thousand population, respectively, compared with an average of twelve for all low-income countries, excluding China and India).

In all these countries with exceptionally poor population-resource balance ratios, but particularly in those countries that are less able to adjust to critical land resource constraints through increased inputs and improved cultivation practices, extensive soil mining is bringing the margin of threatened survival closer.

The remaining nineteen Group 3 countries are relatively better off than those in Groups 1 and 2, although the populations of four of them (Gambia, Mozambique, Sierra Leone, and Tanzania) will reach capacity at low input levels in fewer than thirty years. This grace period could be longer if they achieve widespread agricultural transformation within the next twenty years. It could be shorter, however, if not all potential agricultural land can be taken under cultivation within the same period, as in fact seems likely. In Mozambique, for example, only 5 percent of potential agricultural land was under cultivation in 1981, and in Tanzania only 6 percent was covered. The situation was a bit less dramatic in Sierra Leone and the Gambia, where 29 percent and 42 percent, respectively, of potential agricultural land was under cultivation.[2] Nevertheless, given present rates of expansion in land used for agriculture of less than 1.5 percent per year in these countries, it is not likely that complete coverage will be achieved in any of them within that short period.

Most of the untapped land resources of Sub-Saharan Africa are, in fact, concentrated within Group 3 countries. For these countries, growth in agriculture depends largely on the rate at which expansion into new lands can occur. Consisting mostly of dense tropical forest lands, much of the unopened lands are the region's most fertile but also the most difficult to clear. In addition, they are plagued with tropical diseases such as malaria, trypanosomiasis (both human and animal forms), and onchocerciasis (Wawer 1984). Spontaneous movement of human populations into these areas has been slow and, although likely to accelerate with increasing population, may not expand quickly enough to compensate for the expected pressures on land in more dense areas caused also by rapid population growth. It may become increasingly necessary for governments to help accelerate expansion by providing the large investments in infrastructure (including transportation and health services) needed in these areas.

Table 2-3 suggests that these differences in population-resource balance lead to differences in agricultural output. For purposes of this table, Group 3 countries have been split into two subgroups: countries whose population will exceed potential by 2030 (Group 3a, with nine countries) and countries whose population will not exceed potential by 2030 (Group 3b, with ten countries).

Except for the last group, growth in agricultural production increases sharply as the population-resource balance improves: from an average of 1.1 percent per year for Group 1, to 2.2 percent for Group 2, to 3.5 percent for Group 3a. There is then a sudden drop in average growth rate to 1.5 percent for the last set of countries, Group 3b. It is reasonable to hypothesize that

Table 2-3. *Average Annual Growth Rates of Agricultural Production, by Severity of Population-Resource Balance*

Population-resource balance group	Agricultural growth rate
Group 1: Countries whose actual 1982 population exceeded potential population-supporting capacity	1.1
Group 2: Countries whose projected 2000 population will exceed potential population-supporting capacity	2.2
Group 3a: Countries whose projected 2030 population will exceed potential population-supporting capacity	3.5
Group 3b: Countries whose projected 2030 population will not exceed potential population-supporting capacity (including Angola, Cameroon, Central African Republic, Chad, Congo, Equatorial Guinea, Gabon, Madagascar, Zaire and Zambia)	1.5

Source: Author's estimates. Based on data on agricultural growth in World Bank (1984a).

some economies of scale remain to be achieved through continued population growth in this last group of countries. For the first three groups, however, the implication is that agricultural growth is already slowing down in areas with limited land resources.

Figure 2-2 illustrates the same results graphically using simple averages, by group, of population-resource balance ratios and agricultural growth rates. Read from right to left, the graph reflects a pattern consistent with the hypothesis of marginal returns to labor that first increase and then decrease and are reflected in increasing and then decreasing rates of growth of agricultural output.

The above data, though based on cross-country comparisons, could also reflect regional differences within countries, particularly within the larger ones that span several soil and climatic zones. Sudan, for example, which has vast unused agricultural potential and would not reach its potential supporting capacity at low input levels until 2027, has marked regional differences, with some areas having a poor population-resource balance and others having much excess capacity. The extreme north of Sudan is desert and supports almost no population. North-central Sudan is sparsely populated, like most of the rest of the country. Because of its dry climate and sandy soils, however, this region has begun to experience declining soil fertility. Eastern Sudan is also a low rainfall area and was producing very low yields until the large-scale irrigation schemes were introduced in the area. Population-supporting capacity has increased considerably in the irrigation scheme areas, as

Figure 2-2. *Population-Resource Balance and Agricultural Output*

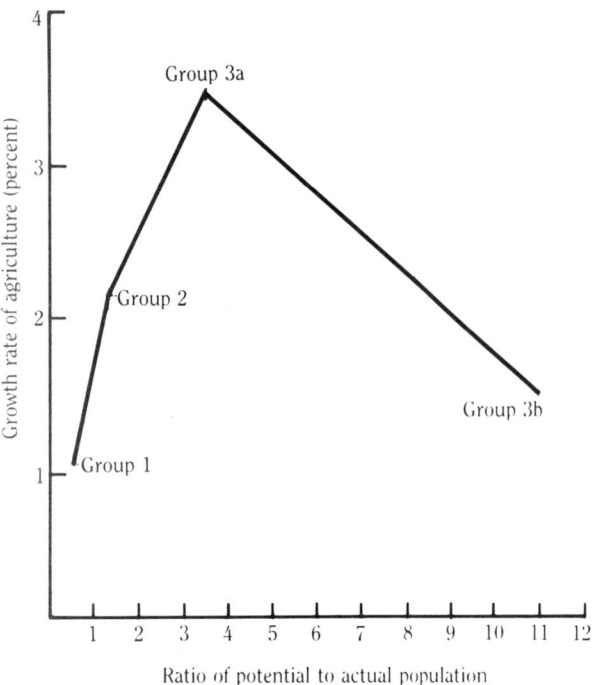

Growth rate of agriculture (percent)

Group 3a

Group 3b

Group 2

Group 1

Ratio of potential to actual population

Source: Tables 2-2 and 2-3.

have actual population densities, which are higher than the rest of the country, but the nonscheme areas in eastern Sudan remain low potential areas. In contrast, south-central and southern Sudan have adequate rainfall and rich soils. Central Sudan has higher densities relative to the rest of the country, consistent with its potential. Southern Sudan, the area with the greatest long-term potential, remains largely untapped and underpopulated. With the appropriate investments in land development and transportation, this region could support much larger populations (Barnes 1985).

Similar regional differences would also be of concern in countries such as Cameroon, Kenya, Nigeria, and Tanzania and should be considered in any country-level analysis of the problems discussed above.

Population Growth, Technological Change, and Agricultural Growth

The FAO estimates of carrying capacity discussed above show that a fourfold increase in carrying capacity could result if agriculture in Sub-Saharan Africa were to shift from low to intermediate levels of technology. As table 2-4 indicates, half of the Group 1 countries discussed in the previous section would have had excess capacity

in 1982 had they been at technology levels equivalent to those found in Asia today, which is at 46 percent of the difference between low and intermediate levels. Clearly, advances in agricultural technology could improve agricultural performance in the region by relieving the pressures on land resources caused by population growth. But is this technological advance occurring quickly enough in Sub-Saharan Africa to offset population pressure? What happens to productivity as population grows if technology does not advance appropriately?

To answer these questions, it is necessary to understand the intimate relationship between population growth and the evolution of farming systems. On the one hand, population growth generates changes in the agricultural ecology that could lead to declines in agricultural productivity. On the other, these same pres-

Table 2-4. *Changes in Population-Resource Balance with Improvements in Technology, Countries in Groups 1 and 2*

Country	Ratio of potential to actual population, 1982		
	Low inputs	Inputs at present Asian levels	Intermediate inputs
Group 1[a]			
Rwanda	0.1	0.33	0.6
Burundi	0.2	0.57	1.0
Niger	0.2	0.34	0.5
Kenya	0.3	0.48	0.7
Somalia	0.3	0.44	0.6
Lesotho	0.4	0.68	1.0
Ethiopia	0.5	1.24	2.1
Maruitania	0.5	0.91	1.4
Namibia	0.6	1.20	1.9
Nigeria	0.6	1.43	2.4
Uganda	0.8	1.90	3.2
Botswana	0.9	2.69	4.8
Senegal	0.9	2.05	3.4
Burkina Faso	0.9	2.37	4.1
Group 2[b]			
Malawi	1.1	2.30	3.7
Swaziland	1.1	2.94	5.1
Togo	1.4	3.75	6.5
Zimbabwe	1.5	3.85	6.6
Benin	1.7	4.41	7.6
Ghana	1.7	4.28	7.3
Mali	1.3	3.00	5.0

Note: Asian levels are assumed to be 46 percent of the difference between low and intermediate levels.

a. Countries whose actual 1982 population exceeded potential population-supporting capacity.

b. Countries whose projected 2000 population will exceed potential population-supporting capacity.

Source: Author's estimates. Calculated from data in FAO (1982b) and World Bank (1984a).

sures on land resources stimulate the development and spread of new technology that could prevent productivity declines. The answer lies in the outcome of this race between ecological degradation and technological advance—both related to population growth.

Population Growth, Farming Intensity, and Soil Fertility

Historical and cross-regional comparisons of food supply systems show that the evolution of agriculture from the earliest stage of hunting and gathering to the most intensive stage of multiple cropping is determined principally by increases in population density (Boserup 1965, 1981; Pingali and Binswanger 1984a; Ruthenberg 1980). Before agriculture replaced hunting and gathering as man's principal economic activity, much more of the earth's land area was covered with forests than at present. With the introduction of agriculture, some of the forest area was cleared for crop cultivation. The agricultural method most appropriate at such low population densities is a system of forest fallow, where land that has been cleared is planted for one or two years and is then abandoned to allow regrowth while cultivation proceeds in another part of the forest. At times, the original forest area is not replanted for an entire generation.

As population increases over time, however, there is a gradual shortening of the period of fallow between croppings, so that forest density is reduced and larger trees are replaced by bush and smaller growth and, subsequently, by grasses. Eventually, fallows disappear, and further increases in population density lead to conversion of larger and larger areas to permanent cropland and then, as in many parts of the developing world, to multicropped land producing as many as three crops in one calendar year.

A number of factors other than population density affect progress through the agricultural transition, the most important of which are the climatic and soil characteristics of the local area. In the humid climatic zones, leaching and water erosion could rapidly degrade soil quality as agriculture evolves into more intensive farming systems. Agriculture in much of Central Africa, for example, which is still predominantly forest or bush fallow, could not undergo transition to more intensive food cropping systems in the absence of technological development to maintain soil fertility. No such technology is available at present for this type of ecology. Historically, the response to increases in population density in these areas has been a shift to tree crop production or expansion to new lands (or out-migration). Arid areas such as the marginal zones of the Sahara and the low-rainfall, semiarid regions of East or

Southern Africa cannot advance much beyond marginal crop production and will support only pastoral systems of food production, supplemented occasionally by cultivation when the rains permit (Ruthenberg 1980). On the other hand, more fertile lowland areas are often left uncultivated until later in the transition because of difficulties of preparing the heavy soils and controlling water and drainage. It is in the semiarid, semihumid, and high altitude zones, where more intensive farming systems are feasible and potentially productive, that the transition process usually takes place in full.

The shorter fallow period that marks the agricultural transition alters not only the vegetation but also soil characteristics. The disappearance of the forest cover to provide material for soil regeneration, the shorter period in which such regeneration could occur, and increased leaching (in humid areas), soil erosion, and dessication (in less humid or arid areas) resulting from the reduced vegetative cover all reduce soil fertility even before fallow periods decline to zero years. This reduction in soil fertility as fallow periods decline in response to increased population density lies at the heart of the relationship between population growth and soil productivity.

Evidence exists to show that parts of Africa are experiencing just such declines in soil fertility as fallow periods decline. In eastern Nigeria, for example, maize yields are two tons in areas of long fallow, slightly over one ton as the length of the cropping period approaches that of the fallow period, and less than a ton when the cropping period begins to exceed the fallow period (Ruthenberg 1980). In Sierra Leone (FAO 1980) a nationwide sample of 562 farmers with a mean length of fallow of 8.8 years was asked to compare yields in the past and the present. Sixty-seven percent of the sample reported that yields were higher in the past than at present, 19 percent reported comparable yields, and 14 percent reported yields lower in the past. It is difficult to explain the reported decline in yields other than through a decline in soil fertility resulting from shorter fallow periods.

Results from four farming system studies from different regions of Sudan (Barnes 1985) show how the relationship between changing fallows and changing yields will vary, depending on soil and climatic conditions. In the northern Kordofan, which has a dry climate and sandy soil, fallow periods of four to ten years (with 37 percent of arable land cultivated) are not long enough to maintain soil fertility, and yield declines are common. Richer soils and better rainfall in the Nuba Mountain area in southern Kordofan permit shorter fallow periods of two to four years without yield declines. Fallows are much longer in the sparsely populated areas of southern Sudan, and no fallow declines are reported for grain crops; hence, yields remain high. In the White

Nile Province of eastern Sudan, where the large-scale irrigation projects are located, both fallows and yields are declining in the traditional (nonirrigated) areas where farming must rely on very little rainfall. These examples illustrate how the threshold levels of farming intensity (that is, the points at which yields start to decline) could differ in different ecologies.

Farming Intensity, Technological Change, and Labor Productivity

Farmers have responded in different ways to declining soil fertility caused by more intensive use of land: they use more of the inputs already in use, such as labor; they replace old inputs with better ones, for example switching from the hoe to the plow at the bush fallow or the short fallow stage; they introduce new inputs, such as new seeds and fertilizers (organic fertilizers in the earlier stages and chemical fertilizers later on); and they combine their inputs in different ways.[3] The response varies, depending on soil and climatic conditions affecting input effectiveness; on farmers' knowledge about various inputs, and on physical and financial accessibility of the inputs. Of all the options, an increase in labor inputs is a universal response; as numerous farm studies in Sub-Saharan Africa have shown, none of the others necessarily follows immediately.

Replacement of the hoe with the plow would improve labor efficiency and restore soil fertility through better land preparation. Decreasing labor productivity, however, does not immediately lead to a shift from the hoe to the plow. This shift reflects an economic decision based on expected returns to investment rather than on technological considerations alone. The farmer must conclude that the expected gains in yield and in reduced work effort would more than offset the cost of acquiring and maintaining a plow and draft animals, and he must have access to the capital needed to acquire the new technology.

Table 2-5 shows the changes in labor time per hectare required when farming intensity increases without a change in technique. All four cases presented involved the hoe as the main tool for land preparation and cultivation; fertilizer was not used in any of the cases. Despite a 64 percent difference in labor input per hectare between the Liberia and Côte d'Ivoire examples, output per work-hour increases by only 10 percent (from 1.26 to 1.38). Continued increases in labor input in the more intensive systems are not sufficient even to maintain output per work-hour; output declines to 1.03 and then to 0.48 with greater farming intensity.

Regressions on a sample of twenty-one rice- and maize-growing farms in Sub-Saharan Africa show a significant reduction (at 5 percent level of significance) in output per work-hour with increasing farming intensity, given no change in technique. All farms in this sample used the hoe as farm implement, and farming intensity ranged from $R = 20$ to $R = 111$.[4] The estimated elasticity of output per work-hour with respect to farming intensity was 0.5.[5] In contrast, results from a separate set of regressions on fifty-two farms (in several developing countries) that included hoe, animal traction, and tractor users did not yield a significant coefficient for farming intensity when the mechanization variable was included in the equation (Pingali and Binswanger 1984a). Increased farming intensity apparently leads to reduced labor productivity in the absence of a change in technique; the loss in productivity can be reversed by a shift from the hoe to the plow or tractor.

Table 2-5. *Examples of Labor Use with Changing Farming Intensity*
(hours per hectare)

Item	Country, region, and intensity of farming[a]			
	Liberia, Gbanga, 11	*Côte d'Ivoire, Man, 24*	*Ghana, Begora, 40*	*Cameroon, Bamunka, 100*
Land clearing	418.4	300.8	665	—
Land preparation	—	—	—	714
Sowing and planting	107.2	142.4	207	536.8
Fertilizing and manuring	—	—	—	—
Weeding	36.8	292	276.8	113
Plant protection	44	222	—	1,393
Harvesting	164	218.4	280	264
Threshing		84		280
Total	770	1,260	1,429	3,301

—Data not available.
a. Farming intensity is measured by the percentage of time in a rotation cycle that a plot of land is devoted to cropping.
Source: Pingali and Binswanger (1984a).

Figure 2-3. *Population Growth, Technological Change, and Agricultural Productivity*

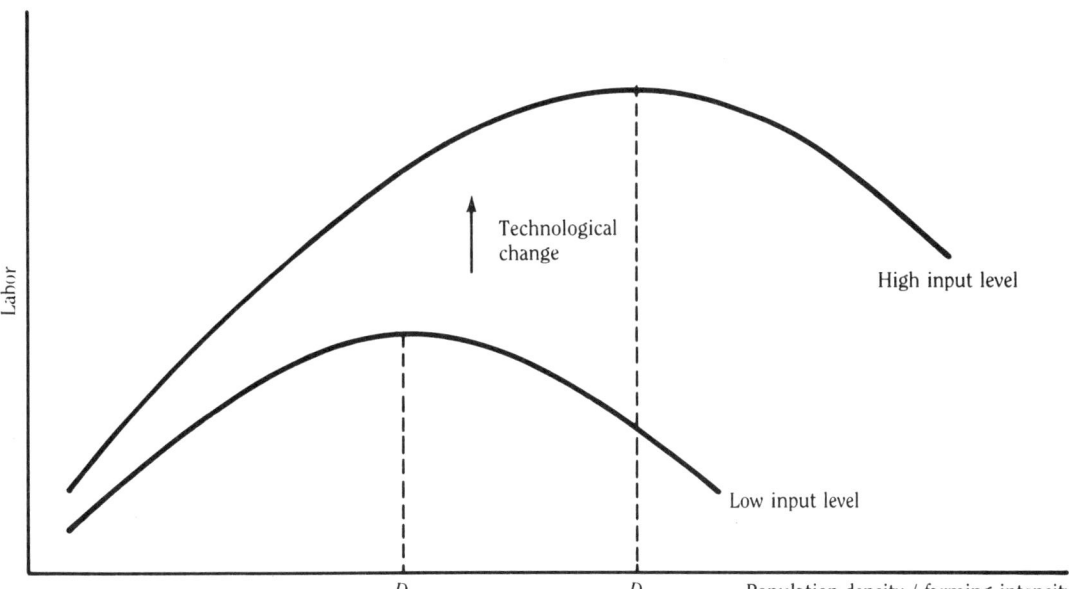

Thus population pressure on land resources may be causing declines in the region's agricultural productivity, even at this early stage of the agricultural transition. Increased population density leads to increased farming intensity, which, in turn, leads to declining soil fertility. Simply increasing labor inputs to compensate for declining soil fertility may not be sufficient. If changes in technology are not introduced (for example, increased fertilizer use or a shift from the hoe to the plow or other more efficient power sources), agricultural productivity could decline. Changes in technology could fend off declines in productivity if technological change occurs quickly enough to offset the effects of increased population density. Evidence of declining yields, however, suggests that the necessary technological changes have not been occurring in countries of Sub-Saharan Africa.

Figure 2-3 illustrates this hypothesized relationship among population growth, technological change, and agricultural productivity. At low levels of input, the marginal product of labor starts to decline at point D_1. At higher input levels, the point of diminishing returns occurs later, at a higher population density D_2. Outward movement along the horizontal axis (that is, increasing population density) to any point beyond D_1 accelerates the decline in productivity. Movement from a lower curve to a higher one (that is, improvement in technology) delays the decline. Hence agricultural development depends ultimately on the relative rates of growth of population and technological change.

It is appropriate here to draw attention to the positive contributions that population growth can make to agricultural productivity. Two important benefits are the economies of scale enjoyed at the early stages of the transition, particularly with respect to infrastructure development, and the opening of new markets that motivate surplus production and output maximization by allowing specialization and trade.

During the stages of forest and bush fallow, the population generally moves through a large area of land during a single agricultural cycle without setting up permanent domiciles in any specific place. With shortening fallow periods, permanent settlements become more practical, and populations develop not only permanent domiciles but also higher levels of social and physical organization. At this point, investments in transportation and communication facilities as well as storage and processing facilities, all of which contribute to improved productivity, become more economic as the population grows. Investments in social infrastructure, such as health, housing, and education, which improve the quality of the human resources and the quality of life, likewise become more economic with a growing population. In areas where endemic diseases such as malaria or tsetse fly infestation would otherwise discourage settlement, and therefore the use of new land, eradication efforts become economic when large enough populations are subsequently able to settle in these areas. Such positive contributions to productivity occur only in the early stages of population growth, however, and eventually become insignificant, as illustrated in figure 2-3. But as noted above, about one-fourth of Sub-Saharan African countries studied (Group 3b countries in table 2-5) may stand to gain from increased population density.

Equally critical as economies of scale in infrastructure development, if not more so, is the influence that increased population density has on opportunities for trade and specialization. When population groups are relatively isolated, agricultural production is almost exclusively for subsistence purposes. As long as enough is produced to satisfy the group's food and related needs, there is little incentive to expand production. Increased population density facilitates opportunities for trade and specialization, stimulates surplus production, and hence encourages more efficient production. The development of markets and the additional income earned from surplus production allow greater access to new inputs and technologies, thus also increasing productivity, but large-scale capital investment is required to produce these effects.

Effects of Population Growth on Technological Change

The same factor that causes declines in labor productivity—that is, population pressure on limited land resources—leads also to spontaneous changes in agricultural technology that work to offset the initial productivity declines. Boserup (1965) has documented this relationship between population growth and agricultural technology from historical experience in other regions and from cross-sectional comparisons in Sub-Saharan Africa. She has shown that fertilizers and the plow were spontaneously introduced to compensate for declining soil fertility and increased labor requirements in regions (for example, Western Europe) that passed this stage of the transition centuries ago, and she suggests that the same changes should occur in Africa as it goes through this same stage.

In fact, spontaneous change in technology stimulated by population growth is occurring in Sub-Saharan Africa. In much of the region, fertilizer use is increasing, and cultivators are shifting gradually from the hoe to the plow where the latter is available and appropriate. The more relevant issue, however, is whether the change will happen quickly enough to offset the negative effects of population growth on productivity, given present high rates of fertility. The answer to this question is not immediately obvious, but it is possible to speculate on it by looking more closely at the nature of the changes that need to occur and by examining the region's particular situation relative to the historical experience of other regions.

The technological changes that occur at this stage involve not only increased use of inputs but also fundamental changes in economic organization, particularly with respect to the development of markets for both new and old inputs. New or additional tools (plows), draft animals, and fertilizers must be brought in from external markets. Even more important are the changes occurring in markets for the traditional inputs, land and labor: during the transition, communal rights to land must eventually give way to individual ownership as farmland becomes scarce. The early usufructuary system, which still predominates in much of Sub-Saharan Africa, usually exists without a codified set of laws governing ownership. Gradually, a private market in land develops, and pressures on central governments to codify land laws arise. The inevitable conflicts involved in the transition from communal to private ownership give rise to insecurity about land rights, which is a major constraint on agricultural investment in the region. The institutional and social changes involved in this transition will not come easily or quickly.

Fundamental changes are occurrinng in the labor market as well. As agriculture becomes more intensive, particularly during the late bush fallow or short fallow stages, a growing tendency toward sharp seasonal peaks at critical points in a crop cycle emerges. In drier climates, the short period available for land preparation and sowing creates a peak in labor demand; in more humid climates, the peak occurs during harvesting, which must be done quickly to avoid destruction by humidity. At this stage, markets for nonfamily farm labor also start to develop.

Periods of excess labor demand, particularly with short fallow or annual cultivation systems, occur during only a few weeks in the year. Much less field labor is needed during the rest of the growing period, and demand can come to a virtual halt at other times of the year. Thus, despite the high returns to labor during peak periods, average returns to agricultural labor over a year may remain too low to keep workers, otherwise needed during the peaks, from moving out of agriculture altogether. This situation will not be corrected by additions to the agricultural labor force that result from population growth. Access to tools and machines to temper shortages during peak periods, availability of rural-based employment possibilities during the off season, and general improvements in technology to maintain labor productivity in agriculture are more rational alternatives.

Labor shortages in agriculture are even better understood in the light of changing economic opportunities in sectors other than agriculture. The appeal of higher wages in mining and industry as well as in a generally overextended government sector draws labor away from agriculture. As a result of this competition, wage demands by the small hired labor force in agriculture during peak seasons rise to levels far in excess of the average return to agricultural labor and are often simply unaffordable for farmers. Hence, even as labor markets start to develop in response to the emergence of peak periods of demand in the crop cycle, wage demands generally make hired labor inaccessible to most farmers.

The necessary adjustments in the various input markets are likely to take place in time, as they did in other regions of the world. But Sub-Saharan Africa, the last major region in the world to pass through the forest and bush fallow stages of the agricultural transition, faces an unprecedented growth rate of 3 percent. At the time of the transition in the rest of the Old World, by comparison, population was growing at a much slower pace than it is growing in Sub-Saharan Africa today. Until the eighteenth century, the world population was growing at no more than 0.5 percent per year, increasing to about 1 percent per year by the first half of the twentieth century (United Nations 1973).

Sub-Saharan Africa's rapid population growth means that the pressure on agriculture is much more intense than in the historical experience of other parts of the world. One-sixth as much time is available for the technological, attitudinal, organizational, and economic changes that must take place if drastic declines in current agricultural productivity and permanent damage to long-term agricultural potential are to be avoided. This difference in time horizon, brought about by much higher population growth rates, distinguishes the Sub-Saharan African experience from the already completed experiences of other parts of the world and threatens its successful transition from traditional to modern agriculture. For this reason, too, the population-related problems in the region's agriculture could arise not only in areas where population *size* is large relative to potential but also in those areas where population *growth rates* are too high to allow the necessary concurrent technological change.

Conclusions

Sub-Saharan Africa remains one of the least densely populated areas of the world. It has immense potential for increasing agricultural output through extension of agriculture to uncultivated areas; through intensification of land use in areas where fallow systems of agriculture prevail; and through advancements in agricultural technology, which at present consist mainly of primitive slash-and-burn and hoe cultivation techniques. Yet per capita production in agriculture has been declining, with agricultural growth rates remaining significantly below the average for all other regions and population growth rates among the highest in the world.

The promise of great potential has not eliminated short- and medium-term shortcomings in the region's agriculture. The problems of agriculture in Sub-Saharan Africa can be attributed, at least in part, to population pressures on land, despite the presence of vast areas of unused agricultural land. The distribution of population is not congruent with the distribution of natural resources, and African agriculture has not progressed quickly enough beyond simple technologies to forestall reductions in the marginal productivity of labor and land resulting from declining fallow periods.

Even at the present low input levels found in the region, enough land is available to support a population 2.7 times larger than the actual population in 1975. A closer look at individual countries, however, shows a wide variation in the population-resource balance. The rate of growth in agriculture among these countries was found to increase as the population-resource balance improved but to decline sharply in the least densely populated countries where productivity gains from economies of scale could still be attained.

About half the countries exceed, or will exceed by the year 2000, their potential population-carrying capacity at prevailing low input levels. For these countries population growth should immediately be curtailed until significant advances in technology are attained. For another one-fourth of the countries, enough excess capacity remains to allow satisfactory rates of agricultural growth at present, but if current population growth rates persist carrying capacity will be exceeded by 2030. For these countries, moderated population growth rates along with population redistribution programs to support spontaneous movements would maintain agricultural growth rates at the highest possible levels while allowing time for the necessary advancement in agricultural technology. For the last group of countries, which are sparsely populated, current high population growth rates may actually accelerate progress in agriculture, but maintenance of such growth rates can be justified only if present low levels of health, education, and other aspects of the quality of life can be raised as the population grows.

Much of the population-resource imbalance in Sub-Saharan Africa could be eliminated if the agriculture sector advanced to improved agricultural techniques. Studies by Boserup and others of the historical experience in other regions of the world suggest that population growth and its attendant increase in population density inevitably lead to higher levels of technology. Increased density leads to intensification of land use in agriculture (mainly through shortening of the fallow period between crops), which, in turn, leads to soil degradation and to conditions favorable to changes in technology, such as a shift from the hoe to the plow, increased use of fertilizers, and increased labor input.

The change in technology reverses the tendency toward declining yields that would occur otherwise with soil degradation. With shorter fallow periods, larger expanses of land are brought under cultivation, and if yields are maintained, total output increases. Under this scenario, increases in population density result endogenously in increased yield, thus providing a built-in mechanism for maintenance, if not improvement, of per capita output levels.

In Sub-Saharan Africa, however, where population is growing at an unprecedented 3 percent a year—a rate far higher than that of other regions that completed the agricultural transition a century or more ago—there are indications that increases in farming intensity are occurring without the expected technological change and, as a result, that yields are declining in some areas where fallows have shortened below the minimum threshold required for maintaining soil fertility.

In addition to the obvious acquisition and learning costs involved in a change in technology, other fundamental changes are necessary for successful technological advance at this particular stage in the agricultural transition. These include organizational changes in land tenancy arrangements and labor use and the development of markets for new inputs (such as fertilizers, plows, and draft animals) as well as old inputs that are now becoming scarce (that is, land and labor). These changes are in fact occurring but apparently not quickly enough to offset the decreasing productivity resulting from rapid intensification of land use, a direct consequence of rapid population growth.

Stronger evidence is needed to determine that declining yields are, in fact, caused by the shorter fallow periods and the slow advance in technology; to establish a consistent pattern over a wide range of cases; and to quantify the effects of population growth on agricultural growth in order to determine how important it is relative to other factors. Such evidence can be obtained through a closer study of population density and growth data along with data on farming intensity, prevailing technology, land and labor market conditions, and agriculture sector policy for specific locations in the region. Pending the availability of country case studies of this sort, the evidence of unprecedented population growth rates in Sub-Saharan Africa, increasingly intensified land use, and declining yields present a prima facie case in support of the argument that population growth is having deleterious effects on agriculture in Africa.

Useful policy suggestions can be made for both the population and the agriculture sectors on the basis of the tentative evidence presented here. The first and most important recommendation is the initiation of a conscious policy on population control, particularly in (but not limited to) those countries where population-

resource balances have reached or are approaching critical levels. There is a need to establish a capacity to understand the dynamics of population growth and population movements within these countries and their effects on agriculture and other development sectors, and a need to provide and promote family planning services for effective reduction in population growth. Recognizing that population control may be an important factor in the success of their own programs, agriculture planners would do well to be informed on the consequences of population growth for agricultural development and to support actively any plans for an organized population control program.

In all countries, whether or not they have reached critical population-resource balance levels, closer attention to population distribution issues is needed. This statement is especially true for countries with wide regional differences in carrying capacities in population densities. To the extent possible, any population redistribution program should try to facilitate movements that would, in any case, occur spontaneously (usually on a self-selected basis) rather than to uproot large groups of people and transplant them in a totally new place with perhaps a totally new agricultural environment. Population redistribution programs are generally difficult to implement because they require multisectoral cooperation, including participation from the agriculture, transport, and social sectors. In many countries, however, they may be the key to improvements in living standards, and even to the survival, of large segments of the population.

Finally, a conscious effort can be made to target both population control and agricultural assistance programs in those areas where the population-resource balance is most threatened. In both sectors, public programs that provide the appropriate technological knowhow through extension services and support the efficient provision of the necessary supplies are recommended. Cooperation and coordination between the sectors both in the identification of target areas and in service delivery would be ideal.

Notes

1. A low input level uses rain-fed cultivation of a traditional mixture of crops, local cultivars and no fertilizer or chemical control of pests and no long-term soil conservation measures, manual labor with hand tools, high labor intensity, low capital intensity, subsistence production, and fragmented landholdings and does not require access to markets. High-input technology, in comparison, involves rain-fed cultivation of an optimum mixture of crops; optimum fertilizer applications, chemical control of pests, weeds, and disease, and complete conservation measures; complete mechanization, including harvesting; low labor intensity; high capital intensity; com-

mercial production; and consolidated landholdings and requires access to markets.

2. Potential agricultural land includes all land currently under cultivation or planted to tree crops plus permanent meadows and pastures plus forest and woodland. Better land use data are needed for a more correct picture of the size of potential agricultural land, the extent to which it is currently under use, and the relative productive capacities of the unused portions of the land. The data used here (FAO 1982b) give only rough estimates of land use and insufficient information on land quality.

3. The use of the term "intensity" in this context (and in much of the farming systems literature cited in this chapter) differs slightly from the use of the term in the more standard agriculture development literature. In the latter, the term "intensive farming" is used in reference to the increased use of inputs on a given piece of land or the multiple cropping of a piece of land in order to increase output. Intensive farming is usually contrasted with "extensive farming," which covers larger land areas (that is, more pieces of land) in order to increase output. In standard agricultural development literature, extensive farming is believed to occur for as long as some arable land of "good quality" remains uncultivated, after which intensive farming methods then predominate. In this chapter "intensification" refers to the entire process, including the outward expansion in area cultivated (for example, that which results from shorter fallow periods), the increase in input levels, and the multiple cropping of land.

4. *R* represents farming intensity, which is measured here by the percentage of time in a rotation cycle that a plot of land is devoted to cropping. For example, if land is used for two years and left fallow for eight, the *R* value of the system would be 20. This would be the forest or bush fallow system. A system of three crops in each year would have an *R* value of 300, a multicropping system.

5. Unpublished results communicated to the author by Prabhu Pingali.

References

Barnes, Douglas. 1985. "Population Growth and Land Resources in Sudan." PHN Technical Note 19-B. Population, Health, and Nutrition Department, World Bank, Washington, D.C.

Boserup, Ester. 1965. *The Conditions of Agricultural Growth.* Chicago: Aldine.

_____. 1981. *Population and Technological Change.* Chicago: University of Chicago Press.

FAO (Food and Agriculture Organization). 1980. *Bush Fallow in Sierra Leone.* Sierra Leone Land Resources Survey Technical Report No. 6. Freetown: UNDP/FAO.

_____. 1982a. *Food Production Yearbook.* Rome.

_____. 1982b. *Land, Food, and People.* Rome.

Higgins, G. M., A. H. Kassam, L. Naiken, G. Fischer, and M. M. Shah. 1982. *Potential Population Supporting Capacities of Land in the Developing World.* Rome: FAO, UNDP, and IASSA.

Jones, William I., and Roberto Egli. 1984. *Farming Systems in Africa.* World Bank Technical Paper 27. Washington, D.C.

Morgan, W. B. 1969. "Peasant Agriculture in Tropical Africa." In M. F. Thomas and G. W. Whittington, eds., *Environment and Land Use in Africa.* London: Methuen.

Pingali, Prabhu, and Hans P. Binswanger. 1984a. "Population Density and Agricultural Intensification: A Study of the Evolution of Technologies in Tropical Agriculture." Report ARU22. Agriculture and Rural Development Department, Research Unit, World Bank, Washington, D.C.

_____. 1984b. "Population Density and Farming Systems—The Changing Locus of Innovation and Technical Change." Report ARU24. Agriculture and Rural Development Department, Research Unit, World Bank, Washington, D.C.

Pingali, Prabhu, Yves Bigot, and Hans P. Binswanger. 1987. *Agricultural Mechanization and the Evolution of Farming Systems in Sub-Saharan Africa.* Baltimore, Md.: Johns Hopkins University Press.

Ruthenberg, Hans. 1980. *Farming Systems in the Tropics.* 3rd ed. Oxford: Clarendon Press.

United Nations. 1973. *The Determinants and Consequences of Population Trends.* Vol. 1. Department of Economic and Social Affairs, Population Studies No. 50. New York.

Wawer, Maria. 1984. "Factors Influencing Health Status in Sub-Saharan Africa (1984)." Population, Health, and Nutrition Department, World Bank, Washington, D.C.; processed.

World Bank. 1981. *Accelerated Development in Sub-Saharan Africa.* Washington, D.C.

_____. 1984a. *World Development Report, 1984.* New York: Oxford University Press.

_____. 1984b. *Toward Sustained Development in Sub-Saharan Africa.* Washington, D.C.

3

Population Growth, Wood Fuels, and Resource Problems

Douglas F. Barnes

Fuelwood has become increasingly difficult to obtain in both rural and urban areas in many Sub-Saharan African countries. Populations have been growing very rapidly and are therefore using much more wood fuels than in the past. In many regions, the regeneration rate of trees and bush has not kept pace with population growth and the resulting expanding demand for fuelwood. The consequence is deforestation or degradation of the existing tree stocks in some areas.

There are several important reasons for concern about population growth, wood fuel shortages, and deforestation. Wood resources may be overexploited just to maintain current standards of living. When existing resources such as wood fuels are in great demand and yet are not widely traded, the poor are typically most affected by the resulting scarcity. Finally, deforestation may cause significant future problems, such as soil erosion, which takes years to develop. Although the fuelwood crisis in Sub-Saharan African countries specifically is recognized to be a consequence of rapid population growth, most of the solutions offered to improve the situation involve increased production or conservation of wood fuel energy rather than population-related policies.

On the subcontinent, the wood fuel shortages in many regions have three primary causes: an increase in wood fuel consumption; expansion of agriculture into forests or woodlands, which reduces available tree stocks; and overgrazing caused by an increase in the cattle population. Wood fuels are the staple source of household energy in Sub-Saharan Africa, with 90 percent of households using them for cooking. An increase in population translates directly into an increase in demand for wood fuels. As a result, in some parts of Africa the demand for both wood fuels and agricultural land has led to

deforestation and desertification (Myers 1980; FAO/UNEP 1981; Anderson and Fishwick 1984; Gorse and Steeds 1987); in other areas, there has been a substantial increase in the price of wood fuels (Chauvin 1981). In addition, many cities have experienced wood fuel problems because of the highly concentrated demand for wood from the rural areas surrounding them (Chauvin 1981; French 1984). In regions with dense populations, trees are being harvested at a faster rate than they can be replenished by natural regrowth (FAO 1983b). The problem is further exacerbated because many other causes of deforestation are also related to population growth. The growth in the number of cattle and sheep often closely parallels human population growth, and grazing is one of the causes of deforestation (Allen and Barnes 1985).

This chapter focuses on how population growth relates to rural energy, land use, development of rural markets, and the availability of alternative fuels. One might speculate that population growth will cause more intensive use of land for agriculture, a significant development of fuelwood markets in urban areas, and replacement of fuelwood with other energy sources if scarcity persists over time. There are problems, however, and sometimes there are lags in these adjustments. I will address these issues after a more general discussion relating population growth to deforestation in a broad socioeconomic framework.

Population and Deforestation: Conceptual Issues

Population growth in isolation is not enough to cause deforestation or household energy shortages. The distribution of population, land use intensity, agroclimate, carrying capacity of the soils, and the level of economic development are all important in determining whether there are or will be household energy shortages. Population growth in many land-abundant areas, for instance, will result in an expansion of agricultural land along with no decline in fuelwood availability. In many parts of Africa, land is abundant and populations are relatively sparse, and there is no current fuelwood shortage. In other areas, however, population density is quite high or tree regrowth is very low. In these areas, wood resources have been under extensive pressure from growing populations.

Population Distribution and Land Use

The popular image of Africa as a sparsely populated continent with jungles and forests, although inaccurate, does suggest a low intensity of land use that is characteristic of many parts of the subcontinent. Figure 3-1 illustrates the danger of making sweeping generalizations concerning population and land use in Sub-Saharan Africa. The vertical dimension represents population density, whereas the horizontal dimension gives the types of land use and vegetation classification. On the extreme left and right of the figure, the population density is very low. These areas represent the opposite ends of the rainfall spectrum: the tropical forests and the desert. In both cases, geoclimatic conditions limit human settlement in the absence of extensive capital investments. In the desert and sub-desert, there is not enough water to support high levels of human populations. The tropical forests in many cases are in remote locations, and the high levels of rainfall limit the potential of the land for agriculture.

The wide variation in population density in areas between the extremes of the tropical forests and the desert illustrates the fact that historical circumstances, geographical differences, and the productivity of the land can affect the location of human settlements. About 68 percent of the population is living in 28 percent of the land area in Sub-Saharan Africa. Many countries, for example, Gabon and Sudan, have areas that are underutilized, but others, such as Kenya, have high population densities. Because of national boundaries, geography, and poor infrastructure, movement between the more dense and the less dense regions is not always possible. The higher-density agricultural areas tend to have more intensive levels of agricultural inputs, and likewise the lower-density regions have longer fallow periods to restore fertility to the land. The regions with high population density, for instance, include parts of West Africa along the Gulf of Guinea, whereas the lower-population zones are spread throughout areas such as

southern Burkina Faso, Malawi, southeastern Senegal, and many other parts of Africa.

Deforestation and Desertification

Population and resource issues are very complex and involve a combination of climate, soils, topography, kinds of farming systems, population growth, population density, and level of economic development. The six zones represented in figure 3-1 illustrate how the causes of deforestation vary by density of human population, agroclimate, and vegetation zone. Desertification, for instance, is a problem in regions with low population density, which have a very low capacity for agricultural production because of the climate and soils (Gorse and Steeds 1987). These same regions have populations of herders and transhumants, which take advantage of grass that regrows annually. The attempt to move from low-intensity agriculture to more intense levels without the aid of irrigation can lead to severe environmental problems, including desertification.

Farming can become much more intensive in areas with more intermediate levels of rainfall, even without irrigation. Many of these areas in Africa have high levels of population density (top of figure 3-1). These regions can experience loss in soil fertility if fallows are not adequate or if farmers do not use the necessary soil improvement techniques.

In the well-forested regions with high rainfall, deforestation is generally caused not by increased demand for wood fuels but rather by logging or by a decline in fallow periods in forest fallow farming systems (Allen and Barnes 1985; FAO 1983a). Except in the mountainous zones, intense use of the land for agriculture in these areas is generally not possible because the high levels of rainfall leach the soil, so that the land is unsuitable for intensive agriculture. The presence of insects and diseases in many of these regions also keeps human populations from settling in them. The exception is in Burundi, the highlands of Kenya, and Rwanda, where soils are fertile and forests have been depleted because of dense and growing populations.

Agroclimate is also a significant factor in the production of wood fuels for household energy. Regions with a high rate of tree regrowth can meet the needs of a larger number of people than those with low regrowth potential. The regions with wood fuel deficits are generally those with low to moderate rainfall and high population densities. In the areas with very low population density and low rainfall, the demand for wood fuels can outstrip the supply because of the very slow regrowth potential of trees. Where population density is high and rainfall levels are moderate, the prob-

Figure 3-1. *Land Use, Vegetation Zones, and Population Density, 1980*

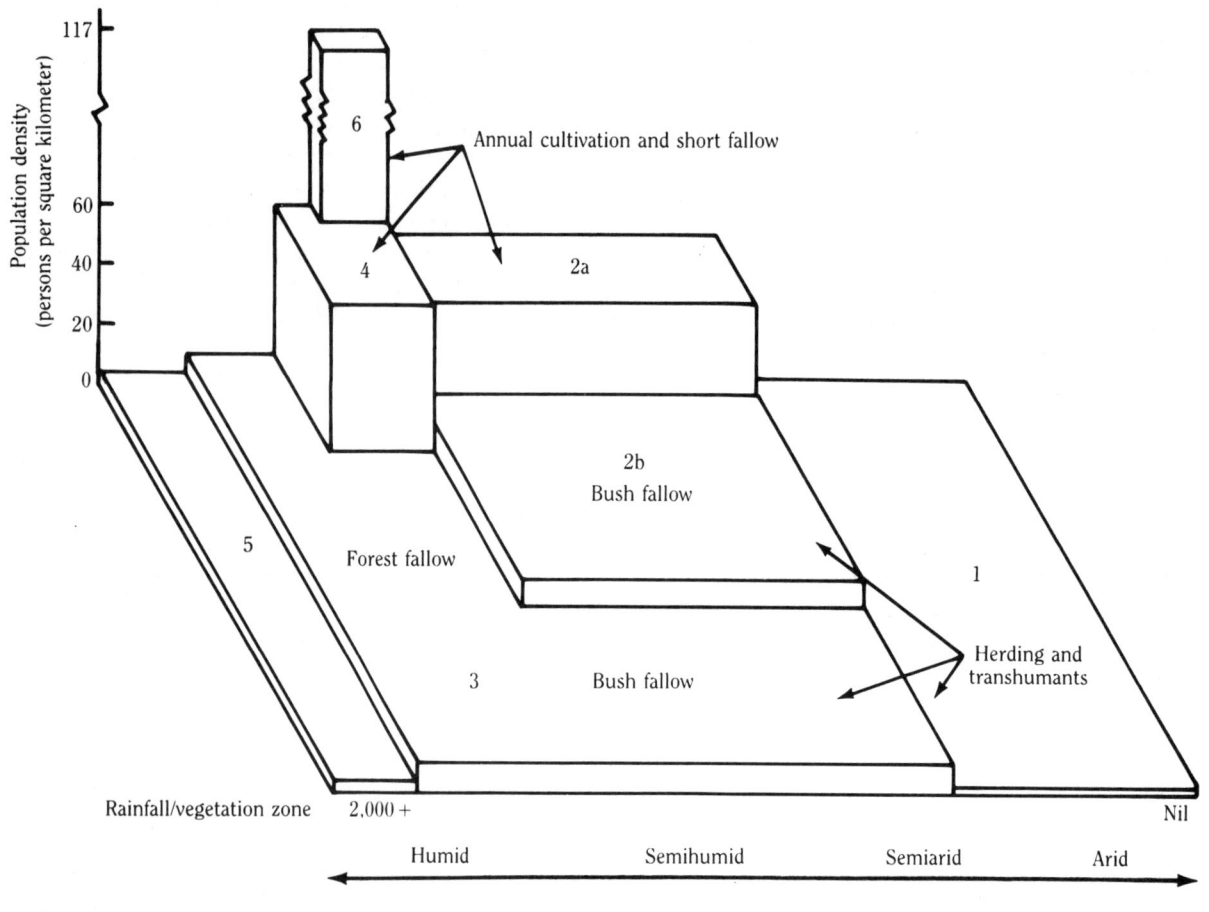

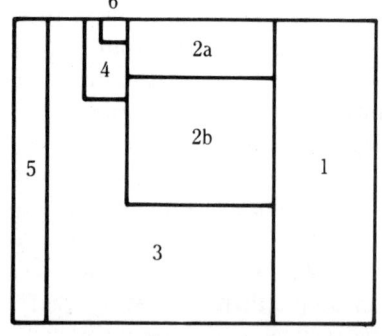

Note: Surface area represents total land area for Sub-Saharan Africa. Population and vegetation zones (percentage of total land area): (1) desert and subdesert (28 percent); (2) heavily populated woods and savanna (25 percent); (3) sparsely populated wooded savanna and forest area (34 percent); (4) heavily populated forests and plantations (3 percent); (5) very sparsely populated forests (9 percent); (6) very heavily populated, mountainous forest area (0.5 percent).

Vegetation zone 2 has been divided according to figures from the FAO *Production Yearbook 1981.* Zone 2a is arable land, according to the FAO definition, and 2b is the remainder of land in the zone. The population densities are estimated based on the assumption that agriculture in zone 2a is more intensive than that in 2b.

Sources: FAO (1983); FAO/UNEP (1981).

lems with scarcity of wood fuels are a consequence of the rapidly growing demand for wood fuels caused by population growth.

Economic Development, Population Growth, and Deforestation

A brief description of the changes in general energy patterns and land use associated with different stages of socioeconomic development can help put the African population and resource issues in perspective. It should be noted, however, that the following model is an oversimplification, and the economic stages can last decades or longer.

Countries at low levels of economic development but with abundant land have a very low intensity of agriculture. In fact, expansion of food production for growing populations is met through an expansion of arable land, which is often cleared forests. Forest products, including wood fuels, are in relative abundance during this stage. The demand for wood fuels can be met fairly easily through regeneration of trees and bush during long agricultural fallow periods.

Most African countries today are moving beyond the very lowest levels of subsistence cultivation and low population density. With economic development and population growth, deforestation can result from the expansion of agricultural land to meet growing demand for food and from the harvesting of trees to meet the growing wood demand for household energy. At this stage, because of the declining base of forests and rapidly increasing populations, the demand for wood fuels changes from low levels met by extensive use of forests to higher levels met by more intensive use of small areas of forests. Energy sources at this stage are mostly wood fuels, agricultural waste, and, in some cases, dung. Because there has not yet been a transition to commercial fuels, in this period high population growth combined with a lag in the development of more intensive tree production causes a severe strain on forest resources.

As forest clearing, population growth, and economic development proceed in the later stages of development for countries such as the United States and the European nations, several things mitigate the rate at which forests disappear. First, increasing urbanization and rising incomes are accompanied by productivity gains in agriculture due to such practices as irrigation, use of improved varieties, and application of fertilizers, pesticides, or herbicides. At some point, most of the highly productive agricultural land has been brought into production, so that continued clearing results in smaller marginal increases in food production. Urbanization, improvement in the agricultural productivity of arable land, and declining agricultural returns on marginal land reduce the demand for newly cleared land and diminish the rate of forest clearing.

In the later stages of development, other factors also relieve the pressure on forests. At some point in development, forest area begins to increase again. For instance, early settlement in the northeastern part of the United States led to cleared forest land for agriculture. During the last eighty years, however, much of the land has been returned to forests. What is the reason? First, birth rates decline with rising income, and population growth rates decline. Low population growth provides the possibility of constant rather than rising demand for arable land and wood products. At the same time, industrialization results in a pattern of energy consumption based on fossil fuels that hardly depends on forests. It should be recognized, however, that, with the exception of Mauritius, African countries will not reach such a level for many years to come. In the meantime, the high rate of population growth is causing deforestation problems for many countries.

Africa is now in the early stages of the development cycle. Population growth rates are high, urban growth rates are even higher, and in many of the countries economic growth has been very slow during the last decade (World Bank 1984a). Thus in Sub-Saharan Africa, population growth has important consequences for land use and rural energy. The following sections analyze the consequences of rural population growth for (1) household energy consumption, (2) wood fuels collection, and (3) biomass and wood fuels production.

Energy Use in Rural Areas

Energy use in Africa reflects the rather low levels of development of most countries. Energy use per person in the Republic of Korea, for instance, is fifteen times higher than in Tanzania (Allen and Barnes 1985), mainly because of the rather low industrial and urban base in Tanzania. Countries with low-income, largely rural populations generally use more traditional fuels, and household consumption takes a larger share of total energy use (Dunkerley and Ramsay 1983). This trend is clearly illustrated in table 3-1. In most of the countries in Sub-Saharan Africa, traditional forms of energy and household consumption dominate total energy use.

The increase in demand for household energy will almost parallel population growth. The typical end uses of energy in Sub-Saharan Africa generally are cooking, heating, lighting, ironing, and some small-scale industrial uses such as tobacco curing and brickmaking. It is sometimes difficult to distinguish between end uses. Cooking with wood fuels generally dominates the energy flows and also provides light and heat. Based on studies in the Sudanian and Sahelian zones, figure

Table 3-1. *Gross National Product and Percentages of Traditional Fuels and Household Consumption in Total Energy Use, Selected Countries, 1980*

Country	GNP per capita	Percentage of traditional fuels in total energy consumption	Percentage of household sector in total energy consumption
Burundi	202	80.1	—
Malawi	233	94.1	40.9
Kenya	418	81.0	82.3
Senegal	452	66.9	68.7
Sudan	470	86.8	81.2
Liberia	527	48.2	55.4
Egypt	582	29.8	26.4
Zimbabwe	627	25.6	30.0
Morocco	864	6.0	23.5
Tunisia	1312	17.9	36.3

— Not available.
Source: Dunkerley and Ramsay (1983).

3-2 shows the dominant role of cooking, which also holds for other countries in Sub-Saharan Africa. Although there will be some switching from wood fuels to commercial fuels, interfuel substitution is not expected to take place on a large scale, at least not in the near future, and population growth will directly affect the need for fuelwood for these activities.

Wood Fuels: Deficit or Surplus?

The fuelwood situation in rural areas of Sub-Saharan Africa is highly location specific (Allen and Barnes 1985; Arnold 1979). In many regions there is a surplus of wood fuels, whereas in other parts severe deficits exist. Even within countries, the situation varies from region to region. In the northern part of Sudan, for instance, the wood fuel crisis is very real, with shortages, rising prices, and environmental degradation. In the south, however, there is a surplus of wood fuels because of the favorable climate and relatively low population densities.

The classification of regions in Africa by population density and vegetation zone allows a more precise statement of the nature of the wood fuels problem. This problem is illustrated in figure 3-3, which breaks down Sub-Saharan Africa by the same zones as figure 3-1. The desert and subdesert cover 28 percent of the land area in Sub-Saharan Africa. Many parts of these arid regions are experiencing acute shortages of biomass, and the situation is not likely to improve by the year 2000. Despite low population densities, the carrying capacity of the land is so low that population growth is not sustainable for either agriculture or wood fuels, and as a consequence there is currently out-migration from the region. This is the situation in the northern part of the Sahel and Sudanian zones, including Chad, northern Mali, Niger, and Sudan.

In the heavily populated savanna zones (zone 2), which include approximately one-quarter of the land area in Sub-Saharan Africa, only 25 to 50 percent of the demand for wood fuels will be met from the yearly regrowth of trees. In spite of favorable conditions for regrowth, the situation is becoming increasingly severe because of rather dense and increasing populations. Included in these zones are parts of central Burkina Faso, Gambia, northern Nigeria, Senegal, and Sierra Leone.

In the less densely populated savanna regions (zone 3) covering 23 percent of the land, the situation is not quite so dramatic. For today at least, these areas have sufficient wood fuels. Without intervention, however, the situation could deteriorate even in these areas by 2000. Such regions include southern Burkina Faso, northern Côte d'Ivoire, southern Tanzania, and central Zaire.

In the central part of Africa, with tropical forests and low population density (zone 5) covering 9 percent of total land area, the ideal tree growth conditions and sparse populations mean that there should be adequate supplies for the year 2000 and beyond. This region includes Angola and northern Zaire along with the Central African Republic and Gabon.

The areas along the Gulf of Guinea, covering 3 percent of land area in Sub-Saharan Africa (zone 4), have satisfactory supplies of wood fuels, but the situation could worsen by 2000. The climate is ideal for growing trees in this region, and many forests have been con-

Figure 3-2. *Energy End Uses in the Sahelian and Sudanian Region, 1980: Wood Energy Dominates Household Energy Flows*

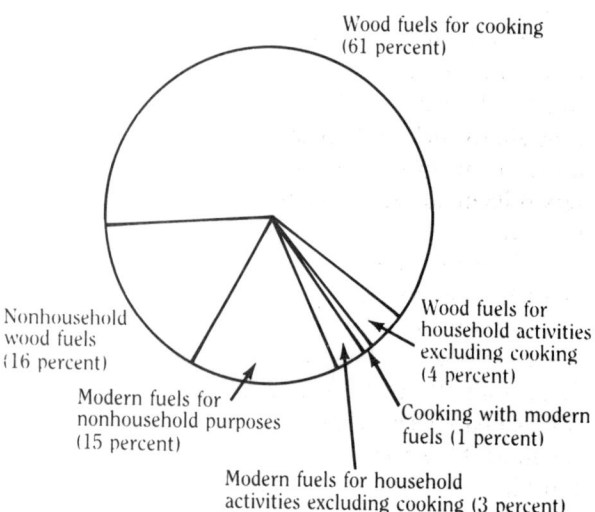

Wood fuels for cooking (61 percent)

Nonhousehold wood fuels (16 percent)

Wood fuels for household activities excluding cooking (4 percent)

Modern fuels for nonhousehold purposes (15 percent)

Cooking with modern fuels (1 percent)

Modern fuels for household activities excluding cooking (3 percent)

Total wood fuels use = 81 percent of energy use

Source: FRIDA (1980).

Figure 3-3. *Accessible Wood Resources and Population Density, 1980 and 2000*

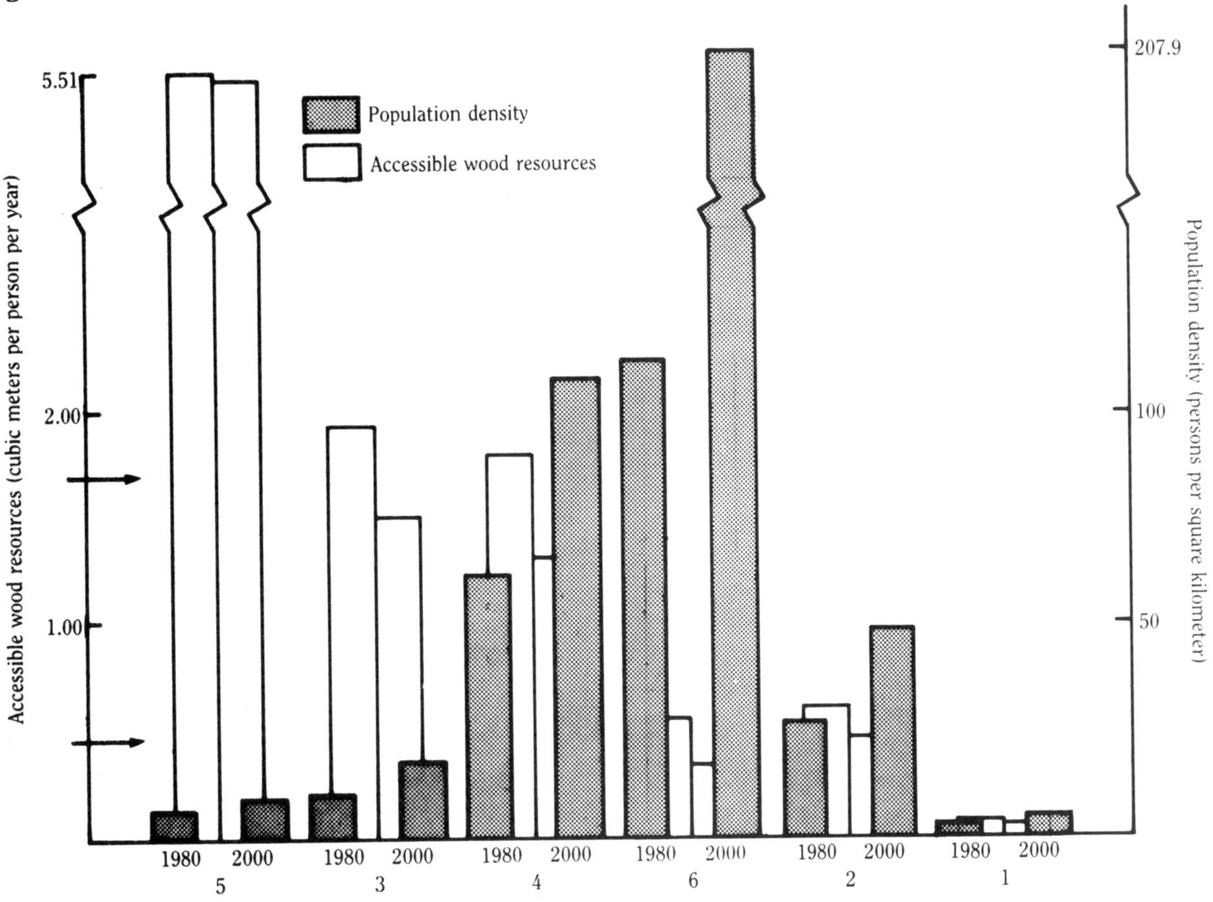

Note: Arrows on left column represent maximum and minimum per capita wood energy needs. Population and vegetation zones (percentage of total land area): (1) desert and subdesert (28 percent); (2) heavily populated woods and savanna (25 percent); (3) sparsely populated wooded savanna and forest area (34 percent); (4) heavily populated forests and plantations (3 percent); (5) very sparsely populated forests (9 percent); (6) very heavily populated, mountainous forest area (0.5 percent).

Source: FAO (1983b).

verted to commercial tree plantations. Therefore people in rural areas will probably not have any shortage of wood fuels even by 2000. Because of large urban concentrations such as those at Abidjan, Accra, and Lagos, however, the growing demand for wood by urban centers is likely to cause regional deficits for twenty years or more.

In the densely populated mountainous areas (zone 6) of such countries as Ethiopia, Rwanda, and Uganda, which cover less than 1 percent of total land area, the wood fuels deficit is likely to continue until 2000. Reforestation efforts in such countries as Burundi and Rwanda have been relatively successful, but even there the efforts have been not able to keep up with population growth.

Economic Growth and Social Class

Population growth, economic growth, and type of social structure can have a substantial impact on the need for wood fuels. Two scenarios for Sub-Saharan Africa illustrate what might happen with different types of economic growth. In the first scenario, rapid population growth is accompanied by significant economic growth, causing increases in real income for Sub-Saharan Africa. The demand for wood fuels would first increase and then decline because of interfuel substitution. For Nigeria, Grut (1972) found that wood fuel consumption increases from the lower class to the middle class and then declines in the high-income classes. Similar trends are found in household expenditure surveys in Botswana, Malawi, and Tanzania.

Population growth within the context of dynamic economic growth would not lead to a worsening of the current wood fuel situation. The opposite situation would be economic stagnation, with a significant expansion of a poor underclass. The expansion of a large underclass would mean an almost constant increase in demand for wood energy. Given the relatively slow economic growth in rural areas of many African countries, wood fuels

Geographisches Institut
der Universität Kiel

will probably remain the staple fuel for many years to come. In this case, the increase in wood fuel use would be directly related to the population growth.

Even under the most liberal assumption, the shortages of wood fuels in deficit regions are not expected to abate by 2000. Moreover, if there is economic growth but the growth is inequitable, the demand for wood fuels would probably not be significantly altered. Thus, economic growth without equity would result in little interfuel substitution, and consequently the pressure on remaining forest and vegetation would continue.

Rural Interfuel Substitution and Energy Alternatives

In rural areas, interfuel substitution generally means a switch to less efficient and lower-value fuels. The most common alternatives to wood fuels in rural areas are agricultural waste and dung. Although wood fuels are preferred fuels in most rural areas, once they become harder to collect or more expensive, rural families turn to whatever is available locally to cook meals. The alternative fuels generally are valuable manure or fertilizers. The detrimental effects of the substitution of agricultural wastes and dung have been vividly described for Ethiopia (Newcombe 1989). The cycle includes deterioration of soil fertility and eventual loss of topsoil. If trees are grown to replace dung, the avoided costs of environmental deterioration and declining yields can be substantial. It has been estimated that, for each additional 1 million people, the resulting demand for the dung and agricultural waste that would replace wood fuels would cost the economy of Ethiopia approximately 102–150 thousand tons of grain production (World Bank 1983). Although the example of Ethiopia is probably an extreme case, it highlights the need for population control or reforestation in some regions.

The impact of interfuel substitution on fertilizer use must be placed in the context of the type of farming system and the agroclimatic conditions. Declining soil fertility is common to the cycle of agricultural intensification. When trees are abundant and population density is low, land is cleared on a rotational basis. The trees and fodder restore the soil's fertility over a period of years. Growing populations put pressure on the system by shortening fallows to grow more food. At this stage, agricultural wastes and dung are worked into the soil to compensate for the declining fallows. The growing demand for wood fuels is accompanied by an intensification of agriculture. Several important questions arise. Will farmers' need for energy take priority over the need for organic fertilizer or other needs? How much agricultural waste can they divert to fuel without reducing agricultural yields? Because food production is obviously very vital to farmers, why would they divert agricultural waste and dung from fertilizer use to cook meals? These are some of the important but unanswered

questions on the interaction between population growth and increasing demand for food and the growing demand for biomass energy.

Informal Rural Energy Markets

The wood markets in rural areas are informal rather than formal. In most cases, wood is gathered by individual households for their own needs. In fairly wood-abundant regions, wood is gathered with little labor from the surrounding bush or woodland. In rural areas with higher population density and slow tree regrowth, wood becomes more scarce; in some cases people must walk long distances to obtain wood for cooking (Hoskins 1979, 1980). In such areas, the bundles of wood sometimes become much larger, and the wood is collected less often because it is not available locally (Skutsch 1983). As a result, an informal market develops. Gradually, the trading of wood fuels becomes more common, and wood may be purchased from neighbors or rural markets. The general principle is that population growth combined with increasing labor specialization and costs and increasing wood scarcity in rural areas lead to the development of more formal wood fuel markets (Dewees 1989), which nevertheless are much less formal than their urban counterparts.

Population growth in combination with the rate of tree regrowth affects the distance that must be traveled for wood and the development of markets for wood in rural areas. Unfortunately, very little information exists on the time necessary for wood collection under different socioeconomic and agroclimatic conditions. In table 3-2, the figures cited for Sub-Saharan Africa on distance traveled for wood fuels are given by country. A travel range from zero to ten kilometers, with very wide fluctuations, shows that fuelwood collection in many locations requires much time. In countries with severe deforestation problems, people are walking long distances to obtain fuelwood.

The methods of fuelwood harvesting and collecting vary according to the region and the demand for fuels. The regions with low population density and high tree regrowth have abundant wood available for rural populations. As a consequence, fuelwood collection is likely to be very casual; it is sometimes gathered around homesteads and on the farm. In such regions, the supply of wood fuels may be greater than the demand for them. In contrast, the regions with high population density and high regrowth potential may still have very informal collection of fuelwood, but longer hours may be required to collect the fuels for daily needs. In this case, women may combine looking for fuelwood with other activities. For instance, in walking to and from farms, people will collect wood fuels and carry them back to the household (French 1984). In such regions, the extent of the problem depends on population density and

Table 3-2. *Distance Walked for Firewood Collection, Rural Areas of Selected Countries*
(kilometers)

Country	Distance[a]	Year	Source
Fuelwood			
Botswana	7.5	1980	Shaik (n.d.)
Cameroon (Yaounde)	2–6	1980	Roy (1980)
Kenya	1.6–7.0	1979	Openshaw (1980)
Malawi[b]	0–3.6	1980	Malawi (1981)
Sudan (Bara)	1–10	1977	Digernes (1977)
Tanzania	1–5	1980	Araya (1981)
Burkina Faso (Boulenga)	5	1977	Ernst (1977)
Burkina Faso (Koudougou)	5–10	1979	Winterbottom (1979)
Charcoal			
Kenya (Machakos)	3	1979	Openshaw (1980)
Sudan (Bara)	16–25	1977–78	Digernes (1977)

a. One-way distance.
b. For 90 percent of population. The remaining 10 percent collected fuelwood at a distance greater than 3.6 kilometers.
Source: Barnes, Allen, and Ramsay (1982).

whether the rate of population growth is exceeding the rate of tree regrowth. In the dryer regions with low population density, people probably have to walk long distances to collect fuelwood. In many cases, they form groups to walk to forest reserves or other areas where trees are known to be plentiful (Hoskins 1980). The result is that available fuelwood supplies are pushed farther away from the rural communities, especially during the dry seasons.

Women are the most common users and collectors of wood fuels in developing countries (Hoskins 1979; Noronha 1980). The adverse consequences of population growth and resulting deforestation are therefore more severe for women than for men. Time spent on other activities, such as gardening, must be curtailed as wood fuels become more scarce. The amount of time spent collecting wood fuels ranges from six hours per week in Kenya, for instance, (Brokensha and Riley 1978) to about fifteen in Burkina Faso (Winterbottom 1979) to more than forty in central Tanzania (Mnzava 1980; Openshaw and Moris 1979). Many of these estimates overstate the actual time, because wood fuel collection can be combined with other activities. Nevertheless, they do demonstrate that, within some regions, women are already spending a significant proportion of their time and energy collecting fuelwood. Population growth without any change in land use would only further increase the time spent collecting fuelwood.

Energy Use in Urban Households

The growing demand of urban populations for all forms of energy presents difficult choices for urban centers in Africa. For countries without the requisite natural resources, the growth of commercial demand for fuels means higher bills for imported oil. The situation is different for wood fuels, which are rarely imported in significant quantities in Sub-Saharan Africa. The projection of urban needs for wood fuels generally involves a scenario of deforested and degraded rings around most urban centers that sometimes extend deep into the rural countryside. In Malawi there is a "pattern of deforestation radiating outward from urban areas" (Malawi 1984), and Chauvin (1981, p. 18) noted that in Burkina Faso the "situation is critical because the tree cover around nearby towns and villages is rapidly disappearing."

Populations in urban regions of Africa are growing at an extremely rapid rate compared both with rural populations of Sub-Saharan Africa and with urban populations in other parts of the world. The average annual urban population growth rate for Sub-Saharan Africa was 6.1 percent during 1970–82, compared with less than 2 percent for rural areas (World Bank 1984b). The degree of urbanization in a country is closely related to the use of commercial fuels for energy. It is true in Africa, as in Asia and Latin America, that a more developed industrial urban base means a higher use of commercial energy (Dunkerley and Ramsay 1983). Despite these well-established relationships, however, wood fuels continue to play an extremely important role within urban households. In many cities, as much as 90 percent of urban households use wood fuels for cooking (French 1984). The traditional model for analyzing urban household energy demand is to predict a country's urban population in a future year and then calculate a demand for energy based on current needs while allowing for some interfuel substitution (table 3-3).

Social Class and Fuel Choice

One difference between urban and rural energy consumption is that urban households in most cases have a wider choice of fuels. There is extensive evidence from

Table 3-3. *Urban Population Growth and Household Energy Projection, Selected Countries*

Country	Annual urban population growth rate		Urban population				Urban household energy demand[a]	
			1980		2000			
	1960–70	1970–82	Millions	Percent	Millions	Percent	1980	2000
Ghana	4.6	5.0	4.3	36	11.7	56	6.8	18.6
Ethiopia	6.5	5.6	5.0	15	16.7	32	5.1	18.6
Kenya	6.4	7.3	2.2	14	8.3	25	4.1	15.5
Nigeria	4.7	4.9	17.0	20	42.6	26	5.0	25.5
Rwanda	5.4	6.4	0.2	4	0.6	6	0.2	0.5
Sudan	6.8	5.8	4.5	25	16.8	54	6.0	23.0
Tanzania	6.3	8.5	2.3	12	12.1	35	4.7	25.2
Uganda	7.1	3.4	1.6	12	6.0	25	4.1	15.8
Zaire	5.2	7.6	9.5	34	38.2	78	6.1	24.6
Zambia	5.2	6.5	2.3	38	6.7	61	3.8	7.9
Zimbabwe	6.7	6.0	1.6	23	5.6	37	1.5	5.2

a. 10^6 cubic meters fuelwood equivalent.
Source: World Bank (1984b).

household energy use surveys that fuel choice varies with household income (FRIDA 1980; Malawi 1984; Barnes 1987; Hosier and Dowd 1988; Leach and Mearns 1988; Malawi 1984; McGranahan, Nathans, and Chubbi 1980; Milukas 1986; World Bank 1988a, 1988b, 1988c, 1988d). Wood fuels are the overwhelming choice of the poorest households in Sub-Saharan Africa, in large part because wood in many areas has not been as scarce as in other parts of the developing world. In Nairobi, Kenya, more than 65 percent of total energy consumption of the poorest households is estimated to come from wood or charcoal (McGranahan and Nathans 1979). This consumption, however, falls off to less than 3 percent in the wealthiest households, which rely mainly on commercial fuels such as electricity and liquefied petroleum gas (LPG). In four urban regions of Malawi, 96 percent of the low-income households use wood fuels for cooking, compared with 19 percent of the highest-income households (Malawi 1984). More than 80 percent of the high-income families use electricity for cooking. Because there are substantially more poor households, approximately 90 percent of all households use wood for cooking. Essentially the same pattern exists in other countries, with wealthy households consuming a greater share of commercial energy.

As incomes rise from lower to middle class, the typical pattern is for wood energy use first to increase and subsequently to decline when kerosene is substituted for wood. As incomes rise from the middle class to the upper class, however, kerosene gives way to electricity and LPG in cooking (see Alam, Dunkerley, and Ramsay 1984). As a result, because a greater variety of commercial fuels is available in urban areas than in rural areas, urban areas have a greater potential for switching from wood fuels to commercial energy. This potential will, however, depend upon the economic growth and income distribution within cities.

Despite the availability of commercial fuels, urban households may prefer wood fuels, even though price per unit of useful cooking energy is sometimes similar. The cost of wood as opposed to commercial fuels depends on the resources available in individual countries as well as on pricing policies. As table 3-4 indicates, wood energy is not always the cheapest fuel, once end use efficiency is taken into consideration. Estimates of comparative prices should be made with caution, however, because factors other than price enter into household energy choice. Wood fuels are generally easier to obtain than many other energy sources; biomass can be collected or purchased; wood fuel stoves are cheap though not very efficient; heat from wood fuels cooking is used for warmth in regions with colder seasons; and the smoke from wood fires in some cases is a deterrent to pests.

Although commercial fuels can be very convenient, intermittent supply has plagued some countries. During the past ten years, for example, there have been sporadic shortages of commercial fuels, such as kerosene. Electricity supplies at peak demand periods also are not always reliable. The sometimes unreliable supply complicates cooking with commercial fuels, however convenient it may otherwise be. Nevertheless, the dramatic increase in the use of commercial fuels among higher-income classes in urban areas in Sub-Saharan Africa is testimony to their desirability. As lower-income families move up the income ladder in urban areas, they will consume more commercial fuels. Wood fuel use will probably first increase with a rise in income and then decrease as incomes reach higher levels (Grut 1972).

Urban Wood Fuel Prices

Compared with the informal trade in the rural areas, the wood markets in urban areas are well developed.

Table 3-4. *Relative Costs of Fuelwood, Charcoal, and Commercial Energy for Cooking, Selected Countries*

Energy source	Cameroon	Senegal	Northern Nigeria	Niger	Ethiopia
Relative costs[a]					
Fuelwood	1.0	1.0	1.1	1.0	1.0
Charcoal	3.4	0.9	2.4	1.4	1.6
Kerosene	10.0	1.7	0.6	1.7	0.7
Liquified petroleum gas	—	1.3–1.9	2.0	2.0	1.1
Electricity	11.1	3.3	1.1	2.8	2.0
Fuelwood costs[b]	4	9	11	9	26

— Not available.
a. All costs are adjusted for thermal efficiencies and include cost of appliances.
b. Cents per kilowatt hour of useful heat absorbed by the pot.
Source: Anderson and Fishwick (1984, p. 30).

The price of wood fuels in urban markets has increased dramatically during the last fifteen to twenty years. According to Wardle and Palmieri (1981), the delivered price of wood fuels for developing countries increased by about 12 percent a year between 1970 and 1979 (figure 3-4). The increase in the price of wood fuels is parallel to but somewhat lower than the increase in the price of oil for the same period. Once wood fuel prices are adjusted for the inflation rate, there is only a small real price increase of about 1.5 to 2.0 percent per year for the same period. This general trend, however, masks the fact that, in specific urban markets, wood fuel prices have taken a dramatic jump, although in other markets prices have remained relatively flat or even declined somewhat, a disparity that once again highlights the location-specific nature of deforestation and wood fuel problems. In Burkina Faso, for instance, the real price of wood fuels has jumped from $2.50 per cubic meter to $5.14 in just nine years, a real annual compound growth rate of more than 9 percent (Barnes and others 1982). In a survey conducted in four towns in Malawi, the three larger towns with insufficient natural resources surrounding them had higher wood fuel prices than the smaller town with better resources. The stock around the smaller town had not yet been significantly degraded, and households could obtain wood at roadside markets just outside the town (Malawi 1984). Rapidly growing cities or towns, and especially those with climates not conducive to the growing of trees, are thus likely to have higher wood fuel prices and larger degraded rings surrounding them.

The price rise is illustrated graphically in figure 3-5. In Phase 1, population growth causes agricultural expansion, shorter fallows, and increasing demand for wood fuels, which means that trees and bush are harvested from common and private land without replanting. At this stage, the most common source of energy for sale in urban markets is fuelwood. In Phase 2, the prices flare up because the tree stocks have been severely eroded with the rapid growth of demand. Fuelwood availability is pushed farther from the city, and charcoal begins to replace wood in urban markets. Deforested rings may begin to appear around the city. Farmers and others begin to perceive the fuelwood scarcity, but trees continue to be harvested from savanna and farms to meet wood fuel needs, and there is still no replanting. Finally, in the third phase, the price

Figure 3-4. *Mean Yearly Price for Fuelwood in Nineteen Countries: Current and Real Prices*

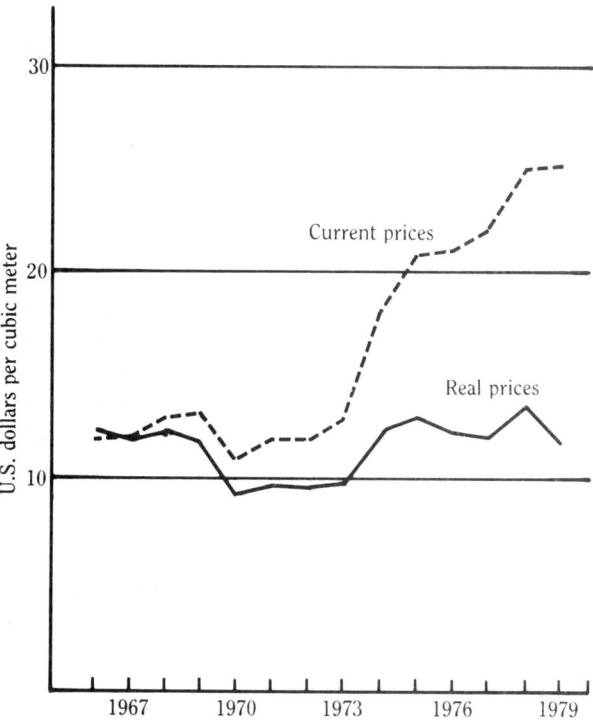

Note: Real prices were calculated using the U.S. Consumer Price Index.

Source: FAO (1981).

Figure 3-5. *Relationship between Energy Prices and Wood Scarcity*

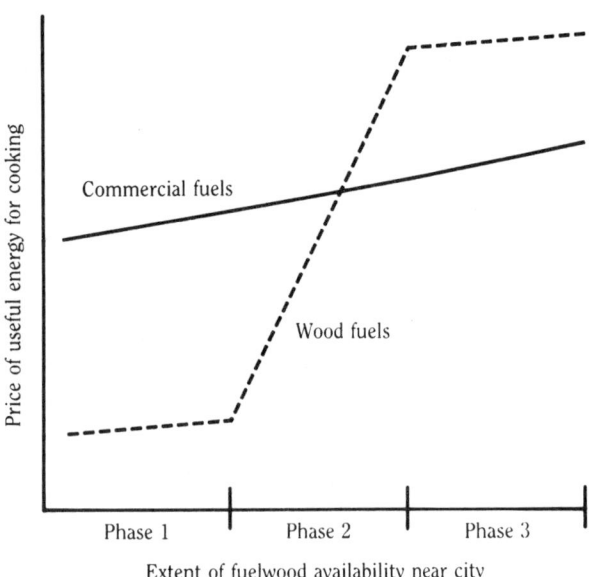

Note: Phase 1 is relative abundance. Phase 2 is growing scarcity. Phase 3 is significant scarcity.

Source: Barnes (1985).

of charcoal and fuelwood exceeds that of the alternative commercial fuels, and people begin to switch to commercial fuels. Because wood fuels can be supplemented with gathered wood, the price probably stabilizes somewhere above the commercial alternatives. At this stage, farmers have more of an incentive to plant trees for wood fuels and other tree products. There is no adequate information on producer prices for trees or other factors to enhance understanding of the incentives for farmers to grow trees, an issue that I examine in the next section.

Markets and Transport: Links between Producers and Consumers

The most poorly understood aspect of urban household energy in Sub-Saharan Africa is the link between producers and consumers, a link involving collection, transportation, and marketing that is well developed in many countries. As indicated, people in urban areas commonly purchase wood fuels, whereas those in rural areas generally collect them from the natural woodlands or their own farm plots. Therefore, retailers either organize wood collection themselves or, more likely, purchase it from an intermediary who transports it from rural areas or regions in close proximity to the city. The seller in urban areas can be an individual, a small

neighborhood shop, a friend or neighbor, a large retail market, or, in rare instances, a producer. At the point of sale, the price of wood fuels depends on the costs of production or collection, transportation, and marketing and distribution and includes a profit markup for each transaction along the way. The distribution system can be very elaborate, depending on the quantities of wood fuels necessary for the growing urban population. The difference between the farm-gate or "stumpage" price and the price in the urban market can be quite substantial.

In most countries, the majority of wood fuels are harvested from bushland or private farms rather than from forest reserves. The producers collect fuelwood or make charcoal and transport it by some simple mechanism to the city (Chauvin 1981; French 1984). There are generally many pickup points along roadsides, and the transport of wood fuels can be very informally arranged between producers and truck or donkey cart drivers or others.

In the context of such a transport and marketing structure, rapid population growth in urban areas leads to a rapid increase in demand for wood fuels. The deforested rings or degraded forests surrounding the growing city then expand steadily outward as the available trees are harvested from the points closest to the city and closest to the roads leading into the city. Since fuelwood is heavy and bulky, most cities with trees within 50–100 kilometers have fuelwood in the marketplace. Transport costs dictate that, beyond this point, fuelwood is transformed into charcoal (with energy being lost in the conversion), which can be transported more cheaply into the city because it is very light (Chauvin 1981).

The costs of transporting wood fuels from rural to urban areas are not well known. In a recent study by French (1984), transport costs are estimated to be about one-third of the total urban price of wood fuels, whereas the price paid to producers is a mere one-fifteenth of its urban price. According to French, the producer prices are so low that it is possible to harvest existing wood fuels, but the costs of planting, growing, and maintaining trees may be too high in the context of current prices.

Production of Wood Fuels and Intensity of Land Use

The rapid growth of urban and rural populations has had an impact on regional agricultural development. Agriculture is more intensified and labor and input costs are higher near urban areas than in more distant rural areas. As demand for agricultural products increases, high-value crops replace some of the staple grain crops in the farming system. Rather than grow sorghum or some other low-value grain crops, the areas around cities will grow vegetables, rice, and other high-value crops, depending on the agroclimatic conditions. The intensification of agriculture is also accompanied by a shortening of fallow periods and perhaps even annual cropping. Additional inputs such as labor, fertilizers, and manures are applied to the land to produce higher yields. Similar changes in predominantly rural areas have taken place on a smaller scale.

In the past, the fallow system of agriculture combined with low population density allowed the land to produce more than enough wood for cooking and other energy uses. Wood fuels have traditionally been readily available from fallow land and wasteland in Sub-Saharan Africa. Because of the low population density and long fallows, trees had a chance to regenerate with little active management by rural people. The situation varied by climate and geographic region, of course. Very long fallow periods are required in the dry regions to restore moisture and fertility to the soil. In the zones more suitable for agriculture, trees can regrow in shorter periods of time, and in these regions, fallows can be shorter. Trees grow very fast in the tropical forests, and population densities there have been very low.

Land under Production: Food or Fuel?

Some of the deforestation observed around urban centers in Sub-Saharan Africa may be caused in part by an increasing intensification of agriculture. As the fallow periods shorten, the wood and bush are cleared from the land and sold to urban markets at fairly low prices. Trees and bush may even be viewed as an obstacle to agricultural production. Agricultural intensification near cities makes perfect sense, as food is necessary for the growing urban markets. Still, the question may be asked: why is tree production different from food production? Why is there no intensification of tree production?

As I have indicated, part of the reason is that, in the early stages of land intensification, the price of wood fuels is not competitive with the price of food commodities, but other factors are also involved. The price of wood fuels at the farm gate may admittedly be too low to support tree production. The price of transport can be quite high, however, and profit margins for intermediaries such as sellers are also high. There may be no inherent tradeoff between food and tree crops, because in many locations trees would be more suitable than food crops. Trees could easily be grown on open fields, along roads, beside crops, and in other locations. Thus the question really is: why is there not both agricultural and tree production near the cities?

The model adopted in this chapter suggests that an increase in the intensity of agriculture is not initially accompanied by an increase in tree planting incentives. With a few exceptions, trees were never really managed in the earlier stages of development but rather were simply allowed to regrow on fallow ground. In fact, some have argued not only that the concept of growing trees is unfamiliar but that trees are viewed as a constraint to cultivation activities (see, for example, Openshaw and Moris 1979; Skutsch 1983). When population densities were low, no real need existed to manage tree growing extensively. With an increase in population density, the demand for wood fuels increases, and trees continue to be harvested from fallow ground. Because sufficient quantities are initially available from cleared agricultural land, the increase in the intensity of tree production lags behind agriculture. Only in the later stages of the cycle are the consequences of deforestation and degradation recognized. At that time, the incentive for growing trees increases; wood fuels become more scarce, prices rise, and markets develop.

The increase in population density in the short term leads to expansion of land-extensive systems of agriculture; over the long term, it leads to agricultural intensification. Over the short term, as more land is brought under cultivation, there is actually an excess supply of trees and biomass harvested from cleared land. Once this short-run supply has been consumed or sold to urban markets, the harvested stocks are not replanted. As a consequence, over the long there is a decrease in the growing stock, and wood fuels may become more scarce. The long-run decline in forests and wood fuels is well documented (Myers 1980; FAO/ UNEP 1981; World Bank 1983; see Allen and Barnes 1985 for a review). The present problem is thus that people in many African countries are mining the existing stocks of trees, and private incentives for managing them for the future are lacking.

A Problem of the Commons?

The deforestation and fuelwood problems are often attributed to the harvesting of wood from ground held in common, so that there is no incentive for individuals to replant the trees. Communities or individuals have no incentive to protect the land from deforestation because no one really owns the trees or the land. Individuals overuse the common land for short-term private gains, and in the long run society suffers from a declining volume of tree stocks.

One problem with such an analysis is its assumption that the common land is available to anyone who wants it. In actuality, there is informal agreement over rights to use of common land by various populations even in sparsely populated areas. The problem of the commons occurs only after population growth or other changes have precipitated conflicting claims of private or communal right to manage the land (Repetto and Holmes 1983; Noronha 1984).

The relevance of this discussion for population growth is that the land traditionally used for fallow or grazing will increasingly be managed by farmers for use in agriculture. Land not under cultivation is stripped of trees by people selling wood fuels. Wood fuels are thus harvested at very low cost. This is what is commonly described as overuse of common property resources. In reality, the overuse results from a situation in which population density and intensity of land use for agriculture have increased, whereas the rules and customs governing rights to own or manage trees have become outmoded (Thomson 1981).

The process described in the previous section has often been characterized as a problem of the commons. Under conditions of low population density and growth, land is abundant, and ownership of land is not really an issue because the value of land is very low. Someone belonging to a community who wants to cultivate new land simply clears it, farms it for a few years, and then returns it to fallow. This is the case in southern Sudan and many other countries. In a sense, the phrase "communal land" in such cases really means that the land cannot be claimed by outsiders. As a consequence the commons are not really communally managed but rather include land to which community members have rights, whereas others outside the community do not. This statement clearly defines community rights, but it says nothing about who manages the land. Land may be managed by an entire group, by a representative of a group, or by an individual tribal or family leader within the group (see Noronha 1984 for a review).

Conflicts between agriculturalists and herders also arise because of the growth of both human and animal populations. As fallows shorten, land rights of individual farmers generally take precedence over the rights of herders. With agricultural expansion, herders are forced into more marginal land, and within a short time the bush and pasture begin to degrade because of overgrazing. Expansion of the population of herders and animals further complicates the problems.

The reaction of herders to an increase in their herds and a decrease in available pasture has differed, depending on the region. In Sudan, the relatively wealthy herders obtain the rights to tenancies in the irrigation schemes and are settled while part of their families continue to herd. Other, less wealthy herders hire themselves out as agricultural laborers during the peak agricultural season. In Somalia, the strategy for coping has been to have one family member as a herder, another in trade, and others in government service (Noronha 1984). In other areas, pastoralists have been forced to settle. The question of what should happen to pastoralists and transhumants in Sub-Saharan Africa is still

unsettled, with some advocating range management and others stressing the need to integrate livestock management into small farms. Whatever the solution, the rights of pastoralists are typically abused under conditions of agricultural intensification and population growth.

Farm-Level Incentives to Grow Trees

From the perspective of the producer-harvester of wood fuels, the incentives for harvesting without planting are currently greater than the incentives for doing both. In the context of rapidly growing urban demand for food, farmers near urban centers are producing food, which has a higher value than wood. There is no reason, however, why private farms cannot produce wood fuels on land that is not being used for crops. Trees often produce environmental benefits that would enhance agricultural yields. Also, expansion of agricultural land should not be considered an unequivocal degradation of the land. In fact, a certain amount of tree loss near cities is to be expected. The issue is not whether trees are being harvested near the cities, but how to obtain the maximum social and economic benefit from the land under changed socioeconomic conditions.

The farm-level incentives to grow trees depend on a complex interaction between population growth, prices, institutions, climate, and stage of deforestation. As indicated, population growth is related to the incentives for planting trees, but unfortunately a time lag may be involved. The growth in the demand for wood fuels eventually results in scarcity. If the price of wood fuels rises or more labor is required to collect fuelwood, then farmers would have greater incentives to grow trees for themselves and perhaps for a market (Skutsch 1983; French 1984). In regions with low rainfall where trees provide important environmental benefits, greater incentives for managing trees would be expected because they would be indirectly linked with agricultural production. Rising prices alone are probably not sufficient to sustain spontaneous tree planting. Other programs, such as seedling distribution and forestry extension, may be necessary. The regions in which deforestation has reached a more advanced stage are probably more likely to offer farmers greater incentives to plant trees (Skutsch 1983). Because of the time lags involved in creating the incentives, the situation may become very severe before enough incentives develop to stimulate tree planting. Until tree stocks are depleted and biomass energy becomes unavailable locally, or until stumpage fees rise to more realistic levels, people will continue to harvest "free" wood fuels for their household energy needs (Spears 1983).

A number of obstacles may block the growing of trees for urban consumption on farms near urban areas. Trees will not be grown in regions where they are abundant on common land. Farmers in most African countries are accustomed to harvesting trees or bush from fallow land, without the need for replanting (Spears 1983). Though they are familiar with traditional agricultural techniques, the planting and maintenance of trees for a wood fuel market is for the most part a rather new concept, even though trees may be planted for a variety of other reasons. Another difference is that trees require a long period in which to reach maturity, which may represent a severe constraint for farmers who are trying to produce income in the current year rather than ten years down the road. In many countries institutional support, including forestry extension for smallholder tree farming, is nonexistent.

The key to understanding the incentives to grow trees on common property is that agricultural systems have not kept pace with altering circumstances. By the time the issues of common property resources are recognized, past solutions to land use management have become outmoded and new solutions are required. Africa is just now encountering the limits of growth for its traditional system of agriculture. The new methods of resource management that evolve in the coming years will involve not just the protection of existing resources but also the participation of African farmers and herders.

Conclusions

Rural energy consumers in many parts of Sub-Saharan Africa are experiencing shortages of wood fuels. Because of poor infrastructure and markets for commercial fuels, interfuel substitution in rural areas means moving from wood to agricultural wastes and dung, which are lower-grade fuels and also valuable fertilizers. Rural energy markets, which are fairly informal, rely mostly on women's and children's labor for collecting wood. Although regional variation is significant, population growth generally means that wood fuels become increasingly scarce, and women must walk long distances to collect them. Population growth in the context of limited supply of wood fuels means that a more formal market for wood fuels should develop. Currently, however, the production of wood fuels generally receives low priority compared with the production of food. Areas where the intensity of agriculture has increased have often not experienced a similar growth in the intensity of tree production. Meanwhile, traditional forestry reserves and trees on fallow land are harvested without replanting.

Often overlooked in evaluating the deforestation problem is the fact that high population density does not cause all of the problems associated with deforest-

ation. In fact, cities or countries with high population densities may benefit from economies of scale that are not possible in sparsely settled countries and cities; markets can be more efficient and infrastructure less expensive per person. The population growth rate rather than population density causes the problems associated with deforestation. Agricultural systems over the long term change to accommodate the higher levels of population density by use of fertilizers, new inputs, and new technologies to increase both agricultural and tree production. Still, it takes time for the land use system to adjust to growing population pressure. Most of the land-extensive cultivation systems in Sub-Saharan Africa are reaching their production limits. The critical problems occur when increasing population pressure pushes the present agricultural techniques and system of land use to the limits of their ability to produce additional food. In other words, rapid population growth puts pressure on the traditional methods of cultivation and tree production and, except in very arid areas, is not really limited by the potential of the land itself.

In the face of high rates of population growth, no one doubts that there needs to be more land under cultivation to produce more food or that people need more fuelwood for cooking. The important point is that such needs are being met in an environmentally unsound way in many regions and that something should be done about it. Although many areas have location-specific problems, the general problems are population growth, poor land use practices in the face of changing situations, outmoded land tenure systems, and conflicts between private incentives for farmers and larger social goals.

Population growth as a key to increases in household energy use and expansion of agricultural land should be explicitly recognized as part of both the problem and the solution. There are short- and long-term solutions to the deforestation problem. Over the short term, energy conservation and the substitution of modern for wood fuels are the two most promising ways to remove pressure on the natural resource base in affected regions. In critical areas, such as the Sahel, a policy to encourage out-migration from the most severely affected regions may be appropriate. Over the long term, the promotion of appropriate agricultural practices, the development of methods to reinforce local management of bushland and natural forests, the increase in private tree production, the promotion of family planning programs, and general economic development would all take pressure off forests and wood fuels. Such programs can improve human productivity and the quality of rural life in countries or regions most affected by population growth and ameliorate the present or impending fuelwood crisis in Sub-Saharan Africa.

References

Alam, Manzoor, Joy Dunkerley, and William Ramsay. 1984. *Fuelwood in Urban Markets: A Case Study of Hyderabad.* New Delhi: Concept Publishing.

Allen, Julia, and Douglas Barnes. 1985. "The Causes of Deforestation in Developing Countries." *Annals of the Association of American Geographers* 25 (2).

Anderson, Dennis, and Robert Fishwick. 1985. *Fuelwood Consumption and Deforestation in African Countries.* World Bank Staff Working Paper 704. Washington, D.C.

Araya, Z. 1981. "Village Forestry in Tanzania: Problem Context and Organizational Proposal for Sustained Development." Report prepared for the Forest Division Ministry of Natural Resources and Tourism, Dar-es-Salaam, Tanzania, January.

Arnold, J. E. M. 1979. "Wood Energy and Rural Communities." *Natural Resources Forum* 3: 229–52.

Barnes, Douglas. 1985. "Understanding Fuelwood Prices in Developing Nations." World Bank Agriculture and Rural Development Department. Washington, D.C. Processed.

———. 1987. "Household Energy and Interfuel Substitution in Tanzania and Malawi." Paper prepared for FAO. Rome.

Barnes, Douglas F., and Julia Allen. 1983. "Forestry-Population Interactions in Sudan and Tanzania." Paper presented at Population Association of America Annual Meeting, Pittsburgh, Pa., April.

Barnes, Douglas, Julia Allen, and William Ramsay. 1982. "Social Forestry in Developing Nations." Discussion Paper D73-F. Washington, D.C.: Resources for the Future, April.

Brokensha, David, and Bernard Riley. 1978. "Forest, Foraging, Fences, and Fuel in a Marginal Area of Kenya." Paper presented at the USAID Africa Bureau Firewood Workshop, Washington, D.C., June 12–14.

Cecelski, Elizabeth, Joy Dunkerley, and William Ramsay. 1979. "Household Energy and the Poor in the Third World." Research Paper R-15. Washington, D.C.: Resources for the Future.

Chauvin, Henri. 1981. "When an African City Runs Out of Fuel." *Unasylva* 33 (133): 11–21.

Dewees, P. A. 1989. "The Woodfuel Crisis Reconsidered: Observations on the Dynamics of Abundance and Scarcity." *World Development* 17, no. 8 (August): 1159–72.

Digernes, Turi H. 1977. "Wood for Fuel-Energy Crisis Implying Desertification: The Case of Bara, The Sudan." Major thesis in geography at the University of Bergen, Norway.

Dunkerley, Joy, and William Ramsay. 1983. "Analysis of Energy Prospects and Problems of Developing Countries." Report prepared for U.S. Agency for International Development/PPC, Washington, D.C., August.

Ernst, E. 1977. "Fuel Consumption among Rural Families in Upper Volta, West Africa." Ouagadougou, Upper Volta: Peace Corps.

FAO (Food and Agriculture Organization of the United Nations). 1981. *Forest Product Prices, 1961–80.* Rome.

———. 1983a. *FAO Production Yearbook, 1981.* Rome.

———. 1983b. "Fuelwood Supplies in the Developing Countries." FAO Forestry Paper 42. Rome.

———. 1987. "Wood-Based Fuels and Substitution Among Fuels in Africa." Rome. Processed.

FAO/UNEP (Food and Agriculture Organization of the United Nations and U.N. Environment Program). 1981. *Tropical Forest Resources Assessment Project: Forest Resources of Tropical Africa.* Rome.

French, David. 1984. "African Farmers' Behavior in Tree Planting: Sociological and Economic Variables in Reforestation." Paper presented at the Agriculture and Rural Development Department Sociological Workshop Series, World Bank, Washington, D.C., October.

FRIDA (Fund for Research and Investment for the Development of Africa). 1980. "Domestic Energy in Sub-Saharan Africa: The Impending Crisis, Its Measurement, and the Framework for Practical Solutions." London.

Gorse, Jean, and David R. Steeds. 1987. *Desertification in the Sahelian and Sudanian Zones in West Africa.* World Bank Technical Paper 61. Washington, D.C.

Grut, Michael. 1972. "Nigeria: The Market for Firewood, Poles, and Sawnwood in the Major Towns and Cities in the Savanna Region." UNFAO/UNDP Technical Report 6. Rome: FAO, 1972.

Hosier, R. H., and J. Dowd. 1988. "Household Fuel Choice in Zimbabwe: An Empirical Test of the Energy Ladder Hypothesis." *Resources and Energy* 9: 347–61.

Hoskins, Marilyn. 1979. "Women in Forestry for Local Community Development." Report prepared for the Office of Women in Development, U.S. Agency for International Development, Washington, D.C.

———. 1980. "Community Participation in African Fuelwood Production, Transformation, and Utilization." In *Energy in Africa.* Washington, D.C.: U.S. Agency for International Development.

Leach, G., and R. Mearns. 1988. *Bioenergy Issues and Options in Africa.* A Report for the Royal Norwegian Ministry of Development Cooperation. London: International Institute for Environment and Development.

McGranahan, Gordon, R. Nathans, and S. Chubbi. 1980. "Patterns of Urban Household Energy Use in Developing Countries: The Case of Nairobi." *Energy and Environment in East Africa* (Proceedings): 178–231.

Malawi. 1981. *Malawi Rural Energy Survey.* Lilongwe, Malawi: Energy Unit, Ministry of Agriculture.

———. 1984. *Malawi Urban Energy Survey.* Lilongwe, Malawi: Energy Studies Unit, Ministry of Forestry and Natural Resources. September.

Milukas, Matthew V. 1986. "Energy Flow in a Secondary City: A Case Study of Nakuru, Kenya." Ph.D. thesis, University of California, Berkeley.

Mnzava, E. M. *Report on Village Afforestation: Lessons of Experience in Tanzania.* Rome: FAO, 1980.

Myers, Norman. 1980. *Conversion of Tropical Moist Forests.* A report prepared for Committee on Research Priorities on Tropical Biology of the National Research Council, National Academy of Sciences, Washington, D.C.

Newcombe, Kenneth J. 1989. "An Economic Justification for Rural Afforestation: The Case of Ethiopia." In Gunter Schramm and Jeremy J. Warford, eds., *Environmental Management and Economic Development*. Baltimore, Md.: Johns Hopkins University Press.

Noronha, Raymond. 1980. "Sociological Aspects of Forestry Project Design." Agriculture and Rural Development Department Technical Paper. World Bank, Washington, D.C.; processed.

———. 1984. "A Review of the Literature on Land Tenure Systems in Sub-Saharan Africa." Paper prepared for Agriculture and Rural Development Research Unit, World Bank, Washington, D.C., November.

Openshaw, Keith. 1980. "Rural Energy Consumption with Particular Reference to the Machakos District of Kenya." University of Dar-es-Salaam, Morogoro, Tanzania; processed.

Openshaw, Keith, and J. Moris. 1979. "The Socio-Economics of Agroforestry." University of Dar-es-Salaam, Morogoro, Tanzania, July; processed.

Repetto, Robert, and Thomas Holmes. 1983. "The Role of Population in Resource Depletion in Developing Countries." *Population and Development Review* 9 (4).

Roy, S. 1980. "Case Study on Fuel Wood Collection and Problems of Rural Women." In "Collected Papers from a Seminar on the Role of Women in Community Forestry," held December 4–9 at the Forest Research Institute in Dehra Dun, India. Processed.

Shaik, Asif, with Patricia Carson. n.d. "The Economics of Village-Level Forestry: A Methodological Framework." Paper prepared for Africa Bureau, U.S. Agency for International Development, Washington, D.C.

Skutsch, Margaret. 1983. "Why People Don't Plant Trees: Village Case Studies, Tanzania." Resources for the Future Discussion Paper D-73P. Washington, D.C.

Spears, John. 1983. "Sectoral Paper on Forests: Executive Summary." World Resources Institute, Washington, D.C.

Thomson, James. 1981. "Public Choice Analysis of Institutional Constraints on Firewood Production Strategies in the West African Sahel." In *Public Choice and Rural Development*. Washington, D.C.: Resources for the Future.

United Nations Development Programme/World Bank. 1984. *Ethiopia: Issues and Options in the Energy Sector*. Report of the joint UNDP/World Bank Energy Assessment Program. Washington, D.C.

Wardle, Philip, and M. Palmieri. 1981. "What Does Fuelwood Really Cost?" *Unasylva* 33(131): 20–23.

Winterbottom, Robert. 1979. "Upper Volta Koudougou Agricultural Development Project." U.S. Agency for International Development, Appraisal Report for the Forestry Subprogram, Ouagadougou, August.

World Bank. 1983. *Energy Transition in Developing Countries*. Washington, D.C.

———. 1984a. *World Development Report 1984*. New York: Oxford University Press.

———. 1984b. *Toward Sustained Development in Sub-Saharan Africa*. Washington, D.C.

———. 1988a. *Cape Verde: Household Energy Strategy Study*. Report of the Joint UNDP/World Bank Energy Sector Management Assistance Program, October. Washington, D.C.

———. 1988b. *Mauritania: Household Energy Strategy*. Report of the Joint UNDP/World Bank Energy Sector Management Assistance Program, November. Washington, D.C.

———. 1988c. *Senegal: Urban Household Energy Strategy*. Report of the Joint UNDP/World Bank Energy Sector Management Assistance Program, June. Washington, D.C.

———. 1988d. *Niger: Household Energy Conservation and Substitution*. Report of the Joint UNDP/World Bank Energy Sector Management Assistance Program, January. Washington, D.C.

4

Absorbing a Rapidly Growing Labor Force

Stein Hansen

Because of the record high rate of population growth, the labor force of Sub-Saharan Africa is projected to increase by almost 80 percent between 1980 and 2000, the equivalent of an average annual growth rate of 2.9 percent (World Bank 1986a). This labor force projection, combined with the low rates of economic growth forecast for the rest of this century, suggests that creating sustainable employment is one of the principal challenges of development.

The creation of sustainable employment requires efficient use of labor, capital, and land. Physical capital and administrative and organizational capabilities are scarce in Sub-Saharan Africa, whereas unskilled labor appears to be abundant. Therefore, production techniques that are at the same time labor-intensive (low capital-labor ratios) and efficient users of capital (low capital-output ratios) are required to generate sustainable growth. Most new labor force entrants in Sub-Saharan Africa will come from rural areas and city slums and thus will be poor and unskilled. Their number and lack of skills mean that, in most countries, real income for the great majority of workers will not increase because of the pressures of population growth.

The problem in an increasing number of countries is exacerbated by declines in the amount of cultivable land available per worker, declines in land productivity because of cultivation beyond sustainable capacity, and cultivation of land of lesser quality. In addition, a number of Sub-Saharan African countries have in the past adopted—and many still follow—development strategies that foster economic dualism, with capital being allocated to large-scale capital-intensive projects. Such

The author is grateful for valuable comments and criticism by Trygve Haavelmo, Ronald G. Ridker, Jeremy J. Warford, Odd Ystgaard, and the staff of the Population, Health, and Nutrition Division of the World Bank.

strategies were based on the belief that economic growth was a direct function of the growth in the capital stock and that labor would be employed in fixed proportion to capital. At the same time, peasant agriculture and other rural activities were to provide employment and consumer goods without drawing on the scarce capital of other sectors.

In practice, such strategies neglected smallholder agriculture and the rural sector, even though that neglect was not intentional. The unforeseen difficulties of operating large-scale, capital-intensive industries at the required high levels of capacity utilization with inadequate investments in supporting physical and organizational infrastructure resulted in slower economic growth and lower than expected savings and reinvestments. At the same time, the extremely small amount of capital allocated to developing the rural sector neither produced the consumer goods nor mitigated poverty to anywhere near the extent anticipated (Mellor and Johnston 1984).

Resource endowments and population-supporting capacities vary substantially in Sub-Saharan Africa (see chapter 2 in this volume). With political stability and proper public policies and management, population-absorption prospects look bright for countries in Central Africa, where population-supporting capacity is estimated to exceed projected populations for the year 2000 by factors far in excess of five (FAO/UNFPA/IIASA 1982). At the same time, these countries have relatively high domestic savings per new labor force entrant by Sub-Saharan African standards. At the other end of the spectrum, Sahelian and East African countries have severely limited potential population-supporting capacities and low or negative domestic savings.

This chapter focuses on the following questions:

- What are the employment-creation prospects for meeting the projected 80 percent increase in labor supply by 2000 if there is no change in development strategies and employment policies?

- To what extent can unemployment, underemployment, and below-subsistence productivity be reduced or eliminated if the recommended changes in strategy and policy are implemented in an increasing number of Sub-Saharan countries?

- To what extent are Sub-Saharan land resources sufficient to produce the food requirements of projected future populations, given the limited potential of many countries for nonagricultural exports to finance food imports?

- What are the capital costs of creating sustainable jobs in different sectors and with different techniques in Sub-Saharan Africa? How do these costs coincide with the domestic savings per new labor force entrant?

In considering these questions, country-specific examples are used to illustrate issues of general validity to parts or all of Sub-Saharan Africa. Reference is made to some countries more frequently than to others simply because the relevant data and research on population growth and employment creation vary greatly in availability from one part of Sub-Saharan Africa to another.

The Macroeconomic Setting

Gross domestic investments (GDI) per new entrant into the labor market vary enormously between rich and poor countries. Whereas France, which has a slow-growing labor force, was able to invest more than US$250,000 per new labor force entrant in 1975, Ethiopia had little more than US$1,000 available (Squire 1981).

The differences with respect to gross domestic savings (GDS) are even greater. In 1984, eleven Sub-Saharan countries had negative GDS, and another twelve had less than US$2,000 GDS per new labor force entrant. In Norway, the comparable figure for 1981 was about US$2 million. Clearly, slower population growth can account for only a fraction of the difference in absolute amounts available. Differences in national income and savings rate account for the bulk of the difference. Norway does not have a set of viable employment-creation options several thousand times those of half the countries of Sub-Saharan Africa, as the respective GDS rates imply. In fact, a high-income country may face very limited opportunities for viable job creation because of wage rigidities, labor immobilities, and low levels of international activity (Johansen 1982). With the present excess supply of unskilled labor in Sub-Saharan Africa, if labor force growth rates were reduced from the projected 2.9 percent toward the projected 0.7 percent of

industrial market economies, the amount available for investments per new labor force entrant would increase manyfold and, other things being equal, would provide greater scope for absorbing entrants in a sustainable way.

The share of GDI available for the creation of employment in Sub-Saharan Africa is also negatively affected by the pressures of rapid population growth on such social investments as primary education and health (World Bank 1984). More important, the share of GDI financed by GDS is remarkably low in oil-importing economies of Sub-Saharan Africa (World Bank 1986b). Although the GDI share of gross domestic product (GDP) has increased slightly in the low-income economies of Sub-Saharan Africa, the GDS share has declined over the past two decades to such low levels that virtually no net savings take place. In other words, actual domestic investments have become increasingly dependent upon foreign aid. It is therefore of interest to look at GDS per new labor force entrant as an indicator of the ability of a country to finance workplaces and provide for technical progress through domestic capital formation. This simple indicator is useful as long as the economic situation of the countries in question severely constrains the options for absorbing the new labor force entrants in an economically viable way. Table 4-1 ranks Sub-Saharan African countries by this indicator. When compared with the capital costs of creating employment in different sectors of an economy and with different technologies, resource availabilities, growth potentials constraints on employment creation can be traced in a crude way.

The data in table 4-1 suggest that the problem for Sub-Saharan Africa is not finding outlets for domestic savings but simply determining whether the annual supply of goods and services per head will rise or fall. It is a race between population growth and available production power (Haavelmo 1961).

In a simple economic growth model where labor and capital constitute the two input factors in the net national product, the development of per capita income depends only on the sum of the so-called partial elasticities of production with regard to capital and labor and on observable values of net national product, labor, and capital and their rates of change at a given time.

It is not unreasonable to assume increasing returns to scale in some manufacturing processes and in public infrastructure (Laumas and Williams 1984). Even at the macro level, it is possible to envisage a newly settled continent, for example, Australia, with such a sparse population relative to natural resources and capital availability that increasing returns prevail—at least in the early stages of development (Pitchford 1974).

In Sub-Saharan Africa, however, the lack of skilled labor, public managerial and physical infrastructure,

Table 4-1. *Estimated Gross Domestic Savings per New Labor Force Entrant, 1984*

Above US$10,000	US$5,000– 10,000	US$2,500– 4,999	US$1,000– 2,499	Below US$1,000	Negative
Gabon[a]	Nigeria	Liberia	Malawi	Mozambique[b]	Mali
Congo	Swaziland[b]	Guinea	Rwanda[b]	Togo	Sudan
Cameroon	Angola[b]	Zambia	Niger	Ethiopia	Benin
Botswana	Zimbabwe	Madagascar	Senegal		Gambia
Mauritius		Kenya	Sierra Leone		Chad
Côte d'Ivoire		Zaire[a]	Burundi		Lesotho
			Uganda		Somalia
			Ghana		Mauritania
			Tanzania		Guinea-Bissau
					Burkina Faso
					Central African Republic

a. 1983.
b. 1979.
Sources: Computed from data in World Bank 1986b or annex tables in earlier editions of *World Development Report.*

and capital availability are severe constraints on development. Unskilled labor is the rapidly growing abundant resource, whereas renewable natural resources such as forest cover, genetic species, and cultivable soils are being depleted. Furthermore, these constraints combined with rapid population growth could hamper efficient use of whatever technical potential is found in a country and could thus delay or altogether prevent discoveries of new resources. Too little becomes available for investments in modern sectors, and insufficient capital is generated for proper education and training (Schultz 1971).

These negative effects of population pressure also exacerbate the problems and costs of planning and managing the development process. In fact, it has been claimed that rapid population growth in the above combination of circumstances and relative factor endowments, which is rather typical of Sub-Saharan Africa today, could be a serious obstacle to the technical progress that accounts for half of total economic growth in the industrial market economies (Leibenstein 1971). Developing the bureaucracy and institutional services required to implement modern sector projects on a scale proportional to the rapid rate of population growth could thus prove difficult.

In sum, the unequal availability of input factors (indeed, the severe limitations on some were observed all over Sub-Saharan Africa) suggests macro production functions such that returns to scale are at best equal to one and in many cases are less than one (Haavelmo 1977). Per capita income is then constant or increasing over time if and only if the net domestic savings ratio over the incremental capital-output ratio is equal to or higher than the rate of population growth. On the basis of alternative values of these two ratios, one can construct a matrix to show the maximum rates of population growth that will not cause a decline in output per head (table 4-2).

Although year-to-year observations reveal large fluctuations, it seems reasonable to assume that the incremental capital-output ratio (ICOR) is high (above 4) in slow-growing economies typical of Sub-Saharan Africa. In Tanzania, for example, the five-year ICOR average increased from 3.8 in 1969–73 to 4.5 in 1973–77 and to 13.8 in 1976–80 (NORAD 1984). At the same time, GDS in Sub-Saharan African countries has been very low: 12 percent for all of Sub-Saharan Africa in 1983, 13 percent for middle-income oil-importing countries, and only 7 percent for low-income countries (World Bank 1986a). In table 4-2, one sees that with the not

Table 4-2. *Maximum Permissible Rates of Population Growth under Constant Returns to Scale*

Incremental capital-output ratio	Net domestic savings rate				
	0.05	0.10	0.15	0.20	0.25
2.0	0.0250	0.0500	0.0750	0.1000	0.1250
3.0	0.0167	0.0333	0.0500	0.0667	0.0833
4.0	0.0125	0.0250	0.0375	0.0500	0.0625
5.0	0.0100	0.0200	0.0300	0.0400	0.0500
10.0	0.0050	0.0100	0.0150	0.0200	0.0250

Note: Net domestic savings rates are five to ten percentage points less than gross domestic savings rates; for example, if the gross domestic savings rate is 15 percent, then the net domestic savings rate will be 5–10 percent.
Source: Haavelmo 1961.

unrealistic assumption of ICOR equal to 5 and net domestic savings rate equal to 0.05, average annual population growth cannot exceed 1 percent if a decline in per capita income is to be avoided. With decreasing returns to scale, the situation is even less favorable.

Gradual technological changes, if they can be assumed to improve production, can clearly replace significant rates of capital accumulation. But the setting for such technological changes must be properly established in Sub-Saharan Africa before their impact can be expected to counter rapid population growth.

Two other means remain: drastically changed behavior or massive increases in foreign aid. Neither seems to be a very realistic possibility and cannot therefore be counted on to counter the impact of population growth on per capita income development in Sub-Saharan Africa.

The Costs of Employment Creation

Direct investments to create a job vary substantially with the type of job as well as with the sector in question. There are, however, significant social costs resulting from an inability to absorb an increasing labor force. Any skills that a smallholder or worker in the informal sector possesses when becoming unemployed depreciate in the absence of opportunities to practice and improve. Malnutrition and starvation reduce labor productivity, the number of healthy days, and the ability to acquire work. Although allocations to offset such conditions can significantly reduce costs and stimulate growth, I shall deal in this section with the direct capital costs of creating jobs.

Even with this limited scope, discussion is hampered by measurement problems. When comparing the costs of creating comparable jobs in the formal and informal sectors of an economy, one must bear in mind that, in practice, output and capital are not necessarily homogeneous commodities. Foreign investors, for example, tend to look at the convertible cash return potential of a project. Their supply of capital is not necessarily available for the types of informal-sector investments identified below.

Data on comparative costs in Sub-Saharan Africa show that creation of formal-sector employment requires substantially more capital per job than does the creation of similar employment in the informal sector. Some studies further indicate that capital is used more effectively to create jobs in the informal sector, even when such economic activities are obstructed and discriminated against by the government. Several conclusions may be drawn from the results of a series of sector studies in Cameroon, Côte d'Ivoire, Ghana, Kenya, Mauritania, Sierra Leone, Tanzania, Togo, and Zambia

(Byerlee and others 1983; Demol and Nihan 1982; Ghai 1980; House 1984; ILO 1973, 1976; ILO/JASPA 1981a, 1981b, 1982; Nihan and Jourdain 1978; Steel 1981; World Bank 1978):

- Labor-intensive construction creates ten (or more) times as many jobs as modern construction methods.
- Informal sector repair and maintenance services create from four to seven times more jobs than the same tasks carried out in the formal sector.
- Informal small-scale manufacturing creates five to thirty times more jobs than modern large-scale manufacturing.
- Informal small-scale manufacturing creates three to eleven times more jobs than medium-sized modern manufacturing.
- Export manufacturing creates 1.5 times more jobs than import substitution manufacturing.

The costs of creating employment through settlements or agricultural development programs also vary substantially. Direct comparisons between different projects are often obscured, however, by different cost concepts, cost coverage, and inclusion or exclusion of downstream impacts.

For any such project to be compatible with maximum income generation, its economically computed net present worth must be positive, assuming appropriate resource prices on the relevant inputs and outputs. Unit costs for World Bank–assisted settlement projects and other agricultural development projects in Sub-Saharan Africa, summarized below, have been adjusted to 1980 prices for purposes of comparison with the cost figures given above for the formal and informal sectors (ILO/ JASPA 1982; McCarthy and Mwangi 1982; World Bank 1978b, 1981). The cases covered in the above references suggest that the development unit costs of large-scale irrigated agriculture are about ten times those of rain-fed schemes and perhaps more than twenty times higher than labor-intensive rain-fed projects. The cost per workplace implicit in the development costs can be crudely estimated by assuming 0.64 workplaces per hectare of smallholdings and 0.09 workplaces per hectare of large mixed farms and gap farms (McCarthy and Mwangi 1982).

The employment-creation costs in irrigated schemes are largely comparable to those of medium- to large-scale modern manufacturing, whereas employment costs in rain-fed schemes are similar to those of small-scale manufacturing. The employment-creation costs in labor-intensive rain-fed schemes are comparable to those of informal sectors. Table 4-3 summarizes the comparative costs per workplace for Sub-Saharan Africa adjusted to 1980 prices using the national inflation rates

Table 4-3. *Approximate Capital Costs per Workplace, 1980*

Compared investments	Thousands of U.S. dollars
Medium/large-scale modern manufacturing and large-scale irrigation schemes	15–40
Small-scale manufacturing/rain-fed schemes	1.5–6
Informal sector/labor-intensive rain-fed schemes	0.1–1

Sources: World Bank 1978a, 1978b, 1980, 1981; ILO 1973, 1976; ILO/JASPA 1981a, 1981b, 1982; Ghai 1980; House 1984; Demol and Nihan 1982; Nihan and Jourdain 1978; Steel 1981; Byerlee and others 1983; McCarthy and Mwangi 1982.

published annually by the World Bank in the *World Development Report* annexes.

Potential for the Creation of Agricultural Employment

Seventy-three percent of the population of Sub-Saharan Africa is classified as nonurban (World Bank 1986b), and 70 percent of the labor force is engaged in agriculture, with skills appropriate for peasant farming and associated informal activities. A natural focal point is therefore the employment-creating potential of the agricultural sector. Although the average population density of Africa is less than one-fifth of Asia's, some Sub-Saharan African countries are becoming crowded, at least relative to their limited potential for the production of food. This is one of the main findings of the "Land Resources for Populations of the Future" project (FAO/UNFPA/IIASA 1982), which provides country-specific estimates of the potential population-supporting capacities (PPSC) determined by soil and climate conditions and levels of farm technology. The study compares three levels of technology (low, intermediate, and high) for rain-fed cultivation. The low input level is described as subsistence-level farming, and no conservation measures are then assumed. A full rate of soil loss and the sharpest decrease in productivity therefore results. Through investments in conservation, this loss is reduced 50 percent in the intermediate alternative and becomes what is termed an "acceptable loss level" in the high input category.

The results if the subsistence scenario prevails in Sub-Saharan Africa are striking: the area of rain-fed cropland will decrease by 16.5 percent, whereas the rain-fed crop productivity will decrease by 29.4 percent. Total land productivity in Africa's rain-fed regions will decrease by almost 25 percent. The role of irrigated production in Sub-Saharan Africa is projected to be

marginal on physical grounds, to say nothing of the economic obstacles to large-scale irrigated development.

At the aggregate level, the agricultural sector of Sub-Saharan Africa is projected to have the physical capacity to support at least 1.6 times its projected population in 2000 with no more than subsistence level of agriculture. With the intermediate rain-fed alternative, this ratio increases to 6.3.

Heavy population pressure on scarce agricultural land and limited physical scope for employment creation in agriculture is generally found in eighteen countries in Sub-Saharan Africa, which are projected to have some 345 million inhabitants (World Bank 1986a), or more than 50 percent of the total population of Sub-Saharan Africa projected for 2000. These countries include: Ethiopia, Kenya, Malawi, Nigeria, and Uganda.

Of the remaining countries, ten have moderately strong population pressures and a somewhat broader physical scope for employment absorption in the agricultural sector. Their projected total population for 2000 is 121 million. Burkina Faso, Ghana, Mali, Tanzania, and Zimbabwe are in this group.

Eighteen countries projected to have some 207 million people in 2000 are considered high-potential countries with moderate to high potential for physical-employment absorption in the agricultural sector and low or no population pressure. This group includes Angola, Cameroon, the Central African Republic, the Congo, Gabon, and Zaire in Central Africa; Madagascar, Mozambique, Sudan, and Zambia in East Africa; and Côte d'Ivoire in West Africa.

Land Use Intensification

The rapid population growth and the estimated PPSCs of Sub-Saharan Africa suggest that future projects for agricultural production and employment should be based on strategies that emphasize sustainable intensification of land use. Increases in farming intensity lead to declining labor productivity (Eicher and Baker 1982; Pingali and Binswanger 1983). The progression from hand to animal to tractor cultivation results in positive shifts in labor productivity but not in yields per hectare. At a given intensity of farming, shifting to animal traction reduces labor use by 64 percent and increases yields per work-hour by 71 percent. A further shift to tractor use reduces labor use by an additional 35.5 percent and yields per work-hour by 61 percent. Labor-saving benefits are the primary reason for switching to higher levels of mechanization. Mechanization is thus chosen by private farmers for economic reasons, and the choice between tractor-mechanized and labor-intensive farming systems, and thus the scope of additional agricultural and rural employment, depend critically on the outlook for policy changes that will stimulate more intensive labor use.

A recent World Bank econometric analysis based on data covering fifty-three specific locations in Africa, Asia, and Latin America (Pingali and Binswanger 1983) found that a 10 percent increase in farming intensity caused a 4.4 percent increase in yields and a 3.4 percent rise in labor use per hectare, regardless of the type of tools used.

Intensification of smallholder agriculture through more widespread use of fertilizers, pesticides, improved seeds, and so forth has been identified as a potential means of increasing yields and improving the degree of food self-sufficiency in the region. Comparison of the development in yields per hectare for major crops in Sub-Saharan Africa with that of all developing countries reveals the following trends (World Bank 1981, 1983):

- Yields are significantly lower for most crops in Sub-Saharan Africa than in other developing regions.
- In 1973–84, most yields decreased in Sub-Saharan Africa but increased in other developing regions.
- Per capita agricultural production in Sub-Saharan Africa decreased by 1.9 percent per year in 1973–84, although it increased elsewhere.
- Fertilizer consumption per hectare of arable land is much lower in Sub-Saharan Africa than in other developing regions and has decreased in most of Sub-Saharan Africa in 1973–84, although it increased in other developing regions.

It is not the farmers' technical ability to raise yields with the use of fertilizers, but rather the general marketing and provision of fertilizers to smallholders, that has limited the increased use of fertilizers. Lack of credit and distance from sources of supply constrain smallholders' use of fertilizers, pesticides, and so forth. Creation of agricultural employment in Sub-Saharan Africa is thus reduced.

The scope for increased labor use through intensification could be substantial, amounting in Kenya to an estimated 750,000 jobs, or 16 percent of agricultural employment in 1980 (McCarthy and Mwangi 1982). In Kenya fertilizer use per hectare is already one of the highest in Sub-Saharan Africa, but only half the average of developing countries in other parts of the world (World Bank 1983). Similar estimates for the employment-generation impact of intensification have been derived for southern Sudan (Norconsult A.S. 1978). It seems reasonable to assume that most countries in Sub-Saharan Africa have substantial relative potential for labor absorption through intensification because of their very low present use of fertilizer, pesticides, and improved

seeds. But a broad range of changes, with regard to both the political and the supply situation, must be introduced before this potential is realized.

Land Redistribution

There is increasing evidence that small farms have, on average, both higher employment and higher output per hectare than large farms using land of comparable quality (World Bank 1981). The scope for employment creation through land redistribution, however, varies substantially with the crops that are grown (McCarthy and Mwangi 1982). Whereas large, mixed farm crops other than pyrethrum, root crops, and vegetables require very little labor input per hectare, the dominant plantation crops other than sisal are rather labor-intensive. Large-scale livestock, however, requires relatively little labor. Substantial employment gains from redistribution are possible when large-scale cultivation of cereals is replaced by small-scale farming of virtually any crop except pulses and sorghum.

Between 1963 and 1974, hybrid maize replaced traditional varieties, and at the same time, tea and coffee acreage expanded in the Central Province of Kenya. As a result of this change in cropping pattern, the World Bank estimated a 28 percent increase in labor demand, or 2.3 percent per year. Meaningful diversion to the most labor-intensive crops has obvious limitations, however, including:

Tenure and local sovereignties over land

Tribal claims and loyalties

Quality of land

Patterns of demand for and consumption of products

Farm systems adaptations

Inadequacy of extension services, especially for women

International cash crop agreements

Peak demand for farm labor.

The impact of these factors can be modified by government policies. Changes in market prices and consumer preferences can also have a significant effect. The absolute employment-creating potential in Sub-Saharan Africa from such land redistribution also depends on the present share of large farms and tribal lands in the total agricultural land area. In this respect, the situation is not overwhelming because landlords and landless classes are not present in most of Sub-Saharan Africa as they are in Asia and Latin America.

A substantial proportion of agricultural investments over the past two decades has gone to large-scale, government-operated estates using mechanized and irrigated technologies (both capital-intensive): irrigation in Nigeria; state farms in the Congo, Ethiopia,

Ghana, Sudan, and Zambia; and sugar schemes in Côte d'Ivoire.

Capital-intensive rice production would increase output by moderate amounts but would drastically reduce the demand for labor, as occurred in Ghana (Winch 1976); labor-intensive hand cultivation can almost double the demand for labor, as in Sierra Leone rice production (Byerlee and others 1983). The Kenya experience, furthermore, confirms that the subdivision of large farms and gap farms into new smallholdings would provide an additional 0.55 work-years of employment per hectare (McCarthy and Mwangi 1982).

Irrigation and Drainage

Although the economic outlook for large-scale irrigation is rather poor in Sub-Saharan Africa, the potential for low-cost, small-scale irrigation schemes is far from exhausted. Such developments have grown rapidly in Côte d'Ivoire, Liberia, Nigeria, Senegal, and Sierra Leone. It has been estimated that in Nigeria informal irrigation schemes have contributed more to total food production than the formal irrigation schemes, and there are 2 million more hectares suitable for such development (World Bank 1981). The employment-absorptive capacity of such development could be another 1.5 million agricultural jobs, equal to two years' growth in the agricultural labor force of Nigeria.

Kenya's technical potential for irrigated farming is one of the highest in Sub-Saharan Africa. So far, less than 5 percent of this potential has been developed (McCarthy and Mwangi 1982). Although the technical potential is substantial, the required capital costs and the complex logistics make this choice questionable. Drainage, in contrast, can be developed at a fraction of the cost of irrigation development and promises environmentally sustainable and economically feasible development of another 1 million jobs (McCarthy and Mwangi 1982; Ruthenberg 1978).

Expansion of Cultivated Areas

The Sub-Saharan African countries in which expansion of agricultural land is possible and feasible correspond roughly to those with high PPSC ratios. The total land area of Angola, the Congo, Zaire, and Zambia is some 465 million hectares. The total 1980 population of these four countries was 43 million and is projected to grow to 74 million by 2000 (World Bank 1986a). The agricultural labor force, about 15.7 million in 1980, is expected to reach 25 million by 2000. The total PPSC of these four countries will be 342 million in 2000 with subsistence-level farming and about 1,500 million with the intermediate level of inputs (FAO/UNFPA/IIASA 1982).

With an average density of 0.5 jobs per hectare on the high-potential soils in these countries (compared with 0.64 for smallholders in Kenya), 50 million hectares of agricultural land will be required to absorb the agricultural labor force in 2000. This is no more than 11 percent of the total land area of these four countries, which have the bulk of the 93 million hectares of the most easily developed farmland in all of Sub-Saharan Africa (Buringh and others 1975). The availability of land suitable for cultivation will thus not be a constraint on rural labor force absorption in these four countries for many decades or perhaps centuries to come. In contrast (for example, in the case of Nigeria), the supply of cultivable land is more acute in the Sahel and the more populous parts of West Africa as well as in Ethiopia, rapidly growing Kenya, and the landlocked small East African countries of Burundi, Malawi, and Rwanda. Potential population-supporting capacities in terms of food production constrain the ability of agriculture in these countries to absorb future entrants into the rural labor force.

The bulk of empirical evidence shows that countries that have been successful in producing cash crops have also been among the most successful in expanding food production (World Bank 1981). The reason for this complementarity is that benefits from a changing dynamic agriculture are not restricted to a single crop or sets of crops. When change accelerates, the productivity of the whole farming system also increases (Cleve 1974).

Most countries in Sub-Saharan Africa have distinct comparative advantages in export crop production (World Bank 1981). If this export advantage is sacrificed for self-reliance in food supply, it may be at the expense of income and workplaces. In many countries, however, established gender roles and rights, combined with more recent patterns of migration, leave women behind to farm and to feed the family without the proper managerial and decision-making authority. Extension services, credit facilities, and agricultural policies have not been tailored to serve this role structure, so that the development of new sustainable agricultural and rural employment is hampered.

Rural Nonfarm Employment

The rural nonfarm sector is an important source of employment and income in Sub-Saharan Africa. Measuring its role poses certain problems because of the effect of seasonal variation in farm employment on nonfarm employment. It seems reasonable to assume that between 20 and 30 percent of the rural labor force is primarily engaged in nonfarm work, and the nonfarm labor force appears to grow at a faster rate than rural agricultural employment (Anderson and Leiserson 1980).

Females are strongly associated with employment in manufacturing and small-scale production (Steel 1981). Productive absorption of women into the industrial sector hence depends on expanding demand for products of small-scale enterprises. There is no homogeneous role of women in African employment activities, however. Whereas their role in trading has been pervasive in West Africa, trade in East Africa has been male dominated, with women more active in farming activities there.

Peasant farmers in Asia typically spend 40 percent of increments to income on locally produced, nonagricultural goods and services, but such linkages seem to be weaker in Sub-Saharan Africa (Mellor and Johnston 1984). The reason is the very low average productivity of agricultural labor, the consequent lesser differentiation of the rural economy, the less developed infrastructure, and a particularly suboptimal pattern of nonagricultural investments. Yet there are important links between rural income generation and income redistribution, on the one hand, and employment generation in the rural nonfarm sector, on the other (Byerlee and others 1983).

The expansion of small-scale sector outputs has also been found to have an indirect employment effect larger than that derived from large-scale sectors. Input-output data for Sierra Leone, for example, have shown that backward linkages to other, small-scale nonagricultural sectors and agriculture are much stronger than when large-scale sector output is expanded (Fatoo 1977).

The future size of the rural nonfarm sector will thus depend heavily on the future growth of the agricultural sector and the choices of levels of mechanization. If new cash crops or technologies are introduced into the agricultural sector, the increased agricultural production will create two effects: an indirect "income effect" that could increase demand for rurally produced consumer goods, and a direct "output effect" that could increase the demand for rurally produced agricultural inputs and provide opportunities for local processing of agricultural output (Liedholm 1983).

The Potential for Job Creation in the Formal Sector

The formal sector is dominated by the public sector and modern industry with more than ten employees and US$10,000 or more invested per workplace. Nonagricultural wage employment in the public sector and modern industry is about 20 percent of the total labor force of Sub-Saharan Africa, of which 12 percent is employed in industry.

Wage employment in the formal sector typically grows at 4 percent per year, although substantial variation in this growth rate has been observed over the period 1973–84, from a low 1.1 percent in Zambia through an "average" 3.9 percent in Kenya to more than 8 percent in Botswana, Cameroon, and Malawi. In oil-exporting Gabon and Nigeria, these growth rates have been even higher.

Within the wage employment sectors, the public sector has grown much faster than the private sector and, in about 1980, accounted for between 40 and 75 percent of formal-sector employment (World Bank 1981). The increasing food deficit and the trend toward lower domestic savings rates and reduced savings per new labor force entrant suggest that it will be increasingly difficult to sustain such growth rates with capital-intensive wage employment.

As noted earlier, creation of formal-sector jobs requires substantially more capital per job than creation of similar employment in the informal sector. The difference in capital costs per worker explains, at least in part, why the employment-absorption ability of the industrial sector of Sub-Saharan Africa has been poor for the past ten to fifteen years. Even in Côte d'Ivoire, one of the most successful African economies, this ability has declined rapidly since the early 1970s. Whereas a 10 percent increase in industrial output led to a 7 percent increase in employment up to 1971, the employment response dropped to 4 percent in 1972 and further to 1.6 percent in 1974 (Monson 1981).

With such low employment-absorption responses to rises in industrial output, the increases in urban labor forces will far outpace the demand for wage employment by the industrial sector. With the prevailing rural-urban migration flows and the observed unemployment and underemployment, unskilled labor is virtually perfectly elastic in supply. If the minimum-wage requirements were removed (equivalent to a 20 percent wage reduction) and if demand for unskilled labor were to grow at the same rate as industrial output, unskilled employment in the modern sector in Côte d'Ivoire would increase by 20,000, or 20 percent over its 1972 level. This jump is equal to a 10 percent increase in total modern-sector employment. Unskilled labor would increase twice as much in exportables as in importables (Monson 1981).

The negative impact on employment creation of minimum-wage regulations, overvalued local currencies, capital subsidies to import substitution industries, and other market distortions are probably worse in other African countries than in Côte d'Ivoire. The removal of such distortions would have significant labor-absorption impacts in the modern sector and—depending on the rural-urban migration effect—could reduce the depressing effects on remuneration in the urban informal sectors. As a consequence, income inequalities would be reduced.

Because the industrial sector in most places constitutes only 5 to 10 percent of the labor force, however, the immediate overall labor-absorption impact of a doubling of its employment growth rates would be very limited. It is in the rural and urban informal sectors that the labor forces will continue to grow for many years to come. A few examples will illustrate this point.

Over the past ten years, there has been virtually no growth in modern manufacturing employment in Zambia. The 0.1 million modern-sector jobs growth projected by 2000 is insignificant when compared with the 2 million increase in the total labor force (ILO 1981b). These new labor force entrants must compete for informal-sector jobs and agricultural employment. Fortunately, a very high cultivable land-to-man ratio makes it technically possible for the modernization of agriculture to proceed without the expulsion of labor from the rural areas.

In contrast, Nigeria, which has by far the largest population in Africa (an estimated 96 million in 1984 and projected to reach 163 million by 2000), has rather limited scope for the creation of agricultural employment relative to the massive labor force growth projected. Although the total employment is estimated to have grown from 24 million to 28 million from 1970 to 1975, agricultural employment increased by only 1 million. Even fewer people (0.75 million) were absorbed in the modern, or formal, sector, of which more than half were absorbed by the public sector. The remaining labor force entrants, totaling 2.25 million, were absorbed by the informal sector. During the five-year oil boom of Nigeria, when there was an impressive 14.5 percent annual growth in employment in the private modern sector, no more than 0.3 million, or 8 percent of the increase in the national labor force, were absorbed in this sector. Since 1975 the employment growth rate of the modern sector has slowed considerably, and it is likely to remain well below the growth rate projected for formal-sector output.

The Nigerian labor force is projected to increase by almost 30 million between 1980 and 2000, with one-third of this increase in the urban labor force. From the above discussion, it is clear that the absorptive capacity of the modern manufacturing sector must increase enormously to play any significant part in meeting this tremendous challenge.

The output of modern manufacturing grew by an impressive 15 percent from 1965 to 1973, but slowed to 8.5 percent from 1973 to 1984 (still impressive by African standards, World Bank 1986a). Even with a high elasticity of employment with respect to output of 0.6 (compared with 0.16 in Côte d'Ivoire in the mid-1970s), maintenance of such a high growth rate for output would yield no more than 5 percent annual growth in the modern manufacturing labor force. Manufacturing would thus absorb approximately 1.3 million new entrants over the 1980–2000 period, equal to 4 percent of the projected increase in the labor force or to 13 percent of the increase in the urban labor force. The service sector showed a similar decelerating trend. Although its output grew by 8.8 percent annually from 1965 to 1973, the growth rate dropped to 3.2 percent between 1973 and 1984. Continuation of this growth rate until 2000, combined with a unit employment elasticity, would yield a total of 1.5 million new workplaces in the service sector over the twenty-year period, equal to 15 percent of the increase in the urban labor force.

This scenario would leave 72 percent, or 7.2 million, of urban labor force entrants to find employment in the informal sector in urban Nigeria between 1980 and 2000. Add to this the 20 million new rural labor force entrants and the projected absorptive capacity of the agricultural and rural sectors, and it seems obvious that Nigeria, in spite of its oil wealth, is forced to consider seriously its primary abundant resource—unskilled labor—in its development strategies.

The high capital costs per workplace of modern manufacturing and large-scale irrigated farming (US$10,000 to US$40,000 at 1980 prices) far exceed the GDS per new labor force entrant in the mid-1980s of US$7,500. Consequently, labor-intensive infrastructure, services, maintenance, informal-sector activities, and labor-intensive sustainable developments in agriculture are the only options with any scope for creating enough jobs to absorb the tremendous growth in the labor force. Smallholder intensification probably holds by far the greatest potential for absorbing Nigeria's additional workers before the turn of the century.

Malawi's labor force, estimated at 3 million in 1980, is increasing at a rate of 2.7 percent, or 85,000, a year. Wage employment in the manufacturing sector was estimated at 5 percent of the labor force. Even if it grows at a rate of 6.5 percent (equal to that of the 1970s), the sector cannot absorb more than 12 percent of the annual labor force increase. In Tanzania, wage employment constituted no more than 5 percent, or 0.4 million, of a labor force estimated at 8 million in 1980. Manufacturing employed 100,000, or 25 percent of the wage earners, and had increased at an annual rate of 5.4 percent during the second half of the 1970s (NORAD 1984). Even so, this annual average absorption of some 4,000 workers contributed only marginally toward providing sustainable employment to the 200,000 new entrants into the labor force each year (ILO/JASPA 1982).

The Role of the Informal Sector

The informal sector absorbs a major portion of urban entrants and has attracted increasing attention over the past decade. Without this sector, open unemployment would have reached enormous proportions in Sub-Saharan Africa.

What precisely is the informal sector? It is difficult to delineate because this sector is largely based on non-registered, nonpermit, or nonauthorized operations. The heterogeneity of informal-sector output is as wide as the final and intermediate consumption observed in low-income and squatter sectors of urbanized areas in Africa. Repair and maintenance of modern-sector manufactures, locally invented products made from scrapped and recycled materials, sidewalk cafes and bars—all these are typical informal-sector activities (House 1984). Common characteristics are the small scale of operation and the low level of capital required per workplace, which is often less than 10 percent of that required for similar activities in the formal sector (table 4-3). The modest amount of upstream linkage to the formal sector follows partly from institutional and political barriers to markets and credit facilities and partly from the segmented market orientation of most informal-sector participants.

Informal-sector workers' salaries and remuneration in kind (for example, in the case of apprentices) are sensitive downward to the free entry of labor into this sector. Productivity of labor and remuneration tend to be far below legally enforced minimum wages in the formal sector, so that the demands for the output from the informal sector are limited. With increasing excess urban labor supply, one experiences an increasing dichotomy between the formal sector and the informal in Sub-Saharan Africa. This dichotomy could have politically destabilizing effects and could thereby contribute to the delay of much-needed stimuli into African economies.

Studies of the urban informal sector conducted by the ILO in Burkina Faso, Cameroon, the Gambia, Ghana, Kenya, Liberia, Mauritania, Nigeria, Senegal, Sierra Leone, Tanzania, and Togo establish that in its employment-creating role this sector provides some 60 to 70 percent of all urban employment of Sub-Saharan Africa (Selhuraman 1977).

Wage employment in the formal sector of Nigeria is increasing too slowly to absorb the growth in the urban labor force. The urban informal sector, accounting for more than 50 percent of Lagos's employment and perhaps as much as 70 percent of Nigeria's total urban employment (ILO/JASPA 1981a), absorbs the majority of new urban labor force entrants and thus prevents them from being totally unemployed.

In Nouakchott, Mauritania, modern informal-sector employment accounts for 35 percent of the jobs provided by the corresponding formal sector (Nihan and Jourdain 1978). The informal sector of Nouakchott has contributed to a rapid rise in employment of a type

probably better suited to recent rural-urban migrants than that provided in the formal sector. The overall increase in urban, informal-sector employment has averaged 13.8 percent per year; the services subsector leads with 16.4 percent of this total. Even informal-sector manufacturing employment grew at an impressive annual 12.7 percent during the 1970s.

In Kenya between 1980 and 2000, more than 1 million new labor force entrants will have to seek employment in the informal sector, but the importance of the Kenyan informal sector will accelerate after 2000 because of the limited scope for further employment creation in agriculture combined with a continued record high growth rate in the labor force. Between 2000 and 2020, another 13.2 million new labor force entrants will compete for 1 million agricultural jobs and perhaps 2–3 million formal-sector jobs. This competition will exert tremendous pressure on remuneration in the rapidly growing informal sector as well as in subsistence farming, accelerating new nonsustainable subsistence settlements on marginal lands, and will reduce the scope for maintaining or increasing per capita income. The accelerating depletion of land and forest cover following present uncontrolled population growth will reduce Kenya's job-creation potential relative to a situation with a lower rate of population growth.

During the 1970s, informal-sector employment in Tanzania increased at a rate of 7 to 8 percent annually (ILO/JASPA 1982). Discrimination against this sector, to the benefit of larger firms, took the form of absence of credits, nonallocation of inputs, zoning regulations, outright police persecution, and so forth—a pattern found all over Sub-Saharan Africa. A study of this pattern in Tanzania concluded: "Just benign neglect could well be a great help to many informal activities!" (ILO/JASPA 1982, p. 77).

In Malawi, the informal sector appears to be relatively unimportant (less than 10 percent of the urban labor force) compared with the typical pattern found throughout Sub-Saharan Africa. The sector's share could increase rapidly, however, because of Malawi's limited absorption possibilities in agriculture and its rapid rate of population growth (Kaluwa 1981). Malawi's labor force is projected to grow by almost 5 million between 2000 and 2020, and the informal sector will become the major source of employment for these new entrants. Immediate measures to reduce population growth could ease the inevitable remuneration pressure considerably.

With economic growth less than in the 1970s, when these ILO surveys were conducted, it is anticipated that the informal sector will become increasingly important in African labor markets in the years to come. In addition to creating jobs and entrepreneurial opportunities for new small-scale establishments, this sector offers important vocational training through its apprenticeship system. Approximately one-third of those employed in this sector are absorbed as apprentices and are given on-the-job training in crafts and skills.

The Scope of Employment Creation: Summary and Conclusions

Labor absorption rates in the formal sector have not kept pace with the rapid growth of the urban labor force in Sub-Saharan Africa. Given the overwhelming role of the rural and agricultural sector, it is logical to concentrate on the growth rates of agricultural output that are required to absorb the growth in the rural labor force.

Countries are ranked below by their ability to absorb future rural labor force entrants on the assumption that past growth in agricultural output will continue. Growth rates of the national labor force are used as the basis for these computations, though it is acknowledged that they are marginally higher than those of the rural labor force. It is assumed that labor is absorbed at a rate of 7.7 percent for each 10 percent increase in yields (Pingali and Binswanger 1983).

Land-Abundant Countries

Only ten Sub-Saharan African countries have a "subsistence" level of agriculture with PPSC above three times the projected population in 2000 (see table 4-4; FAO/UNFPA/IISA 1982). All but the Central African Republic and Madagascar have US$2,500 or more in GDS per new labor force entrant. Output growth rates have been in excess of projected labor force growth rates only in Côte d'Ivoire and Gabon; in the remaining countries in this group, agricultural output growth has been substantially slower.

Among these countries, only Côte d'Ivoire has reached the necessary agricultural growth rate, whereas Gabon is marginally behind. The greatest relative improvements are required in Angola and Guinea.

Moderately Land-Abundant Countries

A second group of six countries in Sub-Saharan Africa is moderately land abundant, in the sense that their PPSCs are between one and three times the projected population for 2000. All of the countries in this group except Liberia have very low GDS (below US$1,000) or negative GDS per new labor force entrant, and all have an agricultural growth performance that is insufficient to match their projected labor force growth rates (table 4-5).

Without substantially improved agricultural performance, the pressures on the informal sector will become gradually more severe in the years to come.

Table 4-4. *Land-Abundant Countries: Growth in Agricultural Output Required to Absorb the Projected 1980–2000 Rural Labor Force Increase with Labor-Intensive Land Use*
(percent)

Country	Agricultural output growth rate, 1973–84	Required agricultural output growth	Share of future increase in rural labor force not absorbed with past output performance
Côte d'Ivoire	4.3	4.3	0
Gabon	1.4	1.6	12
Zaire	1.9	3.6	47
Congo	2.2	4.8	54
Central African Republic	1.1	3.1	65
Madagascar	1.3	3.8	66
Cameroon	0.6	3.9	85
Zambia	0.6	4.0	85
Guinea	0.2	2.3	91
Angola	−2.5	3.5	>100

Note: All of these countries can expand their cultivable land areas in addition to or instead of land intensification or redistribution.

Source: Computed using World Bank statistics.

Land-Scarce Countries

There are twenty-two countries in Sub-Saharan Africa that have an estimated subsistence-level PPSC below their projected population in 2000 (table 4-6). In terms of GDS per new labor force entrant, as well as agricultural output performance, this is a rather mixed group of countries. Eight of these countries (Burkina Faso, Ma-

Table 4-5. *Moderately Land-Abundant Countries: Growth in Agricultural Output Required to Absorb the Projected 1980–2000 Labor Force Growth with Labor-Intensive Land Use*
(percent)

Countries	Agricultural output growth rate, 1973–84	Required agricultural output growth	Share of future increase in rural labor force not absorbed with past output performance
Tanzania	2.8	4.2	33
Chad	1.7	3.0	43
Liberia	1.2	3.3	64
Sudan	1.3	3.6	64
Gambia	−1.4	2.9	>100
Mozambique	−2.2	3.1	>100

Source: Computed using World Bank statistics.

Table 4-6. *Land-Scarce Countries: Growth in Agricultural Output Required to Absorb the Projected 1980–2000 Labor Force Growth with Labor-Intensive Land Use*
(percent)

Countries	Agricultural output growth rate, 1973–84	Required agricultural output growth	Share of future increase in rural labor force not absorbed with past output performance
Swaziland	5.1	4.2	0
Rwanda	4.9	4.0	0
Niger	5.3	3.9	0
Mali	3.4	3.1	0
Mauritania	2.8	2.7	0
Burkina Faso	2.3	2.2	0
Nigeria	3.5	4.0	12
Malawi	3.0	3.5	14
Ethiopia	2.3	3.3	30
Benin	2.1	3.4	38
Togo	2.3	3.8	39
Sierra Leone	1.5	2.5	40
Chad	1.7	3.0	43
Somalia	1.8	3.4	47
Kenya	2.4	4.6	48
Mauritius	0.9[a]	2.7	67
Burundi	1.2	3.6	67
Uganda	1.3	4.2	69
Zimbabwe	0.9	4.4	80
Botswana	− 1.2	3.8	>100
Senegal	− 0.3	3.1	>100
Ghana	− 2.1	4.6	>100

a. 1970–82.
Source: Computed using World Bank statistics.

lawi, Mali, Mauritania, Niger, Nigeria, Rwanda, Swaziland) experienced a higher growth rate for agricultural output in 1973–84 than that projected for the labor force in 1980–2000. Except for Nigeria and Swaziland, however, these countries have had a low or negative GDS (Burkina Faso, Mali, Mauritania) per new labor force entrant in recent years. Among the remaining fourteen countries, insufficient PPSC to feed the projected population in 2000 is combined with a recorded history of growth of agricultural output that has been less than that of the labor force.

In seven of these countries, agricultural output over the past decade has been rather poor, and if this trend continues, less than half of the rural labor force will be absorbed in the rural labor market. Except for Botswana and Mauritius, the GDS per new labor force entrant is too low for the formal sector or irrigated large-scale agriculture to assume any significant role in labor absorption.

Although this land-scarce group is heterogeneous, the countries share a common need for the careful evaluation and control of agricultural area expansion, whether planned or spontaneous, to ensure sustainable rural development. Intensification rather than area expansion is the technical solution to be sought in these countries. The pressures on the informal sector, especially in urban areas, will be enormous in the years to come unless policies and priorities are directed toward massive improvements in labor-intensive agriculture and complementary rural production takes place.

This analysis has shown that no more than ten countries of almost forty in Sub-Saharan Africa have anywhere near the ability to absorb projected rural labor force increases by 2000 without significant changes in labor market policy. Another nine countries face moderate policy challenges in order to raise the agricultural and rural output enough to absorb the rural labor force increase, whereas the third and largest group of countries must initiate significant policy changes so that sufficient rural labor absorption will be feasible until 2000, let alone after the turn of the century. Most of these countries cannot expect much labor absorption through cultivation of new land. Once their land intensification potential has been realized, other sectors of the economy will have to relieve agriculture of the role of creating sustainable employment.

Past trends suggest a very limited capacity for labor absorption in the formal sector for decades to come. Therefore, the surplus labor will enter the informal sector, which is already producing at a subsistence level in most of Sub-Saharan Africa. Alternatively, people will settle on new marginal land and apply nonsustainable cultivation practices. Since unemployment compensation is not feasible in these countries, governments should immediately remove the barriers to efficient performance in the informal sectors so as to maximize this sector's labor-absorptive potential. Creating more competition between formal- and informal-sector activities is likely to reduce the capital-labor ratio and the capital-output ratio in the formal sectors, thus increasing labor-absorptive potential. Until the turn of the century, however, smallholder agriculture and rural nonfarm activities should continue to absorb the large majorities of new entrants into the labor force. Rapid increases in informal urban employment are likely to be a sign of stagnation rather than of a healthy structural change unless government policy toward this sector changes drastically.

The strongest message from this analysis is that, even in the most efficiently operated Sub-Saharan African countries with limited PPSCs, the long run (after 2000) labor-absorptive capacities look frightfully inadequate, even with the best domestic economic policies at present conceivable.

References

Anderson, Dennis, and M. M. Leiserson. 1980. "Rural Non-farm Employment in Developing Countries." *Economic Development and Cultural Change* 28(2): 227–48.

Buringh, P., G. J. Staring, and D. J. Van Heemsk. 1975. *Computation of the Absolute Maximum Food Production of the World.* Wageningen, Netherlands: Agricultural University.

Byerlee, Derek, C. K. Eicher, Carl Liedholm, and D. S. C. Spencer. 1983. "Employment-Output Conflicts, Factor-Price Distortions, and Choice of Technique: Empirical Results from Sierra Leone." *Economic Development and Cultural Change* 31(2): 315–36.

Cleve, T. H. 1974. *African Farmers: Labor Use in the Development of Smallholder Agriculture.* New York: Praeger.

Demol, Erik, and Georges Nihan. 1982. "The Modern Informal Sector in Yaoundi." *International Labour Review* 121:77–88.

Eicher, C. K., and D. G. Baker. 1982. *Research on Agricultural Development in Sub-Saharan Africa: A Critical Survey.* International Development Paper 1. East Lansing: Michigan State University.

Fatoo, Habib. 1977. "Macroeconomic Analysis of Output, Employment, and Migration in Sierra Leone." Ph.D. diss., Michigan State University.

FAO/UNFPA/IIARA (Food and Agriculture Organization of the United Nations, United Nations Fund for Population Activities and International Institute for Applied Research Analysis.) 1982. "Potential Population Supporting Capacities of Lands in the Developing World." Technical Report FPA/INT/513.

Ghai, Dharam. 1980. "Basic Needs: From Word to Action—With Illustrations from Kenya." *International Labour Review* 119(3): 367–79.

Haavelmo, Trygre. 1961. "The Race between Population and Economic Progress." In *Institute of Economics Memorandum of March 10, 1961* (in Norwegian). Oslo, Norway: University of Oslo.

———. "Critical Remarks to the Theories of Economic Growth." 1977. In *Institute of Economics Memorandum of April 22, 1977*, edited by A. Hervik (in Norwegian). Oslo, Norway: University of Oslo.

House, W. J. 1984. "Nairobi's Informal Sector: Dynamic Entrepreneurs or Surplus Labour?" *Economic Development and Cultural Change* 32(2): 277–302.

ILO (International Labour Organisation). 1973. *Employment in Africa: Some Critical Issues.* Geneva.

———. 1976. *Growth, Equity, and Employment: A Comprehensive Strategy for the Sudan.* Geneva.

ILO/JASPA (International Labour Organisation/Jobs and Skills Programme for Africa). 1981a. *Nigeria—First Things First.*

———. 1981b. *Zambia: Basic Needs in an Economy under Pressure.* Addis Ababa.

———. 1982. *Basic Needs in Danger: A Basic Needs Oriented Development Strategy for Tanzania.* Addis Ababa.

Johansen, Leif. 1982. "A Note on the Possibility of an International Equilibrium with Low Levels of Activity." *Journal of International Economics* 13:257–65.

Kaluwa, B. M. 1981. *Location and Extent of Future Employment Opportunities: Lilongwe, 1980–83.* Lilongwe: University of Malawi.

Laumas, P. S., and Martin Williams. 1984. "Economies of Scale for Various Types of Manufacturing Production Technologies in an Underdeveloped Economy." *Economic Development and Cultural Change* 32(2): 401–12.

Leibenstein, Harvey. 1971. "The Impact of Population Growth on Economic Welfare: Nontraditional Elements." In *Rapid Population Growth: Consequences and Policy Implications*, edited by R. Revelle. Baltimore, Md.: Johns Hopkins University Press.

Liedholm, Carl. 1983. "Research on Employment in the Rural Non-Farm Sector in Africa." Department of Economics, Michigan State University, East Lansing.

McCarthy, F. D., and W. M. Mwangi. 1982. *Kenyan Agriculture Towards 2000.* Laxenburg, Austria: International Institute for Applied Research Analysis.

Mellor, J. W., and B. F. Johnston. 1984. "The World Food Equation: Interrelations among Development, Employment, and Food Consumption." *Journal of Economic Literature* 22:531–74.

Monson, Terry. "Trade Strategies and Employment in the Ivory Coast." 1981. In *Trade and Employment in Developing Countries*, edited by Anne Krueger and others. Chicago, Ill.: University of Chicago Press.

Nihan, Georges, and Robert Jourdain. 1978. "The Modern Informal Sector in Nouakchott." *International Labour Review* 117(6): 709–19.

NORAD (Norwegian Agency for Development). 1984. *Review of Norwegian Financial Assistance to Tanzania.* Mission Report. Oslo.

Norconsult, A. S. 1978. "Kenya-Sudan Road Link: Economic and Engineering Appraisal." Oslo.

Pingali, P. L., and H. P. Binswanger. 1983. "Population Density, Farming Intensity, Patterns of Labour Use, and Mechanization." Discussion Paper, Report ARU 11. Agricultural and Rural Development Department, World Bank, Washington, D.C., September; processed.

Pitchford, J. D. 1974. *Population in Economic Growth.* Amsterdam: North Holland.

Ruthenberg, Hans. 1978. "Outline of a Strategy for Agricultural Development in Kenya." Processed.

Schultz, T. P. 1971. "An Economic Perspective on Population Growth." In *Rapid Population Growth: Consequences and Policy Implications*, edited by R. Revelle. Baltimore, Md.: Johns Hopkins University Press.

Selhuraman, S. V. 1977. "The Urban Informal Sector in Africa." *International Labour Review*, no. 116 (3): 343–52.

Squire, Lyn. 1981. *Employment Policy in Developing Countries: A Survey of Issues and Evidence.* New York: Oxford University Press.

Steel, W. F. 1981. "Female and Small-Scale Employment under Modernization in Ghana." *Economic Development and Cultural Change* 30(1): 153–67.

Winch, F. 1976. "Cost and Returns of Alternative Rice Production Systems in Northern Ghana: Implications for Output, Employment, and Income Distribution." Ph.D. diss., Michigan State University, East Lansing.

World Bank. 1978a. *Employment and Development of Small Enterprises.* World Bank Sector Policy Paper. Washington, D.C.

———. 1978b. *Agricultural Land Settlements.* A World Bank Issues Paper. Washington, D.C.

———. 1981. *Accelerated Development in Sub-Saharan Africa: An Agenda for Action.* Washington, D.C.

———. 1983. *World Development Report 1983.* New York: Oxford University Press.

———. 1984. *World Development Report 1984.* New York: Oxford University Press.

———. 1986a. *Financing Adjustment with Growth in Sub-Saharan Africa, 1986–90.* Washington, D.C.

———. 1986b. *World Development Report 1986.* New York: Oxford University Press.

5

Accommodating Urban Growth in Sub-Saharan Africa

Mark R. Montgomery and Edward K. Brown

The urban populations of Sub-Saharan Africa are growing at remarkable rates. Urban growth has negative consequences that are readily apparent to politicians and planners alike; not surprisingly, the public sector has often responded to growth with restrictive measures designed to displace new arrivals and discourage further rural-to-urban migration. We shall argue that this type of antiaccommodationist response is ineffective as well as inappropriate. Policies to restrict urban growth by means of checks and controls on movement are far more likely to hinder economic development than to promote it. A more promising strategy would be an emphasis on family planning to reduce the rate of urban increase, combined with a set of intervention policies narrowly focused on the urban labor market and the provision of infrastructure. We will attempt to make the case for such a strategy, which we would term "accommodationist," for Sub-Saharan Africa.

The accommodationist rationale rests on several points. First, experience suggest that policies designed to keep people out of large cities are rarely feasible without massive exertions of political will. There are surely better ways to expend scarce political capital (Laquian 1981; Simmons 1981). Second, such policies are ineffective against natural increase, a source of city growth that rivals migration in importance. Third, a sensible population distribution policy must take into account the close connection between urbanization and economic development. The economic benefits that arise from concentration of firms, labor, and consumers in cities are impressively documented, even if still poorly understood (Henderson 1986; Montgomery 1988). A distribution policy that attempts to bring urban growth to a halt would be most difficult to justify on economic grounds. A carefully designed policy, in contrast, would seek to eliminate market imperfections and policy distortions so as to encourage efficient locational decisions on the part of individuals and firms. Such a policy might well attempt to divert urban growth from large cities to secondary cities and industrial estates, although the case for doing so is not always compelling.

Much of the concern about urban employment conditions rests with the supply side of the labor market. Yet the contribution that family planning can make in restraining the growth of the urban labor force does not seem to have been fully appreciated in Sub-Saharan Africa. The largest contributor to urban growth rates in developing countries is the rate of natural increase in urban areas—on average, it accounts for almost 61 percent of total urban growth (United Nations 1980). Levels of urbanization are lower in Sub-Saharan Africa than in much of the developing world, however, and rural-urban migration accounts for 40 to 60 percent of urban growth there. The benefit from urban-oriented family planning programs is immediate in the sense that school-age cohorts are smaller than they would be in the absence of fertility limitation, and there may also be an effect on the demands for urban health services. Family planning efforts directed at rural areas yield longer-run benefits in that they reduce the number of migrants who will eventually contribute to city growth.

If policies designed to keep people out of large cities will not necessarily improve urban standards of living, neither will family planning programs by themselves. A complementary set of policies is required, one that focuses directly on urban labor markets and urban investments in infrastructure. The economic rationale for providing infrastructure is especially clear-cut. As will be seen, much of the debate in this area concerns the appropriate quality of services.

The costs of accommodating urban growth will be severe for many countries in Sub-Saharan Africa. It is

74

74

important to give these costs a realistic appraisal. Accommodationist policies place special stress on urban public administration—on the design and implementation of revenue instruments and the planning for and management of urban investments in infrastructure and interventions in the labor market. In each of these areas, the shortage of skilled civil servants creates bottlenecks and weakens the capacity of the public sector to guide or respond to urban growth. These administrative weaknesses pose the most serious obstacles to an accommodationist policy.

Urbanization and Urban Growth

This overview of urbanization in Sub-Saharan Africa begins with a brief historical review, considers data from recent censuses and other sources, and then discusses likely paths of urban growth up to the year 2000. Three features of urbanization are considered: urban proportions, the rate of growth of urban populations, and the level of primacy.

Historical Review

Although it was not until the latter part of the nineteenth century and the beginning of the twentieth that many major urban centers emerged, urbanization in Sub-Saharan Africa is not an entirely modern phenomenon. Precolonial urbanization extended across the Sudan savanna and forest zones of West Africa, where such notable towns as Gao, Timbuktu, and Djenne along the Niger River flourished. Kano, the biggest city in today's northern Nigeria, first appeared in the late tenth century; Benin also dates from this period. Other precolonial towns that have become important centers today include Kumasi, Porto Novo, Ibadan, and Abeokuta. The majority of these precolonial towns were essentially agrarian communities, although in some there existed significant social differentiation, with extensive occupational division of labor, skills, and political positions (Hanna and Hanna 1981).

In Central and East Africa, precolonial urbanization was less prevalent, although in the former the capitals of some kingdoms (for example, Luanda in the Kongo Kingdom) had an unquestionably urban character. The interior of East Africa possessed no major towns prior to European infiltration, the main centers of the region being the coastal town of Mombasa and the island of Zanzibar, where Arabs had established trading links.

The process of urbanization did not gather momentum in Sub-Saharan Africa until World War II. The need for strategic resources, which could be satisfied through local raw materials and industries, created employment opportunities in the colonial administrative and commercial centers. The rate of rural-urban migration as well as intercountry migration accelerated with the demand for resources. Independence seems to have stimulated further urban growth, particularly in capital cities, in a number of countries.

In short, urban growth in Sub-Saharan Africa is the product of both traditional and modern developments. The lack of uniformity in urban structure across regions (evident in data presented below) reflects a diversity in indigenous cultures and politics as well as differences in material resources and the types of European intervention.

Levels and Rates of Urbanization

A comparison of levels and rates of urbanization is made difficult by variations in the definition of urban areas. There are nearly as many definitions of urban places as there are countries in Sub-Saharan Africa. Because data collection in the region began relatively recently and statistical methods continue to be improved, there is an additional problem of intertemporal change in definition for many countries. Although the 1950 Sudan census defined urban centers as some sixty-eight identified towns, for example, the 1973 and 1983 censuses used a cutoff point of 5,000 or more inhabitants. Hence it is difficult to be precise about either cross-country comparisons or within-country trends. Changes in city boundaries also make comparisons difficult.

General tendencies concerning the level of urbanization can be discerned in census data. Table 5-1 shows the urban percentages and average annual growth rates of urban populations in various African regions and in other regions of the world for 1950–80.

Four observations can be made about Sub-Saharan urbanization. First, the urban proportions are low in comparison with those in much of the developing world. With the exception of Central Africa, which resembles East Asia in urban proportions, the other subregions— East and West Africa—are among the world's least urbanized, with one-sixth and one-fifth of their 1980 populations, respectively, living in urban areas. Although North Africa and the Republic of South Africa are more urbanized, the level of urbanization for Africa as a whole is still below the norm. Only South Asia compares with Africa as a whole in urban proportions.

Second, although the average level of urbanization is low, there is marked country-specific variation. In East Africa, for example, countries such as Somalia and the Sudan display urban proportions considerably higher than the average for the subregion. At the other extreme are two neighboring countries, Burundi and Rwanda, with very low levels of urbanization (4.5 percent each in the late 1970s). Recent estimates for Uganda are also rather low (9 percent, 1980), whereas the Kenyan 1979

Table 5-1. *Percentage of Population in Urban Areas and Annual Urban Growth Rates, Major Areas and Regions, 1950–80*

Region	Percentage of population in urban areas					Annual urban growth rate			
	1950	1960	1970	1975	1980	1950–65	1960–70	1970–75	1975–80
World total	29.0	33.9	37.1	39.3	41.3	3.35	2.91	2.84	2.93
More developed regions	52.5	58.7	64.7	67.5	70.2	2.44	2.05	1.75	1.68
Less developed regions	16.7	21.9	25.8	28.0	30.5	4.68	3.94	3.95	4.06
Africa	14.5	18.1	22.9	25.7	28.9	4.42	4.85	4.97	5.10
East	5.5	7.5	10.7	13.2	16.1	5.37	6.06	6.95	6.87
Central	14.6	18.1	25.2	29.7	34.4	4.07	5.71	5.56	5.40
Southern	37.3	41.7	43.8	44.8	46.5	3.52	3.38	3.17	3.62
West	10.2	13.5	17.3	19.6	22.3	4.97	4.87	5.10	5.34
North	24.5	29.8	36.6	40.1	43.8	4.33	4.71	4.57	4.59
Latin America	41.2	49.5	57.4	61.2	64.7	4.57	4.21	4.01	3.86
East Asia	16.7	24.7	28.6	30.7	33.1	5.46	3.09	3.06	3.03
South Asia	15.7	17.8	20.4	22.0	24.0	3.37	3.91	4.01	4.33

Source: United Nations 1980.

level, at 13 percent, is much closer to the norm for the subregion. Similar country variation is evident in West Africa, a region in which the coastal countries display higher levels of urbanization than do those of the Sahel.

A third salient feature of urbanization in Sub-Saharan Africa is perhaps the most dramatic: the extremely high rates of city growth. Although these rates are not entirely without historical precedent—the cities of tropical Latin America and South Asia experienced a similar pace in the 1950s—growth is occurring at rates that considerably exceed those experienced by currently developed countries at a comparable period in their histories (that is, 1875–1900).

For almost all Sub-Saharan Africa countries, recent average annual intercensal urban growth rates are higher than 5 percent, and a significant number display rates of 10 percent or above. Tanzania's 1967–78 intercensal average annual growth rate was 11.6 percent, suggesting that its urban population doubled in six years. Kenya's 1967–79 average intercensal annual growth rate was 6.4 percent, Zambia's was 6.5 percent (1969–80), Rwanda's was 7.4 percent (1970–78), and that of the Côte d'Ivoire was 8.2 percent (1970–80). All these rates imply doubling in a decade or less.

The fourth important feature of African urbanization is the prevalence of "primate cities"—single towns or cities constituting the bulk of the total urban population in the country. Deficiencies of data, particularly regarding the definition of urban areas, must temper our conclusions here. Yet without doubt, in most of the countries of the region, the capital city is the largest, accounting for perhaps 30 to 50 percent of the total urban population (see table 5-2). In many cases, the capital is at least twice the size of the second largest city.

These levels of primacy contrast with the pattern in North Africa, South Asia, and Latin America at com-

parable levels of development. Within North Africa a downward trend in primacy is apparent, and with the exception of Egypt, primacy levels are below 30 percent. In South Asia, the level of primacy is also lower and has been relatively stable over the last two decades.

The importance of large towns in Sub-Saharan Africa is further evident in the size distributions for urban areas. In most countries more than half of the urban population lives in towns of at least 50,000 inhabitants. (The majority of countries have no more than six cities of this size.) Another 10 to 30 percent live in centers with between 10,000 and 50,000 inhabitants. An analysis of trends shows that the urban population continues to gravitate toward the few large cities. Malawi in 1977 had 68 percent of its total urban population in two towns with more than 50,000 inhabitants. Senegal in 1976 had three-quarters of total urban population in the six cities with more than 50,000 inhabitants.

Overall, these data suggest that three-quarters or more of the Sub-Saharan Africa urban population lives in towns of at least 10,000 inhabitants, and the majority in agglomerations of at least 50,000. The typical African urban dweller inhabits a respectably sized city that is growing at an exceedingly fast pace. This high urban concentration in a few towns and the rapid rate of urban growth are perhaps the two distinctive features of urbanization in the region.

Urbanization and Income Levels

The connection between urban proportions and income levels can be examined further using cross-national data from the World Bank (1984). We consider a regression equation of the following general form:

$$U = \beta_0 + \beta_1 y + \beta_2 y^2 + \beta_3 D_s$$
$$+ \beta_4 D_s y + \beta_5 \text{Den} + \beta_6 r.$$

Table 5-2. *Percentage of Urban Population Living in Largest City*

	First period		Second period	
Country	Year	Urban percentage	Year	Urban percentage
East Africa				
Burundi	1979	33.3		
Ethiopia	1968	31.5	1980	37.0*
Kenya	1962	46.9	1979	57.0
Somalia	1975	33.0	1980	34.0*
Sudan	1956	28.8	1980	31.0
Tanzania	1957	29.1	1978	31.2
Uganda	1959	37.8	1980	52.0
Zaire	1958	13.9	1980	30.0
Zambia	1963	17.2	1980	35.0
West Africa				
Angola	1960	43.9	1980	64.0
Benin	1961	55.3	1980	63.0*
Burkina Faso	1975	33.7	1980	41.0*
Cameroon	1960	26.0	1980	21.0*
Central African				
Republic	1959	56.0	1980	36.0
Chad	1963	37.7	1980	39.0*
Congo	1960	69.7	1980	56.4**
Côte d'Ivoire	1965	35.9	1980	32.6*
Gabon	1961	38.8		
Gambia	1976	100.0		
Ghana	1960	21.8	1980	35.0*
Guinea	1955	27.9	1980	80.0*
Liberia	1962	40.3	1974	38.8
Mali	1960	31.6	1980	24.0*
Mauritania	1965	21.4	1977	42.2
Niger	1977	21.7	1982	31.0*
Nigeria	1953	8.6	1980	17.0*
Senegal	1960	53.1	1980	65.0
Sierra Leone	1963	30.3	1980	47.0*
Togo	1960	57.6	1980	60.0*
Southern Africa				
Botswana	1964	21.3	1981	39.6
Lesotho	1966	43.8	1976	40.4
Malawi	1966	54.2	1977	47.2
Mozambique	1970	82.4	1981	83.0
Namibia	1960	29.2	1970	32.6
South Africa	1951	17.0	1970	13.8
Swaziland	1966	51.7	1976	30.7
Zimbabwe	1962	32.9	1969	37.9

Sources: Single asterisk (*) denotes World Bank 1984; double asterisk (**), United Nations 1980; otherwise, various censuses and surveys.

where the dependent variable U is the percentage urban in 1982, and explanatory variables include the level of income per capita (y) in 1982, national population growth rates (r) and density levels (Den), and a dummy variable for the countries of Sub-Saharan Africa (D_s). The data are restricted to developing countries. The sample includes countries with income per capita of US$6,840 or less in 1982. The mean urban percentage for the sample is 37.8; for Sub-Saharan countries it is 24.3 (1982 figures). The regressions are to be viewed as descriptive in the sense that they trace out empirical associations (rather than causal relations) between the urban percentage and levels of income per capita when other factors such as population density are held constant.

The first column of table 5-3 confirms that the association between urban proportions and income per capita is positive. If the coefficient estimate is taken at face value, each increase of $100 in per capita income is associated with a one-point gain in the urban percentage. Coefficients on the variable D_s, introduced to account for shifts in the regression intercept and slope in Sub-Saharan Africa, suggest that Sub-Saharan Africa is less urbanized than other developing regions when

Table 5-3. *Percentage of Urban Population and Income Levels: Descriptive Regressions*

Item	Model (1)	Model (2)	Model (3)	Model (4)
Constant	23.8	29.2	29.8	3.0
	(9.8)	(9.2)	(0.9)	(0.7)
Income per capita, 1982	1.1×10^{-2}	1.0×10^{-2}	1.0×10^{-2}	3.1×10^{-2}
	(8.7)	(7.1)	(6.7)	(8.7)
Income per capita squared				-4.0×10^{-4}
				(6.6)
D_S^a		-9.9	-13.6	0.3
		(2.5)	(2.6)	(0.1)
D_S times income per capita			6.0×10^{-3}	-6.0×10^{-3}
			(1.1)	(1.1)
Population density				6.3
				(2.4)
Population rate, 1960–70				3.9
				(1.9)
R^2	0.49	0.53	0.53	0.72

Note: t-statistics appear in parentheses.
a. Dummy variable denoting country in Sub-Saharan Africa.
Source: World Bank 1984.

income per capita is held constant (column 3). The fourth column of the table, however, in which a curvilinear relationship between per capita income and urbanization is examined, shows no discernible difference between Sub-Saharan Africa and the remainder of the developing world in urbanization once population density levels have been included in the equation.

In sum, the countries of Sub-Saharan Africa seem neither more nor less urbanized than their counterparts elsewhere in the developing world if income per capita is taken into account. This finding begs an important question concerning the causal relations between urbanization and income per capita, to which we return below.

Projections

Recent estimates suggest a leveling off of urban growth rates and the possibility of a decline in rates of growth in some countries (United Nations 1980). Nonetheless, projections for 1980–2000 indicate that Sub-Saharan Africa will continue to have the fastest rate of urban growth among major regions of the developing world until the end of the century. Average annual urban growth for the whole of Africa will likely remain over 4 percent, with East and West Africa continuing to display rates of 5 percent. The U.N. projection (United Nations 1980) indicates that the urban population of Africa as a whole will grow by a factor of 10.9, which is exceptionally high in comparison with Latin America (6.9), East Asia (7.2), South Asia (7.5), and the more developed countries (2.4). These enormous increases are now all but inevitable. In spite of this rapid growth,

all other regions of the world are likely to attain an urban majority by 2000, whereas both East and West Africa will probably retain their rural majority—an indication of lower initial levels of urbanization.

Urbanization and Economic Development

The cross-national data presented above help document the positive association between urbanization and income per capita. Economic theory can provide a general explanation that emphasizes the importance of cities to economic growth. As will be seen, however, the application of the theory to Sub-Saharan Africa may be limited.

The explanation begins with the proposition that income elasticities for manufactured goods and for services exceed those for primary products. Therefore, as per capita incomes begin to rise, there is a greater shift in the demand for secondary and tertiary products than for primary products. The production of manufactured goods, in particular, is thought to be subject to agglomeration economies; that is, there are downward shifts in the average cost curves of individual firms that result from clustering with like firms, service and repair establishments, and consumers of final products. Clustering may also generate lower unit input costs, especially for inputs that exhibit economies of scale (for example, electricity) and have relatively high transport or distribution costs. In short, the transport and communication costs incurred in manufacturing are minimized in agglomeration economies. There may be a dynamic element present as well. Firms in close proximity to other firms may find it less expensive to innovate, in the sense that it is less costly to test a market reaction to a new product; demonstration effects, perhaps more visible when firms are spatially clustered, may then spread innovations across firms more rapidly. The resulting technological change induces income growth, and the process begins to build upon itself.

This rather stylized economic rationale for urbanization involves both the minimization of communication and transport costs at a point in time and technological change over time. It assigns the lead role to manufacturing, although innovations may also diffuse within the service sector, and some service industries may themselves be closely linked to manufacturing. In general, however, services play a subsidiary role in the argument; in the extreme, the bulk of service employment would exist simply to meet the needs of the manufacturing labor force.

When we apply the framework sketched above to Sub-Saharan Africa, three questions immediately arise. First, how well established is the empirical evidence for agglomeration economies? Second, if the urbanization rationale rests on manufacturing and on the links between manufacturing and services, how strong do such linkages appear to be? Third, if the realization of agglomeration economies requires public-sector investment in infrastructure, what policy options are available to minimize the adjustment costs involved? We touch on the first two of these issues in this section and reserve the third for later discussion.

The connection between income levels and the demand for manufactured goods and services, relative to primary products, is well established. Table 5-4 presents a descriptive analysis of labor force shares. The dependent variables for the regressions are the percentages of the labor force in agriculture, industry, and services, and the explanatory variables include levels of income per capita, a dummy variable for the countries of Sub-Saharan Africa, population density, and the population growth rate.

Table 5-4 confirms what other analyses have shown, namely, that there is an increase in both the manufacturing and services share as income levels rise, with a corresponding decrease in the proportion of the labor force found in agriculture. Given its levels of per capita income, Sub-Saharan Africa exhibits somewhat lower levels of employment in services and (perhaps) in industry than does the remainder of the developing world.

Although there is a little hard evidence concerning agglomeration economies in developing countries, existing studies of agglomeration effects come to a remarkably uniform conclusion: there are clear productivity advantages associated with urbanization (see Montgomery 1988 for a review). The results of Henderson (1986) for Brazilian manufacturing are especially instructive. He distinguishes between two sources of agglomeration economies: those arising from the clustering of firms within a given industry ("economies of localization") and those that are the result of the location of a firm, whatever its industry, within a large urban area, as opposed to a smaller urban or rural location ("economies of urbanization"). Economies of localization reflect intraindustry specialization, the reduction of search costs for firms looking for workers with specific types of training, the within-industry diffusion of innovations, and economies of scale in the provision of public sector inputs specifically tailored to given industries. Urbanization economies, in contrast, arise from the overall size of the labor market that a

Table 5-4. *1980 Labor Force Shares and Income Levels: Descriptive Regressions*

Item	Percentage in agriculture	Percentage in industry	Percentage in services
Constant	81.3	10.4	8.3
	(14.1)	(3.8)	(1.9)
Income per capita, 1982	-2.7×10^{-2}	0.9×10^{-2}	1.9×10^{-2}
	(9.0)	(6.0)	(7.8)
Income per capita squared	2.8×10^{-6}	-0.8×10^{-6}	-2.0×10^{-6}
	(5.3)	(3.2)	(4.8)
D_S^a	8.6	-2.6	-6.0
	(2.7)	(1.7)	(2.5)
Population density	-1.5	3.9	-2.5
	(0.6)	(3.3)	(1.3)
Population growth rate, 1960–70	-1.8	-0.5	2.3
	(0.9)	(0.5)	(1.5)
R^2	0.79	0.72	0.71

Note: t-statistics appear in parentheses.
a. Dummy variable denoting country in Sub-Saharan Africa.
Source: World Bank 1984.

firm might tap and general economies of scale in the provision of public services.

Henderson concludes that localization economies are quite significant in Brazilian manufacturing. That is, manufacturing firms that are in proximity to other firms in their industry appear to be more productive. With minor exceptions, productivity differences arising from city size alone do not appear significant in the Brazilian case. There are potentially important lessons here for population distribution in Africa. The key point is that the level of industrial employment at which localization economies are exhausted varies by industry. For some industries, no extra productivity benefit is derived from clustering in large agglomerations. To extract the productivity benefits of clustering, therefore, such industries could be located in a range of smaller towns. Firms in industries that require large agglomerations to derive productivity benefits could be grouped in the larger towns and cities. The existence of localization economies provides one economic rationale for the decentralization of urban populations.

No study similar to Henderson's has been conducted in Sub-Saharan Africa. A careful investigation of localization economies by industry could provide important information for policy. Henderson's central conclusion—the greater importance of localization economies than urbanization economies in developing countries—has been challenged, however, in a study by Shukla (1984), who finds that urbanization economies bring larger benefits in Indian manufacturing.

The relatively small size of the manufacturing sector in Sub-Saharan Africa has long been a concern of policymakers. Can the existence of agglomeration economies in manufacturing provide a rationale for current levels of urbanization in the region? To what extent might agglomeration economies in manufacturing generate additional benefits by expanding employment in services?

Table 5-5 provides a framework for considering the issues. The dependent variable considered here is the percentage of the labor force in service employment. The question is whether a measure of industrial output—the share of industry in gross domestic product—is associated with the share of the labor force in services. A positive association might suggest backward linkages between manufacturing and services, although other interpretations are possible.

As noted above, both service and manufacturing employment tend to rise with income per capita. The regressions in table 5-5 indicate that, when income per capita is held constant, an increase in industry's share of gross domestic product (an output measure for industry) is associated with an increase in the share of employment going to services. We regard the positive coefficient as reflecting derived demands for service jobs

Table 5-5. *Percentage of the Labor Force in Services: Descriptive Regressions*

Item	Full sample	Sub-Saharan African countries
Constant	8.8	8.2
	(2.3)	(2.3)
Income per capita, 1982	6.5×10^{-3}	17.3×10^{-3}
	(5.5)	(1.9)
Share of industry in gross domestic product	0.39	0.01
	(2.6)	(0.0)
R^2	0.55	0.29

Source: World Bank 1984.

that arise from increases in industrial output. If this is a reasonable interpretation, then the second column of table 5-5 suggests that the links between the industrial sector and services are very weak in Sub-Saharan Africa. The coefficient on industry's share in this regression is insignificantly different from zero.

Although on their own these results are scarcely conclusive, they do point to one persistent concern about the levels of urbanization in Sub-Saharan Africa. The economic rationale for urbanization rests on the existence of agglomeration economies in manufacturing, for the most part, and on demands originating in manufacturing for services. The small size of the manufacturing base in African cities, when coupled with (apparently) weak links to the service sector, makes it difficult to establish a case for the economic rationality of present levels of urbanization. Our results suggest not necessarily that urbanization ought to be restrained but rather that the links between urban manufacturing and services might be better cultivated. We will return to the linkage issue later in the chapter.

If the conventional view of urbanization and agglomeration economies is difficult to sustain for Sub-Saharan Africa, additional factors may be incorporated in an accommodationist argument. These have to do with connections between the urban economy and the agricultural sector that arise through short-term migration and urban-to-rural remittance networks. There is substantial evidence, particularly for Kenya, on the size and direction of urban-rural remittance flows (see Johnson and Whitelaw 1974; Knowles and Anker 1981). Both Stark (1976) and Collier and Lal (1980) have argued that remittances provide a source of capital to the rural sector that might not otherwise be available, given the limited penetration of formal capital markets into rural areas. They go on to suggest that the infusion of funds leads to increased agricultural investment and a greater willingness to undertake technological change in the agricultural sector. In essence, the transfer of labor from rural to urban areas is accompanied by a reverse flow of capital, acting to improve average rural incomes over time.

The link between remittance flows (or the return of "target" migrants with their accumulated capital) and investment in agriculture is not well documented. Certainly the survey responses on the use of remittance funds do not suggest that agricultural investments are a first priority (Rempel and Lobdell 1978), although the availability of remittance income may free other funds for investment purposes. The response that does appear in the surveys has to do with the use of remittances to finance the education of a migrant's younger siblings or nephews, that is, with human capital investments.

Even if remittances do not stimulate investment in agriculture, they may reduce the net variability in incomes accruing to a rural-based extended family (Montgomery 1983). An extended family receiving remittance income from its migrant members has at least one source of income that may be more stable than the incomes available in agriculture. Remittance transfers could have an insurancelike function, increasing in years in which drought or other factors intensify the difficulties in agricultural production. For these reasons, actions that improve earnings prospects in urban areas may well generate benefits for the rural sector.

Decentralized Urban Development

Population distribution policies, in Sub-Saharan Africa and elsewhere, have often tried to divert urban growth toward smaller urban centers and secondary cities (Abumere 1981). The notion of localization economies discussed above provides one economic rationale for diverting growth. Yet the incentives arising from localization and urbanization economies must be balanced against other factors: the transport costs of inputs and of final products; land rents and wage levels, which theory and empirical evidence suggest will tend to decline outside large urban centers; and, particularly if governmental interventions are pervasive, access to public sector decisionmakers. Economic theory cannot provide specific guidelines for the optimal distribution of city sizes. A number of writers (for example, Hamer 1984) have argued that in the early stages of development one might expect levels of primacy to be high. Over the longer term, however, rising wages and land costs will create a market incentive for some firms to relocate to the urban periphery. If these economic incentives for decentralization are accompanied by infrastructure policies that funnel investment funds toward promising secondary cities, a less centralized urban system may begin to emerge.

The World Bank's experience in São Paulo suggests that it may be difficult for location policies to spur the decentralization process along. One might think that the most natural starting point for policy would be to encourage firms in the central metropolitan area to open branches or to transfer to new locations, especially given the lower land rents and wages in the periphery. In fact, a small proportion of employment decentralization in the São Paulo study region resulted from either branching or transfers. The bulk of employment decentralization arose from stationary expansion of firms already in place and the birth of new firms. Worries about the availability of public services—particularly electricity and telecommunications—tended to discourage firms in the metropolitan area from looking very far into the urban periphery. Declines in wage levels did not appear to provide much of an incentive for relocation, whereas land rents, which declined more steeply with distance, emerged as more significant.

From these findings we conclude that, once the underlying economic incentives for decentralization have emerged, Sub-Saharan governments should make firms aware of such opportunities (Hamer's review suggests that urban firms have surprisingly limited information about alternative locations), provide the necessary infrastructure, and attempt to promote local entrepreneurship and selected local firms as the key to secondary-city growth. There is certainly a role for the public sector in monitoring the evolution of wages and land rents by location and in contingency planning for relatively rapid provision of services once economic incentives point toward particular secondary cities. Decentralization of government authority, certainly a slow process in its own right, may help (Henderson 1982). All these are policy options for the long term; developing-country experience shows that efforts to develop industrial estates or to promote secondary-city alternatives rarely meet with speedy success.

Urban Labor Markets

Are urban employment conditions deteriorating in Sub-Saharan Africa? Few would suggest otherwise. High rates of urban labor force growth, arising from natural increase and in-migration, must put some downward pressure on earnings and some upward pressure on rates of unemployment. The common perception, reinforced by economic models (Todaro 1969), is that deterioration has occurred. Without doubt, the economic declines of the 1980s have reduced incomes across the board, and urban incomes, as well as rural ones, have suffered. Yet it is surprisingly difficult to marshal empirical data in support of the view that, over the long term, shifts in the supply of labor to cities must dominate shifts in the demand for that labor. In this section we consider data on the sectoral composition of labor, unemployment, and earnings. Our data do not extend into the 1980s, and therefore our conclusions must be somewhat circumscribed. Nevertheless, although the data certainly do not suggest an overall improvement in urban employment conditions in the decades before the 1980s, neither do they reinforce the view that conditions unambiguously deteriorated. The picture is mixed. We conclude that despite the rapidity of shifts in urban labor supply in Sub-Saharan Africa, they do not necessarily dominate the shifts in demand.

It is often argued that the service sector acts as a repository for low-skill employment, particularly for migrants who fail to gain jobs in the urban modern sector (Todaro 1969). Sabolo (1975) discusses trends in the sectoral composition of labor in Sub-Saharan Africa, dividing overall service employment into "modern" services, including banking and financial services, and residual, or "informal" services, representing commerce, construction, and unidentified activities. Sabolo's data on trends in employment shares do not suggest large increases in the informal service component relative to modern services during a period of rapid urban growth in Sub-Saharan Africa. There is a similar finding in the United Nations' (1980, chapter 5) detailed breakdown of trends in urban service employment for a sample of developing countries outside Sub-Saharan Africa. (See Gregory 1986 for an analysis of employment in Mexico City that reaches the same conclusion.) The findings are consistent with results from other studies (Mazumdar 1976) on the employment found by rural-urban migrants. Migrants do not appear to be disproportionately located in informal service jobs or in services relative to manufacturing. Although much more detailed research on the question is in order, these aggregate data do not reinforce the view that urban growth in Africa has been accompanied by large increases in the share of low-skill service employment.

The findings on open unemployment rates are equally mixed. The levels of open unemployment rates within Sub-Saharan Africa cited by Sabolo (1975) are high relative to rates found elsewhere in the developing world. Nevertheless, Sabolo's data do not reveal alarming increases in unemployment rates during the 1960–73 period. Gregory's (1980) very careful assessment of unemployment trends in developing countries finds erratic changes in unemployment rates and little evidence for clear positive or negative time trends in the data. (Gregory's sample does not include countries from Sub-Saharan Africa.)

On the most important labor market issue—trends in real urban earnings in Sub-Saharan Africa—there are scarcely any data to consider. Berg (1976) has investigated levels of earnings prevalent in the Sahelian countries during a period that covers the Sahelian drought and cityward migration. His figures suggest a decline in the real earnings levels of urban unskilled wage earners in some countries but not in all of them; the re-

ported declines would seem to have been accentuated during the drought years. Gregory's (1986) analysis of earnings trends in Mexico City may have relevance for the comparably fast-growing cities of Sub-Saharan Africa; he finds an upward trend in real earnings across skill groups in the face of rapid labor force growth.

Whether or not its share of total urban employment is rising, informal employment is an important part of the Africa urban scene (see chapter 4 in this volume). How should this sector be viewed? Is it simply a repository for low-income employment? Could incomes in the sector be improved through more extensive forward linkages to the modern sector?

Sethuraman (1977, p. 347) presents a picture of an African informal sector that is relatively isolated from modern-sector firms:

> In Kumasi . . . direct linkages with formal sector firms are surprisingly limited, only about 10 percent of intermediate inputs being bought directly from the modern sector. However, there is a significant strengthening of such linkages as the size of the informal sector firm increases. In these cases backward linkages with other informal sector enterprises are also much stronger. . . . At least in the case of Ghana, linkages take the form of subcontracting to other informal sector enterprises. For example, certain aspects of automobile repair, metalwork, and shoe manufacture are subcontracted to more specialized enterprises with the necessary equipment or skills. This implies a more efficient use of available capital and other resources. It also partly explains why the informal sector enterprises cluster together. Backward linkages with rural areas are virtually non-existent. Forward linkages are mainly with individuals, households, and other informal sector enterprises and only to a small extent with the formal sector. The reasons for this are to be found partly in the pattern of goods and services produced (mostly consumer oriented) and partly in the inability of informal sector enterprises to reach formal sector customers or to turn out high-quality products.

House (1984) has investigated the pattern of earnings with Nairobi's informal sector, focusing in particular on the incomes accruing to proprietors of informal-sector establishments and the wage earnings of employees and apprentices in the sector. House shows that mean incomes in furniture and metal goods manufacture, restaurants, retailing, and vehicle repair are high relative to those in other occupations; this finding suggests a division of the informal sector into an intermediate category and a very low-income services sector. House estimates that 40 percent of proprietors earn less than the minimum wage in the formal sector.

Among the factors that influence proprietor incomes in the informal sector, one in particular stands out:

firms with subcontracting arrangements generate higher incomes for their proprietors. Most such contracts were to supply inputs or services to the modern sector, mainly furniture and metal goods and vehicle repair. Hence, at least in Nairobi, there appear to be more extensive forward links to the formal sector than Sethuraman suggests is the case in Ghana.

In short, the African informal sector is exceedingly diverse. Although there are differences in mean earnings, the distribution of earnings in the informal sector overlaps that of the modern sector to a surprising degree (Squire 1981). Simple statements about the share of employment found in the informal sector cannot convey enough information for policy decisions. Among the influences on informal-sector incomes that are potentially amenable to policy influence, the density of forward linkages to the modern urban sector is perhaps most significant. Policies that affect the ease with which formal-sector firms can contract for inputs or services from informal-sector enterprises may have an important impact on urban incomes and income growth. Public policy might well concentrate on those informal-sector firms (such as those in vehicle repair and furniture manufacture) that have the potential to meet formal-sector standards of quality.

Public-Sector Investments in Urban Services

The economic rationale for urbanization rests in large part on agglomeration economies, and the delivery of public services is critical if these economies are to be realized. Discussions of urban bias often make it seem as though services are provided solely for the benefit of urban consumers, but urban firms also use public services as inputs and also benefit. Expenditures on communications, transport, water, and electricity may have direct impacts on production and urban incomes. The important question from the policy point of view concerns the appropriate level of quality in service provision. It is seldom feasible or efficient to adopt the standards of Western cities in supplying services to households and small commercial and industrial users, although a forward-looking policy will make provision for upgrades over time.

If budgetary resources are to be conserved, each aspect of government involvement must be carefully justified. Certain items can be moved entirely out of government budgets. There is, for instance, no compelling rationale for government provision of bus services. This type of transport can be adequately provided through the private sector, although there may remain a need for oversight and regulation. There is, similarly, no compelling justification for government construction of housing. The most productive role for government is to stimulate private-sector housing investment—

through the provision of services (of appropriate quality) to low-income areas, through land policy and the regularizing of ownership, and through removal of regulations that encumber financial markets and discourage construction. The experiences of Sub-Saharan African governments with World Bank–sponsored sites-and-services programs are instructive here.

As shown in Cohen and others (1979), it is characteristic of Sub-Saharan Africa that if services are at a low level in the largest cities, they are even less available in secondary cities. The provision of infrastructure in secondary cities often falls well below the minimum levels necessary to encourage economies of agglomeration. In many cases, such cities would appear to be dominated by their large communities of the poor.

Kisumu, a relatively rapidly growing secondary city (1974 population: 46,000) in the midst of Kenya's densely settled, agricultural Western province, is a case in point. The World Bank estimates that more than 50 percent of households in Kisumu are located in squatter areas (as opposed to roughly one-third in Nairobi), and employment growth in Kisumu has been plagued by severe underinvestment in infrastructure. Yet Kisumu would appear to have potential as an agricultural marketing and services center; one aim of the sites-and-services program in Kisumu has been to encourage this line of development. Francistown, Botswana's second largest city (at 23,000 population in 1975) and the location of earlier (1974) Bank assistance, has roughly 60 percent of its population in squatter settlements, whereas in Gabarone the figure is closer to 27 percent. Even in Selebi Phikwe (population 21,000), a newly established city that serves a large copper, nickel, and diamond mining complex in the north, the percentage of the population in squatter housing approaches 40 percent.

Some of the general lessons learned in the course of the Bank-sponsored sites-and-services programs in Sub-Saharan Africa and elsewhere are summarized below, with an eye toward linking infrastructure policies with employment policies for the urban poor. In designing policies that cut across various infrastructure sectors, a general principle behind the Bank's programs has been to make use of user charges whenever possible and to tie these as closely as possible to the long-run marginal costs of service provision. The emphasis on pricing and cost recovery raises the question of how sensitive service demand is to prices and incomes, an issue on which we touch briefly below.

Transport

Transportation issues could not be more central in determining whether resources are allocated efficiently within an urban area. A transport system links one firm to another and thereby affects the extent to which economies of proximity are realized. It connects workers to firms and influences both the time and the money costs involved in labor force participation. It alters the cost of distributing firm output to local consumers. A transport system can be the decisive factor in determining whether and to what extent other public services can be provided to certain areas—in particular, water supply and waste disposal—and in determining the access of both firms and consumers to off-site public services. Transport therefore plays a key role in influencing the allocation of urban resources.

Household demand for transport services is derived demand, based in large part on the location of employment and the housing rent gradient. In general, the choice of transport mode in trips to and from work depends on household income and earnings opportunities; walking trips are perhaps the only option for the poorest groups in the urban population (Linn 1983, p. 106). Even in large cities, walking and cycling can account for some 60 percent of all trips (Linn 1983, p. 91, cites Dar es Salaam, Karachi, and Kinshasa as examples), although as Mills and Song (1979) note for Korea, bus transport becomes an important mode in work trips as incomes improve. The urban poor devote between 1 and 10 percent of their income to transport costs.

One important element of transport costs—the cost of time—depends on the choice of mode and on the level of congestion. The time costs involved in work trips may discourage labor force participation among poor and secondary earners and may clearly reduce the welfare of the poor.

What transport policies should Sub-Saharan governments pursue? In reference to bus services, Linn (1983, p. 115), drawing on Bank work in Jakarta, argues that the public sector has no comparative advantage in service provision. Private bus companies appear to provide efficient service as long as they are not overly regulated. A role for the public sector might remain in subsidizing private firms to provide service to low-income areas.

A number of additional issues involve a regulatory role for the public sector. Congestion costs can be reduced by such simple devices as reserving lanes for buses and bicycles, designating one-way streets, and diverting through traffic around the congested central city areas. The congestion costs generated by private autos—belonging primarily to upper-income groups—can be limited by a system of time-of-day or area license plates or by outright bans on automobiles in certain locations. Both efficiency and equity can be served by improving the access of the poor to employment. Linn (1983, p. 101) suggests that planners in large cities (where work trips are long) give more attention to pedestrian overpasses, neighborhood walkways, and bicycle paths.

Water Supply

Water is both used as an input in production (primarily in manufacturing) and consumed by households. With respect to the latter, there are important externalities involved in supplying treated water to households. The World Health Organization suggests that, on a daily basis, some twenty to forty liters of treated water per person are necessary to meet minimal sanitation standards and prevent the spread of disease.

Where water is priced, household demands are sensitive to income, especially at the low end of the income scale (Meerman 1979). When water is supplied through communal standpipes, the primary cost from the user's point of view is the opportunity cost of time spent drawing water or, in cases where access is difficult, in the fees paid to private water vendors. The time costs involved in drawing water reduce the hours available for market work by women and secondary earners; in addition, as noted in Saunders and Warford (1976, p. 124), water consumption by households that must rely on standpipes often falls well below the levels necessary to ensure minimum health standards.

The significant proportion of total demand for water is from industrial or commercial firms, although the figures cited are imprecise. Warford and Julius (1977) suggest that residential users account for only 40 percent of total consumption in an East African context, whereas the World Bank (1980) gives a range of 40 to 70 percent for residential use. Perhaps the crucial question is the extent to which low-income residential users can be adequately served by communal standpipes rather than through a system of house connections. Because the savings in distribution costs for a standpipe system are considerable, such systems are to be preferred in servicing low-income areas—indeed, a standpipe system may be the only option that is feasible in a budgetary sense. The number and location of standpipes remains important, however, because standpipes that are too widely spaced may generate time costs and discourage consumption.

Pricing decisions are also critical in ensuring that water is used efficiently. Metering is often appropriate for industrial and large-scale commercial consumers; it is seldom appropriate for the small commercial and domestic users (Saunders and Warford 1976, p. 123). Standpost systems are, of course, not easily metered, and in general flat fees for access must be collected from households. Households with connections can be metered (the World Bank has experimented with pricing connection fees at or below cost and with "lifeline" pricing schedules designed to encourage at least minimum consumption), or charges can be levied on the basis of size of connection and number of household fixtures. Saunders and Warford (1976, p. 176–79) suggest that fees be keyed to the long-run incremental costs of providing service—in general, geographically uniform pricing systems (often the result of a consolidation of regional water boards) do not encourage efficient locational decisions.

Sewage Disposal

The supply of water and the collection, treatment, and disposal of waste water and sewage are closely linked. Not only does the level of water supply influence the need for a disposal system—Rovani (1979) notes that, once house connections are made, the daily water flow typically exceeds 100 liters per person and makes a sewerage system necessary—but also the two services have similar health externalities. And as in the case of water supply, a range of low-cost technologies is available for sewerage systems that may help ease the strain on government budgets.

The major distinction to be drawn here is between waterborne sewerage systems—the systems that, in the past, have been favored by developing-country urban engineers—and lower-cost technologies, some of which have been developed only recently, that often involve separate disposal of excreta and waste water (World Bank 1980, p. 22). The lower-cost technologies range from pit latrines and communal toilets to vacuum truck cartage, low-cost septic tanks, and sewered aquaprivies. The World Bank's experience with such technologies suggests that they can provide acceptable levels of sanitation within urban areas, at least outside the central business district (CBD); waterborne systems appear to be required only within the CBD (Linn 1983, p. 149–51, and Linn 1982). There are exceptions, of course; in Abidjan, local flooding and seepage conditions make waterborne systems necessary.

The World Bank has identified a series of systems through which developing-country cities might progress, beginning with low-cost technologies outside the CBD and moving gradually toward waterborne systems. One key point in a low-cost system is typically the collection of excreta by vacuum trucks; hence, access roads to septic tanks or aquaprivies must be provided.

Solid Waste Disposal

The justification for public-sector intervention in the collection of solid waste, beyond the provision of access roads, appears to be limited. Private-sector collection systems seem to work well enough in cities such as Cairo and Alexandria and can be financed through user charges. There is some justification, however, for a public-sector role in disposing of solid wastes. Linn (1982)

suggests that sanitary landfills are often adequate for developing-country cities and that planners should view proposals for capital-intensive composting facilities or incinerators with caution.

Electricity

Technological economies of scale in electricity generation appear to be substantial, with little scope for quality variation or alternative low-cost technologies. Electricity costs are sensitive to the distances between demand centers and to the difficulty of the terrain. As a result, average costs for servicing rural or low-density areas are higher than for urban service delivery.

A large part of electricity consumption can be traced to industrial and commercial users. In one sample these users accounted for more than 60 percent of total consumption. Household demands are sensitive to income, as documented in Meerman (1979, p. 188).

The most efficient systems for electricity pricing, in principle, involve time-of-day or peak-load pricing in addition to regional variation. Unfortunately, sophisticated metering systems are difficult to maintain and are themselves vulnerable to power outages; therefore meters are generally economical only for the larger industrial and commercial users. Residential users can be charged flat rates and given current-limiting devices to restrain consumption.

Land Policy and Housing

In the course of a number of World Bank sites-and-services programs beginning in the early 1970s, a consensus developed that the construction of shelters is best carried out by the private sector as long as the proper incentives are in place to encourage housing investment. There are no apparent economies of scale in construction, and public housing projects have tended to set quality standards that put the units out of reach of most of the urban poor. Key incentives include the availability of services, as discussed above, and, perhaps most important, security of tenure or landownership. The dilemma in housing policy is how best to encourage private investment in housing when many of the low-income population are illegal squatters or are renting from owners who have divided lots in violation of zoning laws.

Several conversion schemes have been explored in the course of the World Bank's sites-and-services and slum-upgrading programs. Regularization of ownership rights is perhaps easiest when squatters occupy publicly owned land; in such cases, ownership can be granted in return for a payment, as in the Bank's Cairo project.

Squatters on private land present more difficult problems. Here the conversion costs are both political and economic—they include meeting owners' objections to public acquisition or expropriation as well as the financial costs of acquisition. Strain on budgetary resources is lessened if payments are required of the new owners and if laws permit the public sector to expropriate land. Ownership gives a low-income household a foothold on capital markets, since land can be used as collateral for construction loans.

Application of marginal cost pricing in the sites-and-services or slum-upgrading programs has been hindered by the fact that, quite often, only the poor or project participants are paying anything close to marginal costs. Upper-income groups in Sub-Saharan cities can rely on the long tradition of heavily subsidized public services. The inequities are obvious to lower-income project participants and are an important source of tension in efforts to rationalize prices.

Urban Public Finance and Administration

Here we briefly discuss the general revenue instruments available to the public sector and then summarize the political and institutional constraints in Sub-Saharan Africa that affect both revenue raising and the implementation of urban infrastructure investments and integrated policies for employment and service provision.

A universal aspect of urbanization is that sites near the city center and along transport routes are bid up in value as a city grows. If urbanization requires substantial investments in infrastructure, then why not finance such expenditures out of revenues drawn from property or site taxation? As Bahl, Holland, and Linn (1983) have pointed out, property and land value taxes are underutilized in developing countries and, even where such taxes are in place, the revenues have not kept pace with growth in the potential tax base. Property listings are often nonexistent. Assessment practices are clearly inadequate in many developing-country cities, in part because of a shortage of trained assessors, difficulties in collection, and, in some cases, taxpayers' resistance. Inflation transforms an already difficult assessment task into one that is exceedingly hard to carry out efficiently or equitably.

Shoup (1979) has identified some additional political considerations that may make administration difficult. Relatively little commercial real estate in urban areas is owned by foreign firms or large domestic corporations, which in some circumstances could be taxed at low political cost. Rather, in many cities the important government officials, their families, and other elites are the major property owners. For obvious political reasons, these assets may not be taxable. Unfortunately, there is often very little middle-class housing or land-ownership as an alternative source of tax revenue. As Shoup (1979) puts it, a gulf exists between the "politically nontaxable mansions and luxury apartments in high-rise structures, on the one hand, and the shanties of the poor that are not worth trying to tax, on the other."

Bahl, Holland, and Linn (1983) argue that, for the near term at least, property taxation cannot be relied upon to produce major new infusions of revenue. Still, few real alternatives present themselves. In some countries there is revenue potential in automobile taxation, but in many, fuel, license, and use taxes are already in place. The development of property and site tax systems in Sub-Saharan Africa could begin with highly simplified systems, in which relatively crude criteria (for example, the number of floors in a structure) are used to determine tax payments.

Perhaps the most vexing long-term problem, touching on both the revenue side of urban public finance and the implementation of urban projects, lies in the shortage of skilled public-sector personnel (Cohen 1982). Although many of the sites-and-services projects have involved the training of local personnel and efforts to strengthen local housing authorities, it is not yet clear whether local administrators can carry on the effort as housing and infrastructure programs move beyond the pilot stage.

Conclusions

This chapter has argued that the rapid growth of Sub-Saharan urban populations is one of a number of factors that make the accommodation of urbanization so difficult. A slower rate of urban growth, achievable in part through concerted efforts toward family planning, would help buy time in which more fundamental reforms could be directed at the root causes of low urban incomes. We have attempted to identify some of these root causes in policy rigidities, labor market imperfections, and deviations from appropriate levels of service pricing and taxation.

We wish to place special emphasis on revenue raising and service delivery. If the cities of Sub-Saharan Africa are to assume their proper role as engines of growth, it is imperative that their systems of public finance be strengthened. The revenue instrument with greatest long-run potential, the property tax, is admittedly demanding of currently scarce public-sector resources. Yet we would argue that the effort to put such a tax in place must begin in earnest, for otherwise the public sector will find itself unable to sustain the investments in service delivery that are essential if economic growth is to proceed.

References

Abumere, S. I. 1981. "Population Distribution Policies and Measures in Africa South of the Sahara." *Population and Development Review* 7: 421–34.

Bahl, Roy W., D. Holland, and Johannes F. Linn. 1983. "Urban Growth and Local Taxes in Less Developed Countries." *Papers of the East-West Population Institute* 89.

Berg, Elliot. 1976. "The Economic Impact of the Drought and Inflation in the Sahel." Discussion Paper No. 315. Ann Arbor: Center for Research on Economic Development, University of Michigan.

Cohen, Michael A. 1982. "The Political Economy of Urban Reform in Africa." Paper presented at the annual meeting of the Canadian Association of Africa Studies, Toronto, May.

Cohen, Michael A., S. A. Agunbiade, Daniele Antelin, and Anne de Mautort. 1979. *Urban Growth and Economic Development in the Sahel.* World Bank Staff Working Paper 315. Washington, D.C.

Collier, Paul, and Deepak Lal. 1980. *Poverty and Growth in Kenya.* World Bank Staff Working Paper 389. Washington, D.C.

Gregory, Peter. 1980. "An Assessment of Changes in Employment Conditions in Less Developed Countries." *Economic Development and Cultural Change* 28: 673–700.

_____. 1986. *The Myth of Market Failure: Employment and the Labor Market in Mexico.* Baltimore, Md.: Johns Hopkins University Press.

Hamer, Andrew. 1984. "Decentralized Urban Development and Industrial Location Behavior in São Paulo, Brazil: A Synthesis of Research Issues and Conclusions." Discussion Paper UDD-29. Water Supply and Urban Development Department, World Bank, Washington, D.C.; processed.

Hanna, William J., and Judith L. Hanna, eds. 1981. *Urban Dynamics in Black Africa.* New York: Aldine.

Henderson, J. V. 1982. "The Impact of Government Policies on Urban Concentration." *Journal of Urban Economics* 12: 280–303.

_____. 1986. "Efficiency of Resource Usage and City Size." *Journal of Urban Economics* 19: 47–70.

House, William. 1984. "Nairobi's Informal Sector: Dynamic Entrepreneurs or Surplus Labor?" *Economic Development and Cultural Change* 32: 227–302.

Johnson, George, and William Whitelaw. 1974. "Urban-Rural Transfers in Kenya: An Estimated Remittances Function." *Economic Development and Cultural Change* 22: 473–97.

Knowles, James, and Richard Anker. 1981. "An Analysis of Income Transfers in a Developing Country: The Case of Kenya." *Journal of Development Economics* 8.

Laquian, Aprodicio. 1981. "Review and Evaluation of Urban Accommodationist Policies in Population Redistribution." In *Population Distribution Policies in Development Planning.* New York: Department of International Economic and Social Affairs, United Nations.

Linn, Johannes F. 1982. "The Costs of Urbanization in Developing Countries." *Economic Development and Cultural Change* 30: 625–48.

_____. 1983. *Cities in the Developing World: Policies for Their Efficient and Equitable Growth.* New York: Oxford University Press.

Mazumdar, Dipak. 1976. "The Urban Informal Sector." *World Development* 4: 665–79.

Meerman, Jacob. 1979. *Public Expenditure in Malaysia: Who Benefits and Why.* New York: Oxford University Press.

Mills, Edwin, and Byung Nak Song. 1979. *Urbanization and Urban Problems.* Cambridge, Mass.: Harvard University Press.

Montgomery, Mark. 1983. "Consumption Risks and Migration as an Economic Strategy in Senegal." Department of Economics, Princeton University; processed.

_____. 1988. "How Large Is Too Large? Implications of the City Size Literature for Population Policy and Research." *Economic Development and Cultural Change.* 36: 691–720.

Rempel, Henry, and Richard Lobdell. 1978. "The Role of Urban to Rural Remittances in Rural Development." *Journal of Development Studies* 14: 324–41.

Rovani, Yves. 1979. "The Problems of Water Supply and Waste Disposal." *Finance and Development* 16: 14–18.

Sabolo, Yves. 1975. "Employment and Unemployment, 1960–90." *International Labour Review* 112: 401–11.

Saunders, Robert J., and Jeremy J. Warford. 1976. *Village Water Supply.* Baltimore, Md.: Johns Hopkins University Press.

Sethuraman, S. V. 1977. "The Urban Informal Sector in Africa." *International Labour Review* 114: 343–52.

Shoup, Carl. 1979. "The Taxation of Urban Property in Less Developed Countries: A Concluding Discussion." In *The Taxation of Urban Property in Less Developed Countries,* edited by Roy W. Bahl. Madison: University of Wisconsin Press.

Shukla, Vishnoo Prasad. 1984. "The Productivity of Indian Cities and Some Implications for Development Policy." Ph.D. diss., Department of Economics, Princeton University.

Simmons, Alan B. 1981. "A Review and Evaluation of Attempts to Constrain Migration to Selected Urban Centres and Regions." In *Population Distribution Policies in Development Planning.* New York: Department of International Economic and Social Affairs, United Nations.

Squire, Lyn. 1981. *Employment Policy in Developing Countries: A Survey of Issues and Evidence.* New York: Oxford University Press.

Stark, Oded. 1976. "Rural-to-Urban Migration and Some Economic Issues: A Review Utilizing Findings of Surveys and Empirical Studies Covering the 1965–75 Period." Working Paper 38. Geneva: World Employment Program, International Labour Office; processed.

Todaro, Michael. 1969. "A Model of Labor Migration and Urban Unemployment in Less Developed Countries." *American Economic Review* 59.

United Nations. 1980. *Patterns of Urban and Rural Population Growth*. Population Study 68. New York: Department of International Economic and Social Affairs.

Warford, Jeremy J., and DeAnne Julius. 1977. "The Multiple Objectives of Water Rate Policy in Less Developed Countries." *Water Supply and Management* 1: 335–42.

World Bank. 1979. *World Development Report 1979*. New York: Oxford University Press.

———. 1980. *Water Supply and Waste Disposal*. Washington, D.C.

———. 1984. *World Development Report 1984*. New York: Oxford University Press.

Part III

Household and Individual Consequences of Reproductive Patterns

Rapid population growth in Sub-Saharan Africa is associated with patterns of reproduction that affect individuals, families, and societies. These patterns include the youthfulness of women at marriage, frequent childbearing at all ages but notably among both teenagers and older women, and short interbirth intervals. These reproductive patterns have grim health consequences for many mothers and children and affect the well-being of the family and household. Maine and others (chapter 6) and Acsadi and Johnson-Acsadi (chapter 7) outline and quantify these consequences and indicate gains that can be achieved by altering these patterns. Correction of unhealthy and harmful reproductive patterns requires great and persistent social effort but small economic investment.

The health-related consequences of high fertility actually increase the demand for births. Anticipation that children will be lost reinforces the desire for large families, thus sustaining rapid population growth. Although most Sub-Saharan African societies have traditionally required behavior that ensured a healthful interval between births, levels of maternal, infant, and early childhood mortality and conditions of morbidity are nonetheless among the most unfavorable anywhere in the world.

From the sparse available information, Maine and others estimate that the level of maternal mortality is possibly forty to sixty times as high as in developed countries. Among other factors, maternal mortality is strongly influenced by conditions that can be controlled by the woman and her family, notably the age at which she gives birth and the number of pregnancies she has. If women who do not want more children were able to limit their families, or if the extremely high average family size of eight children were reduced to six, it is estimated that the lives of every four to twenty women who die as a result of pregnancy or delivery would be saved.

The negative health effects of high fertility are notable for the newborn. Maternal age, birth order, and especially the length of the interval between successive births greatly influence the viability of the child. Short birth intervals are common in some parts of the region and increasingly prevalent in Sub-Saharan Africa. Their deleterious effects persist at least through the first five years of life, and they are associated with very high rates of mortality in infancy and early childhood. If all second and higher-order births were to be spaced at least twenty-four months apart, 12 to 20 percent of infant deaths in Sub-Saharan Africa would be averted. If intervals were as long as four years, the reduction in infant mortality would be even greater.

Acsadi and Johnson-Acsadi document the fact that premature entry into a marital union also has a powerful negative effect upon the health of both mothers and their young children. These authors also show that, if the purpose of early marriage is a harmonious family life that perpetuates and extends the lineage, than the custom of early marriage is self-defeating.

Age at first union generally determines age at first birth because contraception is seldom used early in the marriage. In some Sub-Saharan African countries, 25 to 40 percent of women are married or enter first union before age fifteen and in eight countries well over 50 percent are in a union before age eighteen. Below maternal age eighteen, babies are frequently miscarried or born at below normal birth weight, a common cause of infant death, and may suffer a variety of other abnormalities. The younger the maternal age, the higher the rate of infant mortality.

Of particular interest is the impact of age at marriage upon the health, mortality, and socioeconomic well-being of the woman. Early marriage and the consequent early commencement of childbearing are associated not only with lack of education but also with high fertility and large completed family size. Women who enter a union at the age of fifteen years or less, however, are often barren or subfecund at least temporarily. The lower the median age at marriage in this region, the longer the average interval before the first child and the fewer the children born within the first five years of marriage. Furthermore, when physical injury, infection, or physiological immaturity impairs the fecundity of very young women, infertility may persist until age 35 or later.

The socioeconomic consequences of high fertility for the family and household (reviewed by DeLancey, chapter 8) are more elusive and depend on particular circumstances and a variety of factors. High fertility and large family size may affect the amount as well as the quality of education that children receive, increase the pressure upon family agricultural holdings, may necessitate the intensification or diversification of cultivation, precipitate migration of family members, and influence the economic activity of women.

Accumulation of savings is a critical problem for Sub-Saharan African populations but is said to relate less to number of children than to family structure. Accordingly, extended families are seen to earn more and save less, whereas nuclear families earn less and save more. The extended family is widely prevalent in the region, savings are low, and the pressure upon families is considerable though evidently bearable. Families consider children to be a desirable gain, and the demand for them is high. The demand for children is determined not only by economic factors, however, but also, and perhaps most especially in Sub-Saharan African populations, by culture, religion, and tradition (see particularly chapters 11–13 in part IV).

6

Effects of Fertility Change on Maternal and Child Survival

Deborah Maine, Regina McNamara, Joe Wray, Abdul-Aziz Farah, and Marilyn Wallace

The health situation in Sub-Saharan Africa today is complex. On the one hand, by almost every available indicator—such as mortality under age five or life expectancy at birth—health status there is the least favorable among major world regions. Indicators of socioeconomic and environmental factors that affect health are consistent with this finding. On the other hand, for at least the last several decades, crude and infant mortality rates have declined substantially.

Mortality and fertility are related in dynamic and complex ways. In Sub-Saharan Africa, the decline in mortality has not been offset by decreased fertility. Birth rates have declined minimally, if at all. The result, of course, is rapid population growth. This chapter focuses on one particular aspect of the relationship between mortality and fertility, the direct or short-term effect of fertility on maternal and child survival.[1]

The Overall Risk of Maternal Death

Pregnancy and childbirth are major determinants of women's health. In developing countries, complications of pregnancy and delivery account for about one-quarter of all deaths among women of reproductive age (Chen and others 1974; Williams 1979; Fortney and others 1986). In comparison, in the United States, maternal

The authors acknowledge the generous assistance of Shea Rutstein of Westinghouse Health Systems for help with methodology; Erika Royston and Jane Ferguson of the Division of Family Hygiene, World Health Organization, Geneva, and Judith Fortney and Barbara Janowitz of Family Health International for sharing their information on maternal mortality; and Nicholas Prescott of the World Bank for comments on statistics.

deaths constitute less than 1 percent of total deaths among women aged fifteen to forty-nine (United States 1984).

From an epidemiological viewpoint, the effect of fertility on mortality among women can be measured in at least two ways: (1) the overall risk of maternal mortality, that is, the average risk of death associated with becoming pregnant; and (2) the relative risk associated with pregnancy among various groups of women, for example, maternal mortality among women of different ages. The public health importance of relative risk depends, in part, on the proportion of women in the population who are in high-risk groups, that is, the level of exposure to risk. Using data on risk and exposure, it is possible to estimate the impact of family formation patterns on maternal mortality.

By far the most common sources of information on maternal mortality in Africa are hospital studies, that is, reports on the number of maternal deaths in a hospital compared with the number of deliveries there during a specified period. Reliable rates, however, cannot be derived from these studies because the population from which the patients are drawn cannot be identified; most women in Africa deliver at home. Some researchers provide separate statistics for women who received prenatal care at the hospital ("booked" cases). The advantage of information on booked cases is that women who come for prenatal care can be considered to be a population within which some deaths occur. Doing so reduces the bias that results from a heavy concentration of complicated deliveries. Mortality among unbooked patients is often ten or more times that among booked cases in the same facility (Akingba 1977).

Of the dozens of African hospital studies examined, only nine provide separate mortality rates for booked patients. In these, maternal mortality among booked

Table 6-1. *Maternal Mortality in Sub-Saharan Africa*

Type of study	Country	Period	Deaths per 100,000 births	Source
Hospital studies (booked patients)	Kenya	1977	280	Aggarwal (1980)
	Nigeria	1966–72	225	Akingba (1977)
		1966–75	98	Ayangade (1981)
		1970	159	Hartfield (1980)
		1970–71	530	Waboso (1973)
		1971–72	88	Megafu (1975)
		1970–74	142	Okoisor (1978)
		1976–79	130	Harrison and Rossiter (1985)
	Zimbabwe	1976	59	Brown (1981)
Official records	Malawi	1977	103	Bullough (1981)
	Niger	1980	135	Thuriaux and Lamotte (1984)
	Nigeria	1961–69	172	Hartfield and Woodland (1980)
	Uganda	1967	126	Grech and others (1969)
Community studies	Ethiopia	1981–83	566	Kwast and others (1985)
	Ghana	1972	400	Department of Community Health and School of Public Health (1979)
	Senegal	1983–86	590	Garenne (1986)

Note: Rates are usually per 100,000 total births rather than live births.

women ranged from 59 to 530 deaths per 100,000 deliveries (table 6-1). The median is 150. The reasons for the variation are not known, but patterns of "selection" into medical care are probably as important as true difference in mortality. In countries where most women receive no prenatal care, for example, it is likely that booked women are more advantaged than average.

Another source of data is special studies of official records, as distinct from official government reports of vital statistics (which do not exist in most of Sub-Saharan Africa). Typically, in such studies the numerator is derived from surveys of death records from as many sources as possible in a given area, and the denominator is the estimated number of births in the area during the same period of time. Four such studies were found. These reported 103 to 172 maternal deaths per 100,000 live births, with the median being 130 (table 6-1).

A basic assumption in these special studies is that a large majority of maternal deaths (unlike births) either take place in health facilities or eventually come to the attention of the medical personnel. This is, however, a questionable assumption. Recent community studies have demonstrated that, in developing countries, only a fraction of maternal deaths take place in medical facilities (Bhatia 1985; Fortney and others 1985; Alauddin 1986; Khan and others 1986).

By far the best evidence on maternal deaths comes from community studies, but these are rare. Community studies in Ethiopia, Ghana, and Senegal found 566, 400, and 590 maternal deaths per 100,000 live births,

respectively (table 6-1). For comparison, recent community studies in Bali and Bangladesh found 718 and 623 maternal deaths per 100,000 live births, respectively (Fortney and others 1986; Khan and others 1986).

What can be deduced from this relatively meager collection of data? Most of the studies shown in table 6-1 give conservative estimates. Among the studies of booked patients and official records, the median rate of maternal morbidity is 138. The recent community studies (the preferred source of data) show 400–590 deaths per 100,000 live births. Is it credible that maternal deaths in Sub-Saharan Africa are this common? Quite possibly, considering that in 1920, when the life expectancy for women in the United States was fifty-five (somewhat longer than in Africa today), the maternal mortality rate was a staggering 800 for the total population and even higher among minorities (New York Academy of Medicine 1933).

When discussing the risks of childbearing, it is necessary to consider the alternative, namely, the risks of avoiding pregnancy. From results of two decades of research on oral contraceptives and hundreds of studies on IUDs and other methods, it appears that use of modern contraceptive methods by women in developed countries is far safer than pregnancy and childbirth except for use of the pill by older women who smoke (Ory and others 1980, 1983).

Not surprisingly, data from developing countries relative to the side effects of modern methods of contraception are virtually nonexistent, and the issues are complex. On the one hand, it may be that common health problems in developing countries interact with contraceptives to produce side effects that either are not seen or are not common in industrialized countries. This possibility has not been substantiated, however. On the other hand, it may be that use of effective contraception is even more beneficial to women in developing countries whose health is more endangered to begin with. There is some support for this view. Although a community study in Egypt found that women who were taking the pill were more likely than other women to die of cardiovascular disease, for example, "a single pregnancy and delivery . . . carried 48 times the risk of death as a year of contraceptive use" (Fortney and others 1986).

Women in developing countries who resort to illicit abortion in order to avoid having a child are at very high risk of serious complications and death. Tens of thousands of women in these countries die from illegal abortions every year (Liskin 1980; Rochat and others 1980). Although deaths from illicit abortion have been believed to be less common in Sub-Saharan Africa than in other parts of the world, they are certainly not uncommon (Ojo and Savage 1974). In one teaching hospital in Abidjan, for example, an average of thirteen women are treated every day for serious complications of illegal abortions (Welffens-Ekra 1985). Furthermore, clinicians in Sub-Saharan Africa report an increase in young women suffering the effects of illegal abortions (Akingba 1977). Only if birth planning is accomplished by safe methods do the health benefits to women discussed here apply.

Relative Risks of Maternal Mortality and Exposure to Risk

The overall risk of maternal death is largely determined by such factors as era (for example, before or after the invention of antibiotics), country, socioeconomic status, and access to medical care. Unfortunately, there is usually little that an individual or family can do to change these factors. Other factors that also affect the risk of maternal mortality, however—notably, the age at which women give birth and the number of pregnancies they have—are, to some extent, under women's control. These factors may be considered relative risks.

The importance of these relative risks depends, to a large extent, on the proportion of pregnancies that carry high risk. The high risk associated with giving birth after age forty, for example, has little consequence for public health in the United States because it is no longer a common event. In Sub-Saharan Africa, on the other hand, women generally marry early, have their first

birth soon afterward, and continue to have children until they are in their late thirties or early forties. There is, of course, considerable variation within and among countries.

Maternal Age

Numerous studies spanning continents and decades have shown that adolescents and women thirty-five or older are much more likely than are women in their twenties to die as a result of pregnancy (see, for example, Nortman 1974; Acsadi and Johnson-Acsadi 1986). This relationship is not dependent on socioeconomic status. In fact, Nortman (1974) observed that the effect of age on maternal mortality is stronger in countries that have low rates of maternal deaths (for example, European countries) than in those with high rates. Regardless of the level of maternal mortality, the effect of age is impressive. In Nortman's high-mortality group of countries, women aged twenty to twenty-four had the lowest rates of maternal death. Women younger than twenty were 50 percent more likely to die of complications of pregnancy or childbirth. At age twenty-five the rate began to rise again until women forty to forty-four had a rate nearly five times that of women twenty-to twenty-four.

Maternal mortality by age could be examined in Zaria Hospital in Nigeria during 1976–79 from a series of more than 22,000 deliveries among both booked and unbooked patients (Harrison and Rossiter 1985). The excess of maternal deaths among women in their early teens is clear. Fifteen-year-olds had 6.8 times the rate of maternal death of women aged twenty to twenty-four, and the maternal mortality of sixteen-year-old women was 2.5 times as high. Women on either side of the "ideal" age group (twenty to twenty-four years old)—those aged seventeen to nineteen or twenty-five to twenty-nine—had 30 percent higher rates. Among women aged thirty or older, the risk of dying was 2.6 times that of women aged twenty to twenty-four. These data confirm that maternal mortality in Africa is affected by age in much the same way as in other parts of the world.

Table 6-2 shows the proportion of all births to women in high-risk age groups in nine Sub-Saharan African countries. The proportion of total births involving mothers aged fifteen to nineteen ranged from 10 percent in Benin and Kenya to 23 percent in Cameroon. There was less variation in births to older women: 8–15 percent at ages thirty-five to thirty-nine; 5–13 percent among women forty to forty-nine. As the last column of table 6-2 shows, the proportion of all births that occur among women aged thirty-five and older ranges from 25 percent in Benin to 38 percent in Kenya.

Table 6-2. *Percentage of All Births to Women in Various Age Groups*

Country	15–19	20–24	25–29	30–34	35–39	40–49	35–49
Benin	10	28	29	18	10	5	25
Cameroon	23	28	21	14	8	6	37
Côte d'Ivoire	19	30	23	13	8	6	34
Ghana	15	27	23	16	11	9	34
Kenya	10	21	22	18	15	13	38
Lesotho	14	30	23	16	10	7	31
Nigeria	18	25	25	18	8	6	33
Senegal	19	25	24	15	11	6	36
Sudan	11	24	32	16	11	5	27

Sources: Benin (1984); Cameroon (1983); Côte d'Ivoire (1984); Ghana (1983); Kenya (1980); Lesotho (1981); Nigeria (1984a); Senegal (1981); Sudan (1981).

Parity

For decades, studies have consistently shown that maternal mortality varies with parity as well as with maternal age. In general, maternal mortality is slightly elevated among women having their first birth, is lowest among women having their second or third child, and increases sharply thereafter (Nortman 1974; Maine 1981). This relationship has been documented in a wide variety of settings and over time, as maternal mortality rates declined dramatically during this century. The available information indicates that Africa is no different from the rest of the world in this respect (Correa and others 1978).

Because women necessarily age with increased parity, some of the observed effect of either age or parity may be due to the other factor. In several studies in which the effects of age were controlled while those of parity were examined (Chen and others 1974; Nortman 1974), age and parity were found to influence maternal mortality independently.

Unless pregnancies are very widely spaced, continuing childbearing into their late thirties and early forties is a sign that women are attaining very high parities. This is the case in Africa, where fertility is higher than in other parts of the world. One measure of fertility is the total fertility rate (TFR); this represents the number of children an average woman would have during her lifetime if she conformed to the age-specific fertility rates current at the time of the survey. The United Nations (1985) estimates that, during 1980–85, in Asia and Latin America, the TFRs were 3.5 and 4.1, respectively, compared with 6.3 in Africa. Kenya had the world's highest TFR, 8.1. The TFR, however, does not fully indicate how large the families of many African women are. On the basis of results of the World Fertility Survey (WFS), it can be estimated that among women who had, for the most part, completed childbearing (that is, were aged forty-five to forty-nine), the following proportions had borne seven or more children: Cameroon and Le-

sotho, 37 percent; Sudan, 49 percent; Ghana and Côte d'Ivoire, 57 percent; Kenya, 73 percent.

In some societies, family size in one's grandparents' generation seems large by current standards. It is important to remember, however, that the large families cited above are not relics of the past; there is no evidence that completed family size has been declining substantially in these countries.

Birth Interval

As evidence of an effect of birth spacing on infant mortality has accumulated, people have speculated about a similar effect on maternal mortality. Having children very close together must be hard on women, especially poor women, the reasoning goes. It has been hypothesized that this strain on the mother's body, named the "maternal depletion syndrome" by Jelliffe (1966), might increase a woman's risk of maternal death. As sensible as this seems, no evidence of an effect of birth spacing on maternal mortality has been found. Preliminary results of a population-based study in Matlab, Bangladesh, and of a multicenter, hospital-based case/control study, for example, showed no birth-spacing effect on maternal survival (Fortney 1988; Koenig and others 1986).

The Potential for Averting Maternal Deaths

A number of researchers have estimated the proportion of maternal deaths that might be averted with a given change in childbearing patterns (Nortman 1974; Trussel and Pebley 1984). Some models used the assumption that women thirty-five or older have no further births but did not consider whether such births are wanted. The WFS, however, provided data on the number of women in each age group who said that they wanted no more children. It is therefore possible to use women's own fertility desires to estimate the proportion of births that could be averted in the future if women who

Table 6-3. *Percentage of Women Who Want No More Children and Percentage of Such Women Not Currently Using an Efficient Method of Contraception*

Country	Percentage of currently married, fecund women who want no more children	Percentage of those who want no more children not using efficient contraception
Cameroon	10	94
Côte d'Ivoire	4	96
Ghana	12	83
Kenya	17	83
Lesotho	15	84
Nigeria	5	96
Sudan	17	84

Source: World Fertility Survey first country reports (see table 6-2).

wanted no more children used contraception. Although these data have shortcomings, it seems preferable to use women's stated desires rather than the alternatives.

The proportion of women who say that they want no more children is much higher in North Africa (47 and 53 percent in Tunisia and Egypt, respectively) than in Sub-Saharan Africa (4–17 percent; see table 6-3). The proportion of women who, at the time of the WFS inquiries, were using an efficient method of contraception among those who said that they did not want more children is 4–17 percent in the seven Sub-Saharan African countries, compared with 46–48 percent in Egypt and Tunisia.

If all women who say they want no more children (and are not currently using an efficient method of contraception) realized their desires and had no more births, it is estimated that the number of maternal deaths would be reduced by the following proportions: Côte d'Ivoire, 5 percent; Nigeria, 6 percent; Ghana and Kenya, 15 percent each; Lesotho and Sudan, 18 percent each. In Egypt and Tunisia, where much higher proportions of women say they want no more children, the reductions would be larger (28 and 26 percent, respectively). Although the estimated beneficial effect of family planning on maternal health is weaker in Sub-Saharan Africa than in North Africa, it is not insignificant, especially in view of the high incidence of maternal deaths in these countries.

The method of estimation used has a number of problems.[2] It both inflates and underestimates the potential effect of contraception on maternal mortality. On the one hand, it assumes perfect contraception, which is neither humanly nor technically possible. The effect is thus inflated. On the other hand, it is quite likely that there are many women who will not say to a stranger (an interviewer) that they want no more children, even though that is the case. Furthermore, some women

would use contraception to postpone their first birth from their teens into their twenties, thus averting some of the maternal deaths associated with extreme youth. The effect is then underestimated.

Another way to conceptualize the reduction in maternal deaths possible through the use of family planning is to focus on the risk to an individual woman. Although infant death is a one-time risk, women face the risk of maternal death repeatedly. Consequently, even if the increasing risk per pregnancy with age and birth order is ignored, a women's chances of dying are multiplied by the number of births she has. If the maternal mortality rate in Kenya is 500, for example, and the total fertility rate is eight, the average woman has about one chance in twenty-five of a maternal death. Reducing the average completed family size in Kenya from eight to six children would reduce the number of maternal deaths by at least one-quarter.

The Risk of Infant and Child Death

In 1982, infant mortality in Sub-Saharan Africa ranged from 77 deaths per 1,000 live births in Kenya, to 190 in Sierra Leone, with most countries having rates between 100 and 140 (World Bank 1984). Child mortality rates (deaths at one to five years) ranged from 13 deaths per 1,000 children per year in Kenya, to 39 in Angola, with most countries having rates of 20 to 30. These rates mean that, in many Sub-Saharan African countries, one-fifth to one-quarter of children die before their fifth birthday.

Although these rates are among the highest in the world, they are considerably lower than they were two decades ago. In about one-half of thirty-two Sub-Saharan African countries, infant mortality declined by 20–30 percent during 1960–82. Child mortality declined by at least 40 percent in two-thirds of these countries.

Birth Order and Maternal Age

Traditionally, studies examining the relationship of birth order to infant mortality have shown U-shaped, J-shaped, or reverse J-shaped curves. That is, mortality is lowest among second and third children (Wray 1971; Nortman 1974; Maine 1981; Acsadi and Johnson-Acsadi 1986). The relationship between infant and child mortality and family formation patterns in Sub-Saharan Africa has been explored with WFS data for nine countries (Rutstein 1984). The familiar pattern emerges, as figure 6-1 shows. In these countries, infant mortality is generally lowest among second- and third-order children, whereas seventh- and higher-order children generally have the

Figure 6-1. *Infant Mortality by Birth Order*

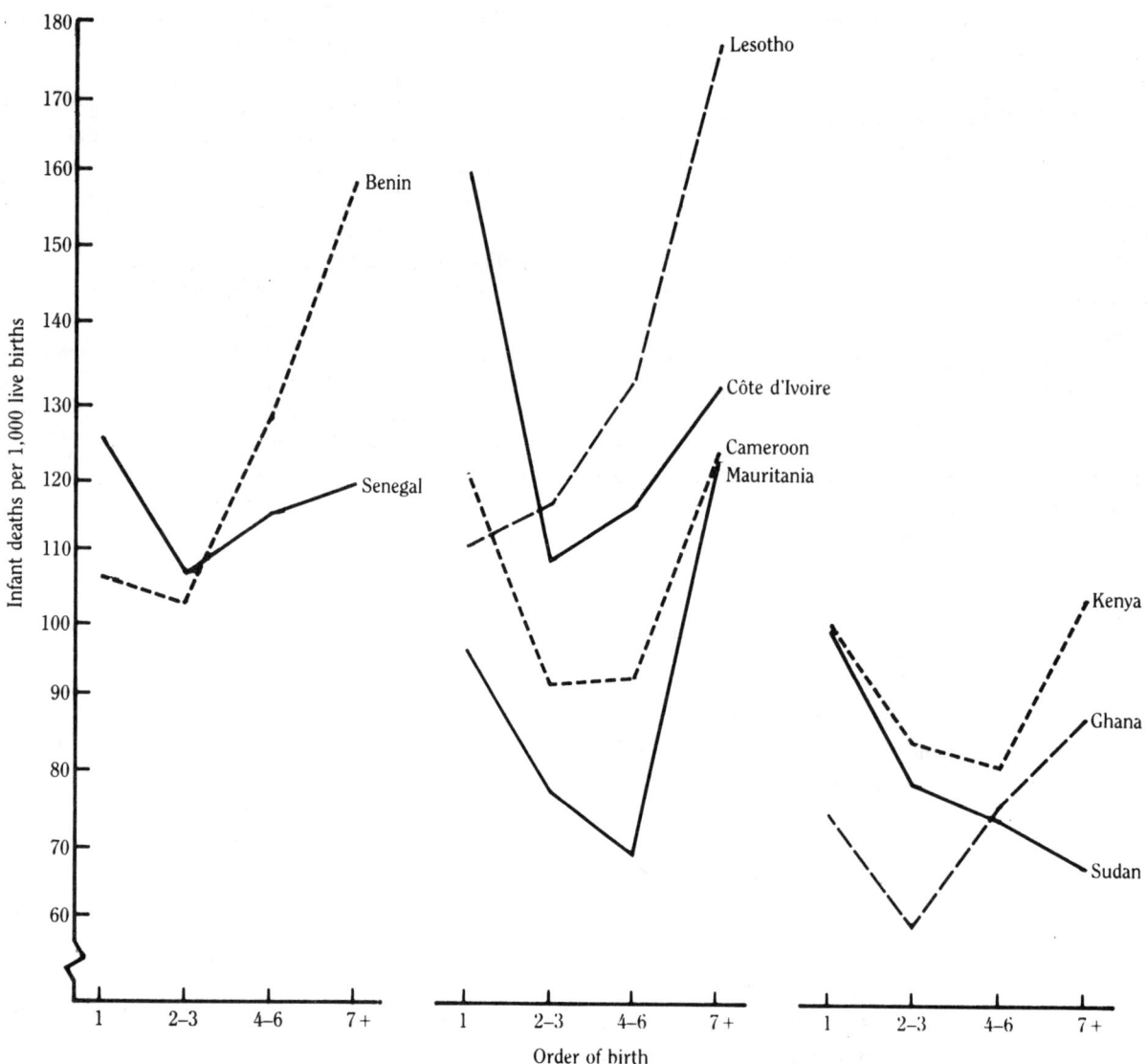

Source: Rutstein (1984).

highest mortality rates. In Mauritania and Kenya, however, infants of birth order 4–6 have the lowest mortality rates. In Sudan, infant mortality appears to decline steadily with birth order, a very unusual pattern. After the first year of life, birth order has no consistent effect on mortality.

The relationship of maternal age to infant mortality is also roughly what would be expected from the findings of previous studies: mortality is lowest among infants born to women aged twenty to twenty-nine years and highest among those born to women at either end of the childbearing ages. Among women under twenty and those forty and over, some differences in infant mortality also exist. Infants born to women aged sev-

enteen or younger, for example, are generally at much higher risk than those born to the relatively more mature eighteen- and nineteen-year-olds.

Until a few years ago, birth order and maternal age were the main demographic factors studied for effects on infant well-being. Now the trend seems to be to discount the importance of birth order and age. When the effects of maternal education, infant's sex, birth order, and interbirth interval are controlled, the effect of maternal age on infant mortality is often reduced and, in some countries, disappears (Hobcraft and others 1984). It is a mistake, however, to discount maternal age and birth order on the strength of such findings. A difference exists between research conducted to discover etiology and research done to shape policy and programs. Controlling for various other factors while examining the effect of birth order, for example, makes it possible to search for the root "cause." Still, no simple cause really exists. Many variables are strongly correlated, as are age and parity. To individual women or the program personnel who have contact with them, age and birth order are still extremely useful markers, indicating the need for special counseling and care.

The same argument may be made in response to the idea that completed family size is a more important influence on infant mortality than birth order (Gray 1984). Midwives, physicians, and health educators, when faced with an individual woman, do not know what the size of her completed family will be (and neither does she). They can know only her current age and parity. If statistical analysis is to help policymakers, the models should incorporate relevant markers such as these that are of use to programs.

Length of Preceding Birth Interval

The WFS data confirm results of earlier research in developed countries that a short birth interval adversely affects both the preceding and the succeeding child. Figure 6-2 shows for nine countries the relationship between infant mortality and the length of the preceding birth interval. This relationship is expressed as the relative risk of death among infants born at the end of a short birth interval (less than twenty-four months). Infants born at the end of a medium interval (twenty-four to twenty-seven months) serve as the baseline group.

A short birth interval is associated with an increase in infant mortality in each of the nine countries. The relative risk ranges from 1.3 in Senegal (that is, excess deaths of 30 percent) to 2.1 in Ghana. The figure also shows that, in all nine countries, being born at the end of a long interval (forty-eight or more months) confers greater protection against infant mortality than does a medium interval.

Figure 6-2. *Relative Risk of Infant Mortality by Length of Preceding Birth Interval*

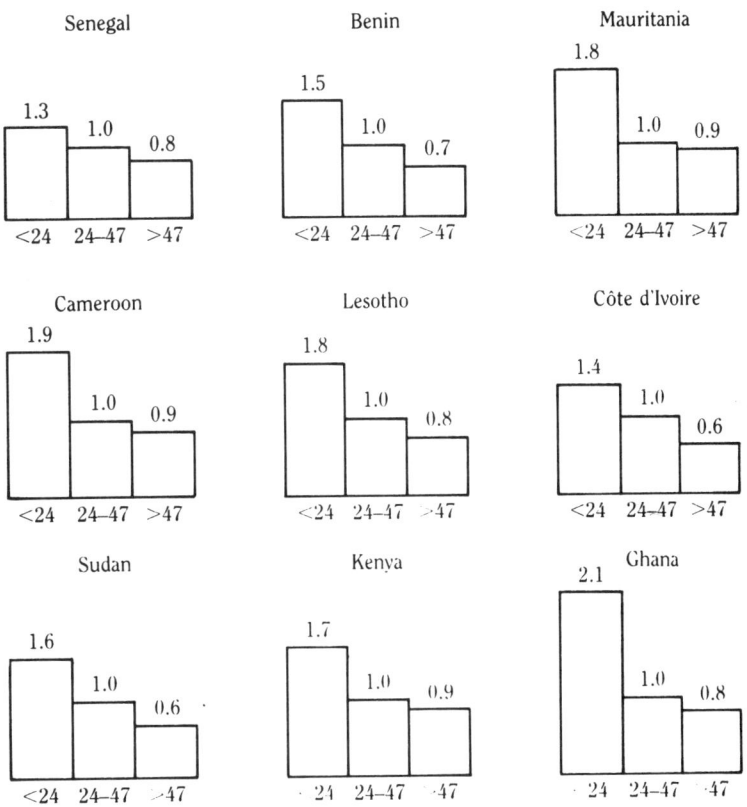

Note: Bars show relative risk of infant mortality. Numbers above bars express risk. Numbers below bars show length of preceding birth interval (in months).

Source: Rutstein (1984).

Preliminary WFS data revealed that in Nigeria, which has one-fifth of the population of Sub-Saharan Africa, a short birth interval carries a substantial excess risk of childhood mortality. Relative risk of infant mortality at intervals of less than twenty-four months, compared with twenty-four to forty-seven months, was 1.6. When the interval was longer than forty-seven months, the relative risk fell to 0.7.[3]

WFS data on births in the fifteen years before the survey in Cameroon, Ghana, and Kenya allowed the separation of birth intervals into finer categories. This analysis shows that infants with preceding birth intervals of three years (thirty-six to forty-seven months) have substantially lower death rates than infants with preceding intervals of two years (twenty-four to thirty-five months). No "threshold" in birth intervals appeared above which risk of death stabilizes. On the contrary, the beneficial effect of lengthening birth intervals is incremental, at least up to six years.

Among toddlers (children twelve to twenty-three months old) in Côte d'Ivoire, Mauritania, and Senegal, a short preceding birth interval was not associated with increased mortality. In Benin, Cameroon, Ghana, Kenya, Lesotho, and Sudan, however, toddlers born at the end of short intervals were 24–58 percent more likely to die than those born at the end of a medium interval. The meaning of the inconsistencies that appear among these nine Sub-Saharan countries is not clear. Three community studies of child spacing in Sub-Saharan Africa have not found evidence of excess child mortality associated with short intervals (Cantrelle and Leridon 1971; Doyle and others 1978; Boerma and van Vianen 1984). But the additional benefit of a long interval (forty-eight or more months) is even more pronounced among toddlers than among infants. Intervals of at least four years were associated with the lowest mortality in Benin, Cameroon, Côte d'Ivoire, Ghana, Kenya, Mauritania, Senegal, and Sudan though not in Lesotho. In a number of countries, mortality among toddlers born after such long intervals was about half that among those born after a medium interval; in Nigeria, it was about one-third.

As for deaths at two to five years, there is no consistent excess of deaths among children born after short intervals.

Length of Subsequent Birth Interval

The widespread and strong tradition of child spacing in Africa generally has, as its stated purpose, the survival and development of the child already born (Williams 1938). For a woman to become pregnant before that child is on its feet (literally and figuratively) is an occasion for shame in many parts of Sub-Saharan Africa

(Lesthaeghe and others 1981). Premature weaning is obviously hazardous to a child's health. After the birth of another child, the preceding child may receive much less maternal attention and is commonly given into the care of an older child.

Using WFS data, Hobcraft and others (1983) analyzed the effect of subsequent birth interval on deaths at ages one to five in Ghana, Kenya, Lesotho, and Sudan. When children for whom both the preceding and subsequent birth intervals were long are compared with children who had either a short preceding birth interval or a short subsequent interval, it appears that, for toddler mortality, a short subsequent interval is more harmful than a short preceding interval. This finding seems to confirm folk wisdom about the importance of subsequent interval to the well-being of the weanling.

In a later analysis, Hobcraft and others (1984) analyzed the risks of toddler death associated with subsequent birth intervals of less than twelve months. Relative risks following such short intervals were extremely high, even after the effects of birth order, maternal age, and education were controlled.

For mortality at ages two to five, the results are weaker and more varied. Furthermore, when multivariate analysis was used to control the effects of birth order, maternal age, and education, the effects of subsequent interval on mortality at two to five years disappeared in most of these African countries (Hobcraft and others 1984).

Possible Confounding Factors and Explanations

Ever since studies of the relationship between birth interval and child mortality have been published, questions about their validity have been raised and theories about mechanisms of action have been proposed. The wealth of new data and recent studies allows us to address some of these issues.

Some investigators have raised the possibility that in many cases the birth interval may be short because the first child of the pair died. The death of a young child may hasten the next conception by interrupting lactational amenorrhea, postpartum abstinence, or the use of contraceptives. Children born in such circumstances are likely to be at higher risk because of conditions peculiar to the family, either biological or environmental.

This hypothesis was tested using WFS data for Cameroon, Ghana, and Kenya. As expected, mortality rates are much higher for siblings of nonsurvivors, and in the multivariate analysis the death of an immediately adjacent sibling is a powerful predictor of mortality. When adjustment is made for the survival of the older child of the pair, however, the relative risk of death in the first month of life is reduced only from 3.5 to 3.0 in Cameroon. In Ghana and Kenya, differences due to this adjustment are even smaller.

Other factors that might confound the relationship between birth interval and mortality are maternal age, birth order, and socioeconomic status. If short-interval births are concentrated among high-risk women (those who are poor, at either extreme of their reproductive years, and with high parity), the apparent excess of deaths among children with short birth intervals might be due to these other factors. Logistic regression was therefore used to estimate the relative contribution of these several factors to risk of mortality. It was found that the effects of birth interval are clearly independent of maternal education (an indicator of socioeconomic status), maternal age, and birth order. When these three factors are introduced into a logistic regression, relative risks of death are virtually unaffected.

One popular theory about the birth spacing effect (both in folk wisdom and among researchers) is that, when children in a family are born too close together, they compete for the family's resources, such as food and parental attention. Despite the commonsense appeal of this theory, the WFS data indicate that competition within the family is not a major factor in the birth spacing effect. First, families of higher socioeconomic status would seem to be able to provide enough food and care for several young children. As we have seen, however, controlling for maternal education does not materially change the relative risks of death associated with short birth intervals. Second, if the older child of a closely spaced pair dies in infancy, and the competition is thus ended, the risk of death for the younger child associated with the short interval should be reduced. Again, this is not the case.

Another hypothesis about the hazards of short birth intervals is that they are a characteristic of high-risk families and that this intrafamilial risk (rather than short interval) is the reason for the apparent effect of birth spacing on child survival. Although the death of an older sibling seems a reasonable marker for high-risk families, the effects of birth spacing are not appreciably greater in such families than in those where the older sibling survived.

Finally, there is the "maternal depletion" theory, according to which the physical strain on the mother exerted by closely spaced pregnancies adversely affects the children. This might explain some of the effect on newborns, but it is a less likely explanation for risk to older children.

In truth, each of the factors implicated by these hypotheses may play a part in the effect of birth spacing. Even when they are taken together, however, they do not appear to account for the entire effect, from birth

through the first five years of life, on both children in a pair. Furthermore, the persistence of the birth spacing effect after adjustment for maternal education, maternal age, and birth order, and across countries and decades, indicates that much remains to be learned about its causes.

Exposure to Risk of Infant and Child Death

As noted in the section on maternal mortality, very large families (seven or more children) are common in Sub-Saharan Africa. Births at young and old ages are also common. Among the women aged twenty to thirty-four at the time of interview, 39 percent in Kenya and 29 percent in Ghana had had their first birth before they were eighteen. As shown in table 6-2, childbearing among women in their forties is also relatively frequent in Sub-Saharan Africa.

Anthropological studies show that people in traditional societies all over the world have long perceived the advantages of long birth intervals. This has certainly been the case in Sub-Saharan Africa, where prolonged postpartum sexual abstinence and breastfeeding have been the rule (Schoenmaeckers and others 1981). This review also indicated that patterns of postpartum abstinence are changing and, in fact, have probably been changing for many years. The authors observed, for example, that because Islam imposes abstinence only during the first forty days postpartum, this standard has been adopted in a number of Sub-Saharan societies where it was probably much longer in the past. Urbanization and education of women beyond the primary level will probably also shorten breastfeeding and postpartum abstinence durations (Acsadi and Johnson-Acsadi 1986). Unless these traditional practices are replaced by use of modern contraceptives, the result will be shorter birth intervals.

Information on the proportion of births preceded by intervals of less than two years is available for five Sub-Saharan African countries (Hobcraft and others 1983). The five countries fall into two distinct groups: in Ghana, Lesotho, and Senegal, less than 20 percent of births follow short intervals; in Kenya and Sudan, on the other hand, at least 35 percent of births are preceded by short intervals.

It is surprising to find that, in three countries, short birth intervals are apparently becoming less common rather than more so. When the fertility histories reported by women are divided into births that took place ten to fourteen years and zero to five years before the survey, the proportion of births with short preceding intervals decreased over time: from 34 to 29 percent in Cameroon; from 25 to 20 percent in Ghana; and from

Table 6-4. *Percentage of Children with Preceding Birth Intervals of Less Than Two Years, by Maternal Age*

Country	Maternal age		
	<20	20–29	30+
Cameroon	45	32	27
Ghana	39	22	21
Kenya	52	42	36

Source: World Fertility Survey; standard recode data tapes.

44 to 38 percent in Kenya. These declines were apparent in each maternal age group. One possible explanation is that, because infant deaths have become less common, lactational amenorrhea is less often interrupted. This is, however, pure conjecture. More research is needed on trends in birth spacing and the reasons for such trends.

Examination of the WFS data for Cameroon, Ghana, and Kenya clearly shows that women younger than twenty are particularly likely to have short birth intervals. As table 6-4 shows, in Ghana short birth intervals were almost twice as common among the youngest mothers as among older women. In these countries, birth spacing showed no clear relationship to either maternal education or area of residence.

Detailed local studies contribute to the understanding of birth spacing patterns and trends in Sub-Saharan Africa, and some of the evidence is hopeful. Caldwell and Caldwell (1981a, 1981b) found that the upper educational groups in Nigeria have begun to substitute modern contraceptives for postpartum abstinence. Data from Ghana on recent births indicate longer intervals among younger women and among those with secondary education and especially long intervals among women in the largest urban centers (Gaisie 1984). Such intervals are probably evidence of the effective use of contraception.

The Potential for Averting Infant and Child Deaths

The information presented above allows us to estimate the effect on infant mortality of various possible changes in fertility patterns in Africa. Using WFS country-specific data on the proportions of births that follow short intervals and on the risks associated with such intervals, it may be estimated that, if all preceding intervals less than twenty-four months long became twenty-four to forty-seven months long, the proportion of infant deaths averted would be 22 percent in Cameroon, 17 percent in Ghana, 20 percent in Kenya,[4] 12 percent in Lesotho, 5 percent in Senegal, and 19 percent in Sudan. If in-

tervals were extended to four or more years, the reductions would be even greater.

The methodology used does not control for sibling death, maternal age, birth order, or maternal education, factors found to have a measurable but not large effect on relative risk. Direct effects of longer birth intervals on infant and child deaths may therefore be overstated, but a number of other points about the above estimates are noteworthy. First, they refer only to infant mortality, whereas the WFS data clearly indicate that the deleterious effects of a short birth interval persist for at least the first five years of life. Also, the estimates do not account for excess fetal mortality due to short spacing (Acsadi and Johnson-Acsadi 1986). Second, they represent only the effects of the preceding birth interval, whereas it seems that in the second year of life the subsequent interval is more important. Third, in Africa, where women generally bear children as long as they are able, the extension of birth intervals would undoubtedly result in a decline in fertility. This decline would, in turn, reduce the number of high-order births and would thereby further reduce infant mortality. In short, for a number of reasons the estimates of deaths prevented by improved birth spacing are probably too low.

The proportion of women who say they want no more children is smaller in Sub-Saharan Africa than in other parts of the world. Even so, if such women had no more births, it is estimated that there would be smaller, but still substantial, reductions in infant deaths; 8–11 percent in Ghana, Kenya, Lesotho, and Sudan. These estimates are based on the proportion of women of various parities who say they want no more children and on country-specific relative risks of infant death by birth order.[5]

Conclusions

Discussions of health and population policy in developing countries often bog down in arguments about the reciprocity of fertility and mortality. The ostensible object of these arguments is to establish priorities among various kinds of programs. We believe that consideration of family planning as a health intervention obviates most of these arguments. One such argument is that reducing mortality without first reducing fertility will, in the long run, aggravate health problems through uncontrolled population growth. This argument simply does not apply to family planning, which reduces mortality and fertility at the same time.

According to the available evidence for Sub-Saharan Africa, few initiatives have the potential to decrease both fertility and mortality. Increases in urbanization, income, education, and employment of women are all associated with reductions in infant mortality. Studies in various parts of the world have associated these same factors with declines in fertility, but (at least so far) the data from Africa are conflicting. Although urbanization is generally associated with smaller family size, for example, in Sub-Saharan Africa it is also linked to the deterioration of traditional birth spacing practices, so that birth intervals become shorter. This may be a temporary effect. But even if this transitional phase lasts only a generation, any rise in the already high levels of fertility in Africa has serious implications for health.

Thus, whether the objective is prompt improvement of maternal or child health or long-term balancing of fertility and mortality in order to bolster development efforts, an essential component of development efforts in Sub-Saharan Africa should be programs that (1) educate families about the health risks associated with unfavorable reproductive patterns, and (2) provide access to modern methods of contraception so that couples can put into practice their knowledge and desires.

Notes

1.   The discussion must focus on survival rather than on health per se because of the paucity of morbidity data, even in developed countries. In Africa, more than anywhere else in the world, one must rely on mortality data because many people have little or no contact with the modern medical system and special health surveys are rare. With specific attention to Africa, the chapter summarizes the considerable literature showing that changes in childbearing patterns and declines in fertility can lead to substantial reductions in maternal and child mortality.

"Direct" and "short-term" are relative terms. An example of a short-term effect is the increased likelihood of maternal death with increasing birth order. An example of an indirect or long-term effect might be that high birth order spurs population growth, thereby increases the load on the medical system, and perhaps lowers the quality of obstetric care, so that more maternal deaths occur.

2.   The potential for averting maternal deaths through family planning was determined as follows. Using country-specific data from WFS first country reports, the proportion of all women in each five-year age group was multiplied by the relevant age-specific fertility rate (ASFR). (So that numbers would be sufficient to permit work, the product was also multiplied by 1 million.) This procedure gives the number of births per year in each age group for a cohort of women conforming to the age and fertility patterns of the country.

The number of births to women in each age group was then multiplied by an arbitrary maternal mortality rate (0.002). Note that the rate of maternal mortality used here does not

effect the results, as the proportion of deaths averted, not the number, is being determined. The product is multiplied by the relative risk of maternal mortality in that age group, derived from Nortman's data for high-mortality countries (Nortman 1974, table 2). The result is the number of maternal deaths expected, given current fertility patterns. As a next step, the proportion of women who want no more children and are not using efficient contraceptives was derived by multiplying the percentage of women who want no more children by the proportion of these women who were not using an efficient method of contraception. This is multiplied by the number of maternal deaths expected in that age group, producing the number of deaths averted under these conditions and assumptions. This process is repeated for each age group, and the deaths averted are summed. The total is divided by the total number of expected deaths to derive the proportion of deaths averted.

If women in an age group are assumed to have no more children, then all deaths occurring in the age group (rather than just those among unprotected women who want no more children) are added to the numerator.

Example: Women aged thirty-five to thirty-nine in Lesotho

0.048 = proportion of all women 35–39 at time of survey
0.169 = their age-specific fertility rate

$0.048 \times 0.169 \times 1,000,000 = 8,112$ births per year

0.002 = arbitrary overall maternal mortality rate
3.17 = relative risk of maternal death at 35–39

$8,112 \times 0.002 \times 3.17 = 51$ maternal deaths

0.275 = proportion of women 35–39 in Lesotho who want no more children
0.203 = proportion of these women currently using an efficient method of contraception

$0.275 \times 1 - (0.203) = 0.219$ = proportion of women 35–39 who want no more children and are not using an efficient method of contraception

$0.219 \times 51 = 11.2$ = deaths averted if these women had no more births.

This process is repeated for each age group, and the deaths averted are summed and divided by the total deaths to give the proportion of deaths averted.

3.   The WFS data tape for Nigeria was not generally available at this writing, but Shea Rutstein kindly provided the results of some preliminary analyses in a personal communication dated June 1985.

4.   This was determined as follows. It was assumed that no woman really wants a short interval, or that, conversely, no woman would mind waiting a few extra months to become pregnant again and consequently that no more short-interval births take place. Given the proportion of births that followed short intervals (less than twenty-four months) (Hobcraft and

others 1983) and the mortality rates among infants born after short and long intervals (Rutstein 1983, 1984), the percentage risk attributable to short intervals was calculated using the following formula:

$$\frac{I_0 - I_n}{I_0,}$$

where

I_0 = infant mortality rate in the total population = $W_n I_n$ + $W_s I_s$

I_n = infant mortality rate after long interval (24–48 months)

I_s = infant mortality rate after short intervals (< 24 months)

W_n = proportion of births at long intervals

W_s = proportion of births at short intervals

Example: Kenya

$W_n = 0.65$ $W_s = 0.35$
$I_n = 68$ $I_s = 117$

$I_0 = 0.65(68) + 0.35(117) = 85.15$
Percentage of deaths averted: $(85 - 68) \div 85 = 20\%$

5.   To estimate the proportion of infant deaths that would be averted by reducing birth order, a synthetic cohort was constructed similar to that used to estimate maternal mortality except that women are grouped by parity, not age. Unfortunately, the published WFS data are not arranged to make this a simple process.

The distribution of ever-married women by number of children ever born was used to determine the order of their last birth. From a cross-tabulation of age by parity, the parity distribution of (last) births in each age group was derived. This was multiplied by the total number of births to women in that age group in the synthetic cohort (see first step estimating maternal mortality in note 2 above), which yielded the number of births by age and parity. When summed across parity, the aggregate was the parity distribution in the synthetic cohort, with the age distribution and age-specific fertility rate of the country taken into account.

The number of births in each parity group is then multiplied by the overall infant mortality rate and the relative risk associated with parity in that country (Rutstein 1983, 1984). This procedure gives the number of infant deaths by birth order.

The remaining steps are similar to the third and fourth steps of the maternal mortality calculations. The proportion of women at various parities who want no more children was multiplied by the proportion of those women who are not using efficient methods of contraception. One slight difference is that the proportion of women who want no more children was figured using parity at last birth minus one. The proportion of women whose last birth was their seventh, for example, was multiplied by the proportion of women who, at parity six, said they did not want another child. The product was then multiplied by the number of infant deaths in that parity group, derived above.

References

Acsadi, G. T., and G. Johnson-Acsadi. 1986. *Optimum Conditions for Childbearing.* London: International Planned Parenthood Federation.

Aggarwal, V. P. 1980. "Obstetric Emergency Referrals to Kenyatta National Hospital." *East African Medical Journal* 57: 144–49.

Akingba, J. B. 1977. "Abortion, Maternity, and Other Health Problems in Nigeria." *Nigerian Medical Journal* 7: 465–71.

Alauddin, Mohammed. 1986. "Maternal Mortality in Rural Bangladesh: The Tangail District." *Studies in Family Planning* 17: 13–21.

Ayangade, S. O. 1981. "Maternal Mortality in a Semi-Urban Nigerian Community." *Journal of the National Medical Association* 73: 137–40.

Benin. 1984. *Enquête Fécondité au Benin, 1982: Résumé de Résultats.* World Fertility Survey Summary of Findings, No. 48. Voorburg, Netherlands: International Statistical Institute, June.

Bhatia, J. C. 1985. "Maternal Mortality in Ananthapur District, India: Preliminary Findings of a Study." Doc. No. FHE/PMM/85.9.16. World Health Organization, Geneva.

Boerma, J. T., and H. A. van Vianen. 1984. "Birth Interval, Mortality, and Growth of Children in a Rural Area in Kenya." *Journal of Biosocial Science* 16: 475–86.

Brown, I. M. 1981. "Perspectives in Obstetric Care for Zimbabwe." *Central African Journal of Medicine* 27: 37–41.

Bullough, C. H. W. 1981. "Analysis of Maternal Deaths in the Central Region of Malawi." *East African Medical Journal* 58: 25–36.

Caldwell, J. C., and P. Caldwell. 1981a. "Cause and Sequence in the Reduction of Postnatal Abstinence in Ibadan City, Nigeria." In H. J. Page and R. Lesthaeghe, eds., *Child-Spacing in Tropical Africa: Traditions and Change.* London: Academic Press.

Caldwell, Patricia, and J. C. Caldwell. 1981b. "The Function of Child-Spacing in Traditional Societies and the Direction of Change." In H. J. Page and R. Laesthaeghe, eds., *Child-Spacing in Tropical Africa: Traditions and Change.* London: Academic Press.

Cameroon. 1983. *Enquête Nationale sur la Fécondité du Cameroun, 1978: Rapport Principal.* Vols. II, 1 and 2. *Tableaux Statistiques.* World Fertility Survey. Yaounde, Cameroon: Direction de la Statistique et de la Comptabilité Nationale, Ministère de l'Economie et du Plan.

Cantrelle, Pierre, and Henri Leridon. 1971. "Breastfeeding, Mortality in Childhood, and Fertility in a Rural Zone of Senegal." *Population Studies* 25: 505–33.

Chen, L. C., M. C. Gesche, S. Ahmed, A. I. Chowdhury, and W. H. Mosley. 1974. "Maternal Mortality in Rural Bangladesh." *Studies in Family Planning* 5: 334–41.

Correa, Paul, Fadel Diadhiou, Jeanne Lauroy, M. D. Bah, and F. A. Adanlete. 1978. "Mortalité maternelle au cours de la parturition à la clinique gynecologique et obstetricale de

Dakar." *Bulletin de la Société Médicale d'Afrique Noire de Langue Française* 23: 262–69.

Côte d'Ivoire. 1984. *Enquête Ivoirienne sur la Fécondité, 1980–81: Rapport Principal*. Vol. 1. *Analyse des Principaux Résultats*. Vol. 2. *Tableaux Statistiques*. World Fertility Survey. Abidjan, Côte d'Ivoire: Direction de la Statistique, Ministère de l'Economie et des Finances.

Department of Community Health, University of Ghana Medical School, and School of Public Health, University of California, Los Angeles. 1979. "Health Status at Baseline." In *The Danfa Comprehensive Rural Health and Family Planning Project, Ghana: Final Report*. Accra, Ghana.

Doyle, Pat, David Morley, Margaret Woodland, and Jane Cole. 1978. "Birth Intervals, Survival, and Growth in a Nigerian Village." *Journal of Biosocial Science* 10: 81–94.

Fortney, J. A. 1988. Personal communication, August 11.

Fortney, J. A., and others. 1985. "Maternal Mortality in Indonesia and Egypt." Doc. No. FHE/PMM/85.9.13. World Health Organization, Geneva.

Fortney, J. A., I. Susanti, S. Gadalla, S. Saleh, S. M. Rogers, and M. Potts. 1986. "Reproductive Mortality in Two Developing Countries." *American Journal of Public Health* 76: 134–38

Gaisie, S. K. 1984. "The Proximate Determinants of Fertility in Ghana." World Fertility Survey Scientific Report, No. 53. International Statistical Institute, Voorburg, Netherlands.

Garenne, Michel. 1986. Personal communication to Nadine Burton, Family Health International, September 6.

Ghana. 1983. *Ghana Fertility Survey, 1979–1980, First Report*. Vol. 1. *Background, Methodology, and Findings*. Vol. 2. *Statistical Tables*. World Fertility Survey. Accra, Ghana: Central Bureau of Statistics.

Gray, R. H. 1984. "Maternal Reproduction and Child Survival." *American Journal of Public Health* 74: 1080–81.

Grech, E. S., J. Galea, and R. R. Trussell. 1969. "Maternal Mortality in Uganda." *International Journal of Gynaecology and Obstetrics* 7: 263–78.

Harrison, K. A., and C. E. Rossiter. 1985. "Maternal Mortality." In K. A. Harrison, ed., *Child-bearing and Social Priorities: A Survey of 22,774 Consecutive Births in Zaria, Northern Nigeria*. Oxford: Blackwell Scientific.

Hartfield, V. J. 1980. "Maternal Mortality in Nigeria Compared with Earlier International Experience." *International Journal of Gynaecology and Obstetrics* 18: 70–75.

Hartfield, V. J., and M. Woodland. 1980. "Prevention of Maternal Death in a Nigerian Village." *International Journal of Gynaecology and Obstetrics* 18: 150–52.

Hobcraft, John, J. W. McDonald, and S. O. Rutstein. 1983. "Child-Spacing Effects on Infant and Early Child Mortality." *Population Index* 49: 585–618.

——. 1984. "Demographic Determinants of Infant and Early Childhood Mortality: A Comparative Analysis." World Fertility Survey Technical Report, No. 2370. International Statistical Institute, Voorburg, Netherlands.

Jelliffe, D. B. 1966. *Assessment of the Nutritional Status of the Community (with Special Reference to Field Surveys in Developing Countries)*. Geneva: World Health Organization.

Kenya. 1980. *Kenya Fertility Survey, 1977–1978, First Report*. Vols. 1 and 2. World Fertility Survey, Nairobi, Kenya: Central Bureau of Statistics.

Khan, A. R., F. A. Jahan, and S. F. Begum. 1986. "Maternal Mortality in Rural Bangladesh: The Jamalpur District." *Studies in Family Planning* 17: 7–12.

Koenig, Michael, A. I. Chowdhury, V. Faveau, and J. Chakraborty. 1986. "Maternal Mortality in Matlab, Bangladesh." Paper presented at the annual meeting of the Population Association of America, San Francisco, California, April 2–5.

Kwast, B. E., W. Kidare-Mariam, E. M. Saed, and F. G. R. Fowkes. 1985. "Epidemiology of Maternal Mortality in Addis Ababa: A Community-Based Study." *Ethiopian Medical Journal* 23: 7–16.

Lesotho. 1981. *Lesotho Fertility Survey 1977, First Report*. Vols. 1 and 2. World Fertility Survey. Maseru, Lesotho: Central Bureau of Statistics.

Lesthaeghe, R., P. O. Dhadike, and H. J. Page. 1981. "Child-Spacing and Fertility in Sub-Saharan Africa: An Overview of Issues." In H. J. Page and R. Lesthaeghe, eds., *Child-Spacing in Tropical Africa: Traditions and Change*. London: Academic Press.

Liskin, Laurie. 1980. "Complications of Abortion in Developing Countries." *Population Reports*, ser. F, no. 7.

Maine, Deborah. 1981. *Family Planning: Its Impact on the Health of Women and Children*. New York: Center for Population and Family Health, Columbia University.

Megafu, Uchenna. 1975. "Causes of Maternal Deaths at the University of Nigeria Teaching Hospital, Enugu, 1971–1972." *West African Medical Journal* (April): 87–91.

New York Academy of Medicine. 1933. "Maternal Mortality in New York City: A Study of all Puerperal Deaths, 1930–1932." Commonwealth Fund, New York.

Nigeria. 1984a. *Nigeria Fertility Survey, 1981/82: Principal Report*. Vol. 2, *Statistical Tables*. Lagos, Nigeria: National Population Bureau.

——. 1984b. *Nigeria Fertility Survey, 1981/82: A Summary of Findings*. World Fertility Survey Summary of Findings, No. 49. Voorburg, Netherlands: International Statistical Institute.

Nortman, Dorothy. 1974. "Parental Age as a Factor in Pregnancy Outcome and Child Development." Reports on Population/Family Planning, No. 16. Population Council, New York.

Ojo, O. A., and V. Y. Savage. 1974. "A Ten-Year Review of Maternal Mortality Rates in the University College Hospital, Ibadan, Nigeria." *American Journal of Obstetrics and Gynaecology* 118: 517–22.

Okoisor, A. T. 1978. "Maternal Mortality in the Lagos University Teaching Hospital: A Five-Year Survey, 1970–1974." *Nigerian Medical Journal* 8: 349–54.

Ory, H. W., J. D. Forrest, and R. Lincoln. 1983. *Making Choices:*

Evaluating the Health Risks and Benefits of Birth Control Methods. New York: Alan Guttmacher Institute.

Ory, H. W., A. Rosenfield, and L. C. Landman. 1980. "The Pill at Twenty: An Assessment." *International Family Planning Perspectives* 6: 125–30.

Rochat, R. W., D. Kramer, P. Senanayake, and C. Howell. 1980. "Induced Abortion and Health Problems in Developing Countries." *Lancet* 2: 484.

Rutstein, S. O. 1983. "Infant and Child Mortality: Levels, Trends, and Demographic Differentials." *World Fertility Survey Comparative Studies: Cross-National Summaries*, No. 24. Voorburg, Netherlands: International Statistical Institute.

——. 1984. "Demographic Differentials in Infant and Child Mortality." *World Fertility Survey Studies: Cross-National Summaries*. Preliminary tables. Voorburg, Netherlands: International Statistical Institute; processed.

Schoenmaeckers, R., I. H. Shah, R. Lesthaeghe, and O. Tambashe. 1981. "The Child-Spacing Tradition and Postpartum Taboo in Tropical Africa: Anthropological Evidence." In H. J. Page and R. Lesthaeghe, eds., *Child-Spacing in Tropical Africa: Traditions and Change*. London: Academic Press.

Senegal. 1981. *Enquête Sénégalaise sur la Fécondité 1978: Rapport National d'Analyse*. Vol. 1. World Fertility Survey. Dakar, Senegal: Division des Enquête et de la Démographie, Direction de la Statistique, Ministère de l'Economie et des Finances.

Sudan. 1981. *The Sudan Fertility Survey, 1979: Principal Report*. Vols. 1 and 2. World Fertility Survey. Khartoum, Sudan: Department of Statistics, Ministry of National Planning.

Thuriaux, M. C., and J. M. Lamotte. 1984. "Maternal Mortality in Developing Countries: A Note on the Choice of Denominator." *International Journal of Epidemiology* 13: 246–47.

Trussell, James, and A. R. Pebley. 1984. "The Potential Impact of Changes in Fertility on Infant, Child, and Maternal Mortality." *Studies in Family Planning* 15: 267–80.

United Nations. 1984. *Demographic Yearbook, 1982*. New York: United Nations.

——. 1985. *United Nations World Population Chart, 1985*. ST/ESA/SER.A/98/Add.1. New York: United Nations.

United States. 1984. National Center for Health Statistics. *Vital Statistics of the United States, 1979*. Vol. 2. *Mortality*. Pt. A. Washington, D.C.: U.S. Public Health Service.

Waboso, M. F. 1973. "The Causes of Maternal Mortality in the Eastern States of Nigeria." *Nigerian Medical Journal* 3: 99–104.

Welffens-Ekra, Christiane. 1985. "Towards the Integration of Family Planning into Mother and Child Health Care Services in Ivory Coast." Paper presented at a workshop on preventing maternal deaths in Sub-Saharan Africa at the Nongovernmental Organizations (NGO) Forum, Nairobi, Kenya, July.

Williams, Belmont. 1979. "Maternal Mortality in Sierra Leone." Freetown, Sierra Leone: Ministry of Health.

Williams, C. D. 1938. "Child Health in the Gold Coast." *Lancet* 1: 97–102.

World Bank. 1984. *World Development Report 1984*. New York: Oxford University Press.

Wray, J. D. 1971. "Population Pressure on Families: Family Size and Child Spacing." *Reports on Population/Family Planning*, No. 9 (August).

7

Effects of Timing of Marriage on Reproductive Health

George T. F. Acsadi and Gwendolyn Johnson-Acsadi

The family of procreation ordinarily begins with marriage or with a marital union that is expected to be of long or lasting duration. Thus marriage norms, such as those relevant to the timing of entry into marriage or to the prevalence of marriages, are intricately interwoven with fertility and family size. High fertility is closely associated with early marriages, and early marriages have dire consequences for reproductive health.

In Sub-Saharan Africa, marriage has diverse meanings (Van de Walle 1968; Huzayyin and Acsadi 1976; Adegbola and Page 1982). In addition to civil marriages that are established by law and are performed and registered by a civil servant, there are also church marriages and Moslem weddings and—probably the most widespread kind of marriage—socially and often legally recognized traditional marriages, which may or may not be preceded by cohabitation. Traditional marriage is a complex process that consists of a series of events spread out over time, sometimes years. The elements of this process may vary among cultures but usually include a step of arranging the marriage and a step of betrothal or engagement. Another important element of marriage is the financial arrangement between the bridegroom (and his kinsmen) and the bride (and her kinsmen) concerning gifts, services rendered, dowry, or cash payment (such as bride-wealth, bride-price, and mahr), either in one sum or in installments. Fulfillment of these obligations, performance of the customary rites and ceremonies, cohabitation, pregnancy, and confinement may all be considered as elements of marriage. Traditional marriages as well as consensual, de facto marital unions and free casual unions may also be followed by a religious or civil marriage. Under such conditions, it is difficult to tie the date of marriage to a particular event and to determine the age of the bride at marriage.

The World Fertility Survey (WFS), from which the most recent comparative data on this topic are available, made, as a rule, no distinction between marriages and other sexual unions. It considered as marital unions all more or less stable cohabitations of a woman and a man, whether sanctified by religion, law, or custom or simply a "marriage" of convenience. In this chapter, therefore, all sexual unions will be considered and described as marriages. The WFS did not, however, consider the birth of a child as evidence of a marital union. For many women, a first birth is tabulated as occurring before marriage (see table 7-1). Thus, the age of a woman at first marriage as reported in the WFS may be higher than her actual age at entering a de facto sexual union.

In a modern society, individuals or couples can choose the age at which they marry, whether they should have children, how many children to have and at what intervals, and the age at which they will cease childbearing. In a traditional society, on the other hand, individuals have little room for decisionmaking in these matters; the proper ways are prescribed by cultural norms and are enforced by the kinship circle or community. In Sub-Saharan Africa, these norms and customs favor both early marriage and high fertility.

The proportion of adolescents among married females varies greatly among developing countries and, depending on local traditions, their problems and the perception of these problems also vary from country to country. Nevertheless, some consequences of early marriages are common in all countries and may cause the same concern everywhere (Acsadi and Johnson-Acsadi 1986a). The WFS surveys verified, for example, that early marriages are associated with premature childbearing and large completed families. The data also imply that very early marriage is counterproductive from the view-

Table 7-1. *Age at First Marriage, Birth, and Menarche: Percentages of Early Marriages and Premarital Conceptions, Selected Countries, around 1980*

	Ever-married women aged 25–29 years				Percentage of ever-married women whose first birth occurred:		
Country	Median age at first marriage (1)	Median age at first birth (2)	Percentage ever-married at age 16 (3)	Mean age at menarche[a] (4)	Before marriage (5)	0–7 months after marriage (6)	Combined (7)
Benin	18.1	19.6	22.7	14.7	15.2	16.1	31.3
Cameroon	16.9	19.3	39.2	14.2	17.9	10.2	28.1
Côte d'Ivoire	17.4	18.8	30.8	14.1	16.7	12.2	18.9
Ghana	18.3	19.9	22.2	15.0	7.8	7.5	15.3
Kenya	18.1	18.8	24.7	14.4	20.2	15.6	35.8
Lesotho	18.9	20.9	13.7	14.6	4.8	5.8	10.6
Mauritania	15.3	18.8	57.1	13.7	2.7	—	—
Nigeria	16.5	19.0	37.9	14.0	12.1	11.3	23.4
Senegal	16.3	18.6	46.9	—	3.9	4.0	7.9
Sudan (North)	17.0	19.4	42.7	13.2	1.7	2.9	4.6

— Not available.

a. All ever-married women.

Sources: Ebanks and Singh (1984), pp. 30 (col. 1) and 43–53 (col. 3); Singh (1984), p. 23 (cols. 1–2); Smith (1980), pp. 14–18; Singh and Ferry (1984), pp. 36–37 (col. 4); Nigeria (1984), pp. 63, 80–81, 139 (cols 1–4); WFS standard recode tapes (cols. 5–7).

point of ensuring high fertility because adolescents are often barren and may later become infecund.

Prevalence of Early Marriages

The average age at which a woman first enters a marital union varies widely among countries and within them according to culture, rural-urban residence, and other factors.

As measured by the singulate mean age at marriage (SMAM; Hajnal 1953), women in Sub-Saharan Africa marry earlier than their counterparts in other continents—with the exception of a few Asian countries, such as Afghanistan, Bangladesh, Nepal, and Yemen, where child marriages are the rule rather than the exception. Women marry or are compelled to marry earliest in the Moslem-dominated areas of the Sudano-Sahelian region in West Africa (for example, female SMAM is less than eighteen years in Burkina Faso, the Central African Republic, Chad, Guinea, and Niger), in several countries of East Africa (for example, Ethiopia, Malawi, Mozambique, and Uganda), and in Central Africa (Angola, Gabon). As figure 7-1 shows, female SMAM is 20 years or more in only a few countries (United Nations 1988).

An alternative measure is the median age at marriage, the age at which one-half of the women in a group are married. This indicator was calculated for several WFS countries for women aged 25–29 years at the time of the interview, who had passed the customary marriageable age. Only 2–5 percent of these women were not yet married, and the median age at marriage of this age group reflects the most recent marital behavior. In the ten countries for which data are shown in table 7-1, this indicator varied widely. Women married earliest in some West African countries (Mauritania, Nigeria, Senegal), many probably before reaching adolescence. In most countries, half of the women were already married about one or two years younger than the singulate mean age at marriage in figure 7-1 indicates.

Child marriages, judging from this generation's experience, were not unusual in these countries: 31 to 46 percent of the women married when they were only 15–17 years old (table 7-2). Even in countries where median age at marriage is relatively late, it is common for some women to marry before reaching age 15. In other countries where median age at marriage is lower (for example, Nigeria and North Sudan), the most frequent age at marriage is less than 15. It is evident that, in Sub-Saharan African countries, a sizable proportion of women enter into marital unions at the onset of the reproductive life span and are exposed to pregnancy risks while still very young and perhaps even physiologically immature for mating and childbearing.

In the Sub-Saharan WFS countries, mean age at menarche is between 13 and 15 years. Large proportions of women (from 9 to 40 percent of those who had ever married) were married before age 15, a fact suggesting that sexual intercourse before puberty may not be uncommon. The WFS findings on premarital conceptions suggest that age at the beginning of de facto sexual unions is even younger than at first marriage, so that

Figure 7-1. *Singulate Mean Age of Women at Marriage, Most Recent Census and Survey Data*

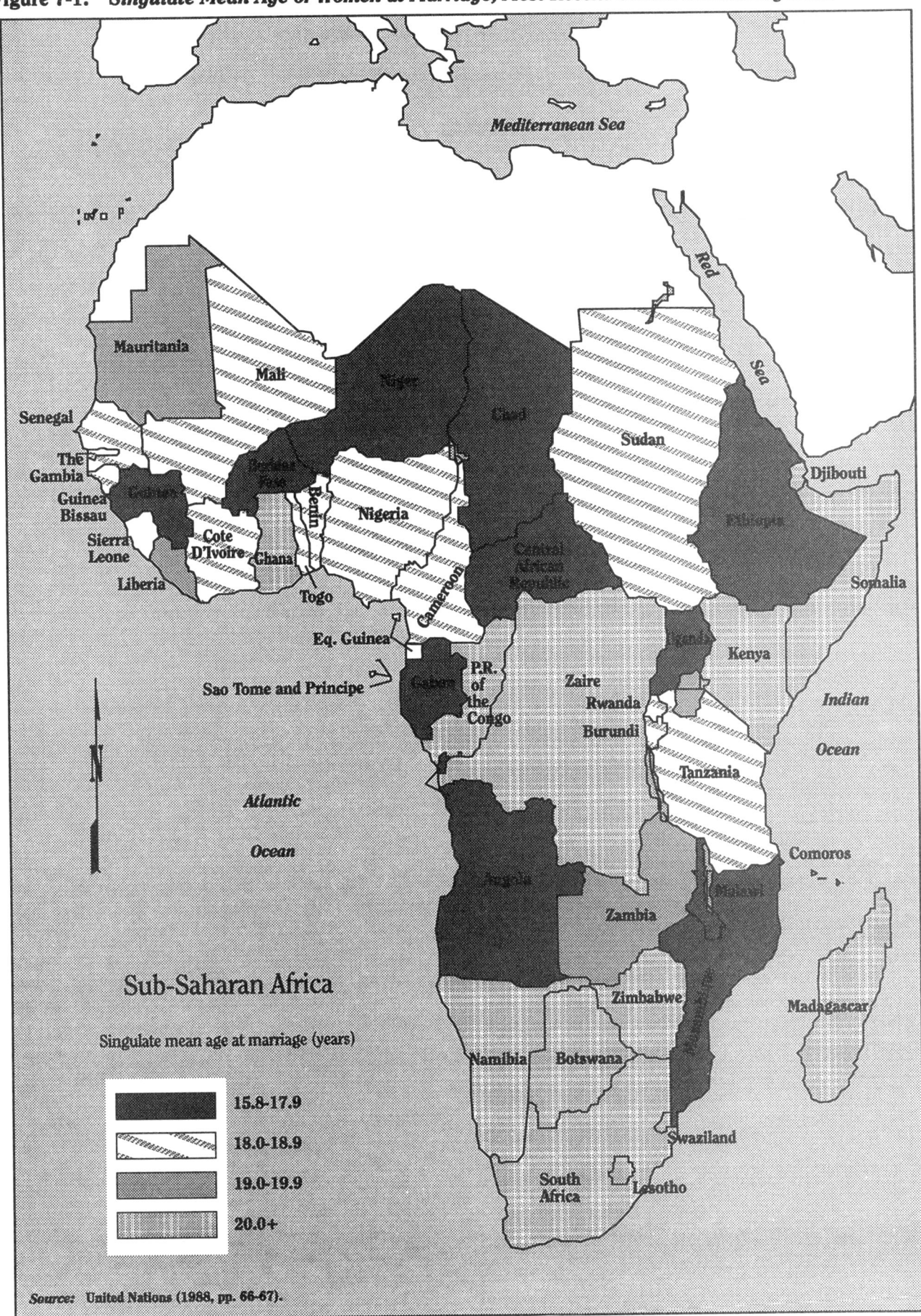

Sub-Saharan Africa

Singulate mean age at marriage (years)

■	15.8–17.9
▨	18.0–18.9
▨	19.0–19.9
▨	20.0+

Source: United Nations (1988, pp. 66–67).

Table 7-2. *Percentage Distribution of Ever-Married Women, by Age at First Marriage, Selected Countries, around 1980*

Country	Total	<15	15–17	18–19	20–21	22–24	25 +
Benin	99.9	11.5	37.4	25.0	12.8	15.6	5.0
Cameroon	99.9	25.8	39.5	15.0	7.9	5.6	5.9
Côte d'Ivoire	100.0	19.6	45.6	17.7	8.5	5.0	3.6
Ghana	99.9	12.3	41.5	22.9	11.6	7.8	3.0
Kenya	100.0	18.7	37.2	21.8	12.9	7.1	3.1
Lesotho	100.0	8.7	38.0	29.6	13.4	8.8	3.5
Nigeria	100.0	37.0	33.5	12.8	8.7	4.6	3.4
Senegal	100.0	34.7	43.3	11.9	5.6	3.0	1.5
Sudan (North)	100.0	39.5	30.7	13.5	7.2	5.7	3.4

Note: Data are based on WFS surveys conducted in Sub-Saharan African countries in 1977–82. "Marriage" refers to any kind of union involving a more or less stable cohabitation of a woman with a man, whether sanctified by religion, law, or custom or simply a "marriage" of convenience. In principle, age at marriage refers to the age of a woman when she started living with her husband (or mate).
Source: WFS standard recode tapes.

the commencement of marital life before menarche may be even more common than indicated by the data on age at first marriage.

Age at First Marriage and High Fertility

In Sub-Saharan Africa, where family planning is rarely practiced prior to the birth of the first child, the timing of first marriage bears directly upon fertility patterns, and these patterns determine, at least in part, the viability of the offspring; fetal, infant, and childhood mortality conditions; and maternal health.

Age at marriage determines in large measure age at first birth. In most WFS counties, among the women who were aged 25–29 years when interviewed, median age at first marriage was between 15.3 and 18.9 years and age at first birth between 18.6 and 20.9 years (table 7-1). It is notable, however, that in countries where median age at first marriage was less than 17 years, the interval between median ages at first marriage and first birth was considerably longer (2.3–3.5 years) than in countries where women married later (0.7–2.0 years). The fact that timing of first birth is closely related to age at first marriage is documented in figure 7-2. Among thirty-nine developing countries that participated in the WFS, median age at first marriage and median age at first birth among women aged 25–29 years are strongly correlated.

A consequence of early marriage is the lengthening of the period that women are married and sexually active, which, without birth control or infecundity, results in higher completed fertility. Except where marriage occurs at a very young age, the earlier a woman marries, the younger she is when she bears her first child, and the more children she has when she reaches the end of her reproductive years, other things being equal (table

7-3). In thirty-nine WFS developing countries, the number of children born to a woman during her childbearing years was, on average, 7.0 children if she married at age 17 or earlier, 6.1 if the marriage occurred at age 20–21, and only 4.2 if she was older than 24 years when first married (Acsadi and Johnson-Acsadi 1985a).

The data in table 7-3 show the same basic tendency among Sub-Saharan African countries, with some variations. In Ghana, the younger women marry, the higher their number of children ever born by age 45–49 years. In Kenya and Lesotho, completed family size is highest among women who married at ages 15–17; in Cameroon, Nigeria, and Senegal, among those who married at ages 18–19. Because family size affects maternal and child health, age at first marriage should be considered an important variable from the aspect of possible policy intervention.

Adolescent Sterility and Initial Infecundity

Although figure 7-2 shows a strong association between age at first marriage and age at first birth, no such relationship appears to exist between the ages of 15 and 18 years. In a group of sixteen countries, seven of them in Sub-Saharan Africa, median age at first marriage was between 15.2 and 18.3 years and median age at first birth fell in the range of 18.6–19.9 years, with little association between the two. In fact, table 7-1 shows that in Sub-Saharan Africa the lower the median age at first marriage, the more time elapses before the first birth (across countries the correlation $r = -0.69$).

Thus, very early marriages tend, as a rule, to be barren at least for a while. This phenomenon is usually termed adolescent sterility or sometimes adolescent subfecundity, with reference to a condition in which the physiological capacity to produce live born children

Figure 7-2. *Median Age at First Marriage and at First Birth in Developing Countries, Women Aged 25–29 Years*

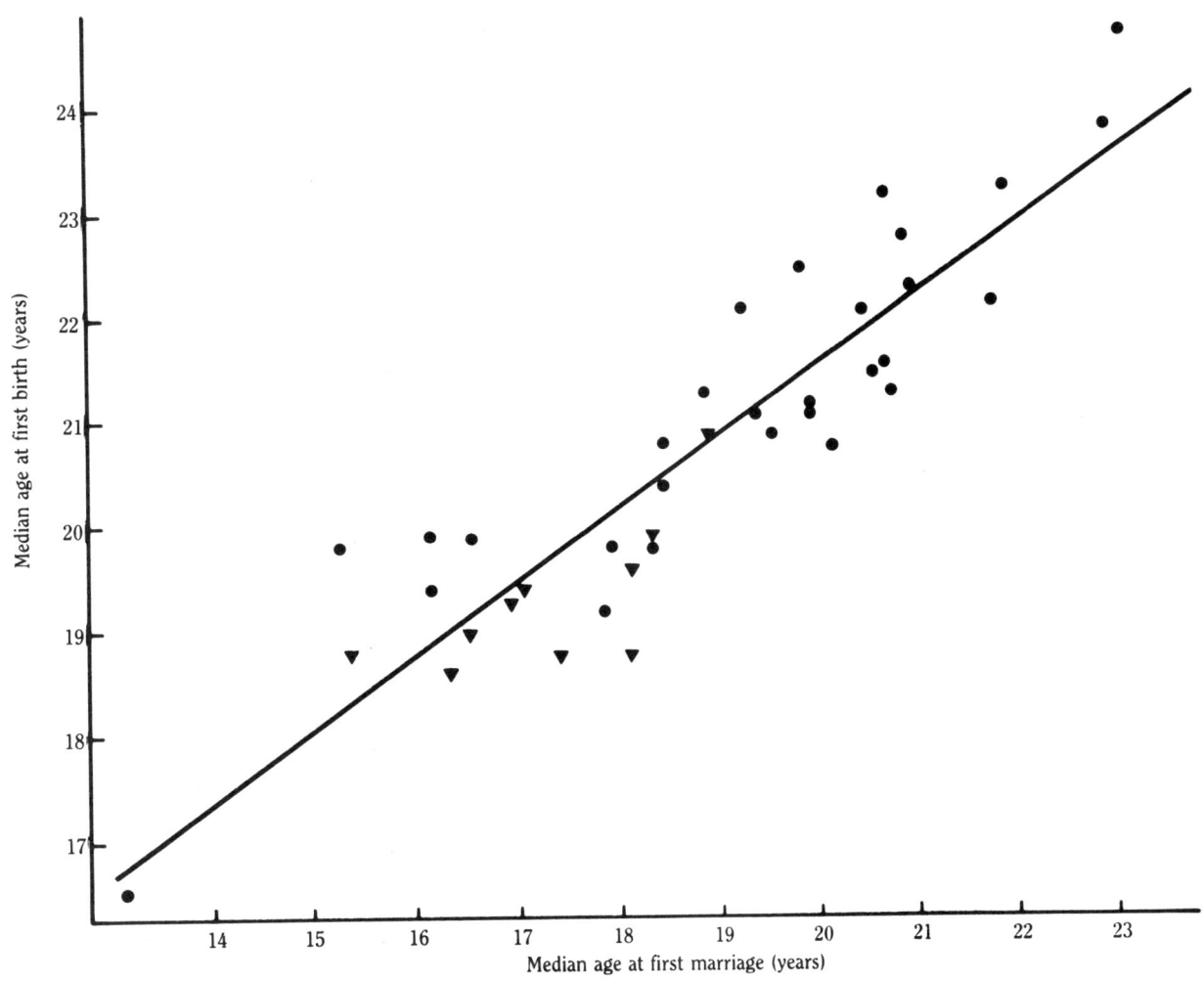

Key: ▼ Sub-Saharan African countries.　● Other developing countries.

Note: Mean $X = 18.7$; mean $Y = 20.7$. $Y = 7.61 + 0.70X$; $R = 0.91$.

Source: WFS data.

has not yet risen to its maximum adult level (Grebenik and Hill 1974). It is uncertain whether the long conception delay between first marriage and first birth among adolescents is due to subfecundity, to fecundity below the standard adult level, or to sterility or infecundity, a physiological incapacity to produce a live born child.

Adolescent sterility or subfecundity is also indicated by the length of the first birth interval—that is, the interval between marriage and first birth. Table 7-4 shows that the first birth interval among ever-married women who had a positive first interval (that is, who gave birth after marriage) was invariably longest among women married at age 14 or younger. The first birth interval declines gradually with increasing age at marriage.

Another indicator of adolescent sterility or subfecundity is the number of children born in the first five years of marriage (table 7-5). In each Sub-Saharan African country, the most children were born during the first five years of marriage to women who married at age 18 years or older. Below age 18, the mean number of children born is considerably lower, especially in the case of women who married younger than 15 years.

One possible explanation is that those who marry earlier may have more premarital births, excluded from the computations, than those who marry later. The proportion of premarital births is relatively high in Sub-Saharan Africa (table 7-1). However, the proportions of women with a premarital conception were lowest among those who married youngest and increased gradually

Table 7-3. *Mean Number of Children Ever Born per Woman Aged 45–49 Years by Age at First Marriage, Selected Countries, around 1980*

Countries	<15	15–17	18–19	20–21	22–24	25+
Cameroon[a]	4.3	4.9	5.8	5.3	4.9	4.6[b]
Ghana	7.8	7.3	7.2	6.2	5.9	5.2[b]
Kenya	7.9	8.4	8.1	7.4	7.6	6.5
Lesotho	5.5	5.7	5.6	5.1	4.8	2.8
Nigeria	6.1	5.9	6.6	6.0	4.9	4.9[b]
Senegal	6.9	7.4	7.9	5.6	—	—
Sudan (North)	6.5	5.6	6.2	6.0	7.3	4.5

— Fewer than 10 cases in cell.
a. Women aged 45 and over at the time of the survey.
b. Age at first marriage 25–29 years.
Sources: Lightbourne, Singh, with Green (1982), p. 27, and WFS first country reports.

with age at first marriage. Thus the observed subfecundity of those who married young is not due to the exclusion of premarital births, which diminished rather than exaggerated the differences in the number of children born in the first years by age at first marriage.

Initial infecundity can be scrutinized more closely by looking at those who had failed to produce a live born child five years after marriage. In principle, this failure may be either voluntary or involuntary, but voluntary postponement of the first birth and avoidance of childbearing altogether are practically nonexistent in Sub-Saharan Africa. Table 7-6 shows the precentages of women initially infecund among women 25–34 years old. Regardless of age at marriage, some women in each country suffered initial infecundity. The highest proportions initially infecund, however, were among those who married very young, especially under 15.

Initial infecundity is naturally more frequent in areas where early marriage is the norm. In addition, when the proportions of initially infecund women who married before age 15 are regressed on the proportions married before this age in twenty-seven developing countries, a positive correlation ($r = 0.67$) is obtained

(Acsadi and Johnson-Acsadi 1985b). In countries where child marriages are widespread, more of the young brides are physically immature than in countries where lower proportions of women, presumably those who are reproductively more mature, enter into union at young ages.

Later Infecundity as a Consequence of Early Marriage

Initial infecundity may be temporary but is often long lasting, as is indicated by cross-national analysis, which shows a relationship between early marriage and later infecundity.

Acsadi and Johnson-Acsadi (1986b) analyzed self-reported infecundity as well as behavioral infecundity (defined as being continuously married for five years prior to the survey, not having used contraception, and having had no birth during that interval; Vaessen 1984). They found significant differences among populations in twenty-seven developing countries in the proportion of women infecund at ages 20–24, when fecundity and

Table 7-4. *Mean Length of First-Birth Interval (Months) by Age at First Marriage, Selected Countries, around 1980*

Country	Total	Age at first marriage (years)					
		<15	15–17	18–19	20–21	22–24	25+
Benin	23.3	40.9	22.5	18.8	19.9	18.6	23.7
Cameroon	38.7	52.8	36.8	26.1	26.6	25.6	31.0
Côte d'Ivoire	25.7	31.4	24.3	23.9	22.3	22.6	24.3
Ghana	24.5	29.8	24.4	23.1	25.6	18.6	20.9
Kenya	24.2	34.1	22.1	20.6	19.5	20.2	22.9
Lesotho	26.2	39.3	27.9	24.0	20.5	20.3	21.7
Nigeria	38.7	49.2	34.9	30.2	29.9	21.9	22.4
Senegal	26.9	32.1	25.2	19.9	24.9	19.1	17.0
Sudan (North)	34.4	41.7	32.3	26.9	25.6	28.0	22.7

Note: Based on responses given by ever-married women with a positive first birth interval (that is, women who had a first birth after first marriage). Women whose first birth occurred before marriage and those who have had no first birth are excluded. First birth interval is the interval between first marriage and first birth.
Source: WFS standard recode tapes.

Table 7-5. *Mean Births in First Five Years of Marriage, by Age at First Marriage, Selected Countries, around 1980*

Country	Total	<15	15–17	18+
		Age at first marriage (years)		
Benin	1.8	1.4	1.9	2.0
Cameroon	1.5	1.0	1.5	2.1
Côte d'Ivoire	1.8	1.5	1.7	2.1
Ghana	1.7	1.5	1.6	1.7
Kenya	2.1	1.6	2.0	2.4
Lesotho	1.5	1.2	1.4	1.6
Nigeria	1.5	1.2	1.6	1.8
Senegal	1.5	1.4	1.6	1.8
Sudan (North)	1.5	1.4	1.6	1.7

Note: Based on responses given by ever-married women who had spent five years or more in union.

Source: WFS standard recode tapes.

fertility are usually at their peak. The frequency of infecundity was associated with the frequency of early marriage. The higher the percentage of women ever married at exact age 16, the greater the proportion infecund at ages 20–24 ($r = 0.75$). Conversely, the later the median age at first marriage, the smaller the proportion infecund at ages 20–24 ($r = -0.77$).

At the micro level, an open birth interval (that is, the interval between the birth of the last child, or marriage if there is no child, and the interview) of 48 months or longer, during which contraception was not practiced, can be used as a indicator of current infecundity. Data on this point appear in table 7-7. Because the open birth interval tends to lengthen with age, the data are only for women aged 25–34 years. Current infecundity is shown, in most countries, to be much more frequent among those who married young, especially under age 15.

The malefic effects of early entry into conjugal unions therefore include not only long initial infecundity but often long-lasting or permanent sterility. Early pregnancy has a high probability of producing a nonviable fetus, a stillborn, or a low birthweight baby with impaired viability after a long and painful labor (Acsadi and Johnson-Acsadi 1988). It may also cause physical injury to the woman, leaving her not only sterile but also a social outcast (for example, if she suffers a vesicovaginal fistula). Very young women also have less resistance to sexually transmitted diseases, which may lead to permanent sterility. Initial and permanent infecundity, a scourge of women in Sub-Saharan African countries, therefore follows early marriage naturally and perhaps more frequently than has been thought.

Other Consequences of Early Marriage

Early marriage also has a marked and harmful impact on the viability of offspring. As the previous chapter demonstrated, the risk of dying in the first year of life is higher for infants born to mothers who are closer to the lower and upper limits of the reproductive period than to those who are in the prime of their childbearing years. Collaborative World Health Organization (WHO) studies in the early 1970s (Omran and Standley 1976, 1981) and later the World Fertility Survey documented

Table 7-6. *Percentage of Initially Infecund Women Aged 25–34 Years, by Age at First Marriage, Selected Countries, around 1980*

Country	Total	<15	15–17	18–19	20–21	22+
			Age at first marriage (years)			
Benin	9.1	24.1	9.2	5.8	5.6	3.4
Cameroon	24.9	45.3	23.2	10.4	11.5	9.3
Côte d'Ivoire	10.2	17.0	10.3	8.3	5.2	4.6
Ghana	8.6	13.2	9.8	6.5	7.8	6.3
Kenya	7.5	15.4	8.2	4.7	4.3	0.4
Lesotho	10.3	18.6	10.6	11.0	8.4	4.4
Mauritania	25.5	32.8	11.8	14.9	13.0	13.6
Nigeria	21.1	34.2	17.1	11.9	11.1	0.0
Senegal	11.6	16.6	10.3	7.1	12.3	3.8
Sudan (North)	15.4	22.2	12.5	12.2	7.0	7.3
Sub-Saharan Africa (10 samples)	14.9	28.1	13.1	8.7	8.0	4.6
Developing countries (27 samples)	13.7	29.2	11.6	8.0	7.3	4.7

Note: Initial infecundity is the failure, whether voluntary or involuntary, to produce a live birth within five years of first marriage (or union) or prior to it. It is based on responses given by ever-married women aged 25–34 years at the time of the survey. Women without a live birth who married fewer than five years prior to the survey are excluded.

Source: WFS standard recode tapes.

Table 7-7. *Percentage of Currently Infecund Women Aged 25–34 Years, by Age at First Marriage, Selected Countries, around 1980*

Country		Age at first marriage (years)				
	Total	<15	15–17	18–19	20–21	22+
Benin	14.9	16.3	15.2	15.6	13.4	13.8
Cameroon	32.2	42.9	27.6	23.9	31.3	35.8
Côte d'Ivoire	17.3	15.1	18.9	17.1	17.1	15.0
Ghana	18.5	23.6	20.2	19.8	11.0	13.8
Kenya	15.9	23.1	16.7	13.4	12.1	8.6
Lesotho	23.9	36.5	26.8	22.6	22.9	9.0
Nigeria	27.7	33.7	26.3	21.9	30.0	10.5
Senegal	19.8	23.4	18.5	17.0	22.4	12.1
Sudan (North)	19.7	27.1	15.8	15.9	13.3	9.1
Sub-Saharan Africa (9 samples)	22.6	30.2	21.8	19.0	19.9	15.1
Developing countries (25 samples)	22.4	27.9	22.2	20.8	20.5	14.9

Note: Current infecundity is the failure, whether voluntary or involuntary, to produce a live birth in the past four or more years, indicated by an open birth interval of forty-eight months or longer. It is based on responses given by ever-married women aged 25–34 years at the time of the survey who did not use any contraceptive method in the open birth interval. Excluded are women pregnant at the time of the survey and never-married women who had not borne a child.

Source: WFS standard recode tapes.

that, in developing countries, maternal age has a considerable effect upon the probability that a child will survive infancy and early childhood and that infants born to teenage mothers suffer considerably higher risk than those born at maternal ages 20–39 years (Rutstein 1984; Acsadi and Johnson-Acsadi 1985a, 1986b).

In thirty-nine developing countries that carried out WFS surveys, the mortality rate of infants born to women less than 20 years old was, on the average, 126 per 1,000 live births, 42 percent higher than for those born to women aged 20–29 years. In ten Sub-Saharan WFS countries, the proportion of babies dying within the first month of life was 50 percent higher and post-neonatal mortality was 25 percent higher when the mother was under age 20 than when she was 20–29 at the time of the birth (chapter 10 in this volume).

Specific studies conducted in developed countries and time series of reliable current vital statistics also show that mortality of infants born to teenage mothers is higher than that of babies of more mature women (Nortman 1984; Acsadi and Johnson-Acsadi 1986b). The relationship between maternal age and infant mortality may change, however, with the reduction of the general level of infant mortality. It can be hypothesized that, during the transition from high to low levels of infant mortality, the lowest mortality risk tends to shift to babies of somewhat younger mothers, and the curve depicting infant mortality by maternal age tends to change from a reverse-J shape associated with high mortality to a U shape in conditions of moderate mortality before assuming the J shape when mortality reaches lower levels.

Sources of the greater hazards for infants born to teenagers are held to be the physiological immaturity of the mothers; their social immaturity and inexperience with child care; and impoverishment with respect to formal schooling and overall living conditions. The effects of biological and physiological factors are predominant during the pregnancy and in the perinatal period. After the neonatal period, however, the effects of socioeconomic factors increase and gain preponderance. Socioeconomic factors then play a dominant role in later mortality (that of toddlers and children). The findings of the World Fertility Survey support the view that, although the overall level of infant mortality is governed in good measure by socioeconomic factors (including public health and medicine), the relationship between maternal age and infant mortality is mainly biologically determined.

Some researchers have disputed the contention that maternal age itself is responsible, through its biological effects, for differences in child health and mortality. The deleterious effect of young maternal age does not disappear, however, if other variables (principally birth order) are controlled. Indeed, the high mortality of infants born to young mothers and, consequently, that of firstborn babies may be explained, at least partly, by low birth weight. As observed in developed countries (Acsadi 1959), birth weight is lowest for babies whose mothers are 16 years old or younger at birth. Average birth weight according to maternal age can be described by a convex second-degree curve. The birth weight of newborn infants, either male or female, first increases steeply with maternal age up to about age 25 years (on the average by 300 grams), then increases more slowly to about age 35, when it reaches its zenith and begins to decrease. Corresponding patterns can be observed by birth order (Loeb 1965).

Variations in average birth weight by maternal age correspond to proportions of underweight, premature babies, whose chances of survival are less favorable than others (Hungary 1970; Selvin and Garfinkel 1972; Chakraborty and others 1975). The relationship between maternal age and birth weight is one factor underlying the relationship between maternal age and child survival. Low birth weight usually indicates premature births that are also often immature births. Thus infants with low birth weight are less viable than infants born with normal weight: both fetal and perinatal mortality rise steadily with decreasing birth weight. Low birth weight is associated not only with high perinatal mortality but also with a much higher risk of dying during later infancy, especially for a male child. Children of below-normal birth weight who survive infancy may also be subject to more health problems during childhood than those born with normal weight (WHO 1979).

Early marriage also affects the health and mortality of the woman. In every country that publishes relevant national statistics, evidence shows that maternal age has a strong effect on maternal mortality, with a much higher risk of maternal death (due to both obstetric causes and abortion) for those near the limits of the childbearing period than for those in their prime childbearing ages (chapter 6 in this volume). In many countries, maternal mortality is distressingly higher among young teenage mothers than among mothers of any other age.

Conclusions

Very early marriage is counterproductive from the viewpoint of ensuring the intended reproductive goal because it has as its concomitants adolescent sterility and often permanent infecundity. In addition, it endangers the health of the woman and the viability of her offspring and causes high infant, child, and maternal mortality. Not only does it preclude the possibility of education for women and thus of their obtaining higher social status and contributing to development efforts, but it also adversely affects family health and family life. In countries where the custom of early marriage is widespread, policymakers therefore have the task and responsibility to initiate population education (both for those coming into the marriageable age and those who may arrange their marriages, where such is the norm) regarding the advantages of delaying marriages. It is important to begin building a public consensus about an acceptable marriageable age and, if necessary, to enact or revise marriage laws to minimize the harmful effects of early marriage. Proper sanctions against early marriage are needed and should be enforced.

References

Acsadi, George. 1959. "Az újszülöttek súlyának alakulása az anya korával kapcsolatban." [Relevance of Maternal Age to the Trend of Birthweights.] Demográfia (Budapest) 2(4): 58–86.

Acsadi, George T. F., and Gwendolyn Johnson-Acsadi. 1985a. "Perspectives on Family Planning in Developing Countries: Some Lessons Learned from the WFS [World Fertility Survey]." London: International Planned Parenthood Federation; processed.

———. 1985b. "Health Aspects of Early Marriage and Reproductive Patterns." [International Planned Parenthood Federation] Medical Bulletin 19(4): 2–4.

———. 1986a. *Policy Relevance of Findings of the World Fertility Survey for Developing Countries.* ST/ESA/SER.R/59. New York: United Nations.

———. 1986b. *Optimum Conditions for Childbearing.* London: International Planned Parenthood Federation.

———. 1988. "Early Entry into Marital Union as a Determinant of Infertility and Infecundity in Developing Countries, with Special Emphasis on Sub-Saharan Africa." Paper presented at the seminar "Biological and Demographic Determinants of Human Reproduction." Baltimore, Md., January 4–8. Liège, Belgium: International Union for Scientific Study of Population; processed.

Adegbola, O., and H. Page. 1982. "Nuptiality and Fertility in Metropolitan Lagos: Components and Compensating Mechanisms." In L. T. Ruzicka, ed., *Nuptiality and Fertility.* Liège, Belgium: Ordina.

Chakraborty, R., M. Roy, and S. R. Das. 1975. "Proportion of Low Birth Weight Infants in an Indian Population and Its Relationship with Maternal Age and Parity." *Human Heredity* 25(2): 73–79.

Ebanks, G. E., and Susheela Singh. 1984. "Socio-economic Differentials in Age at Marriage." WFS Comparative Studies: Cross-National Summaries. Preliminary tables. Voorburg, Netherlands: International Statistical Institute; processed.

Grebenik, E., and Althea Hill. 1974. *International Demographic Terminology: Fertility, Family Planning, and Nuptiality.* Liège, Belgium: International Union for Scientific Study of Population; processed.

Hajnal, John. 1953. "Age at Marriage and Proportions Marrying." *Population Studies* 7: 111–32.

Hungary. 1970. *A koraszülöttek adatai.* [Data on Premature Infants.] Budapest: Központi Statisztikai Hivatal.

Huzayyin, S. A., and G. T. Acsadi, eds. 1976. *Family and Marriage in Some African and Asiatic Countries.* Cairo Demographic Centre Research Monograph Series, No. 6. Cairo: S.O.P. Press.

Lightbourne, Robert E., Susheela Singh, with Cynthia P. Green. 1982. "The World Fertility Survey: Charting Global Childbearing." *Population Bulletin* 37(1). New York: Population Reference Bureau.

Loeb, J. 1965. "Weight at Birth and Survival of Newborn, by Age of Mother and Total Birth Orders." *Vital and Health Statistics*, ser. 21, no. 5.

Nigeria. 1984. *The Nigeria Fertility Survey 1981/82*. Principal Report. Vol. 1. Lagos, Nigeria: National Population Bureau/ World Fertility Survey.

Nortman, Dorothy. 1974. "Parental Age as a Factor in Pregnancy Outcome and Child Development." *Reports on Population/Family Planning* 16. New York: Population Council.

Omran, Abdel R., and C. C. Standley, eds. 1976. *Family Formation Patterns and Health*. Geneva: World Health Organization.

————. 1981. *Further Studies on Family Formation Patterns and Health*. Geneva: World Health Organization.

Rutstein, Shea O. 1984. "Infant and Child Mortality: Levels, Trends, and Demographic Differentials." Rev. ed. wfs *Comparative Studies: Cross-National Summaries*, No. 43. Voorburg, Netherlands: International Statistical Institute.

Selvin, S., and J. Garfinkel. 1972. "The Relationship between Parental Age and Birth Order with the Percentage of Low Birthweight Infants." *Human Biology*, 44(3): 501–10.

Singh, Susheela. 1984. "Assessment of Nuptiality Data." Paper presented at the symposium "World Fertility Survey, 1972–1984," London; processed.

Singh, Susheela, and Benoit Ferry. 1984. "Biological and Traditional Factors That Influence Fertility." wfs *Comparative Studies: Cross-National Summaries*, No. 40. Voorburg, Netherlands: International Statistical Institute.

Smith, D. P. 1980. "Age at First Marriage." wfs *Comparative Studies: Cross-National Summaries*, No. 7. Voorburg, Netherlands: International Statistical Institute.

United Nations. 1988. *First Marriage: Patterns and Determinants*. st/esa/ser.r/76. New York: Department of International Economic and Social Affairs.

Vaessen, Martin. 1984. "Childlessness and Infecundity." wfs *Comparative Studies: Cross-National Summaries*, No. 31. Voorburg, Netherlands: International Statistical Institute.

Van de Walle, Etienne. 1968. "Marriage in African Censuses and Inquiries." In W. Brass and others, eds., *The Demography of Tropical Africa*. Princeton: Princeton University Press.

World Health Organization. 1979. "Maternal and Child Health: Report by the Director General." Paper Presented at the Thirty-second World Health Assembly, Geneva.

8

Socioeconomic Consequences of High Fertility for the Family

Virginia DeLancey

High fertility and close child spacing affect both health and socioeconomic conditions. Health consequences— fetal, infant, child, and maternal mortality, morbidity, nutrition, and other factors—have been covered in previous chapters. Socioeconomic consequences include effects on income, savings, expenditures, education, labor supply, occupation, population pressure, land tenure, and migration. The consequences may be either positive or negative. To the extent that they are positive, the demand for children should be high; to the extent that they are negative, the demand for children should be low. In addition, the consequences differ throughout the world, depending upon variables such as family structure and government social welfare systems.

As suggested above, it is more difficult to generalize about the socioeconomic consequences of high fertility and close child spacing than about the health-related consequences. In addition, even within Sub-Saharan Africa, the socioeconomic consequences differ greatly from one ethnic group to another and from one geographic location to another, depending upon the related family structure or government social welfare system, for example. Thus, from society to society, the consequences may be negatively or positively related to the causal variables, or there may be no consequences at all.

It is also difficult to generalize because the studies are not completely comparable. The most important variable, fertility, is defined and measured in different ways in different studies. Although it is often measured by the number of surviving children, it is sometimes measured by the number of children ever born. Because many of the studies were carried out for reasons other than those considered here, the independent variable is sometimes measured by family or household size, or even by the quantity of work time expended by children,

rather than by the number of children in the family. Similarly, the economic variables such as income and savings are sometimes measured in terms of totals, and sometimes in terms of per capita figures.

As a result of the variability of consequences from society to society, as well as differences in measurement of the important variables, especially fertility, but also the economic variables, the results are largely inconclusive. That is, there is no evidence that the socioeconomic consequences of high fertility and close child spacing are always negative. However, there is also no evidence that the consequences are always, or nearly always, positive.

At the household level, high fertility may have consequences for total income, savings, and expenditures, as well as for per capita income, savings, and expenditures. It may affect the amount, and perhaps also the quality, of education that the children receive as well as the number of children who obtain access to basic education. Depending upon the availability of land, the tenure system, and inheritance laws, the consequences of high fertility and closely spaced children may be pressure upon the arable land available for family use. If pressure occurs, there may be more intensive or diversified cultivation or migration and changed occupations. High fertility may also affect the supply of female labor. Depending upon the type of work and employment location, as well as the sector of the economy, it may increase or decrease the supply of that labor—or it may have no effect.

The socioeconomic consequences of high fertility and close child spacing differ greatly from one ethnic group to another and from one geographic location to another. From society to society, the consequences may be negative or positive, or there may be no consequences at all. The net effect is therefore difficult to determine.

That is, there is no evidence that the socioeconomic consequences are always negative. There is also no evidence, however, that they are always, or nearly always, positive.

Income

The consequences of high fertility and close child spacing for household income are indeterminate in Sub-Saharan Africa. A negative effect has been hypothesized by some scholars and a positive one by others. Chernichovsky (1979), for example, suggested that the presence of children, irrespective of their number, may decrease family income in developed countries because of the negative effect upon the mother's labor supply, but the opposite may be true in developing countries. Children are likely to increase family income as a result of the increased land that is made available to larger families; the increase in the father's labor supply resulting from attempts to cope with financial pressures caused by the greater demand of larger families for consumption goods and education; and the direct contribution of children to household income.

Using non-African data, Birdsall (1980) showed that the relationship between population growth and poverty depended upon the way household income was measured. For total household income, three middle-income groups had the highest average number of children. For per capita income, the poorest 20 percent of households had the highest average number of children. In Birdsall's opinion, per capita income is the more important measure; although children need less food than adults, they still increase a family's overall needs, especially for health care and education.

Birdsall concluded that a disproportionate number of poor children come from large families, who are least able to respond with increased educational opportunities and health care:

> Numerous children per family compound the problem of low income by reducing the resources put into each child's education and, probably, into nutrition, health care, and other basic needs. Poorly nourished children are likely to have trouble with schooling later on. And children who receive less education are likely to have many children themselves. From one generation to the next, large family size, low investments in children, and inequality in incomes and skills are bound together in a way that helps perpetuate poverty. (Birdsall 1980, p. 24.)

Whether these same relationships hold throughout Sub-Saharan Africa is difficult to ascertain; the answer depends upon the cost of children as well as upon the contributions of children to household income.

The consequences of high fertility and closely spaced children may depend upon whether the household is urban or rural. The two settings offer different employment opportunities for both parents and children as well as different potential for a conflict between the roles of mother and of income producer that results from the presence of children.

In urban areas, where income is often earned as wages or salaries or from self-employment in business, children may find little opportunity to contribute to family income. Total income may be unaffected by family size, but per capita income may decline. The potential contribution of children should not be discounted entirely, however, because children may assist their families in looking after a family business. Even small children may help sell articles in petty trade or may vend the food that their mothers prepare at home. Whereas children may or may not contribute to family income, urban settings often emphasize the high cost of children. This cost may encourage parents to increase their work hours, take second jobs, or seek alternative ways of earning money.

In rural settings, children may contribute to total family income by working on the family farm. In some societies, farm plots are distributed according to family needs—the larger the family, the greater the quantity of land allotted by the traditional land tenure system. The additional labor may allow more intensive or more diversified cultivation if land is scarce or more extensive cultivation if additional acreage is available. Depending upon the productivity of the children, the additional labor may permit either increased consumption or increased production of food or crops for cash sale, or both.

When older children, in either urban or rural locations, leave home, especially if they find employment for wages, they may be expected to continue to contribute to their parents' income by sending money home periodically. This contribution may increase total family income or may help to maintain it as parents become older and are less able to work.

The few research projects that have attempted to examine the relationship between fertility and income in Sub-Saharan Africa include studies in Kenya and Botswana. In Kenya, Kelley (1976) found that the effect of surviving children on household income was positive. In a later article, however, Kelley and Swartz (1979) hypothesized that the influence of children on income and work force participation is uncertain: children may prevent the mother from participating in the labor force, add directly or indirectly to the family's income, or induce adults to work longer and harder to support their children.

Kelley and Swartz tested their income model with empirical data collected in 1968–69 by the Central Bureau of Statistics for the Urban Household Budget Sur-

Table 8-1. *Percentage Distribution of Holdings by Holding Size and Household Members, Kenya, 1974–75*

Holding size (hectares)	Household size (members)							
	1	*2–3*	*4–5*	*6–7*	*8–10*	*11–15*	*16+*	*Total*
<0.5	8.81	15.32	14.53	15.33	13.83	10.94	13.01	13.91
0.5–0.9	13.90	28.58	17.60	19.12	14.14	13.66	12.92	17.92
1.0–1.9	46.54	18.94	31.79	25.83	25.17	28.83	20.03	26.99
2.0–2.9	19.89	12.03	12.36	18.31	15.19	16.29	9.51	15.11
3.0–3.9	6.34	4.31	10.25	6.89	11.85	11.17	10.06	8.89
4.0–4.9	0.03	14.17	7.37	5.47	0.67	4.63	12.36	7.22
5.0–7.9	3.90	4.41	3.44	5.95	8.88	8.51	16.59	6.50
8.0+	0.60	2.25	2.66	3.10	4.27	5.97	5.53	3.47
Total	100.00	100.00	100.00	100.00	100.00	100.00	100.00	100.00
Average per capita holding	1.80	0.82	0.45	0.32	0.25	0.20	0.19	0.30
Mean income (Kenya shillings)								
Per household	1392	1934	2892	3499	4028	4932	6022	3484
Per member	1392	774	643	538	448	397	335	498

Source: Integrated Rural Survey 1 (1974–75), Kenya Central Bureau of Statistics; cited in World Bank (1980), pp. 60–61.

vey in three urban areas of Kenya (Kisumu, Mombasa, and Nairobi). The sample consisted of 1,146 households, mostly African, mainly from the upper- and middle-income groups, divided into three categories: nuclear, near-nuclear, and extended. They concluded that the impact of children on income varied by household structure. Children in extended households exerted a positive and significant impact on income. Children in nuclear households and children per se did not exert a significant impact.

A World Bank (1980) country study of Kenya also found evidence that larger households had higher total incomes. Per capita incomes, however, were lower (table 8-1). The data were collected in 1974–75 by the Central Bureau of Statistics for rural smallholder households that had no more than twenty acres of land. According to the report, the larger the household size, the larger the total number of hectares held but the smaller the per capita holdings.

In Ghana, Dutta-Roy (1969, cited in Addo 1970) found a positive association between income of household head and larger family sizes. High fertility, however, did not cause an increase in income; high income caused an increase in family size although not necessarily in fertility. That is, the more highly educated the household head, the more likely he/she was to earn higher income, and according to custom, the larger the number of individuals he/she was expected to support, though they were not necessarily his/her own children. In another study in Ghana, a survey of preschool children, Kpedekpo and Addo (1970, cited in Addo 1970) found a weak positive relationship between income and family size for the three towns covered in the survey.

Mueller (1982) provided some insight into the consequences of fertility for income in Botswana through an analysis of time use data. The effect of children was measured by the quantity of work time expended, not by the number of children in the family. The data, collected as part of the Botswana Rural Income Distribution Survey, produced a file of 1,765 households, of which 1,115 households farming under traditional land tenure systems were actually interviewed. Children's labor made a significant contribution only in cattle-owning households; the job of looking after the cattle is often allocated to children. The work of children was insignificant in affecting total family income in female-headed households without prime working-age males, probably because female-headed households owned fewer animals than male-headed households (World Bank 1980). Thus the effect of child labor time depended upon the role of children within the family and the type of tasks normally assigned to them.

In summary, the empirical studies showed varying results, depending upon whether total family income or per capita income was calculated and on whether the children were in extended or nuclear families, rural or urban settings, cattle-owning or non-cattle-owning families, and male- or female-headed households.

Income Transfers

In addition to affecting the size of family income, fertility may also affect the transfer of income, particularly among family members separated by migration. Johnson and Whitelaw (1974) estimated a remittance function using data from a 1971 survey of 1,140 males employed in Nairobi. The authors found that the more children the men had living with them in Nairobi, the lower were their urban-rural remittances. The more children they had living in their rural home area, however, the greater were their urban-rural remittances.

Using data from the 1974 ILO/University of Nairobi Household Survey for 1,515 households, Knowles and Anker (1977) found that 29 percent had transferred some income during the preceding twelve months. Number of children did not significantly affect the decision to transfer income but did affect the amount and proportion of income transferred. The number of children living away from the household head increased the amount of income that rural household heads transferred, and the proportion of income that urban household heads transferred. This finding was consistent with the idea that school fees in Kenya are an important motive for income transfers.

Savings

Very few studies analyze whether high fertility and closely spaced children have consequences for savings. This topic may have been neglected because, in the past, it was often believed that little saving occurs at the household level in Sub-Saharan Africa. Yet recent studies of traditional savings and credit associations and credit unions (DeLancey 1978, 1981, 1983) have shown that individuals often save a considerable portion of their incomes.

It is uncertain whether having many children encourages families to try to save more, particularly for future education costs, or whether the current costs of those children prevent families from saving. Savings may vary greatly from location to location, depending upon the opportunities to earn a cash income and the costs of important expenditures such as education. It is also important to differentiate between total and per capita saving. Not only the number of children but also their spacing and their ages matter. Very young children contribute little to household income but add to medical, food, clothing, and shelter expenses. Older children may be able to contribute more to income but also cost more to educate. Still older children may contribute even more as they complete their education. Thus the particular mix of ages within the household is crucial

to determining the effect upon income as well as upon savings.

In his study of personal savings and family size and composition, Chernichovsky (1979) cited two examples from Sub-Saharan Africa. Each of them used family size as an explanatory variable but did not consider family composition and life-cycle issues. Their results differed. Snyder (1974a), using a sample from Sierra Leone, found that household size did not affect the probability that households will have positive savings, but Waldorf (1977) found a negative effect of family size on household savings in Uganda.

The World Bank country study of Kenya (1980) reported that household savings as well as household size rose with increases in landholding (table 8-2). The net effect of household size on savings could not be determined, however, and direction of causation could not automatically be assumed.

Kelley and Swartz (1979) estimated two sets of savings models. The first involved the net direct impact of household structure upon savings; the second concerned the various effects of the extended family's demographic structure on savings. In neither set of equations did the number of children in the household influence the level of total or financial savings when income and household structure were controlled, although they did exert a significant, positive effect upon the level of savings for investment in human capital. The study showed, in general, that nuclear families earned comparatively less but saved more, whereas extended families earned more but saved less. It was hypothesized that extended families offer security to members, which decreases the importance of savings, whereas the nuclear family must accumulate savings for its own protection. Thus the number of children may be less critical than the structure of the family (World Bank 1980).

Expenditures

Expenditures fall into several major categories, including medical care, clothing, housing, food, and education. Education expenditures are discussed in a separate section because of their importance in respects other than cost.

Table 8-2. *Household Characteristics by Holding Size, Kenya, 1974–75*

Household characteristics (Kenya shillings)	Holding size (hectares)			
	<2.0	2.0–3.9	4.0–7.9	8.0+
Mean household income	3,127	3,704	4,937	5,755
Mean household consumption	3,079	3,580	4,590	4,362
Mean household saving	48	124	347	1,393
Mean household size (persons)	6.8	7.4	7.6	8.4

Source: Integrated Rural Survey 1 (1974–75), Kenya Central Bureau of Statistics; cited in World Bank (1980), p. 62.

Food

When food is purchased for cash, it may be expected that, for any given income, the greater the number of children, the greater the budget strain. There may be several results. For a given income, either less food may be purchased, per capita or in total, or lower-quality food may be purchased. In either case, nutrition will suffer, with undesirable health consequences, or resources may be shifted from other expenditures to food expenditures, so that the total quantity of food purchased increases but not necessarily per capita.

When food is produced on the family farm, the effect of a large family may be very different. Where land is sufficient, children may assist in increasing production of food for consumption and possibly also for cash sale. Where land is not plentiful, however, marginal productivity may decrease to zero or may even become negative, so that there is less food per capita and nutritional problems occur.

A study of the interrelationships between family structure and resources was carried out by Mudambi (1980) in eastern Nigeria. Interviews with members of 200 urban and rural families showed that families with the lowest food allowances also had a large number of children (between eight and eighteen) to support. The conclusion of the study was that the larger the family, the lower the food allowance per individual. A study of this phenomenon in Ghana (Idusogie 1972, cited in Mudambi 1980) also showed a scaling down in the quality of food rations to cope with an increase in household size. In another study carried out in Ghana, however, Kpedekpo and Addo (cited in Addo 1970) found a positive correlation between family size and food expenditures, particularly when there were large numbers of children and old relatives. They assumed that the rise in size of household was closely associated with an increasing number of children. In the three towns surveyed, 63, 64, and 81 percent of income was being spent on food.

A study of the relationship between household size and consumption patterns in Kenya conducted by the Central Bureau of Statistics in 1972 (World Bank 1980) showed that an increase in household size would cause a shift in expenditures from nonfood items such as transport, recreation, clothing, and housing, and a significant shift from alcohol and tobacco, toward basic foodstuffs.

Medical Care

It was not possible to find specific studies of household medical expenditures in Sub-Saharan Africa. Wray (1971), however, found that, throughout the world, medical care expenditures, unlike food costs, decrease as family size increases in spite of the fact that the need for medical care increases. Thus, large families may deprive themselves of medical care to meet other needs, possibly for food.

Housing

Total housing outlay may increase as the number of children increases, may remain the same within a fixed budget, or may decrease if resources must be shifted to the food budget. Mudambi's study (1980) in eastern Nigeria reported that 71 percent of those who were inadequately housed were large families from lower socioeconomic and rural segments of the sample. Addo (1970) provided more comprehensive data on housing expenditures in Ghana from the 1966 Migration Survey of the Accra Capital District and the Eastern Region. He found that, although the occupied room space increased as the size of the household expanded, the number of household members per room also rose. Number of rooms per unit increased only slightly as the size of the household increased, so that overcrowding occurred and grew worse as the household grew larger (table 8-3).

It should be recalled that the study of household size

Table 8-3. *Mean Number of Rooms Occupied, by Number of Persons in Household and Education of Head*

Persons in household	Education of head, Accra capital district (urban)			Education of head, Eastern Region (urban)		
	None	Elementary or middle	Beyond middle	None	Elementary or middle	Beyond middle
1	1.06	1.21	1.45	1.27	1.13	1.65
2	1.14	1.21	1.65	1.57	1.38	1.67
3–4	1.28	1.40	2.39	1.57	1.67	1.62
5–9	1.64	1.86	3.02	2.34	2.23	3.47
10+	2.75	3.87	—	4.40	4.00	—
All households	1.41	1.64	2.18	2.09	1.82	2.21

—Too few cases.
Source: Addo (1970), p. 51.

and consumption expenditures of the Central Bureau of Statistics in Kenya found shifts in expenditures away from certain categories, including housing, toward basic foodstuffs. Although the shift was not statistically significant at the 0.01 level, it does support the findings of Mudambi and Addo.

Clothing

Total clothing expenditures may increase or remain the same as the number of children increases. They may even decrease if resources must be shifted to food expenditures. Per capita clothing expenditures are unlikely to increase as number of children increases, but it is uncertain whether they remain the same or decrease as a result of budget constraints. Mudambi's study (1980) of family resources in eastern Nigeria found no sharp distinctions among three urban socioeconomic segments in the quantity of clothing that children had and concluded that families preferred to clothe their children well even if doing so meant that they could not provide good food. The study did not compare the quality and cost of clothing, however. The study of household size and consumption expenditures by the Kenya Central Bureau of Statistics (cited in World Bank 1980, p. 58) indicated that, as family size increases, expenditures shift away from clothing and certain other categories toward basic foodstuffs. The shift from clothing, however, was not statistically significant at the 0.01 level.

Education Expenditures

Much evidence shows that education affects fertility. In addition, fertility may affect the education of women and children. In many societies, motherhood often terminates a young woman's education. This statement holds true particularly if she becomes pregnant while she is still a student at the primary or secondary school level. Mott (1974), for example, reported that, in the Nigerian village of Ebendo, young women with children had difficulty continuing their education unless they were able to engage a mother substitute. Many young women attempted to stay in school by resorting to illegal abortions.

High fertility may also affect the education of children. The costs (tuition, school uniforms, books, and so forth) may prevent many families from educating all of their children. The first male child often receives highest priority. Later children, and especially girls, may receive lower priority. High fertility, however, may also have a positive effect on children's education: if direct education costs are low, and if there is a demand for child labor in the home and on the farm, it may be easier for children from larger families to attend school when the work load is divided among them.

Close spacing of children may also make it more difficult to educate them. If children are widely spaced, the constraint may not be so great because of the operation of "sibling chains of assistance." That is, the first child to complete his or her education and obtain employment is obligated to assist a younger sibling. This assistance continues until all siblings have been educated with the help of older brothers and sisters.

Mueller (1983) has argued that the direct costs of education in Sub-Saharan Africa may be very low and may thus have less of a negative effect upon fertility than in industrialized countries. The indirect costs, the child's labor forgone, may be more significant than the direct costs. But families with many children may be more able to spare some from farm work to go to school. If school begins to interfere with child labor, however, attendance may become irregular, depending upon the price elasticity of demand for education.

Furthermore, according to Mueller, parents may view education of children as an investment that will increase their earning power and their future remittances to the home. If earnings in agriculture are low compared with urban earnings, then the expected payoff from raising children may be large, so that there is no tradeoff between quantity and quality of children. The difficulty in determining the relationship is that the investments in education must be made a considerable time before the return from the investment is received. It may be difficult for low-income families to educate many children if they are unable to borrow. Yet in some cultures social mechanisms ease this burden; for example, relatives may help, or there may be sibling chains of assistance.

Ssennyonga (1975) observed that, in Kenya, children's education may be so important that some farmers are willing to go without necessities, such as sugar and salt, just to raise the money for school fees and uniforms. To assure that at least one son performs successfully in school, parents often delay the education of other children, particularly daughters. They hope that, upon graduation, the older sons will then help support their younger siblings.

Mueller (1983) presented empirical findings on the tradeoff between quality and quantity of children from throughout the world, including some examples from Sub-Saharan Africa. In the first example, Snyder (1974a) showed a positive association in 1968–69 data, mostly urban, from Sierra Leone between children's education and number of children born after controlling for other variables. The relationship was most significant for women under thirty-five; it became weaker at older ages. In the second example, the Rural Income Distribution Survey conducted in Botswana in 1974–75 also indicated a positive relationship. Mueller's analysis of time use (1982) revealed that, as the number of children in the household increased, economic work per child was reduced, whereas average school hours per child rose. That is, with more children, it was easier to send some to school and still obtain the needed child labor for cattle tending and farm work.

Using the same data base, Chernichovsky (1981) gave a somewhat different interpretation. He noted that, in Botswana, children play a role in the household economy, and therefore the indirect costs of schooling may still be substantial. Those costs, in combination with the direct costs of transportation, uniforms, and school fees, might prohibit schooling for many families. Chernichovsky, however, indicated that the larger the number of children of primary school age in the household, the greater the probability of their enrollment, which may be explained by the falling (marginal) productivity of labor and the consequent reduction of indirect costs of schooling. He also found that the larger the number of primary-school-aged children in the household, the higher the level of education. In general, the more persons available in the household, the lower the (per capita) demand for child labor and therefore the lower the indirect costs of formal education.

The findings for Botswana were particularly interesting because of the large number of young men who migrate to South Africa to work in the mines; parents can receive appreciable remittances from uneducated children as a result. The opportunity cost of school attendance may thus play an important role in the decision to opt for quantity or quality of children (Mueller 1982).

In the third example, Anker and Knowles (1982) analyzed the tradeoff between quantity and quality separately for urban and rural areas of Kenya. They claimed that, in the rural areas, "higher levels of school attainment seem to have a stimulative effect on fertility. It appears that parents view education for their children as a good investment" (cited in Mueller 1983, p. 24). The positive relationship between education and fertility is consistent with the two other findings, but one must wonder whether or not the direction of causation might be the opposite of that suggested by Anker and Knowles. It is possible that parents struggled to provide education for their children in spite of the increasing number of offspring because they believed that education was a good investment.

In urban areas, in contrast, Anker and Knowles found that neither the actual school enrollment rate nor the wife's expectations regarding her children's education were significantly related to fertility. These findings should also be contrasted with those of Kelley and Swartz (1979), who found that, in three urban locations in Kenya, number of children had a positive influence on the level of human capital savings for investment in children's education.

Mueller concluded that, despite the empirical evidence of a quantity/quality tradeoff in some developing countries, theoretical as well as empirical support exists for the idea that rising educational aspirations may not lead to a decline in the demand for children.

Labor Supply

Female labor force participation and fertility, it is widely hypothesized, are inversely related and are simultaneously and jointly determined. Both are highly dependent on the wife's wage, which has both an income effect and a price effect, which measures the opportunity cost of children in terms of the value of a woman's time. On one hand, the wage has a positive income effect; as it increases, labor force participation as well as the demand for children increase. On the other hand, the wage has a negative price (or substitution) effect; as it rises, the value of a woman's time increases, and therefore the cost of staying home to care for children rises. The higher the cost of children (that is, the greater the earnings a woman must forgo to care for children), the lower will be the demand for children. The negative price effect generally outweighs the positive income effect in developed countries and is partly responsible for the inverse relationship between fertility and the participation of women in the labor force.

Empirical work in developed countries has confirmed the inverse relationship. Studies at the household level in Sub-Saharan Africa come to varying conclusions, however, depending on whether employment is in the urban or rural sector, whether fertility is a decision variable, and especially whether employment is compatible with child rearing or whether child care alternatives are available (DeLancey 1980).

Reasons can be found why the relationship between female labor force participation and fertility in Sub-Saharan Africa should be negative, positive, or nonexistent, with causation, if any, going in either direction. A negative relationship might be expected in urban, modern-sector wage or salary employment, where women with low fertility may find it easier to work than women with high fertility. Similarly, women who are in the labor force may decide to have smaller families in order to avoid potential conflicts between the roles of worker and mother or because they find work a rewarding substitute for children. Thus, current labor force participation may be a consequence of past fertility or a determinant of future or lifetime fertility, or both may be simultaneously and jointly determined and dependent on the value of women's time.

A positive relationship between female labor force participation and fertility may also be expected in some instances: when women who work can afford more children or when increased numbers of children encourage the parents to work harder. Jobs compatible with child care or inexpensive child care alternatives—inexpensive household help or help from members of the extended family—would be necessary to produce a positive relationship. Under similar circumstances, when work and child rearing are compatible and women do not have to choose between motherhood and employment, fertility and female participation in the labor force may also show no relationship.

Micro-level research on the relationship between fertility and participation of women in the labor force in Sub-Saharan Africa provides a variety of findings, most of them supporting a positive relationship and emphasizing the compatibility of jobs and child care. I will review studies by country, from West to East to Southern Africa.

West Africa

In Sierra Leone, Snyder (1974b) attempted to test a version of the economic theory of fertility (Easterlin 1973; also see 1975). Using data from 717 households from surveys conducted in 1966–69, he found a positive relationship between fertility and the current labor force status of women. It was significant, however, only in the oldest group of women. Unfortunately, the fertility variable that Snyder employed was the number of children ever fathered by the household head. In order to approximate the number of surviving children of a woman, he reduced the original sample of 3,071 to 717 by eliminating households on many bases, including the presence of multiple wives. Thus, he eliminated most cases in which the male fertility variable differed from female fertility, but he may have had to work with a culturally biased, atypical group of respondents.

A study by Uyanga (1976) of 145 couples from Jos, Nigeria, also found a positive relationship between number of surviving children and a woman's current employment status. He also found education to be positively related to employment and inversely related to

fertility, however, and concluded that education explained the relationship. Uyanga's comparison of current labor force status with past fertility weakens the validity of his conclusion.

Another study was carried out by Arowolo (1978) in Ibadan, Nigeria. Using survey data from the 1973 Changing African Family Project, the author maintained that no relationship existed between number of children and female labor force participation, either because of the lack of conflict between the roles of mother and wage earner or because of adaptive mechanisms that reconcile the traditional belief in large families with the demands of urban employment. In order to uncover those adaptive mechanisms, he conducted further research in Ibadan with a sample of 957 respondents (Arowolo 1977). Throughout the analysis, he viewed labor force participation as a determinant of fertility rather than as a possible consequence, even when he related current labor force participation to fertility. He found a positive relationship. Employed women in many age groups had more children than unemployed women and unpaid family workers (table 8-4). When the sample was differentiated by rural-urban origin, the most fertile group was of employed women born outside Ibadan, followed in descending order of fertility by unemployed women born outside Ibadan, unemployed women born inside Ibadan, and employed women born inside Ibadan. Arowolo found no substantial differences in fertility by occupational class or by type of work done. He concluded that such differentials had not yet emerged, although the broad categories might have concealed actual differences. The results might also have been affected by the availability of child care alternatives, because 58 percent of the women had resident relatives. Among all respondents, 22 percent relied on such relatives to care for their children. An even larger group (27 percent) employed housemaids, and a few used neighbors, cotenants, nannies, and so

Table 8-4. *Mean Children Ever Born, by Employment Status of Woman and Her Place of Birth, Ibadan, Nigeria, 1974*

| | Gainfully employed | | | | Unemployed/unpaid family work | | | |
| | Born in Ibadan | | Born elsewhere | | Born in Ibadan | | Born elsewhere | |
Age group	Mean live births	Cases	Mean live births	Cases	Mean live births	Cases	Mean live births	Cases
15–19	1.0	3	1.8	6	0.9	9	1.2	5
20–24	1.9	25	1.7	44	1.4	8	1.8	18
25–29	2.0	46	2.5	130	2.1	18	2.2	34
30–34	3.5	32	3.8	107	2.2	22	3.3	29
35–39	3.5	21	4.1	86	3.8	12	3.9	30
40–44	4.4	25	5.2	62	3.1	15	4.8	16
45–49	3.6	22	5.2	25	5.3	7	5.0	10

Source: Arowolo (1977), app. B, p. 61.

forth. Less than half of them (41 percent), mostly the unpaid family workers, claimed that they did not use any child care surrogates.

A study conducted in Lagos, Nigeria (Adewuyi 1980), examined compatibility of roles by analyzing current employment status of 952 mothers by age of youngest child. The presence and age of children rather than the number of children were considered the important determinants of labor force participation. The employment rate of mothers whose youngest child was in preschool (73 percent) was only one percentage point lower than that of mothers whose youngest was in primary school, but the rates of those whose youngest child was in primary school were four percentage points lower than those whose youngest child was in secondary school or higher. Another classification of the same data, however, reveals more clearly the importance of the presence of household help. The employment rate of mothers with preschool children (77 percent) differed only slightly from that of mothers with older children (79 percent) if the mother had household help. For those without household help, only 51 percent of mothers with preschool children were employed, versus 68 percent of those with school-age and older children. Irrespective of the age of the youngest child, mothers without help had much lower participation rates than those with help.

Standing and Sheehan (1978b) obtained results for Nigeria from a survey conducted by the Human Resources Research Unit of the University of Lagos in 1973–74, which sampled 2,700 women from four areas of Nigeria. The survey understated participation in rural areas because most women were excluded if they produced subsistence goods or worked in family enterprises and thus said that they did not work for pay or did not earn money. Although the number of children did not have a significant effect, the presence of children had a positive relationship with female participation in the labor force, although it was significant only in rural areas. The authors explained that "children do not greatly inhibit women's work" but instead increased women's income needs (p. 135). From this study and other studies in Ghana and Kenya (1978a), they rejected the conventional inverse relationship for Sub-Saharan Africa despite contradictory results in Sudan (to be considered below).

Ware's (1977) generalizations from a series of studies in the Yoruba area of western Nigeria during the Changing African Family Project help to explain the above-mentioned findings. She claimed that women, although varying in other characteristics, shared three attributes: they hoped to have large families of five to six children, could not imagine not working, and did not see any conflict between working and childbearing. In fact, the major problem in analyzing the data from these studies

was to find a group of economically inactive housewives in Ibadan. Nevertheless, Ware found that the more children women had, up to seven, the more likely the women were to be working, although differences occurred mainly among petty traders.

The Ghanaian study cited by Standing and Sheehan (deGraft Johnson and others 1975) suggested a positive relationship of employment and fertility. The authors found a peak female activity rate for ages 50–54 and explained it as indicating the completion of the "family building" period (Standing 1981). A later Ghanaian investigation, although not at the household level, by deGraft Johnson (1978) found that more women were leaving their roles as homemakers, substituting market work for household work, and that the number of female students was increasing substantially.

Smock (1977) concluded that high rates of female economic activity had been compatible with high fertility in Ghana, primarily because women were engaged in traditional economic pursuits, such as trading and farming, which did not interfere with childbearing and child rearing. Also, the availability of servants had made it possible for elite women to combine a career with a family. Oppong's study (1975) of 184 married nurses in Accra indicated similar findings for women employed in the modern sector. She also noted that arranging for the day-to-day care of infants and young children is not as great a problem as it is for Western women because child minders and housekeepers are readily available.

For Abidjan, Côte d'Ivoire, Lewis (1982) found no relationship between fertility and female participation in the labor force in cross-tabular analysis of data from a sample of 880 women. She concluded that the roles of mother and worker were compatible enough to allow the women to work as well as bear children. Child care needs were met by inexpensive household help and the extended family system. Yet tests of significance showed that the mean number of surviving children of salaried women in particular, as well as the mean number of children ever born to them, were significantly less than they were for inactive women aged 25–34.

In Cameroon, DeLancey (1980) conducted a survey among 220 married women employed for wages at the Cameroon Development Corporation plantations and a control group of women not employed for wages. Labor force participation was a decision variable for most of the women interviewed, but fertility was not. In multivariate models, no significant relationship was found between number of surviving children and current wage employment, but a significant positive relationship was found between number of children ever born and lifetime wage employment when the researchers controlled for age of the woman. Furthermore, measures of compatibility (use or potential use of unpaid, substitute child care) had significant positive relationships with both current and lifetime wage employment, which indicates that women were able to assume the roles of both mother and wage earner at the same time.

East Africa

In East Africa, studies have been reported for Kenya, Sudan, and Tanzania. For Kenya, Mosley and others (1982) reported from World Fertility Survey data that nearly all married women work in the rural agricultural sector, but only a few do so in the formal labor sector. They found that the fertility of women in salaried work was 15 percent lower than that of other women (table 8-5). The difference, according to the authors, was the result of contraceptive practice, although this may be a tenuous assertion with current labor force status related to past fertility.

Anker and Knowles (1978) reported on the 1974 International Labour Organisation/University of Nairobi Household Survey. In the rural sample (1,215 women), number of live births had little effect on female labor force participation since marriage. In the urban sample (341 women), neither the presence of a child 0–5 years old, nor the presence of another woman 15 years or older in the household (who could assist with child care), nor the presence of another wife in the household was significantly related to female labor force participation in the last twelve months. Anker and Knowles concluded that "the child care burden does not significantly affect female labor force participation in Kenya" (p. 159).

The results for Sudan (Sheehan 1978) contrast with this finding. The sample was 2,614 currently married women in the greater Khartoum area. Bivariate analysis showed that the presence of children in the household depressed female participation in the labor force. The presence of one child had little effect, but two children under age 5 or three under age 14 significantly reduced

female participation in the labor force. Multivariate regression analysis confirmed this result, showing the effect was statistically significant but small.

For urban Tanzania, Shields (1980) found that women do not necessarily withdraw from the labor force during the reproductive years. Multivariate logit analysis of data for 663 urban women confirmed that the relationship between number of dependents and female employment status was negative. For most age groups, mean number of children was smaller for the employed than for the unemployed (table 8-6). Furthermore, the mean number of children of wage-earning women was less than that of the self-employed. Among wage earners, however, professional, technical, managerial, and administrative workers had more children than most other groups. According to Shields, this difference may reflect the higher income of this group and a consequent ability to purchase surrogate care.

Southern Africa

Mueller's (1982) study of time use in Botswana accommodates a different view. She found that the presence of a baby in the house made a difference in the use of time by mothers. The amount of time allocated to housework by each woman aged 20–64 increased when a baby was present, whereas leisure and economic work decreased. Women's economic work increased to about age forty-two, as child rearing gradually took less time. Men's leisure time was also curtailed when there was a baby present, whereas household time and economic work time rose.

Population Pressure on Land and Migration

High fertility may result in population pressure on the land, which may lead to rural-rural or urban-rural mi-

Table 8-5. *Fertility Measures, Birth Interval Components, and Contraceptive Use, Kenya, 1978*

	Current work status	
Measure	Working	Not working
Marital fertility rate[a]	273	321
Pregnancy progression ratio[b]	0.76	0.81
Estimated mean (months)		
Live birth interval	33	30
Duration of breastfeeding	15	17
Duration of postpartum amenorrhea	10	11
Percentage using effective contraception	16	4
Sample size	304	4,857

Note: Work status groups are age adjusted.

a. Marital fertility rate = fertility rate for married women, that is, the number of live births per 1,000 married women.

b. Pregnancy progression ratio = proportion of married women who will progress to another pregnancy. Among married women who do not use contraceptives, it may be used as an estimate of fecundity.

Source: Mosley and others (1982), p. 16.

Table 8-6. *Mean Number of Children, by Age Group and Economic Activity, Urban Women in Tanzania*

	Economic activity	
Age group	Employed	Unemployed
<15	0.5	0.1
15–19	0.6	0.5
20–24	1.1	1.7
25–29	2.2	2.7
30–34	2.8	3.4
35–39	3.5	3.4
40–44	3.3	3.6
45–49	2.8	3.4
50–54	2.0	3.9
55–59	2.7	3.3
60–64	1.4	2.4
65–87	1.8	3.2
All ages	2.0	2.2
Number of cases	481	1,982

Note: Economic activity means had wage employment within the past week or nonwage employment at any time.
Source: NUMELIST (1971), cited in Shields (1980), p. 66.

gration. The relationship is quite complex, however. Much depends upon the balance of certain push-and-pull factors, such as the availability of arable land, the system of land tenure, the kinship system, access to farmland in other locations, and opportunities for further education or alternative employment.

If land is a scarce resource, the larger the family of the present generation, the less land there will be per capita. Diminishing returns may set in as more and more family members cultivate a fixed quantity of land. According to economic theory, marginal productivity may eventually drop to zero; it may even be possible to remove some of those who work the land without any loss of total product. Migration may be a necessity. Gugler (1976) emphasizes that, in tropical Africa, some peasants have little choice but to move out of agriculture when it no longer provides them with bare subsistence. In addition to diminishing returns, Spengler (1964) noted the additional problem of depletion of soil fertility as fallow time is reduced with increased population pressure. Migration may be either long-term, relatively permanent migration of the entire family or short-term, seasonal male migration, sometimes called "labor circulation," with women and children left behind to cultivate the land and support those remaining with them.

When migration occurs, it is not always because of a per capita shortage of land. Mabogunje (1977) pointed out that, in Sub-Saharan Africa, population pressure generally involves not an absolute shortage of land per capita but a recurring threat of famine or crop failure, sometimes because of inadequate equipment or faulty methods of cultivation. Riddell (1978) noted that the majority of urban migrants in West Africa are not formerly landless peasants. He claimed that the most im-

portant reason for migration is that the rural population is so disadvantaged that individuals are anxious to leave, no matter how long it may take to find a job. Byerlee (1974) denied that migrants come from poor households and substantiated this contention with Caldwell's (1969) findings from Ghana. He maintained that unfavorable rural-urban income differentials are the most important determinants of migration. Population pressure on the land, however, might be one cause of such income differentials.

West Africa

In West Africa, much Nigerian research and some Ghanaian research has been conducted on the consequences of high fertility for population pressure on land and migration. In eastern Nigeria, the Ibos have high fertility and one of the highest population densities in that country. According to Onwuazor (1975), the man-to-land ratio has been reduced to an average of about 0.15 acres under cultivation per household of about 5.6 persons. Onwuazor noted that this reduction has forced many people out of agriculture, the traditional mainstay of the economy, but claimed that high population density does not necessarily mean population pressure.

The interaction of high fertility and decreasing mortality may lead to circulatory labor migration, a type of seasonal migration described by Dema (1968) in eastern Nigeria. Farmers in that densely populated area have attempted to remain self-sufficient in food production by practicing intensive mixed cropping. Dema found that men who had greater food crop acreage per person had better diets, which led to more robust physical development of their children; they were not tempted to migrate. Men who had less food crop acreage per person attempted to augment their incomes by migrating seasonally. They worked for wages on farms or as laborers in the timber and tree crop areas elsewhere in southern Nigeria, and even as far away as the plantations on Fernando Po, and sent home remittances. Dema cited a 1963 study of Maku (Awgu), which showed that the adult sex ratio varied from 68 males per 100 females in April to 86 per 100 in August of the same year. Men who intended to migrate completed the farm work of clearing and tilling the land early in order to leave by April. In their absence, the farms were tended by the women and children. The men returned in about August to help harvest the yams.

Goddard (1974) also studied labor circulation, identified land shortage as a cause, and cited references to it for Burkina Faso, Ghana, Nigeria, Tanzania, Togo, and Zimbabwe. He noted that labor circulation had been a comparatively small phenomenon in Sokoto, in northern Nigeria, before the 1930s but had developed in association with a rapid increase in rural population and the resultant pressure on land resources and the indigenous agricultural system. Although the land tenure system had traditionally been communal, the demand for land was resulting in permanent landholdings and in the sale of land. In addition, inheritance laws encouraged subdivision and fragmentation of holdings; the average size of a holding was decreasing as population densities were increasing. In some of the villages, the higher densities resulted in more intensive farming. Net farm incomes were decreasing in spite of intensification, however, and diminishing returns from traditional inputs meant that less time was being spent on farms. Labor circulation was the option chosen by many.

In the town of Dorayi in northern Nigeria, where there is extreme pressure of the population on farm land, Hill (1975, 1977) found very little migration of men whose fathers were still alive. At the time of the research, the average size of farm plots in Dorayi was one acre, and it had greatly decreased within the memory span of people there. Although farm acreage per capita was becoming smaller and more fragmented, Hill noted a remarkably close economic relationship between fathers and sons as a direct consequence of the persistent and intensifying pressure. There was very little migration of sons and almost invariable coresidence of fathers and sons in very large compounds inhabited by seven or more married men and their dependents. Hill suggested that the search for security in that environment had caused fathers to cling to their sons and had led most resident brothers to remain together after their father's death.

Hill (1978) also described certain Fante food growing villages near Cape Coast in southern Ghana, where the rate of migration was so high that one village had no

fathers with resident married sons and another only three. The result was a high average age of farmers. Such migration had been going on for a half a century or more but was not a consequence of land shortage.

East Africa

Responses to high fertility vary in East Africa, just as they do in West Africa. The response to rising population density in the Kilimanjaro area of Tanzania has been diversification and intensification of agriculture (Kocher 1979). Here, too, the increasing scarcity of land meant that landholdings were broken up so that most sons could inherit land; in consequence land litigation among kinsmen increased, and the value of land in the highlands rose by an estimated 700 percent (Maro 1974, cited in Kocher 1979). Evidence of this trend appears in a 1973 survey in which about three-quarters of the respondents said that their landholdings were smaller than those of their fathers. As a result of these changes, many residents of the area had taken nonagricultural jobs.

The pressure of population on land resources has had similar consequences in Kenya. Ominde (1968a, 1986b) noted that it has been a factor inducing people to move to other rural areas or to urban ones, particularly where densities of more than 500 persons per square mile have been reached. He claims, however, that the initial impetus for these movements has come more from past economic policy, including the demand for labor on modern farms, and the urbanization associated with economic development, which has tended to intensify the attraction of urban areas.

Bernard and Thom (1981) describe a problem relevant to many locations. In the Machakos and Kitui districts of Kenya, the inheritance system provides registered tenure to only one son. This provision has created much landlessness in succeeding generations. Even when inheritance systems allow land to be bequeathed to more than one son, difficulties arise.

As in West Africa, however, one must be careful not to assume that migration occurs because of population pressure alone. The World Bank (1980) country study for Kenya found that migration from rural districts to urban centers of population greater than 10,000 was determined more by perceived opportunities in the towns than by the characteristics of the districts of origin. Greater land availability had a negative but statistically insignificant relationship to rural out-migration. Another study in Kenya focused on the twenty-two main smallholder districts that contained more than 85 percent of the population living outside the urban centers of Nairobi and Mombasa (Wasow 1981). The sex ratio in the working ages (ages 20 to 40), used as a measure of the net impact of migration on a district, was not significantly related to any of the physical land pressure variables. Land pressure from widespread inequality in landholdings, however, measured by the prevalence of small plots of land, was significantly and negatively related to the sex ratio among people of working age and cannot be rejected as a cause of migration.

Southern Africa

In Southern Africa, a study in Botswana was designed to examine rural push and urban pull factors associated with migration (Bryant and others 1978). In a survey of 930 adults, respondents were asked why they had left their home village and why they had come to Gaborone. The reasons cited were predominantly economic; for example, 83 percent of the males and 47 percent of the females migrated to find a job or take one that had been arranged in advance, whereas 42 percent of the females migrated to accompany a relative although not necessarily a husband. The attraction of urban services did not appear to be a significant pull factor except for educational opportunities. It is unclear whether the large percentages of men and women who claimed that they migrated in order to find or take a job were influenced by push factors (for example, because of land scarcity) or by pull factors.

In summary, the consequences of high fertility may be scarcity of land, land fragmentation, and eventually migration. Land may become fragmented into small plots as a result of inheritance systems that divide the land among the heirs, generation after generation. It is difficult to determine the true reasons for migration, which is often a consequence of several factors. Migration might not occur even when it would be expected to act as a safety valve for pressure on the land. As Hill cautions, population density and the incidence of migration are not necessarily closely related.

Conclusions

The socioeconomic consequences for the family of high fertility and the close spacing of children are less clear than the health consequences. The effects of fertility upon income depend upon whether total or per capita income is being measured and whether families are extended or nuclear, rural or urban, whether they own or do not own cattle, and whether the family head is male or female. The effect of high fertility and close child spacing upon savings varies greatly. The few studies conducted on this topic showed that fertility and child spacing had either no effect or a negative effect upon savings, although one study did show a positive effect upon human capital savings for investment in education.

The effect of fertility on food expenditures depends upon whether food is purchased for cash or is grown on the family farm. Increasing numbers of children caused food purchases to decrease in quantity or quality, particularly per capita purchases, although sometimes greater numbers of offspring increase total food production on the family farm. Increasing numbers of children also cause transfers of expenditures from other categories, such as clothing or housing, to food. One study showed that the effect of fertility upon housing expenditures was an increase in the number of rooms occupied, although overcrowding increased overall as family size grew. No significant relationship is found between family size and clothing expenditures, but the number of studies is inadequate. The effect of fertility and child spacing on education is surprising. Although it may not be possible to educate all children in some large families with large numbers of children, there is also considerable evidence of a positive relationship between fertility and education. It is believed that this is the result of "sibling chains of assistance" or of a family's ability, with a greater number of children, to obtain the needed labor and still send some children to school.

High fertility and close child spacing also affect the supply of labor, particularly that of women. The effect depends greatly, however, upon whether employment is in the urban or rural sector and in the modern or traditional sector, whether fertility is a decision variable, and especially whether employment is compatible with the role of mother.

The consequences of fertility with respect to population pressure on the land and migration are also elusive. The micro and macro consequences seem to merge, and it is difficult to find evidence of the effects at the household level alone. Depending upon the land tenure system and inheritance laws, however, high fertility appears to lead to land fragmentation and cultivation of increasingly small farm plots or even to landlessness. In some instances, the result has been intensification or diversification of cultivation, or off-farm employment and "labor circulation," or more permanent rural-rural or rural-urban migration.

The net socioeconomic consequences of high fertility and close child spacing are therefore difficult to determine. They may be negative, may be positive, or may not even exist under particular circumstances. There is one concept which has not been fully explored in this paper: the "value of children," especially its psychological aspects. I have mentioned that children are valued for their labor contribution and their assistance in educating siblings, but they are also highly valued in Sub-Saharan Africa for their social security role. Thus, another consequence of high fertility may be the sense of security that parents obtain that their many children will be able to care for them in their old age or in times of adversity. In conclusion, at the household level in Sub-Saharan Africa, the demand for children may remain high because, when families consider the consequences of high fertility, they do not presently calculate a negative net balance, although in time they may do so.

References

Addo, N. O. 1970. "Household/Family Size and Socio-Demographic Variables: The Ghanaian Experience." Paper presented at the Symposium on Implications of Population Trends for Policy Measures in West Africa, University of Ghana; processed.

Adewuyi, A. A. 1980. "Childcare and Female Employment in a Nigerian Metropolis: The Role of the Under-Six's." *Nigerian Journal of Economic and Social Studies* 22(July): 197–218.

Anker, Richard, and Knowles, J. C. 1978. "A Micro-Analysis of Female Labour Force Participation in Africa." In G. Standing and G. Sheehan, eds., *Labour Force Participation in Low-Income Countries.* Geneva: International Labour Office.

———. 1982. *Fertility Determinants in Developing Countries: A Case Study of Kenya.* Liège, Belgium; Ordina.

Arowolo, O. O. 1977. "Fertility of Urban Yoruba Working Women: A Case Study of Ibadan City." *Nigerian Journal of Economic and Social Studies* 19(March): 37–66.

———. 1978. "Female Labour Force Participation and Fertility: The Case of Ibadan City in the Western State of Nigeria." In C. Oppong, G. Adaba, M. Bekombo-Priso, and J Mogey, eds., *Marriage, Fertility, and Parenthood in West Africa.* Canberra: Australian National University.

Bernard, Frank E., and Derrick J. Thorn. 1981. "Population Pressure and Human Carrying Capacity in Selected Locations of Machakos and Kitui Districts." *Journal of Developing Areas* 15(April): 381–406.

Birdsall, Nancy. 1980. "Population Growth and Poverty in the Developing World." *Population Bulletin* 35 (December).

Bryant, Coralie, Betsy Stephens, and Sherry MacLiver. 1978. "Rural to Urban Migration: Some Data from Botswana." *African Studies Review* 21(September): 85–99.

Byerlee, Derek. 1974. "Rural-Urban Migration in Africa: Theory, Policy, and Research Implications." *International Migration Review* 8: 543–66.

Caldwell, J. C. 1969. *African Rural-Urban Migration: The Movement to Ghana's Towns.* New York: Columbia University Press.

Chernichovsky, Dov. 1979. "Personal Savings and Family Size and Composition: The Unresolved Issue." In *Economic and Demographic Change: Issues for the 1980s, Helsinki 1978.*

Vol. 1. Liège, Belgium: International Union for the Scientific Study of Population.

———. 1981. "Socioeconomic and Demographic Aspects of School Enrollment and Attendance in Rural Botswana." Discussion Paper 81–47. Population and Human Resources Division, World Bank, Washington, D.C., October.

DeGraft Johnson, K. T. 1978. "Factors Affecting Labour Force Participation Rates in Ghana, 1970." In G. Standing and G. Sheehan, eds., *Labour Force Participation in Low-Income Countries.* Geneva: International Labour Office.

DeGraft Johnson, D. T., K. Ewusi, and R. Appiah. 1975. "The Determinants of Labour Force Participation Rates in Ghana." Geneva: International Labor Office; processed.

DeLancey, Virginia. 1978. "Women at the Cameroon Development Corporation: How Their Money Works." *Rural Africana*, n.s., no. 2(September): 9–33.

———. 1980. "The Relationship between Female Wage Employment and Fertility in Africa: An Example from Cameroon." Ph.D. diss., University of South Carolina, Columbia.

———. 1981. "The Role of Credit Unions in Development for West African Women." Paper presented at the African Studies Association Annual Meeting, Bloomington, Indiana, October 21–24.

———. 1983. "Report on the Base-line Data Survey for the Camccul/woccu/usaid Credit Union Development Project (631-0044, pvo/opg) in Cameroon." Report prepared for the World Council of Credit Unions and the Cameroon Cooperative Credit Union League, July.

Dema, I. S. 1968. "Some Reflections upon the Nutritional Problems of Dense Farm Populations in Parts of Nigeria." In J. C. Caldwell and C. Okonjo, eds., *The Population of Tropical Africa.* London: Longmans.

Dutta-Roy, D. K. 1969. *The Eastern Region Household Budget Survey.* Technical Publication Series, No. 6. Legon: Institute of Statistical, Social, and Economic Research.

Easterlin, R. A. 1973. "Fertility and the Theory of Household Choice." Paper presented at the annual meeting of the Population Association of America, New Orleans.

———. 1975. "An Economic Framework for Fertility Analysis." *Studies in Family Planning* 6(March): 54–63.

Goddard, A. D. 1974. "Population Movements and Land Shortages in the Sokoto Close-settled Zone, Nigeria." In S. Amin, ed., *Modern Migrations in Western Africa.* London: Oxford University Press for the International African Institute.

Gugler, Josef. 1976. "Migrating to Urban Centres of Unemployment in Tropical Africa." In A. H. Richmond and D. Kubat, eds., *Internal Migration: The New World and the Third World.* Beverly Hills: Sage.

Hill, Polly. 1975. "Some Socio-economic Consequences of High Population Density in Rural Areas near Kano City." In R. P. Moss and R. J. A. R. Rathbone, eds., *The Population Factor in African Studies.* London: University of London Press.

———. 1977. *Population, Prosperity, and Poverty: Rural Kano 1900 and 1970.* Cambridge, Eng.: Cambridge University Press.

————. 1978. "Food Farming and Migration from Fante Villages." *Africa* 48(3): 220–30.

Idusogie, E. O. 1972. "The Relation of Population and Nutritional Health Problems in African Communities." Special Paper No. 7. Joint Food and Agriculture Organization/World Health Organization/Organization of African Unity Regional Food and Nutrition Commission for Africa. Cited in Mudambi, 1980.

Johnson, G. E., and W. E. Whitelaw. 1974. "Urban-Rural Income Transfers in Kenya: An Estimated Remittance Function." *Economic Development and Cultural Change* 22(April): 473–79.

Kelley, A. C. 1976. "Interactions of Economic and Demographic Household Behavior." Paper presented at the National Bureau of Economic Research Conference on Population and Economic Changes in Less Developed Countries, Philadelphia, October.

Kelley, A. C., and C. Swartz. 1979. "The Impact of Family Structure on Microeconomic Decision Making in Developing Countries: A Case Study of Nuclear and Extended Families in Urban Kenya." In *Economic and Demographic Change: Issues for the 1980s, Helsinki 1978.* Vol. 1. Liège, Belgium: International Union for the Scientific Study of Population.

Knowles, J. C., and R. Anker. 1977. "An Analysis of Income Transfers in a Developing Country: The Case of Kenya." World Employment Programme, Population and Employment Working Paper No. 59. International Labour Office, Geneva.

Kocher, J. E. 1979. "Rural Development and Fertility Change in Tropical Africa: Evidence from Tanzania." African Rural Economy Paper No. 19. African Rural Economy Program, Department of Agricultural Economics, Michigan State University, East Lansing, and Bureau of Resource Use and Land Use Planning, University of Dar es Salaam.

Kpedekpo. G. M. K., and N. O. Addo, eds. 1970. "A Survey of Pre-School Children in La Bone, Nima and James Town of Accra." Community Health Reports, Project II. Accra, Ghana.

Lewis, Barbara. 1982. "Fertility and Employment: An Assessment of Role Incompatibility among African Urban Women." In E. G. Bay, ed., *Women and Work in Africa.* Westview Special Studies on Africa. Boulder, Colo.: Westview Press.

Mabogunje, A. L. 1977. "The Urban Situation in Nigeria." In S. Goldstein and D. F. Sly, eds., *Patterns of Urbanization: Comparative Country Studies.* Vol. 2. Dolhain, Belgium: Ordina.

Maro, P. S. 1974. "Population and Land Resources in Northern Tanzania: The Dynamics of Change, 1920–1970." Ph.D. diss., University of Minnesota, Minneapolis.

Mosley, W. H., L. H. Werner, and S. Becker. 1982. "The Dynamics of Birth Spacing and Marital Fertility in Kenya." Scientific Reports No. 30. International Statistical Institute, Voorburg, Netherlands, and World Fertility Survey, London.

Mott, Frank. 1974. *The Dynamics of Demographic Change in a Nigerian Village.* Human Resources Research Unit,

Faculty of Social Sciences, Research Project No. 5. Research Bulletin No. 5/001. University of Lagos, Nigeria; processed.

Mudambi, Sumati. 1980. "Interrelationships between Family Structure and Family Resources in Eastern Nigeria." *Journal of Family Welfare* 26: 13–26.

Mueller, Eva. 1982. "The Value and Allocation of Time in Rural Botswana." Discussion Paper No. 81-44. Population and Human Resources Division, World Bank, Washington, D.C., November.

————. 1983. "Income, Aspirations, and Fertility in Rural Areas of Less Developed Countries." Paper presented at the Conference on Rural Development and Human Fertility, Pennsylvania State University, University Park, April 11–13.

Ominde, S. H. 1968a. *Land and Population Movements in Kenya.* Evanston, Ill.: Northwestern University Press.

————. 1968b. "Some Aspects of Population Movements in Kenya." In J. C. Caldwell and C. Okonjo, eds., *The Population of Tropical Africa.* London: Longmans.

Onwuazor, Sammy. 1975. "Population Growth, Modernisation, and Social Status among the Igbo of Nigeria." In T. S. Epstein and D. Jackson, eds., *The Paradox of Poverty: Socio-Economic Aspects of Population Growth.* New Delhi: S. G. Wasani for the Macmillan Company of India.

Oppong, Christine. 1975. "Pilot Study of Family System Planning and Size in Accra: The Case of Married Nurses." Reported Submitted to the National Family Planning Program, Accra, Ghana.

Riddell, J. B. 1978. "The Migration to the Cities of West Africa: Some Policy Considerations." *Journal of Modern African Studies* 16(2): 241–60.

Sheehan, Glen. 1978. "Labour Force Participation Rates in Khartoum." In G. Standing and G. Sheehan, eds., *Labour Force Participation in Low-Income Countries.* Geneva: International Labour Office.

Shields, Nwanganga. 1980. *Women in the Urban Labour Markets of Africa: The Case of Tanzania.* World Bank Staff Working Paper 380. Washington, D.C., April.

Smock, A. C. 1977. "Ghana: From Autonomy to Subordination." In J. Z. Giele and A. C. Smock, eds., *Women: Roles and Status in Eight Countries.* New York: John Wiley.

Snyder, D. W. 1974a. "Econometric Studies of Household Savings Behavior in Developing Countries: A Survey." *Journal of Development Studies* 10(January): 139–53.

————. 1974b. "Economic Determinants of Family Size in West Africa." *Demography* 11(November): 613–27.

Spengler, J. J. 1964. "Population Movements and Problems in Sub-Saharan Africa." In E. A. G. Robinson, ed., *Economic Development for Africa South of the Sahara.* New York: St. Martin's Press.

Ssennyonga, J. W. 1975. "Cost/Benefit versus Parental Immortality: Family Size in Rural Kenya." In T. S. Epstein and D. Jackson, eds., *The Paradox of Poverty: Socio-Economic Aspects of Population Growth.* New Delhi: S. G. Wasani for the Macmillan Company of India.

Standing, Guy. 1981. *Labour Force Participation and Development* 2d ed. Geneva: International Labour Office.

Standing, Guy, and Glen Sheehan. 1978a. *Labour Force Participation in Low-Income Countries*. Geneva: International Labour Office.

———. 1978b. "Economic Activity of Women in Nigeria." In G. Standing and G. Sheehan, eds., *Labour Force Participation in Low-Income Countries*. Geneva: International Labour Office.

Uyanga, Joseph. 1976. "Family Size and the Participation of Women in Labor Force: A Nigerian Case Study." *African Urban Notes* (African Studies Center, Michigan State University) 2(Spring): 59–72.

Waldorf, H. W. 1977. "A Comparison of Savings Rates in Uganda: Africans, Asians, and Europeans." *Journal of Development Studies* 13(April): 228–37.

Ware, Helen. 1977. "Women's Work and Fertility in Africa." In *The Fertility of Working Women: A Synthesis of International Research*. New York: Praeger.

Wasow, Bernard. 1981. "The Working Age Sex Ratio and Job Search Migration in Kenya." *Journal of Developing Areas* 15(April): 435–44.

World Bank. 1980. *Kenya: Population and Development*. A World Bank Country Study. Washington, D.C.

Wray, J. D. 1971. "Population Pressure on Families: Family Size and Child Spacing." In *Rapid Population Growth: Consequences and Policy Implications*, edited by the National Academy of Sciences. Vol. 2, Research Papers. Baltimore: Johns Hopkins University Press for the National Academy of Sciences.

Part IV

The Context and Causes of High Fertility

Among Sub-Saharan African countries, levels of fertility vary markedly, with total fertility rates ranging from 4.1 in Gabon to 8.1 in Kenya. This wide range cannot be explained by the timing of a secular decline of fertility because the decline seems not to have begun in any of these countries. Nor do levels of socioeconomic development explain the wide variations in fertility levels. Differences in contraception are only partly responsible for fertility variation. More important are other proximate determinants that affect fertility, which are described by Bongaarts, Frank, and Lesthaeghe (chapter 9).

The principal such determinants in this region are lactational amenorrhea due to breastfeeding, postpartum sexual abstinence, and involuntary pathological sterility. The relative importance of these determinants depends upon culture and tradition and the extent to which tradition is eroded by modernization (as argued by Acsadi and Johnson-Acsadi in chapter 11 and by Caldwell and Caldwell in chapter 13). Breastfeeding is virtually universal but continues for varying lengths of time. Similarly, customs of postpartum abstinence are not and never have been everywhere uniform. Among nine countries of the region, average duration of postpartum abstinence varies from three months in Kenya to more than fifteen months in Benin. Within countries, too, custom and habit vary. These variations account in good measure for fertility differences among Sub-

Saharan African countries. Because of current changes in breastfeeding and postpartum abstinence, in many countries fertility will possibly stagnate at high levels or even rise before secular decline starts.

Differences in fertility by residence and level of education are not so marked as to suggest the imminent decline of fertility, and particularly of marital fertility, as shown by Cochrane and Farid (chapter 10). The classic relationship between lower fertility and higher education is not evident in some Sub-Saharan countries and, where it does appear, is often weak. The primary reason is near uniformity in desired family size and low levels of contraceptive use among urban residents and the better educated. In fact, as urban and better educated women dispense with lengthy breastfeeding and extended postpartum abstinence, which are increasingly incompatible with their economic activities and urban residence, their fertility will rise if they do not compensate with contraception (chapters 9 and 11).

The desire for large families permeates the societies of Sub-Saharan Africa and is common among all classes. Very few women want to cease childbearing before age 35 or before they have borne five, six, and sometimes more children. Urban and educated women are only slightly more likely to terminate childbearing at a particular family size than their rural and less educated counterparts. The traditional fabric of these societies mandates behavior for both men and women that is consonant with the bearing and rearing of large numbers of children and provides for punitive measures where there is evidence of deviant behavior (chapters 11 and 13). The desire is widespread for a healthful interval between births, usually achieved by extended postpartum abstinence and lengthy breastfeeding, but this serves health purposes and does not aim to limit the number of births.

Large numbers of women appear to be unaware that they can limit births, and most others have not wanted to do so (Frank makes this argument in chapter 12; see also chapter 11). Although some small groups limit fertility, there is no general demand for contraception or for the restriction of family size. This is evident whether demand is measured by the incidence of induced abortion, by infanticide, by avoidance of pregnancy, or by child abandonment (chapter 12). The burdens of child rearing are lightened through redistribution of child care among family members and through specific mechanisms such as fostering, which is widely prevalent throughout the region. These strategies lessen the impact of an additional child upon family resources.

The traditions and cultures of Sub-Saharan Africa promote early and continual childbearing in many ways: through religion, where traditionalism even invades Christianity and Islam; through imposed obligations to dead ancestors and other relatives; through inheritance patterns and the perception of children as wealth; through notions of reincarnation; through emphasis on the duties of a man to his lineage; through the stress on the role of children as validating adult status. The woman's role is to bear children and to continue her husband's lineage; except as wife and mother, in most societies, she has no status (chapter 13).

Barrenness and subfecundity subject a woman to ridicule, abuse, ostracism, and divorce. If a woman's child dies, she may be considered cursed and held responsible, and her husband may take another wife. Her well-being is assured only as long as she produces children. In such circumstances, it is to the woman's social advantage to continue to bear children at expected intervals (chapters 11 and 13).

These cultural patterns do not augur well for early receptivity to fertility control on any appreciable scale. In traditional societies in other regions, the introduction of organized family planning activities has facilitated acceptance of the small family norm and has led people to change their fertility behavior. There is no substantial evidence as yet in this region that family planning activities have precipitated a change in attitudes toward desired number of children or have been responsible for a reduction in demand for them. Nonetheless, the widespread belief in the necessity of healthful child spacing may support acceptance of family planning, at least for spacing purposes.

9

The Proximate Determinants of Fertility

John Bongaarts, Odile Frank, and Ron Lesthaeghe

Levels of fertility vary widely among countries in Sub-Saharan Africa. The total fertility rate ranges from a high of 8.1 in Kenya to 4.1 in Gabon (United Nations 1982). This impressive range is not unusual: similar differences in fertility are found among countries of Asia and Latin America. Africa is unique, however, in that the lowest levels of fertility have not been achieved through declines in fertility. Countries with relatively low fertility in Latin America and Asia have experienced rapid declines in fertility that correlate strongly with socioeconomic development and organized efforts to reduce the birth rate. In contrast, except for Mauritius, no country in Sub-Saharan Africa has experienced a significant reduction in fertility, and there is no significant correlation between development indicators and fertility. The processes that gave rise to fertility differentials in Sub-Saharan Africa are therefore very different from those found elsewhere.

In addition to variations in fertility among nations, there are within countries large differences among geographic regions and ethnic and socioeconomic groups. These differentials are all the more remarkable because only a small percentage of women deliberately control their fertility through contraception or induced abortion. Explanations for these findings must therefore be found largely elsewhere. The present chapter addresses this task.

The Determinants of Fertility

Any detailed and comprehensive analysis of factors influencing fertility requires a distinction between two

classes of determinants: proximate variables and socioeconomic and environmental "background" variables. The latter include social, cultural, economic, institutional, psychological, health, and environmental variables, and the former consist of all the biological and behavioral factors through which the background variables must operate to affect fertility (Davis and Blake 1956; Bongaarts and Potter 1983). The principal characteristic of a proximate determinant is its direct influence on fertility. In contrast, socioeconomic variables can affect fertility only indirectly by modifying the proximate determinants.

One of the most important advantages of including the proximate variables in the study of the fertility process is that it improves understanding of the operation of the socioeconomic determinants. In general, a socioeconomic variable can have negative fertility effects through one set of proximate variables (such as education's effect on use of contraception) and positive effects through another set (such as education's effect on length of breastfeeding). The overall net effect of a socioeconomic variable on fertility can therefore be positive, negative, or insignificant, depending on the relative contributions of the positive and negative effects of the proximate determinants. These offsetting effects of proximate determinants on fertility levels play an especially crucial role in Sub-Saharan Africa, but before we consider this subject further, it is necessary to discuss the proximate determinants in some detail.

The proximate determinants are:

1. Proportion of women married or in sexual unions
2. Frequency of intercourse
3. Postpartum abstinence
4. Lactational amenorrhea
5. Contraception
6. Induced abortion

This chapter is a revised and shortened version of a paper published in *Population and Development Review*, 10, 3 (September 1984): 511–37.

7. Spontaneous intrauterine mortality
8. Natural sterility
9. Pathological sterility.

All variation in fertility is by definition attributable to variation in one or more of these variables.

Pattern of Marriage and Sexual Unions

Although a woman could, in principle, bear children throughout her reproductive life, from the age of about fifteen to about forty-five, few women do so because overall exposure to childbearing is limited to the total amount of time during which a woman is actually cohabiting or is in a union (for simplicity, the word "marriage" as used here denotes any such regular sexual union). In any society, the total time spent in unions for all women depends on the age at first marriage, the proportion of women who never marry, the frequency of divorce and widowhood, the frequency of remarriage, and the age at which sexual activity comes to an end (if it does so before menopause). These various factors are summarized in the proportions of all women married at any point in time. Consideration of the role of marriage in limiting the exposure of women to childbearing must also take some account of the level of extramarital exposure of young women before marriage and of older women who never married or are divorced or widowed. Even within marriage, the particular forms marriage takes can affect exposure to childbearing, principally through the patterns of sexual activity that tend to be associated with it. Arranged marriages, for example, tend to be associated with lower frequencies of intercourse than romantic marriages (Rindfuss and Morgan 1983), and polygynous marriages tend also to be associated with lower sexual activity (of each woman) than monogamous ones. All the marriage factors have relevance in the African context. The role of polygyny, however, will be discussed under patterns of sexual activity.

The average age at which women in Sub-Saharan Africa enter their first union varies regionally from under seventeen years to about twenty-two.[1] Overall, age at marriage is at the low end of the range in West Africa, at the high end in parts of East Africa, and in the middle of the range in Central Africa and in the coastal areas around the Bight of Benin and the Gulf of Guinea in the west and the Indian Ocean in the east. Age at marriage is higher in urban areas than in rural ones in association with higher levels of education for urban women.

These differentials in age at first marriage seem to reflect true differences in regional and ethnic practices rather than a cross-sectional picture of a continental

transition in the age at first marriage because there is little evidence that age at marriage has substantially increased in Sub-Saharan African national populations over the last twenty or thirty years. An exception is Kenya, where relatively better data at several points in time show the average age at first marriage rising by more than a year and a half, from just over 18.5 to over 20 between 1962 and 1979. It is also possible that northern Sudan has experienced some increase in the average age at first marriage.

The Sub-Saharan African range of age at first marriage is more narrow than the range in Asia, as measured by World Fertility Surveys in the mid to late 1970s, but the two regions differ in two other important respects. First, no African population of significant size has as early an age at first marriage as Bangladesh in 1975 (about sixteen years). Second, data for the large majority of Asian countries show that current levels of ages at first marriage result from fairly widespread increases in age at marriage since the 1950s.

Marriage is for all intents and purposes universal in Sub-Saharan Africa. The proportion of women still unmarried is only about 5 percent or less in the age group 25–29 and declines to 3 percent or less thereafter. Marital instability due to both voluntary dissolution (divorce) and involuntary dissolution (widowhood) is high throughout Sub-Saharan Africa. Very high rates of remarriage and good accessibility to husbands through polygyny, however, mean that few women are not in unions at any point in time relative to the incidence of marriage dissolutions. Table 9-1 gives the average proportions of first marriages that ended in divorce or widowhood by duration of the first marriage for women currently under age fifty and is based on data for six African countries. The proportions of first marriages ending in divorce range from more than 7 percent for marriages of very short durations (zero to four years) to nearly 20 percent for the longest duration (thirty or more years). The incidence of widowhood is much lower for shorter durations (when husbands are younger and have lower mortality) but increases rapidly and reaches the incidence of divorce at the longest durations of marriage. Among women married less than five years, some 8 percent have experienced the end of a first union, either through divorce or widowhood; among women married thirty years or more, the proportion is greater than 40 percent. For all durations of first marriage except thirty or more years, which essentially applies to women past childbearing, divorce is by far the major cause of dissolution and would therefore be the major reason for any time lost to childbearing associated with an unmarried state.

As a result of high rates of remarriage, however, comparatively few women are in fact currently widowed or divorced at any time. For the same six countries (table

Table 9-1. *Percentage of First Marriages Ending in Divorce or Widowhood, by Years since First Marriage, for Women Aged 15–49: Average Schedule for Six African Countries, 1977–79*

	Years since first marriage						
Cause of dissolution	0–4	5–9	10–14	15–19	20–24	25–29	30+
Divorce	7.4	13.9	16.7	17.1	18.0	18.3	19.5
Widowhood	0.8	2.1	4.6	8.0	11.5	15.0	21.0
Total	8.2	16.0	21.3	25.1	29.5	33.3	40.5

Source: Lesthaeghe (1984).

9-1), only 5 to 10 percent of women aged 20–39—the entire range of peak childbearing years—will be found unmarried at any time. If we take into account dissolution of marriages and remarriage after dissolutions and consider all forms of conjugal unions, women in Sub-Saharan Africa, once they enter their first union, will spend more than 90 percent of their remaining reproductive life in a union (see table 9-2).

Over time, the incidence of widowhood has probably declined steadily with reduced adult mortality. The risks of widowhood among African women are more sensitive to mortality declines at earlier ages among women than in many other regions of the world, because the age differences between spouses are typically large (van de Walle 1968). The median age gap, for example, ranges from about six to eight years for all once-married women married less than ten years up to fifteen or twenty years or more for women who are second and third wives in polygynous unions (Casterline and McDonald 1983). With any further reductions in adult mortality, the incidence of divorce, which already plays the major role in marital dissolution, will increasingly determine the incidence of marital dissolution, whereas the current incidence of remarriage will continue to maintain the proportion of unmarried women at a very low level.

Exposure to childbearing outside marriage, particularly before first marriage, is appreciable in Africa and must be considered alongside women's formal exposure to childbearing, as represented by the proportion of

women's lives during which they are in one or another form of conjugal union. The incidence of extramarital exposure, however, varies considerably. Its level is therefore difficult to characterize for the entire region, but probably around 5 to 10 percent of all births occur to unmarried women (Lesthaeghe 1984).

Patterns of Sexual Activity

The previous section showed how total time spent in marriage was important in assessing the amount of time a married woman could spend bearing children. Duration of married time, however, is not necessarily equivalent to the total duration of exposure to pregnancy within marriage. Within marriage, exposure to pregnancy depends on the pattern of sexual activity. The three most important factors here are frequency of intercourse during cohabitation of spouses, abstinence between cohabiting spouses, and separation of spouses.

There is strong evidence that real differences in coital frequency are associated with marriage forms. Thus polygynously married women have lower fertility than monogamously married women, and lower frequency of intercourse is probably one important determinant. Polygyny lowers fertility not only because time with the husband is shared but also because polygynously married women beyond the first wife tend to have even older husbands than monogamously married women

Table 9-2. *Percentage Currently Divorced or Widowed and Percentage of Time Spent in Sexual Union, by Age: Average Schedule for Six African Countries, 1977–79*

	Age group						
Item	15–19	20–24	25–29	30–34	35–39	40–44	45–59
Percentage of all women currently divorced or widowed	2.4	5.1	5.6	7.7	10.3	13.9	—
Percentage of time since first marriage spent in sexual unions, all ever-married women	96.8[a]	95.6	95.2	94.2	93.7	92.7	91.4

—No data.
a. Under age 20.
Source: Lesthaeghe (1984).

and because polygynously married women not infrequently each have a separate household, sometimes at great distances from each other.

Polygyny is associated with two other factors that account for lower fertility of polygynous wives. First, polygynous wives are more often infertile than monogamous wives because a monogamously married man will more frequently take a second wife if his first wife is childless than if she is not. We will discuss this topic in greater detail later. Second, polygyny facilitates the practice of postpartum abstinence, or abstinence from intercourse following birth, which is a major proximate determinant of Sub-Saharan African fertility.

Of the various possible types of sexual abstinence, postpartum abstinence is the most notable and widely practiced form in Sub-Saharan Africa. Where long periods of abstinence are observed, their duration is generally tied to ongoing breastfeeding, which is recognized as essential to the health and normal development of the infant and young child. It is possible that at one time a period of abstinence extending throughout lactation, sometimes beyond, was practiced in most of Africa. This is supported by frequent reports from groups observing short periods today that the practice was more prolonged in the past. From whatever levels the duration of abstinence has declined, considerable variation in the practice can be recognized in contemporary Africa from information on abstinence in the last twenty or thirty years. Geographically by ethnic group, the different durations display a high level of consistency (Schoenmaeckers and others 1981). Reported durations of forty days or less cluster in the lake regions of central East Africa and in scattered parts of the Sahel (among some Islamicized West African groups) and of southeastern Africa. Reported durations exceeding forty days and up to one year cluster remarkably in East Africa (generally east of the lake regions) but occur also in West Africa (Ghana). Finally, postpartum abstinence periods of more than one year (and sometimes of two years or more), comprising by far the largest proportion of all reports, are found throughout Sub-Sahelian West and Central Africa.

The potential impact of postpartum abstinence on fertility depends critically on its duration in relation to the duration of lactational amenorrhea. In assessing the quantitative effect of postpartum abstinence on duration of exposure, it is useful to introduce the concept of the nonsusceptible period, which equals the total duration of absence of risk of conception, whether the protection is provided by lactational amenorrhea or by abstinence. It is then also necessary, however, to analyze separately the effects at the level of the individual and of the population. For individual women, the duration of the nonsusceptible period equals the duration of abstinence or the duration of amenorrhea, whichever

is longer. On the population level, given the substantial variation around the mean durations of abstinence and amenorrhea, the average duration of the nonsusceptible period will be longer than the average duration of either abstinence or amenorrhea (Lesthaeghe 1984).

Because breastfeeding in Sub-Saharan Africa tends to be practiced far longer than a year in the majority of rural and traditional societies, the impact of the longest durations of abstinence has the greatest relevance to fertility. In fact, there is ample evidence that, among groups in which abstinence exceeds one year, its duration is purposefully tied to the duration of breastfeeding and customarily lasts until weaning (in some groups, such as the Yoruba of Nigeria, abstinence exceeds breastfeeding at all durations). As a result, in the majority of societies practicing extended abstinence, women do not begin to be exposed to conception until after their most recent child is weaned, which can mean that successive children are spaced as much as four years apart.

Nevertheless, close scrutiny of the distribution of all durations of abstinence in Sub-Saharan Africa, and in particular examination of the most recent surveys, quickly reveals that this distribution not only is related to differentials in customary practices but also reflects the erosion of these practices, which is occurring at varying speeds across the continent. A complete engagement of the erosion process at a national level can be inferred in Tanzania, but its results are possibly best observed in Kenya. In Tanzania in the 1970s, reported duration of abstinence showed varying levels and mixed practices but rarely exceeded six months. In Kenya (Republic of Kenya 1980), the fertility survey of 1977–78 revealed an average duration of abstinence of about four months. The decline of the abstinence duration in Kenya can be presumed to have played a role in the country's overall fertility increase, which will be examined later. Finally, often large differentials between rural and urban practices and between women of different educational groups, such as those found in recent surveys, portend other national trends toward abandonment of the practice if they indeed indicate the first step in the process, as researchers strongly suspect.

Long periods during which spouses are separated can appreciably reduce women's overall exposure to conception. Such separations are principally due to male labor migration and are particularly widespread in southern Africa. Labor migration is a phenomenon of considerable importance in West Africa also but tends to involve longer-term migration of unmarried men and has tended consequently to bolster polygyny rather than to result in widespread separation of spouses. In southern Africa, polygyny is less common, and the majority of migrating married men will be absent for several months or even a few years. Such absences may drastically reduce the overall frequency of intercourse in a married lifetime.

The impact on fertility of this reduction in exposure time can be strongly tempered by the timing of spousal separation. In some areas, husbands are reported to leave once their wives are pregnant, and the periods of absence are intended to coincide with the pregnancy and the child's early life. Unexpectedly long durations of postpartum abstinence found in the Lesotho fertility survey of 1977 (Kingdom of Lesotho 1981) illustrate this timing effect on a national scale. Because of large-scale labor migration of males to the Republic of South Africa, the surprisingly long abstinence probably reflects the customary absence of husbands in the postpartum period rather than abstinence between cohabiting spouses per se.

Breastfeeding and Lactational Amenorrhea

Because the biological feedback of suckling effectively blocks ovulation for a period of time, the length and intensity of breastfeeding have a potentially large influence on the period of time that a woman is exposed to conception. The length of time during which ovulation is blocked by lactation (lactational amenorrhea) falls short of the total duration of lactation because frequency and intensity of suckling decline as weaning approaches, but lactational amenorrhea lasts for a large part of the breastfeeding period at all breastfeeding durations. Amenorrhea lasts for about two months following delivery in the absence of any lactation. The average duration of lactational amenorrhea increases in proportion to the average length of breastfeeding, lasting for about 60 to 70 percent of the duration of breastfeeding where breastfeeding lasts two years and more. For the longest breastfeeding durations, amenorrheic periods of up to two years occur (Bongaarts and Potter 1983).

Breastfeeding is evidently universal throughout Sub-Saharan Africa. Its duration varies substantially between countries, however, and reflects to a large extent both differences in practice and the negative effects of modern influences. The mean duration of breastfeeding is about 19 months in Lesotho, 18 months in Ghana, and 16.5 months in Sudan and Kenya. The average nonsusceptible periods due to lactational amenorrhea for these breastfeeding durations are about 13 months in Lesotho, 12 months in Ghana, and 11 months in Sudan and Kenya. These are minimal estimates of the average duration of nonsusceptibility, however, because abstinence effects are not included (see the discussion above). To illustrate, the added effect of abstinence would raise the mean nonsusceptible period to 18 months in Lesotho, 17 months in Ghana, 12

months in Sudan, and 13 months in Kenya (Casterline and others 1983).

Use of Birth Control

Birth control that is intended to limit family size includes both the contraception and induced abortion. Contraception still plays a very limited role in determining fertility in Sub-Saharan Africa (chapter 12 in this volume). On the one hand, knowledge levels are very low: the proportion of ever-married women who report never having heard of any method to delay or avoid a pregnancy ranges from 12 percent in Kenya, 32 percent in Ghana, 35 percent in Lesotho, 40 percent in Senegal, and 49 percent in Sudan to 66 percent in Cameroon. On the other hand, even better levels of knowledge are not necessarily associated with higher use: current use of any method of contraception (including traditional methods and sterilization) among all currently married women in about 1980 ranged from about 9.5 percent in Ghana to 5–6 percent in Kenya, Nigeria, Sudan, and Lesotho, and below 5 percent in Senegal. Taking account only of women who are currently exposed to conception, current use is higher (12.4 percent in Ghana, 9.2 in Kenya, 7 percent in Lesotho, 6 percent in Sudan and Nigeria, and 5.2 percent in Senegal), but a third and more of the respondents are using ineffective methods (in Senegal the majority).

Data on induced abortion are very rare in Sub-Saharan Africa as in other regions. Overall, abortion is probably used in a number of urban areas among the very youngest women before marriage, but otherwise the practice appears to be infrequent. The urban phenomenon is variously reported to represent an increasing health problem, but at the regional level, induced abortion probably has a negligible impact on fertility.

Fetal Loss

Intrauterine mortality includes both spontaneous abortions, which comprise the bulk of pregnancy losses, and stillbirths (mortality after the twenty-eighth week of pregnancy). There are good reasons to believe that overall intrauterine mortality is similar in all human populations and is probably about 20 percent (Bongaarts and Potter 1983). Stillbirths, although they may be more frequent in Africa than elsewhere, constitute so small a proportion of intrauterine mortality as to have a negligible effect on the total.

Evidence exists that epidemic malaria may be associated with higher levels of intrauterine mortality. Malaria is widespread in much of Africa but is highly endemic, and its transmission is stable. Stable transmission may mean a lower overall effect on fetal loss than is seen in regions where malaria is epidemic. Notwithstanding the absence of the data needed to make a better determination, the effect on fertility is deemed negligible relative to the order of magnitude of expected levels of fetal loss (Lancet 1983).

Sterility

Sterility arises from both natural and pathological causes. In this discussion, the prevalence of sterility is measured by its results, that is, the level of infertility. The natural maximum duration of reproductive life in women is from menarche to menopause. Both terms denote a process rather than a well-defined event. The onset of first menstruation is followed by a period during which anovulatory or otherwise incomplete cycles occur with decreasing frequency, so that populations of women experience a period of naturally occurring relative infertility for a number of years in the earliest portion of the reproductive span, the actual years of age involved depending on the age at menarch. Average age at menarche in the 1960s and 1970s has been found to range from about 12 to 18 years for various populations for which there are relevant data. Existing data for Africa range nearly as widely in the same time period: from about thirteen years among affluent or urban groups in Uganda and Nigeria to more than seventeen among rural Hutu in Rwanda. Average age at menarche evidently depends on a number of both genetic and nutritional factors, although the role of any one factor is not well known (Gray 1979).

In menopause, the final point in a process of several years' duration, the frequency and regularity of ovulation decline until ovulation ceases. Evidence from a number of studies suggests that in a population of women the process begins in the thirties, half of the women are menopausal at the end of their forties, and all women are menopausal by the middle to end of their fifties. It is clear, however, that the onset of infertility precedes menopause by a number of years. The reason is that, in addition to irregular and infrequent, even rare, ovulation, aging of the reproductive system is associated with a higher frequency of early spontaneous abortions, and older women tend to have a lower frequency of intercourse. Most important, therefore, the process translates into a mean age at last birth of about forty in populations that do not intentionally stop childbearing at an early age (Bongaarts and Potter 1983). The resulting pattern of natural infertility with age provides us with a lower bound for probable levels of infertility that is essential to the analysis of pathological infertility in Africa. Thus the age at which natural infertility is at its lowest level, 3 percent in the early

twenties, provides us with the lowest proportion of women whom we would expect to be childless for life in a society where virtually all women are exposed to the risk of conception. This standard level of childlessness is confirmed by the lowest proportion (about 3 percent) of ever-married women ending their reproductive years childless in a number of populations.

Chlamydia and gonorrhea cause both primary and secondary infertility in many parts of Sub-Saharan Africa. For any level of primary infertility or childlessness, there is an accompanying larger proportion of women who have incurred secondary infertility: these women are unable to have additional children, sometimes very early in their childbearing life. The proportion of women childless after the end of childbearing (say, ages 45–49) makes it possible to gauge the ultimate weight of primary infertility and to have a very good indication of the extent of accompanying secondary infertility.

The highest levels of infertility (20 percent and more of women aged 45–49 definitively childless) are found across a large area of Central Africa. Lower levels (between 12 and 20 percent childless among women aged 45–49) are found in interspersed areas of Central Africa and in East Africa. In general, much lower levels, but which still exceed expected infertility (3 to 12 percent childless among women aged 45–49) are found across West Africa, although higher infertility is found among a number of Sahelian groups of upper West Africa and in some coastal areas. The relationship between definitive childlessness and total fertility for the subpopulations of eighteen countries shows that infertility accounts for about 60 percent of variation in total fertility and that each 9 percent increment in the proportion of women aged 45–49 who are childless translates into a drop in total fertility of one live birth. Average childlessness for twenty-one countries of Sub-Saharan Africa is as high as 12 percent (weighted for population sizes): in other words, after discounting natural infertility of 3 percent, on average, women have a shortfall of one live birth across these countries because of pathological infertility alone (Frank 1983a).

Estimating the Fertility-Inhibiting Effects of the Proximate Determinants

The principal proximate determinants (age at first union, lactational amenorrhea due to breastfeeding, decreased exposure to conception due to postpartum sexual abstinence, and pathological, involuntary infertility due to gonorrhea) depend, for their fertility effect, on behaviors that are susceptible to modern influences in Africa, especially those of education and urbanization. Thus educated, urban women, although they tend to marry later, generally abstain sexually for shorter periods after delivery and tend to replace breastfeeding earlier or altogether with alternative milk or solid foods. Recourse to contraception could compensate for the positive effects these changes have on fertility, but use of contraception is clearly lagging. In Kenya, for example, fertility is increasing among young, educated, married urban women. The same phenomenon has been observed in several studies in Nigeria, and the Nigeria Fertility Survey confirms that current fertility is higher among women with primary education compared with women who have less or no education and among women with an urban residence (Federal Republic of Nigeria 1983). Broad extension of education for women in rural areas can bring about these effects at national levels, but some erosion of abstinence and breastfeeding durations can be anticipated even in the absence of substantial increases in women's education.

A convenient approach to quantifying the effects of the proximate determinants is to consider them as inhibitors of fertility. In other words, delayed entrance into the first sexual union, marital disruption, breastfeeding, postpartum abstinence, and infertility are all factors that reduce fertility to levels below those that would prevail in the absence of the effects of these proximate variables. As noted earlier, their consequences for overall reproductive performance can be substantial. Prolonged breastfeeding, for example, may result in a period of lactational amenorrhea of eighteen months. In a population with a mean birth interval of three years (not unusual for Africa), in other words, nonsterile women could spend half the birth interval and hence half their married life within amenorrheic periods. The impact of breastfeeding in this example is clearly important, but in order to compare it with the fertility effects of other proximate variables, it is necessary to use a mathematical model that quantifies the relationship between fertility and its proximate determinants. A detailed description of the model used here can be found in Bongaarts and Potter (1983). This model basically translates a measure of each proximate variable into its proportional effect on fertility as measured in the total fertility rate.[2]

The following fairly typical values for the principal proximate determinants in Sub-Saharan Africa in the 1970s may be used to illustrate an application of this model:

- Proportion of reproductive years not living in union (weighted average): 0.15
- Proportion practicing contraception among women in union: 0.05
- Duration of postpartum nonsusceptible period: 16 months
- Proportion childless at end of the reproductive years (an indicator of the incidence of pathological sterility): 0.10.

The model can be used to estimate from these measures the percentage increase in fertility that would occur if the fertility-inhibiting effect of each of these proximate variables were removed. The results plotted in figure 9-1 indicate that the elimination of breastfeeding and postpartum abstinence would produce a 72 percent increase in fertility. The effects of the other variables are much smaller: 18 percent for time spent outside unions, 12 percent for pathological sterility, and 5 percent for contraception. Expressed in births per woman, the average observed total fertility rate of 6.6 would increase to 11.4 without breastfeeding and postpartum abstinence, and if the inhibiting effects of nonexposure to unions, pathological sterility, and contraception were also removed, fertility would reach more than fifteen births per woman. Obviously, the proximate variables, especially the postpartum nonsusceptible period, have a powerful negative effect on fertility in Sub-Saharan Africa. Figure 9-1 also shows the effects of the proximate variables in other continents. This comparison indicates that the effects of marriage or union exposure and of

Figure 9-1. *Estimated Percentage Increase in Fertility Associated with Elimination of Fertility-Inhibiting Effect of Different Proximate Variables, by Region or Continent*

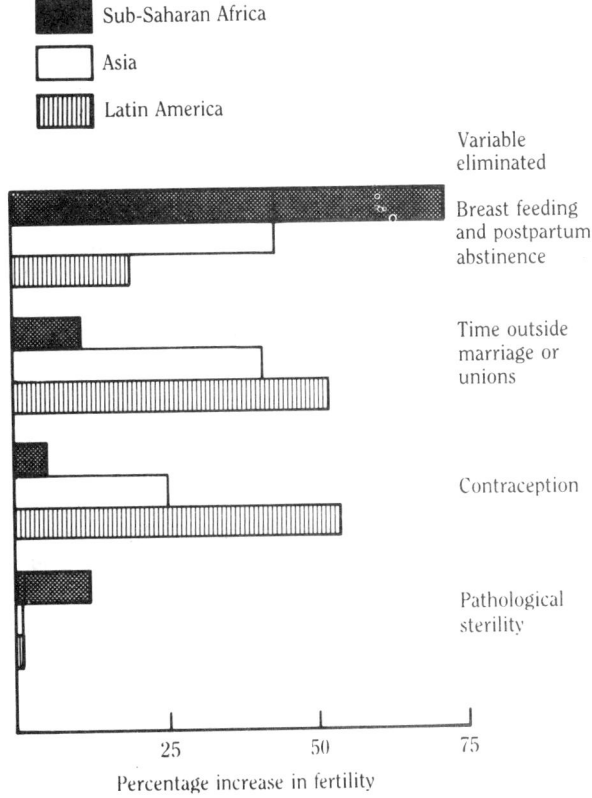

Percentage increase in fertility

Sources: For Sub-Saharan Africa, see text; for Asia and Latin America, Casterline and others (1984).

contraception are considerably greater in Latin America and Asia than in Africa. On the other hand, in Sub-Saharan Africa the fertility-inhibiting effects of postpartum nonsusceptibility and of pathological sterility substantially exceed those observed elsewhere.

Differentials in Fertility and the Proximate Variables

By definition, the variations in fertility among countries, among regions and socioeconomic strata within countries, and among individual women reflect the effects of one or more of the proximate variables. Unfortunately, owing to a paucity of data for some proximate variables, it is not possible here to provide a detailed and comprehensive explanation of the sources of the national, subnational, and individual variations in fertility. Instead, a few examples will be given to illustrate the principal causes of some fertility differentials.

As noted above, total fertility rates of countries in Sub-Saharan Africa range from 8.1 in Kenya to 4.1 in Gabon. Two crucial clues as to the cause of the gap in fertility between these two countries were provided in the earlier discussion of the proximate determinants: Kenya has one of the shortest durations of the postpartum nonsusceptible period found in Sub-Saharan Africa, and Gabon has very high levels of childlessness, which is indicative of a high prevalence of pathological sterility. To determine to what extent the set of factors can account for the difference in fertility between Kenya and Gabon, a simple two-step calculation is made with the model used in the previous section. First, an estimate is made of the decline in total fertility that would occur if Kenya's nonsusceptible period were lengthened from its current duration of thirteen months to a more typical sixteen months. Second, the increase in Gabon's fertility following the elimination of pathological sterility is estimated. The rise in the nonsusceptible period in Kenya reduces its total fertility rate from 8.1 to 7.4, whereas Gabon's total fertility rate rises from 4.1 to 7.3 after corrections have been made for the higher prevalence of childlessness. These simple adjustments have cut the fertility difference between Kenya and Gabon from 4 to a negligible 0.1 births per woman. Although there are undoubtedly differences in other proximate determinants between these two countries, it appears safe to conclude that the relatively short duration of the nonsusceptible period in Kenya and the high incidence of pathological sterility in Gabon are the principal proximate determinants of the large gap in observed total fertility rates for these two countries.

To carry out a similar exercise on the subnational level requires more detailed measures of the proximate determinants than are currently available, but a few generalizations about a few countries can be made.

First, the regional differences in fertility in Cameroon are largely caused by variations in levels of childlessness, which ranged (in the 1960s) from 29 percent in the Southeast to 7 percent in the West (Frank 1983b). The elimination of pathological sterility would, according to the model, raise the total fertility rate from 4.3 to 7.1 in the Southeast and from 6.5 to 6.9 in the West. Thus, after adjusting for the effect of pathological sterility, fertility levels in these two regions of Cameroon are virtually equal.

Second, the lower fertility rates among better educated and urban women in Ghana, Kenya, Lesotho, Senegal, and northern Sudan are primarily caused by later age at first union and by higher prevalence of contraceptive practice. Higher levels of education and urban residence, however, are also associated with shorter durations of postpartum abstinence and breastfeeding and perhaps with lower levels of pathological sterility. This association tends to offset the fertility-inhibiting effects of later marriage and the greater extent of contraceptive practice. In fact, as noted earlier, this offsetting effect can be so large as to result in a rise in fertility with increasing education in some strata (Casterline and others 1984).

The proximate determinants are also responsible for the very large variations in children ever born among individual women. The simple fertility model used thus far on the aggregate level is inadequate to account for individual differences. Instead an analysis with complex computer simulation models would be required to study this topic in detail, a task that falls outside the scope of the present chapter (see Bongaarts and Potter 1983 for applications of such models). A few relevant observations can be made, however. In general, both behavioral and biological factors are involved in determining the number of children a woman will have. Behavioral variables include the age at first union, the use of contraception, the pattern and duration of breastfeeding, and the frequency of intercourse. Behavioral factors account for some of the individual variation in fertility, but in the absence of differences in behavior, the number of children ever born would still range from zero to more than ten. This wide range indicates the crucial role played by biological factors at the individual level. Natural sterility, for example, which at the aggregate level has little explanatory power, is a major cause of variation among individuals, because a woman who is sterile when she enters her first union will remain childless, whereas a woman who remains fertile until age 50 will have several decades of reproductive life, sufficient to produce ten or even fifteen births. In addition, the spacing between births ranges from about a year to several years even among women with the same breastfeeding and intercourse patterns because durations of lactational amenorrhea, occurrences of spontaneous abortions, and waiting time to conception are to a large extent randomly determined. The role played by chance is one of the more important causes of the large range in the number of children ever born among individual women by the end of the reproductive years.

Implications for Future Trends in Fertility

The preceding analysis constitutes a basis from which some implications for future fertility trends can be derived. Naturally, any discussion of the demographic future of Sub-Saharan Africa must in large part be speculative because of the absence of reliable measures of current and past trends in fertility and the proximate determinants. The fact that the outlook for economic development is very unclear adds further uncertainty, but it is assumed here for simplicity that Sub-Saharan Africa will (slowly) follow the general pattern of modernization and development found elsewhere in the world.

Future trends in fertility are entirely determined by trends in the proximate determinants. The proximate determinants can be divided into two general classes, those that can be expected to exert upward pressure on fertility in the future and those that will tend to reduce fertility:

- Fertility-enhancing trends: shortening of breastfeeding and postpartum abstinence; decline in pathological sterility
- Fertility-reducing trends: rise in age at first union; higher prevalence and effectiveness of contraception.

These are the main variables that are likely to determine the overall trend in fertility, even though some other proximate determinants (for example, induced abortion, frequency of intercourse) may play a significant role in some societies or subgroups. Whether fertility will rise or fall in the near future therefore depends on the balance of the fertility-enhancing and fertility-reducing trends in the proximate determinants.

Past fertility trends in Sub-Saharan Africa provide an important indication of what might lie ahead. Although most countries have not experienced a significant change in fertility in recent decades, in Kenya, one important exception, the total fertility rate rose from 6.6 in 1950–55 to 8.1 in 1975–80 (United Nations 1982). Although it is possible that the estimate for the earlier period is not entirely accurate, there can be little doubt that fertility has increased significantly. This increase occurred despite a rise in age at marriage; the postpartum nonsusceptible period was shortened because of reductions in traditionally long periods of breastfeeding and postpartum abstinence. Kenya's fertility is bound to decline below its present very high level eventually, but if its past experience is any guide to what lies ahead for

other countries, then a rise in fertility in many countries of Sub-Saharan Africa may be inevitable. This statement is especially true in countries where the durations of breastfeeding and postpartum abstinence are still long or where the prevalence of pathological sterility is high. Moreover, the mere presence of infertility in a society will impede the acceptance of contraception, because the risk of becoming sterile makes childbearing uncertain, which in turn tends to weaken individuals' interest in controlling their fertility.

Support for a possible upward trend in fertility is found in cross-sectional studies that correlate socioeconomic indicators of regions with levels of fertility and the proximate variables. Lesthaeghe (1984), for example, has collected estimates of three proximate variables (marital exposure, contraception, and postpartum nonsusceptibility) for a large set of regions for which a measure of literacy was also available. As expected, marital exposure and duration of postpartum nonsusceptibility were lowest, and the prevalence of contraception was highest in regions with the highest levels of literacy. Using a model to estimate the fertility effect of these trends, fertility in the least literate regions was found to be less than that in regions with higher degrees of literacy for most of the observed range. Only after literacy reached levels above 70 percent of women of reproductive age did fertility decline as the effect of increasing contraception and later age at first union outweighed the effect of shorter breastfeeding and postpartum abstinence. Although, as Lesthaeghe noted, one cannot simply use such cross-sectional analysis to predict trends over time, this finding confirms that there is a potential for a significant rise in fertility in Sub-Saharan Africa.

Another demonstration of the formidable changes in reproductive behavior that will be required to achieve declines in fertility can be made with a model that projects future fertility levels from trends in the proximate determinants. This exercise will be simplified by examining the effect on marital fertility of two proximate determinants crucial to the reduction of fertility: the postpartum nonsusceptible period and the prevalence of contraception. Table 9-3 provides an illustra-

Table 9-3. *Model Estimates of Levels of Contraceptive Prevalence Required to Obtain Different Reductions in Marital Fertility by the Year 2000, by Duration of the Nonsusceptible Period*

Percentage reduction in marital fertility by the year 2000	Duration of postpartum nonsusceptibility	
	16 months	8.5 months
0	5	29
10	15	37
20	26	45
30	36	53

tion of two projections of the levels of contraceptive prevalence required to reach specified reductions in fertility by the year 2000. In the first projection, it is assumed that current contraceptive prevalence among married women of reproductive age is 5 percent and that the duration of nonsusceptible period is sixteen months. The second column of table 9-3 provides estimates of the contraceptive prevalence levels needed to reduce marital fertility by 10, 20 and 30 percent, respectively, assuming no change in breastfeeding or postpartum abstinence. A 20-percent reduction, for example, will require a contraceptive prevalence of 26 percent in the year 2000. The last column of table 9-3 gives the required levels of contraceptive prevalence if the duration of the nonsusceptible period were reduced to eight and a half months (such a reduction may well occur in substantial parts of Africa by the year 2000). In this second projection, contraceptive prevalence will have to rise to 29 percent just to prevent an increase in marital fertility. A modest 20 percent reduction in marital fertility will require that no fewer than 45 percent of married women engage in contraception. The projections are plotted in figure 9-2.

A dramatic rise in contraceptive prevalence is unlikely to occur in most of Sub-Saharan Africa before the end of the century. Desired family size is higher in Sub-Saharan Africa than anywhere else in the world, and no evidence exists that traditional reproductive norms are changing. What little contraceptive use exists is predominantly among older, high-parity women; only a very small proportion of low-parity women deliberately want to stop childbearing. Large declines in fertility will not occur until these traditional patterns of reproductive behavior are modified. It is difficult, therefore, to be optimistic about future trends in fertility in Sub-Saharan Africa.

Notes

1. Unless otherwise stated, the data for African countries to which reference is made in this chapter are derived from analyses carried out by Lesthaeghe (1984) of World Fertility Surveys in Sub-Saharan African countries. The six countries and the survey dates are Cameroon (1978), Ghana (1979), Kenya (1977–78), Lesotho (1977), Senegal (1979), and Sudan (1979). Full citations appear in the references.

2. The existing version of this model quantifies the proportional fertility-inhibiting effects of four proximate variables: the marriage pattern, contraception, induced abortion, and postpartum infecundability. In the present analysis, a fifth proximate variable, pathological sterility, is introduced. Its effect on fertility is measured with an index, I_p, which is estimated from the percentage of childless women at the end of the reproductive years (s) using the equation $I_p = (7.63 - 0.11 \times s)/7.30$. This equation is based on the results of a regression of the total fertility rate on proportion childless presented by Frank (1983a).

Figure 9-2. *Estimated Contraceptive Prevalence Levels Required to Obtain Different Reductions in Marital Fertility by the Year 2000, by Duration of the Nonsusceptible Period*

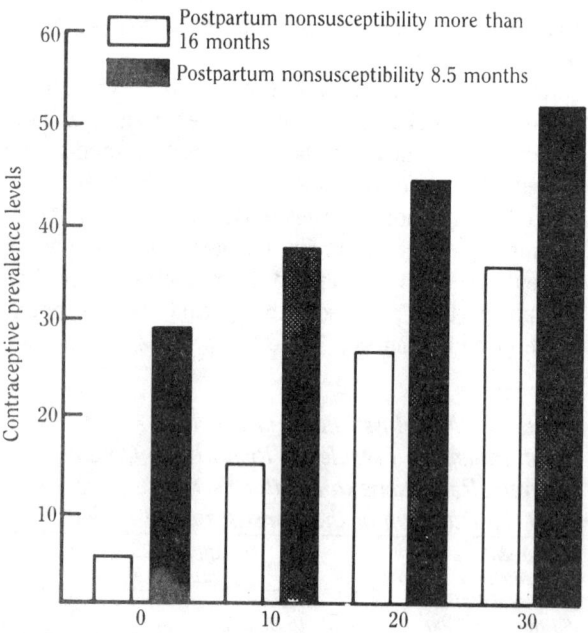

Source: Table 9-1.

References

Bongaarts, J. P., and R. G. Potter. 1983. *Fertility, Biology, and Behavior: An Analysis of the Proximate Determinants.* New York: Academic Press.

Casterline, J. B., and P. F. McDonald. 1983. "The Age Difference between Union Partners." Technical Paper No. 2070. London: World Fertility Survey; processed.

Casterline, J. B., S. Singh, J Cleland, and H. Ashurst. 1984. "The Proximate Determinants of Fertility." *World Fertility Survey Comparative Studies: Cross-National Summaries*, No. 39.

Davis, Kingsley, and J. Blake. 1956. "Social Structure and Fertility: An Analytic Framework." *Economic Development and Cultural Change* 4(4): 211–35.

Democratic Republic of Sudan. 1982. *The Sudan Fertility Survey, 1979: Principal Report.* Khartoum, Sudan: Department of Statistics, Ministry of National Planning.

Federal Republic of Nigeria. 1983. "Nigeria Fertility Survey, 1981–82." Preliminary Report. National Population Commission, Lagos, Nigeria, and World Fertility Survey, London.

Frank, Odile. 1983a. "Infertility in Sub-Saharan Africa: Estimates and Implications." *Population and Development Review* 9(1): 137–44.

————. 1983b. "Infertility in Sub-Saharan Africa." Center for Policy Studies Working Paper No. 97. Population Council, New York.

Gray, R. H. 1979. "Biological Factors Other Than Nutrition and Lactation Which May Influence Natural Fertility: A Review." In H. Leridon and J. Menken, eds., *Patterns and Determinants of Natural Fertility*. Liège, Belgium: Ordina.

Kingdom of Lesotho. 1983. *Lesotho Fertility Survey, 1977: First Report*. Maseru, Lesotho: Central Bureau of Statistics, Ministry of Planning and Statistics, 1981.

Lesthaeghe, R. O. 1984. "Fertility and Its Proximate Determinants in Sub-Saharan Africa: The Record of the 1960s and 1970s." Interuniversity Program in Demography Working Paper 1984-2. Vrije Universiteit Brussels, Belgium.

"Malaria in Pregnancy." *Lancet* 2(8341): 84–85.

Republic of Ghana. 1983. *Ghana Fertility Survey, 1979–1980: First Report*. Accra, Ghana: Central Bureau of Statistics.

Republic of Kenya. 1980. *Kenya Fertility Survey, 1977–1978: First Report*. Nairobi, Kenya: Central Bureau of Statistics, Ministry of Economic Planning and Development.

République du Sénégal. 1981. *Enquête Sénégalaise sur la Fécondité, 1978*. Dakar, Senegal: Direction de la Statistique, Division des Enquêtes et de la Démographie, Ministère de l'Economie et des Finances.

République Unie du Cameroun. 1983. *Enquête Nationale sur la Fécondité du Cameroun: Rapport Principal*. Yaounde, Cameroon: Direction de la Statistique et de la Comptabilité Nationale.

Rindfuss, R. R., and S. P. Morgan. 1983. "Marriage, Sex, and the First Birth Interval: The Quiet Revolution in Asia." *Population and Development Review* 9(2): 259–78.

Schoenmaeckers, R., I. H. Shah, R. O. Lesthaeghe, and O. Tambashe. 1981. "The Child-Spacing Tradition and the Postpartum Taboo in Tropical Africa: Anthropological Evidence." In H. O. Page and R. O. Lesthaeghe, eds., *Child-Spacing in Tropical Africa: Traditions and Change*. London: Academic Press.

United Nations. 1982. *Demographic Indicators of Countries: Estimates and Projections as Assessed in 1980*. New York.

Van de Walle, E. 1968. "Marriages in African Censuses and Inquiries." In W. Brass and others, eds., *The Demography of Tropical Africa*. Princeton: Princeton University Press.

10

Socioeconomic Differentials in Fertility and Their Explanation

Susan H. Cochrane and Samir Farid

Current fertility in Sub-Saharan Africa is extremely high. For the ten countries of Sub-Saharan Africa for which World Fertility Surveys (WFS) have been conducted (table 10-1), the total fertility rate (TFR) is 6.71, substantially higher than the rates in Asia (5.00), Latin America (4.84), and North Africa (5.82) but slightly lower than rates found in the average of four countries of the Middle East, Jordan, Syria, Turkey, and the Yemen Arab Republic (Cochrane and Farid 1989).

Sub-Saharan Africa's fertility has always been high. Measures of cumulative fertility, that is, of children ever born, show that, for women 45–49 years old, fertility in Sub-Saharan Africa is close to or just below that in other developing regions. This pattern also holds for

women over 35. For women under 35, especially under 30, however, the number of children ever born is substantially higher in Sub-Saharan Africa than elsewhere.

The high current fertility in Sub-Saharan Africa arises from a pattern of early and virtually universal marriage and very low use of contraception. It would be even higher but for near universal and prolonged breastfeeding and considerable postpartum abstinence. Table 10-2 summarizes the contribution of these factors to fertility in Africa and other developing regions. The most striking difference between Sub-Saharan Africa and other regions is the very low usage of contraception. The index of contraception of 96 percent shows that contraception reduces fertility by only 4 percent from

Table 10-1. *Cumulative Fertility for Women Forty-five to Forty-nine, Current Fertility, and P/F Ratios*

Country	Cumulative fertility (P)	Current fertility (F)	P/F ratio
Benin	6.27	7.08	0.89
Cameroon	5.18	6.40	0.81
Côte d'Ivoire	6.84	7.36	0.92
Ghana	6.71	6.47	1.04
Kenya	7.88	8.25	0.96
Lesotho	5.29	5.76	0.92
Mauritania	6.00	6.25	0.96
Nigeria	5.84	6.34	0.92
Senegal	7.16	7.15	1.00
Sudan (north)	5.98	6.02	0.99
Sub-Saharan Africa (10 countries)	6.31	6.71	0.94
North Africa (3 countries)	6.69	5.82	1.15
Middle East (2 countries)	7.45	6.99	1.07
Asia (10 countries)	6.24	5.00	1.28
Latin America (12 countries)	6.30	4.84	1.35

Note: Cumulative fertility is the number of children ever born to women aged forty-five to forty-nine years. Current fertility is the total fertility rate zero to four years prior to each survey. Regional means are based on countries that participated in the World Fertility Survey.
Source: World Fertility Survey (1984).

144

Table 10-2. *Total Legitimate Fertility and Total Fecundity Rates and Indexes of Three Main Proximate Determinants of Fertility*

Country	Observed total fertility rate (legitimate)	Index of marriage	Index of contraception	Index of postpartum infecundability	Total fecundity rate
Benin	7.08	0.840	0.881	0.637	15.03
Cameroon	6.40	0.802	0.981	0.668	12.17
Côte d'Ivoire	7.36	0.840	0.979	0.670	13.36
Ghana	6.22	0.820	0.923	0.666	12.35
Kenya	7.40	0.790	0.944	0.695	14.27
Lesotho	5.27	0.741	0.958	0.645	11.52
Mauritania	6.25	0.749	0.994	0.702	11.96
Nigeria	6.34	0.862	0.968	0.637	11.92
Senegal	6.90	0.859	0.980	0.661	12.39
Sudan (north)	6.02	0.762	0.962	0.694	11.83
Sub-Saharan Africa (10 countries)	6.52	0.807	0.957	0.668	12.68
North Africa (3 countries)	5.68	0.697	0.790	0.712	14.57
Middle East (2 countries)	7.54	0.749	0.817	0.797	15.50
Asia (10 countries)	4.92	0.704	0.800	0.680	13.18
Latin America (12 countries)	4.54	0.656	0.652	0.842	12.80

Note: Total fertility rates, based on births occurring within union only, are derived using Bongaarts's (1978) methodology.

Source: North Africa estimates are based on WFS tabulations for Egypt, Morocco, and Tunisia. Other regional estimates are from Casterline and others (1984), table 7.

the biological maximum attainable, given marriage patterns and postpartum infecundity.

In other regions, contraception reduces fertility by 18 to 35 percent. Sub-Saharan Africa's marriage pattern is not very different from the pattern found in the Middle East, and its postpartum infecundity is not very different from that of Asia. Various factors other than marriage, contraception, and postpartum infecundity of course affect fertility. There is, for example, some extramarital fertility in Sub-Saharan Africa (the total legitimate fertility rate is 6.52, whereas the TFR based on all births is 6.71). In addition, the total biological potential of legitimate fertility estimated using the Bongaarts method (table 10-2) is only 12.68, a figure substantially below that for North Africa, the Middle East, and Asia and slightly below that for Latin America. The implication is that other factors may be suppressing fertility in Sub-Saharan Africa and also perhaps in Latin America. Spousal separation and, especially in Sub-Saharan Africa, pathological sterility have been proposed as partial explanations of this phenomenon.

Given this brief summary of African fertility, what can be expected in the future? No definitive answer to this question is possible, but an examination of the socioeconomic differentials in fertility from World Fertility Survey data in ten Sub-Saharan countries provides some insight into potential changes that may occur in fertility in the course of development. Examination of socioeconomic differences in the proximate determinants of fertility, discussed in the preceding chapter, provides additional insight into the potential dynamics of fertility.

Socioeconomic Differences in Fertility

It has generally been hypothesized that more "modern" individuals (those living in urban areas, those who are well educated, those working in the modern sector) have lower fertility than more traditional individuals (those who are rural, uneducated, agricultural). It has been well documented that, at least with respect to education, this is not always the case (Cochrane 1979, 1983). The present chapter will first examine how well this pattern fits in Sub-Saharan Africa and will then consider the socioeconomic patterns in the proximate determinants of fertility.

Tables 10-3 and 10-5 summarize differences in current fertility by the residence and education of women. Three measures of current fertility are used here: (1) the total fertility rate (TFR) for women aged fifteen to forty-nine; (2) the total marital fertility rate (TMFR) for women 20–49; and (3) the total marital fertility rate for marital durations of zero to twenty-four years. The first rate is well known. The second may be interpreted as the mean number of births to a woman who remained within a union during the ages 20–49 and who experienced the observed within-union fertility schedule. The third rate is obtained by the cumulation of duration-specific marital fertility rates to durations of twenty-five years.

Urban-Rural Differentials

For Sub-Saharan Africa as a whole, the expected pattern of urban-rural differentials appears in table 10-3: fer-

Table 10-3. *Fertility Rates, by Residence and Country*

Country	Total fertility rate, age 15–49				Total marital fertility rate, age 20–49			Total marital fertility rate, 0–24 years married		
	All	Major urban	Other urban	Rural	Major urban	Other urban	Rural	Major urban	Other urban	Rural
Benin	7.08	5.75	6.70	7.40	6.55	6.52	6.86	6.02	6.35	6.82
Cameroon	6.40	5.30	6.70	6.51	5.70	6.15	5.83	5.40	5.99	5.79
Côte d'Ivoire	7.36	6.42	6.86	7.72	6.09	6.31	6.95	6.07	6.31	6.82
Ghana	6.47	5.41	6.26	6.79	5.79	6.43	6.59	5.41	5.82	6.30
Kenya	8.25	5.90	6.08	8.48	6.21	5.97	8.01	6.86	6.27	8.03
Lesotho	5.76	4.79	—	6.23	5.41	—	5.96	5.27	—	5.86
Mauritania	6.25	6.25	6.13	6.28	6.53	6.81	6.45	6.31	6.78	6.81
Nigeria	6.34	6.73	5.88	6.39	6.41	5.83	5.91	6.60	6.07	6.01
Senegal	7.15	6.76	6.32	7.47	7.08	6.37	6.66	7.20	6.70	7.02
Sudan (north)	6.02	4.80	5.68	6.43	5.71	6.09	6.64	6.46	6.52	6.91
Sub-Saharan Africa (mean)	6.71	5.81	6.29	6.97	6.15	6.28	6.59	6.16	6.31	6.64

— No data.
Source: WFS tabulations.

tility is lowest in major urban areas and highest in rural areas. For the individual countries of Sub-Saharan Africa, deviations from this pattern occur. In particular, Cameroon and Nigeria show rural fertility by all three measures below fertility in at least one urban category. This pattern may arise from subfecundity due to poor health in rural regions of these countries. In Senegal, also, marital fertility in rural areas is below that for major urban areas. Outside Sub-Saharan Africa, no country shows rural fertility below urban fertility for all three measures of fertility, but Guyana, Indonesia, and Pakistan show lower rural than urban fertility on two of the three measures.

Table 10-4 summarizes regional averages in fertility from WFS survey data and the differentials across residence. On average, the TFR in major urban areas is higher in Sub-Saharan Africa than elsewhere, and except for the Middle East, marital fertility is also higher in Sub-Saharan Africa than in other regions. For "other urban areas," all measures of fertility are highest in the

Table 10-4. *Fertility Rates, by Residence and Region*

Residence	Sub-Saharan Africa (10)	North Africa (3)	Middle East (3)	Asia (10)	Latin America (13)
Total fertility rate, age 15–49					
Major urban	5.81	4.15	5.51	3.95	3.51
Other urban	6.29	4.81	7.46	4.40	4.30
Rural	6.97	6.70	9.03	5.30	6.14
Difference	1.16	2.55	3.52	1.35	2.63
Difference (%)	17	38	39	25	43
Total marital fertility rate, age 20–49					
Major urban	6.15	5.31	6.55	5.06	4.42
Other urban	6.28	6.08	8.01	5.36	5.09
Rural	6.59	7.27	9.15	5.80	6.64
Difference	0.44	1.96	2.60	0.74	2.22
Difference (%)	6	27	28	13	33
Total marital fertility rate, 0–24 years married					
Major urban	6.16	5.29	6.97	4.88	4.06
Other urban	6.31	6.19	8.21	5.42	4.87
Rural	6.64	7.41	9.07	5.94	6.61
Difference	0.48	2.12	2.10	1.06	2.55
Difference (%)	7	29	23	18	39

Note: Parenthetical numbers in column heads are numbers of countries.
Sources: WFS tabulations for Sub-Saharan Africa and North Africa; Ashurst and Casterline (1984) for others.

Middle East, followed by Sub-Saharan Africa. For rural areas the pattern is different. Rural marital fertility in Sub-Saharan Africa is well below that in the Middle East and North Africa and close to the level in Latin America. The total fertility rate in rural Sub-Saharan Africa is below that in North Africa and the Middle East, above the level in Latin America, and far above that in Asia. These findings can be summarized by looking at base levels of fertility in rural areas and differentials across residence. Asia has low base levels compared with those in other regions, and countries of Sub-Saharan Africa have high base levels but not as high as those in the Middle East. Base-level marital fertility is as high in Latin America as it is in Sub-Saharan Africa, which has the smallest differences across residence by all measures of fertility. North Africa, the Middle East, and Latin America all have large differentials—in excess of two children on all three measures of current fertility. If percentage differentials are examined, those in Sub-Saharan African countries are the lowest, in Asia the second lowest, and in Latin America the highest.

Educational Differentials

It is hypothesized that, as education increases, fertility declines. This statement is generally but not universally true. In countries with low levels of literacy and urbanization, women with a small amount of schooling often have higher fertility than women with no schooling (Cochrane 1979, 1983). Table 10-5 shows a pattern of an increase in fertility with education prior to a decrease in the TFRs and TMFRs of Benin, Cameroon, Côte d'Ivoire, Kenya, Nigeria, and Senegal. In Ghana and Lesotho, more irregular patterns are observed. Only in Sudan is an inverse pattern seen, and this pattern does not hold when the fertility of those married zero to twenty-four years is observed. In Sub-Saharan Africa, the general pattern of fertility across education groups is consistent with that found among essentially rural and illiterate populations, that is, an increase in fertility with education is found at low levels of education. Regional averages in table 10-6 show that the curvilinear relationship between current fertility and education exists only for Sub-Saharan Africa and Asia, but the differences between those with no education and those with one to three years of school are much smaller in Asia than in Sub-Saharan Africa. That is, fertility increases more with a small amount of schooling in Sub-Saharan Africa than elsewhere.

Among the least educated, fertility is lowest in Asia and highest in the Middle East (table 10-6). Sub-Saharan Africa, North Africa, and Latin America show intermediate values. Among the most educated, Latin American women have the lowest fertility. Middle Eastern women have the highest marital fertility rates among the most educated, followed by Sub-Saharan African women. On TFRs, Sub-Saharan Africa has slightly higher values than the Middle East.

Differentials in fertility across education groups show the same pattern that has been found for differentials across residence. Differentials, particularly percentage

Table 10-5. *Fertility Rates, by Wife's Education and Country*

Country	Total fertility rate, age 15–49 per years of education				Total marital fertility rate, age 20–49 per years of education				Total marital fertility rate, 0–24 years married per years of education			
	0	*1–3*	*4–6*	*7+*	*0*	*1–3*	*4–6*	*7+*	*0*	*1–3*	*4–6*	*7+*
Benin	7.35	8.50	5.77	4.26	6.80	7.95	6.20	5.64	6.75	7.22	5.94	5.26
Cameroon	6.38	6.98	6.77	5.18	5.59	6.57	6.50	5.26	5.47	6.23	6.27	5.16
Côte d'Ivoire	7.45	8.02	6.36	5.83	6.75	6.91	5.82	5.65	6.60	7.06	5.66	6.84
Ghana	6.84	6.67	6.96	5.49	6.48	6.99	7.02	5.66	6.18	5.74	6.05	5.33
Kenya	8.28	9.21	8.43	7.34	7.43	8.53	7.90	7.83	7.48	8.33	8.13	7.69
Lesotho	6.24	5.63	5.97	4.76	5.76	5.45	6.00	5.96	5.41	5.54	5.88	5.88
Mauritania	—	—	—	—	6.56	—	6.47	—	6.89	—	6.00	—
Nigeria	6.58	6.88	7.59	4.20	5.69	5.85	7.68	5.40	5.78	6.30	7.03	5.36
Senegal	7.32	9.44	6.31	4.47	6.64	8.96	6.42	5.96	6.95	7.28	6.80	6.11
Sudan (north)	6.47	5.56	4.98	3.37	6.42	6.23	5.82	5.31	6.74	7.35	6.88	5.13
Sub-Saharan Africa	6.99	7.43	6.57	4.99	6.41	7.05	6.58	5.85	6.43	6.78	6.46	5.86

— Not available.

Source: WFS tabulations.

Table 10-6. *Fertility Rates, by Wife's Education and Region*

Wife's education (in years)	Sub-Saharan Africa (10)	North Africa (3)	Middle East (3)	Asia (10)	Latin America (13)
Total fertility rate, age 15–49					
None	6.99	—	8.90	5.81	6.62
1–3	7.43	—	6.91	5.89	6.04
4–6	6.57	—	5.98	5.66	4.71
7+	4.99	—	4.79	3.70	3.19
Difference	2.00	—	4.11	2.11	3.43
Difference (%)	29	—	46	36	52
Total marital fertility rate, age 20–49					
None	6.41	6.79	8.83	5.64	6.76
1–3	7.05	6.06	7.13	5.66	6.21
4–6	6.58	5.85	6.41	5.77	5.16
7+	5.85	5.27	6.14	4.93	4.37
Difference	0.56	1.52	2.69	0.71	2.39
Difference (%)	9	22	30	13	35
Total marital fertility rate, 0–24 years married					
None	6.43	6.96	8.84	5.91	6.76
1–3	6.78	5.93	8.32	5.98	6.17
4–6	6.46	5.99	7.58	5.94	5.18
7+	5.86	4.10	6.70	4.49	3.79
Difference	0.57	2.86	2.14	1.42	2.97
Difference (%)	9	41	24	24	44

Note: Parenthetical numbers in column heads are numbers of countries.
— Not available.
Source: WFS tabulations for Sub-Saharan Africa and North Africa; Ashurst and Casterline (1984) for others.

differentials, are smallest in Sub-Saharan Africa, followed by Asia, and are highest in Latin America.

Thus, regional differentials in fertility by the socioeconomic characteristics of residence and education show three distinct patterns for the major regions: (a) high base-level fertility and small differentials in Sub-Saharan Africa; (b) high base levels and large differentials in Latin America; and (c) low base levels and medium to small differentials in Asia. In the Middle East, very high base levels and differentials slightly below those in Latin America are observed. North Africa has a more mixed pattern, depending on whether residence or education is the measure of development. Whether these cross-sectional differentials can predict movements in fertility in the course of development depends very much on their explanation.

How can these patterns be explained? Socioeconomic differentials in fertility arise primarily from socioeconomic differentials in marriage, postpartum infecundity, and contraceptive use. Casterline and others (1984) explored socioeconomic patterns in a Bongaarts framework using the measures c_c, c_m, and c_i for countries for which WFS data were available at that time, but they did not attempt to explain regional patterns in socioeconomic differentials in fertility. The socioeconomic differentials in the proximate determinants are discussed below.

Socioeconomic Differences in Age at Marriage

In the European experience, changes in marriage behavior initiated the first fertility decline. Socioeconomic differentials in age at marriage may well be predictive of future declines and may in part explain current socioeconomic differences in fertility.

Urban-Rural Differences

Marriage in Sub-Saharan Africa is both early and universal. Table 10-7 summarizes the differences between urban and rural areas in age at marriage. For both urban and rural areas, age at marriage is lower in Sub-Saharan Africa than in the other regions, in terms both of the proportion ever married in various age groups and of the singulate mean age at marriage. In fact, the age at marriage is so low in Sub-Saharan Africa that, in urban areas, it is lower than age at marriage in the rural areas of the other regions for which data are available.

Differentials in age at marriage in Sub-Saharan Africa are smaller than in the other regions. The greatest differentials, particularly in teenage marriage, are found in North Africa, followed by Asia and then Latin America. Part of the smaller urban-rural differences in fertility in Sub-Saharan Africa can thus be explained by

Table 10-7. *Percentage of Women Ever Married, by Age, Residence, and Region and Singulate Mean Age at Marriage, by Residence and Region*

Age group and residence	Sub-Saharan Africa (10)	North Africa (3)	Asia (9)	Latin America (8)
	Percentage ever married			
Age 15–19				
Urban	31.9	6.0	15.4	22.0
Rural	46.1	22.4	24.7	31.8
Difference	14.2	16.4	9.3	9.8
Difference (%)	31	73	38	31
Age 20–24				
Urban	74.0	44.4	51.8	61.2
Rural	86.2	67.7	65.4	73.5
Difference	12.2	23.3	13.6	12.3
Difference (%)	14	34	21	17
Age 25–29				
Urban	92.4	79.7	79.5	82.5
Rural	95.8	89.6	87.6	88.7
Difference	3.4	9.9	8.1	6.2
Difference (%)	4	11	9	7
	Singulate mean age at marriage (years)			
Urban	19.1	23.5	22.9	21.6
Rural	18.4	21.0	21.1	20.0
Difference	0.7	2.5	1.8	1.6
Difference (%)	4	11	8	7

Note: Parenthetical numbers in column heads are numbers of countries.
Source: WFS tabulations for Sub-Saharan Africa and North Africa; McCarthy (1982) for Latin America and Asia.

smaller urban-rural differences in age at marriage. In other regions, however, the urban-rural differences in age at marriage do not correspond to the pattern of urban-rural differentials in fertility.

Educational Differences

It is generally hypothesized that the more education a woman has, the older her age at marriage, on average. The data presented in table 10-8 on regional averages indicate that uneducated women are more likely to be married at age 15–19 and 20–24 and have a lower singulate mean age at marriage than those with seven or more years of schooling. A uniform pattern of education is not, however, observed for all regions and all levels of education. Only for Sub-Saharan Africa does age at marriage increase uniformly with education. In addition, the differentials in age at marriage across education groups are greater in Sub-Saharan Africa than elsewhere.

Therefore, the pattern of age at marriage by education for the three major regions is different from that observed for fertility. The small differentials in fertility across education groups cannot be explained by smaller differences in age at marriage by education groups in Sub-Saharan Africa than elsewhere.

Socioeconomic Differences in Breastfeeding Patterns

In Sub-Saharan Africa, breastfeeding patterns have been shown to be a major factor suppressing fertility below its biological maximum. These breastfeeding patterns may help explain socioeconomic differences in fertility. In particular, if urban, more educated women abandon universal, prolonged breastfeeding, their fertility would tend to be higher than patterns of marriage might otherwise suggest.

Urban-Rural Differences

Table 10-9 indicates that duration of breastfeeding varies inversely with urban residence. In rural areas, breastfeeding is shortest in Latin America and longest in Asia, with Sub-Saharan Africa very close to Asia and the Middle East close to Latin America. In major urban areas, breastfeeding is shortest in Latin America and far longer in Africa than it is even in Asia. Differentials in breastfeeding duration across residence groups are very large for Latin America and Asia (being almost identical in percentage terms) and much smaller in Sub-Saharan Africa. The relatively small urban-rural differences in

Table 10-8. *Percentage of Women Ever Married by Age, Wife's Education, and Region, and Singulate Mean Age at Marriage, by Wife's Education and Region*

Age group and wife's education (in years)	Sub-Saharan Africa (9)	Asia (5)	Latin America (8)
Percentage ever married			
Age 15–19			
None	64	34	39
1–3	46	41	40
4–6	32	37	32
7+	16	12	17
Difference	48	22	22
Difference (%)	75	65	56
Age group 20–24			
None	89	73	75
1–3	91	76	81
4–6	81	66	74
7+	56	40	52
Difference	33	33	23
Difference (%)	37	45	31
Singulate mean age at marriage (years)			
None	17.3	20.3	20.0
1–3	18.3	19.6	18.7
4–6	19.5	20.7	20.1
7+	22.5	24.0	22.1
Difference	5.2	3.7	2.1
Difference (%)	30	18	11

Note: Parenthetical numbers in column heads are numbers of countries.
Source: WFS tabulations for Sub-Saharan Africa; McCarthy (1982) for Asia and Latin America.

fertility in Sub-Saharan Africa do not appear to be explained by drastic reductions in breastfeeding among urban women.

Educational Differences

The generally hypothesized inverse relationship between duration of breastfeeding and education seems to hold without deviation for all regional averages in table 10-10. Levels of breastfeeding among those with no schooling are longest in Asia, followed closely by Sub-Saharan Africa, and are shortest in the Middle East, followed closely by Latin America. Among the most educated, breastfeeding is shortest by far in Latin America and longest in Sub-Saharan Africa, followed by Asia.

Differentials across education groups are greatest in Latin America and smallest by far in Sub-Saharan Africa. As with urban-rural differences in breastfeeding, this suggests that the pattern of substantial abandonment of breastfeeding with education does not explain the smaller fertility differentials in Sub-Saharan Africa than elsewhere.

Socioeconomic Differences in Contraceptive Use

Of the three major determinants of fertility (marriage, breastfeeding, and contraceptive use), only contraceptive use is primarily motivated by a desire to control fertility. It is, therefore, the proximate determinant most likely to correspond to and change with fertility aspirations. Differentials in contraceptive use are therefore expected to correspond to differentials in family size preferences.

Urban-Rural Differentials

Contraceptive use is very low in Sub-Saharan Africa. Table 10-11 shows that, among women living in major urban areas, contraceptive use is far lower in Sub-Saharan Africa than among the rural women of other regions, especially when use of efficient methods is examined. Although percentage differentials in contraceptive use are large in Sub-Saharan Africa because of the low base levels, absolute differences are extremely small. Thus, a major determinant of smaller urban-rural

Table 10-9. *Mean Duration of Breastfeeding, by Residence and Region*
(months)

Residence	Sub-Saharan Africa (9)	Middle East (2)	Asia (10)	Latin America (12)
All live-born children				
Major urban	15.1	9.6	10.2	5.8
Other urban	15.4	11.1	14.2	8.1
Rural	18.2	12.3	19.5	11.2
Difference	3.1	2.7	9.3	5.4
Difference (%)	17	22	48	48
Surviving infants				
Major urban	16.0	9.9	10.0	5.9
Other urban	16.7	11.6	15.4	8.5
Rural	20.0	13.0	21.3	11.9
Difference	4.0	3.1	11.3	6.0
Difference (%)	20	24	53	50

Note: Parenthetical numbers in column heads are numbers of countries.
Sources: WFS tabulations for nine countries of Sub-Saharan Africa; Ferry and Smith (1983) for other regions.

differentials in fertility is probably the very small urban-rural differentials in use of contraception, especially efficient contraception.

Educational Differentials

Unfortunately it is difficult to find data on educational differentials in contraceptive use that are directly comparable to those available from the WFS for Sub-Saharan African countries. For a small sample of countries (seven from Asia and eight from Latin America), Mamlouk (1982) provided estimates for educational categories that are roughly equivalent to less than three years, primary, and secondary. Using weights, primary and secondary education groups can be combined into a category roughly equivalent to four or more years of education. Mamlouk's estimates are age standardized but are not available separately for efficient methods. Table 10-12 summarizes these limited data. Contraceptive usage does increase with education, but usage among the most educated in Sub-Saharan Africa slightly exceeds usage among the least educated in North Africa. Usage of those with the highest level of education is substantially below that of those with no school or one to three years of

Table 10-10. *Mean Duration of Breastfeeding, by Wife's Education and Region*
(months)

Wife's education (in years)	Sub-Saharan Africa (9)	Middle East (2)	Asia (10)	Latin America (12)
All live-born children				
None	18.7	12.8	20.0	13.7
1–3	16.6	12.6	17.6	11.0
4–6	15.9	10.1	16.4	8.0
7+	14.0	8.3	11.0	5.0
Difference	4.7	4.5	9.0	8.7
Difference (%)	25	35	45	64
Surviving infants				
None	20.4	13.4	22.2	14.7
1–3	18.3	13.0	19.2	11.8
4–6	17.3	10.6	17.4	8.7
7+	15.0	8.6	11.3	5.1
Difference	5.4	4.8	10.9	9.6
Difference (%)	26	36	99	65

Note: Parenthetical numbers in column heads are numbers of countries.
Sources: WFS tabulations for nine countries of Sub-Saharan Africa; Ferry and Smith (1983) for other regions.

Table 10-11. *Percentage Currently Using Contraception, by Residence and Region*

Residence	Sub-Saharan Africa (9)	North Africa (3)	Asia (10)	Latin America (8)
Efficient methods				
Major urban	6	35	30	41
Other urban	3	32	24	35
Rural	1	13	17	27
Difference	5	22	13	14
Difference (%)	83	63	43	34
All methods				
Major urban	10	42	38	52
Other urban	7	39	32	45
Rural	5	14	23	32
Difference	5	28	15	20
Difference (%)	50	67	39	38

Note: Parenthetical numbers in column heads are numbers of countries.
Sources: WFS tabulations for nine countries of Sub-Saharan Africa; Lightbourne (1980) for other regions.

school in Asia and Latin America. It is not possible to compare size of differentials across education groups between regions, given differences in the education groups, but in absolute size differentials in Sub-Saharan Africa are much smaller than in North Africa.

An analysis of Casterline and others (1984) has only five Sub-Saharan African countries, but it can provide some insight into educational differentials in c_c (Bongaart's measure of overall usage and efficiency of methods used). These data appear in the second panel of table 10-12. This indicator shows that usage of contraception among the most educated in five Sub-Saharan African countries is below that of the least educated in Latin America and Asia (that is, the values for c_c are higher). Differentials in c_c correspond with those ob-

served in fertility differentials: they are highest in Latin America, lowest in Sub-Saharan Africa, and intermediate for Asia.

Although the data on educational differentials in contraceptive use are rarer than data on other differentials, they do suggest that, among the three major proximate determinants of fertility, contraceptive use is the only one that can explain in part the smaller educational differentials in fertility found in Sub-Saharan Africa than in Asia and Latin America.

The cause of small differentials in contraceptive use in Sub-Saharan Africa is probably the smaller differentials in knowledge of, access to, and motivation to use contraception. Unfortunately data are not available on differentials in knowledge and access, but some data

Table 10-12. *Current Use of Contraception, by Wife's Education and Region*

Wife's education (in years)	Sub-Saharan Africa	North Africa	Asia	Latin America
Population currently using (age standardized)				
None (%)	4	14		
1–3 (%)	8	39	} 29	} 34
4–6	9	43		
7+	19	56	} 43	} 52
Difference	15	42	14	18
Difference (%)	375	300	48	53
No. of countries	10	3	7	8
Bongaart's c_c				
None	0.976	—	0.845	0.781
1–3	0.865	—	0.792	0.694
4–6	0.940	—	0.777	0.637
7+	0.862	—	0.703	0.552
Difference	0.114	—	0.142	0.229
Difference (%)	12	—	17	29
No. of countries	5	—	10	12

Sources: Top, WFS tabulations for Africa and Mamlouk (1982) for other regions; bottom, Casterline and others (1984).

are available on differentials in motivation as reflected in desired family size.

Desired Family Size

Family size preferences have been shown elsewhere to be important determinants of contraceptive use. Desired family sizes are higher in Sub-Saharan Africa than elsewhere, and the patterns of differential for several groups are unique.

Urban-Rural Differences

Table 10-13 summarizes the available statistics on urban-rural differences in desired family size (chapter 11 in this volume; Kent and Larson 1982). Unfortunately, the statistics are not directly comparable because the data for Sub-Saharan Africa have two categories of urban residence, whereas figures for the other regions combine all urban residents into one category.

Despite these differences in categories, the data illustrate dramatically the preferences in Africa for very large families. Desired family size in major urban areas of Sub-Saharan Africa is one child greater than in rural Latin America and 1.7 greater than in rural Asia. The differentials across residence are larger in Sub-Saharan Africa than elsewhere. In part, the reason is the compressed urban categories used in Asia and Latin America. What is clear is that very high desired family size, even among the most urban, suppresses motivation for the use of contraception. Comparisons of desired family size with TFRS for all ten Sub-Saharan African countries show that, in all residence categories, desired family size exceeds TFRS. Therefore even without mortality, on average, there would be little motivation for limiting fertility.

Table 10.13. *Desired Family Size, by Residence and Region*

Residence	Sub-Saharan Africa (7)	Asia (9)	Latin America (10)
Major urban	5.93	} 3.8	} 4.1
Other urban	6.65		
Rural	7.44	4.2	4.9
Difference	1.51	0.4	0.8
Difference (%)	20	10	16

Note: Parenthetical numbers in column heads are numbers of countries.
Sources: Chapter 11 of this volume for Sub-Saharan Africa; Kent and Larson (1982) for other regions.

Table 10-14. *Desired Family Size, by Wife's Education and Region*

Wife's education (in years)	Sub-Saharan Africa (7)	Asia (10)	Latin America (10)
None	7.72	} 4.50	} 5.33
1–3	6.88		
4–6	6.22	4.01	4.54
7–9	5.63	} 3.42	} 3.60
10 +	5.16		
Difference	2.56	1.08	1.73
Difference (%)	33	24	32

Note: Parenthetical numbers in column heads are numbers of countries.
Sources: Chapter 11 of this volume for Sub-Saharan Africa; Kent and Larson (1982) for Asia and Latin America.

Educational Differences

Data from Acsadi and Johnson-Acsadi (chapter 11 in this volume) and from Kent and Larson (1982) can be compared for educational categories (see table 10-14), but the categories are not completely identical in the two sources.

The very high desired family size is illustrated by the fact that the desired family size among the most educated in Sub-Saharan Africa exceeds that of the uneducated in Asia but is slightly below the least educated in Latin America. Among the least educated, desired family size is greater than in Asia by more than three children and greater than in Latin American by more than two children.

Absolute differences in fertility across education groups are larger in Sub-Saharan Africa than elsewhere, in part because of the smaller number of education categories elsewhere. Thus it appears that the very low motivation to use contraception among even the most educated in Sub-Saharan Africa reflects not the lack of differentials in desired family size but the extremely high demand for children among all education groups. Comparisons of desired family size with TFRS indicate that, for the most educated and the least educated, desired family size exceeds TFRS. For intermediate levels, the converse is true. This implies that the greatest potential unmet need for family planning may be for women with an intermediate level of education.

Conclusions

The very high fertility in Sub-Saharan Africa is explained by fertility levels among the rural population and least educated women; these levels are higher than in any other region except the Middle East by differentials across residence and education groups that are smaller than elsewhere, as well as by the composition of the population, in which the very high fertility groups weigh heavily. Asia and Latin America, with lower fertility, have very different patterns. In Asia, fertility is relatively low among the rural and least educated groups, and differentials are almost as small as in Africa. In Latin America, base levels of fertility are relatively high, but differentials are very large.

The Sub-Saharan African pattern of small socioeconomic differentials in fertility is explained in part by small differentials in and very low usage of contraception, even among the most educated. This, in turn, is explained by very high levels of desired family size, which, even among urban residents and the most educated women, exceed TFRs. Marriage patterns explain part of the small urban-rural differences in fertility but do not explain small educational differentials in fertility. Patterns of breastfeeding do not explain small urban-rural or educational differentials in fertility because there does not yet appear to be substantial abandonment of breastfeeding among educated and urban women, at least with respect to the categories used in this analysis.

Future levels of fertility in Sub-Saharan Africa are difficult to predict. Fertility has the potential to rise if more educated and urban women adopt the breastfeeding patterns of Asia and Latin America without adopting modern contraception. Fertility also has the potential to decrease as education and urbanization occur, because desired family size, though high in all groups, at all levels, does differ across them. Whereas the above discussion presents a comprehensive picture of regional patterns, different patterns exist for countries within various regions. Within Sub-Saharan Africa, the patterns are fairly similar among countries, but this situation may change as different patterns of growth and development occur.

References

Ashurst, Hazel, and J. B. Casterline. 1984. "Socio-economic Differentials in Current Fertility." WFS *Comparative Studies: Cross-National Summaries*. Additional Tables. London; processed.

Bongaarts, John. 1978. "A Framework for Analyzing the Proximate Determinants of Fertility." *Population and Development Review* 4(1): 105–32.

Casterline, J. B., S. Singh, J. G. Cleland, and Hazel Ashurst. 1984. "The Proximate Determinants of Fertility." WFS *Comparative Studies: Cross-National Summaries*, No. 34.

Cochrane, S. H. 1983. "Effects of Education and Urbanization on Fertility." In *Determinants of Fertility: A Summary of the Knowledge*. Washington, D.C.: National Academy of Sciences.

———. 1979. *Fertility and Education: What Do We Really Know?* Baltimore, Md.: Johns Hopkins University Press.

Cochrane, S. H., and S. M. Farid. 1989. *Fertility in Sub-Saharan Africa: Analysis and Explanation*. World Bank Discussion Paper 43. Washington, D.C.

Ferry, B., and D. P. Smith. 1983. "Breastfeeding Differentials." *World Fertility Survey Comparative Studies: Cross-National Summaries*, No. 23.

Kent, M. M., and A. Larson. 1982. "Family Size Preferences: Evidence from the World Fertility Surveys." Reports on the World Fertility Survey. No. 4. Population Reference Bureau, Washington, D.C., April; processed.

Lightbourne, R. E., 1980. "Urban-Rural Differentials in Contraceptive Use." *World Fertility Survey Comparative Studies: Cross-National Summaries*, No. 10.

Mamlouk, M. 1982. "Knowledge and Use of Contraception in Twenty Developing Countries." Reports on the World Fertility Survey, No. 3. *Population Reference Bureau*, Washington, D.C., February.

McCarthy, J. 1982. "Differentials in Age at First Marriage." *World Fertility Survey Comparative Studies: Cross-National Summaries*, No. 19.

World Fertility Survey. 1984. *Major Findings and Implications*. Oxford: Alden Press.

11

Demand for Children and for Childspacing

George T. F. Acsadi and Gwendolyn Johnson-Acsadi

In the great ethnic mosaic of Sub-Saharan Africa, there is little room for generalizations. In all agricultural societies such as those that predominate in Africa, however, children are the natural and necessary source of farm labor. In general, children were, and in many Sub-Saharan cultures still are, considered to be a source of wealth and prestige. Historically, sons assured the father (as well as the family, clan, or tribe) of social, political, and economic strength, of a voice in many aspects of community life, and of continuation of the lineage; the bride-price paid for daughters increased family wealth.

A woman's status was enhanced by the regular birth of children; barrenness or few children subjected her to scorn and ridicule, whereas many children assured respect. Moreover, daughters lessened her physical burdens of child care and work, and sons might ensure that she retained her home and property upon the death of her husband.

Children provided security in old age, performed funeral and other rites, commemorated ancestors, and at a very early age, began work on the land or at animal husbandry. They protected family property from intruders, and they were sometimes considered proof that the ancestors has bestowed favor upon the couple.

Throughout Sub-Saharan Africa, many of these cultural elements survive, particularly among rural populations and illiterate people, as articulated desires for many children, even in the more modern segments of these societies, attest. The conditions that nourished many of these elements are changing, however. Relatively recent laws requiring universal school attendance up to a specified age, for example, have reduced the perceived economic utility of children and have called

The authors express their thanks to Susan H. Cochrane of the World Bank and to Michael Vlasoff of the U.N. Economic Commission of Latin America for helpful critical comments.

attention to their costs; improved health conditions have enhanced child survival; and modern urbanization has undermined many elements of the social fabric that supported the traditional family and the long-standing reproductive norms.

In all of these societies, there were and continue to be social as well as biological constraints against unlimited fertility. Extended periods of breastfeeding and postpartum abstinence were and still are customary; in some societies, postpartum abstinence may last for several years, although in others, it is becoming shorter. Sexual intercourse is also avoided ritually in many cultures in connection with certain occasions, dates, and events. Timing, conditions, and forms of marriage, familial roles, and duties, circumstances involving temporary absence of mates, and customs concerning widowhood and remarriage may also impose restraints on fertility. Widespread illness, nutritional deficiencies, and infertility in some areas may also seriously restrict fertility.

Cultural norms concerning procreation vary widely, even in Sub-Saharan Africa (and always have), but traditional societies in Africa, like societies elsewhere, regulated replacement in light of the socioeconomic situation and environment (Lorimer 1954). The main channel through which society—spontaneously or consciously—influences replacement is a fertility regulatory system of social norms, values, customs, laws, and institutions relating to family and kinship, sexual relationships, marriage (a term that we use to encompass any marital union), children, fertility, and related matters that embody many important aspects of life (Acsadi 1972, 1976, 1979). The system is an inseparable part of culture, supported by particular religious beliefs, ideology, or morality. Its elements are usually sustained by incentives, but may also be sanctioned by tradition and customary or codified law and are enforceable by the kinship circle, a larger social group, or the state.

The elements of a fertility regulatory system, however, are not consistent in their demographic effect; some promote fertility, and others limit it. Components such as late marriage, celibacy, sexual taboos, extended breastfeeding, lengthy abstinence, and polygyny limit or depress fertility, whereas others, such as early and universal marriage, acceptance of premarital relations and of children born out of wedlock, child fostering, condemnation of barrenness, and banning of birth control practices, may increase or maintain fertility at a high level. The system keeps the diverse effects in balance.

Modern socioeconomic development affects both those factors that limited fertility and those that promoted it. During the transition of the fertility regulatory system, the balance between the two sets of factors may theoretically be maintained, or the limiting factors may even prevail. Often, however, those components of the system that moderated fertility (for example, customs assuring reasonable childspacing) are eclipsed more quickly. Thus, although low fertility is usually associated with a high level of socioeconomic development, the initial stage of modern development—almost as a rule—induces transitory fertility increase.

The reason for the ostensible contradiction is that the relevant norms, values, and beliefs that support fertility are deeply embedded in the social consciousness and are less susceptible even to radical social, economic, or political changes than are the components that limit fertility. Economic and social development undermines and destroys the old customs and taboos that primarily moderated fertility, but couples do not necessarily use modern birth control in their place. Use of powdered milk and baby formulas may shorten or displace breastfeeding, old sexual taboos may vanish, and couples may be increasingly less willing to observe traditional abstinence. Other concomitant factors of development, such as improved nutrition, better health conditions, and elimination of diseases causing infertility, also contribute to the increase of fertility. Infant and child mortality may decrease, and more children may survive to adolescence and young adulthood than before, but the coming generations need considerable time in which to perceive the changes and to recognize that less frequent childbearing can assure the same effective reproduction. Because the socioeconomic changes do not affect each social, regional, or ethnic group equally or simultaneously, it is possible that their impact will be manifest only or largely in the most affected—that is, the urban, educated, young, nonagricultural—segments of the population, causing "unexpected" differentials if the disappearing fertility constraints are not replaced by modern equivalents. For a while, the elements of the traditional and emerging systems may coexist and may govern different segments of the same society.

In the study of demand for children and childspacing, another important theoretical consideration is the individual's attitudes and decisionmaking capacity regarding childbearing and family size. An essential difference between traditional and modern fertility regulatory systems is that, in the former, at least as far as the woman is concerned, hardly anything is left to individual preferences or decisionmaking, whereas in a modern system, individual attitudes and decisionmaking play a decisive role.

In a traditional society, with few exceptions, marriages were arranged by parents or kin, according to their choice at an age predetermined by custom or according to strict rules that prescribed the circle of men to whom a bride could be offered for marriage (and a circle of men whom she could not marry), but the marriageable woman (frequently only a child) might not even know her future husband before marriage. In many cases, remarriages were governed by the rules of levirate or sororate and often also of inheritance. Marriage necessarily involved cohabitation, with the natural consequence of procreation. Children came as they came (or as they were given by God or by ancestral spirits); women did not count them. The number of offspring was limited only by natural conditions and by spacing of births, mostly through abstinence for a prescribed long period after birth and prolonged breastfeeding that might last until a certain determined stage of child development. Though abstinence and breastfeeding were in the interest of mothers and their children, whether or not and how long she would abstain or breastfeed were not matters about which a woman could decide. Certainly, spacing effectively limited fertility and family size; however, it was never perceived as a measure through which fertility could be controlled but rather as a natural way of life, the sole attitude, behavior, and conduct that should be assumed in the given situation. In the traditional system, the individual did not "control" fertility or harbor any thoughts of an ideal family size (in numerical terms); the system's "built-in" ideal family size and fertility control prevailed.

Nonetheless, as a society becomes increasingly modern, individuals gain a greater role in selecting their mates or the choice may be entirely theirs. They are also freer to break up a marriage and to remarry. Cohabitation does not necessarily involve procreation if birth control is used. Couples may postpone their first birth until a time when they expect to be better off and in a position to raise children. They usually have relatively clear ideas about how many children they want (albeit such plans may be flexible), and with the help of modern contraception, they can achieve not only the planned family size but also the preferred spacing between births, or they can stop bearing children altogether. The birth is basically elective, the result of decisionmaking by the individual or by the couples jointly.

The Demand for Children: Desires and Expectations

It has generally been accepted that information on desired family size and on trends in the number of children wanted by women is useful for the design of policy instruments aimed at altering the patterns and course of fertility. The statistics upon which discussions in this and subsequent sections of this chapter are based were gathered in the World Fertility Survey (WFS 1984), in surveys of knowledge, attitudes, and practice (KAP) of family planning, and in demographic and health surveys.

Concepts

Though there is certain inconsistency in the various surveys and in use of the terminology, basically two kinds of questions are asked.[1] One group of questions inquires about the desire for future birth(s), asking whether or not the respondent wants more children and, if she wants more, how many more. By adding the additional number of children wanted to the number of living children, the total number of children wanted (or desired family size) can be obtained.

The term "desired family size" implies realistic desires; in other words, it is presupposed that respondents intend to have the number of children stated and implicitly assume not only present conditions (for example, concerning knowledge and the practice of birth control) but also a foreseeable course of future family life that can be expected under normal circumstances. As is the case with the WFS surveys, however, such questions are usually asked of currently married and "fecund" women. In WFS terminology, "fecund" women excludes those with a fertility impairment but includes women who have been sterilized for contraceptive purposes. The latter category, and women who "want no more children," constitute those whose additional number of children wanted is zero.

A different aspect of the attitudes toward family size may be approached through other kinds of questions relevant to the cognate ideas of "ideal" or "desired" family sizes. These terms do not necessarily imply that respondents intend to realize them or can do so. Questions in this group may address the opinions rather than the intentions of the respondents, usually under certain specified conditions. They may relate to the respondents or to others and may be formulated in a prospective or retrospective manner.

In the WFS practice, the question concerning ideal or desired family size ("If you could choose exactly the number of children to have in your whole life, how many children would that be?") was put to all women because everyone may have an opinion about the ideal number of children to have. Consequently, by being asked of all women, the WFS measure of desired family size or its equivalent, the number of "total children desired," expresses less a realistic demand for children than the prevailing social values or some kind of broader public opinion molded not only by social norms but also by the lifetime experiences of the older respondents and the expectations of younger women.

In developed countries, the reliability of data relevant to attitudes toward and preferences regarding childbearing and family size is not contested; only the value of these attitudes for forecasting actual future fertility is sometimes called into question. Even though individual ideals and plans may change considerably, a generation's attitudes remain remarkably constant during its life, and its average desires for children are more or less realized. On the other hand, some doubt is cast on similar data originating in developing countries, where not only the validity and value of individual statements but also the utility of summary data is disputed. Questions about reliability and validity of these data arise, first of all, from the respondents' lack of familiarity with the concepts, a phenomenon that has its roots in the culture (that is, in the traditional fertility regulatory system, which does not accommodate individual desires and decisionmaking). In such situations, the questions may confuse the respondents, who may become evasive and reluctant to answer ("not stated" category) or may cause the respondents to give answers that will be categorized as "don't know" and "undecided" (Acsadi 1982).

In a society where a traditional fertility regulatory system prevails or coexists with modern systems, it is relatively easy to elicit an affirmative answer from almost everybody to the question of whether the respondent wants a child sometime in the future. Indeed, as table 11-1 shows, in most Sub-Saharan African countries, at least two-thirds of women questioned wanted to have more children.

There is a widespread tendency among the peoples of Sub-Saharan Africa to attribute to God or some other supernatural power, for example, dead ancestors, the number of children that they have. Thus although the desire for children is widespread and readily articulated, questions put by an interviewer concerning the additional or total number of children that the respondents would like to have may elicit a variety of nonnumerical responses, such as "what God gives," "it is up to God,"

Table 11-1. *Percentage Distribution of Women by Desire for More Children*

Country	Survey year	Wanted more children	Wanted no more children	Undecided	Total	Percentage giving nonnumerical responses of the total
WFS surveys						
Benin	1981–82	74	8	18	100	22
Cameroon	1978	—	3	—	100	26
Côte d'Ivoire	1980–81	91	4	5	100	25
Ghana	1979	78	12	10	100	11
Kenya	1977–78	68	17	15	100	19
Lesotho	1977	84	15	1	100	2
Mauritania	1981	61	11	28	100	31
Nigeria	1981–82	84	5	11	100	43
Senegal	1978	87	8	5	100	29
Sudan (north)	1978–79	77	17	6	100	18
Other surveys						
Botswana	1984	65	33	2	100	—
Chad[a]	1970	65	7	28	100	61
Liberia	1986	75	17	8	100	—
Niger[a]	1970	75	8	17	100	47
Nigeria, southwest	1971	88	8	4	100	45
Nigeria, Ondo	1986	66	23	11	100	—
Zaire[b]	1982	77	19	4	100	67
Zimbabwe	1984	69	24	7	100	—

— Not available
a. Area survey.
b. Area survey. Figures are unwieghted means of urban and rural numbers.
Sources: WFS (1984); United Nations (1987); Benin (1983); Mauritania (1983); Nigeria (1983); WFS standard recode tapes; Acsadi and Johnson-Acsadi (1985); Botswana (1985); Reyna (1975); Liberia (1988); Dankoussou and others (1975); Acsadi (n.d.); Ondo State (1987); Mangani and others (1982); Zimbabwe (1985).

and "as many as possible." As table 11-1 indicates, from one-fifth to two-thirds of respondents in most countries gave nonnumerical answers. Researchers encountered similar situations in other regions but, except for some Asian countries, not as often.

Where the notion prevails that births occur within marriage as a matter of course, the concept of "demand" for children as commonly used may not apply or may exist in the Western cultural sense only when a woman has not borne a child after a reasonable period of exposure to risk or if she has borne fewer than would be expected, given her exposure time. Even then, "demand" may be not for a specified number of children but for the remedy of an abnormal condition. There is no place for individualistic "demand" for children in a traditional society; the "demand" is determined by the relevant components of the fertility regulatory system. Nonetheless, a large proportion of women in Sub-Saharan Africa appear able to specify the number of children that they would prefer to have and even the number of additional children that they have wanted.

The data relevant to the attitudes toward family size are certainly not exempt from errors and distortions as is normally the case with statistics derived from surveys

in developing countries, especially in Sub-Saharan Africa. The main argument, however, that may be brought against their use and utility—that respondents are not familiar with the concepts or cannot even perceive the meaning of the questions—is not acceptable. Perhaps the first and most important step in analyzing the demand for children, in the context of a transitional society in Sub-Saharan Africa, is to identify that portion of the population that has no individual "demand" but represents a demand determined by the traditions and the portion that has an individual "demand."

The Desire to Cease Child-Bearing

The prevalence among women of a desire to cease child-bearing, as determined from KAP surveys, has been used as a barometer of the need for contraceptive supplies and services, particularly where large fractions of the respondents who expressed this preference were not using a contraceptive.

The two demographic variables examined for their possible relationship to desire for no more children are age of the woman and the number of living children that she had at the time of the inquiry. In addition, the prevalence of this preference and of indecision about expressing one are seen in relation to the woman's level of educational attainment, her place of residence, and her place of work since marriage. Another demographic factor found to be associated with a woman's desire to cease childbearing is the number of living sons or daughters that she has. In the countries of Sub-Saharan Africa for which data are presented here, however, percentages of total respondents who did not want to have more children are so consistently small, and the desire for additional children is so general, that sex preference is probably not a major determining factor in the demand for children.

WFS surveys in ten Sub-Saharan African countries (table 11-1) revealed that few women wanted no more children (from 3–5 percent in Cameroon, Côte d'Ivoire, and Nigeria to 17 percent in Kenya and Sudan. Similarly, few women were undecided above having more children (from 1 percent in Lesotho to 28 percent in Mauritania).

Other surveys carried out in Botswana, Chad, Liberia, Niger, Nigeria, Zaire, and Zimbabwe also disclosed that relatively few women of reproductive age wanted to cease childbearing altogether, the range being from 7 percent in Chad to 33 percent in Botswana. These surveys are not strictly comparable with the WFS inquiries or with each other. Nonetheless, they do tend to confirm a widespread desire to continue having children or a reticence on the part of many African women either to eschew further childbearing or to articulate such a desire. In contrast, according to WFS surveys (WFS 1984), the wish not to have more children was expressed by about one- to two-thirds of women (32 to 63 percent) in thirteen countries of Latin America and the Caribbean, by 30 to 72 percent in eleven countries of South and East Asia and the Pacific, by about every second woman in three North African countries (42 to 54 percent) and also by large proportions (19 to 59 percent) of women in four countries in West Asia.

Fertility preferences are conditioned by many factors, as noted earlier. From the data in table 11-2, it is evident that younger women do not wish to stop having children. Indeed, except in Botswana and Zimbabwe, not until the age group 40–44 years did as many as one-third of the women state this preference. With minor exceptions, the wish to have no more children increases in prevalence with the age of the woman.

The increasing prevalence of the desire to cease childbearing may be due, at least in part, to the relationship between age and the number of living children. It may

Table 11-2. *Percentages of Women Wanting No More Children or Undecided, by Age*

Country	<20	20–24	25–29	30–34	35–39	40–44	45+	Total
				Wanted no more children				
WFS surveys								
Benin	2	1	4	8	14	26	38	8
Côte d'Ivoire	2	2	2	5	9	14	13	4
Ghana	0	3	5	11	22	34	39	12
Kenya	2	4	11	19	26	40	42	17
Lesotho	1	6	12	23	28	30	27	15
Nigeria	2	1	2	5	5	13	21	4
Senegal	1	3	2	14	28	31	40	8
Sudan (north)	2	8	13	20	27	29	35	17
Other surveys								
Botswana	14	19	24	37	47	56	71	33
Liberia	1	7	9	20	25	35	48	17
Zimbabwe	8	4	10	19	42	73	82	25
				Undecided				
WFS surveys								
Côte d'Ivoire	3	3	6	7	7	6	10	5
Ghana	3	5	8	12	18	17	15	10
Kenya	6	8	15	19	23	21	23	15
Lesotho	1	1	0	1	1	1	3	1
Liberia	10	5	7	9	10	8	5	8
Nigeria	6	5	11	11	18	19	29	11
Senegal	2	3	7	6	4	31	20	5
Sudan (north)	4	4	6	6	8	6	8	6

Note: Data exclude currently unmarried or infecund women and a small number of "not stated" cases. In Senegal, only pregnant women were queried about their attitudes.

Sources: WFS standard recode tapes; Benin (1983); Nigeria (1983); Botswana (1985); Liberia (1988); Zimbabwe (1985).

also be attributable, however, to the fact that, in some societies, many older women consider themselves beyond the age where childbearing is proper, for example, if a daughter is married, if a married son is sharing the living quarters, or if the woman has a grandchild (Molnos 1973; Okediji and others 1976). Conversely, women over age 30 were more indecisive than younger ones about a preference for more children, in part because they were loath to flaunt tradition and in part because the question appeared obtuse.

To a considerable extent in these countries, the desire for more children depends upon the number of children that the woman has. With a few minor exceptions, the percentage wanting no more increases with the rise in effective family size.[2] Among the countries for which statistics are available (table 11-3), there were pronounced differences in the incidence of indecision about wanting more children. Indecision is more common among women who have many children.

In the six countries for which data are available, educational attainment is not found to be consistently related to desire for no more children (table 11-4). This is not remarkable, however, as the better educated women in Sub-Saharan Africa are younger and thus have achieved comparatively smaller families. Looking only at women with five surviving children in western Nigeria, researchers found a positive relationship: 24 percent of illiterate women wanted no more children, as contrasted with 33 percent of women with primary education and 55 percent of women with secondary education (Okediji and others 1976).

Place of residence, however, has a more consistent influence upon wanting no more children than do the other socioeconomic variables examined here (table 11-4). Urban life evidently summarizes more succinctly the effect of modernization in the Sub-Saharan African context than do the other explanatory variables. Except in Côte d'Ivoire, the wish to terminate childbearing was

Table 11-3. *Percentages of Women Wanting No More Children or Undecided, by Number of Living Children*

Country	Number of living children							
	0	1	2	3	4	5	6	7+
	Wanted no more children							
WFS surveys								
Benin	0	1	3	6	10	12	20	29
Cameroon	1	2	4	4	3	8	9	27
Côte d'Ivoire	0	1	2	3	3	6	11	19
Ghana	1	1	3	6	15	19	35	49
Kenya	2	1	4	7	16	18	25	45
Lesotho	0	3	8	15	26	42	45	57
Nigeria	4	2	2	4	5	7	5	8[a]
Mauritania	3	4	7	11	13	16	15	23
Senegal	0	2	1	1	5	8	18	40
Sudan (north)	1	4	8	11	17	22	32	41
Other surveys								
Botswana	4	15	24	30	40	41	54	57[a]
Liberia	2	2	6	10	23	33	57[b]	—
Zimbabwe	2	6	12	13	27	31	44	56[a]
	Undecided							
WFS surveys								
Côte d'Ivoire	3	2	4	5	7	6	11	9[a]
Ghana	2	5	9	11	13	19	16	25[a]
Kenya	4	7	10	13	17	24	27	21[a]
Lesotho	1	1	1	1	0	1	1	4[a]
Liberia	4	6	7	9	11	9	8[b]	—
Nigeria	5	6	11	12	15	13	16	21[a]
Senegal	3	3	3	8	5	12	9	18
Sudan (north)	3	3	6	7	7	9	6	9[a]

— Not available.

Note: Data exclude currently unmarried or infecund women and a small number of "not stated" cases. In Senegal, only pregnant women were queried about their attitudes.

a. Seven children alive.

b. Six or more children alive.

Sources: United Nations (1987); WFS standard recode tapes; Benin (1983); Nigeria (1983); Botswana (1985); Liberia (1988); Zimbabwe (1985).

Table 11-4. *Percentages of Women Wanting No More Children by Wife's Education, Residence, and Place of Work since Marriage*

Wife's education, residence, place of work	Côte d'Ivoire	Ghana	Kenya	Lesotho	Senegal	Sudan (north)
Wife's education						
No schooling	4	12	16	15	8	16
1–3 years	2	15	24	16	(2)	21
4–6 years	4	13	16	15	(17)	20
7+ years	6	10	15	15	(0)	22
Residence						
Major urban	5	17	18	—	12	29
Other urban	5	12	16	19	8	22
Rural	4	11	17	15	7	14
Workplace						
Family farm	4	11	(33)	(0)	7	13
Other farm	5	14	23	(26)	(25)	12
At home	7	14	20	18	(17)	15
Away from home	5	13	24	24	(13)	17
Didn't work	4	5	16	13	7	18
Total	4	12	17	15	8	17

— Not applicable.
Note: Percentages in parentheses are based on fewer than 50 cases. Data exclude currently unmarried or infecund women and a small number of "not stated" cases (between 1 and 28). In Senegal, only pregnant women are included.
Source: WFS standard recode tapes.

in all cases more widespread in major urban centers than in "other urban" communities and, except in Kenya, where there was almost no difference, more prevalent in "other urban" areas than in rural areas.

Whether a woman works and the setting in which she works can influence the extent to which she finds childbearing convenient or inconvenient. Except in the Sudan, the wish to have no more children was voiced with relatively greater frequency among "working" women than among "nonworking" women. That no pattern was consistent in respect to place of work may be attributed to several factors, for example, the compatibility of women's work with fertility; the varying importance of women's roles as family farmer or hired laborer; whether she lived in a nuclear or extended family household; differences among the groups in composition by age, level of education, and achieved family size; and intercountry incomparability of definitions of work and place of work.

Additional Children Desired

Clearly, desire for additional children is widely prevalent among women in these countries. Excluding those who did not want more children, in five of the six countries listed in table 11-5, women who gave numerical responses most often wanted two children in addition to those they already had. In Côte d'Ivoire, however, five additional children was the most frequent answer. Sim-

ilarly, in Senegal, where only pregnant women were asked this question, four and five more children were preferred by almost as many women as wanted two more. Use of the plural in the question "How many more children do you want to have?" may have exerted some influence on the responses, at least with respect to women's preference for two more children rather than for one additional child.

The distribution of women by the number of children that they said they wanted in addition to the number living shows a marked digit preference. In addition to the zero-five digit preference, the preference for even numbers over odd ones (except five) is also noticeable. Disregarding these anomalies, the percentages more or less consistently decrease from two additional children onward, so that relatively few women want an unrealistically large number of additional children, lending some credence to the responses.

The relative trustworthiness of responses relevant to additional children desired, which can be considered as indicators of demand for children—at least by those who gave numerical answers—also appears from the negative association with the number of living children. With the exception of some means that were computed from too few cases, the mean number of additional children desired decreases consistently with an increase in the number living (figure 11-1). There are great differences among these countries, however, in the demand for children. Although the range of the mean

Table 11-5. *Percentage Distribution of Women by Additional Children Wanted*

Additional children wanted	Côte d'Ivoire	Ghana	Kenya	Lesotho	Senegal	Sudan (north)
0	5.4	14.6	22.8	15.7	9.6	19.3
1	6.9	14.7	7.8	14.4	5.7	12.4
2	13.5	24.4	16.3	20.5	15.5	18.5
3	13.3	18.8	13.2	14.5	11.6	14.9
4	12.0	13.4	13.2	14.0	15.3	12.5
5	15.4	5.1	8.6	7.0	14.6	7.9
6	9.8	4.9	6.8	5.8	6.6	4.6
7	4.3	1.3	1.8	1.8	4.3	3.0
8	5.3	1.2	2.4	1.5	5.2	1.7
9	2.5	0.7	0.6	0.5	2.3	0.5
10	10.3	0.9	4.8	3.5	7.5	3.6
11 +	1.5	0.3	1.6	0.5	1.7	1.0
Total	100.0	100.0	100.0	100.0	100.0	100.0
N	3,381	3,243	3,786	2,576	439	2,169

Note: Data exclude unmarried or infecund women. Women who gave a numerical answer are included, as are those who wanted no more children or were sterilized for contraceptive purposes. In Senegal, only pregnant women are included.
Source: WFS standard recode tapes.

number of additional children desired by women at different effective parities is very wide in Sub-Saharan Africa, it is well above the range of demand for children in eight Asian and eight Latin American and Caribbean countries.[3] It should be noted that the range of the mean number of additional children desired at different effective parities is almost as wide in Asia as in Sub-Saharan Africa, whereas Latin America and the Caribbean seem to be more homogeneous with respect to the demand for additional children.[4]

There is little difference in the mean wanted family size between childless women and those who have only one living child in each of seven countries (table 11-6). In each country, however, wanted family size increases notably with each successive parity above the third.

The demand for children begins to weaken only after women have at least four, five, or six living children. Though the proportion of women who want no more children becomes considerable after seven or eight living children (see table 11-3), the mean wanted family size surpasses the number of living children by one or two. Cell sizes at these parities are too small to permit generalizations, but it seems that, in many Sub-Saharan African countries, the desire for more children begins to subside only after there are eight living children. The more detailed WFS data, however, suggest that, in the more traditional societies or the more traditionalist segments of these populations, among women with six or more living children the wish to have additional children may depend little on the number of children living, and wanted family size in this range may therefore rise with each additional living child.

In general, in the Sub-Saharan African countries for which data are available, women on average wanted nearly as many again or even more children than they already had (table 11-7). The highest mean numbers of additional children desired were reported in West Africa, but even in southern African countries, where the mean numbers of additional children desired were lowest, the demand was for about as many or more children as actual family size.

In a large sample of non-African countries (Lightbourne and MacDonald 1982), there was not one in which the women's desires even approached the expressed wishes of African women for additional children desired. In seventeen Asian, Latin American, and Caribbean countries, the difference between the mean wanted family size and the mean number of children living varied between 0.4 and 2.0. In summary, if the result of these comparisons can be generalized, it seems that, indeed, the demand for children among all regions of the world is greatest in Sub-Saharan Africa.

The Desire for Children

As is evident from the preceding discussion, the total number of children desired by a woman (that is, desired family size) in Sub-Saharan Africa in general is higher than the number of living children and the number of additional children desired combined (that is, wanted family size). The WFS and Westinghouse surveys revealed a general desire for large families, ranging from 6.1 to 8.7 children (see table 11-7), which is consistent with the results of earlier surveys (including Sierra Leone,

Figure 11-1. *Mean Number of Additional Children Desired, by Number of Their Living Children*

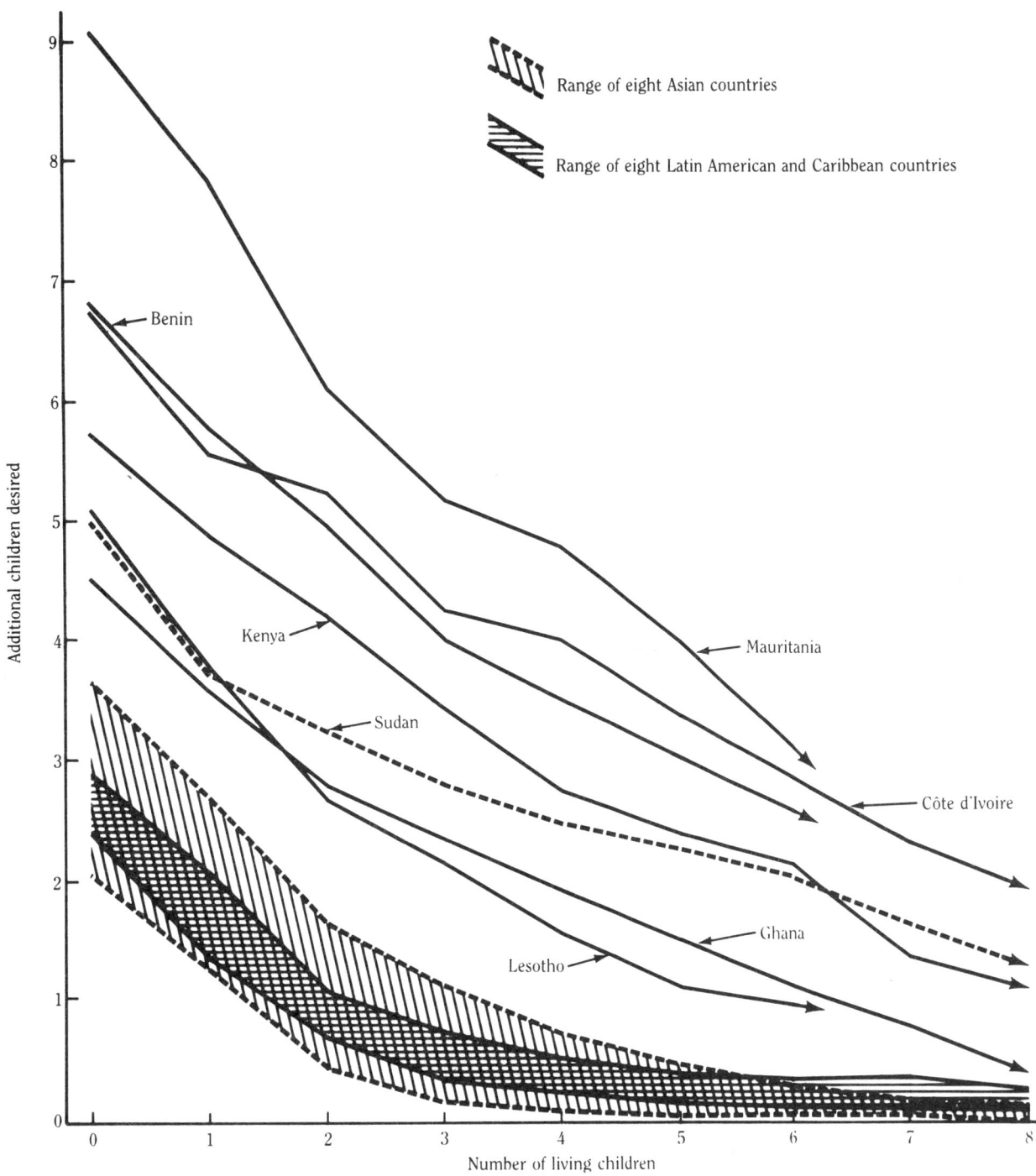

Sources: WFS standard recode tapes; Lightbourne and MacDonald (1982).

Table 11-6. *Mean Wanted Family Size by Number of Living Children*

Number of living children	Côte d'Ivoire	Ghana	Kenya	Lesotho	Nigeria	Senegal	Sudan (north)
0	6.8	4.6	5.8	5.2	7.5	6.3	5.1
1	6.6	4.6	5.9	4.8	7.3	7.0	4.8
2	7.3	4.9	6.3	4.7	7.5	6.6	5.3
3	7.3	5.4	6.5	5.2	8.0	6.6	5.8
4	8.1	5.9	6.8	5.6	8.4	6.8	6.5
5	8.4	6.5	7.4	6.1	8.9	(6.9)	7.3
6	8.9	7.1	8.2	7.0	9.7	(8.1)	8.1
7	9.3	7.8	8.4	7.6	11.0	(7.6)	8.7
8	10.0	8.4	9.1	8.6	9.8	(8.0)	9.3

Note: Data exclude unmarried or infecund women. Figures in parentheses are based on fewer than 50 cases. In Senegal, only pregnant women are included.

Sources: WFS standard recode tapes; Nigeria (1984).

1969–70; rural Kenya, 1966; Zaire, 1973–76; and several Nigerian surveys in 1965–66, 1967, 1971–73, 1974). Except in three West Asian countries (Jordan, Syria, and Yemen), desired family size varied from 3.2 to 4.9 children in twenty-five developing countries in other regions (figure 11-2), well below levels in Sub-Saharan Africa (United Nations 1987).

It is difficult to predict whether family size preferences will be reduced in Sub-Saharan Africa and, if so, when. Using expectation of life at birth as a proxy for level of development (with due regard for its inability to reflect all components of modernization) and for infant mortality, which is one of its main components, we may hypothesize that, concomitantly or in tandem with modernization, the demand among Sub-Saharan African couples for large families will lessen. But because the two variables are only very loosely associated,

a change in one will not necessarily bring a change in the other.

As figure 11-2 shows, if life expectancy can be regarded as a proxy variable for socioeconomic development, then development appears to have little direct effect on the desire for children. It does not matter whether expectation of life at birth is low or high, except in the Sub-Saharan African and West Asian countries. Desired family size is in the range of three to five children in all countries, and there is no hint of any association between the two variables. The marks representing Sub-Saharan African countries are clustered in the upper left corner of the figure, and thus there is a very slight indication of a tendency toward decreasing ideal family size, as the arrow on the graph shows. The arrow points toward the zone of desired family size of three to five children and suggests that, with further

Table 11-7. *Mean Number of Children Living, Additionally Desired, Total Wanted, Desired, and Ever Born to Women Aged 40–44*

Country	Living	Additional wanted	Total wanted	Total desired	Ever born to women aged 40–44
Benin	2.5	4.4	6.9	7.5	6.1
Botswana	3.1	2.8	5.9	—	6.4
Cameroon	—	—	6.1	8.0	5.2
Côte d'Ivoire	2.8	4.2	7.0	8.5	6.7
Ghana	2.9	2.7	5.6	6.1	6.1
Kenya	3.7	3.2	6.9	7.2	7.6
Lesotho	2.2	3.1	5.3	6.0	5.3
Liberia	—	—	—	6.5	6.9
Mauritania	3.1	3.7	6.8	8.7	5.9
Nigeria	2.5	5.2	7.7	8.4	5.2
Senegal	2.4	4.4	6.8	8.4	6.8
Sudan (north)	3.4	3.0	6.4	6.4	6.2
Zimbabwe	3.4	2.6	6.0	—	7.0

— Not available.

Sources: WFS standard recode tapes; WFS (1984); Botswana (1985); Liberia (1988); Zimbabwe (1985). Cleland and Hobcraft (1985).

Figure 11-2. *Mean Desired Family Size by Expectation of Life at Birth*

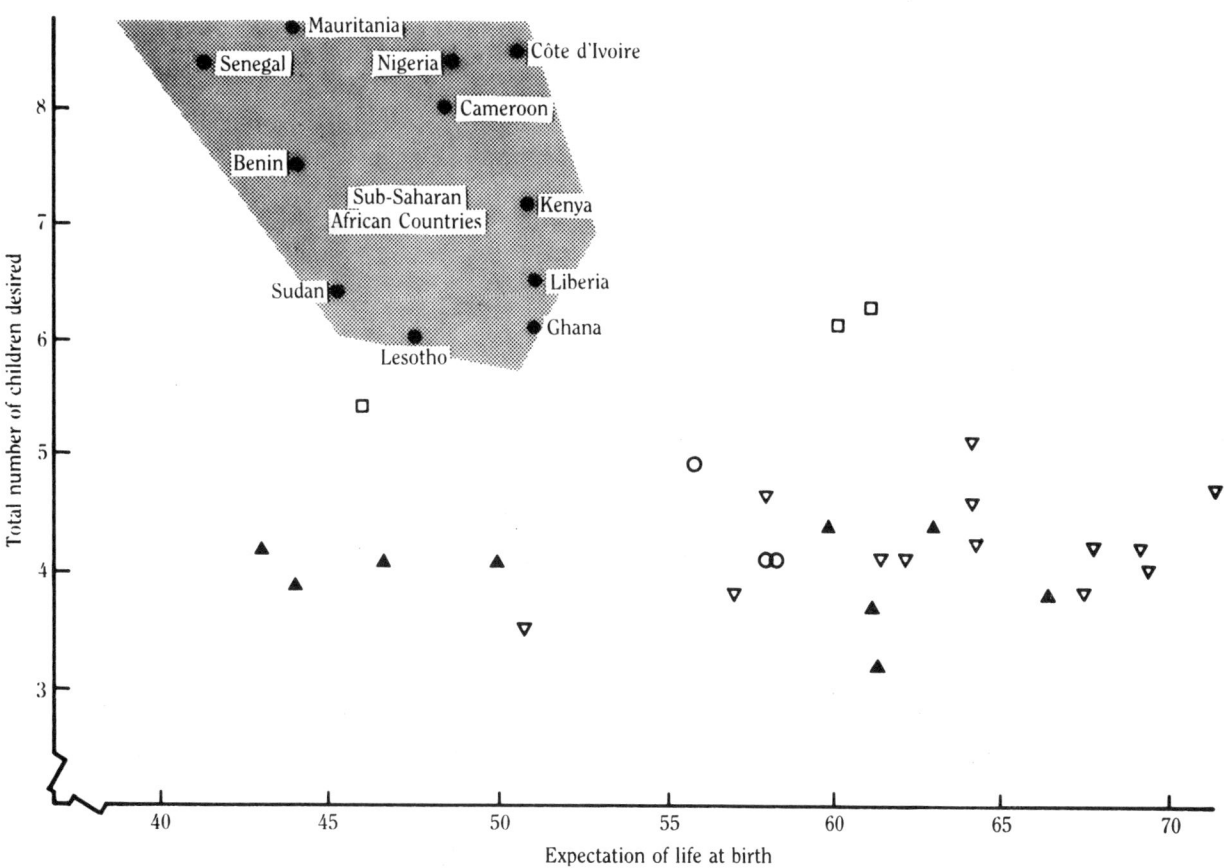

Key: ● Sub-Saharan Africa; ○ North Africa; □ Western Asia; ▲ other parts of Asia; ▽ Latin America and Caribbean.

development (represented by an increase in life expectancy to a level of 55–60 years), the ideal family size may decrease to this level.

Although recent surveys permit such conjecture, they do not support it sufficiently. The regional differences in family size preferences reflect not only differences in modernization but also in historical circumstances, including sociocultural and political conditions. Furthermore, the introduction of a national family planning program in most Asian countries and in many Latin American and Caribbean countries either induced or precipitated the alteration of family size norms and preferences. Such programs have had little impact in Sub-Saharan Africa.

If we compare the reported large family size desired by women in Sub-Saharan Africa with the preferences for considerably smaller families in Asia and Latin America, it is tempting to hypothesize that Sub-Saharan Africa perhaps represents an earlier stage in the demographic transition and that, consequently, the desire

for children will decline soon to the level observed in most other developing countries. In view of the earlier findings, however, there seems to be less evidence to support this hypothesis than an equally possible one, namely, that family size preferences are culture-bound phenomena, that Sub-Saharan African cultures nurture a desire for a particularly large family in the absence of moderating interventions, and that such a phenomenon may resist socioeconomic changes for a long while.

On the basis of these interregional comparisons, it appears that the prospect for a modification of family size ideals in the short run is bleak, though the possibility for such changes cannot be excluded either. It is likely that, with further development and loosening of the grip of the traditional system, more and more women will have a notion as to the "desired" family size that they individually wish to realize. Greater changes, however, cannot be reasonably expected without pronounced alterations in the cultural determinants of family size ideals.

Some Factors Affecting the Desire for Children

With a few minor deviations due possibly to sampling errors, available data show that mean number of children desired increases with the woman's age (table 11-8) as it does in many other developing countries (Lightbourne and MacDonald 1982). This increase does not necessarily indicate a trend among younger women toward a desire for fewer children because women tend to rationalize the number that they have or to state slightly more than they have as the number that they want or consider desirable, and the number that they have is positively associated with their age.

Where desired family size is an individual preference more or less consciously reached, it may be influenced not only by demographic traits but also by other personal attributes as well as by the sociocultural and economic environment. How a woman's education influences her desired family size depends upon a variety of factors, including the general level of education in her community or country (Cochrane 1979; United Nations 1983). Illiteracy is still widespread throughout most of Sub-Saharan Africa. Among the eight countries listed in table 11-8 for which data are available, proportions of the total samples of women who had had no schooling ranged from an anomalous 8 percent in Lesotho to more than 80 percent in Sudan, Senegal, and Mauritania. A sizable proportion of the women had had seven or more

years schooling only in Ghana, Lesotho, and Kenya (from 24 to 38 percent).

In general, desired family size was lowest in the three countries in which the largest fractions of women had completed seven or more years schooling and in Sudan. The negative association of education with desired family size in these countries may reflect several factors. The number of children desired increases with the age of women. At the same time, illiteracy ("no schooling") is much more prevalent among older than younger women. It may also be noted that the gap in desired family size between the women with no schooling and those with seven or more years does not appear to be closely related to their aggregate level of education.

Urban life is generally associated with ideas and patterns of behavior that are more modern than those found among rural populations. Urban inhabitants are usually better educated than rural people; in towns and cities new ideas are comparatively more easily disseminated by the more sophisticated means of communication found there; controls of family and clan are usually weaker; and the power of culture as a regulatory force is more often less pervasive. There are great differences in the definition and quality of "urban," however, and these disparities may be of consequence for a comparative assessment of demand for children.

Percentages of women living in major or "other" urban places in eight African WFS surveys for which data

Table 11-8. *Mean Desired Family Size, by Age, Wife's Education, and Residence*

Age, wife's education, residence	Côte d'Ivoire	Ghana	Kenya	Lesotho	Liberia	Mauritania	Senegal	Sudan (north)
Age								
–19	7.5	4.8	5.8	5.6	5.2	8.4	7.5	5.4
20–24	7.8	5.0	6.1	5.4	5.5	8.5	7.5	5.3
25–29	8.2	5.4	6.5	5.5	5.9	8.8	8.1	6.0
30–34	8.7	6.2	7.2	5.9	6.2	9.3	8.6	6.9
35–39	9.1	6.8	8.0	6.5	6.9	10.1	8.5	7.1
40–44	9.3	7.2	8.1	6.8	7.4	9.5	8.7	7.2
45–49	9.4	7.3	8.6[a]	6.9	7.5	10.0[a]	8.6	6.7
Wife's education								
0 years	8.7	6.6	7.6	6.6	—	9.5[b]	8.4	6.6
1–3 years	8.0	5.6	6.9	6.5	—	} 8.4[b]	6.7	5.9
4–6 years	7.2	5.5	6.4	6.0	—		4.9	5.1
7–9 years	6.5	4.9	6.0	5.5	—	} 6.5[b]	} 5.2[c]	4.9
10+ years	5.6	4.7	5.1	4.7	—			4.5
Residence								
Major urban	7.1	5.1	5.5	} 5.3	} 4.5	} 9.4	6.4	5.6
Other urban	7.6	5.4	5.8				6.9	6.1
Rural	8.9	6.0	6.9	6.0	5.9	9.1	8.7	6.5

—Not available.

a. Includes wives 50 years of age.

b. The education groups for Mauritania are defined as: cannot read, less than six years, and six or more years.

c. Seven or more years; mean calculated from a sample of fourteen women.

Sources: WFS standard recode tapes; Liberia (1988); Mauritania (1983).

on desired family size by residence are available vary greatly. Across countries, the mean number of children desired is unrelated to the level of urbanization. Côte d'Ivoire, for example, has both one of the most urbanized populations and one of the largest mean desired family sizes. Within each of these countries except Mauritania, however, the number of children desired is inversely proportional to the degree of urbanization of the woman's place of residence (table 11-8). The differences between urban and rural women in mean total number of children desired are considerable. This result, however, may represent not the relaxation of traditionalism in the large cities but ethnic differences because the population of a city or town ordinarily has a disproportionate number of a single ethnic group. Such may be the case in Mauritania, where, according to preliminary data, the mean number of children desired was somewhat lower in the two rural strata of the sample than in the stratum that consisted of Nouakchott and other urban places (Mauritania 1983). A model constructed for twenty-two countries that controlled age and age at first union showed that education affects fertility preferences independently of urban-rural residence but that, on average, the effect is somewhat greater in rural areas than in urban ones (United Nations 1983). Among countries, however, the pattern varied greatly: in both Kenya and Lesotho—the two African countries included in the analysis—the effect of education was more pronounced in urban areas than in rural ones, with both a greater effect and a wider rural-urban disparity in Lesotho than in Kenya.

To reevaluate the effect of education, replicated series of analysis of variance (ANOVA) and multiple classification analysis (MCA) were carried out using the WFS standard recode tapes for six Sub-Saharan African countries. The replicated model used in the United Nations study served as a basis for analyzing the relationship between education and desires regarding family size, with the difference that education was subdivided into four rather

than five groups because two of the samples included very few women who could have been classified as having ten or more years of education.

Table 11-9 presents the results of this analysis. It includes the beta values, which, though not comparable among the countries, illuminate the relationship in each individual country. When adjusted for age at first marriage and the age of the respondent, the influence of education on desired family size diminishes, an indication that part of the educational differential is due to differentials by age and age at marriage. The results of the analysis of the data from the six African surveys correspond to the findings of the U.N. study inasmuch as the influence of education on desired family size appears to be weaker after adjustment. The effect of education on the number of children desired, however, is still considerable.

The pattern of the relationship makes it appear that, except in Lesotho, there is in each country a sizable difference in the number of total children desired between women who never attended school and those who had one to three years of schooling. In Senegal, education seems to have the greatest reducing effect on the family size desired by those with four to six years of schooling, whereas in Ghana and Kenya, the same amount of education has no more impact; in effect it has somewhat less than completion of one to three years of schooling. On the other hand, in these two countries as well as in Côte d'Ivoire, Lesotho, and Sudan, completion of seven or more years of education seems to be crucial from the viewpoint of the desired family size.

The differences among countries in the amount by which a given level of schooling lowers desired family size may be attributed, at least in part, to the importance people attach to education and to certain educational levels; to the content of the educational process at different levels; and to the status that a particular level of educational attainment confers upon a woman. In gen-

Table 11-9. *Effect of Wife's Education on Desired Family Size: Results of Multiple Classification Analysis*

Years of schooling	Côte d'Ivoire	Ghana	Kenya	Lesotho	Senegal	Sudan (north)
Overall mean	8.37	6.03	7.18	5.96	8.28	6.32
			Deviations adjusted for independents and covariates			
Education						
No schooling	0.24	0.46	0.34	0.43	0.20	0.18
1–3 years	−0.15	−0.19	−0.26	0.32	−0.95	−0.20
4–6 years	−0.85	−0.13	−0.25	0.02	−2.75	−0.85
7+ years	−1.97	−0.74	−0.52	−0.34	−1.75	−1.12
Beta	0.18	0.25	0.12	0.09	0.18	0.13
Multiple R^2	0.076	0.216	0.084	0.063	0.057	0.073

Note: Dependent variable: number of total children desired; factor: wife's education in four groups; covariates: age at first marriage, age in completed years. Significance of F (joint effect): 0.000.
Source: WFS standard recode tapes.

eral, women who have not attended school are more traditional-minded than those who have obtained some education; therefore the former nurture traditional ideas for a large family and the latter tend to form individual ideas about the definitive, and smaller, family size. Depending on the cultural features, the educational system, and the level of general education, the effect of education on individual fertility preferences may also be rather gradual, as in Côte d'Ivoire or Sudan, or the pattern of the relationship may be somewhat erratic at certain points and may coincide with the particular conditions relevant to education in a country, as the examples of Ghana, Kenya, Lesotho, and Senegal suggest.

Although the moderating effect of education on the number of children desired is obvious in each of the six countries investigated, this influence should not be overestimated. The effect that may be attributed to education after eliminating the effect due to age and age at marriage is rather small; even women with seven or more years of schooling desire a completed family of between 5.2 and 6.7 children! The beta values and the multiple R^2 values for each country also show that education and the covariates explain, except perhaps in the case of Ghana, only a very small proportion of the variation in the number of children desired by women in these countries.

To examine the relationship between urban-rural residence and desired family size, the model was expanded to include, as another factor, the domicile of the respondents (in three groups: major urban, other urban, and rural places; except in Lesotho, where only two—

urban and rural—categories were used). Education was kept in the model, in order to clarify the effect of both residence and education adjusted for each other. The model was further expanded by including the number of living children as a variable. As discussed earlier, this is highly relevant to desired family size, and it was changed by replacing age at first marriage with the variable years since first marriage.

The results of this second series of analyses appear in table 11-10. If the adjusted deviations are compared with those in table 11-9, it appears that with the inclusion of residence and the number of living children, except for Lesotho and Kenya, the influence of education upon desired family size further weakens. The direction of the effect of education on the desired family size remains consistent in all countries, however, and there is still a sizable difference in the expressed desires between uneducated and highly educated women (0.8 to 1.7 children).

The differences between the mean numbers of children desired by urban and rural women also decrease when the deviations are adjusted for education and for the three covariates (from the range of 0.7–1.9 to 0.4–1.6), and the direction of the effect remains the same. Like education, residence—through what it represents (occupations, housing and living conditions, exposure to mass media, and so forth)—has an impact on family size preferences. The differences in desired family size appear not only between the major urban and rural places but—surprisingly, in view of the uncertainties and inconsistencies in the definition "urban" and the often rural characteristics of some "other urban" set-

Table 11-10. *Effects of Wife's Education and Residence on Desired Family Size: Results of Multiple Classification Analysis*

Wife's education and residence	Côte d'Ivoire	Ghana	Kenya	Lesotho	Senegal	Sudan (north)
Overall mean	8.37	6.03	7.18	5.96	8.28	6.32
Deviations adjusted for independents and covariates						
Education						
No schooling	0.19	0.43	0.39	0.48	0.12	0.15
1–3 years	−0.20	−0.25	−0.36	0.36	−0.41	−0.24
4–6 years	−0.75	−0.25	−0.35	0.00	−1.94	−0.78
7+ years	−1.47	−0.66	−0.50	−0.34	−1.00	−0.76
Beta	0.14	0.22	0.13	0.10	0.12	0.11
Residence						
Major urban	−1.00	−0.25	−0.79	—	−1.18	−0.57
Other urban	−0.53	−0.19	−0.68	−0.50	−0.83	−0.15
Rural	0.42	0.11	0.10	0.04	0.39	0.13
Beta	0.18	0.07	0.09	0.06	0.19	0.08
Multiple R^2	0.154	0.325	0.129	0.105	0.089	0.123

—Not applicable.

Note: Dependent variable: number of total children desired; factors: wife's education in four groups, type of place of residence; covariates: age in completed years, years since first marriage, number of living children. Significance of F (joint effect): 0.000.

Source: WFS standard record tapes.

tlements—also between the "other urban" and rural places.

This analysis shows that education and urban-rural residence individually affect desired family size and that the effects are comparable. The adjusted means of the number of children desired by women living in major urban areas are by 0.3 to 1.2 children lower than the overall mean, whereas that of the best-educated women is lower by 0.3 to 1.5. With regard to the beta values, the moderating influence of urban life appears to be more important than that of education in Côte d'Ivoire and Senegal; in the other countries—especially in Ghana—the effect of education is stronger. Thus both education and urbanization have an effect on desired family size, and they may be considered as parts of the modernization process that is slowly changing the traditional system and its values with respect to the demand for children.

Desired Family Size, Effective Fertility, and Contraceptive Use

Variations among Sub-Saharan African countries in the demographic factors of age and number of living children partly explain the differences among them in desired family size. Furthermore, both desired family size and effective family size have been found to influence the frequency and pattern of contraceptive use (United Nations 1981).

As the populations of these countries subscribe less and less to the traditional means of regulating family size, a corollary of the modernizing trend, contraceptive use may become the preference of increasing numbers of women. Logic would dictate that women who have as many children as they want or more would seek a means of preventing further births and that those who have fewer than they desire, but who want their additional children at preferred intervals (not achieved by abstinence or prolonged breastfeeding), would adopt a contraceptive.

In six WFS surveys carried out in Sub-Saharan African countries, very few respondents desired fewer children than they had, by far the largest percentage (8.9) being in Sudan. In the other five countries, the proportion of such women varied between 0.5 (Côte d'Ivoire) and 3.8 percent (Kenya). The percentages of women who were satisfied with the number of children they had and desired exactly the same family size was somewhat higher; it ranged from 3.0 in Senegal to 10.1 in Kenya. The overwhelming sentiment expressed by the great majority of respondents was a desire for more children than were living (from 63 to 86 percent).

Acknowledgments by respondents that they had more children than they desired rose in prevalence as effective family size increased (table 11-11). Women do not frequently acknowledge anywhere, and especially not in Sub-Saharan Africa, that they have more children than they desire, as this confession might be interpreted as expressing a dislike of one or more of their children. Therefore, in a culturally more traditional country, such as Côte d'Ivoire, very few women expressed the view that, if they could, they would have a smaller family than they had, even with eight, nine, or more living children. Expressed desires for fewer than the effective number of children was also rarely stated in Ghana. In the other four countries, such desires were expressed somewhat more often by women who had many living children. In all six countries, however, only 0 to 4 percent of women with four children thought that their effective family size was too large.

If findings from the six WFS inquiries are at all representative for Sub-Saharan Africa, they would appear to confirm that contraceptives have little appeal in the region. Proportions of respondents who were currently using any contraceptive method ranged from a high of 15.6 in Ghana to a low of 3.7 percent in Côte d'Ivoire (table 11-12). Recent demographic and health surveys taken in Burundi, Liberia, Mali, Ondo state (Nigeria), and Senegal disclosed similarly infrequent (3–7 percent) current use of contraceptive methods; the only exceptions seem to be Botswana and Zimbabwe, where 24 and 38 percent, respectively, of the respondents were using a method at the time of the survey.

Although the failure to use a method may be attributed in part to lack of knowledge or means, it appears unlikely that, among women in these surveys, ignorance of contraception would be so pervasive. One study (Johnson-Acsadi and Szykman 1984) revealed, for example, that 93.4 percent of Kenyan women who were exposed to the risk of pregnancy and wanted no more children but were not using contraception knew at least one method of contraception.

It may be observed from table 11-12 that, in Ghana and Lesotho especially, large fractions of the (small numbers of) women who had more children than they desired were using a contraceptive. It is hazardous to suggest that the current users among women whose family size was more than or equal to their preferred number of children were attempting to cease childbearing; some may have been attempting to achieve longer interbirth intervals. Still, the users among those who had fewer children than they desired (from 4 percent in Côte d'Ivoire to 13 percent in Ghana) may almost certainly have adopted contraception for spacing or postponing purposes.

Indeed, it appears that the vast majority of contraceptive users were spacing births. The lower panel of table 11-12 shows that from 59 to 81 percent of all women using a contraceptive method were in this cat-

Table 11-11. *Percentage Distribution of Women by Desire for Fewer or More Than Number of Children Currently Living*

Country	\multicolumn{10}{c}{Living children}

Country	0	1	2	3	4	5	6	7	8	9+
\multicolumn{11}{c}{Desired fewer than living}
Côte d'Ivoire	—	0	1	1	0	1	1	1	5	1
Ghana	—	0	0	0	0	3	3	9	7	10
Kenya	—	0	0	1	3	7	6	13	14	20
Lesotho	—	0	0	1	4	8	14	25	29	35
Senegal	—	0	0	1	2	6	9	9	14	29
Sudan (north)	—	1	1	5	4	12	17	23	34	40
\multicolumn{11}{c}{Desired equal to living}
Côte d'Ivoire	0	1	1	2	3	7	8	12	11	31
Ghana	0	1	2	9	18	17	34	29	39	42
Kenya	0	1	3	7	15	20	21	27	29	28
Lesotho	1	2	6	10	17	18	21	16	21	33
Senegal	0	1	2	2	4	7	9	11	12	10
Sudan (north)	0	4	7	9	17	13	13	13	10	21
\multicolumn{11}{c}{Desired more than living}
Côte d'Ivoire	72	78	74	70	66	65	59	61	58	41
Ghana	91	89	88	80	69	71	50	53	46	39
Kenya	83	86	83	75	65	51	49	41	33	27
Lesotho	97	97	92	86	76	72	63	58	46	32
Senegal	78	75	77	63	62	55	48	41	41	23
Sudan (north)	83	80	75	72	62	56	46	38	33	22

— Not available.

Note: Categories do not add up to 100 because "other answers" and "not stated" are not included.

Source: WFS standard recode tapes.

egory (that is, desired more children but were using a method, evidently to achieve acceptable birth intervals).

The Demand for Spacing

Fertility in Sub-Saharan Africa, though probably the highest among major world regions, is well below the level of fecundity. Even though a great many women want as many children as possible, the expressed desires with respect to number of children are tempered by a certain realism that modifies this demand so that it amounts, in effect, to the number that can be achieved under certain well-defined cultural conditions. These conditions require practices that enable individuals (within a context of high infant and early childhood mortality)

Table 11-12. *Percentage Using Contraception, by Desired Family Size Relative to Number of Living Children*

Desired number of children relative to living children	Côte d'Ivoire	Ghana	Kenya	Lesotho	Senegal	Sudan (north)
\multicolumn{7}{c}{Percentage of women currently using contraception}
Desired < living	—	28.6	13.3	30.0	8.3	14.5
Desired = living	12.9	22.3	20.7	20.3	12.0	13.5
Desired > living	4.0	12.6	8.3	5.7	5.0	5.6
Desired not given	2.2	3.2	5.6	2.2	2.3	2.2
Combined	3.7	15.6	9.4	7.2	5.2	6.4
\multicolumn{7}{c}{Percentage distribution of current users}
Desired < living	—	2.3	5.4	9.0	4.8	18.5
Desired = living	6.2	14.4	24.1	12.2	7.3	16.9
Desired > living	79.1	80.5	59.6	74.2	71.8	59.2
Desired not given	14.7	2.8	10.9	0.6	16.6	5.4
Total	100.0	100.0	100.0	100.0	100.0	100.0

— Not available.

Source: WFS standard recode tapes.

to fulfill desires with regard to family size. It is useful to identify these practices that at once limit fertility and enable women to have the children that they want. These practices include both modern and traditional means. The latter are emphasized here because, at present, they are more important in the Sub-Saharan African context.

In accordance with long-established societal prescriptions, the principal mechanisms by which the people of Sub-Saharan Africa regulate fertility is the maintenance of "reasonable" intervals between births (see chapter 9 in this volume). Birth spacing is aimed to protect the well-being of the mother and the health of the baby. Pregnancy is known to affect breastfeeding unfavorably and thus to make the suckling child susceptible to kwashiorkor or other life-threatening maladies. The woman is therefore obligated to avoid conceiving another child for some acceptable period, and in many societies failure to do so can bring social sanctions (Mabogunje 1981). Increasingly, birth spacing has been emphasized also for the well-being of the mother, who, in addition to bearing and rearing children, frequently assumes important economic responsibilities.

Cultural norms in traditional societies within Sub-Saharan Africa specify behavior patterns that have the effect of regulating fertility but in the minds of the individuals may not necessarily be associated with the control of reproduction. These norms include marriage customs, sexual taboos, breastfeeding, and customary postpartum abstinence (often involving a return of the woman to her maternal home that is ostensibly for care at confinement and help with the young child but in fact enforces abstinence; Molnos 1973; Acsadi 1976; Mabogunje 1981; Page and Lesthaeghe 1981). In addition to these customs, which are inherent elements of the social fabric, the peoples of the region have many traditional methods of deliberately preventing conception. Most KAP surveys report the use of rhythm, douche, withdrawal, locally made sponges and suppositories, and other methods that do not require the assistance of a physician or the purchase of a manufactured product. Herbal medicines and potions, womb turning, and a variety of abortifacients as well as charms and magic may also be applied when a pregnancy is not wanted (Acsadi 1972, 1976; Acsadi and others 1972; Molnos 1973; Morgan 1975).

By and large, the rules laid down by these societies that affect the spacing of births and widespread adherence to these rules are the primary reasons why fertility is below the level of fecundity. Some of the norms affect fertility by limiting the period during which women are exposed to childbearing (for instance, norms about marriage and marriageable age that determine the entry into the childbearing period or norms that prescribe cessation of procreation under given circumstances); others do so by controlling the interval between successive deliveries. Childspacing is governed mainly by customs relevant to breastfeeding and postpartum abstinence.

Breastfeeding and Amenorrhea

From the viewpoint of spacing, the importance of breastfeeding lies in the biological consequences of lactation on women, which—to a certain degree and under given conditions—suppresses ovulation and extends postpartum amenorrhea (Gray 1981) and, thus, diminishes fecundity. Extended breastfeeding can increase the length of the interval between consecutive births (Jain and Bongaarts 1981).

Nearly all women in twelve Sub-Saharan African countries for which data are available breastfed their babies, and eight or nine out of ten were still doing so at six months (table 11-13). In all countries, except in Liberia, at least one-third of women breastfed for one and a half years; in most countries, about one-half continued breastfeeding for that long. Moreover, about one-third of the women in Benin and Lesotho were still breastfeeding when the child was two years old. A few women continued the practice even after the child's fourth birthday.

Because breastfeeding affects ovulations, such differences in the length of breastfeeding, other things being equal, should cause considerable variation in the length of the intervals between consecutive births and, consequently, in levels of fertility. Breastfeeding thus affects fertility through its impact on ovulation. The duration of the anovulatory period is roughly equal to the duration of postpartum amenorrhea, though ovulation may occur before the return of menstruation.

Comparisons of proportions of women amenorrheic with proportions breastfeeding after specific periods (figure 11-3) suggest that the two phenomena are associated, although there are essential differences in their tendencies. In all four countries selected to represent the relationship between breastfeeding and amenorrhea, the proportion of women still breastfeeding decreases slowly, and the curves depicting them run convex courses.[5] The convexity is clearly recognizable until one and a half to two years. Thereafter the curves tend to approach the horizontal axis in a concave fashion. On the other hand, the proportion of women still amenorrheic decreases rapidly, and the curves assume or approach a concave shape. Thus the curves of breastfeeding and amenorrheic women are of a different character, which implies that the relatively close association between breastfeeding and amenorrhea does not mean that the duration of the former strictly determines the length of the latter (or the length of the anovulatory period).

Table 11-13. *Percentage of Women Breastfeeding, by Months since Birth*

Country	Total breastfed	Length of breastfeeding (months)							Mean months
		3	6	12	18	24	30	36	
		Current status							
Benin	98	90	90	76	50	34	8	8	19.3
Cameroon	98	92	90	77	45	20	10	2	17.6
Côte d'Ivoire	98	87	84	78	52	22	10	5	17.5
Ghana	98	91	90	72	44	19	11	3	17.9
Kenya	98	86	82	67	35	17	6	3	15.7
Lesotho	96	93	89	76	66	33	12	3	19.5
Mauritania	98	91	86	67	45	10	6	0	15.8
Senegal	98	94	94	82	59	22	5	0	18.5
Sudan (north)	98	91	86	72	39	14	4	3	15.9
		During the open birth interval[a]							
Botswana	98	96	93	73	49	16	—	11	18.9[b]
Liberia	—	87	75	61	27	13	4	—	17.0
Zimbabwe	98	98	96	84	47	9	—	—	18.8[b]

— Not available.

a. For all women with a birth within 36 months prior to the survey.

b. Median length.

Sources: Ferry and Smith (1983), which also provides a detailed description of current status rates; Balkaran and Smith (1984); Botswana (1985); Liberia (1988); Zimbabwe (1985).

The divergence of the breastfeeding and amenorrheic curves is important from a demographic viewpoint because the gap between the two curves (the shaded area of figure 11-3) represents the proportion of women for whom breastfeeding does not afford protection against conception. This gap seemingly widens during the first year of lactation, when about one-third to three-fourths of the breastfeeding women are left unprotected.

From the discussion above, it is clear that breastfeeding offers very uncertain protection against conception in individual cases and that it is inadequate for total populations. Part of the seemingly close association between breastfeeding and amenorrhea may be partly due to a simple coincidence between the two phenomena, inasmuch as practically all women in these countries breastfeed their infants for at least three or six months but wean at some point. Similarly, whether they breastfeed or not, all women are amenorrheic following confinement and practically all will resume menstruating.

Statistics for five African countries show that, though there is obviously some connection between breastfeeding and amenorrhea (because the mean duration of amenorrhea generally increases with the duration of breastfeeding), the relationship is not straightforward and strong. As the data in table 11-14 suggest, there is hardly any difference in the duration of amenorrhea among those who did not breastfeed in the last closed pregnancy interval, or who breastfed only for a short while (that is, for zero to two months) and among those who breastfed for four or five months or for half a year. The women who breastfed for two or three years were

protected for an average of only eleven months or—as a maximum—one year and a half.

Whether we focus on the mean durations of breastfeeding and amenorrhea or on the proportions of women still breastfeeding and amenorrheic, it appears that the degree of contraceptive protection provided by breastfeeding varies greatly from country to country. Breastfeeding is most universal and endures for the longest period in Lesotho, where the shortest mean duration of amenorrhea was reported. Indeed, the shortest mean duration of breastfeeding, in Kenya, was associated with a somewhat longer mean duration of amenorrhea than in Lesotho, where the mean duration of breastfeeding was the longest.

These findings on the uncertain effect of breastfeeding upon postpartum amenorrhea cannot be considered anomalous; they are compatible with earlier findings (Gray 1981) that the precise relationship between breastfeeding and amenorrhea is disputable. The inconsistency of the relationship—both individually and on the aggregate level—can be explained, at least partly, by differences in breastfeeding practices and patterns.

In the past, there might have been differences among ethnic groups as to the mean duration of breastfeeding. There is little doubt, however, that the duration of breastfeeding is decreasing and that the large differences found in these surveys mainly reflect the varying tempo of this trend in the individual countries, as is illustrated by the differences in the mean duration of breastfeeding among selected socioeconomic groups in six Sub-Saharan African countries (Ghana 1983; Kenya 1980; Lesotho 1981; Liberia 1988; Nigeria 1984; Sudan

Figure 11-3. *Percentage of Women Still Breastfeeding, Abstaining, or Amenorrheic by Months since Birth*

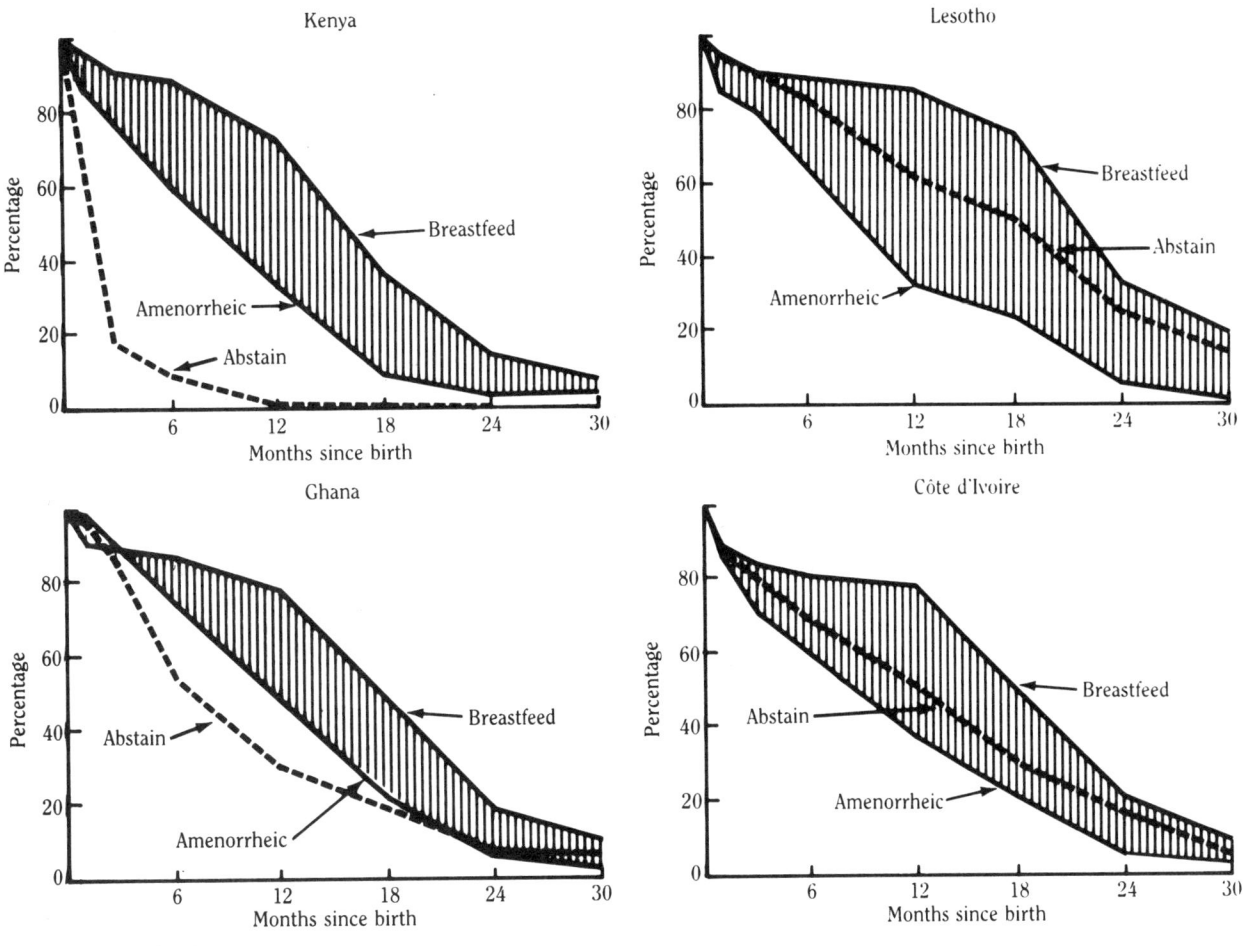

------ Abstain

Source: Singh and Ferry (1984).

1979). Even in countries where there are hardly any regional differences in the duration of lactation, for example in Lesotho, there are differences by urban-rural residence, husband's occupation, and especially woman's an's level of education. In general, urban and more educated women tend to shorten the duration of breastfeeding, as do women whose husbands have occupations that require more education and are practiced mostly in urban settlements. The duration of breastfeeding also declines from generation to generation (see table 11-19).

Breastfeeding and Spacing Preferences

As an explanation for the individual and aggregate differentials in the duration of breastfeeding, it may be hypothesized that prolonged breastfeeding is a means of assuring the desired childspacing, and the differentials arise from variations in childspacing demands or

to the extent to which other applied means affect the intended spacing pattern. It is questionable, however, whether the differences in the duration of breastfeeding reflect conscious behavior on the part of the women to achieve a certain pattern of spacing and an intended family size. Although it is theoretically possible that people manipulate spacing (and fertility) through deliberate modification of breastfeeding patterns, such behavior is improbable in a traditional society. Breastfeeding is an instinctive, natural element of the feeding and rearing of children. It provides the exclusive nourishment for infants up to an age when other foods are introduced into their diet and is a supplementary aliment until the child is weaned. Although there is evidence that the need for breastfeeding and its beneficial effect on the child's health are widely recognized, there is no indication that its impact on fecundity is well known.[6]

Table 11-14. *Mean Duration of Amenorrhea in the Last Closed Pregnancy Interval by Duration of Breastfeeding (months)*

Duration of breastfeeding (months)	Ghana	Kenya	Lesotho	Nigeria	Sudan (north)
Nonlive birth	3.7	} 3.9	3.1	8.0	5.2
Not breastfed	5.9				
0	7.3			8.1	
1	6.1	} 5.3	3.6	5.6	} 5.5
2	7.1			7.2	
3	8.3	4.5	4.6	6.2	4.3
4–5	7.8	4.6	4.5	5.6	4.3
6	8.7	5.9	3.9	6.9	5.3
7–8	8.9	6.1	5.6	6.1	5.0
9–11	9.0	6.9	5.8	7.5	6.6
12	10.4	9.0	7.5	9.2	9.3
13–17	11.3	10.5	8.4	10.4	11.3
18	12.4	12.1	8.9	11.1	13.3
19–23	12.1	12.0	10.1	11.9	16.9
24	14.1	14.5	10.8	13.6	17.3
25–29	18.5	17.1[b]	} 11.8	13.5	14.1[b]
30	16.7	—		11.8	—
31–35	13.6[a]	—	12.9	11.7[a]	—
36	18.2	—	13.3	15.7	—
Mean duration of amenorrhea	10.5	8.8	8.3	10.4	11.5
Mean duration of breastfeeding	15.1	13.0	19.8	16.3	16.6

— Not available.
Note: Data relate to women with at least two pregnancies; in Nigeria, the mean duration is measured in the last closed birth interval.
a. Fewer than ten cases.
b. 25 months and more.
Sources: Ghana (1983); Kenya (1980); Lesotho (1981); Nigeria (1984); Sudan (1982).

The question of whether spacing is manipulated by the length of breastfeeding presupposes that women have ideas regarding desirable spacing patterns. Anthropological and demographic evidence indicates that the vast majority of Sub-Saharan women have a definite idea about the length of healthful or desirable childspacing. Two earlier surveys from Nigeria and Togo and recent surveys from Botswana and Zimbabwe revealed that most women had an idea as to the most healthful or desirable interval between successive births. As table 11-15 shows, in six southwestern Nigerian states and in Togo, the mean length of childspacing considered "healthy" or "desirable" was more than two and a half years. Most frequently, women thought that children should be spaced at three-year intervals. A sizable proportion of women in Nigeria, however, especially those living in metropolitan Lagos and Ibadan or in other urban areas, preferred two-year intervals. Mainly in rural areas, three or more years was the most desirable interval. According to recent surveys, the "ideal" birth intervals seem to be longer in Botswana and Zimbabwe than in the West African countries. In Zimbabwe, the mean "ideal" interval was 2.9 years. The mode was two

years, but in urban areas, the most popular preference was for intervals of three or more years. In Botswana, most women preferred four years or more between births, and more urban women than rural women wanted intervals of this length.

The earlier Nigerian findings suggested a gradual erosion of traditional spacing patterns as a consequence of urbanization and its modernizing influences. The more traditional, rural women adhered more to the idea of a longer more healthful birth interval than did their less traditional counterparts in urban areas. The shortest mean interval thought to be healthful, reported from the metropolitan areas of Lagos and Ibadan, was followed by gradually longer preferences in other urban areas and in the countryside. On this basis, one may infer a gradual erosion of a traditional spacing as a consequence of urbanization. On the other hand, the comparatively widespread literacy and schooling among urban women in Botswana and Zimbabwe and the spread of family planning activities in those countries may account for their recognition of the value of certain reproductive ideals for health, especially of children.

Table 11-15. *Percentage of Women Preferring Particular Birth Intervals*

Country and residence	Mean length	Length of birth interval (years)					
		0–1	2	3	4+	Not sure	Total
Botswana	3.3	5	25	30	39	1	100
Urban	3.5	3	19	33	45	0	100
Rural	3.3	6	26	30	37	1	100
Nigeria, South-West	2.6	6	37	41	7	10	100
Metropolitan	2.4	8	50	36	3	4	100
Other urban	2.5	6	43	38	6	8	100
Rural	2.7	5	29	44	9	13	100
Togo, Maritime	2.8	8	23	50	17	2	100
Zimbabwe	2.9	3	39	33	24	1	100
Urban	3.2	2	31	33	34	0	100
Rural	2.7	3	44	33	19	1	100

Note: The date relate to the "ideal" interval between births in Botswana and Zimbabwe, to the "most healthy interval" in the six Nigerian states south-west of the River Niger, and to the "desired" interval in Togo.
Sources: Botswana (1985); Acsadi (n.d.); Kumekpor (1975); Zimbabwe (1985).

The considerable variance among the six Nigerian states, however, also called attention to probable regional differences that may be due not only to developmental factors but also to cultural or ethnic diversity. In Bendel state, for example, where mainly members of the Edo and Urhobo ethnic groups were interviewed, more than one-quarter of the women stated no opinion about a healthy birth interval, whereas in the other states, where the majority of respondents were Yoruba, it was exceptional if a woman did not state an opinion, and the stated preference was usually for three or more years. Thus, although urbanization and modernization affect the traditional way of thinking about spacing, it is also clear that population subgroups may have different traditional ideas about spacing or no views at all.

Postpartum Abstinence

The question remains: if population groups following traditions in Sub-Saharan Africa have definite opinions about a desirable pattern of spacing, how do they establish it without resorting to contraception or abortion more frequently than is reported and without being aware of the effect of breastfeeding on spacing? Women recognize a longer period of postpartum amenorrhea while lactating. The effect of breastfeeding upon amenorrhea varies from place to place (and possibly among individuals), however, and the relationship between the two depends not only on the length of breastfeeding but also on the lactation practices. Women may also have realized that conception can take place during postpartum amenorrhea, because there can be ovulation before the first menses occur. Traditional societies understood not only that breastfeeding alone is not sufficient to protect against pregnancy but also that pregnancy has adverse effects on lactation and thus endangers the health or life of the child that is being breastfed (Talbot 1969, II, 356–57). As a logical consequence, the custom of postpartum abstinence was established to maintain adequate lactation for a lengthy period between the last child and the next conception in the interest of the child's health.

The beneficial effect of childspacing on the mother's health may also be one of the supportive motives for forming ideas about a desirable spacing pattern. Such a pattern cannot be assured by breastfeeding alone; however, postpartum abstention, if fully observed, guarantees the maintenance of the desired interval. Thus, the traditional custom of long postpartum abstinence, once quite general in Sub-Saharan Africa, has a very important secondary effect on fertility through the corollary childspacing pattern (Caldwell and Caldwell 1977). As was recognized well before World War II, the relatively low birth rates in Africa were "due to the maintenance of an ancient custom which keeps the family small—the custom of abstaining from intercourse until the child has been weaned, and weaning may be postponed for a long time. The length of time differs from tribe to tribe, but the practice does effectively keep the successive children spaced out and makes large families of living children impossible" (Carr-Saunders 1964, pp. 302–3).

Postpartum abstinence has been vulnerable to modernization, however, partly because the spread of urbanization diluted the practice of postpartum spousal separation according to which the wife returned to her maternal home for as long as she was breastfeeding. At the same time, acceptance of substitutes for mother's milk has begun to undermine the custom of breastfeeding and, hence, to negate the need for abstinence to maintain healthful lactation. In areas dominated by Islam, however, which does not prescribe a long absti-

Table 11-16. *Mean Length of Postpartum Abstinence in Last Closed Pregnancy Interval, by Duration of Breastfeeding (months)*

Duration of breastfeeding (months)	Ghana	Kenya	Lesotho	Nigeria	Sudan (north)
Non-live birth	4.4	—	3.4	0.0	1.8
Not breastfed	6.3	2.6	6.0	8.3	0.0
Months					
0	5.9	3.0	3.1	8.9	2.9
1	6.0	2.8	4.3	6.2	2.1
2	5.4	4.0	6.1	7.7	3.6
3	7.2	3.5	6.1	8.8	2.5
4–6	6.6	3.2	6.9	8.1	4.4
7–8	6.5	3.6	6.3	8.6	4.9
9–11	6.4	3.6	8.2	9.3	5.6
12	7.4	4.2	10.8	12.1	6.2
13–17	8.6	4.1	12.0	12.4	6.4
18	9.0	3.6	13.6	14.5	6.7
19–23	13.7	4.3	15.0	15.3	7.4
24	14.6	5.6	19.4	20.4	7.3
25–29	22.5	4.6	22.0	22.3	5.8
30–35	20.7	8.1	22.9	28.1	4.7[a]
36+	26.1	14.1	27.9	24.5	—
Until child died	—	2.8	—	—	—
Total	8.9	4.0	13.9	14.1	5.9

— Not applicable.

Note: The data relate to women with at least two pregnancies (including any current pregnancy). Except in Kenya, the response "until child died" was converted to age at death.

a. 30 months or more.

Sources: Ghana (1983); Kenya (1980); Lesotho (1981); Nigeria (1984); Sudan (1982).

nence period after confinement, erosion of the custom of postpartum abstinence has not affected the breast-feeding pattern; thus, even without abstinence as a backup, breastfeeding can provide some lengthening of interbirth intervals in these areas.

There is a close link between breastfeeding and postpartum abstinence in countries where traditional abstinence is practiced (table 11-16). In Lesotho and Nigeria, for example, the mean length of postpartum abstinence rises with the duration of breastfeeding so markedly that prolonged lactation of three years or more is associated with more than two years of abstention. Thus in these countries postpartum abstinence provides significantly longer protection than does amenorrhea associated with the same duration of breastfeeding (8.3 and 10.4 months, respectively).

Results of WFS inquiries indicated that, in Sub-Saharan Africa, the region in which postpartum abstinence is perhaps most widely used for long periods, the practice is not widely recognized as a means of avoiding pregnancy. In only one of six surveys was knowledge of postpartum abstinence for "several months or longer" and with the "purpose of avoiding pregnancy" reported to be pervasive.

This seeming incongruence has its genesis in the traditional purpose of postpartum abstinence, a fact that

is reflected in findings from the Westinghouse survey conducted in Botswana. Among women who knew at least one family planning method, 80 percent considered abstinence to be "customary," and of these, 75 percent thought that the custom protects the health of the baby; 13 percent thought that it was to benefit the mother's health; and 10 percent thought that abstinence protects the health of the mother and child or of the father (Botswana 1985).

The Length of Postpartum Abstinence

Information suggestive of the normative length of customary postpartum abstinence is scant indeed. Some earlier studies provided data on the norms relevant to the length of abstinence period, however. In the 1971 Nigerian FFFP Study (Acsadi and others 1972), for example, wives were asked their opinion as to the length of healthy childspacing, and thus indirectly about the length of the abstinence period, and the husbands answered the question: "How many weeks after the termination of a pregnancy should a woman resume sex relations with her husband?" The appropriate abstinence period (asked of husbands) should obviously be shorter than the healthy interval between successive deliveries (asked of wives) by about one year. Thus the

Table 11-17. *Percentage of Nigerian Husbands Preferring Particular Lengths of Postpartum Abstinence, by Residence and Ethnic Group*

Residence, ethnic group	Mean length (years)	0–1 month	2–11 months	1 year	2 years	3+ years	No response	Total
Nigeria, Southwest[a]	1.5	5	30	29	14	13	9	100
Six Yoruba cities[b]	1.3	6	32	33	12	10	7	100
Rural Yoruba districts[c]	1.8	3	17	31	19	18	12	100
Residence								
Lagos and Ogun state								
Urban	1.4	3	28	36	12	7	14	100
Rural	1.8	2	16	35	15	20	12	100
Oyo state								
Urban	1.6	7	15	26	26	7	19	100
Rural	1.7	5	19	28	19	16	13	100
Ondo state								
Urban	1.7	5	21	38	16	15	5	100
Rural	2.0	1	12	35	26	17	9	100
Kwara state								
Urban	1.7	3	21	36	14	17	9	100
Rural	2.2	4	11	20	22	35	8	100
Bendel state								
Urban	0.9	3	55	29	3	3	7	100
Rural	0.8	5	66	15	5	3	6	100
Ethnic group								
In Kwara state								
Yoruba	1.8	6	28	15	15	27	9	100
Igbirra	2.0	5	5	50	6	34	0	100
Nupe	2.3	3	4	19	29	30	15	100
Other	1.5	1	30	37	17	9	6	100
In rural Bendel								
Edo of								
Ivbiosakon	1.6	0	28	38	17	12	5	100
Iyekuselu	0.4	2	88	2	1	1	6	100
Central Ishan	0.4	29	62	2	0	0	7	100
Urhobo/Jeremi clan	0.6	2	74	16	0	0	8	100
Others	0.6	11	64	9	9	0	7	100

a. Six states southwest from the River Niger; FFFP Study 1971–73, Western Phase; 2,855 husbands of women under fifty years (Acsadi and others 1972).

b. Settlements with more than 100,000 population in 1963; includes Ibadan, Oshogbo, Iwo, Ede, Oyo, and Ilorin. These cities are excluded from urban areas in Oyo, Ondo, and Kwara states.

c. All rural subsamples in Lagos, Ogun, Ondo, and Oyo states with almost exclusively Yoruba populations.

Source: Acsadi (n.d.)

mean length of postpartum abstinence of 1.5 years that should be observed according to the husbands (table 11-17) approximates the mean healthy spacing favored by the wives (2.6 years) if the time needed for conception and pregnancy is taken into account.

The data in table 11-17 support earlier observations that the custom of abstinence was neither uniform among peoples of southern Nigeria nor equally observed by all (Talbot 1969). The shortest mean period of abstinence was reported from the rural districts of Bendel state. In the region of the Yoruba ethnic group, the shortest length of postpartum abstinence was reported from the six cities of predominantly Yoruba population (1.3 years). The period of postpartum abstinence thought to be proper

is somewhat longer in other urban areas of five states with Yoruba majority and longer in the rural areas of the same states. In the latter, the mean length of abstinence varied between 1.7 and 2.2 years, which is congruent with the finding that the majority of women in the same rural areas think three or more years is the healthful interval between births (table 11-15).

A comparison of wives' opinions on childspacing with husbands' notions about abstinence supports the view that husbands, particularly in a monogamous relationship, urge an end to the abstinence period, whereas the wives, lacking knowledge of and access to modern contraceptives, are more insistent upon maintaining a period of the customary length. In Nigeria, this thesis was found to be particularly applicable in the larger cities and, especially, in Bendel state, where few husbands favored even a one-year period of abstinence. In the selected rural areas of Bendel state, for example, fewer than one-quarter of the husbands thought that a woman should not resume sex earlier than one year after delivery; the majority favored less than six months of abstinence, whereas most of the female respondents considered two or more years of childspacing to be preferable, and one-quarter of them did not have an opinion (or did not want to declare it openly).

Although the foregoing supports the thesis that the abstinence custom is eroding, the current known regional diversity indicates an earlier variance in its pattern among regional or ethnic groups. Talbot (1969), for example, reported that, in about the 1920s, the Yoruba breastfed for about 2.5 years and abstained during suckling, whereas women in the Edo-Bini group (in Bendel state) often breastfed even longer, but cohabitation was forbidden only for a year.

Results of the WFS surveys conducted in the countries of this region have corroborated on a wider scale the earlier findings of regional diversity in the observance of postpartum abstinence. Its length in the last closed interbirth interval, as reported by women interviewed in the inquiries, varied widely in five countries, possibly because of the variations in tempo or timing of the changes but perhaps also because of the earlier variance in the abstinence pattern. As seen from tables 11-18 and 11-19, the mean length of postpartum abstinence ranged from four (Kenya) to fourteen (Nigeria) months. Among the recent Westinghouse surveys, adherence to the custom of postpartum abstinence in Botswana (1985)

seems to be similar to that in Lesotho and Liberia (1988) to that in Nigeria (for mothers whose last child was at least two years old, the median period of abstinence was about one year in Botswana and the mean period was seventeen months in Liberia). The cumulative proportion of women still abstaining at different elapsed times after a birth indicates how widely the length of postpartum abstinence has varied among women in these surveys, so much so that, for many couples, traditional norms appear to have been of little import. Among the seven countries for which data are available, the custom seems to have declined most markedly in Kenya.

The differences in the abstinence pattern in the last closed interval can also be seen in figure 11-3. Postpartum abstinence is more strongly associated with breastfeeding than is amenorrhea, at least in countries such as Lesotho and Côte d'Ivoire, where women still breastfeed for long durations and where a still considerable proportion of them observe the custom of traditional postpartum abstinence. In such countries, abstinence plays a larger role in spacing and has a greater impact on fertility than breastfeeding through its effect on lengthening the period of amenorrhea. If the custom of long, traditional postpartum abstinence is nonexistent or adherence diminishes or disappears, of course, the effect of breastfeeding will be more important if abstinence is not replaced with other contraceptive practices (see, for examples, Ghana and Kenya in figure 11-3).

Because traditional postpartum abstinence is practiced in the interest of breastfeeding, its observance or length should naturally decline as the proportion of breastfeeding mothers decreases or as the duration of

Table 11-18. *Percentage Distribution of Women by Length of Postpartum Abstinence*

Length of abstinence	Ghana	Kenya	Lesotho	Nigeria	Sudan (north)
	Percentage of women				
0–1 month	1.5	24.8	9.7	1.6	11.1
2–5 months	36.0	56.0	14.9	17.6	35.7
6–11 months	34.7	11.6	15.7	21.3	44.1
12–17 months	15.3	5.4	25.1	23.3	7.5
18–23 months	3.9	0.7	11.7	12.7	1.3
2 years	6.9	1.1	18.3	20.4	0.4
3+ years	1.6	0.6	4.6	2.9	—
Total	99.9	100.2	100.0	99.8	100.1
Mean length (years)	0.7	0.3	1.2	1.2	0.5
	Percentage abstaining at specified durations				
3 months or more	95.7	52.1	85.7	94.2	85.5
6 months or more	62.4	19.4	75.4	80.8	53.3
1 year or more	27.7	7.8	59.7	59.5	9.2
1.5 years or more	12.4	2.4	34.6	36.2	1.7
2 years or more	8.5	1.7	22.9	23.5	0.4

— Not applicable.
Note: Data relate to women with at least two pregnancies (including any current pregnancy).
Sources: Ghana (1983); Kenya (1980); Lesotho (1981); Nigeria (1984); Sudan (1982).

Table 11-19. *Mean Durations of Breastfeeding and Postpartum Abstinence in Last Closed Pregnancy Interval, by Age of Woman*

Current age (years)	Ghana	Kenya	Lesotho	Nigeria	Sudan (north)
	Duration of breastfeeding (months)				
–19	14.3	11.7	15.8	17.2	13.1
20–24	14.5	12.1	17.7	16.1	14.7
25–29	14.6	12.7	19.6	16.2	15.6
30–34	15.1	13.4	20.2	16.3	16.3
35–39	15.4	13.2	20.2	16.4	16.9
40–44	15.8	14.0	20.9	17.9	17.2
45 +	15.4	13.6	20.6	17.6	17.6
Total	15.1	13.0	19.8	16.6	16.2
	Length of abstinence (months)				
–19	7.3	—	9.7	12.0	4.6
20–24	8.4	—	11.9	13.0	5.6
25–29	8.5	—	13.1	13.6	5.9
30–34	9.1	—	14.2	14.4	6.1
35–39	9.5	—	14.3	13.8	5.9
40–44	9.0	—	15.5	15.1	6.0
45 +	9.3	—	15.1	15.7	6.2
Total	8.9	4.0	13.8	14.1	5.9

— Not available.
Sources: Ghana (1983); Kenya (1980); Lesotho (1981); Nigeria (1984); Sudan (1982).

breastfeeding becomes shorter. The data in figure 11-3 also suggest, however, that the abstinence custom may recede prior to the decline of breastfeeding or that the former may proceed more rapidly than the latter.

Although husbands probably play an important role in abandonment of the custom of postpartum abstinence or in shortening its length, so generally do younger, urban, and educated wives.[7] As the statistics in table 11-19 attest, women over forty (and their spouses) generally adhere more to the traditions and abstain longer than do the younger ones. In Nigeria and Lesotho, where the mean length of postpartum abstinence is still longer than a year, a gradual erosion of the custom from generation to generation can be observed. On the average, women over forty abstain longer than fifteen months, women in their thirties for about fourteen months, those in their twenties for twelve or thirteen months, and those in their teens for only one year or less. In Ghana and Sudan, where the mean length of abstinence is shorter, the pattern is more uniform among women over thirty, suggesting that the custom of a shorter abstinence period (about nine and six months, respectively) was established long ago and has been maintained for decades. Recently, however—about ten or fifteen years before the surveys—a new trend of shortening the period began.

Differentials in postpartum abstinence are very similar to those found in breastfeeding. A much longer period of postpartum abstinence is observed by women who never attended school than by those who attained some higher level of education. There are also differ-ences in the length of abstinence among women who live in urban and rural areas and among those whose husbands belong to different occupational categories. The shortest period of abstinence is practiced by women who live in urban areas and whose husbands have professional or clerical occupations, and the longest by wives of agricultural workers or other manual workers who live in the countryside.

There are considerable differences in the length of abstinence not only among countries but, as mentioned before, among smaller regions and ethnic groups within nations. These differences are greater than those found between urban and rural dwellers. In Ghana (1983), for example, the mean length of postpartum abstinence was about three or four times greater in the Upper region (20.8 months, where the mean duration of breastfeeding was also the longest, 23.2 months), than in the Ashanti and Central regions (5.7 and 5.8 months, respectively), where the mean duration of breastfeeding was also shorter (13.0 and 10.9 months, respectively). Similar differences appeared among ethnic groups as well.

Marital customs, naturally, may be closely related to the length and observance of traditional postpartum abstinence. Polygyny, a widespread family form in Sub-Saharan Africa, for instance, tends to decrease fertility (van de Walle 1968), and its negative effect can probably be attributed, at least in part, to the fact that it facilitates the observance of a long abstinence period. From another viewpoint, if proper childspacing is accomplished by abstinence, husbands are prompted to have another wife (Whiting 1964). In either case, the two phenomena are, obviously, interconnected. The association of marriage type with abstinence was recently supported by the findings of the Ghana Fertility Survey conducted within the framework of the WFS, which collected data on the duration of abstinence by the type of current marriage. It has been reported (Ghana 1983) that the mean duration of abstinence was two months shorter for women in monogamous marriages (8.3) than for those in polygynous marriages (10.3).

More detailed information on the relationship is available from the earlier FFFP survey conducted in the six Nigerian states, where husbands who had only one wife reported a somewhat shorter mean normative abstinence period (1.40 years) than those who had two or more wives (1.54 years). The length of the abstinence period or the proportion of husbands who permitted three or more years of abstinence, however, did not increase consistently with the number of additional wives.

When ethnicity and urban-rural residence were taken into account, the association did not hold everywhere; for instance, among the Edo in Bendel state, the abstinence custom was weak or almost nonexistent. The observance of the custom was also only loosely associated with the frequency of polygynous families. Polygyny was very general in the surveyed Nigerian states (38 percent of the husbands interviewed had two or more wives), but its frequency greatly varied among selected subsamples and ethnic groups. Polygyny was also less frequent in the cities than in the countryside.

In the final analysis, though polygyny is supportive of the custom of abstinence, the former is not the cause of the latter. In a society where polygyny is widespread, monogamy for a husband in many cases is only the first, temporary stage in polygyny. Certain wealth is necessary to establish a polygynous household, and time is needed to gain wealth. Though there is real monogamous family life, monogamy frequently means only a specific stage in the life cycle of a polygynous man. Therefore, "monogamous" husbands on the average are younger and polygynous husbands older. The traditional custom of abstinence was equally the norm for men and women in a group, irrespective of the type of family in which they lived. If the customary postpartum abstinence is eroding among urbanites and younger people, as is the case in the areas noted above, then "monogamous" husbands should be those who observe it less and for a shorter period.

Patterns of Contraceptive Use: Indication of Demand for Spacing

In the climate of increasing modernization, breastfeeding and postpartum abstinence are decreasing in frequency and duration; some women are beginning to use contraceptives instead or to attempt to halt reproduction altogether (Mabogunje 1981). As noted earlier, however, relatively few of the respondents in the Sub-Saharan African surveys wanted to terminate reproduction even when they had six and seven children. Thus, in these societies, as in others, contraceptive use may have different purposes and may follow varied patterns.

A design for analyzing patterns of contraceptive use proffered by the WFS permits examination of patterns of use among women who were using or had used contraception and of attitudes toward use among those who had never done so. It also makes possible an assessment of prevalence in the open interval among both current users and those who had been using contraceptives but had stopped and were still exposed to the risk of pregnancy (WFS 1977b). Table 11-20 indicates that the majority of those who had never used contraceptives did not intend to do so in the future, especially in Côte d'Ivoire, Nigeria, Senegal, and Sudan. Whether this attitude was based upon a desire for additional children cannot be determined, but many of the women obviously fall into that category. Relatively large numbers in three countries—Ghana, Kenya, and Lesotho—did anticipate future use but whether for spacing or stopping is not known.

The relative number of exposed women who had used a contraceptive method at all in the open interval was much higher than the percentage of current users. Large fractions of these open interval users were probably spacers who had discontinued contraceptive practice for the purpose of having a child.

In an earlier study of this phenomenon (Acsadi 1979a), it was suggested that added insight would be gained if the purpose of contraceptive use became the main criterion of classification. This scheme distinguishes "spacers" who used or were using a method of birth regulation (among both past and current users who had at least one child and wanted more); "stoppers" who desired to terminate childbearing (those who were sterilized and those who were using some other method of contraception and wanted no more children); and "postponers" who wanted to delay for an indeterminate period the birth of the first child (past and current nulliparous users). It would also be possible to separate among the "never users" those who were "potential users" (those who intend to use a contraceptive method) classified according to their desire for a child as "potential spacers" (those who want more children) and "potential stoppers" (those who want no more).

Results of the classification of exposed women by this scheme are in table 11-21. What emerged is revealing indeed; in each Sub-Saharan African country, spacers far outnumbered current users. In Côte d'Ivoire, the country with apparently the most traditional level of

Table 11-20. *Percentage Distribution of Women by Pattern of Contraceptive Use*

Pattern[a]	Côte d'Ivoire	Ghana	Kenya	Lesotho	Nigeria	Senegal	Sudan (north)
Never used (excludes infecund)							
Intends future use	1.3	16.7	13.8	25.0	1.9	1.2	7.4
Intends no future use	26	54.8	63.7	71.9	83.9	87.3	85.2
Nonuser but previously used	95	69.5	78.3	65.2	97.7	98.6	91.3
In open interval	21.3	6.6	3.3	9.6	1.6	2.9	2.0
In last closed interval	29.0	13.4	5.7	3.7	2.7	2.2	} 7.7
Earlier	20.9	15.5	20.1	9.1	6.6	3.4	
Sterilized	—	0.5	1.1	0.9	0.1	0.0	0.3
Current user	2.8	9.2	6.1	4.8	5.1	4.2	4.8
Total	100.0	100.0	100.0	100.0	100.0	100.0	100.0
In open interval:							
Total users[b]	24.1	16.3	10.5	15.3	6.8	7.1	7.1
Percentage that stopped using	88.4	40.3	31.4	62.6	23.5	41.2	27.8

a. WFS classification.
b. Total past but not current users in the open interval, sterilized and current users.
Source: WFS standard recode tapes. Nigeria (1984).

demand, more than two-thirds of the exposed women were spacers, whereas only 3.2 percent of them were currently using a contraceptive method. It is evident that, in each of the countries, larger percentages of women had used a contraceptive during the open birth interval but, at the time of the interview, had suspended the practice, very likely in order to conceive. These women should therefore be categorized as spacers, not nonusers.

The scheme also makes it possible to identify women who were postponing their first birth. This group comprises only a small fraction of the exposed women because relatively few were childless and because it is not customary in traditional societies for women to use a contraceptive before their first live birth (see United Nations 1981). Also, in numerous Sub-Saharan African societies, there is pressure upon women to demonstrate fecundity, and the arrival of the first child is eagerly awaited (see, among others, Molnos 1968).

In Sudan, large fractions, and the overwhelming majority in Senegal of never users, stated in reply to a direct question that they did not intend to use a contraceptive at any time in the future. Sizable proportions in Ghana, Kenya, and Lesotho, however, did intend future use, and except in Senegal, the aim of these "potential users" was probably to space the additional children that they wanted to have. The frequency of stoppers among the potential users was very small.

The motivation for spacing, which is an intrinsic part of these cultures, is widespread and strong, but termination of childbearing by any means but natural processes has little appeal. This point is especially clear from the comparison of the Sub-Saharan African patterns with those in Asia and Latin America, which are

Table 11-21. *Percentage Distribution of Women by Contraceptive Use and Purpose*

Country	Spacers	Postponers	Stoppers	Potential users	Never users[a]	Total
Africa						
Côte d'Ivoire[b]	69.9	0.9	3.2	1.3	24.7	100.0
Ghana	37.7	0.8	6.7	16.7	38.1	100.0
Kenya	28.4	0.4	7.5	13.8	49.9	100.0
Lesotho	21.0	0.3	6.8	25.0	46.9	100.0
Senegal[b]	11.1	0.2	1.4	1.2	86.1	100.0
Sudan (north)	10.3	0.4	4.1	7.4	77.8	100.0
Other regions						
Sri Lanka	10.8	0.5	38.0	21.7	28.9	100.0
Panama	23.2	1.8	51.7	14.0	13.3	100.0

a. Intending no use.
b. Partly estimated percentages.
Sources: Acsadi (1979); WFS standard recode tapes.

represented in table 11-21 by Sri Lanka and Panama. Although the Sub-Saharan African pattern can be characterized in general by predominance of spacers (and of never users) over those who wanted to stop childbearing, the pattern is dominated both in Panama and Sri Lanka by the stoppers. (Postponers, probably a more frequent type in developed countries, lack importance in any of the developing countries investigated.) The diagonally opposite patterns of contraceptive use in Sub-Saharan Africa compared with populations in other major world regions, particularly the readiness for spacing, have significant policy implications and make plain the need for the development of specific approaches to population programs in the region.

Conclusions

The peoples of Sub-Saharan Africa have in common a desire for large families. The essence of the traditional fabric of these societies involves mandatory behavior for both women and men that is consonant with the bearing and rearing of large numbers of children and is often supported by sanctions against deviants. The individual must subscribe to the behavioral norms and thus is not given an option about the number of children to have. To the extent that these behavior patterns, imposed by the society, characterize the behavior of all women of reproductive age and of their partners, the observed average completed family size indicates the society's demand for children.

This description is of a traditionalist society, and some changes have been taking place, particularly in the modern sectors. However, because the vast majority of these people live in rural areas and in towns that are barely urban, and because even urban people frown upon the infraction of mores, individuals are subject to the surveillance of kin and community, traditionalism is widespread, behavior tends to follow the pattern prescribed by the culture, and an individual approach to reproduction is not common. Thus, only relatively infrequently within these countries will a woman of childbearing age express, for personal reasons, the wish not to have more children.

When they are about age 40 and their older children marry, women tend to want to cease childbearing, not because they want no more children, but because of the social implications of bearing children along with their daughter or daughter-in-law. The majority of women would like to have more than six living children before they seriously consider terminating reproduction. Although education and urban life modify these attitudes somewhat, in these countries they have not yet created an environment conducive to effective large-scale pro-

motion of family planning among younger women as a means of avoiding future births. Without further and more pervasive social and cultural change, it is unlikely that women will voluntarily cease childbearing until they reach a certain age, have married children, or have the relatively large family that they want. The structures of society, family, and household are such that work, whether involving modern or traditional occupations, at home or away from home, need not have an important influence upon childbearing and the desire for children.

If desired family size can be taken as an indicator of demand for children, it may be said that this demand is highest in Sub-Saharan Africa. Indeed, the level of wanted fertility in this region seems to be unprecedented, not only in comparison with other continents, but, according to available evidence, even in historical context. Furthermore, there is little indication of any decrease in this demand for children triggered by socioeconomic development, at least in the short run.

Although the vast majority of respondents in Sub-Saharan African countries wanted more children than they had, this tendency declined as the number of children living increased—evidence, albeit meager, that there are indeed limits to the number of children that the people consider an ideal family size. The problem confronting policymakers is that of lowering these limits.

As long as Sub-Saharan societies place a high value on having many children, require compliance with customs that produce large families, sanction the nonconformist, and reward those who comply (mainly with high status), the demand for large numbers of children will be strong and pervasive. At present, neither education nor urban residence has a noteworthy depressing effect upon this demand. The implication is that progress in economic and social development alone will not likely bring about lower reproductive ideals in the region; reduction of the demand for children among these people will require changes in the culture itself.

Some family planning services are certainly needed to meet the so-called unmet need of a relatively small number of women who want to cease childbearing as well as to treat infertility, but such a limited effort cannot be expected to have a considerable impact upon aggregate fertility levels. In addition to satisfying the demand for such services, a family planning program should also compensate for the decline of traditional means of fertility control. Where national policy is to regulate population growth and government policy is directed toward facilitating a fertility decline, however, the measures adopted should be aimed not only at promoting spacing but also at making smaller family size norms acceptable, attractive, and achievable.

Notes

1. For a general discussion of these questions, see United Nations (1970), World Fertility Survey (1977), Grebenik and Hill (1979), and Acsadi (1980).

2. Effective family size, or effective parity, in this text, denotes women classified on the basis of their surviving children.

3. The Asian countries represented in figure 11-1 are: Indonesia, Malaysia, Nepal, Pakistan, the Philippines, the Republic of Korea, Sri Lanka, and Thailand; the Latin American and Caribbean countries are: Colombia, Costa Rica, Dominican Republic, Guyana, Jamaica, Mexico, Panama, and Peru.

4. For Sub-Saharan African countries, the means were calculated from data on wfs variable V509 (additional children wanted); for other countries it is the difference between the mean wanted family size (Lightbourne and MacDonald 1982) and the mean number of living children. The demand for children in Jordan, which is not represented in figure 11-1, is about as high as in Ghana and Lesotho in Sub-Saharan Africa.

5. Figure 11-3 is based on current status measures (see Singh and Ferry 1984) and was drafted by using prevalence at some pivotal durations. The curves would assume a more erratic shape if they were drawn on the basis of prevalence at each single month.

6. The western phase of the Nigerian FFFP Survey of 1971–73, for instance, which inquired whether respondents had used breastfeeding to delay or prevent pregnancy, revealed that only 2 percent of the women breastfed for this purpose, but even the sporadic affirmative answers may have been due to a misunderstanding of the question.

7. Usually, the husband decides (in accordance with the loosely stated norms) when to resume marital life. As an Igbirra-Nupe couple from Iboje village (Oka district, Nigeria) stated, "It is for the woman to go and live with her parents when she is carrying a baby. When the child can walk very well, the husband comes to tell his wife that she is now fit for another sex" (Acsadi 1976, p.137).

References

Acsadi, George T. 1972. "Fertility Regulation among the Yoruba." Paper presented at the seminar "Family Planning in West Africa," University of Ibadan, Ibadan, August 7–12, processed.

_____. 1976. "Traditional Birth Control Methods in Yorubaland." In J. F. Marshall and S. Polgar, eds., *Culture, Natality, and Family Planning*. Monograph 21. Chapel Hill, N.C.: Carolina Population Center, University of North Carolina at Chapel Hill.

_____. 1979. "Illustrations of Strategies and Some Tactical Considerations Relevant to Comparative Analysis of wfs Data." U.N. Working Group on Comparative Analysis of wfs Data, 3d meeting. UN/UNFPA/WFS, III/8. Geneva; processed.

_____. 1980. "Review of Characteristics, Measures, and Other Indicators." In *The United Nations Programme for Comparative Analysis of World Fertility Survey Data*. New York: U.N. Fund for Population Activities.

_____. 1982. *Comparative Demographic Analysis: A Manual*. U.N. Working Group on Comparative Analysis of World Fertility Survey Data, 5th meeting. UN/UNFPA/WFS.V/16. Geneva; processed.

_____. n.d. "The Nigerian Fertility, Family, and Family Planning Study, 1971–73." University of Ife, Nigeria. Unpublished data.

Acsadi, George T., A. A. Igun, and G. Z. Johnson. 1972. *Surveys of Fertility, Family, and Family Planning in Nigeria*. Ile-Ife: Institute of Population and Manpower Studies, University of Ife.

Acsadi, George T. and Gwendolyn Johnson-Acsadi. 1985. "Demand for Children and Spacing in Sub-Saharan Africa." PHN Technical Note 85-6. World Bank Population, Health and Nutrition Department. Washington, D.C.; processed.

Balkaran, S., and D. P. Smith. "Socio-economic Differentials in Breastfeeding." *World Fertility Survey Comparative Studies: Cross-National Summaries*. Additional Tables. Voorburg, Netherlands: International Statistical Institute; processed.

Benin. Bureau Central de Récensement. 1983. *Enquête Fécondité au Benin*. Rapport préliminaire; processed.

Botswana. 1985. *Botswana Family Health Survey, 1984*. Gaborone, Botswana: Ministry of Health; Columbia, Md.: Westinghouse Public Applied Systems.

Caldwell, John C., and P. Caldwell. 1977. "The Role of Marital Sexual Abstinence in Determining Fertility: A Study of Yoruba in Nigeria." *Population Studies* 31: 343–69.

Carr-Saunders, A. M. 1964. *World Population: Past Growth and Present Trends*. London: Frank Cass.

Centro Latinoamericano de Demografía and Community and Family Study Center. 1972. *Fertility and Family Planning in Metropolitan Latin America*. Chicago: CFSC, University of Chicago.

Cleland, John, and John Hobcraft, eds. 1985. *Reproductive Change in Developing Countries*. Oxford: Oxford University Press.

Cochrane, S. H. 1979. *Fertility and Education: What Do We Really Know?* World Bank Staff Occasional Papers, No. 26. Baltimore, Md.: Johns Hopkins University Press.

Dankoussou, Issaka, S. Diarra, D. Laya, and D. I. Pool. 1975. "Niger." In J. C. Caldwell and others, eds., *Population Growth and Socio-economic Change in West Africa*. New York: Columbia University Press.

Ferry, B. 1981. "Breastfeeding." *World Fertility Survey Comparative Studies: Cross-National Summaries*. No. 13.

Ferry, Benoit, and David P. Smith. 1983. "Breastfeeding Differentials." *World Fertility Survey Comparative Studies: Cross-National Summaries*, No. 23.

Ghana. Central Bureau of Statistics. 1983. *Ghana Fertility Survey, 1979–1980*. First Report. Vols. 1–2. Accra.

Gray, Ronald H. 1981. "Birth Intervals, Postpartum Sexual Abstinence, and Child Health." In H. J. Page and R. Lesthaeghe, eds., *Child-Spacing In Tropical Africa: Traditions and Change*. London: Academic Press.

Grebenik, E., and Althea Hill. 1974. *International Demographic Terminology: Fertility, Family Planning, and Nuptiality*. IUSSP Papers, No. 4. Liège, Belgium: International Union for the Scientific Study of Population.

Jain, Anrudh, and John Bongaarts. 1981. "Socio-Biological Factors in Exposure to Childbearing: Breastfeeding and Its Fertility Effects." In *World Fertility Survey Conference, 1980: Records of Proceedings*. Vol. 2. Voorburg, Netherlands: International Statistical Institute.

Johnson-Acsadi, Gwendolyn, and M. Szykman. 1984. "Selected Characteristics of Exposed Women Who Wanted No More Children but Were Not Using Contraceptives." In J. A. Ross and R. McNamara, eds., *Survey Analysis for the Guidance of Family Planning Programs*. Liège, Belgium: Ordina.

Kenya. Central Bureau of Statistics. 1980. *Kenya Fertility Survey, 1977–1978*. Vols. 1–2. Nairobi: Ministry of Economic Planning and Development.

Kumekpor, T. K. 1975. "Togo." In John C. Caldwell and others, eds., *Population Growth and Socioeconomic Change in West Africa*. New York: Columbia University Press.

Lesotho. Central Bureau of Statistics. 1981. *Lesotho Fertility Survey, 1977*. Vols. 1–2. Maseru, Lesotho: Ministry of Planning and Statistics.

Liberia. 1988. *Demographic and Health Survey, 1986*. Monrovia, Liberia: Bureau of Statistics; Columbia, Md.: Institute for Resource Development/Westinghouse.

Lightbourne, Robert E. 1985. "Individual Preferences and Fertility Behaviour." In J. Cleland and J. Hobcraft, eds., *Reproductive Change in Developing Countries*. Oxford: Oxford University Press.

Lightbourne, Robert E., and A. L. MacDonald. 1982. *Family Size Preferences*. WFS Comparative Studies: Cross-National Summaries, No. 14. Voorburg: International Statistical Institute.

Lorimer, Frank. 1954. *Culture and Human Fertility: A Study of the Relation of Cultural Conditions to Fertility in Non-Industrial and Transitional Societies*. Paris: U.N. Educational, Scientific, and Cultural Organization.

Mabogunje, Akin L. 1981. "The Policy Implications of Changes in Child-Spacing Practices in Tropical Africa." In H. J. Page and R. Lesthaeghe, eds., *Child-Spacing In Tropical Africa: Traditions and Change*. London: Academic Press.

Mangani, Nlandu, Jane T. Bertrand, and others. 1982. "Results of the PRODEF/Tulane Survey in Bas Zaire." Part 1. "Population Characteristics, Reproductive Ideals, and Fertility Control." November; processed.

Mauritania. Direction de la Statistique et de la Comptabilité Nationale. 1983. *Enquête Nationale sur la Fécondité, 1981: Résultats provisoires*. Ministère de Plan et de l'Amènagement du Territoire.

Molnos, Angela. 1968. *Attitudes towards Family Planning in East Africa*. Munich: Weltforum Verlag; processed.

_____. 1973. *Cultural Source Materials for Population Planning in East Africa*. Vol 3. *Beliefs and Practices*. Nairobi: East African Publishing House.

Morgan, R. W. 1975. "Fertility Levels and Change." In J. C. Caldwell and others, eds., *Population Growth and Socioeconomic Change in West Africa*. New York: Columbia University Press.

Nigeria. 1984. *The Nigeria Fertility Survey, 1981–82*: Principal Report. Vols. 1–2. Lagos, Nigeria: National Population Bureau.

Nigeria. National Population Commission. 1983. "Nigeria Fertility Survey, 1981–1982: Preliminary Report." Lagos. March; processed.

Okediji, F. O. and others. 1976. "The Changing African Family Project: A Report with Special Reference to the Nigerian Segment." *Studies in Family Planning*, 7(5): 126–36.

Ondo State (Nigeria). 1987. *Ondo State of Nigeria: Demographic and Health Survey, 1986*. Akure, Nigeria: Ministry of Health; Columbia, Md.: Institute for Resource Development/Westinghouse; processed.

Page, Hilary J., and Ron Lesthaeghe, eds. 1981. *Child-Spacing in Tropical Africa: Traditions and Change*. London: Academic Press.

Reyna, S. P. 1975. "Pronatalism and Child Labor: Chadian Attitudes to Birth Control and Family Size." In J. C. Caldwell and others, eds., *Population Growth and Socioeconomic Change in West Africa*. New York: Columbia University Press.

Singh, Susheela, and Benoit Ferry. 1984. "Biological and Traditional Factors That Influence Fertility: Results from World Fertility Surveys." *World Fertility Survey Comparative Surveys: Cross-National Summaries*, No. 40.

Sudan. Department of Statistics. 1982. *The Sudan Fertility Survey, 1979*. Vols. 1–2. Khartoum: Ministry of National Planning.

Talbot, P. A. 1926. *The Peoples of Southern Nigeria*. 4 vols. London: Frank Cass.

United Nations. 1970. *Variables and Questionnaire for Comparative Fertility Surveys*. Population Studies. No. 45. ST/SOA/SER. A/45. New York.

_____. 1981. *Variations in the Incidence of Knowledge and Use of Contraception: A Comparative Analysis of World Fertility Survey Results for Twenty Developing Countries*. New York.

_____. 1983. *Relationships between Fertility and Education: A Comparative Analysis of World Fertility Survey Data for Twenty-two Developing Countries*. ST/ESA/SER.R./48. New York.

_____. 1987. *Fertility Behaviour in the Context of Development: Evidence from the World Fertility Survey*. ST/ESA/ SER. A/100. New York.

Van de Walle, Etienne. 1968. "Marriage in African Censuses and Inquiries." In W. Brass and others, eds., *The Demography of Tropical Africa*. Princeton, N.J.: Princeton University Press.

Whiting, John W. M. 1964. "Effects of Climate on Certain

Cultural Practices." In Ward H. Goodenough, ed., *Explorations in Cultural Anthropology*. New York: McGraw-Hill.

World Fertility Survey. 1977a. *Strategies for the Analysis of wfs Data*, wfs Basic Documentation, No. 9. Voorburg, Netherlands: wfs, December.

———. 1977b. *Guidelines for Country Report No. 1*. wfs Basic Documentation, No. 8. Voorburg, Netherlands: wfs, December.

———. 1984. *Major Findings and Implications*. Oxford: Alden Press.

Zimbabwe. 1985. *Zimbabwe Reproductive Health Survey*. Harare: Zimbabwe National Family Planning Council; Columbia, Md.: Westinghouse Public Applied Systems.

12

The Demand for Fertility Control

Odile Frank

All societies limit fertility as a result of customary restrictions on marriage and sexual behavior, and the maximum potential total of about fifteen births per woman is never observed for a population. Accordingly, the total fertility rate of fewer than seven births per woman in Sub-Saharan Africa, although currently the highest for any region in the world, is still below half of the theoretical maximum.

This level of fertility is the product of traditionally strong upward pressures on childbearing offset by customary behaviors that have powerful dampening effects on individual fertility. In addition to being below its maximum potential, fertility is also below levels of natural fertility that have been reached by other pronatalist societies, such as the Hutterites (Eaton and Mayer 1953). It is probable that because of high mortality in a hostile environment, African social patterns and reproductive behavior in the region came to settle at an equilibrium that traded off the very highest fertility for rudimentary supports to child survival, such as breastfeeding protected by abstinence from sexual relations. This chapter focuses on whether any evidence exists of demand for fertility control and for family planning in the region that may at present or could in the future lead to fertility levels lower than those determined by customary restrictions alone.[1]

Fertility Regulation in Sub-Saharan African Culture

Demand for fertility control in Sub-Saharan Africa can be assessed from several practices as well as from discrete and purposeful contraception. Broadly viewed, fertility is regulated through behavior ranging from avoidance of conception at particular points of a woman's reproductive life to reorganization of her child-rearing schedule over her lifetime. The scope of such behavior can be traced in the order in which it arises as an option in the birth cycle:

- Avoidance of pregnancy
- Induced abortion to regulate the outcome of specific pregnancies
- Infanticide to regulate the survival of live-born infants
- Child abandonment to regulate number (and characteristics) of surviving children
- Child fostering to regulate the timing and tempo of child rearing tasks associated with a surviving family size.

All of these behaviors may be used to regulate the total number of surviving children present at any point in a woman's life.

Avoidance of Pregnancy

In Sub-Saharan Africa, traditional methods of avoiding pregnancy are practiced almost exclusively in relation to an earlier birth, that is, in the postpartum period (Page and Lesthaeghe 1981). They are therefore practiced after and only in reference to the birth of a thriving infant and essentially for the purpose of continuing to guarantee that infant's survival. All postpartum practices (extended breastfeeding, abstinence, and coitus interruptus) are oriented to an infant's survival past a certain stage of development rather than to avoidance of a pregnancy per se. This differentiation is critical to a proper understanding of the nature of conception avoidance in Sub-Saharan Africa.

Although these practices serve to reduce fertility beneath levels that would occur otherwise, they are rarely intended for fertility limitation.[2] Moreover, notwithstanding their overall influence on fertility, with the possible exception of coitus interruptus, all the evidence indicates that they have little future potential as chosen means of family limitation. The trends in both postpartum abstinence and breastfeeding are toward declining durations: postpartum abstinence is clearly disappearing throughout East Africa and at least in urban areas across the rest of Africa. Breastfeeding durations tend to decline in urban areas, and even it they do not, lactational amenorrhea may be shortened by earlier and more intense supplementary feeding, which leads to shortened birth intervals when it is not accompanied by abstinence.

Postpartum abstinence can be expected to disappear altogether in Africa in the long term. With increasing exposure to education and to Western values, sexual abstinence is increasingly onerous. There are unlikely to be policies to promote its continuing practice; on the contrary, policies to encourage the education of women and to improve the health level of mothers and children, which will probably seek to eliminate certain customary practices, such as female circumcision, may inevitably influence the erosion of others, such as postpartum abstinence.

Promotion of breastfeeding is feasible, and the economic obstacles to increased effective demand for breast milk substitutes among the mass of African populations will probably retard the abandonment of breastfeeding. Nevertheless, while prolonged breastfeeding will continue to have dampening effects on fertility overall, it could not responsibly be promoted as a means of limiting fertility at the individual level and certainly could not be expected ever to perform better in this regard than it does now.

In sum, although lactational amenorrhea (due to breastfeeding) and postpartum abstinence are powerful constraints on fertility in Sub-Saharan Africa, they are generally not intended for limitation and have no further potential as fertility-limiting methods. Changes in these phenomena at present give no indication of a demand for fertility limitation; in fact, the combined effects of their declining practice are becoming visible as measurable fertility increases, as in Kenya.

Coitus interruptus, on the other hand, has considerable potential as a means of fertility control and probably played a significant role in the secular European fertility decline (Tietze 1968). Unfortunately, information on its practice in Sub-Saharan Africa is rare, so that nothing can be said about whether increasing levels of practice indicate growing demand for fertility control or limitation.

Current Practice of Contraception

It can be shown on the basis of the findings of the World Fertility Survey (WFS) and Contraceptive Prevalence Survey (CPS) that, in effect, few women in this region who are at risk of conception practice contraception, and the record is only slightly better among women, who, in addition, report that they want no more children.

Table 12-1 summarizes the knowledge and practice of modern contraception in Sub-Saharan Africa as recorded by the WFS and focuses on modern contraceptive use among currently married women, self-reported as fecund, who were exposed to the risk of conception (and were not pregnant at the time of the survey).

Of the sample of all women in each country, from 13 to 84 percent of women had heard of at least one modern or efficient method. The proportion of women

Table 12-1. *Knowledge and Use of Modern Contraception, Selected Coutries, about 1980*
(percent)

Country	Ever-married women who knew a method	Ever-married women who had ever used a method	Exposed women currently using contraception	Exposed women wanting no more children and currently using contraception
Benin	13	—	1	—
Cameroon[a]	29	3	1	6
Côte d'Ivoire	20	3	1	4
Ghana	59	18	7	17
Kenya	84	11	6	17
Lesotho	60	6	3	15
Nigeria	21	3	1	4
Senegal	23	1	1	—
Sudan (north)	50	9	5	16

— Not available.

a. These questions were asked of very restricted samples of women in Cameroon, representing only a fraction of all eligible women in each case. For this reason they are not strictly comparable (République Unie du Cameroun 1983).

Sources: République Populaire du Bénin (1983); Republic of Ghana (1983); République de Côte d'Ivoire (1984); National Population Bureau (1984); République du Sénégal (1981); République Unie du Cameroun (1983); Republic of Kenya (1980); Kingdom of Lesotho (1981); Democratic Republic of the Sudan (1982).

who had ever used a modern method drops, however, to a range of 1 to 18 percent, and in the majority of these countries fewer than 10 percent of women reported having ever used a modern, efficient method.

Current use was measured on a smaller base of women, for the most part, those who were currently married and who reported themselves fecund and not pregnant. Despite the smaller denominator, the proportion of women who were currently using a modern contraceptive method at the time of the surveys shrinks further to between 1 and 7 percent.

Current use of a contraceptive method was higher among currently married women who reported themselves fecund and not pregnant and who also reported that they did not want additional children. Between 4 and 17 percent of these women reported current use of a modern, efficient method.

Although women who want no more children display the highest levels of modern contraceptive use among exposed women, the data in table 12-2 reveal that these women often represent a minority of those who practice modern contraception. This table shows that the majority of currently married fecund women who were practicing modern contraception at the time of these surveys wanted more children in five of the seven countries with data. These observations indicate that modern contraception among currently married fecund women tends to be practiced primarily for spacing purposes (see also chapter 11 in this volume). In addition, the fact that exposed women who do not want additional children are outnumbered by those who say they intend to continue childbearing in most of these countries suggests that nonpractice of contraception may be due less to poor availability than to an apparent lack of motivation to use modern contraceptives. The two exceptions are Kenya and Lesotho, where the majority of exposed women practicing contraception reported that they did not want more children. This is consistent with the finding that about half of these women in Kenya and Lesotho had undergone sterilization (see section on sterilization below and table 12-3).

Finally, it is useful to recall what these proportions represent in absolute numbers of women, which are also shown in table 12-2. Thus, against the sizes of the national samples drawn in these surveys, which range from 4,000 to 10,000 women, the numbers of all the women at risk of conception who reported that they wished to cease childbearing and were using a modern, efficient method of contraception range from 2 to 118 women. The behavior of this group of women is not likely to have any measurable influence on overall fertility until its size becomes more substantial. Moreover, despite an apparent overall indifference of women practicing contraception to their number of living children, it is important to note that these women had, on average, between four and five living children in Lesotho, about five in Ghana, between five and six in North Sudan, and about six in Kenya.

The data that I have discussed thus far relate to retrospective information reported between 1977 and 1982. Consequently, it seems reasonable to ask whether the situation has since changed. More recent data are available now from national surveys, conducted under the CPS program, in Botswana, Kenya, Somalia, and Zimbabwe. (A Zaire survey covered only selected subnational regions). Accordingly, these CPS surveys provide information for one country that had been surveyed earlier under the WFS program—namely, Kenya—that invites a comparison of national data reported for 1977–78 and for 1984 (Republic of Kenya 1984, 1986).

Data for the two surveys show 14 percent of all women as having ever used modern methods in 1984 as compared with 11 percent in 1977–78. Similarly, the proportion of exposed women who reported current use of

Table 12-2. *Contraceptive Use among Exposed Women Who Wanted More Children and Who Did Not Want More, Selected Countries, about 1980*

Country	Of women who wanted more, percentage who currently contracept	Of women who did not want more, percentage who currently contracept	Of current contraceptors, percentage who wanted more	Of current contraceptors, percentage who did not want more	Numbers of women who did not want more children and were using an efficient method
Cameroon	1	6	75	17	2
Côte d'Ivoire	1	4	73	23	5
Ghana	7	17	70	27	67
Kenya	4	17	43	48	118
Lesotho	1	15	36	61	47
Nigeria	1	4	59	32	13
Sudan (north)	4	16	52	44	48

Sources: République Populaire du Bénin (1983); Republic of Ghana (1983); République de Côte d'Ivoire (1984); National Population Bureau (1984); République du Sénégal (1981); République Unie du Cameroun (1983); Republic of Kenya (1980); Kingdom of Lesotho (1981); Democratic Republic of the Sudan (1982).

Table 12-3. *Percentage Sterilized among all Ever-Married Women and among Exposed Women, Selected Countries, about 1980*

Country	Women sterilized as a percentage of			
	All ever-married women	All exposed women	Exposed women who want no more children	Exposed women who used an efficient method
Ghana	0.4	0.6	5.3	31
Kenya	0.8	1.2	7.2	42
Lesotho	0.7	1.1	8.1	55
Nigeria	0.1	0.1	1.5	38
Sudan (north)	0.3	0.4	2.7	17

Sources: République Populaire du Bénin (1983); Republic of Ghana (1983); République de Côte d'Ivoire (1984); National Population Bureau (1984); République du Sénégal (1981); République Unie du Cameroun (1983); Republic of Kenya (1980); Kingdom of Lesotho (1981); Democratic Republic of the Sudan (1982).

a modern method rose from 6 to 9 percent. Specifically, between 1977–78 and 1984, the proportion of currently married women using the pill increased one percentage point and the proportion using the IUD over two percentage points.

The fertility results of the 1984 survey give reason for critical scrutiny of these contraceptive prevalence increases. Total fertility based on births in the twelve months prior to the survey is estimated at 7.7, barely down from 7.9 in 1977–78. (The more reliable fertility estimate from the earlier survey, a three-year average for 1975–77, is 8.1; no comparable three-year estimate is available from the 1984 survey.) The age-specific fertility curve of 1984 is strikingly similar to the curve obtained from the 1977–78 survey, suggesting a high degree of stability of behavior (Republic of Kenya 1984). Prevalence rates have risen but not enough to disturb the overall pattern of high fertility.

Another CPS survey, the 1984 Zimbabwe Reproductive Health Survey (Zimbabwe National Family Planning Council 1985), demonstrates the case more strongly. The survey revealed a reported current use level of modern methods (mostly oral contraception) of 27 percent. Such a level of prevalence suggests that a much faster pace of adoption of modern contraception may be possible in some Sub-Saharan countries. Nevertheless, it should be noted that a total fertility rate (based on reported births in the twelve prior months) of 6.5 births per woman is reported from the same survey. On the basis of Bongaart's regression line for total fertility rates and contraceptive prevalence levels of 83 countries in 1980 ($R^2 = .85$), one would expect a total fertility rate of somewhat more than five births per woman (5.2 by calculation) for a prevalence level of 27 percent (Bongaarts 1984). Even the lower total fertility rate estimated from the 1982 census of 5.8 births per woman is too high to correspond to these prevalence levels (Government of Zimbabwe 1984).

Apparently, the assumption of one-to-one correspondence in the translation of prevalence rates into fertility levels is risky for Sub-Saharan Africa. A combination of poor use effectiveness and compensating falls in breastfeeding and postpartum abstinence durations (which, other things being equal, would raise fertility) apparently bears some responsibility. Other factors tending to inflate recorded prevalence rates are the sincere but inaccurate report of "current" pill use by women to whom pills have indeed been distributed at some point by an active community-based distribution program. The misuse of pills is explicitly recognized in the Zimbabwe report (Zimbabwe National Family Planning Council 1985). Accordingly, "acceptance" of oral contraceptives, in particular, may correspond only slightly to actual protection against conception.

Overall, the low levels of contraceptive practice among the most "motivated" women, as operationally defined, and the stability of high fertility are consistent with the pattern of strong fertility desires in Sub-Saharan Africa.

Sterilization

Voluntary surgical sterilization is a clear operational indicator of an unqualified desire to cease childbearing. The prevalence of sterilization can be gauged once again from results of the WFS. Its incidence may also be gauged, however, from information regarding clinical services currently being provided to African women.

The proportions of women sterilized in Sub-Saharan Africa between 1977 and 1982 were minuscule, as is evident from table 12-3, which presents the findings from the World Fertility Survey for those countries in Sub-Saharan Africa with any reported sterilization. The more recent data for Kenya show that 1.9 percent of all women and 2.6 percent of currently married women were sterilized as of 1984 (Republic of Kenya 1984). Still, although women who have been sterilized comprise quite negligible proportions of all women, they represent a measurable proportion of women who are currently married and would be fecund and exposed otherwise but who want no more children; in fact, they comprise as many as half or more of the "exposed" women who practice modern contraception and report that they do not want more children.

The average age and parity of women seeking sterilization deserve attention. Data from clinics providing voluntary surgical contraception in Kenya, Nigeria, Sierra Leone, and Zaire reveal that mean ages of patient groups range between about 33 and 39 years and that their average parity ranges between 4.8 and 6.7 (Association for Voluntary Sterilization 1984). Sterilization is clearly most often used by older women who wish to cease childbearing and, in this area, the prevalence data from the World Fertility Survey and the clinical incidence data are consistent. Both sources provide evidence of a demand for stopping childbearing at older ages and at high parity. The proportions of women involved are very small, however, and more important, the small proportions, high age, and high parity of these women mean that the effect on fertility rates is negligible. Were demand for sterilization to grow, however—and the more recent Kenya data do suggest this possibility—its level could eventually have a substantial demographic effect, by eliminating highest-order births. In Kenya, for example, a completely successful stop-at-six policy would reduce fertility by 34 percent.

Induced Abortion

After conception has occurred, the major means of controlling fertility is by terminating the pregnancy through induced abortion. In theory, induced abortion can be used by women to the point where fertility is highly controlled at the population level. In practice, abortion has been used by some societies at certain times as the major means of family limitation and has resulted in measurable widespread fertility decline. When recourse to induced abortion is not evident in fertility measures at the population level, as in Sub-Saharan Africa, assessment of the nature of demand for fertility control on the basis of the incidence of induced abortion depends very largely on the characteristics of women using this method. A number of recent studies that are reviewed here allow for such a determination.

In Sub-Saharan African countries as a whole, abortion legislation is very restrictive. The laws currently in effect are for the most part unrevised statutes of the colonial regimes at the time the African nations became independent. In over half of Sub-Saharan African countries, abortion is explicitly illegal or legal only on narrow medical grounds (pregnancy as a threat to a woman's life). In table 12-4, these countries are all noted as providing for legal abortion on narrow grounds because the exception to save a woman's life can generally be assumed as implicit where it is not stated.

In the remaining countries, abortion is legal on broader medical grounds (pregnancy as a threat to a woman's health). Only in seven of the last group of countries is abortion legal on any further grounds: in the case of a known genetic or other impairment of the fetus in Ghana, Liberia, Namibia, Zambia, and Zimbabwe; in the case of rape or incest in Cameroon, Ghana, Liberia, Namibia, and Zimbabwe; and for social or social-medical reasons (such as poverty or unmarried status, for example) in only two countries, Burundi and Zambia, since 1981 and 1972, respectively (Tietze and Henshaw 1986). For all intents and purposes, it is only in these two countries that any scale of elective abortion could be expected on legal grounds.

Any demographically meaningful data on induced abortion in Sub-Saharan Africa, therefore, relate to illegal abortion; reported cases of legal abortion are nil in the majority of countries and insignificant in all others. Akinla (1970), for example, reports that there were seven cases of legal abortion in Freetown, Sierra Leone, during 1965, 1966, and 1967 and three cases at the Lagos University Teaching Hospital, Nigeria, in 1967, whereas four to five legal procedures per year were carried out at Mulago Hospital in Kampala, Uganda, in the 1960s. In Zambia, where legal abortion should be more accessible, the number of legal abortions recorded in the University Teaching Hospital of Lusaka was 48 in 1972, 88 in 1973, 133 in 1974, 165 in 1975, and 173 in 1976, whereas the number of admissions associated with extralegal abortion in the same hospital is estimated to have been about 1,000 in 1976 (Liskin 1980). As recently as 1982–83, sequelae of nonmedically induced abortion were responsible for an important fraction of maternal deaths in the hospital (Mhango and others 1986).

Reliable estimates of the incidence of induced abortion in Sub-Saharan Africa are nonexistent. Statements regarding the increased incidence of induced abortion have generally been made on the basis of a rise in the number of admissions for abortion-related complications to a hospital, which assumes that the incidence of spontaneous abortions is constant, and an increase in abortions can be attributed to induced events. Even when the proportions of induced and spontaneous abortions in hospital admissions for abortion complications are known, these figures provide very little information on the incidence of induced abortions. An unknown proportion of women who have an illegal abortion have a range of complications that do not require hospitalization or have no complications. A further unknown is the proportion who become ill, or die, without seeking medical assistance. Lack of knowledge of the incidence of abortion sequelae, and the fact that medical services are widely unavailable, make the numerator indeterminate.

Table 12-4. *Legal Grounds for Abortion, 1986*

Country	Medical, narrow (life)	Medical, broad (health)	Eugenic (fetal defect)	Juridical (rape, incest)	Social, socio-medical
Benin	yes	no	no	no	no
Botswana	yes	no	no	no	no
Burkina Faso	yes	no	no	no	no
Burundi	no	yes	no	no	yes
Cameroon	no	yes	no	yes	no
Central African Republic	yes	no	no	no	no
Chad	yes	no	no	no	no
Congo	no	yes	no	no	no
Côte d'Ivoire	yes	no	no	no	no
Ethiopia	no	yes	no	no	no
Gabon	yes	no	no	no	no
Ghana	no	yes	yes	yes	no
Guinea	no	yes	no	no	no
Kenya	no	yes	no	no	no
Lesotho	no	yes	no	no	no
Liberia	no	yes	yes	yes	no
Madagascar	yes	no	no	no	no
Malawi	yes	no	no	no	no
Mali	yes	no	no	no	no
Mauritania	yes	no	no	no	no
Mozambique	yes	no	no	no	no
Namibia	no	yes	yes	yes	no
Niger	yes	no	no	no	no
Nigeria	yes	no	no	no	no
Rwanda	no	yes	no	no	no
Senegal	yes	no	no	no	no
Sierra Leone	no	yes	no	no	no
Somalia	yes	no	no	no	no
Sudan	yes	no	no	no	no
Tanzania	no	yes	no	no	no
Togo	yes	no	no	no	no
Uganda	no	yes	no	no	no
Zaire	yes	no	no	no	no
Zambia	no	yes	yes	no	yes
Zimbabwe	no	yes	yes	yes	no

Note: Narrow medical grounds are indicated for all countries where narrow grounds are the only ones explicitly allowed, as well as for all countries were no exception to illegality is mentioned, on the assumption that the exception to save a woman's life is implicit.

Source: Tietze and Henshaw 1986.

Even so, a number of recent studies of abortion in Africa do provide valuable information. These studies essentially allow for a fairly clear characterization of groups of women who had an induced abortion.

There have been several comparable studies—in Ghana, Nigeria, Mali, Uganda, and Zaire—of hospitalized patients with induced abortion complications (Akinla 1970; Ampofo 1970a, 1970b; Binkin and others 1984; Lwanga 1977; Nichols and Bongwele 1983, Okojie 1976). On the basis of these studies, a majority of patients who are hospitalized with complications following induced abortion can be characterized as young, single, urban, educated, childless women. The studies in Mali and Zaire show clearly that these women differ in all these characteristics from women with complications due to spon-

taneous abortion. The latter are older (mean age 26.6, as opposed to 26.4 for the former), most often married (only 13 percent were single, widowed, or divorced, as opposed to 17 percent who had never married), of higher parity (only 22 percent had had no live births in Mali, despite the fact that 46 percent had had at least one prior spontaneous abortion), less educated (72 percent in Mali had never been to school), and, most important, had no history of induced abortion (less than 3 percent reported ever having had an induced abortion).

A number of surveys on the sexual experience, contraceptive behavior, and fertility of young unmarried adults being carried out currently in Sub-Saharan Africa confirm such recourse to induced abortion.[3] The results of one of these surveys apply to 841 young (aged 14–

25 years) unmarried women in Ibadan, Nigeria (Nichols and others 1984, 1986). Fully half of this urban group of women were sexually active, about half again were exposed to the risk of pregnancy and became pregnant, and almost all the pregnancies were terminated by induced abortion. These findings suggest that induced abortion is frequent among young unmarried women in urban areas, particularly among the educated.

In order to broaden the information base in the definition of groups who have recourse to induced abortion, it is useful to look at the history of a sample of women who are somewhat more representative—in this case, women who delivered in hospitals and from whom detailed histories were elicited. One such study of obstetric patients was recently conducted in a hospital in Accra, Ghana, by Janowitz (personal correspondence, 1984). Of 12,000 obstetric patients hospitalized during twelve months between 1981 and 1982, 4,990 were interviewed.

The preliminary results of this survey allow for two relevant observations. First, of the women who were delivering after their second pregnancy, and who had been pregnant only once before (17 percent of the sample), about one in three had had an induced abortion following the first conception. Of these women, however, 73 percent were educated to the secondary or university level, and 81 percent had had at least primary schooling. Of all the educated women, about 40 percent had terminated their first pregnancy. Of all women with no schooling, fewer than 5 percent had terminated their first pregnancy.

Second, of the women who were delivering after their third pregnancy (about 15 percent of the entire sample), about 27 percent of those with a primary education, 55 percent of those with a secondary education, and 63 percent of those with a university education reported a previous induced abortion, whereas only 9 percent of the women with no education reported any previous induced abortion. The proportion of women who had terminated both previous pregnancies also rose with education (1 percent with no schooling, 7 percent with primary, 21 percent with secondary, and 31 percent with university-level education).

Although all of the data reviewed here are based on samples of women who are unrepresentative because of their access to medical care and their self-selection for hospitalization or because of research objectives, together they provide a consistent profile of the groups using induced abortion in Sub-Saharan Africa. These data suggest that induced abortion in urban areas is used primarily by young, unmarried women, very often in an educational stream, who are trying to delay marriage and the onset of childbearing.

Because of this particular pattern of abortion behavior in Sub-Saharan Africa, it is safe to conclude that abortion in urban areas now indicates a demand for controlling or changing the pattern of entry into childbearing. The fact that it occurs mostly within a group that represents a small minority of Sub-Saharan African populations indicates that even the delay in starting childbearing is the product not of broad changes but of specific needs, most often to continue and complete an education program.[4]

In sum, the sporadic data on induced abortion in Sub-Saharan Africa evidently signal a grave medical and public health problem but have little relevance as indicators of demand for fertility limitation. In urban areas, young women in pursuit of secondary and higher education are highly motivated to delay marriage and childbearing and often use induced abortion to terminate pregnancies. Not surprisingly, the women who eventually reach the highest levels of education are the most frequent users of contraception within marriage, and many of them may limit their fertility eventually.

Infanticide and Child Abandonment

Both infanticide and abandonment are means of regulating family size as well as the characteristics of surviving children. Historically, they have been used for both purposes at least occasionally in all societies. The highest recorded incidence of these practices occurred in the cities of Western Europe in the eighteenth and nineteenth centuries (Wrigley 1969).

In Sub-Saharan Africa, infanticide has probably been used occasionally in all societies, but there is no documented evidence that it has ever been used on any scale that would approach demographic significance. Reports of the traditional practice of infanticide clearly relate to exceptional cases, such as multiple births, malformed infants, births to uninitiated girls, breech deliveries, or births following a very short interval, and do not indicate that infanticide was mandatory (Carr-Saunders 1922; Lorimer 1954; Wrigley 1969; LeVine and LeVine 1981).

Abandonment of children probably did not and does not exist in traditional Sub-Saharan Africa, because alternative homes for children are easy to find in virtually all societies, and wet-nursing is practiced. The widespread institution of fostering similarly provided for the welfare of orphans until very recently. Children are now being abandoned in the cities of Africa; however: press reports in Zimbabwe suggest increases in abandoned children in Harare as well as cases of rural abandonment, and it was recently found necessary in Lomé, Togo, to establish a facility called SOS for abandoned children. Nevertheless, reports of child abandonment are still sparse and anecdotal, and it is highly unlikely that it is occurring on any appreciable scale. The phenomenon does, however, indicate the social (and ethnic) dislocation of individuals and families in urban areas, particularly among the poorest segments, and the consequent disappearance of traditional support systems that provide relief in times of stress.

Child Fostering

A system whereby alternative homes for children are available for a number of years of childhood in effect provides a means of regulating family size, through manipulation of the number of children present at any one time. In Sub-Saharan Africa, the institution of fostering provides just such opportunities to individual women (Frank 1984).[5] The anthropological evidence and especially the demographic estimates indicate that child fostering is notably widespread. The proportions of women who make alternative arrangements for their children's upbringing for several years of childhood exceed by far the combined proportions of women who practice modern contraception or who seek sterilization or abortion. In the framework of this analysis, fostering is a widely available and long-standing option for making high fertility manageable, thereby mitigating the demand for all other types of fertility control. Fostering opportunities can meet demands to delay, space, or cease childbearing by providing the means to delay, space, or remove many of the consequences of reproductive events. Fostering can also meet demands for family size limitation because women can place their children, quasi-permanently, only with families who, for one reason or another, have had fewer children.

It is not possible to get direct quantitative data on child fostering from any national data source simply because fostering is not measured. Several indirect estimates of the extent of fostering, however, are available in the literature. Isiugo-Abanihe (1983) has estimated from household data that, in Ghana in 1971, 18 percent of all children below the age of 11 were foster children because they did not have parents in the household. Similarly, from census information, he also estimated that the proportion of children who were away from their mothers in Sierra Leone in 1974 ranged from 29 percent for mothers aged 15–19 and to 46 percent for mothers 30–34; the proportion of mothers aged 15–34 who had children away in Liberia in the same years was 40 percent, with little variation by age (39 percent at 15–19; 32 percent at 20–24; 39 percent at 25–29, and 46 percent at 30–34). Using the WFS household questionnaires, Page (1986) has found that the proportion of children under 15 not living with their mothers (according to region) in Cameroon in 1978 was 13–24 percent; 14–27 percent in Ghana in 1979–80; 21 percent in Côte d'Ivoire in 1980–81; 10–16 percent in Kenya in 1977–78; 21 percent in Lesotho in 1977; 9–13 percent in Nigeria in 1981–82; and 4–9 percent

in northern Sudan in 1979. Finally, census data from Botswana reveal that 22 percent of children born to mothers 15–34 years old were not living with their mothers in 1971 (Republic of Botswana 1972).

Information on child fostering is also available for a number of subnational groups or areas. In southeastern Togo, for example, 14 percent of children born to women aged 30–34 were not living with their mothers in 1976 (Locoh 1982). Similarly, Isiugo-Abanihe (1983) estimated the proportion of women aged 15–34 with children away in Nigeria in 1973 to be 22 percent in Ibadan and 24 percent in Western State (now Ondo, Ogun, and Oyo) and in Lagos State.

In addition, many small studies document the practice of child fostering in a number of ethnic groups and suggest its widespread prevalence—among the Hausa of Nigeria in Sokoto, Kano, Zaria, and Ibadan (Trevor 1975; Smith 1981; Schildkrout 1983; Jackson 1985); the Kanuri of Nigeria in Bornu (Cohen 1961, 1967); the Mossi in Burkina Faso and urban Ghana (Skinner 1960, 1964; Lallemand 1976; Gruenais 1981; Schildkrout 1973); and the Baule of Côte d'Ivoire in Bouake (Etienne 1979a, b). The practice has also been observed in Senegal (Garenne 1981) and in several countries of Central and East Africa, including Uganda (Sembajwe 1977), Tanzania (Richards and Reining 1954), Sudan (Modawi 1965), and Zaire (Guest 1978).

It is interesting that for Ghana, where both national and small-survey estimates of the prevalence of child fostering are available, there is good consistency across the estimates. Goody (1982) found the prevalence of fostered children for all ages in two of the four areas of Gonja in the northern region of Ghana to be 18 percent in central Gonja in 1956–57 and 26 percent in eastern Gonja in 1964. Similarly, nine small studies of other Ghanaian ethnic groups yielded estimates ranging from 15 percent to 36 percent (Azu 1974; Fiawoo 1978; Goody 1982), most of these applying to children of all ages.

In effect, this "redistribution" of children takes place not only between women at one point in time, thus providing more children to women who have fewer children or whose children are grown, but also occurs over women's lifetimes, thus reducing the concentration of the task of raising large families in the childbearing years. Young girls will become involved in raising their elder sisters' or their mothers' young children for years before they bear their own, and older women will continue child rearing, of grandchildren, for example, for years after having ceased their own childbearing.

Fostering also provides the major solution in crisis situations where children require other caretakers, as in the case of divorce or the disability or death of a parent. It is especially important as a known option for childbearing women who must consider their children's welfare in view of the risk of their own death in child-birth or its aftermath. In these contingencies, the possibility of foster care greatly relieves individuals of a number of fears regarding potential obstacles to successfully engendering large families.

At present, the institution of fostering is widespread in Sub-Saharan Africa and is probably important in maintaining interest in high fertility. Evidence that it is no longer always there when needed, as in the case of abandoned children in urban areas, is as yet very scant. Past high fertility assures a pool of alternative caretakers, whereas the patterns of traditional spacing of births and the consequent staggered childbearing of siblings and close kin means that within extended families, opportunities for fostering or reciprocation continually arise.

It is not conceivable that the kind of perturbations and dislocations necessary for this institution to break down would come about soon in these societies. Rather, the institution is likely to be undermined as other changes work to make smaller families ideal. Smaller families are likely to be associated with broadly changed conceptions of kinship obligations, which also reduce the availability of alternative foster parents. In particular, nucleation of families has been associated with increased investment in a smaller number of one's own children, reducing the need for and the value placed on other caretakers as well as raising the costs, and the resentment, involved in taking responsibility for others' children. Unless and until changes in desired family size occur, fostering will continue to facilitate high fertility, diluting the meaning and the utility of other forms of regulation.

In summary, fertility regulation in Sub-Saharan Africa is achieved through two means: foremost is avoidance of the next pregnancy through abstinence (or coitus interruptus) in association with lactational amenorrhea subsequent to live births, and second is rearrangement through fostering of the timing and the tempo of raising surviving children. Contraception, abortion, and sterilization are all used to a lesser extent among more or less well defined groups of women. The utilization of all these means (with the possible exception of contraception among more educated urban women) is generally within a framework of desires for high fertility. Even sterilization is used only when few potential births will be averted and conforms with expected "stopping" patterns rather than suggesting unusual limitation.

Constraints on the Adoption of Modern Contraception to Regulate Fertility

Even within the context of desires for high fertility, one might expect contraception to be adopted as a substitute for traditional forms of fertility regulation. Such substitution is apparently not happening, as even while women are abandoning traditional spacing behaviors in urban areas, the uptake of contraception is slow and lagging. There are clearly constraints on the adoption of contraception, quite apart from problems of availability of supplies and services. The constraints have to do with the fact that contraception is in the realm of forward planning, rather than after-the-fact management, which is not an easy matter in the environment of Sub-Saharan Africa.

A number of real uncertainties are associated with the achievement of large, healthy families in Sub-Saharan Africa. First is the risk of sterility. Primary sterility varies greatly but is present almost everywhere (Frank 1983a). After having some live-born children, there is still the risk of secondary sterility, which affects an even larger proportion of women (Frank 1983b). Second, there is a substantial chance that an infant will die after birth, or after weaning, or yet later in early childhood. Third, there is the risk that children will be handicapped or disabled, through a variety of unforeseeable events, such as accidents, poliomyelitis, and loss of sight. Fourth, there is the chance that children will be lost following divorce, particularly for women in patrilineal societies where husbands and their lineages have preeminent claims to children born during marriage, whether or not the children are biologically theirs. In practice, in most cases, women will leave a fertile marriage at best with the very small unweaned children, whom they must return later, or with one child whom they may keep.[6] Finally, spontaneous abortions ("miscarriages") and stillbirths are yet further risks but cannot be mentioned as special risks in the African context because there is no evidence that they occur at higher rates than anywhere else. Nevertheless, the possibility of miscarrying or delivering children who are stillborn compounds all other threats to successful family building.

An operational uncertainty is attached to all of these real risks, whether they are correctly perceived or not. The uncertainty is translated not into conscious individual weighing of childbearing alternatives but into normative reproductive behavior, where high fertility is firmly bound within a network of supporting institutions.

In this environment of risk, a conception is averted only in reference to a successful live birth, and the avoidance is directed by consideration of the infant and its nurturance rather than by negative appreciation of a new pregnancy. In societies where a successful conception, a healthy pregnancy, and the survival of a child are relatively likely, where the risks are better defined, and where the means to overcome risks are available, individuals can afford to delay conception. The uncertainty of building a healthy family in the Sub-Saharan African context is not conducive to the notion of holding fertility in abeyance, and the exigencies of the process of successfully producing a number of healthy children dwarf the importance of discrete fertility events. In these circumstances, averting individual conceptions does not serve fertility objectives well because losses at different postconception stages are anticipated and do occur. Such conditions favor the "banking" of live-born children and the apparent "hoarding" of children through fostering.

Prospects and Policy Implications

As the foregoing discussion has shown, fertility is regulated throughout Sub-Saharan African societies, principally through the postpartum behaviors of abstinence or coitus interruptus in association with lactational amenorrhea due to breastfeeding duration and intensity but also through manipulation of the actual number of surviving children raised. At the same time, childbearing desires are universally high, a minority of women do not want additional children, and a smaller minority take measures to avoid further childbearing.

The demand for additional control of fertility is evident among some groups of women. Young educated women who wish to delay their entry into childbearing often resort to induced abortion, and evidently a group of older women actively seeks to bring on the end of childbearing by opting for surgical sterilization. Neither of these groups is necessarily seeking or achieving parity-specific fertility limitation. Only among highly educated urban women is fertility effectively lowered by delayed entry into marriage and contraceptive use after a comparatively brief but rapidly paced period of family building.

Balanced against the behavior of these groups are declines in the use of traditional spacing methods, which lead to increasing fertility among young women of moderate education, particularly in urban areas, largely without compensation from the adoption of modern family planning methods.

A number of implications can be drawn from this analysis, and several policy directions are suggested. First, for the region as a whole, a "takeoff" in the adoption of modern contraception will probably not occur until there is an underlying shift in the demand for children. Stability of the current total fertility level of eight children in Kenya in conjunction with infant mortality below 100 per 1,000 suggests that, with even more children born and surviving in the region on average than at present, the supply of children will still not be perceived as excessive. There is little reason to expect the demand for children to decline in the absence of any change in economic, social, or cultural conditions

because it is solidly founded in Sub-Saharan African institutions. Yet there is little indication that the types of change that are hypothesized to have moderated fertility ultimately in demographic transitions elsewhere are now occurring or are about to occur among rural populations. Most particularly, the uncertainties associated with raising families are unlikely to diminish substantially, so that constraints on contraception will remain largely unaltered for some time.

Despite these caveats, increasing recourse to fertility regulation through contraception is not implausible, especially in the face of urban consumerist values and lifestyles and the growth of higher education. Studies of differential fertility in Africa by levels of women's education show clear signs of conventional socioeconomic variation, albeit at very high average levels: current fertility is positively associated with education up to the completion of primary school in Nigeria, for example, and drops only thereafter (National Population Bureau 1984; also see chapters 9 and 11 in this volume). Changing socioeconomic conditions for the urban minority could hardly fail to translate into a net increase in demand for fertility regulation through contraception.

It is also reasonable to expect some rural regions to take the lead in increasing the use of contraception for purposes of family limitation because of a cluster of predisposing contextual characteristics. These include areas in which cash-crop incomes provide relatively higher socioeconomic standards (facilitating, in particular, female education), in which infant mortality is relatively lower, in which health services are better, and in which heads of households are predominantly female because of male worker out-migration but households still manage to have thriving agricultural or other enterprises.

Against these general conclusions, a number of tasks could be usefully undertaken in the area of modern family planning that would lay a foundation for later demographic transition. First, the evident interest in delaying first pregnancy that comes with commitment to educational pursuits in urban areas can be addressed by focusing family planning services, information, and education in educational facilities. Many governments at present find it unacceptable to provide contraception to schoolgirls and unmarried women. Nevertheless, there is also widespread preoccupation with the incidence of induced abortion in urban areas, and the problem is recognized by policymakers in capital cities. Also, serious consideration should be given to increasing access to legal abortion for the purpose of reducing the high morbidity and mortality consequent to illegal procedures.

Second, it makes sense at present to concentrate family planning activities more generally first in urban areas, where most women who have had schooling or are employed in the modern sector reside. Elsewhere, in the face of high demand for these services, a common strategy is to reserve foreign assistance for rural programs because government efforts are already providing sufficient coverage (and may, in fact, be concentrated) in urban areas. This strategy does not apply in Sub-Saharan Africa. Foreign assistance for family planning may be necessary in urban areas because scarce local resources may not be directed to much family planning activity anywhere.

Third, in combination with efforts to broaden knowledge, availability, and contraceptive use in urban areas, efforts to promote breastfeeding could be attempted. Although the influence of breastfeeding promotion may in the end be difficult to evaluate, broadly publicized support may help to slow its rate of abandonment.

Fourth, specific family planning services in the urban areas and in large market towns could be designed to attract mainly older women who have large healthy families and can anticipate the end of childbearing with equanimity. The types of contraceptive services made available need not be limited to sterilization, and they may for some time have little fertility effect. Nevertheless, they introduce the notion of deliberate cessation of childbearing, and younger women who will have experienced less child loss may consider the possibility at earlier ages.

Fifth, infertility and its major causes—the incidence of gonorrhea and chlamydia—must be addressed as a public health problem (Frank 1987). Less can be done through the treatment of cases in clinical settings, which can absorb significant resources, whereas public education and mass medication campaigns have been shown to have influenced infertility substantially in the past (Frank 1983b). The direction of education and of broadly and easily available treatment to men is very important in this regard.

Sixth and finally, research must proceed apace on almost every aspect of the present traditional regulation of fertility and its potential future control in modernizing settings. The range of issues is broad, and a few particular areas of work can be singled out. First, coital frequency and, especially, coitus interruptus should be more often and more carefully included as subjects of inquiry in fertility research, because underlying sexual behaviors may signal an interest in more effective methods that ignorance alone precludes recognizing and addressing. Second, special attention needs to be paid to the kinds of contraceptives that are offered in Sub-Saharan African settings. Many oral contraceptives, for example, may be incompatible with successful breastfeeding (Hull 1981). Also, IUDs have been associated with the development of upper genital tract infections (Cramer and others 1985; Daling and others 1985). In consideration of the level of infertility on this continent,

due in large part to pelvic infection with chlamydia or gonorrhea, the potential consequences of the large-scale distribution of IUDs must be weighed. Condoms, on the other hand, can help to control sexually transmitted diseases and AIDS where their use is acceptable.

In conclusion, little evidence exists presently of a generalized demand for contraception and fertility limitation in Sub-Saharan Africa. Nevertheless, particular groups can be identified that have an interest in controlling fertility at specific points in their life cycle or are demonstrably limiting their fertility. During the period of time, of unforeseeable duration, that will be required for the basic social and economic changes to take place that will make fertility limitation relevant to the populations at large, a range of focused but worthwhile activities can be undertaken to address these identifiable needs.

Notes

1.   Fertility regulation is used here to denote all behaviors that deliberately shape and control fertility-related and family size outcomes, one of which may or may not be number of births: fertility will be restrained by regulation even in the absence of any numerical imperative. Fertility control refers to the regulation of fertility that is more specifically aimed at parity reduction or limitation: with fertility control, the numerical criterion comes to outweigh all other considerations.

2.   The only other conception-limiting practice, terminal abstinence (abstinence in the later years of childbearing), which is practiced because of age or grandmaternal status, is not fertility limiting in purpose.

3.   These surveys are being conducted by Family Health International of Research Triangle Park, North Carolina, and associated institutions.

4.   The specific purpose of making it possible to continue a program of study is often explicitly articulated by young African women (see Ampofo 1970a, 1970b). Recourse to abortion in this context is probably made possible by education, which fosters individual initiative and broadens options, as well as being a means of maintaining educational pursuits.

5.   "Fostering" is the preferred term for the African phenomenon because it greatly resembles fostering in Western societies. It generally involves the relocation of children who are weaned or older, into a family of close kin—of the grandparental, parental, or child's generation—where the child is raised for a period of years or until adulthood and marriage. Very rarely are the children in question adopted, either informally or formally: their biological parents do not relinquish rights over them because of such transfers.

6.   They also leave with any children they are fostering, which is a powerful incentive for women to take on foster children in patrilineal (and patrilocal) societies where the risk of divorce is high. The husbands and their lineages are far better served by keeping surviving children from a family than by exposing themselves to all the risks that "starting over"

would entail. As products of a process fraught with risk and waste, surviving healthy children are a valuable good.

References

Akinla, O. 1970. "Abortion in Africa." In R. E. Hall, ed., *Abortion in a Changing World*, vol. 1. New York: Columbia University Press, 1970.

Ampofo, D. A. 1970a. "Cases of Abortion Treated at Korle Bu Hospital: The Epidemiological and Medical Characteristics." *Ghana Medical Journal* 9(3).

————. 1970b. "The Dynamics of Induced Abortion and the Social Implication for Ghana." *Ghana Medical Journal* 9(4):

Association for Voluntary Sterilization. 1984. Subgrant Review. AVS, New York.

Azu, D. G. 1974. *The Ga Family and Social Change*. Leiden.

Binkin, N. J., N. N. Burton, A. H. Toure, M. Lamine Traore, and R. W. Rochat. 1984. "Women Hospitalized for Abortion Complications in Mali." *International Family Planning Perspectives* 10(1).

Bongaarts, John. 1984. "Implications of Future Fertility Trends for Contraceptive Practice." *Population and Development Review* 10(2): 341–52.

Carr-Saunders, A. M. 1922. *The Population Problem: A Study in Human Evolution*. Oxford: Oxford University Press.

Cohen, R. 1961. "Marriage Instability among the Kanuri of Northern Nigeria." *American Anthropologist* 63.

————. 1967. *The Kanuri of Bornu*. London: Holt, Rinehart and Winston.

Cramer, D. W., I Schiff, S. C. Schoenbaum, M. Gibson, S. Belisle, B. Albrecht, R. J. Stillman, M. J. Berger, E. Wilson, B. V. Stadel, and M. Seibel. 1985. "Tubal Infertility and the Intrauterine Device." *New England Journal of Medicine* 312(15): 941–47.

Daling, J. R., N. S. Weiss, B. J. Metch, W. Ho Chow, R. M. Soderstrom, D. E. Moore, L. R. Spadoni, and B. V. Stadel. 1985. "Primary Tubal Infertility in Relation to the Use of an Intrauterine Device." *New England Journal of Medicine* 312(15): 937–41.

Democratic Republic of the Sudan. 1982. *The Sudan Fertility Survey, 1979: Principal Report*. Khartoum: Ministry of National Planning, Department of Statistics.

Eaton, J. W., and A. J. Mayer. 1953. "The Social Biology of Very High Fertility among the Hutterites: The Demography of a Unique Population." *Human Biology* 25(3).

Etienne, Mona. 1979a. "Maternité Sociale, Rapports d'Adoption, et Pouvoir des Femmes Chez les Baoulé (Côte d'Ivoire)." *L'Homme* 19(3–4).

————. 1979b. "The Case for Social Maternity: Adoption of Children by Urban Baule Women." *Dialectical Anthropology* 4(3).

Fiawoo, D. R. 1978. "Some Patterns of Foster Care in Ghana." In C. Oppong, G. Adaba, M. Bekombo Priso, and J. Mogey, eds., *Marriage, Parenthood, and Fertility in West Africa*. Canberra: Australian National University Press.

Frank, Odile. 1983a. "Infertility in Sub-Saharan Africa: Estimates and Implications." *Population and Development Review* 9(1): 137–44.

————. 1983b. "Infertility in Sub-Saharan Africa." Center for Policy Studies Working Paper No. 97. New York: Population Council.

————. 1984. "Child Fostering in Sub-Saharan Africa." Paper presented at the annual meeting of the Population Association of American, May, Minneapolis; processed.

————. 1987. "Sterility in Women in Sub-Saharan Africa." *IPPF Medical Bulletin* 21(1).

Garenne, Michael. 1981. "The Age Pattern of Infant and Child Mortality in Ngayokheme (Rural West Africa)." Population Studies Center Working Paper No. 9. University of Pennsylvania, Philadelphia.

Goody, E. N. 1982. *Parenthood and Social Reproduction: Fostering and Occupational Roles in West Africa*. Cambridge Studies in Social Anthropology No. 35. New York: Cambridge University Press.

Government of Zimbabwe. 1984. *1982 Population Census: A Preliminary Assessment*. Harare: Central Statistical Office.

Gruenais, M. E. 1981. "Famille et démographie de la famille en Afrique." *Collectif de Travail sur la Famille*. Document de travail no. 1. Paris: O.R.S.T.O.M.

Guest, I. 1978. "Special Report: Infertility in Africa." *People* 5(1).

Hull, V. J. 1981. "The Effects of Hormonal Contraceptives on Lactation: Current Findings, Methodological Considerations, and Future Priorities." *Studies in Family Planning* 12(4): 134–55.

Isiugo-Abanihe, U. C. 1983. "Child Fostering in West Africa: Prevalence, Determinants, and Demographic Consequences." Ph.D. diss. University of Pennsylvania, Philadelphia.

Jackson, Cecile. 1985. "The Kano River Irrigation Project." *Women's Roles and Gender Differences in Development: Cases for Planners, 4*. West Hartford, Conn: Kumarian Press.

Kingdom of Lesotho. 1981. *Lesotho Fertility Survey, 1977: First Report*. Maseru: Ministry of Planning and Statistics, Central Bureau of Statistics.

Lallemand, Suzanne. 1976. "Génitrices et éducatrices Mossi." *L'Homme* 16(1).

LeVine, Sarah, and R. LeVine. 1981. "Child Abuse and Neglect in Sub-Saharan Africa." In J. E. Korbin, ed., *Child Abuse and Neglect*. Los Angeles: University of California Press.

Liskin, L. S. 1980. "Complications of Abortion in Developing Countries." *Population Reports*, ser. F, no. 7.

Locoh, Thérèse. 1982. "Demographic Aspects of the Family Life Cycle in Sub-Saharan Africa." In *Health and the Family Life Cycle: Selected Studies on the Interaction between Mortality, the Family, and Its Life Cycle*. Wiesbaden: Federal Institute for Population Research, World Health Organization.

Lorimer, Frank. 1954. *Culture and Human Fertility*. Zurich: United Nations Educational, Scientific, and Cultural Organization.

Lwanga, C. 1977. "Abortion in Mulago Hospital, Kampala." *East African Medical Journal* 54(3).

Mhango, Chisale, R. Rochat, and A. Arkutu. 1986. "Reproductive Mortality in Lusaka, Zambia, 1982–1983." *Studies in Family Planning* 17(5): 243–51.

Modawi, O. 1965. "The Problem of Infertility in Western Equatoria." Medical diss., University of Khartoum, Khartoum.

National Population Bureau. 1984. *The Nigeria Fertility Survey, 1981/82: Principal Report*. Vol. 1, *Methodology and Findings*. Vol. 2, *Statistical Tables*. Lagos: World Fertility Survey, 1984.

Nichols, D. J., and O. Bongwele. 1983. "Hospitalized Pregnancy Wastage in Zaire: A Preliminary Report." Family Health International, Research Triangle Park, N.C.; processed.

Nichols, D., O. A. Ladipo, J. M. Paxman, and E. O. Otolorin. 1986. "Sexual Behavior, Contraceptive Practice, and Reproductive Health among Nigerian Adolescents." *Studies in Family Planning* 17(2): 100–6.

Nichols, D. J., J. M. Paxman, and O. A. Ladipo. 1984. "Sexual Behavior, Contraceptive Practice, and Reproductive Health among the Young Unmarried Population in Ibadan, Nigeria." Family Health International, Research Triangle Park, N.C.

Okojie, S. E. 1976. "Induced Illegal Abortions in Benin City, Nigeria." *International Journal of Gynaecology and Obstetrics* 14(6).

Page, H. J. 1986. "Child-bearing versus Child-rearing: Co-residence of Mothers and Children in Sub-Saharan Africa." Interuniversity Programme in Demography Working Paper, 1986–2. Vrije Universiteit, Brussels.

Page, H. J., and R. Lesthaeghe. 1981. *Child-Spacing in Tropical Africa: Traditions and Change*. London: Academic Press.

Republic of Botswana. 1972. *Report on the Population Census, 1971*. Gaborone: Central Statistics Office.

Republic of Ghana. 1983. *Ghana Fertility Survey, 1979–1980. First Report*. Accra: Central Bureau of Statistics.

Republic of Kenya. 1980. *Kenya Fertility Survey, 1977–1978: First Report*. vols. 1 and 2. Nairobi: Central Bureau of Statistics, Ministry of Economic Planning and Development and World Fertility Survey.

————. 1984. *Kenya Contraceptive Prevalence Survey, 1984: First Report*. Nairobi: Central Bureau of Statistics, Ministry of Planning and National Development and Contraceptive Prevalence Survey Programme.

————. 1986. *Kenya Contraceptive Prevalence Survey, 1984: Summary Report*. Nairobi: Central Bureau of Statistics, Ministry of Planning and National Development with Institute for Resource Development at Westinghouse.

République de Côte d'Ivoire. 1984. *Enquête Ivoirienne sur la Fécondité, 1980–81. Rapport Principal*. Abidjan: Ministère de l'Economie et des Finances, Direction de la Statistique.

République Populaire du Bénin. 1983. *Enquête Fécondité, au Bénin: Rapport Préliminaire*. Cotonou: Ministère du Plan, de la Statistique et de l'Analyse Economique, Institut National de la Statistique et de l'Analyse Economique, Bureau Central de Récensement, 1983.

République du Sénégal. 1981. *Enquête Sénégalaise sur la fécondité, 1978*. Dakar: Ministère de l'Economie et des Finances, Direction de la Statistique, Division des Enquêtes et de la Démographie.

République Unie du Cameroun. 1983. *Enquête Nationale sur la Fécondité du Cameroun. Rapport Principal*. Yaounde: Direction de la Statistique et de la Compatabilité Nationale.

Richards, A. I., and P. Reining. 1954. "Report on Fertility Surveys in Buganda and Buhaya, 1952." In F. Lorimer, ed., *Culture and Human Fertility*, pt. 4. Zurich: United Nations Educational, Scientific, and Cultural Organization.

Schildkrout, Enid. 1973. "The Fostering of Children in Urban Ghana: Problems of Ethnographic Analysis in a Multi-Cultural Context." *Urban Anthropology* 2(1).

————. 1983. "Dependence and Autonomy: The Economic Activities of Secluded Hausa Women in Kano." In C. Oppong, G. Adaba, M. Bekombo Priso, and J. Mogey, eds., *Marriage, Parenthood, and Fertility in West Africa*. Canberra: Australian National University Press.

Sambajwe, I. S. L. 1977. "Socio-Cultural Supports for High Fertility in Buganda." In *The Economic and Social Supports for High Fertility*. Family and Fertility Change: Changing African Family Companion Series No. 2, edited by L. T. Ruzicka. Canberra: Australian National University Press.

Skinner, E. P. 1960. "The Mossi Pogsioure." *Man* 60.

————. 1964. *The Mossi of the Upper Volta*. Stanford: Stanford University Press.

Smith, M. F. 1981. *Baba of Karo: A Woman of the Muslim Hausa*. New Haven: Yale University Press.

Tietze, Christopher. 1968. "History of Contraceptive Methods." In C. B. Nam, ed., *Population and Society*. Boston: Houghton-Mifflin.

Tietze, Christopher, and S. K. Henshaw. 1986. *Induced Abortion: A World Review, 1986*. 6th ed. New York: Alan Guttmacher Institute.

Trevor, Jean. 1975. "Family Change in Sokoto." In J. C. Caldwell, ed., *Population Growth and Socioeconomic Change in West Africa*. New York: Columbia University Press for the Population Council.

Wrigley, E. A. 1969. *Population and History*. London: World University Library, Weidenfeld and Nicolson.

Zimbabwe National Family Planning Council. 1985. *Zimbabwe Reproductive Health Survey, 1984*. Harare: Zimbabwe National Family Planning Council with Westinghouse Public Applied Systems.

13

Cultural Forces Tending to Sustain High Fertility

John C. Caldwell and Pat Caldwell

An understanding of why fertility transition appears to be retarded in Sub-Saharan Africa is impossible without an understanding of fundamental religious beliefs and cultural practices. There are differences in emphasis, but the basic nature of these beliefs and practices varies surprisingly little throughout the whole region.

Traditional Religion and Its Effect on Fertility

Traditional religion still permeates Sub-Saharan African populations except in a small fraction of the elite of unknown size. Perhaps two-thirds of the population is also Christian or Moslem, but much of the traditional religion remains, less changed perhaps in its interpretation of demographic events than in some other areas.

Within Sub-Saharan Africa, there is a concept of a pantheon of gods, and usually of a supreme God, as well as of more personal and family deities (Fortes 1959; Duru 1983; Kuckertz 1983; Offiong 1983). The concept of gods who have a supreme concern for fertility and make little distinction between that of humans and that of the fields has been described well by Talbot (1927) and Meek (1931) in West Africa and by Mbiti (1970) in East Africa. Associated with this concept is a concept of sinful behavior, which can affect not only the guilty individual but the whole community, which is thereby polluted and is liable to be punished (Duru 1983). The social order is ordained by the spirits (Evans-Pritchard 1953), and fertility is central to that order. Children are the gift of God (Mbiti 1973b) or a blessing from heaven (Messing 1973). Indeed, the Edo of Nigeria address God as "the bringer of children" (Mbiti 1970). The role of a wife in complying with this order has been described in the following way: "She cooperates with her husband,

We thank Muriel Brookfield, Wendy Cosford, Daphne Broers-Freeman, Sue Sydlarczuk, and Kae Mardus for their help.

the ancestors, even God, in creating the child" (Raum 1973b, p. 35). There are differences: Fortes (1959) has argued that the role of fate, which he has related to the same concept in ancient Greece, is stronger in West Africa than in East Africa.

The major influence on behavior is not, however, the gods but the living dead or ancestral shades that survive for four or five generations, especially if the proper rites have been performed, and then disappear. The fact that one's living ancestors will one day become such powerful shades strongly reinforces the earthly power of old people. These concepts were reinforced by a belief in reincarnation, whereby the dead were born again to their descendants. Among Christians and Moslems, the latter belief appears to be eroding, although children are still given the names of grandparents or great-grandparents, and a man will often address his son as his father. Among the Kikuyu of Kenya, and widely across the continent, a child who dies is regarded as a temporary visitor, and the next child is given the same name and regarded as a reincarnation of the same ancestral spirit. Should this child also die, its death is regarded as evidence that the ancestor does not want to return (Soyinka 1967; Kershaw 1973). The Kikuyu expect husbands and wives to bring forth their own sets of parents, and so each couple should raise at least two male and two female children to maturity (Kershaw 1973). In West Africa, too, as among the Ga of Accra, every child is considered to be an ancestor born again (Azu 1974). Among the Yoruba, when a father dies, his children are still likely to cut short postpartum abstinence and a fertility competition develops, because the first son born will mean that the grandfather has returned to the living again.

The relationship between the living and their ancestors is complex. Male descendants are necessary to fulfill the priestly duty of pouring libation, without which the ancestral spirits will begin to fade as they are forgotten.

Geographisches Institut
der Universität Kiel

Thus, if a family line comes to an end because it has been unable to reproduce or rear sons, there is no clearer evidence that it has been cursed (Mbiti 1973b). Fortes concluded:

> One inescapable duty rests on children in relation to both parents. This is the duty of filial piety. It requires a child to honor and respect his parents, to put their wishes before his own, to support and cherish them in old age, quite irrespective of their treatment of him. The supreme act of filial piety owed by sons is the performance of the mortuary and funeral ceremonies for the parents. It is felt by the Tallensi [of northern Ghana] as a compulsion of conscience, but there is a powerful religious sanction in the background. To fail in it is to incur the everlasting wrath of the ancestors. For the mortuary and funeral rites are the first steps in the transformation of parents into ancestor spirits, and the worship of the ancestors is in essence the ritualization of filial piety [1959, p. 29].

In most of Africa, the relationship with the ancestors is much more extensive. Ancestors rebuke their descendants not only for the failure to carry out the appropriate rites but also for a great range of sins, impieties, transgressions, and omissions. The anger of the ancestors takes the form of sickness and even death (Middleton 1973). Until relatively recently, much of the sickness and death in Sub-Saharan Africa was explained in terms of ancestral disapproval, but it was usually unclear what the cause of the disapproval was and hence how amends were to be made. Consequently, there was an important class of persons who were particularly gifted, often as a hereditary trait, in divining the cause. Diviners were approached rarely by the afflicted person but usually by close relatives.

Social and economic relations between the generations are controlled not only by the dead but also by the living. If children treat their parents with disrespect, or transgress against them, particularly by failing to look after them adequately in old age, then the parents have the power to curse their children with all the harmful results that flow from a curse with divine backing. "A curse in Meru [Kenya] is greatly feared and children will do everything to avoid their parents' curse" (Mwambia 1973b, p. 67).

Thus the lineage is the fundamental aspect of both society and religion. Each reinforces the other. It has been observed that the lineage is of indeterminate length, stretching back through the dead ancestors and onward through generations yet unborn. The living are but a small segment temporarily responsible for the lineage property, for its good name and morality, and for the fate of those who have died and of those who are yet to come (Meek 1957). Sickness and death, however, may be the product not of ultimately wise ancestral guidance but of the malicious employment of witchcraft by human beings or the action of malevolent spirits. Whereas all traditional African societies believed in the possibility of ancestral intervention, the degree of belief in witchcraft and evil spirits varied enormously, and some societies, such as the Korongo of Central Sudan, have been reported as having no witchcraft beliefs (Nadel 1952). In contrast, Evans-Pritchard (1974, p. 13) reported that "the notion of witchcraft . . . is on the lips of the Azande [south-west Sudan] every day." Witchcraft plays a major role in beliefs about fertility and child death because it is most often practiced against a person by killing not the hated adult but the person's children (Swartz 1969).

Envy regarding fertility and witchcraft is so interrelated that there are strong prohibitions against accurately stating the number of one's living children (Mbiti 1973a). This reluctance produced such difficulties during the Changing African Family Project in the city of Ibadan that the estimates most relied upon were calculated indirectly from a series of questions constructed to avoid this problem.

So great is the pressure to have children that African societies are permeated by a male fear of impotence and a female fear of acquiring an impotent husband, as has been described, for example, among the Creoles of Freetown, Sierra Leone (Harrell-Bond 1975).

More than thirty years ago, Lorimer (1954) related high fertility and resistance to fertility decline to unilineal descent groups, but his explanation tended toward the secular, with the role of religion being explained as supporting social structures. In contrast, after seeking information from a wide range of anthropologists who had worked in East Africa, Molnos (1973, vol. 3, p. 8) concluded: "The paramount objective of having children was that there should always be a living descendant to remember and honor the departed. Children meant the continuation of the lineage and the perpetuation of the family name and spirit. Descendants were needed to perform funeral ceremonies, to ensure that the parents, unlike childless people, be buried, and that the ancestral spirits be commemorated by erecting shrines, pouring out libations, and offering food."

Among some groups, such as the Nupe, witches are always women (Nadel 1952). In much of Africa, however, although women are predominantly associated with witchcraft, it is not exclusively their preserve. Nevertheless, women are widely associated with mystical powers, originating largely in their fecundity; with impurity, related largely to menstruation and hence relevant only to women between menarche and menopause; and even with innate evil (Ngubane 1977). Paulme (1963, p. 13), after surveying the studies of women in tropical Africa that she had collected, concluded: "Men put up with the presence of their wives but continue to regard them as strangers." Evans-Pritchard (1937, p. 16) observed that women, among the Azande, "played no part in public life and were looked upon as child-bearers and servants rather than as companions and equals." And in some cultures, as among the Yoruba in Nigeria, there were two separate societies, male and female, which rarely intersected (Golde 1970).

According to Paulme (1963, p. 13), "this general atmosphere of mistrust arises, in part at any rate, from the horror inspired by blood, and from the feeling that there are magic dangers inherent in menstruation," from which men are only partly protected by circumcision. Nevertheless, the mystery and danger also arise from the fact that fecundity and childbirth are the central fact of existence. "Continued child-bearing is irrefutable evidence of continued femininity. At the menopause, a woman becomes a kind of honorary male" (Fortes 1978, p. 45). Reproduction is regarded as the keystone of God's plan (Harrell-Bond 1975).

In many matters pertaining to sex and reproduction, there are broad similarities across the region. This is not so with regard to premarital sexual relations and even premarital pregnancy and birth, where there is a broad spectrum of attitudes and practices (Mair 1969). Traditionally, there were contrasts even within contemporary national borders. Forde (1951) reported that, among the Yako of southeastern Nigeria, mothers encouraged their daughters to attend night parties from about eleven years of age, well before menarche, even though coitus apparently did not usually occur at first or among the very youngest, and they apparently had means for seeing that pregnancy did not usually take place before betrothal. In contrast, Olusanya (1969) stressed the importance that the Yoruba in southwest Nigeria laid upon the virginity of the bride at marriage. Within one ethnic group much may depend upon religion, and Arens (1973) has described how, among the Mto Wa Mbu of northern Tanzania, Moslem reputation now depends upon the virginity of daughters at marriage, whereas this is of little significance among the Christians of the area. Middleton (1973) has reported that, among the Lugbara of Uganda, there is some feeling that premarital pregnancy should lead to the arrangement of marriage. Indeed, so important is fecundity that, as Brokensha (1973) reported, among the Mbeere of Kenya, it was felt safer to arrange marriage once pregnancy had been achieved. Some groups have moved in this direction, such as the Creoles in Sierra Leone, where there appears to have been an increase in sterility. The real crime, especially in East Africa, is either sexual relations when still uncircumcised (Ndeti 1973) or pregnancy before female initiation rites (Mwambia 1973b; Njeru 1973; Raum 1973b). In Burundi, there is clearly some pressure against premarital births, given that most women who try to achieve a miscarriage are unmarried (Albert 1963). In Ghana, on the other hand, premarital pregnancy or birth carries no moral stigma among the Ga, unless the mother refuses to name the father (Azu 1974), and even such a refusal causes no problem among the Tallensi, as the child is welcomed by the mother's lineage (Fortes 1978). In West Africa, therefore, much depends on the exact concept of the lineage and of descent.

Parenthood is for all African societies the essential mark of manhood or womanhood. A person is not fully developed until he or she becomes a parent. "In West Africa it is also a fulfillment of fundamental kinship, religious, and political obligations and represents a commitment by parents to transmit the cultural heritage of the community" (Fortes 1978, p. 23). In addition, it represents evidence of masculinity. The need to demonstrate male potency has been given as the explanation for high fertility among the Creoles of Sierra Leone (Steady 1978). Among women, fecundity is identified with their essential female nature, as is shown by the fact that prepubescent and postmenopausal females can attend many rituals throughout the region that are forbidden to other women (Fortes 1978).

Barrenness, Subfecundity, and Child Death

Much of the apprehension about family planning in Sub-Saharan Africa can be understood only in the context of attitudes toward infertility, subfertility, miscarriage, and infant death (see chapter 12 in this volume). These phenomena are not clearly separated and are the major indicators of divine or ancestral disapproval or malevolence from humans or spirits. They cannot be taken lightly and inevitably give rise to fear, anguish, and horror. Reporting upon barrenness or subfertility or infant death has always presented problems for African fertility surveys; interviewees resist and may even disappear (Heisel 1968).

The view of the Kikuyu of Kenya holds for much of the region: "Childlessness was a breach of the line of the generation and of a woman's obligations in life" (Kershaw 1973, p. 55). Of northern Ghana, Fortes (1959, p. 37) reported: "In Tale eyes no one is so unfortunate or so unhappy as a woman who has no children. If, as happens only too often, a young wife loses her babies one after another by miscarriage or in early infancy, she becomes chronically miserable and dejected, and her husband too, for that matter. It is then suspected, and diviners soon confirm, that the cause is her evil Prenatal Destiny."

Children are necessary not only for a woman's well-being but also for a man's status. Among the Meru of Kenya, "children changed a man's status considerably.

He could never undergo some ceremonies and rituals unless he had children. Before he could become a Mwa-riki [and this was the measure of a full man], a man had to have grown-up children, some of them married" (Mwambia 1973b, p. 65).

These are demonstrably attitudes that are unlikely to be quickly modified and unlikely to make family planning readily accepted. Southwold (1973, p. 172) wrote of the most urbanized and economically advanced people of Uganda: "Most Baganda are so concerned—often hysterically—about infertility that it would be very difficult to turn them round to think about the opposite problem. Even a person with plenty of children is still apt to think that infertility is a real problem."

The fear of barrenness is compounded by the awareness of what has happened to infertile women. In many societies, they are driven back to their parents' village and even there may not be allowed to live near others, for the presence of such evil is thought to be polluting and may render other women infertile as well as bring more general misfortune on all. Mwambia (1973b, p. 61) reported of the Meru of Kenya that "it was risky to keep a barren wife in the homestead because of the fear that she would use sorcery to kill other wives' children." Even when the childless woman is sent back to her parents, she is not allowed to live in the family homestead but is housed in a specially built hut at a distance from any other dwellings. There are further ramifications; it is difficult to arrange the marriage of any of her sisters in a society where there is no place for the unmarried woman. In one area of Central Kenya, Brokensha (1973, p. 95) found that "several widows live alone, with no grown up sons to care for them, and are both pitied and feared as they are often regarded as witches, or as having no stake in society, and, therefore, not caring whether they break all polite conventions." In West Africa too, such women tend to be excluded from society. Among the Nupe in Nigeria, Nadel (1942, p. 154) observed, "As the barren woman fails by the common standard of marriage and womanhood, she is also exempted from the standards of common morality. Adultery and chastity count less in her than in other women." Men too can be accused of sterility, but proof is more difficult to obtain. Nevertheless, some societies have a mechanism whereby, if the wife accuses the husband of being responsible, one or more of his age set group will try to impregnate her (Njeru 1973). If a man were proved to be sterile, he too might be regarded as a witch and might well regard himself as one (Brokensha 1973). One of the problems associated with sterility is that it negates the major reason for the payment of bride-wealth: the acquisition of reproductive capacity.

The fear of barrenness is reinforced by the treatment of the childless both in life and in death. The barren are despised, feared, and frequently abused, being likened to cockerels or other castrated animals (Harrell-Bond 1975). In West Africa, the childless are slightly better treated by most groups, but among the Tallensi, who believe that it is better to die in poverty than childless (Fortes 1949), childless women are still likely to drift from husband to husband. Everywhere, they are likely to shift for themselves and, from the West African savanna to the Ogaden of Ethiopia, they are identified with traders and prostitutes (Nadel 1942; Messing 1973). The exception, with regard to trading, is the West African coastal and forest region, where trading is the normal occupation of most women.

A continuing fear is the almost universal treatment meted out to the childless after death. Few societies bury the childless. The reason for this maltreatment is that the disorder commonly arises as a punishment from the gods or the ancestors. The latter may be showing disapproval of the nubility rites performed or ignored, the failure to pay the full bride-price, the deficient sacrifice performed when entering a new house, or a more general failure to perform sacrifices (Ngubane 1977). Unlike most visitations of the ancestors, barrenness is more likely to come to a woman through intervention of her in-laws, especially a dead mother-in-law, as was reported by Evans-Pritchard (1974) among the Azande. A wife's father, however, may invoke his ancestors to make his daughter barren in order to punish her husband or his family for mistreatment (Middleton 1973). It is widely believed that barrenness and child death may arise from specific types of offense (Swartz 1969; Raum 1973b; Middleton 1973). Among the Kikuyu of Kenya, for example, "barrenness would first and foremost be attributed to a breach of behavior, either by the woman or by someone in her mbari, which might not be known to her or to anyone else until it became apparent in the form of punishment by barrenness" (Kershaw 1973, p. 54).

When barrenness threatens, people resort first to divination, followed by the appropriate ritual. Some rituals take the form of propitiation of the ancestors and the carrying out of previously neglected duties. Such fertility rites were common in many ethnic groups in West Africa (Meek 1931; Nadel 1942; Azu 1974). Precisely this area has been least affected by modern medicine, and Spring's (1980, p. 132) description of the situation in Zambia probably applies to the region generally: "People believe that only the traditional medical system can cure some illnesses such as barrenness, 'watery and cold vagina,' postpartum weakness, weak penis, 'rotten sperms,' madness, kakale . . . , and some chest and limb ailments."

Usually the parents of a barren woman must either return the bride-wealth or find a substitute to bear the children, although this woman will not usually be regarded as a wife (Wagner 1939; Richards 1950; Albert 1963). Quite frequently the parents send a younger sister. In some societies, barren wives may continue to live with their husbands, provided that additional wives bear children and are not apprehensive of their presence. Sometimes the problem is overcome when the woman begs a sister for one or more of her children (Barnes 1951). This is not unusual in a society where fostering between relatives is common. Finally, there are similar mechanisms in many parts of Sub-Saharan Africa whereby a childless woman may marry another woman and share in her children; in such cases, the family of the barren woman pays the family of the fertile one bride-wealth (Kershaw 1973; Kabwegyere and Mbula 1979).

Miscarriage and child death are both closely related to barrenness. Miscarriage may be identified by the diviner as due to lineage sorcery (Ngubane 1977). Nevertheless, a frequent cause is believed to be jealousy of cowives and the fear that the new baby might become the father's favorite and hence that their children might suffer. Among the Temne of Sierra Leone, cowives are believed to have fed an abortifacient to a wife who miscarries (Dorjahn 1958). The danger could also flow in the opposite direction. Among the Meru of Kenya, a woman, all of whose children had died, was sent away from the homestead in case she used sorcery to kill the other wives' children (Heisel 1968). The husband is frequently in almost as dangerous a position as his wife: "Losing children indicates a doubtful relationship with one's own parents, siblings and others; even if he is declared guiltless, he is under suspicion of not living the fully moral life since this would involve not arousing the hatred, suspicion or envy of those close to him" (Swartz 1969, p. 82). A woman who has repeated miscarriages may believe that she has been possessed by an evil spirit, or it may be thought that she is at least partly responsible for the killing of her children.

Across the continent, a difficult childbirth is believed to be a sure sign of adultery (Mair 1969; Casale 1982) or of punishment by the husband's ancestors for other misdemeanors (Paulme 1963). Death of the infant after birth is related by the Kikuyu more to crimes committed by the husband's ancestors than to crimes committed by the mother herself (Kershaw 1973).

Unlike many traditional societies, those in Sub-Saharan Africa generally had no concept of having enough children. The inability to continue reproducing at any stage bore a sinister resemblance to barrenness and to having been cursed. Any cessation of reproduction could show the presence of pollution or the existence of a source of pollution in the community and, accordingly, might indicate that both human and crop fertility were endangered (Duru 1983). All members of the community regard "having substantial numbers of children as a sign that the parent or parents are 'members in good standing in the moral community' since serious offenses against that community will result in not having these children in the first place or in losing them to disease . . . The having or not having of a fair number of children is unquestionably an indicator of the parents' moral stance. Thus, by continuing to function in the role of parents they demonstrate rectitude and basic goodness" (Swartz 1969, pp. 82–83).

"The mother of many children is regarded as a special person and is respected by all" (Brokensha 1973b, p. 85), whereas women with small families were pitied and ridiculed (Oyemade and Ogunmuyiwa 1981). Among the Lugbara of Uganda, the marriage anointment was specifically to "drive out trouble," which was taken by all to mean anything that might impair fertility (Isichei 1978). Molnos (1973, vol. 3, p. 7) concluded from the reports on East Africa that high fertility was identified with the "proper woman" and the "proper man," and "children constituted the most important signs of success and achievement." Among the Yoruba of Nigeria, children were wealth and usually still are (Caldwell 1982). Women frequently state that their principal work is to produce children (Middleton 1973). There is a "deeply ingrained idea that normal men and women should continue to beget and bear children throughout their fecund years" and a "wish and need to demonstrate continued virility, potency and fecundity" (Fortes 1978, p. 45). Among the Akamba of Kenya, sons are needed to perpetuate the family line, and the greatest of all curses is apparent in the ending of such a line. Children are given by God, and none should be refused (Olusanya 1969; Mbiti 1973b).

Problems arise if progeny are limited. Among the Kikuyu, bride-wealth payments go to different lines of kin, and several children's marriages have to take place before all are satisfied. Children are named after various ancestors, and if only a few survive, not all ancestral names will be given out and not all ancestors will be able to secure rebirth (Kershaw 1973). It is claimed, however, that, among the Meru of Kenya, pressure to produce sufficient children to meet the need to name all appropriate ancestors is declining (Mwambia 1973b). It is also claimed that, among this group, people now ridicule not only the wife with too few children but also the wife with too many, although in the case of the latter, both there and elsewhere in Africa, it is usually related to charges of sexual activity soon after birth and the consequent endangering of children's lives because of short birth intervals (Njeru 1973).

The concept of a person's nature being closely related to her sexuality and ability to reproduce, and fundamentally changing at such times as menarche and menopause, is deeply based in African religion and culture, as is the concept that fertility is a continuous flow of a divine providence. Consequently, the onset of premature sterility, whether from disease or planned operation, is regarded by most Africans with horror. The reaction to abortion is similar, if not quite as strong. Forde (1951, p. 92) wrote of the Yako of southeastern Nigeria: "Abortion is regarded as an offense against the spirit of the woman's matriclan, which endangers the well being of all members of the group." It is widely believed that male sterilization is associated with impotence, which is deeply feared in all African societies, and that abortion inevitably leads to sterility.

Traditionally neither sickness nor death was commonly ascribed to natural causes. The attitude of the Yoruba of Nigeria is probably typical: only an unusually old person could be expected to die unless there had been an intervention, either human or extrahuman, of some kind. According to tradition, one could usually find the cause of death within a limited range of possibilities. In Kenya, for example, one suspected the breaking of tradition, such as the cutting down of trees in a sacred grove; the failure to perform traditional obligations, such as sacrifices to ancestors at the proper time or on the proper occasion; or magical acts performed by enemies (Brokensha 1973).

Infants were particularly in danger, and hence one might anticipate higher death rates than at most other ages. In Ghana, "during the first few months of life a child is extremely vulnerable both physically and mystically" (Fortes 1949, p. 165). Surrounding the infant are likely to be spirits and dangers of every kind, and their presence is amply proved by the baby's death. For this reason, among the Mbeere of Kenya the burning of the hut in which an infant death took place is still common (Brokensha 1973b). Infant deaths are most commonly believed to be caused by cowives, by the intervention of ancestors, or by the commission of sins, especially those against the spiritual or natural order of things by ancestors (Mair 1969; Kershaw 1973; Middleton 1973; Isichei 1978). Even sorcery kills not only by spells but often by the transmission of poisons, which tends to blur the distinction between the mystical and the material (Duru 1983). The identification of diseases induced by witchcraft with bodily wasting as the life soul is consumed means that the origin of infantile diarrheal disease is easily confirmed (Nadel 1952).

In Sub-Saharan Africa, partly because of the existence of polygyny, and hence the link between a child and its mother in a frequently smaller unit than the relationship that holds with the father, child care is largely in the hands of women—the mother and, frequently, the grandmother. For this reason infant and child mortality is much more closely associated with maternal education than with paternal (Caldwell 1979; Caldwell and McDonald 1981). The choice of the cures or medicines to be employed is related to the person's system of

beliefs. Traditional curing and medicines are an integral part of traditional religion, and hence Christians have been shown to be more likely to use modern medicine than followers of the traditional religions (Spring 1980). The same is not true, however, with regard to those "Ethiopian" or apocalyptic churches which deliberately forswear foreign imports in favor of the African tradition.

Changing Beliefs and Culture

Most of the emphasis so far has been on traditional religion and beliefs. In 1972, it was estimated that those who described themselves as adherents solely to traditional religions had fallen in Sub-Saharan Africa to 40 percent, whereas Christians were estimated as 36 percent and Moslems as 24 percent. The number of Christians was believed to have doubled in the previous fifteen years ("L'Afrique chrétienne," 1972). It is likely that the traditional fraction has by now fallen below one-third. Nevertheless, the true position is far more complex than this. Many Africans argue that the only adherents to traditional religion are those living in their native villages. This reasoning has a certain logic, because only on ancestral land can the links with the ancestors be maintained, although for precisely this reason many migrants return at times most auspicious for rites.

The breakdown by religion does not indicate changes in belief systems as far-reaching as the figures might at first imply. Parrinder (1981, p. 80) has written: "Christianity and Islam are making great claims upon the religious allegiance of Africans, and these two religions have the great advantage of literacy, history and international links. There is little doubt that in time they will replace traditional religions in Africa, but many of the old beliefs and attitudes will survive for centuries because the cultural background, of which religion was an integral expression, is still powerful in determining the thoughts and actions even of educated men in modern African towns."

The fundamental questions deal with the extent of change in belief systems and the likely impact on demographic behavior. Extraordinarily little convincing research has been done. In a major study of witchcraft, the editors concluded that they had no idea of the extent of change in the beliefs of the urban elites (Middleton and Winter 1963).

Perhaps to a greater extent than anywhere else in the world, Sub-Saharan Africans have taken on new religions while retaining much of the content and lessons of the old. The explanation lies largely in the almost complete fusion of religion and society in the old beliefs and also in their segmented nature. Most Africans can accept the concept and name of an imported supreme god with little feeling that their whole belief system has crumbled. In fact, the greatest religious battles have been fought over cultural practices not inextricably tied to religion: polygyny, drumming, singing, and dancing. The fact that the old gods had only tenuous links to the ancestral shades, and the more malevolent spirits of the bush and river, meant that those who accepted a new religion usually saw little confrontation, although they were usually aware that the ritual sacrifices would have to be practiced more discreetly and perhaps less frequently and more perfunctorily.

Both beliefs and practices have changed, but the erosion of the old has been slow, with uneven impact. Probably most Christians and Moslems no longer believe that children are reincarnations of the ancestors, although ancestral names continue to be used. Nevertheless, few would test the ancestral contact, and even fewer would risk the curse of a living parent or dead ancestor by transgressing against the rules of filial respect and obligation. Similarly, there is much apprehension regarding the consequences of attacking high fertility or continued childbearing as an undesirable phenomenon. This statement is particularly true with regard to intervention in the form of sterilization, which would change a person's fecundity status and, in the common view, might also imperil male virility or female womanliness. It is possible the Sub-Saharan African societies will resist abortion less firmly than sterilization, but there is still a feeling that once the living spirit moves again toward birth it is impious or unnatural to stop it.

Page and Lesthaeghe (1981) have argued that Christianity and Islam have modified one traditional practice that had a degree of religious sanction, postpartum female sexual abstinence, at least in savanna West Africa and in East Africa. Perhaps what is remarkable is the small impact of these religions in coastal West Africa, in the case of Moslems, in spite of the clear statement in the Koran that forty days of abstinence will suffice.

Among the Ashanti of Ghana, it was found that the strains produced by economic change associated with becoming the world's greatest cocoa producers had led to a proliferation of cults and shrines within the traditional framework but essentially of a new type (Field 1960). The message from the fetish priests of these shrines broadened the attitude toward barrenness. Childlessness was still said to be caused in some cases by God, and hence to be incurable, and in other cases by witchcraft, where successful divination and correcting activities could work. Yet the Ashanti increasingly stressed family strife, asking, "Which do you prefer, quarrels or children?" Even in rural East Africa, Brokensha (1973) reported that barren women were tolerated more by most Christian families than had been

the case in earlier times. He also said that there had been a decline in female circumcision almost entirely among Anglican girls.

Political Leadership and Fertility Control

Unlike the situation in much of Asia, African governments have given either no leadership or uncertain leadership to family planning programs. The reasons lie partly in their newness and partly in the role of traditional government in Sub-Saharan Africa, where smaller numbers of people are governed than are found in the nation-state.

Chiefs did not have the power of kings or parliaments with regard to lawmaking. The law was largely eternal, and transgressions were indicated by sickness or death. Chiefs and others knew what was unnatural, and their successors in modern national assemblies feel it very difficult to legislate in areas where the natural law is well known. Nearly five decades ago, Fortes and Evans-Pritchard wrote:

> In Africa it is often hardly possible to separate, even in thought, political office from ritual or religious office. Thus, in some African societies it may be said that the King is the executive head, the legislator, the supreme judge, the commander-in-chief of the army, the chief priest or supreme ritual head, and even perhaps the principal capitalist of the whole community. But it is erroneous to think of him as combining in himself a number of separate and distinct offices. There is a single office, that of King, and its various duties and activities and its rights, prerogatives, and privileges make up a single unified whole [1940, p.xxi].

This role as keeper rather than creator or modifier of the moral order was emphasized by Richards (1940) in her study of the political system of the Bemba of Rhodesia. The primary allegiance is to family, lineage, and ethnic group. This is not corruption but moral order and eternal priorities. African assemblies are deeply worried about legislation that affects family behavior. Owusu (1979) argued with regard to contemporary Ghana that Africans understand the problems of national politicians but are skeptical of them precisely because they see them as family centered.

With regard to family planning, African politicians and public servants have also repeatedly been attacked on the grounds that population programs are a form of foreign intervention and that they are imperialist, neo-colonialist plots to keep Africa down (Green 1982). The politically aware have readily echoed any charges from black Americans of intended genocide (Gregory 1971). The head of the national family planning program in

Ghana has reported that much of the political and administrative weakness of the program derives from the fact that "it has been controversial because it has been plagued by ideologies that have sought to interpret international and inter-governmental cooperation in the field as colonialist machinations against developing countries" (Armar 1983).

Such charges, however, are not the fundamental reason for opposition to the establishment or extension of family planning programs. The real problem is that politicians, civil servants, and political activists all feel that the programs may run counter to the basic spiritual beliefs and emotions of African society. They feel that there is little public demand for family planning and are conscious of the threat of grass-roots opposition. Furthermore, they are unwilling to be too closely identified with activities that may be culturally doomed to failure. This anticipation of failure and an attempt even by those officially involved in the programs to distance themselves sufficiently, by behavior or argument, from the programs make poor performance almost inevitable. The threat of failure makes the most ambitious or capable seek other fields for their activities.

In addition, Sub-Saharan African governments do not have the same tradition as Asian governments of providing moral leadership in new areas; the moral law, at least with respect to reproduction, is clear, and politicians should preserve it. In some political areas, various Sub-Saharan African governments have provided strong leadership, often unsuccessfully, and usually by force. The mixture of a moral crusade and a governmental bureaucratic program, sometimes with various degrees of coercion, however, which has lowered fertility in parts of Asia, would meet fierce opposition in Africa and would be unlikely to receive ongoing support from either politicians or government officials.

Land Tenure

Until recently all land was communally owned, and in most of Sub-Saharan Africa it continues to be so. Land tenure was communal; land was held by families, and descent could be traced to the first settlers. Nevertheless, more fixed boundaries delimit the territories of clan or tribe, and when these are endangered, the whole community fights for them and not merely the border families (Talbot 1926). Within clan or family territory, land was claimed according to need as men grew to adulthood, and the parents of a large number of surviving sons could live to see the expansion of the territory over which they reigned (Nadel 1942).

Land is not completely separate from lineage and fertility but is almost another facet of these central concerns. "The ancestors are buried on family land, and they continue to inhabit it. They are in constant touch with the living group of kinsmen through its senior members, and they look to their descendants to preserve the mutual heritage, which is the tangible link between the past, present and future generations of the line. Such land has stored up in it the memories and traditions of the past, and its very possession recalls the obligations which the living owe to the dead" (Little 1951, p. 87).

The position is not stable, however. The system may have been well suited to shifting cultivation, still the predominant form of agriculture, but more long-lasting guarantees of tenure were needed if cash crops were to be planted, especially by entrepreneurs from outside. Hill (1963) showed that the Akwapim of Ghana created de facto freehold in great areas of southern Ghana. Where population increases in density, much the same thing could happen, as it did near Kaduna in northern Nigeria, where there developed "a complex system of land ownership and land transfer, which, in the extreme case, amounts to an outright purchase for money" (Nadel 1942, p. 181). In parts of East Africa, freehold tenure with the right of individuals to buy and sell was created. This "altered profoundly the nature of kinship ties and particularly the relation between the Ganda father and his children" (Richards 1966, p. 12).

Thus, only fertility leads to power over more land and indeed the capacity to farm it. Draft animals are relatively uncommon in tropical Africa, and their experimental introduction in Sierra Leone proved that wives and children are still the most economical method of farming in African conditions (Ware 1977). In most parts of Africa, even this source of labor is strained at times of peak demand. Goody (1973, p. 188) found that, in most of rural Sub-Saharan Africa, labor was the dominating factor in the economy and, hence, that "the optimum strategy under these conditions is likely to be maximum fertility." Molnos (1973, vol. 3, p. 9), in summarizing the East African studies, established that more children meant more cultivation, often more land, and greater division of labor. The importance of the latter aspect of high fertility has been stressed by Reyna (1975) in respect to Chad, where only the larger families can send members to earn cash from windfall opportunities, which become available often at considerable distances. In circumstances where land was communally owned and even housing was often lineage property, as in the case of the large Yoruba compounds of Nigeria or the Ga longhouses of Accra, the only real investment that younger parents could make was in children. Where there is scarcity to the point that putting aside savings instead of consuming is difficult and morally suspect, no one disapproves of investing in two or three more children even in circumstances where some extra tightening of the belt is involved (Caldwell 1982).

Several aspects of the society make it more difficult for either economic demographers or African parents to work out a balance sheet of children's costs and benefits. Many of the difficulties arise from a kinship based on the lineage. It is unwise in any economic model to assume a relationship between biological parenthood and economic responsibility for bringing up children. In a rehousing settlement in Lagos, Marris (1961) found that only half of the children resided with both biological parents; in the Changing African Family Project, only one-half were found with either parent (Caldwell 1982), and in the Côte d'Ivoire, Clignet (1970) found fewer than one-half (see also chapter 12 in this volume). Fostering on this scale is evidence not only of the relative unimportance of the nuclear biological family but also of the value of children because they are lent to other relatives to smooth out unevenness in child help caused by the life cycle or by subfecundity. It also means such a weak link between reproductive decisionmaking and parental—especially paternal—dependency burdens that the latter may well not play a significant role in such decisions.

Brokensha (1973) reported that, among the Mbeere of Kenya, most parents aimed at securing as many children as possible, the only economic drawback being seen as the costs of extended education. These costs were identified as problems for the urban elite in Ghana as early as the beginning of the 1960s (Caldwell 1968a). By the late 1970s, in Ghana, which was suffering from massive economic problems, Bleek (1978) reported that in the cocoa-growing area children were increasingly regarded as a burden. If it is true that a long period, during which economic growth opens new economic and social horizons, followed by sustained economic depression, can lead to a desire to control family size (Banks 1954), then Ghana should be the Sub-Saharan African country in which fertility decline is first established. It is, in fact, possible that the country's total fertility rate has declined from close to seven to nearer six over the last twenty years, but the statistical series is hardly reliable enough to be completely convincing.

The Sub-Saharan African Family

The nature of the lineage means that the kind of family economic calculations common in other societies must be severely qualified in the Sub-Saharan African context, except perhaps among the urban elite. Children belong to all older members of the lineage (Fortes 1978). In the villages, it is often difficult to know who is responsible for their feeding, for they wander from one relative's cooking pot to another. Similarly, costs are widely shared, and few Africans feel significantly less responsible for the schooling costs of their nephews and nieces than for those of their own children (Caldwell 1982).

Reproductive decisions are rendered more complex by the payment of bride-wealth, which is, more clearly than in most other parts of the world, from family to family and which is usually specifically understood to be for reproductive capacity. "Marriage is a contract not between individuals, but between families." The "wife is expected to bear many children, thus contributing to the continuity and viability of the extended family" (Fortes 1961, p. 657). There are ethnic groups that return a woman, but not her children, to her lineage of origin at menopause. Mayer (1973, p. 123) reported of the Gusii of Kenya that "the girl's child-bearing capacity was a main, or the main, thing transferred in exchange for cattle. If she died prematurely, the number of cattle reclaimed was reduced proportionately to the number of children she had borne." Fortes (1978) has argued that the right to dispose of a woman's fertility is not hers, although she may dispose of her sexuality. The payment of considerable bride-wealth keeps the control of marriage securely in the hands of the parents and other older members of the lineage. Such payments are necessary if a marriage is to be recognized, and de facto marriage may well result in sickness inflicted by the ancestors (although fear that it may do so is passing, especially in the towns).

One result of a bride-wealth system of such significance is little son preference (Ware 1974). Indeed, a strong feeling about the need for rearing sufficient numbers of each sex to adulthood is a bulwark for high fertility.

A viable analysis of the supports for high fertility or of the failure of pressures that would seem to suggest an economic benefit from lower fertility to become operative must take into account the nature of a society characterized by polygyny on the unique scale that occurs in Sub-Saharan Africa. In many parts of Africa, up to one-half of the men and most women will spend some of their lives in a polygynous marriage. All women must anticipate the possibility and order their family emotions and economy accordingly. In fact, the basic family economic unit is a woman and her children. Often the production of this unit is sold to her husband, compulsorily and at a discount price, before he arranges its marketing (sometimes once again through his wife, as among the Yoruba). In other cases, such as in the Ghanaian fishing industry described by Vercruijsse (1983), the male fishermen sell their catch to their wives, who then market it. Abu (1983) has noted the pronounced separation of spousal economies, residential patterns, and sexual activities (but not reproductive activities) in an Ashanti urban area. Poh (1974, pp. 65–66) investigated the situation in Ghana among the Akuafem, one of the least traditional groups in Ghana because of a century of Christianization and a long period of cocoa farming, and concluded: "The Akan concept of marriage as an economic and procreative contract, rather than as a spiritual union of man and wife, remained unchanged."

At least in rural areas, men form larger economic units by adding wives to the family, to be supplemented in due course by their children. In most of Sub-Saharan Africa, women are the main cultivators and depend on their children to assist them (van der Meeren-Yeld 1973). Indeed, their main access to male help is their growing sons. Clignet (1970) concluded from his study of the Côte d'Ivoire that children reinforced the benefits of polygyny.

In spite of this segmentation of the family, much of the expenditure pattern on children is controlled by the father and other older male relatives. The segmentation does, however, produce a distancing effect between father and children that, together with the fact that the latter are descendants and not ancestors, means that they are treated austerely, cheaply, and even casually (Albert 1963). In some societies, on the grounds that the eldest son must by nature wish to replace his father, the two completely ignore each other according to the dictates of an avoidance taboo (Fortes 1959).

Fortes (1978) has pointed out that the concept of the relationship between husband and wife as the core of the family is Western, not African. More than in most societies, African women are considered different from men, especially after initiation or circumcision, when even their dress, ornaments, and hair style may change (Brokensha 1973), and they continue to be seen as dangerous to males, although the latter are to a considerable extent protected by their circumcision. According to Dorjahn (1958, p. 839), "It is said that a Temne [of Sierra Leone] marries to have children, not women." Not only the father but also the mother shares these sentiments for sound reasons of economy and security: "Most important of all is a mother's right to be supported by her sons from the time that they become capable of farming. Whether she has a husband or not, she will generally live with her son after she gets past the age of child-bearing" (Fortes 1949, p. 139).

The separation between the spouses remains even in matters of sex and reproduction. Wives are expected to show little excitement about sexual relations with their husbands (Olusanya 1969; Raum 1973b) and to feel no deprivation with long periods of postpartum sexual abstinence (Caldwell and Caldwell 1981). Men cannot even be accused of adultery in many societies because they can claim to have been looking for another wife (Njeru 1973).

In spite of the emphasis on reproduction, nearly all studies of African societies establish the extreme diffi-

culty and rarity of discussions between spouses on either sexual relations or family planning (Caldwell 1968b; Mbiti 1973a). Thus, family planning decisions, when they are made, are likely to be either surreptitious decisions by the wife alone or unilateral ones by the husband (Mwambia 1973a). In contrast to reproductive discussions between relatives, which are always likely to be formal at best, discussions are relatively easy and by far the most frequent between age mates of the same sex (Caldwell and Igun 1970; Caldwell and Caldwell 1976; Molnos 1973, vol. 2; Raum 1973a).

"Wealth flows" (Caldwell 1982) can be delineated more clearly in Sub-Saharan Africa than in any other societies. Parental reward is guaranteed by culture and religion. "Filial piety is a parent's unquestioned and inalienable right because he begot you—or, in the mother's case, she bore you" (Adaba 1978, p. 174). This rule is powerfully reinforced by the children's fear of a parental curse, for curses are usually effective only in the appropriate case, and lack of assistance to parents is one of the clearest of cases. In Nigeria, the Yoruba equate children with wealth both in ideas and linguistically (Caldwell 1982), and Swartz (1969) reported the same views for East Africa, where parents have strong and quite explicit views of the services expected from children.

There have been several attempts to quantify the help expected from children. When the findings are compared across the region there appears to have been less concern about infant and child mortality in West Africa than in East Africa in spite of—or perhaps because of—higher mortality in the west (Caldwell 1968b). In both areas, about one-third of all primary responses to the value of children emphasize prestige and other social rewards. On the economic side, current help and assistance in old age are stressed to approximately the same extent. Swartz (1969, p. 85) agrees but argued that "another sort of meaning that children have for their parents is less directly related to the basic structure of their societies than to their overall values and understanding of man and the universe."

Wealth flows at almost every level in African kinship groups. Barley (1983) reported that in rural Cameroon wives expect to receive a reward for sexual relations even in their own marriage, a practice that has infuriated missionaries, who are apt to liken it to prostitution. In fact, this practice conforms with much of the other bargaining that is found within conjugal relations and exists to some degree throughout much of the region.

Perhaps the fundamental problem of Sub-Saharan African fertility control is the profound division between spouses with regard to reproductive matters. Women are deeply aware that, though they may control their own sexuality, their reproduction is solely a matter of their husband and the husband's lineage. This is, of course, a basic premise of the bride-wealth system, although not all women articulate the problem, even to themselves, in this way. Thus husbands, who may bear little of the cost of children, and perhaps none of the cost of additional children, feel no erosion of their rights to make reproductive decisions. On the contrary, their reproductive obligations are to their lineage and ancestry. Reproductive decisions and family economics are largely separated, nor is there much relation between reproduction and female autonomy. Yoruba market women are among the world's seemingly most autonomous women. They support themselves and their children and are often beholden to no man. Yet when asked about their reproduction, they usually say that the decision will be made by their fathers-in-law, the oldest living ancestors of their husbands. In other cases it is the husband's mother, or even the grandmother, who voices the family's interest.

Safety in Numbers

Children have always been seen as a contribution to the safety of the lineage, the clan, and kingdoms such as those of the Ashanti. The level of violence was sufficient until the late nineteenth century to make everyone aware of this function. Armar (1983) believes that the fractionation of Africa has meant that politicians continue to give less than wholehearted support to national family planning programs for this reason. Such beliefs in security continue to have a strong effect on subnational groups such as the Baganda in Uganda (Southwold 1973), the Creoles of Sierra Leone (Steady 1978), and the various ethnic groups of Nigeria (Adepoju 1981). With regard to defense, most communities were well aware that they needed not only sons but daughters as well because the marriage alliance created large networks ensuring safety (van der Meeren-Yeld 1973; Caldwell 1982).

At the individual level this was, and still is, true. Kabwegyere and Mbula (1979) pointed out that when an old man rises in an Akamba (Kenya) meeting to express forcibly a viewpoint, and sometimes that of a minority, one can be sure that he has some hefty sons in the audience. Molnos (1973, vol. 3, p. 10) summarized the reports in her volumes: "Grown-up males protected the family property, especially under conditions of increasing land shortage and where the head of the family was away as a wage-earner in town. . . . In some pastoral areas, access to pasture and water depended on the ability to fight intruders. . . . Survival as well as political status and independence were based on fighting strength."

Prestige

This chapter has tended to avoid the question of prestige, taking it usually to reflect such material matters as power and economic reward. Nevertheless, the special position of women with regard to their fertility is noteworthy. Children earn for a woman the respect of her kin by marriage, and that respect is often roughly proportional to her fertility. Bisilliat (1983, p. 99) concluded from her study of the Songhai-Zarma in Niger that "a woman's only source of power lies in swelling the number of the male line, in bringing children into the world, in reproducing society." In many Sub-Saharan African societies, women have different appellations as they move through different stages of life marked by their marriage and fertility (see, for example, Kershaw 1973). It is frequently true, however, that the full dignity of motherhood is not reached until her first son is circumcised (Brokensha 1973).

Traditionally, that respect has had no ceiling but continues to grow with her family. Among the Kavirondo, "a prolific wife commands more respect from her husband and his kinsmen" (Wagner 1939. p. 10). Among the Meru of Kenya, as elsewhere throughout the continent, women are pleased to be addressed not by their names but as mothers of their children. "If the number of children increases, she gains more social status, especially if they are of both sexes and are 'well-spaced,' since this means that she has followed the traditional marital obligations pertinent to conception, lactation, and sexual life" (Njeru 1973).

Birth Control

Much of the reaction to birth control follows fairly directly from the attitudes toward fertility and sterility, which originate in the traditional religious and cultural beliefs. It might be anticipated that the use of contraception would correlate with almost any index of socioeconomic change; this is true with regard to education, but there is no correlation with the split between wives in monogamous and polygynous marriages (Brown 1981; Caldwell and Caldwell 1981), possibly because any woman can find herself polygynously married.

Attitudes toward conception must be seen in the context of the traditional reliance on marital sexual abstinence. Olusanya (1969) has written that if a Yoruba man did not want a woman to have a child, he simply did not have sex with her. This behavioral reaction may not be the only one in East Africa. Swartz (1969) reported that the three groups he studied all knew of coitus interruptus but rarely practiced it because it was regarded as a hostile act to women, who remain sexually unsatisfied unless filled with semen. The Lugbara of Uganda usually practice withdrawal only with a divorced woman, with a possible future wife, or in the incestuous relations usual in the ritual "death dance" (Middleton 1973). Both the Lugbara and Chaga (Raum 1973b) know of the contraceptive effect of vaginal plugs of grass soaked in sesame oil. In both West and East Africa, however, the most widely known methods of birth control were magical, involving spells, finger and waist rings, womb turning, and herbal preparations (Heisel 1968; Acsadi 1976; Caldwell and Ware 1977). Traditional abortion was known, although it was usually practiced only in circumstances where pregnancy would be horrific, as in the case of incest. Now, more recent preparations are used, such as pills "for female hygiene" manufactured by the same English firms that met the needs of British women during the Industrial Revolution, and washing blue, which is widely used in developing countries (Heisel 1968; Acsadi 1976; Caldwell and Ware 1977).

Throughout the region, the belief is common that contraceptives are likely to have very harmful effects. In a recent study in Kenya, the country with the oldest Sub-Saharan African family planning program, Dow and Werner (1981) reported that 55 percent of women who knew about the pill believed it would make them ill. Most also believed that it would take an inconvenient or uneconomic amount of time to get supplies.

Foreigners are most apt to misinterpret Sub-Saharan Africa in the area of female sexual morality. They note the sexual freedom of males, which is partly related to the long postpartum sexual abstinence of their wives, and relate it to female behavior, not noting that most of the girlfriends are unmarried women, deserted or divorced women, often because of barrenness, or widows. It is true that the region does not control the chastity of unmarried girls or, in many societies, the surreptitious "affairs" of married women in the strict fashion of North Africa, the Middle East, or South Asia (Evans-Pritchard 1974). Emotions may run high in connection with improper sexuality, and wives may even be sent back to their relatives, but punishments in contemporary Africa usually go no further. Yet precisely because such strain is a good deal more likely than in the peasant societies listed above, there is a continuous apprehension of female sexual promiscuity and a determination to resist it. Many African males are much more shocked to find contraception being discussed or advertised in the presence of women, or to find governments promoting it, than their counterparts are in much more straightlaced societies elsewhere.

This attitude is not new and was reported before there was any debate about government involvement in family planning. Nadel (1952. p. 21) reported the deep suspicion among Nupe males in Nigeria that some women

who took to trading on the grounds that they were barren had only feigned this condition with the help of contraception and abortion: "The men are helpless; they can only brand this voluntary sterility as the gravest possible form of immorality." Dorjahn (1958) reported similar fears among the Temne of Sierra Leone, where men believed that women used contraception to appear barren in order either to punish their husbands or to incite them to break up the marriage. It is irrelevant that, in the vast majority of cases, these were almost certainly false and neurotic suspicions, especially in the case of the Temne, where there appears to be a considerable incidence of sterility probably arising from venereal disease (Caldwell and Caldwell 1983). The important point is that contraception and abortion were seen in this way.

Olusanya (1969, pp. 15–16) reflected the view of much of the region when he reported "the feeling that women are so sexually weak that a little freedom for them invariably leads to extramarital intercourse." He pointed out that for this reason wives were supposed to be impassive when having sexual relations with their husbands and were expected to think very little about sexual activities. If they were given access to contraception, they would abuse it; this idea was encapsulated in the answer of one male respondent: "Even when women are not taught this method, it is always hard to keep up their morals. What do you think would happen with the teaching of such useless methods?" Similar fears have been reported from Freetown in Sierra Leone (Harrell-Bond 1975).

The Ghanaian National Family Planning Programme still exhibits sensitivity about advertising contraception (Armar 1983), and articles and letters in Ghanaian newspapers complain of the embarrassment created by radio or television mention of the subject, especially when women are present (Opeku 1980).

Dow and Werner (1981) have reported survey evidence from Kenya showing that reactions varied widely to the idea of women employing contraception in accordance with what was perceived to be their need. In the case of a married woman with six children and severe economic problems, 75 percent of female respondents were prepared to permit family planning, whereas the proportion approving fell to 17 percent for unmarried women with no children. In practice, the tendency to use contraception is the reverse. Interestingly, only 55 percent would approve of a woman with six children using contraception if she were a grandmother, presumably because of the belief that she should be terminally abstaining.

The timing of the onset of terminal abstinence varies considerably and is not always identified with becoming a grandmother or a mother-in-law. Of two neighboring Kenyan societies, it occurs at different times: when the first son is circumcised in one (Kershaw 1973) and usually some time after menopause in the other (Njeru 1973), although the latter may be a recent development in view of the fact that throughout Africa the menses are believed to be necessary to flush out sperm. In East Africa, there appears in recent decades to have been a transition from postpartum sexual abstinence lasting until after weaning to postpartum abstinence for as little as six months (Brokensha 1973; WFS 1980). This change is surprising in view of the adherence to the belief, found across the continent, that sperm poisons the mother's milk; indeed, the Chaga call semen "man's milk" (Raum 1973b).

Nevertheless, contraception is coming into use, although often with apprehension and abandonment as soon as anything at all untoward happens. In Ibadan City, Nigeria (Caldwell and Caldwell 1976; Caldwell and Ware 1977; Caldwell and Caldwell 1981), it was found that only one-tenth of contraceptors employed birth control with any intention of controlling ultimate family size. Contraception is mainly in demand because it allows husbands and wives to shorten the period of postpartum sexual abstinence without demonstrating by pregnancy to their relatives that they have behaved in such an immoral way and without endangering the lives of their children by having them too closely spaced. The major determinant of a shortened abstinence period is the use of contraception. The second most common use of contraception is to enable women to have premarital sexual relations. It is likely that in Nigeria, and reportedly also in Sierra Leone (Harrell-Bond 1975), most men first become familiar with contraception in extramarital relations. The use of contraception in such liaisons does familiarize men with its use but frequently reinforces the attitude that such behavior is clearly not for their wives.

Conclusions

The central factor implicated in Sub-Saharan African high fertility is a culture, molded by religion, that encourages repeated childbearing and abhors sterility at any stage. Fertility is powerfully supported by the unusually high value of children, which arises from a continuing economic flow from the young to the old, and is also grounded in a culture shaped by religion.

In these circumstances, it is likely that fertility will remain higher at every socioeconomic level of development than is the case in most parts of Asia. This result will reflect not only individual attitudes but also lesser, or less efficient, provision of family planning services, because politicians and administrators are also either apprehensive or skeptical of swimming against the cultural current.

The situation will slowly change, and the engine of change will be a secularization of the society arising to a considerable extent from external cultural forces. Lesthaeghe (1977) has shown how the supports for high fertility in Belgium crumbled with secularization, which he measured by the proportion of votes cast for nonreligious political parties. In a study of rural India, Caldwell and others (1983) adduced evidence to show that health and reproductive behavior had changed with the secularization of the community in this century. The meaning of "secularization" here is complex and certainly does not entail the loss of all religious belief. Rather, it means the slow removal from the religious agenda of specific areas of thought and behavior. In India, this result is achieved partly by strengthening the great religious traditions, both Hindu and Moslem, at the expense of the little traditions of the villages, which embodied age-old attitudes toward life and the demographic processes. This was undoubtedly assisted by modernization and schooling. Such secular change is likely to reach Sub-Saharan Africa both by religious change and by directly secular influences.

References

Abu, Katharine. 1983. "The Separateness of Spouses: Conjugal Resources in an Ashanti Town." In C. Oppong, ed., *Female and Male in West Africa*. London: Allen and Unwin.

Acsadi, G. T. 1976. "Traditional Birth Control Methods in Yorubaland." In J. F. Marshall and S. Polgar, eds., *Culture, Natality, and Family Planning*. Chapel Hill: Carolina Population Center

Adaba, Geraldine. 1978. "Rationality and Responsibility in Family Planning in Traditional African Society." In C. Oppong and others, eds., *Marriage, Fertility, and Parenthood in West Africa*. Canberra: Department of Demography, Australian National University.

Adepoju, Aderanti. 1981. "Military Rule and Population Issues in Nigeria." *African Affairs* 80(318): 29–47.

Albert, E. M. 1963. "Women of Burundi: A Study of Social Values." In D. Paulme, ed., *Women of Tropical Africa*. Berkeley: University of California Press.

Arens, William. 1973. "Mto Wa Mbu, a Multi-Ethnic Community in Northern Tanzania." In A. Molnos, ed., *Cultural Source Materials for Population Planning in East Africa*, vol. 2, *Innovations and Communication*. Nairobi: East African Publishing House.

Armar, A. A. 1983. "The Ghana National Family Planning Programme." In E. Satter, ed., *Management Contributions to Population Programmes: Views from Three Continents*. Kuala Lumpur: International Committee on the Management of Population Programmes.

Azu, D. G. 1974. *The Ga Family and Social Change*. Leiden: Afrika-Studiecentrum, and Cambridge: African Studies Centre.

Banks, J. A. 1954. *Prosperity and Parenthood: A Study of Family Planning among the Victorian Middle Classes*. London: Routledge and Kegan Paul.

Barley, Nigel. 1983. *The Innocent Anthropologist: Notes from a Mud Hut*. London: Colonnade, British Museum.

Barnes, J. A. 1951. *Marriage in a Changing Society: A Study of Structural Change among the Fort Jameson Ngoni*. Capetown, South Africa: Oxford University Press.

Bisilliat, Jeanne. 1983. "The Feminine Sphere in the Institutions of the Songhay-Zarma." In C. Oppong, ed., *Female and Male in West Africa*. London: Allen and Unwin.

Bleek, Wolf. 1978. "The Value of Children to Parents in Kwahu, Ghana." In C. Oppong and others, eds. *Marriage, Fertility, and Parenthood in West Africa*. Canberra: Department of Demography, Australian National University.

Brokensha, D. W. 1973. "The Mbeere of Central Kenya." In A. Molnos, ed., *Cultural Source Materials for Population Planning in East Africa*, vol. 3, *Beliefs and Practices*. Nairobi: East African Publishing House.

Brown, J. E. 1981. "Polygyny and Family Planning in Sub-Saharan Africa." *Studies in Family Planning* 12(8/9): 322–25.

Caldwell, J. C. 1968a. *Population Growth and Family Change in Africa: The New Urban Elite in Ghana*. Canberra: Australian National University Press.

———. 1968b. "The Control of Family Size in Tropical Africa." *Demography* 5(2): 598–619.

———. 1979. "Education as a Factor in Mortality Decline: An Examination of Nigerian Data." *Population Studies* 33(3): 395–413.

———. 1982. *Theory of Fertility Decline*. London: Academic Press.

Caldwell, J. C., and P. Caldwell. 1976. "Demographic and Contraceptive Innovators: A Study of Transitional African Society." *Journal of Biosocial Science* 8(4): 347–65.

———. 1981. "The Function of Child-Spacing in Traditional Societies and the Direction of Change." In H. J. Page and R. Lesthaeghe, eds., *Child-Spacing in Tropical Africa: Traditions and Change*. London: Academic Press.

———. 1983. "The Demographic Evidence for the Incidence and Cause of Abnormally Low Fertility in Tropical Africa." *World Health Statistics Quarterly* 36(1): 2–33.

Caldwell, J. C., and A. Igun. 1970. "The Spread of Anti-Natal Knowledge and Practice in Nigeria." *Population Studies* 24(1): 21–34.

Caldwell, J. C., and P. McDonald. 1981. "Influence of Maternal Education on Infant and Child Mortality: Levels and Causes." In *International Population Conference Manila, 1981: Solicited Papers*, vol. 2. Liège, Belgium: International Union for the Scientific Study of Population.

Caldwell, J. C., P. H. Reddy, and P. Caldwell. 1983. "The Social Component of Mortality Decline: An Investigation in South India Employing Alternative Methodologies." *Population Studies*, 37(2): 185–205.

Caldwell, J. C., and H. Ware. 1977. "The Evolution of Family Planning in an African City: Ibadan, Nigeria." *Population Studies*, 31(3): 487–507.

Casale, D. M. 1982. "Women, Power, and Change in Lugbara (Uganda) Cosmology." *Anthropos* 77: 385–96.

Clignet, Rémi. 1970. *Many Wives, Many Powers: Authority and Power in Polygynous Families*. Evanston: Northwestern University Press.

Dorjahn, V. R. 1958. "Fertility, Polygyny, and Their Interrelations in Temne Society." *American Anthropologist* 60: 838–60.

Dow, T. E., and H. Werner. 1981. "Family Size and Population in Kenya: Continuity and Change in Metropolitan and Rural Attitudes." *Studies in Family Planning* 12(6/7): 272–77.

Duru, M. S. 1983. "Continuity in the Midst of Change: Underlying Themes in Igbo Culture." *Anthropological Quarterly* 56(1): 1–9.

Evans-Pritchard, E. E. 1937. *Witchcraft, Oracles, and Magic among the Azande*. Oxford: Clarendon Press.

———. 1953. "The Nuer Conception of Spirit in Its Relation to the Social Order." *American Anthropologist* 55: 201–14.

———. 1974. *Man and Woman among the Azande*. New York: Free Press.

Field, M. J. 1960. *Search for Security: An Ethno-Psychiatric Study of Rural Ghana*. London: Faber and Faber.

Forde, Daryll. 1951. *Marriage and the Family among the Yako in South-Eastern Nigeria*. London: Percy Lund Humphries.

Fortes, Meyer. 1949. *The Web of Kinship among the Tallensi*. Oxford: Oxford University Press.

———. 1959. *Oedipus and Job in West African Religion*. Cambridge: Cambridge University Press.

———. 1961. "Pietas in Ancestor Worship: The Henry Myers Lecture, 1960." *Journal of the Royal Anthropological Institute* 91(1–2): 166–90.

———. 1978. "Family, Marriage, and Fertility in West Africa." In C. Oppong and others, eds., *Marriage, Fertility, and Parenthood in West Africa*. Canberra: Department of Demography, Australian National University.

Fortes, M., and E. E. Evans-Pritchard, eds. 1940. *African Political Systems*. Oxford: Oxford University Press.

Golde, P. 1970. *Women in the Field: Anthropological Experiences*. Chicago: Aldine.

Goody, Jack, ed. 1973. *The Character of Kinship*. Cambridge: Cambridge University Press.

Green, Edward. 1982. "U.S. Population Policies, Development, and the Rural Poor in Africa." *Journal of Modern African Studies* 20(1): 45–67.

Gregory, Dick. 1971. "My Answer to Genocide." *Ebony* 26(12): 66–72.

Harrell-Bond, B. E. 1975. *Modern Marriage in Sierra Leone: A Study of a Professional Group*. The Hague: Mouton.

Heisel, D. F. 1968. "Attitudes and Practices of Contraception in Kenya." *Demography* 5(2): 632–41.

Hill, Polly. 1963. *The Migrant Cocoa Farmers of Southern Ghana: A Study of Rural Capitalism*. Cambridge: Cambridge University Press.

Isichei, P. A. C. 1978. "The Basic Meaning of a Child through Asaba Personal Names." In C. Oppong and others, eds.,

Marriage, Fertility, and Parenthood in West Africa. Canberra: Department of Demography, Australian National University.

Kabwegyere, T. B., and J. Mbula. 1979. *A Case of the Akamba of Eastern Kenya*. Changing African Family Project Series, Monograph No. 5. Canberra: Department of Demography, Australian National University.

Kershaw, Gretha. 1973. "The Kikuyu of Central Kenya." In A. Molnos, ed., *Cultural Source Materials for Population Planning in East Africa*, vol. 3, *Beliefs and Practices*. Nairobi: East African Publishing House.

Kuckertz, H. 1983. "Symbol and Authority in Mpondo Ancestor Religion." *African Studies* 42(2): 113–33.

"L'Afrique chrétienne a doublé en quinze ans." 1972. *Missi* (November): 273–95.

Lesthaeghe, R. J. 1970. *The Decline of Belgian Fertility, 1800–1970*. Princeton: Princeton University Press.

Little, K. L. 1951. *The Mende of Sierra Leone: A West African People in Transition*. London: Routledge and Kegan Paul.

Lorimer, Frank. 1954. *Culture and Human Fertility*. Paris: United Nations Educational, Scientific, and Cultural Organization.

Mair, L. P. 1969. *African Marriage and Social Change*. London: Frank Cass.

Marris, Peter, 1961. *Family and Social Change in an African City: A Study of Rehousing in Lagos*. London: Routledge and Kegan Paul.

Mayer, Iona. 1973. "The Gusii of Western Kenya." In A. Molnos, ed., *Cultural Source Materials for Population Planning in East Africa*, vol. 3, *Beliefs and Practices*. Nairobi: East African Publishing House.

Mbiti, J. S. 1970. *Concepts of God in Africa*. New York: Praeger.

———. 1973a. "The Kamba of Central Kenya." In A. Molnos, ed., *Cultural Source Materials for Population Planning in East Africa*, vol. 2, *Innovations and Communication*. Nairobi: East African Publishing House.

———. 1973b. "The Kamba of Central Kenya." In A. Molnos, ed., *Cultural Source Materials for Population Planning in East Africa*, vol. 3, *Beliefs and Practices*. Nairobi: East African Publishing House.

Meek, C. K. 1931. *Tribal Studies in Northern Nigeria*. Vol. 1. London: Kegan Paul, French, Trubner.

———. 1957. *Land Tenure and Land Administration in Nigeria and the Cameroons*. London: Her Majesty's Stationery Office.

Messing, S. D. 1973. "The Somali of the Ogaden, South-East Ethiopia." In A. Molnos, ed., *Cultural Source Materials for Population Planning in East Africa*, vol. 3, *Beliefs and Practices*. Nairobi: East African Publishing House.

Middleton, John. 1973. "The Lugbara of North-Western Uganda." In A. Molnos, ed., *Cultural Source Materials for Population Planning in East Africa*, vol. 3, *Beliefs and Practices*. Nairobi: East African Publishing House.

Middleton, John, and E. H. Winter, eds. 1963. *Witchcraft and Sorcery in East Africa*. London: Routledge and Kegan Paul.

Molnos, Angela, ed. 1973. *Cultural Source Materials for Population Planning in East Africa*. Vol. 1., *Review of Socio-Cultural Research, 1952–72*. Vol. 2, *Innovations and Communication*. Vol. 3, *Beliefs and Practices*. Vol. 4, *Bibliography*. Nairobi: East African Publishing House.

Mwambia, S. P. K. 1973a. "The Meru of Central Kenya." In A. Molnos, ed., *Cultural Source Materials for Population Planning in East Africa*, vol. 2., *Innovations and Communication*. Nairobi: East African Publishing House.

———. 1973b. "The Meru of Central Kenya." In A. Molnos, ed., *Cultural Source Materials for Population Planning in East Africa*, vol. 3, *Beliefs and Practices*. Nairobi: East African Publishing House.

Nadel, S. F. 1942. *A Black Byzantium*. London: Oxford University Press.

———. 1952. "Witchcraft in Four African Societies: An Essay in Comparison." *American Anthropologist* 54: 18–29.

Ndeti, Kiruto. 1973. "The Kamba of Central Kenya." In A. Molnos, ed., *Cultural Source Material for Population Planning in East Africa*, vol. 3, *Beliefs and Practices*. Nairobi: East African Publishing House.

Ngubane, Harriet. 1977. *Body and Mind in Zulu Medicine: An Ethnography of Health and Disease in Nyuswa—Zulu Thought and Practice*. London: Academic Press.

Njeru, B. K. 1973. "The Egoji Clan of Meru, Central Kenya." In A. Molnos, ed., *Cultural Source Materials for Population Planning in East Africa*, vol. 3, *Beliefs and Practices*. Nairobi: East African Publishing House.

Offiong, David. 1983. "Social Relations and Witch Beliefs among the Ibibio." *Africa* 53(31): 73–81.

Olusanya, P. O. 1969. "Nigeria: Cultural Barriers to Family Planning among the Yorubas." *Studies in Family Planning*, 37: 13–16.

Opeku, V. A. 1980. "New Look at Population Explosion." *Daily Graphic* (Accra) February (12): 5.

Owusu, Maxwell. 1979. "Politics without Parties: Reflections on the Union Government Proposals in Ghana." *African Studies Review* 22(1): 89–108.

Oyemade, Adefunke, and T. A. Ogunmuyiwa. 1981. "Socio-Cultural Factors and Fertility in a Rural Nigerian Community." *Studies in Family Planning* 12(3): 109–11.

Page, H. J., and R. Lesthaeghe. 1981. *Child-Spacing in Tropical Africa: Traditions and Change*. London: Academic Press.

Parrinder, Geoffrey. 1981. "The Religions of Africa." In *Africa South of the Sahara*. 10th ed. London: Europa.

Paulme, Denise. 1963. "Introduction." In D. Paulme, ed., *Women of Tropical Africa*. Berkeley: University of California Press.

Poh, M. A. K. 1974. "Church and Change in Akuapem." In C. Oppong, ed., *Domestic Rights and Duties in Southern Ghana*. Legon Family Research Paper No. 1. Legon: Institute of African Studies, University of Ghana.

Raum, O. F. 1973a. "The Chaga of North-Eastern Tanzania." In A. Molnos, ed., *Cultural Source Materials for Population Planning in East Africa*, vol. 2, *Innovations and Communication*. Nairobi: East Africa Publishing House.

————. 1973b. "The Chaga of North-Eastern Tanzania." In A. Molnos, ed., *Cultural Source Materials for Population Planning in East Africa*, vol. 3, *Beliefs and Practices*. Nairobi: East African Publishing House.

Reyna, S. P. 1975. "Pronatalism and Child Labor." In J. C. Caldwell, ed., *Population Growth and Socioeconomic Change in West Africa*. New York: Columbia University Press.

Richards, A. I. 1940. "The Political System of the Bemba Tribe—Northern Rhodesia." In M. Fortes and E. E. Evans-Pritchard, *African Political Systems*. Oxford: Oxford University Press.

————. 1950. "Some Types of Family Structure among the Central Bantu." In A. R. Radcliffe-Browne and D. Forde, eds., *African Systems of Kinship and Marriage*. London: Oxford University Press.

————. 1966. *The Changing Structure of a Ganda Village*. Nairobi: East African Publishing House.

Southwold, Martin. 1973. "The Baganda of Central Kenya." In A. Molnos, ed., *Cultural Source Materials for Population Planning in East Africa*, vol. 2, *Innovations and Communication*. Nairobi: East African Publishing House.

Soyinka, Wole. 1967. *Idanre and Other Poems*. London: Methuen.

Spring, Anita. 1980. "Faith and Participation in Traditional versus Cosmopolitan Medical Systems in Northwest Zambia." *Anthropological Quarterly* 53(2): 130–41.

Steady, F. C. 1978. "Male Roles in Fertility in Sierra Leone: The Moving Target." In C. Oppong and others, eds., *Marriage, Fertility, and Parenthood in West Africa*. Canberra: Department of Demography, Australian National University.

Swartz, M. J. 1969. "Some Cultural Influences on Family Size in Three East African Societies." *Anthropological Quarterly* 42(2): 73–88.

Talbot, P. A. 1926. *The Peoples of Southern Nigeria*. Vol. 3, *Ethnology*. London: Oxford University Press.

————. 1927. *Some Nigerian Fertility Cults*. London: Oxford University Press.

van der Meeren-Yeld, Rachel. 1973. "The Kiga of South-Western Uganda." In A. Molnos, ed., *Cultural Source Materials for Population Planning in East Africa*, vol. 2, *Innovations and Communication*. Nairobi: East African Publishing House.

Vercruijsse, E. V. W. 1983. "Fishmongers, Big Dealers, and Fishermen: Co-operation and Conflict between the Sexes in Ghanaian Canoe Fishing." In C. Oppong, ed., *Female and Male in West Africa*. London: Allen and Unwin.

Wagner, Gunter. 1939. *The Changing Family among the Bantu Kavirondo*. London: Oxford University Press.

Ware, Helen. 1974. *Ideal Family Size*. Occasional Paper No. 13. Voorburg: International Statistical Institute and World Fertility Survey.

————. 1977. "Economic Strategy and the Number of Children." In J. C. Caldwell, ed., *The Persistence of High Fertility*. Canberra: Department of Demography, Australian National University.

World Fertility Survey. 1980. *The Kenya Fertility Survey, 1978: A Summary of Findings*. No. 26. Voorburg: International Statistical Institute and WFS.

Part V

Programs to Reduce Fertility

Within the region, population growth is both a political and an economic issue. The division of opinion on this issue has much to do with colonial heritage, and the debate is not entirely over. Cochrane, Sai, and Nassim (chapter 14) examine rapid population growth as an economic issue in a particular demographic and political context.

One view held by some policymakers and others is that population growth yields substantial economies of scale, increases market size, justifies investments in infrastructure, and allows the exploitation of natural resources. The realization of these economies depends upon a number of factors, however, including greater division of labor, an optimum balance between population density and resources, and access to the required technology. Thus the realization of development goals depends not only on population size and growth, which by themselves can create difficulties in the accumulation of savings. More and more, government policymakers are concluding that the conflict between increasing the supply of savings for development, on the one hand, and improving welfare and enhancing basic living standards, on the other, may be exacerbated by rapid population growth rates.

Chapter 14 tracks the development of population policies and family planning programs in Sub-Saharan Africa. Prior to the 1974 World Population Conference, policymakers did recognize negative consequences of population growth but still expressed satisfaction with population growth rates and showed little inclination to intervene to reduce fertility. The conference pro-

duced a dialogue on the subject that included wide international discussion of family planning. The opinions expressed at the conference favored social and economic development as the means of regulating fertility and reducing population growth. Family planning did gain acceptance as a policy alternative but mainly as a health and human rights measure.

By 1986, however, most governments had revised their views on population growth, and a large proportion accepted the demographic rationale as a basis for population policy: 74 percent were providing family planning services directly, and 13 percent were supporting private family planning agencies. Only 13 percent gave no support to family planning. The change in official perspectives between the 1974 and 1984 international population conferences may be attributed to increased information on and analysis of conditions in the region, to the work and support of international agencies and nongovernmental organizations, and, more recently, to the work of Sub-Saharan African organizations and conferences. In spite of the progress, however, the implementation of family planning programs in the region faces political, legal, technical, and cultural problems and continues to be handicapped by administrative and managerial difficulties, the lack of trained manpower, and inadequate funds.

With the differences among these countries in population size, density, and urban concentration, as well as their immense cultural diversity, many approaches to family planning are worth exploration. Ross (chapter 15) reviews various approaches that have been tried in

215

Sub-Saharan Africa, including integrated programs, community-based distribution, social marketing, the use of traditional birth attendants, the postpartum approach, incentives and disincentives, special urban programs, and such other programs as mobile teams, women's organizations, and outreach to military groups, unions, and factories.

Experiments with these approaches point to community-based distribution of contraceptives as one of the most promising means of altering contraceptive behavior in largely rural populations. Males need to be educated as to their roles and responsibilities in respect to family planning: this approach, and all others, depend upon them for success. Household distribution of contraceptives is found to achieve levels of awareness that other approaches do not. Furthermore, where health services are locally available, integration with these services facilitates family planning but in urban areas is not essential. Finally, the success of any approach requires respect for certain cultural norms and an understanding of cultural imperatives.

The Development of Population and Family Planning Policies

Susan H. Cochrane, Fred T. Sai, and Janet Nassim

Africa presents a complex challenge to all development initiatives, including initiatives in the fields of population and family planning. The region south of the Sahara is composed of forty-nine countries. They range from geographically large countries with giant populations, such as Nigeria (land area 924,000 square kilometers, population 98 million), to large countries with relatively small populations, such as the Sudan (2.5 million square kilometers, population 22 million), to small island states with tiny populations. The majority, however, have populations that are small by world standards (see chapter 1 in this volume). Geographically, too, many countries are very small, the arbitrary nature of national boundaries in general being a legacy of the colonial past.

Observers tend to lament the slowness of the Sub-Saharan African response to population growth in the region: the critics' reactions do not take sufficient account of Africa's turbulent economic and political history and its cultural diversity and varied demographic circumstances, factors that give rise to widely differing views and are responsible for much sensitivity and uneasiness among Africans and their governments over the issues of population and family planning.

The Demographic Situation

Population is growing more rapidly in Sub-Saharan Africa than anywhere else in the world. The annual rate of population growth increased from 2.45 percent in the early 1960s to 2.9 percent in the early 1980s and is expected to peak at just over 3 percent around the turn of the century, thirty or forty years later than in other parts of the developing world (United Nations 1986). The population of Sub-Saharan Africa doubled in size between 1950 and 1978; at 3 percent per annum it will double again in 20 to 25 years. The question being debated by policymakers is whether these rates of population growth constrain economic and social development, and what combination of demographic or other forms of development intervention constitute the most appropriate response.

The problem is compounded by the wide variation among individual countries. Population growth rates, for example, range from less than 2 percent to more than 4 percent annually (World Bank 1986), and population densities vary from one inhabitant per square kilometer to more than 200 on the mainland and to more than 500 on the island of Mauritius (World Bank 1987). The wide areas of sparse habitation in the Sahel, the forest areas of West and Central Africa, and the western desert areas of southern Africa are probably responsible for the widespread perception that Africa is in no danger of overpopulation.

The Political Situation

Politically, the region's ability to deal with issues of population growth and economic development in a coherent manner has been hampered by its colonial heritage. The French, the British, the Portuguese, and, to some extent, the Spanish all imposed their own languages, religions, and legal and political systems upon the indigenous people in their colonies, and these systems gave rise to important differences in the region that are often indicated by the classification into francophone (French-speaking), anglophone (English-speaking), and lusophone (Portuguese-speaking) areas.

The arbitrary division of Sub-Saharan Africa by the European powers, sometimes described as the balkanization of Africa, has been an important limiting factor. Efforts to create viable states from diverse ethnic groupings, some split across the borders of two or more countries, have engaged the minds of leaders for a long time. Some of these groupings were held together simply by the colonial powers, and their departure occasionally led to interethnic wars. Elsewhere, ethnic rivalries for power created prolonged political unrest. In one or two instances, the problems remain. In addition, the need for accelerated development in all fields in the face of resource and manpower shortages, as well as Africa's involvement in some of the major international ideological conflicts, such as the east-west political conflict and the north-south trade and resource distribution conflict, seem to take much of the time and energies of Africa's leadership and development personnel. In the face of all these obstacles, the small but accelerating development efforts in the population and family planning field could be seen as reason for hope rather than pessimism.

Economic Issues

The discussion of the consequences of rapid population growth has generated considerable anger and frustration in Sub-Saharan Africa. This was evident at conferences early in the postcolonial period, and some of the individuals concerned have maintained their positions to this day (Amin and Okediji 1971; Eraj 1987). In recent years, however, there has also been widespread recognition of the serious problems associated with rapid population growth. At the heart of the debate has been the issue of the primacy of rapid population growth as an obstacle to development and the priority to be given to population control. The lack of clear-cut evidence to support many of the hypothesized economic consequences of population growth and political issues determined in part by the region's colonial past has complicated the debate.

The fundamental flaw in the argument that population growth is the bête noire of development—especially from the African perspective—is that it assumes a single causation model of development and focuses on very partial analyses. During the 1974 World Population Conference, Zambia summarized this position succinctly: "It would be highly erroneous to jump to the conclusion that Zambia's economic failures were due to rapid population increase" (Cochrane 1985, p. 7). In fact, it is possible to document cases in which rapid development has occurred with rapid population growth, and only fifty years ago Keynes (1937) was suggesting that increased population growth would increase income levels by stimulating demand.

To address the legitimate frustrations of those Sub-Saharan African thinkers who hotly reject the link be-

tween population growth and development, one needs to understand the complexity of the process of economic growth. Yet evidence is lacking in many important respects in the African situation. The relationship of population growth to growth in per capita income—one of the most basic indicators of economic development—is uncertain, because knowledge is lacking on

1. The complex relationship between inputs and outputs in the productive process; in particular, there is lack of understanding of economies of scale
2. The growth of capital and the effect of population growth on the accumulation of capital
3. How input/output relationships change over time through technological change and in particular how population growth stimulates or retards technological change.

These specific gaps in our knowledge of the process of growth and development can briefly be discussed, and various alternatives can be examined. For several serious reasons, however, African policymakers widely reject the standard discussions of developmental consequences of population growth and its implications or view them with hostility.

First, many are skeptical about who will benefit from improvements in productivity brought about by reduced population growth or by any other mechanism. This is the well-known concern of developing countries—particularly primary producers—about adverse movements in terms of trade.

Second, many reject the legitimacy of the worldwide distribution of capital and contend that redistribution should in some way be proportional to need.

Third, many believe that much economic hardship is the result of a faulty distribution of wealth within a country. The poverty of the majority should be alleviated by a redistribution of resources rather than by a reduction in the number of the poor. This view is perhaps most prevalent in countries where the "haves" are of European origin or of any different ethnic or easily identifiable class.

Fourth, the quality of resources is as important as their quantity, but the discussions of population's effect on development rarely focus on the quality/quantity tradeoff. Although reduced quantity can increase quality in some ways, for example, through improved education, improvements in quality achieved through improvements in the health of infants and children will actually increase quantity. Population activities that focus on fertility and seem to ignore mortality tend to be interpreted by some Africans as indifference or hostility to reductions in mortality, a major concern of African governments.

Fifth, it has been argued in Sub-Saharan Africa, as it was in Europe in the 1930s, that a young population is dynamic. This was the Guinea delegate's position at the World Population Conference of 1974, as well as that of Togo at the International Labour Organisation Regional Conference in Nairobi in 1977 (ILO 1977).

Sixth, even if there were complete accord that reduction in the rate of population growth would increase a country's per capita income, there is recognition that there may be very little possibility of reducing fertility in many African countries in the short run. An extension of this argument is the idea that for the present, development is the best contraceptive in Sub-Saharan Africa. "Africa must choose development today and perhaps the pill tomorrow" (Senegal Country Statement at the 1974 World Population Conference, quoted in Cochrane 1985, p. 9).

Seventh, whereas most discussions focus on overall population size and growth rates, the population problem seen by most Africans involves faulty distribution. This is manifested by rapid urban growth, overpopulation in some rural areas, and underpopulation in others.

It is beyond the scope of this chapter to deal with the redistribution of capital or the distribution of the benefits of improved productivity through changes in terms of trade. It is essential, however, to address the other reasons why many Africans reject reduction of population growth as the focal point of development policy in the region.

Economies of Scale

In Sub-Saharan Africa, as in Latin America in earlier periods, the perception exists that substantial economies of scale can be reaped from population growth. According to van de Walle (1975, p. 138), for example, "Abdoulaye Wade supports 'Adam Smith's optimism about the existence of a positive correlation between population and economic activity,' and concludes that a large population will permit further division of labor resulting in higher productivity. Wade also states that 'quantitative demographic insufficiency has been recognized as one of the obstacles in the industrial development of Black Africa.'" Several kinds of economies of scale may be facilitated by population growth: the bringing into production of unused natural resources; increases in market size; and increased manufacturing capacity through shared overhead, particularly in higher returns to investments in infrastructure. Yet on none of these points is the evidence unequivocal.

The availability of unused land or natural resources does not guarantee constant or increasing returns to scale unless the quality of the unused resources and the costs of bringing them into production are, respectively, sufficiently high and sufficiently low.

The economies of scale to be reaped from increased division of labor depend on whether increased population size leads to increased market size. Only if per capita income remains constant or increases will market size expand. In addition, there are ways other than population growth to increase market size—improved transportation and reduction of tariff and other barriers to trade, for example (see chapter 5 in this volume). In Sub-Saharan Africa, one of the major obstacles is the lack of convertible currency.

The economies of scale to be reaped from shared overhead are perhaps particularly important with regard to public utilities. In this case, and in the case of other kinds of social overhead capital, population density reduces overhead per capita more than population size does. Early recognition of this fact in some quarters is evident in a statement at the 1968 University of Ghana symposium on population and socioeconomic development in Ghana: "The existence of these vast empty spaces poses a problem for the economic development of the country. It renders inviable projects of road construction, water and electricity supply to rural areas, and thus retards development of these areas" (Nyarko 1971). This is a major consideration in the "villagization" programs in Tanzania. Optimal population density for shared overhead must be balanced against optimal density, given the productivity of resources. The latter obviously varies by ecological region, and many marginal areas, such as the Sahel, have far exceeded the optimum even at very low densities.

Growth of Capital

Although substantial literature exists on the subject, there is considerable uncertainty concerning the effect of population growth on capital accumulation. In the 1930s, the Keynesians saw population growth as a major stimulant to investment. Most developing countries, however, do not see the lack of investment opportunities as the major constraint on capital accumulation. Rather, the lack of savings is the major concern of developing countries.

The various sources of savings—households, domestic businesses, national governments, foreign private investment, and foreign assistance—bear different and uncertain relationships to population growth.

With regard to household savings, few believe that larger families save more. The effect of population growth on domestic private investment depends on whether it increases market size even if income does not increase. Rapid population growth may also stimulate investment, particularly foreign investment, by lowering wages. Cheap labor has often been an attraction to foreign investment, but today the attraction is more likely to be cheap skilled labor than cheap raw labor. It is harder to train labor, of course, as population grows more rapidly. In addition, investments that are attracted by cheap labor in particular will result in larger transfers of the benefits of improved productivity outside the country. Therefore, with regard to private investment, there must indeed be concern for the group that benefits from population growth and with the degree to which it is benefited. With regard to foreign assistance, the link with population growth is far more political than economic, and one can probably dismiss any notion that the link has implications for the effect of population size on capital growth.

The final source of savings, and a major one in developing countries, is government, on which the most analysis has been done, leading to the clearest consensus among Africans that population growth can create problems. Government savings depend on revenues and expenditures on current account. Revenues can be expected to rise with increases in per capita income but not with population growth by itself. Few governments are sufficiently confident of the positive effects of population growth on per capita income to expect revenues to rise in the short run.

A national goal of improved welfare in the face of rapid population growth directly conflicts with the goal of making increased government savings available for directly productive investment. The more strongly the government commits itself to filling the basic needs of its population, the more likely it is to worry about the costs of population growth.

The prospect of this conflict caused Ghana and Kenya to adopt policies early to reduce fertility, and the experience of this conflict has caused many other nations subsequently to change their policies on population growth. This concern is well expressed in the opening remarks of the vice chancellor of the University of Ghana at the 1968 symposium on population and socioeconomic development in Ghana: "Ghana is fortunate not to be overcrowded on its land surface. Indeed, Africa in general is in this respect more fortunate than the countries of Asia, where population pressures are explosive. Our problem here, however, is not really one of absolute numbers; it is more a question of an adequate means of feeding the people, of improving the quality and standard of living of the people" (Kwapong 1968).

Technological Change

In addition to issues of economies of scale and savings, the issue of technological change is critical for an understanding of the link between population growth and development. The effects of population size, growth, and density on technological change have received considerable attention from pronatalists such as Simon (1981), who argue that more people generate improved technology because they increase the probability of producing a genius (presumably each genius more than compensates for all the extra people) or because the increased hardship stimulates individuals to be more

creative in order to preserve their standard of living—an old belief linking motherhood, necessity, and invention!

In Sub-Saharan Africa, choice of technology rather than invention or innovation is the dominant concern. Some believe that labor scarcity in the region blocks the adoption of agricultural technologies that would increase per capita productivity. This argument, which stems from the work of Boserup (1965, 1981), is basically that the shift from slash and burn to intensive agriculture, represented by multiple year-round cropping, depends upon the availability of labor.

Van de Walle (1975, p. 142), however, reviewing evidence from West Africa, concluded that "it would seem wrong to assume that higher population densities lead necessarily to more intensive forms of cultivation." Even if this assumption were right, there are alternative ways to increase labor supply—through increased use of existing members of the population, either by increased labor force participation or by increased numbers of hours worked, or through relocation of the labor force, through migration or resettlement schemes. Considerable study of agricultural experience in Sub-Saharan Africa is needed to determine the extent to which productivity per worker or per unit of labor is kept abnormally low by (1) lack of sufficient labor, (2) lack of capital, (3) lack of technologies appropriate to the particular ecologies, (4) poor practices by farmers, or (5) deficient or lacking governmental policies. Only in this context can the impact of population growth on agricultural technologies be assessed.

Balancing the Consequences

In trying to determine whether slower or more rapid population growth would be desirable on economic grounds in any context, we should keep a few points in mind.

First, certain consequences are short run and fairly certain, such as those from expenditures to achieve educational goals, whereas others are more likely to be long run and less certain, such as economies of scale achieved by the division of labor or by technological change.

Second, and less obvious, is the fact that even though substantial economies of scale may exist, it may be desirable for population to grow at less than maximum possible rates if the increases in capital as well as population will also increase per capita income and if population growth, at its maximum rate, slows the rate of capital accumulation. (Cochrane 1973 offers a theoretical model of this process.)

Third, the appropriate population policy depends not only on the rate of population growth that will maximize the rate of increase in per capita income but also on the economic, political, and human costs of deliberately shifting the rate of population growth. This cost is frequently neglected, which frustrates and angers (in some cases even frightens) those thinkers who do not trust the antinatalists. This is a particular problem in areas with very high mortality, because a focus on reducing population growth rather than on reducing mortality has been interpreted by some as implying that mortality reductions should be forgone—a very high cost indeed!

Economic Setbacks

Political problems in Sub-Saharan Africa have exacerbated the difficulties of balancing demographic and economic responses, and at least over the last ten to fifteen years, the overall economic situation has deteriorated in important respects. The terms of trade have moved further against primary producers; debt repayment is a heavy burden; and the rate of economic growth has slowed—dropping from 3.9 percent per annum in the 1960s to 2.9 percent in the 1970s. The slowdown in economic growth was in large measure due to the poor performance of the agricultural sector, on which 70 percent of the labor force depends for a living. Table 14-1 gives an indication of the region's problems with regard to income and food production. The economic setbacks have made the burden of population growth more difficult for governments to bear and have been partly responsible for changes in perceptions of the consequences of population growth.

Population Policies and Family Planning Programs

It is useful to view the evolution of population policies and family planning programs against this background of the debate on population consequences. The changing attitudes can usefully be described with reference to the world population conferences held in Bucharest in 1974 and in Mexico City in 1984. These conferences represent major watersheds in the history of family planning.

Although no easy way exists to determine governments' or individuals' perceptions of the relationship between population and well-being, bits and pieces of information do lend insight. The earliest consistent cross-national data on attitudes toward population come from a series of sample surveys conducted around 1965 (Stycos 1971). These surveys covered the urban and generally literate populations in several developed and developing countries. The majority of those interviewed in the three Sub-Saharan African countries—Nigeria, Kenya, and Senegal—felt that a large population would be good for the country, but so did citizens in urban

Latin America and in several cities in Asia and Europe. They did differ substantially, however, in their views on family planning programs. In the African countries, 54 percent of the composite sample approved of family planning, a far smaller proportion than in other regions. In predominantly Roman Catholic Latin America, 74 percent approved of such programs; in the Near East, 74 percent; and in the Far East, 82 percent.

Other, perhaps more relevant information on perceptions of the consequences of population increase has been obtained by examining development plans for Sub-Saharan African countries for the period prior to the 1974 World Population Conference. Plans for Benin, Chad, Mali, Niger, and Togo in West Africa and Ethiopia, Malawi, and Zaire in East and Central Africa made no mention of negative consequences of population growth. Other countries demonstrated some recognition of negative consequences, either simple recognition that national income must grow faster than population to raise per capita income or recognition of problems of employment, education, and nutrition and the more indirect problems of urbanization (Cochrane 1985).

Thus substantial recognition of negative consequences of population growth for development existed even prior to the 1974 conference. We should not conclude that the countries that recognized negative consequences considered them serious enough to justify family planning programs. In Sub-Saharan Africa at the time of the 1974 conference, only Botswana, Kenya, Ghana, and Mauritius had explicit, government-supported family planning programs designed to influence population growth rates (Nortman 1974).

World Population Conference 1974

The positions on population issues of the Sub-Saharan African countries represented at the 1974 conference covered the entire range from strong belief in the positive consequences of larger populations to concerns about a country's capacity to meet population needs. Some countries did not explicitly discuss consequences but mentioned family planning programs and even growth targets, whereas others expressed their population concerns in terms of reducing mortality and improving children's health. Other themes included the importance of national sovereignty in population policy and of individual sovereignty in determining family size. One of the major themes, however, was the rejection of population as the major development problem, for many of the reasons outlined earlier in this chapter.

Many delegates from Sub-Saharan African countries either cosponsored or supported resolutions reflecting the conviction that economic development would be furthered by increased trade and equity in economic relations between developed and developing nations.

Table 14-1. *Income and Food Indicators of the Economic Situation*

| Country | GDP growth (percent) | | Food adequacy[a] | Average food production per capita, 1979–81[b] |
	1969–70	1970–81		
Chad	0.5	—	74	96
Ethiopia	4.4	2.2	76	87
Mali	3.3	4.3	85	88
Malawi	4.9	5.6	94	96
Zaire	3.4	−0.2	94	87
Uganda	5.6	−1.6	83	86
Burundi	4.4	3.2	96	100
Burkina Faso	3.0	3.6	95	94
Rwanda	2.7	5.3	88	104
Somalia	1.0	3.9	100	65
Tanzania	6.0	5.1	83	91
Guinea	3.5	3.0	77	87
Benin	2.6	3.3	103	96
Central African Republic	1.9	1.6	94	102
Sierra Leone	4.3	1.9	89	81
Madagascar	2.9	3.1	109	93
Niger	—	—	92	73
Mozambique	1.3	4.1	70	102
Sudan	3.5	3.2	101	90
Togo	2.1	−0.2	95	74
Ghana	5.9	5.8	88	85
Kenya	2.5	2.0	88	76
Senegal	6.7	1.7	100	77
Mauritania	5.1	1.3	97	95
Liberia	5.2	8.4	114	86
Lesotho	5.0	0.4	107	92
Zambia	—	—	93	81
Angola	—	—	83	—
Nigeria	3.1	4.5	91	91
Zimbabwe	4.3	1.8	86	92
Cameroon	3.7	6.3	106	101
Congo	2.3	5.1	94	92
Côte d'Ivoire	8.0	6.2	112	110
Low-income countries	4.6	4.5	97	—
China and India	4.5	4.8	99	—
Other	4.7	3.6	92	—
Middle-income countries				—
Lower-middle	5.0	5.6	106	—
Upper-middle	6.4	5.6	115	—

— Data not available.
Note: Countries are in ascending order of GNP per capita in 1981.
a. Daily per capita calorie supply as a percentage of minimum requirements in 1980.
b. 1969–71 = 100.
Source: World Bank (1983), tables 2, 6, and 24.

This conviction was, of course, shared by many other countries represented at the conference. The consensus that emerged, and in which the Sub-Saharan African delegates joined, recognized: "The basis for an effective solution of population problems is, above all, socioeconomic transformation. A population policy may have a certain success if it constitutes an integral part of socioeconomic development" (United Nations 1975, p. 3). Distinguishing between aggregate and individual fer-

tility, however, and recognizing that national views on aggregate fertility might not always accord with individual fertility desires, the conference agreed that "all couples and individuals have the basic right to decide freely and responsibly the number and spacing of their children and to have the information, education and means to do so" (United Nations 1975, p. 7). The development of family planning programs therefore does not necessarily indicate that governments believe that

Table 14-2. *Perceptions of Population Growth and Fertility and Policies to Influence Fertility, West and Central Africa*

Country	Perception of population growth		Perception of current fertility		Policy to influence fertility	
	1976	1986	1976	1986	1976	1986
French, Portuguese, and Spanish-speaking						
Benin	OK	OK	OK	OK	none	none
Burkina Faso	OK	OK	OK	OK	none	none
Cameroon	low	high	low	high	none	none
Central African Rep.	low	high	low	high	none	none
Chad	OK	OK	OK	OK	none	none
Congo	OK	low	OK	low	none	none
Côte d'Ivoire	low	OK	OK	OK	maintain	raise
Gabon	low	low	low	low	raise	raise
Guinea	OK	OK	OK	high	none	none
Mali	OK	OK	OK	OK	none	maintain
Mauritania	OK	OK	OK	OK	none	none
Niger	OK	OK	OK	OK	none	none
Senegal	high	high	high	high	none	lower
Togo	OK	OK	OK	OK	none	maintain
Zaire	OK	OK	OK	OK	none	none
Cape Verde	OK	OK	OK	OK	none	none
Guinea-Bissau	OK	OK	OK	OK	none	none
São Tomé and Principe	OK	OK	OK	OK	none	maintain
Equatorial Guinea	low	low	low	low	none	raise
English-speaking						
Gambia	OK	high	OK	high	none	lower
Ghana	high	high	high	high	lower	lower
Liberia	high	high	high	high	none	none
Nigeria	OK	high	OK	high	none	lower
Sierra Leone	high	high	high	high	none	none

Note: Comparability between different dates was intended, but the range of government policy options covered in the monitoring report may not be exactly the same.

Sources: United Nations (1979), tables 56 and 67; United Nations (1986), tables 3.5 and 6.4.

fertility levels are too high or that it is appropriate to intervene. In fact, as documented below, the development of family planning programs in Sub-Saharan Africa owes more to recognition of the health and human rights rationale for family planning than to acknowledgment of demographic needs.

The 1974 conference mandated the United Nations, under whose auspices it was held, to monitor progress on conference resolutions. The first monitoring report, based on 1976 inquiries (United Nations 1979), provided information about policies on, and perceptions of, population growth, national fertility levels, and family planning programs. The majority of governments in Sub-Saharan Africa reported themselves satisfied with their rates of population growth (tables 14-2 and 14-3). Of the forty-three countries responding, twenty-three did not consider their rates of population growth a constraint on development. The majority of the remainder that viewed their rates as a constraint considered them too high, but a substantial minority (six) felt that their low growth rates were a problem. The situation was similar with regard to perceptions of fertility, with twenty-four countries (56 percent) regarding their fertility levels as satisfactory. The majority of countries took a laissez-faire attitude toward fertility, reflecting contemporary doubts about the appropriateness or feasibility of government intervention.

This overall picture, however, obscures substantial variation between regions of Sub-Saharan Africa, variation foreshadowed by statements at the 1974 conference. Table 14-4 reveals considerable differences by geographic area, differences further compounded by language (the official colonial language, except, most notably, for Ethiopia and Somalia). In West and Central Africa, pronatalist perceptions were more common than in East and southern Africa, and laissez-faire attitudes were more in evidence. These tendencies were strongest among the French-speaking countries (as well as the Portuguese-speaking and Spanish-speaking countries, which resemble them in attitudes and will be grouped with them in the discussion) in West and Central Africa. The francophone countries in East and Southern Africa were

Table 14-3. *Perceptions of Population Growth and Fertility and Policies to Influence Fertility, East and Southern Africa*

Country	Perception of population growth		Perception of current fertility		Policy to influence fertility	
	1976	1986	1976	1986	1976	1986
French and Portuguese-speaking						
Burundi	OK	high	OK	high	none	lower
Comoros	high	high	high	high	none	lower
Djibouti	—	OK	—	OK	—	none
Madagascar	high	OK	high	high	none	none
Rwanda	OK	high	high	high	none	lower
Angola	—	OK	—	OK	—	none
Mozambique	low	OK	OK	OK	maintain	none
English-speaking						
Botswana	high	high	high	high	lower	lower
Kenya	high	high	high	high	lower	lower
Lesotho	high	high	high	high	lower	lower
Malawi	OK	high	OK	high	none	none
Mauritius	high	high	high	high	lower	lower
Seychelles	high	high	high	high	lower	lower
South Africa	high	high	high	high	lower	lower
Swaziland	high	high	high	high	lower	lower
Tanzania	OK	high	OK	high	none	none
Uganda	high	high	high	high	lower	lower
Zambia	OK	high	OK	high	none	none
Zimbabwe	—	high	—	high	—	lower
Ethiopia	OK	high	OK	high	none	none
Somalia	OK	OK	OK	OK	none	none
Sudan	OK	OK	OK	OK	none	none

— Not available.

Sources: United Nations (1979), tables 56 and 67; United Nations (1986), tables 3.5 and 6.4.

not as pronatalist as their counterparts in West and Central Africa but were less likely than their anglophone neighbors to consider intervention appropriate.

Government positions on access to family planning services in 1976 showed similar variation. Table 14-5 indicates that, although nearly half of all governments supported family planning directly, countries in East and southern Africa gave more direct support—providing family planning services through government facilities and not just through financial assistance to private family planning organizations—than did those in West and Central Africa (63 percent and 33 percent, respectively). These differences are magnified further when anglophone and francophone countries are compared. The effect of their different cultural, legal, and religious heritages can be seen in the table. Whereas about 80 percent of anglophone countries offered government family planning services, only 20 percent of francophone countries did so. The majority of people in Sub-Saharan Africa, however, lived in countries giving direct support to family planning, because all the countries with populations of more than 10 million, except for Ethiopia, were in this category.

Government Perceptions in 1986

By 1986, the situation as described in the latest monitoring report (United Nations 1986) had changed considerably. By this date, as indicated in table 14-4, most countries in Sub-Saharan Africa viewed their rates of population growth as too high, and even more saw their levels of fertility as too high. Only three of the forty-six Sub-Saharan countries responding to the inquiry saw their rates of growth and their fertility as too low. Many more countries were disposed to intervene to lower fertility levels—34 percent as compared with 21 percent a decade earlier. Differences persisted between West and Central Africa, on the one hand, and East and Southern Africa, on the other, and between francophone and anglophone countries, but in all cases there was a greater perception that population growth rates and fertility levels were too high, and there was less willingness to take a laissez-faire approach.

Government support for family planning programs also grew over the decade. By 1986, 74 percent of governments were providing family planning directly, 13 percent supported private family planning agencies, and

Table 14-4. *Number of Countries by Perceptions of Population Growth and Fertility and Policies to Influence Fertility, 1976 and 1986*

Government perception or policy	Total	West and Central Africa		East and Southern Africa	
		Francophone	Anglophone	Francophone	Anglophone
1976					
Government perception of rate of population growth					
Too low	6	5	0	1	0
Satisfactory	23	13	2	2	6
Too high	14	1	3	2	8
Government perception of current fertility level					
Too low	4	4	0	0	0
Satisfactory	24	14	2	2	6
Too high	15	1	3	3	8
Government policy to influence fertility					
Raise	1	1	0	0	0
Maintain	2	1	0	1	0
Lower	9	0	1	0	8
No intervention	31	17	4	4	6
Number of countries	43	19	5	5	14
1986					
Government perception of rate of population growth					
Too low	3	3	0	0	0
Satisfactory	19	13	0	4	2
Too high	24	3	5	3	13
Government perception of current fertility level					
Too low	3	3	0	0	0
Satisfactory	17	12	0	3	2
Too high	26	4	5	4	13
Government policy to influence fertility					
Raise	3	3	0	0	0
Maintain	3	3	0	0	0
Lower	16	1	3	3	9
No invervention	24	12	2	4	6
Number of countries	46	19	5	7	15

Sources: United Nations (1979), tables 56 and 67; United Nations (1986), tables 3.5 and 6.4.

only 13 percent provided no government assistance at all. No government now actively limits access to contraception to all users, not even those governments that consider the country's fertility levels too low (that is, the Congo, Gabon, and Equatorial Guinea). Again, geographic regions were substantially different, with 90 percent of governments in East and southern Africa giving direct support, compared with 58 percent in West and Central Africa. In East and southern Africa, only Malawi offered no support at all, as opposed to 21 percent of countries in West and Central Africa. Malawi, in fact, has recently changed its position and is now supporting family planning. In all, 85 percent of the population of Sub-Saharan Africa in 1986 lived in countries with direct government support of family planning, though in the francophone countries of West and Central Africa, less than half the population had governments that provided service (table 14-5).

Between the World Population Conferences in 1974 and 1984, therefore, official perceptions and policies changed substantially, though the perception that intervention is feasible grew more slowly than the perception that population growth rates, and specifically fertility rates, are too high. The greatest changes may be observed in support for family planning, with almost 90 percent of countries now supporting it either directly

Table 14-5. *Number of Countries and Distribution of Population by Government Position on Access to and Support for Family Planning, 1976 and 1986*

Government position on family planning (access, support)	Total	West and Central Africa		East and Southern Africa	
		Francophone	Anglophone	Francophone	Anglophone
Number of countries, 1976					
Access allowed, direct support	20	4	4	1	11
Access allowed, indirect support	8	4	1	1	1
Access allowed, no support	12	8	0	3	1
Access limited	3	3	0	0	1
Total countries	43	19	5	5	14
Percentage distribution of population, 1976					
Access allowed, direct support	68.3	41.6	99.3	36.2	71.7
Access allowed, indirect support	15.9	16.0	0.7	31.4	22.0
Access allowed, no support	12.6	36.0	0	32.4	2.5
Access limited	3.2	6.4	0	0	3.8
Population (millions)	307,271	76,422	77,998	25,530	127,321
Number of countries, 1986					
Access allowed, direct support	34	11	3	6	14
Access allowed, indirect support	6	3	2	0	1
Access allowed, no support	6	5	0	1	0
Access limited	0	0	0	0	0
Total countries	46	19	5	7	15
Percentage distribution of population, 1986					
Access allowed, direct support	84.5	43.2	95.0	99.2	97.5
Access allowed, indirect support	11.5	39.3	5.0	0	2.5
Access allowed, no support	4.1	17.5	0	0.8	0
Access limited	0	0	0	0	0
Population (millions)	465,550	107,396	119,150	45,588	193,416

Sources: United Nations (1979), tables 67 and 72; United Nations (1986), table 6.6; United Nations (1987).

or indirectly, as compared with 55 percent 10 years earlier. Many more countries support family planning than intervene to influence fertility. These countries support family planning for its contribution to maternal and child health and as an individual human right.

Regional Variations

Although variations between regions therefore persist, geographical divisions alone cannot explain the observed differences. As stated earlier, Africa has been subjected to foreign cultures, which have interacted with the local social and cultural situations to produce mixes that will perhaps more easily explain important differences.

Among the legal issues, perhaps the most important is the anticontraceptive law that was passed in France in 1920. The law has since been repealed in France but not necessarily in the francophone African countries; although it is widely disregarded, its existence is like a sword of Damocles over the heads of those who advocate family planning. It was repealed in Mali in 1972, in Senegal and Cameroon in 1980, and in Côte d'Ivoire in 1981, but remains on the statute books in about fifteen former French colonies. Both France and Portugal have

advocated pronatalist policies that are still being followed in some of their former colonies. The presence or absence of these laws and policies accounts for important differences between the francophone and the anglophone countries.

With the imperialist powers came several religions. Of these, Roman Catholicism is predominant in francophone and lusophone countries. The Roman Catholic Church opposes all forms of family planning except natural planning, sometimes called the rhythm method.

Finally, there is no tradition of voluntary organizations of consequence in the French system. Therefore, the stimulating relationship between governmental and nongovernmental organizations, which appears in the anglophone countries to be so important in the field of population and family planning, is not present in the francophone system.

Factors Contributing to Changing Perceptions and Policies

Despite continuing anglophone-francophone differences, however, there is a general movement toward greater understanding of the interactions between population and development and the role of family planning in health as well as a desire to influence those interactions. Various factors have affected this process.

Increased Information and Analysis

A considerable body of work on the consequences of population growth for countries in Sub-Saharan Africa dates back long before the 1974 World Population Conference in Bucharest. Much of this work by individual researchers inside and outside the region has been presented in seminars and conferences sponsored locally with support in many cases from the Population Council, the International Planned Parenthood Federation (IPPF), and the United Nations Fund for Population Activities (UNFPA). The International Labour Organisation also sponsored a series of national and regional conferences beginning in 1971. These conferences were cosponsored in many cases by the Organization for African Unity (OAU) and were supported by African institutions with a high degree of African participation. This research is not readily accessible, however, because publication has not always been feasible (see Cochrane 1985 for a review of these conferences), which may explain why the work on consequences of population conditions in the region is so little known and why the perception exists among those outside the region that little thought has been given to these problems.

Other bodies of work also exist outside the conference record, for the most part produced outside the region. The two most systematic efforts to deal with these problems have been UNFPA needs assessments studies and the project "Resources for the Awareness of Population Impacts on Development" (RAPID) of the Futures Group. The UNFPA studies for countries of the region have frequently contained a section on the problems generated in the country by population size, growth, distribution, or other related problems. These sections have not in general included new analysis but have pulled together existing material. RAPID has concentrated exclusively on the consequences of alternative rates of population growth, generally focusing on the two-child versus the three-child family. These two bodies of work are very important in creating an awareness of population problems in the countries, but the extent to which they reflect, or have had impact on, the thinking of Africans is difficult to assess without a careful case-by-case review.

The demographic data for analysis of population consequences have improved greatly over the past twenty years (see chapter 1 in this volume). Until independence, very few countries had complete censuses or were establishing vital registration systems. The need for demographic data constituted the main topic of the first African Population Conference held at the University of Ibadan in 1966 (Caldwell and Okonjo 1968). Without data on population size, distribution, and growth, it is of course impossible to do more than speculate about consequences. Demographic data vary greatly in availability in the countries in the region. Both Ghana and Kenya had early and very good censuses prior to the mid-1960s. Perhaps for this reason population consequences received attention in these countries very early, and these countries became the first to adopt national family planning programs.

The need for demographic data for national planning purposes became evident to the many countries that gained their independence in the 1960s. Many countries undertook censuses in the 1970s, usually with financial or technical assistance from the United Nations Africa Census Programme or from individual donor countries.

In addition, important information on fertility levels and trends was gained by many countries from their participation in the World Fertility Survey, which took place from the mid-1970s through the early 1980s. This study documented not only fertility experience but fertility desires, behavior to regulate fertility, and marriage patterns. An extremely important outcome was the documentation of the strong links between fertility and child health; the survey provided evidence of the need for the inclusion of family planning in health services.

International and Nongovernmental Organizations and Governments

I have already mentioned the contribution of the United Nations, including the UNFPA, to needs assessment and data gathering. Other important population activities of the United Nations in Sub-Saharan Africa include the establishment and support of regional demographic centers in Accra and Yaounde and of an international demographic center in Cairo. In addition, UNFPA supports a program of training in family planning techniques in Mauritius and collaborates in the support of demographic training at the Institut du Sahel in Bamako. These are now important centers of population research, training of health and administrative personnel for population and family planning programs, and support for population-related working groups, seminars, and activities. All of these activities help build consensus on the importance of population issues. Above all, however, UNFPA has been involved in the establishment and support of family planning programs.

Other agencies in the United Nations system have played a role in drawing attention to population and family planning issues, including the World Health Organization (WHO), ILO, the World Bank, and the U.N. Children's Fund (UNICEF). WHO has become progressively more active in stressing the importance of family planning as a maternal and child health measure and in urging its incorporation in health services. Some of the changes in francophone countries were probably influenced by this approach (Hamand 1986).

Nongovernmental agencies have played a vital role in the development of family planning programs in anglophone countries. Because family planning is an emotional and sensitive issue the world over, and particularly in Africa, and also because many governments could not see why they should give high priority to family planning, the initial groundwork was undertaken by nongovernmental family planning associations. In the English-speaking world, nongovernmental organizations have had the traditional role of tackling sensitive issues, fostering new ideas, and creating a climate for acceptance of activities in a way that governments cannot. In the Gambia, Ghana, Kenya, Lesotho, Uganda, and other English-Speaking countries, this has been the pattern.

Botswana and Swaziland were different. In both countries the government showed concern about population growth, the availability of arable land, and the problems related to the provision of education and health services. The governments sought external assistance and became affiliated with the IPPF. In the case of Swaziland, a nongovernmental family planning association has now been formed to deal with education and information and sensitive issues, such as adolescent sexuality and voluntary sterilization. This association is now the IPPF affiliate.

In Mauritius, too, the government was the first to express concerns about population in relation to the economy, particularly to unemployment. It did little, however, apart from setting up committees until private family planning associations were formed that helped to desensitize the issue of population control. The government was then able to establish policies and programs that made for better coverage of the population.

The francophone countries, as stated earlier, have no real tradition of voluntary organizations. Although efforts have been directed toward the establishment of family planning associations, these have not been as effective as in the anglophone countries. By and large, therefore, governments have had to be involved right from the start. At the very least, government involvement would ensure that there would be no prosecutions under the 1920 anticontraceptive law. In Zaire, a parastatal organization was formed instead of a voluntary association; in Senegal, efforts to form an association failed until the government itself permitted the formation of one under its wings, as it were. Perhaps the Togolese association is closest to those of the English system.

IPPF, an international organization with its roots in the countries served through its members, the individual family planning associations, has been active in Af-

rica. In 1971, an IPPF regional council and office was formed to give impetus to its work in the area. There are now IPPF affiliates in twenty-seven Sub-Saharan countries, ten of which are francophone, whereas in 1971, at the founding of the IPPF regional council, there were only eight national associations as affiliates, none of which was in francophone countries.

Regional Population Conferences

During the decade 1974–84, two important conferences provided opportunities for African governments to discuss population growth and development. They were the OAU conference held in Lagos in 1980 and the second U.N. African Population Conference held in Arusha, Tanzania, in January 1984.

At the Lagos Conference, heads of state and governments adopted the Lagos "Plan of Action for the Economic Development of Africa, 1980–2000." The main thrust of the plan of action was toward strategies "to achieve national and collective self-reliant economic and social development for a new international economic order" (OAU 1981). It included several recommendations on population and the need to incorporate population variables in development planning as a means to furthering this end.

The outcome of the 1984 Arusha Conference, attended by forty-four countries, was the Kilimanjaro Programme of Action on Population and Self-Reliant Development. This program formed the basis of African delegates' positions at the International Population Conference at Mexico City. Many background papers explored the relationships between population and development in the African situation, and the recommendations urged again the integration of population considerations into development planning. The program stressed the importance of achieving "population growth rates that are compatible with . . . desired economic growth and social development goals" and recommended that governments "review and amend legislation relating to population issues" (United Nations 1984). In addition, the conference recommended that governments make available family planning services and education and allocate adequate resources for these purposes.

Developments since the 1984 International Population Conference

The two regional conferences reflect the now considerable concern among African governments about the effects of population on development aspirations. Although the recommendations of regional and international conferences are generally neutral about the exact nature of the interrelationships between population and development, and bow to national sovereignty in determining these interrelationships, it is clear that many African governments hold the view that current rates of increase are "excessive." They joined with most other developing countries in rejecting the view of the U.S. government in 1984 that population growth in itself is a neutral phenomenon. In fact, in 1985, heads of government of eleven Sub-Saharan African countries were members of a group of forty developing countries that presented a "Pact to Curb Population Growth" to the secretary general of the United Nations. The pact calls on national leaders to promote effective policies and programs in the realization that, if the "unprecedented population growth continues, future generations of children will not have adequate food, housing, medical care, education and employment opportunities" (Global Committee of Parliamentarians 1985).

In 1986, former elected members of national governments or administrators of thirty-one African countries met in Harare at the African Conference of Parliamentarians on Population and Development and produced one of the most forthright documents yet, the Harare declaration. This declaration included statements recognizing that current and projected growth frustrates the achievement of social and economic goals and pledged the participants "to formulate and implement national population policies and programmes that will reduce high rates of population growth in Africa in an effort to attain a balance between resources and the needs and opportunities of our people" (African Conference of Parliamentarians 1986).

Nigeria, one of the regions's most populous states and home to one in five people in Sub-Saharan Africa, adopted a formal population policy in February 1988. Until a few years ago, its official view was that its annual population growth rate of 3.4 percent was neither too high nor too low. Now, however, it considers the rate too high and wishes to lower it. "The Government now recognizes, more than ever before, the fact that the overall rate of growth has to be brought down to the level which will not impose an excessive burden on the economy in the long run. The Government plans to

achieve this through an integrated approach to population planning." Sudan, too, has now formulated (as of October 1987) a population policy, though it has not been officially promulgated, and Ethiopia, another of the most populous countries, is moving toward an official policy. Viewed from this perspective, the perceptions and policies of a few countries have great impact on the vast majority of the population in the region, and at present the movement is toward greater perception of the harmful effects of rapid population growth and the need for action. Of the other Sub-Saharan African countries with populations of more than 20 million, Kenya has long had a population policy. Tanzania and Zaire still do not. Tanzania, however, has recently changed its perception of its population growth rate and level of fertility from satisfactory to too high. Zaire continues to view both its population growth rate and its fertility as satisfactory. Both, however, provide support to family planning though indirectly in the case of Zaire.

Twelve countries, in addition to Nigeria and Kenya, have explicit population policies, either as separate policy documents (Ghana and Burundi) or integrated in national development plans. Table 14-6 shows the countries and their regional distribution.

Given that in 1974 only four countries—Botswana, Ghana, Kenya, and Mauritius—had established population policies and that some of these were not being acted upon, the process of change is clear.

Problems of Evolution and Implementation of Family Planning Programs

This review of development perceptions and policies in Sub-Saharan Africa has shown a considerable increase in recognition of the constraints imposed by rapid population growth and growing intervention to reduce fertility. Given the short time frame involved, and indeed the short time since independence, and in light of the difficulties confronting most African countries, the record of government commitment—if not yet achieve-

Table 14-6. *Countries with Explicit Population Policies, 1987*

	West and Central Africa		East and Southern Africa	
	Francophone	*Anglophone*	*Francophone*	*Anglophone*
	Cameroon	Ghana	Burundi	Botswana
	Senegal	Nigeria	Rwanda	Kenya
		Gambia		Lesotho
				Mauritius
				Swaziland
				Uganda
				Zambia

Source: Heckel (1986) and World Bank staff.

ment—is encouraging. The greatest gains have been in acceptance of family planning. Though the reasons for this acceptance have often been health and human rights rather than demography, these reasons also reflect a commitment to development, even if it is social rather than economic.

Many problems and barriers, however, remain to impede the evolution, planning, and implementation of population policies and family planning programs. The major problems fall into five categories: political, legal, administrative, technical, and resources (manpower and financial).

Political Problems

As indicated earlier, the implications of population for development in Africa need further evaluation. Even where the effects of population growth are not seen as negative, political support for family planning should be sought for its contribution to family health and welfare. Even some of those who have consistently been skeptical of the role of population growth as an impediment to development are strong supporters of family planning (for example, Eraj 1987). When a program does have demographic goals, these should be carefully explained, and program aims should be shared by the whole population.

As previously noted, many Sub-Saharan African countries are multiethnic states. Leaders are often sensitive to the potential for conflict that strong advocacy of birth control may provoke. In several countries, the dominant ethnic group cannot be expected to curb its growth willingly for fear that it may lose its power base. Other ethnic groups also wish to grow. Where national resources are allocated on a population base, provinces or regions cannot be expected to curtail their population growth rate for fear of losing a portion of the national pie. Nigeria is, of course, a classic example of this phenomenon, but the degree to which the result is more rapid growth of particular groups rather than only of their reported numbers is unclear.

Apartheid, and statements by some South African leaders calling for rapid growth of the white minority and family planning for the black majority, create a backlash in Sub-Saharan Africa. The Catholic church and its current push for natural family planning have an adverse effect upon some fragile programs. Moreover, in many parts of Africa, representatives of the church are opposed to family planning altogether, even though the church officially sanctions natural methods. Natural methods are difficult to practice, however, even under the best of circumstances, and they have very high failure rates.

The most serious political problem is the lack of overt, sustained political support for family planning.

Except in Kenya and Zimbabwe, national leaders do not speak out enough, even for programs and policies that they have themselves propounded. The role of the African elite, especially in francophone countries, is also a source of difficulty. Many members of this elite oppose family planning programs for obscure reasons.

Bad news in the family planning field travels fast. The international media's fondness for exaggerating adverse findings about contraceptives has created many problems for African programs. The recent media debate over injectable contraceptives has led to their withdrawal from some programs. Yet the United Kingdom's decision to permit use of the drug has not received comparable media exposure. Similarly, the pill is widely perceived to be very dangerous.

Legal Problems

As has been stated earlier, the anticontraceptive law of 1920 is still on the books in much of francophone Africa. Laws restricting the sale and distribution of contraceptives to medical practitioners thwart efforts to expand services to rural areas. Some laws are interpreted to exclude unmarried adolescents and minors generally. In addition, abortion laws that have been repealed in France and the United Kingdom remain on the statute books in their former colonies and prevent the institution of safe abortion services. Efforts are urgently needed to assess the effect of such laws and to advocate needed change.

Administrative and Managerial Problems

Even where policies have been clearly enunciated, as in Ghana and Kenya, and organizational principles laid down, actual management may make a program stall. In the case of Kenya, the location of the program within the Ministry of Health did not encourage participation of other ministries. The head of the program was assigned other responsibilities in rural health and thus could not give full attention to the family planning program. Generally, ministries of health in this region are under so many other pressures that they cannot give family planning the priority it needs. The Kenyan situation has improved with the creation of the National Council for Population and Development, which is now responsible for the overall population program.

The Ghana program, located in the Ministry of Finance and Economic Planning, has fared no better. Personality problems and difficulties with coordination and the proper roles of various participating agencies have blocked progress. Coordination with nongovernmental efforts may also prove problematic. National coordination councils set up to provide the machinery for coordination have not proved very successful.

Technical Problems

Other problems relate to the technologies available for family planning and to delivery systems. The contraceptive methods currently available have many drawbacks in the Sub-Saharan African situation. The IUD requires too much medical backup, and the pill requires too much sustained motivation. Depo-Provera has come under severe international attack, and some good programs based on this method have been curtailed in Ghana, Kenya, and Zimbabwe. Surgical contraception is yet to be emphasized in any of the national programs. The Association for Voluntary Sterilization has made small beginnings in a few countries.

The region is in great need of methods that are long-acting, reversible, inexpensive, and not dependent on easy access to medical services. The potential for such methods exists, but major efforts are needed for its realization, and at present the situation is not promising. Historically, the United States has been the main supporter of contraceptive research and development, but recent adverse developments have had international impact. The stance of the U.S. administration in the 1980s on population questions; the growing product liability risks to contraceptive manufacturers; the length and expense of the regulatory process; and the withdrawal of private industry from the field all give rise to concern.

Despite their recognized shortcomings, the existing technologies can have far greater impact if the delivery systems are made more relevant. A delivery system based on health services cannot achieve coverage beyond those services. Thus in much of the region, family planning services will not reach more than 25 percent of those in need unless health services are expanded or delivery systems are changed. The possibilities for change include community-based distribution systems, which can be handled in villages by trained village personnel, and social marketing systems, which make for greater acceptability and cause fewer problems for clients (see chapter 15 in this volume). There is much talk of primary health care in Africa. If primary health care systems, based on thorough decentralization, community participation, and inexpensive approaches, were fully implemented, then integration of family planning in the system would also aid outreach. The overall philosophy should be to demystify family planning and make it accessible, acceptable, and affordable.

Resource Problems

Trained manpower is in short supply. There is therefore a need to undertake more intensive training for family planning workers and to diversify personnel to include members of the community to be served. True community participation is necessary if programs are to expand.

Both national and international family planning funds are also in short supply; the latter, in particular, have been decreasing for a long time. With the renewed call from the United Nations, the World Bank, and the international development community generally for an emphasis on Africa, it is to be hoped that funding for population activities will increase. Many African governments that permit family planning do not provide any funds for them. Without such funds, the psychological support for programs is lacking, and their survival and incorporation within national plans cannot be assured.

Future Directions

The tasks facing the family planning community in Sub-Saharan Africa are the following:

1. Changing attitudes of leaders in countries so that they may provide family planning to their people at least for welfare and human rights reasons

2. Encouraging all countries to include population and family planning considerations within their overall socioeconomic goals

3. Assisting with the development and implementation of comprehensive family planning programs that have effective outreach services and are accessible geographically, socially, and financially

4. Encouraging suitable population and family planning education for all individuals, including men, the unmarried, and adolescents

5. Promoting research into program strengths and weaknesses and finding approaches that work best in specific situations; conducting research into the acceptability, suitability, and safety of contraceptives; and researching personnel needs and training facilities and their usefulness

6. Seeking more international and national resources.

This chapter has reviewed some of the reasons for the reluctance of many Africans to accept population growth as a principal obstacle to development—for reasons to do with the region's colonial past, the absence of concrete evidence of a link between population growth and development, and a questioning of why, if economic growth occurred with population growth in the developed world, it should not do so in the developing world. No developed country, however, ever had to contend with the rates of population growth that many Sub-Saharan African countries are currently facing. In addition, no developed country at a comparable stage of development had made the same compact with their people to provide free education, health care, and other social services that many Sub-Saharan African governments did at the time of independence.

This chapter has also documented the significant shift toward a perception that population growth, and high fertility specifically, is a constraint on development, though there is not a consensus that it is feasible to do something about it. There is, however, good evidence from other developing regions to suggest that fertility change can be initiated in advance of marked improvements in economic circumstances. One estimate is that the timing of fertility decline may be advanced ten to twenty years by the institution of family planning programs (Retherford and Palmore 1983). Where population is pressing against resources as it is in many Sub-Saharan African countries (see chapters 2–5 in this volume), and is doubling, on average, every twenty-three years, such an advance may provide significant benefits. Discussion of development in terms of per capita income, however, important though it is to policymakers, tends to obscure the important contribution to social development that can be made by community-based family planning at the local level. Finally, family planning can make a vital contribution to individual health and reproductive freedom and should be supported as a universal human right.

Non-African economic and social development personnel and the Western European and the U.S. media are still too overtly involved in advocacy of controlling population growth and of family planning. It is time for African leaders to become more openly and forcefully involved in building population and family planning considerations into their development programs.

References

African Conference of Parliamentarians. 1986. Proceedings of the African Conference of Parliamentarians on Population and Development, Harare, Zimbabwe, May 12–16.

Amin, S., and F. O. Okediji. 1971. "Land Use, Agriculture and Food Supply, and Industrialization." In P. Cantrelle and others, eds., *Population in African Development*. Liège: Ordina.

Boserup, E. 1965. *The Conditions of Agricultural Growth*. London: G. Allen.

————. 1981. *Population and Technical Change: A Study of Long Term Trends*. Chicago: University of Chicago Press.

Caldwell, J. C., and C. Okonjo, eds. 1968. *The Population of Tropical Africa*. London: Logmans.

Cochrane, S. H. 1973. "Population and Development: A More General Model." *Economic Development and Cultural Change* 21(3):409–22.

————. 1985. "Development Consequences of Rapid Population Growth: A Review from the Perspective of Sub-Saharan Africa." PHN Technical Note 85-8. World Bank, Population and Human Resources Department, Washington, D.C.

Eraj, Y. A. 1987. "The Difference between Population Control and Family Planning." *Africa Health* (June–July): 14–15.

Global Committee of Parliamentarians. 1985. *Statement on Population Stabilization by World Leaders, 1985*. New York: CCP.

Hamand, Jeremy. 1986. "WHO: A More Positive Stance: Interview with Dr. G. Monekosso." *People* 13(3): 15–16.

Harrison, P. 1987. *The Greening of Africa*. London: Paladin Grafton Books.

Heckel, N. J. 1986. "Population Laws and Policies in Sub-Saharan Africa, 1975–1985." *Studies in Family Planning* 12(4): 122–24.

International Labour Organisation. 1977. Papers presented at the National Seminar on Population, Employment, and Development Planning in Nigeria, Ibadan, July 4–7.

Keynes, J. M. 1937. "Some Economic Consequences of a Declining Population." *Eugenics Review* (Edinburgh) 29(1): 13–18.

Kwapong, A. A. 1968. "Opening Remarks to the Symposium on Population and Socioeconomic Development in Ghana, 1968." *Ghana Population Studies* No. 2.

Nortman, D. 1974. *Population and Family Planning Programs: A Factbook*. Reports on Family Planning No. 2. New York: Population Council.

Nyarko, K. A. J. 1971. "The Case against Family Limitation in Ghana." *Ghana Population Studies* No. 3: 157–67.

Organization for African Unity. 1981. Lagos. *Plan of Action for the Economic Development of Africa, 1980–2000*. Geneva: International Institute for Labour Studies.

Retherford, R. D., and J. A. Palmore. 1983. "Diffusion Processes Affecting Fertility Regulation." In R. A. Bulatao and R. D. Lee, eds., *Determinants of Fertility in Developing Countries*. New York: Academic Press.

Simon, J. 1981. *The Ultimate Resource*. Princeton, N.J.: Princeton University Press.

Stycos, J. M. 1971. *Ideology, Faith, and Family Planning in Latin America: Studies in Public and Private Opinion on Fertility Control*. New York: McGraw-Hill.

United Nations. 1975. *Report of the United Nations World Population Conference, 1974*. New York.

————. 1979. *World Population Trends and Policies: 1977 Monitoring Report*. New York.

————. 1984. *Report on the Debate at the International Conference on Population*. New York.

————. 1986. *World Population Trends and Policies: 1987 Monitoring Report*. Preliminary Version. New York.

————. 1987. *Global Review and Inventory of Population Policies, 1987*. New York. (Database available on diskette)

United Nations. Economic Commission for Africa. 1984. Report of the Second African Population Conference, Arusha, United Republic of Tanzania, January 9–13.

Van de Walle, E. 1975. "Population and Development." In J. C. Caldwell and others, eds., *Population Growth and Socioeconomic Change in West Africa*. New York: Columbia University Press.

World Bank. 1983. *World Development Report 1983*. New York: Oxford University Press.

———. 1986. *Population Growth and Policies in Sub-Saharan Africa*. Washington, D.C.

———. 1987. *Social Indicators of Development*. Washington, D.C.

Family Planning Pilot Projects

John A. Ross

Throughout Africa, national planners are confronted with rapidly growing urban and rural populations and exceedingly high mortality rates for infants, children, and mothers in childbirth. In many areas, one-third to one-half of all deaths are to infants. Large proportions of higher-order births increase health and mortality risks for both mother and child, and excessive fertility rates almost everywhere carry negative social and economic consequences, which were discussed in earlier chapters. Clearly, the long-range tasks of family planning and related health efforts are to bring fertility and mortality into balance at low levels.

Operations research and pilot projects carried out in Sub-Saharan Africa provide guidelines for the design of large-scale programs to expand acceptance and use of family planning and related health care. Although these projects by no means answer all questions, for those they address they offer evidence well worth considering.

This chapter reviews the projects undertaken and summarizes certain lessons learned from them. The substantive focus is on family planning, but attention is also paid to related health interventions because in Africa ill health is interwoven with high fertility—each reinforcing the other—and corrective actions for them should be simultaneous.

In addressing problems of fertility and mortality, planners should review a wide range of policy options before zeroing in on those most appropriate for a particular ministry or department. Figure 15-1 is a list of possible fertility measures, developed and improved over the years by Berelson (1977) (slightly modified by me). The options are divided into those intended to enhance the supply of fertility control services and those intended to increase general demand for services.

These basic measures for reducing fertility have evolved during recent decades. Some are controversial, but others are well accepted and proven. None is individually adequate, and some raise questions of cultural acceptability. With all their limitations, however, these strategies represent essentially the universe of experience with manipulating fertility; each government will necessarily have its own criteria and will necessarily be selective.

This chapter is also selective, choosing to treat chiefly those strategies that imply implementation through health channels. In the African context, this is by common agreement the most realistic way to approach family planning concerns as well as problems of morbidity and mortality. Commercial channels and social marketing approaches will also be examined, however. The following, then, is an attempt to sketch out the probable best ways to provide family planning and related primary health care to large African populations. There is no typical population group in Sub-Saharan Africa, of course, but it is nevertheless worthwhile to seek those general conclusions that appear to have emerged while also paying attention to important exceptions.

Constraints on the Implementation of Family Planning Strategies

As a region, Sub-Saharan Africa encompasses incredible diversity. The innumerable cultural groups and fragmented national units make strategy choices immensely difficult. Numerous conditions act as serious constraints to the implementation of any strategies chosen. Three features alleviate these difficulties, however. First, there is a very uneven pattern of population density, which places sizable populations together and leaves

The author wishes to thank Regina McNamara and Tessa Wardlaw of the Center for Population and Family Health, Columbia University, for their extensive help in the preparation of this chapter.

Figure 15-1. *Possible Fertility Measures*

I. *Measures to Affect Supply*

A. Improve access to modern means of fertility regulation, both quantitatively (to more people) and qualitatively (with better services)

1. Traditional family planning programs, in various forms and with currently available contraceptives (pill, IUD, condom)	Provision of information, supplies and services for voluntary fertility regulation via modern contraception and various delivery systems; many examples operating today.
2. . . . plus sterilization	. . . and adding sterilization, male and/or female.
3. . . . plus abortion	. . . and adding induced abortion, on an equivalent basis, for example, as in China.
4. Community-based distribution of current contraceptives	Emphasizing contraceptive distribution through local agents and depots, including mothers' clubs, and so forth.
5. Social marketing schemes, stimulation of the commercial sector	Subsidy arrangements to encourage sale of contraceptive measures to ease import restrictions, help local manufacture, remove legal barriers.
6. Postpartum arrangements	. . . systematically providing information and services in connection with institutionalized delivery, for example, as in the Population Council-assisted program in 138 hospitals in twenty-one countries.
7. Integration with maternal and child health programs	. . . organized as an integral part of maternal and child health.
8. Integration into general health programs	. . . organized as an integral part of total health infrastructure.
9. Integration into community development programs	. . . organized as part of rural improvement and community development.

B. Improve the product, that is, the acceptability, continuity, and/or effectiveness of new means of fertility control

Research programs directed toward that end now under way in both private and public sectors, for example, drug companies, WHO Expanded Programme, and ICCR, to develop and test better methods, for example, an implant, an IUD free of side effects, a safer or more convenient pill, a non-surgical method for termination of pregnancy.

II. *Measures to Affect Demand*

A. Promote basic socioeconomic determinants of fertility, or the most likely presumed determinants ("thresholds"), singly or together.

1. General development; modernization, social change, socio-cultural transformation . . . away from the traditional (high fertility) society	Reliance on social change, modernization, development, social-structural transformation, "new economic order" to reduce fertility rates "automatically" in the process.
2. Popular education; for example, a goal of six to eight years of schooling for all	. . . with special reference to extending popular education, particularly for girls.
3. Infant-child mortality; for example, toward an infant mortality rate of 50 per 1,000 or below	. . . with special reference to reducing infant and child mortality as a means of lowering desired family size.
4. Income; for example, toward $500 per capita or, better yet, $800 (and perhaps more equitable income distribution)	. . . with special reference to poverty reduction, particularly at the bottom of the income pyramid.
5. Industrialization; for example, toward one third or less of the labor force in agriculture	. . . with special reference to industrial development, and its consequences for family, kinship, modern attitudes.
6. Women's status; toward liberation from traditional childbearing and rearing, through education and employment	. . . with special reference to emancipation of women from traditional status, particularly via education and gainful employment.
7. Urbanization; toward 25 percent living in large cities (100,000 +)	. . . with special reference to urban development, with its implication for housing, diminished economic value of children, etc.

B. Inform and educate. To persuade people to lower fertility through messages, arguments, appeals, reasons provided, through:

1. Mass media (radio, TV, newspapers, poster)	Provision of energetic propaganda for smaller families, including encouragement by respected national figures and political leaders.
2. Person-to-person communication, individually (for example, door-to-door field work) or collectively (for example, group meetings, including special interest groups)	. . . the same through personal contact, including via residential or occupational communities.
3. Formal school systems ("population education")	Incorporation of population materials into primary and secondary curricula, for long-term effect.

C. Manipulate incentives/disincentives

1. Housing and job opportunities	Adjustment of incentives/disincentives, in money or in kind, in antinatalist direction, e.g., as in Singapore, Taiwan, Indian Tea Estates, state provision of welfare to the aged in order to reduce need for children (sons) for that purpose.
2. Maternity costs, leaves, etc.	
3. Child allowances, fees, and so forth	
4. Social security system	
5. Money, gifts	
6. Provision of communal benefits in return for specified fertility behavior	Communal incentives, for example, schools, water supply, for collective fertility performance at appropriate level.

(Figure continues on the following page)

Figure 15-1 *(continued)*

D. Manage community change to develop an antinatalist consensus, via

   1. Youth corps, or equivalent work program, to break traditional bonds with the home community

   2. Community education to discourage higher-order births

E. Impose legal sanctions, via

   1. Increase in age at marriage

   2. Restriction of outmigration from villages

   3. Direct limitation on family size

Source: Berelson (1977).

Proposals for collective employment and instruction of young people, both male and female, away from home ties, in order to delay marriage and modernize attitudes and information.
Organized and systematic efforts to develop community consensus in antinatalist direction.

Increase in minimum age of marriage for women, to at least 18 and preferably beyond.
Limitations in mobility, such that villages cannot export local unemployment to cities but must face up to support of their own excess reproduction.
Governmental imposition of a limit to childbearing, for example, as in recent tendencies in China.

large open spaces. Second, some cities have a surprisingly large concentration of people. Finally, a few large countries predominate (see chapters 1 and 5 in this volume).

Population Density

To a remarkable extent, settlement patterns can determine program choice as well as operational costs. A density map of Africa depicts extreme variations. The vast and unsettled expanse of the Sahara is a dominant feature; below the desert is Sub-Saharan Africa with some countries of low density and others that are thickly settled. For mass programs, the key is to note the areas that are both populous and dense. These exist primarily along the coastline from Côte d'Ivoire through Nigeria and around to Cameroon and also in the countries around Lake Victoria and areas along the Nile toward southern Sudan.

The empty areas are found especially in the southwest and in certain other zones. Few areas are as sparsely populated as the band of countries across the great Sahara Desert, but sizable spaces elsewhere in the region also have very small populations.

Urban Concentrations

Programs for large cities must be different from those for villages, and Sub-Saharan Africa has a substantial number of large urban concentrations. In Zaire, for example, the five largest cities contain 14 percent of the country's population, or one person in seven. In Senegal, Dakar alone has perhaps one-fifth of the total population. Cities of more than a half million inhabitants make up about 5 percent of the total populations of Ethiopia, Nigeria, Sudan, and Tanzania: these are the largest countries in the region, and these big cities therefore account for a considerable share of the total population.

National Populations

The population of Sub-Saharan Africa is divided among forty-nine countries (United Nations 1986). Nigeria alone has one-fifth of the region's population. The largest five countries contain about half the population, the largest ten about two-thirds, and the top fifteen more than three-fourths. The remaining thirty-five countries contain only 22 percent of the population. Thus, in a regional strategy for resource allocation, and in selecting locations for key demonstration projects, there is a strong argument for giving weight to a few large countries.

Furthermore, there are natural groupings among the largest fifteen countries. Experts always stress such major divisions as anglophone/francophone, West/East/Central, and Moslem/non-Moslem, and the following clusters based on geographic proximity and rough cultural similarity combine these criteria:

1. West African anglophone: Nigeria and Ghana (105 million population)
2. West African francophone: Côte d'Ivoire and Cameroon (16 million)
3. Sudan and Ethiopia (56 million), which are contiguous but should probably be considered separately
4. East African anglophone: Kenya, Tanzania, Uganda, and Zimbabwe (65 million), a natural grouping, which can be linked with the extremely high-density areas of Burundi and Rwanda
5. Mozambique (9.7 million), of Portuguese background, and farther south, South Africa (31.6 million), which for obvious reasons is kept aside
6. Zaire in Central Africa (32.0 million)
7. Residual: the large island of Madagascar (9.7 million) and Angola (8.5 million), formerly Portuguese.

These fourteen countries (excluding Burundi, Rwanda, and South Africa from the count) will control future fertility and mortality rates and health levels of Sub-Saharan Africa. If fertility control is to be achieved, it must be accomplished in these countries. Indeed, the five largest countries will tell half of the story.

In short, the surface disarray of Sub-Saharan Africa is greatly simplified by recognizing natural groupings of countries and by noting that most of the population lives in a very few countries, that large clusters exist in a few cities, and that much of the population lives in zones of high density. All of these considerations can lead to crucial planning decisions in the struggle to lower the region's disease, mortality, and fertility levels.

Program Choices

The major program alternatives among which planning officials within each country can choose are discussed below. Choices among these approaches take priority; subordinate actions follow from them.

Seven major strategies for strengthening family planning and related health programs in Africa are considered; see the appendix to this chapter for seven detailed examples. These strategies have survived the last two decades of world experience and have been tried to a greater or lesser extent in Africa itself. They are organized here roughly according to the essential problems that they pose for service outreach.

A major shortcoming of the health system in most developing countries is the failure to direct resources to low-cost measures that will have maximum effects on large populations. Present systems are overly clinical, curative, physician oriented, and passive when they should be grounded in ordinary workers who reach out to villages to implement changes that are known to affect vital rates. Neglected channels outside the health ministry should also be used. Much can be accomplished by applying what is already known, whereas some is a matter of learning quickly through field trials what additional approaches will work best.

Community-Based Distribution

It has become clear that the most effective programs to reduce fertility and early childhood mortality fall under the general heading of community-based distribution (CBD). The key words are "community" and "distribution." The first signifies that, above all else, the program must have a strong presence at the local level, and the second signifies that simple commodities and services must be actively delivered. CBD programs often, but not always, involve workers who appear on each doorstep, at least for a few rounds. CBD programs also require local depots, which people are encouraged to visit for contraceptives, oral rehydration therapy (ORT) packets, antimalarial medicines, and so forth, and they

often use village meetings along with, or instead of, personal contacts. In these programs, however, workers invariably go beyond the clinics and offices to visit communities and thereby achieve the basic outreach that passive, clinic-based systems can never attain. A remarkable case for the rural sector of an entire country—Zimbabwe—is described in the appendix.

The chief argument for CBD in Sub-Saharan Africa is that, without it, the large rural populations cannot be served. One worldwide summary finds that "in the last 12 years more than 70 community-based family planning programs have been undertaken in at least 40 countries. . . . An objective they all share, however, is to improve access to family planning services by removing some of the geographic, financial, bureaucratic, cultural, and communication barriers that limit use of these or any health services. Greater availability is an important goal of all community-based services" (Kols and Wawer 1982, p. 77).

CBD experience is reassuring at the national level in Zimbabwe and in projects in Kenya, Nigeria, Sudan, and Zaire (see cases 1–4 in the appendix). Despite many differences among them, these projects have usually had two features: home visits by lower-level personnel and inexpensive local resupply points. Items distributed, with accompanying efforts to encourage their use, have included contraceptives, ORT, dietary supplements, antimalarials, and antiparasite preparations. The CBD approach is quite flexible and can adapt to different local conditions. Actual and potential variations in approach include:

1. Home visits: sometimes one only, sometimes two or three, rarely repeated indefinitely
2. Stimulus: information, samples or supplies, persuasion; sometimes with interviews to gather data, with queries about recent use; discussion of income-generating activities
3. Commodities and services: pills, condoms, foam; ORT; antimalarial, antiparasite medications, iron, vitamins, and so forth; referral for IUDs, sterilization, inoculations
4. Personnel: volunteers, paid lay workers, fieldworkers, regular staff reassigned to home visits, regular "itinerant" rural staff given new duties, midwives, others
5. Resupply points: small depots in homes, health "huts," outlying small clinics, mothers' clubs
6. Charges: supplies given at home, almost always free, or at depots, sometimes for a fee; charges are meant partly to ensure voluntarism and to reduce courtesy acceptances
7. Training and supervision: highly variable, depending chiefly upon the kind of agency and the scope of the pilot project.

This list can be expanded but is sufficient in its present form to show that numerous combinations of features are possible. The form of each CBD program will be determined largely by local conditions and preferences. The overriding objectives must be wider coverage of the population and realistic adaptation to the available resources, including limited funds and personnel.

CBD programs are eminently suitable for meeting latent demand for family planning, whether in rural villages or in urban slums. Given even modest demand, a CBD program helps make modern contraceptives more acceptable over time both to individual families and to the community at large. The cases reviewed show that household distribution and local resupply can work. The need now is for wider implementation and for more demonstrations in contexts that are representative of large population groups.

Integrated Programs

The question of integration presents many issues, some of which appear to have been clarified in field experiments. Note, however, that field trials with integration often have been large, multipurpose undertakings that have encountered the high risks and exceptional difficulties of trying to follow a fixed research protocol over several years with complex institutional arrangements.

"Integration," in the sense of offering multiple services (for example, contraception and ORT) in one home visit, can work well, as shown recently in Bas Zaire (case 4 in the appendix), the Sudan, and numerous other sites in Africa. Services must work well together as companionable offerings, and such coordination is a complex matter. Where the goal is good results in two programs, for example, family planning and nutrition, the merger may prove cost effective, even though neither one does quite as well as it does when implemented alone. But if the goal is good results in family planning alone, any second program may become a brake on family planning output and reduce its cost effectiveness. In a larger sense, it is always possible that the family planning effort will be helped, not hurt, if several services join forces.

In the Sub-Saharan African context, political factors will usually require household distribution schemes to combine family planning with other interventions, making the issue of integration moot. Nevertheless, care should be taken not to burden workers with too many duties. Training should be simplified, and workers should not try to do too much during any one visit. Countries should also consider adaptations of the Training and Visit System in agriculture, now used in more than forty projects in about twenty countries and adopted by thirteen Indian states (Heaver 1984).

Most Sub-Saharan African countries will wish to supplement family planning with related health activities,

at least in many of their programs. If the combinations are well chosen and worker duties are kept manageable, such programs can be effective, and they can address fertility and mortality concerns simultaneously at the family level. Important features of both integrated programs and CBD programs are illustrated in cases 2–4 in the appendix.

Social Marketing

The commercial sector is another avenue for achieving large-scale effects outside the clinic system. It is a separate channel that contacts many people who do not patronize health facilities, and it reaches out into the countryside through small shops and entrepreneurs. The key is to stimulate the commercial sector to sell the products of interest.

One review of worldwide experience found strong evidence that social marketing—the application of commercial marketing techniques to achieve social objectives—can improve contraceptive availability, increase sales of contraceptive products, spread knowledge of and stimulate wider use of the methods promoted, and provide a substantial measure of protection against unwanted pregnancy at a cost below that of most other programs (Altman and Piotrow 1980). It is too early to tell whether the same will be true for Sub-Saharan Africa because Kenya (case 5 in the appendix) and Ghana are the only African countries in which social marketing has been tried and, at best, partially evaluated. The results were mixed in both cases, not because the public reacted badly, but because of difficult political conditions and inconsistent government support.

The question is how much energy and resources should go into experiments with social marketing, which is a hybrid across profoundly different institutions and therefore may be peculiarly fragile where governments change frequently or bureaucratic caution is strong. Yet it offers the possibility of a powerful distribution network, reaching into most parts of the country, for simple contraceptives. Caution is perhaps the best policy, together with openness where key figures from both the government and commercial sectors are strongly committed to the effort and expert market analysis is encouraging. In the right circumstances, social marketing can make a major difference.

Traditional Midwives

Traditional birth attendants (TBAs) are a program possibility on which there has been rather little formal experimentation with objective data. Nevertheless, enough has been done to indicate that the TBA approach works very well in some cases.

One comprehensive review summarizes the potential of TBAs:

Traditional midwives can learn new concepts if they are presented in an appropriate way; they do influence their own clients and encourage some to adopt family planning. On the other hand, they are rarely active recruiters outside their own clientele, and they cannot serve as the principal agents of change in a national program. But, as attitudes shift, traditional midwives can help to meet the growing need to distribute family planning supplies especially to women who are not well served by other programs [Simpson-Hebert and others 1980].

In Oyo State, Nigeria (case 3 in the appendix), the record is encouraging. Illiterate midwives, selected to serve as volunteer workers under supervision, have performed well in providing illness treatments, prenatal pill disbursements, contraceptive distribution, and health talks. In the Danfa project, however, where both female traditional midwives (*matrones*) and males were trained, the result was only partly favorable. They were observed to be handling an increasing proportion of deliveries and to be seeing more postpartum women than did the untrained midwives and the health center. A few matrones were especially active and the rest much less so, however, and on average, they referred only about one new family planning acceptor per year. One study recommended that they be given fuller administrative and professional support to use and protect their new skills. This suggestion is echoed in other writings on TBAS.

Some 900 TBAs trained between 1956 and 1976 are credited with having reduced neonatal tetanus in Liberia. Use of TBAS (*bundo mamies*), who received three weeks of training that included a family planning component, yielded discouraging results in Sierra Leone as far as referring women to clinics for contraception was concerned. They still possess tantalizing potential: they attend 70 percent of deliveries; they are firmly entrenched; and they have been given increasing de facto recognition. As elsewhere, however, they also have sobering drawbacks: they are very independent, not especially desirous of classroom instruction, and preoccupied with their own primary concerns.

TBAs may best be regarded as simply one among several resources in any rural program. Certainly, more field experimentation involving TBAS is merited. The keys to their effectiveness include their status in the community and the exact set of new functions expected of them, along with careful selection, effective training, supervision or light monitoring, and remuneration.

The Postpartum Approach

Postpartum distribution of contraceptives is a well-proven and thoroughly established approach for increasing family planning use in Asia and Latin America (Castadot and

others 1975). Its narrow acceptance in Sub-Saharan Africa is not primarily the consequence of the low percentage of deliveries in medical facilities; that limitation exists generally in the developing world and is accepted as one boundary. The special factors in Sub-Saharan Africa are the customs of extended breastfeeding and sexual abstinence after childbirth, which to some extent reduce both interest in and need for contraception shortly after delivery. One experiment in Lagos, for example, found little interest in postpartum services, and it consequently stressed other approaches.

Nevertheless, there are ample reasons for encouraging postpartum programs everywhere in Africa. One is the presence of population subgroups that will not practice postpartum abstinence or prolonged breastfeeding and will thus be exposed to unwanted pregnancy. These subgroups will grow as traditions weaken and as bottle feeding spreads. A further reason is to establish attractive services for groups other than delivering women—for those with septic abortions and for "indirect" acceptors, those hearing of the services by word of mouth and coming during later stages of the birth interval, when many have terminated abstinence or breastfeeding. In the postpartum programs in Nigeria and Ghana (case 6 in the appendix), indirect acceptors made up 61 and 58 percent, respectively, of all acceptors. Postpartum programs have some additional advantages: in urban medical facilities they engage a country's medical leadership, and they provide a training base for other personnel.

The original rationale for postpartum programs holds as well now as it did in the mid-1960s, when the International Postpartum Program, established by the Population Council, grew rapidly from some 25 hospitals to about 140. Fundamentally, the approach makes very efficient use of preestablished facilities; it can offer every contraceptive method, and it does so at a time when birth planning, either spacing or stopping, may be of paramount importance in the mother's thinking.

Postpartum activity therefore continues to be one of the most attractive approaches to fund and to institutionalize. In addition to the logistical advantages in providing services where women are already present, a postpartum program affords a special opportunity to offer sterilization. One weakness in initiating ordinary contraception soon after a birth—the overlap with amenorrhea—is not an issue with sterilization because it is permanent (whereas with the IUD or pill, wastage occurs as the normal duration of use duplicates other protection). In addition, women may favorably associate the opportunity for sterilization with hospital delivery. Postpartum medical facilities are sometimes the only auspices under which female sterilization can be officially introduced. It is becoming a more acceptable approach, given the simplified methods of minilaparotomy and laparoscopy, which permit the use of local anesthesia and outpatient services at the six-week checkup visit or later.

Besides sterilization, semipermanent methods also deserve consideration at delivery or at the six-week checkup. Long-acting IUDs are now available, and progesterone injectables have been suggested (they appear not to impair the flow of breast milk, but possible progesterone effects on the infant require further study). In sum, the postpartum approach has been used less in Africa than elsewhere in the world, and much unrealized potential for it exists in both urban and rural areas.

Incentives and Disincentives

Incentives are by no means untried in Sub-Saharan Africa, but experience with them is scattered and poorly documented. In Botswana, Ghana (case 7 in the appendix), Mauritius, and Zimbabwe, special payments have been given to doctors or family planning workers for contraceptive or sterilization acceptors (Jacobsen 1983; Barnett 1984). Mauritius has offered small, one-time payments to contraceptive and vasectomy acceptors. There are also other kinds of reported incentives (or disincentives):

- Employed mothers receive maternity benefits for no more than three births in Ghana
- Paid maternity leave is allowed only once every three years in Tanzania
- Child allowances (income supplements usually paid to government employees) are paid for a maximum of three children in Ghana
- Income tax deductions for dependent children were eliminated in Tanzania (Jacobsen 1983, p. 21, citing Financioglu 1982); and tax allowances are limited to four children in Kenya (Barnett 1984).

(Nonmonetary incentives will be tested in the Corat project of Johns Hopkins University.)

These are local examples of intervention whose effects cannot be measured and may apply to only a modest proportion of the population (those employed in government or large firms or paying taxes). As Singapore's leaders stressed in regard to incentives there, however, such measures can signal new directions to the population and can act as important symbols, speeding the creation of new norms in family size.

The category of incentives is very broad. As noted earlier, incentives may be given to both individuals and communities, over the short term or the long term, directly or indirectly. For high-level government planners, one or more of these alternatives may offer potential for signaling new norms and encouraging new behavior.

Special Urban Programs

Some countries (notably Indonesia, outside Africa) have tried to create special programs for cities because the mechanisms available there differ so greatly from those in villages. Selecting the largest five to ten cities for intensive attention can offer significant advantages. As noted earlier, 5 to 15 percent of the population in certain African countries live in a few urban centers. There are other reasons to develop programs specifically for cities: in the capital city, leaders can be engaged and persuaded of the importance of family planning. In regional cities there may be teaching hospitals or other training centers, with the accompanying medical leadership. Model family planning activities should be established to take advantage of the special resources these facilities offer. Moreover, each major city has its own hinterland and can be a point of diffusion for program action. Programs can build on such components as postpartum efforts, mass media, training efforts involving medical facilities, the testing and manufacture of contraceptives, and social marketing. Demonstration clinics can also be created to illustrate better practices (such as access at convenient hours and provision of a full range of methods) than those that usually prevail in government health centers.

Other Programs

Mobile teams are useful when they are well administered. They have frequently been used but seldom on a large scale or as a complete program. Thus no formal field trials of mobile teams were found. They appear to deserve support where local personnel are capable and a clear need exists. They can, however, be wasteful of both personnel and funds, and they are especially risky when large, costly vehicles are involved. Strong administrative discipline and good supervision are necessary for consistently good performance.

A few other field experiments have been found on some topics that are of interest for future program planning. These include work through factories and unions, military groups, women's organizations, religious groups, and a variety of channels that offer opportunities within each country for useful education or service; a judgment should be made in each case whether the channel can have a significant effect.

Conclusions

A number of conclusions can be drawn from activities in Sub-Saharan Africa, some of them providing more detail on the basic program approaches noted above and others cutting across them. These conclusions are summarized below, with the focus on issues of concern for planning and administration.

First, the Zimbabwe national experience (case 1 in the appendix) and the Bas Zaire experiment (case 4 in the appendix) have yielded findings that are typical for community-based distribution, which is clearly the most promising method for attaining the outreach needed to change behavior in large rural populations. Bertrand and others (1984) derive the following lessons:

- The household distribution of contraceptives is acceptable, provided that certain cultural norms are respected.
- The promotion of family planning services is facilitated by integration with child health services, but integration does not seem to be essential in urban areas.
- Emphasis in family planning programs should be placed on child spacing, not family limitation.
- In an area where trained health personnel are scarce, the use of paraprofessionals to distribute contraceptives is acceptable to community officials and to the general population.
- Household distribution of contraceptives achieves levels of awareness and initiation of use that would take much longer to achieve if the methods were simply made available in service outlets.

Second, attempts to involve males have yielded varying results. Some investigators have found male workers to be quite acceptable in personal contacts with women. The need to educate males as to their roles and responsibilities in regard to family planning is widely recognized. Some have found that male villagers were open-minded and would attend meetings, whereas others found them unresponsive and uninterested. Furthermore, different projects have obtained varying results on the acceptability of the condom. It must be concluded that no general rule has emerged but that males are important everywhere, and programs should be persistent in discovering ways to gain their approval and involvement.

Third, the pill is the only contraceptive method not frequently neglected in the projects reviewed. It is clearly of first importance in CBD trials and deserves continued emphasis.

The IUD has not been the subject of special experimentation except perhaps in one Kenyan study (Cuca and Pierce 1977). It has usually been viewed as a medical method. Nevertheless, it has been included as a referral method in African CBD projects. Much more could be done to establish precedents for insertion by paramedics and away from fixed clinics. Indeed, government midwives in Sudan are being trained to insert IUDs and have

been successful in doing so safely. Many programs outside Africa use paramedics for IUD insertion.

There is little to say regarding the condom except that it is indispensable in programs directed to males, and male programs have been underutilized. Especially with the AIDS epidemic, condoms should be added to more programs and used more vigorously. They have evidently been offered with some success in both Kenya and Ghana. They can be offered in both the private and public sectors and can be imported or manufactured locally; both approaches can usefully absorb donor assistance. Much the same can be said of other barrier methods, although international evidence shows them to have high failure rates and usually low acceptability. Bas Zaire may be a partial exception to this rule, or the African pattern may be genuinely variable.

Injectable contraceptives are a promising option. They are used by about 6.5 million women in more than 100 countries, and recent large studies lay to rest the concerns about their possible impairment of fecundity (Liskin and Rutledge 1984; Liskin and others 1987). Injectables are typically a clinical method, but the way would seem open to careful trials of paramedic injection with a checklist of contraindications, outside the clinic, as in the Matlab project in Bangladesh. The implant is also a very promising method. It is now at the stage of field trials and deserves the closest attention (Liskin and Rutledge 1984; Liskin and others 1987).

Sterilization, both male and female, is probably the most neglected method and the most able to absorb special funding, particularly in combination with post-partum programs, which can also absorb funds. Female sterilization has often been a part of the projects reviewed here. In household visits it has been a referral method along with the IUD. No trials were found that were devoted to sterilization alone, but it is available in many established programs, and it deserves continued emphasis as a one-step option for stopping childbearing.

With respect to vasectomy, it seems clear from non-African experience that provider constraints can be as serious as a lack of male interest. As trials in presumably unfavorable areas have shown, expert prognostications are simply unreliable. Public response cannot be gauged until good service, with proper counseling, is actually established and publicized. Vasectomy is both cheaper and safer than female sterilization and can be done at any time in the birth interval and by less sophisticated medical personnel. There are good reasons to add it to both old and new programs.

Fourth, cost effectiveness is a difficult but important subject. Good cost data are rare everywhere, and Africa is no exception. Costs per user for ten Sub-Saharan African countries have been estimated for 1980 in an extensive and original analysis (Sirageldin and others

1983) which emphasized that there are many sources of error in such estimates. This analysis, however, sets the order of magnitude, suggests further lines of work, and draws several implications for donor and regional planning. In ten countries, the range in cost per user was from US$6.60 in Zaire to US$76.10 in Liberia.

Within a particular country, useful cost data will be uncommon. More to the point, estimates in money terms will usually be only one consideration and often not the most salient one in shaping new programs. The selection of supervisory personnel is often more critical than a budget increase, and liaison with community groups may be a key to improvement. The cost per acceptor or user, or the cost per increment in contraceptive prevalence, is quite likely to be less in cities than in villages, because of the logistical expense of deploying a program in rural areas. That does not necessarily mean, of course, that the program should concentrate only on the cities. Rural needs must be met, and they may well require the use of more cumbersome and expensive methods.

On the other hand, village culture may make possible a network of effective volunteer workers and mothers' groups, which provides a high level of effectiveness at low cost, or underemployed health workers may add contraceptive distribution to their duties with little increase in real costs. The thrust of these observations is simply that costs and cost effectiveness should be approached creatively, with unremitting attention to means of improving both efficiency and effectiveness. In addition, given the defective data common in this field, planners should not involve themselves with cost judgments without knowing how they were derived and how the real resources at hand can be exploited.

Finally, as regards project development, it is useful to note the conclusions of Rosenfield (1964, p. 5), quoted below, which summarize a considerable body of experience:

- Such projects are best developed in a relatively small project area with members of the community and of the health care agency involved in the planning, implementation, and evaluation efforts. Winning the trust of the community and demonstrating that the program is indeed geared to their needs is an essential first step. Without this collaborative effort from the onset the project is faced with major difficulties.

- The evaluation should be geared towards intermediate outcome measures such as services accepted or drugs and commodities distributed. Reasonable conclusions can be drawn from these intermediate measures in an 18 to 24 month period, a period which is too short for longer term objectives such as changes in fertility, mortality, and morbidity.

- One must be ready, despite the research design, to discontinue components of the project which appear not to be working at an early stage in the project or to make significant modifications, as indicated. One advantage of the operations research approach is the lack of rigidity of research design, allowing for such modifications so that the effort remains practical in orientation.

- In some projects, quasi-experimental research designs are possible. In others, a simple demonstration project involving an approach tried elsewhere is worthwhile.

There are, of course, many other issues, indeed, an almost endless list of particular questions and decisions, and their resolution becomes more individual as the level of detail increases. Efforts to set general rules quickly degenerate into speculations and qualifications that are not particularly helpful to national planners. To researchers, it is humbling but true that answers to many questions lie beyond their methods and that they will forever know less about many things than do the village leaders and provincial directors.

Appendix: Illustrative Projects

Case 1: The Zimbabwe CBD Program

Type, Time, and Place. The Zimbabwe CBD program has involved community-based distribution for the rural sector of Zimbabwe in 635 catchment areas from approximately 1983 to the present.

Institution. The Zimbabwe National Family Planning Council implements the project and works through provincial offices and a network of local supervisors.

Objectives. There are two objectives: (1) to deliver oral contraceptives and condoms to the rural population and (2) to perform certain primary health care functions.

Intervention. Each CBD area is an underserved location with a radius of about fifteen kilometers and a population of roughly 3,200, and each has access to a nearby health center. A full-time worker, chosen from the area, follows certain routes repeatedly to visit homes in the area every three weeks. Pill users are given three cycles at a time, condom users are given supplies according to individual need. Both pills and condoms are also supplied to local voluntary organizations. The workers carry equipment to check the blood pressure of pill applicants and also use a list of contraindications to screen them. Some community education is performed through group meetings, and the workers actively encourage the use of contraceptives in addition to supplying them.

Some attention is also given to instruction concerning immunizations, rehydration therapy, and breast-feeding. Workers are fully salaried as regular government employees, with limited vacation, maternity, and retirement benefits. They are closely supervised in groups of eight to ten by a group leader, who was formerly a CBD worker (all promotion is from within). A provincial supervisor, equipped with a Landrover, is in charge of this staff and meets monthly with the group leaders to develop detailed work plans. All CBD workers have bicycles, and group leaders have light motorcycles. There are flexible targets for both new acceptors and numbers of revisits for resupply each month.

A well-defined record system enables the worker to track the resupply experience of each client, with summaries flowing to the supervisory, provincial, and national levels.

Results. The catchment areas include about 2 million people, or 29 percent of the total rural population of Zimbabwe. About 380,000 cohabiting women of childbearing age live in these areas, to whom the program in 1987 distributed about 2.7 million cycles of pills and 2.2 million condoms, representing about 232,000 couple years of protection. Ignoring wastage, this amounts to coverage of more than 60 percent of cohabiting women of childbearing age in the areas, an unprecedented achievement in Sub-Saharan Africa. More than 40 percent of all rural contraceptive users were covered by this program in the 1984 national survey.

Clients in the Zimbabwe program are remarkably young, have small families, and are interested primarily in spacing. Moreover, they use oral contraception almost exclusively. The uptake of condms is small, which represents only about 7 percent of the couple years of protection provided.

One limited study of acceptors showed that three-fourths were below age thirty, and more than half below age twenty-five. Moreover, half had only one or two living children, and one-fourth had three or four. Ninety percent of acceptors said that their objective was to space childbirths or to delay the next pregnancy. All these characteristics agree with more comprehensive data in the 1984 and 1986 national surveys (which were, of course, dominated by the large rural sector). The overall prevalence rate of nearly 40 percent in 1984 and 43 percent in 1988 clearly establish the fundamental transition in Zimbabwe from traditional family-building patterns, particularly among the younger generation.

The primary limitations of the program are the costs of full-time salaried workers and a relatively high density of supervisors; these factors make the addition of more catchment areas difficult. A further, unfortunate limitation is that this is essentially a single-method program, so that apart from the small condom component, little recourse is offered to clients who find the pill unsatisfactory.

Many nonclients in the CBD areas are in touch with the workers. In the 1984 national survey, more than one-third of rural women not using a modern method knew of the CBD program as a possible source, and more than 20 percent of women in the entire rural sector had been visited by a CBD worker.

(References: Zimbabwe National Family Planning Council 1984, 1988; Dow and others 1986; Boohene and Dow 1987.)

Case 2: Health for the Family

Type, Time, and Place. The project involves integrated community-based distribution from 1974 to the present at Chogoria Hospital in Kenya.

Institution. The institution concerned is the Presbyterian Church of East Africa, with funding from Family Planning International Assistance, Church of Scotland, Ford Foundation, and Swedish International Development Authority.

Objectives. There are two objectives: (1) To conduct community-based and clinic activities in order to increase acceptance of family planning among men as well as women. (2) To expand the family life/sexuality education program for young adults by training new group leaders and conducting seminars on preparation for marriage and preparation for employment for school dropouts.

Intervention. Project activities include integrated, curative, and maternal and child health/family planning (MCH/FP) service delivery at twenty-five delivery points and six mobile clinics; also a CBD and a youth program. Youth program leaders make contact with both students and youths who are not in school and who do not belong to any organizations. Contact is often made at informal gatherings, in marketplaces, at weddings, and so forth. Other outreach activities bring family planning information and services to hard-to-reach areas through volunteer health workers, teachers, and peer group opinion leaders. By using "satisfied users" as volunteers, Chogoria Hospital is able to provide services at a low cost. Eventually, the hospital plans to bear this cost independently.

Results. Preliminary results from a Centers for Disease Control evaluation indicate that an estimated 27–30 percent of all eligible women in the area are now active users. By January 1984, more than 30,000 new family planning acceptors had been served. Since 1978, more than 500 voluntary sterilizations have been performed.

(Reference: Family Planning International Assistance 1984.)

Case 3: Oyo Community-Based Delivery, Health, and Family Planning Project

Type, Time, and Place. Integrated community-based distribution from 1981 onward in Oyo State, Nigeria.

Population. Population in the pilot area was roughly 85,000 and in the expanded area was roughly 150,000.

Institutions. The project was implemented by the University College Hospital, Ibadan; State Health Council, Ministry of Health, Oyo; Center for Population and Family Health, Columbia University; and the Pathfinder Fund.

Objectives. There were two objectives: (1) to demonstrate and test the effectiveness of low-cost rural health and family planning services provided by trained community volunteers under the supervision of the existing government MCH program, and (2) to introduce family planning to rural areas of Oyo State in a manner that was acceptable to the community.

Subobjectives. There were four subobjectives: (1) to develop and test appropriate training programs for the community field workers and their supervisors, (2) to assess community receptivity to the services provided, (3) to determine which individual and community characteristics differentiate effective from ineffective fieldworkers, and (4) to evaluate the cost effectiveness of alternative systems of field worker motivation, home visiting, field supervision, and community participation.

Research Design. The design included pre- and post-project surveys; evaluation of service statistics and monitoring of disbursements of drugs and contraceptives; and special studies of specific issues (for example, types of field workers, methods of supervision, and fee and incentive systems).

Interventions. In the pilot area, 165 volunteers were selected by the communities and were trained to provide basic health services (health and family planning education; referrals; treatments for malaria, diarrhea, worms, cough; first aid for cuts and bruises; and distribution of vitamins, iron, and contraceptives). Although the project was initially administered by the University College Hospital, the field workers were supervised by the

nurse midwives from the existing government MCH program, and services were integrated with those of the maternity/health centers. Two-thirds of the workers were TBAs, and one-third were male voluntary health workers.

In the expanded area, volunteer workers, also selected by the communities, were trained to carry out the same services in the remaining health areas in Oyo State, and the government gradually took over administrative responsibility. Workers in the pilot area had received a monetary incentive when the project was initiated, but the practice was discontinued, and no monetary incentive was given to the workers in the expanded area. Small service fees were charged, and the funds were administered by a village committee for community projects.

Results. A baseline survey in the pilot area found that only 36 percent of the respondents' families had used any government health service in the previous year. In its first full year of operation (1982), the community-based workers provided 33,788 illness treatments, 2,051 prenatal pill disbursements, 6,662 contraceptive disbursements, 575 deliveries, and almost 5,000 health talks. The system did not allow for collection of client data, but estimates of use from disbursement of contraceptives indicate that about 25 percent of the women of reproductive age used modern contraception, with current use estimated at 10 percent. Preprogram survey estimates were 2.5 percent for ever use and 1.5 percent for current use.

Local dissemination of information on the University College Hospital pilot project led to a demand from other areas of Oyo State for similar services and resulted in prompt replication of the program by the state government.

Remarks. The major lessons from this community-based project are several.

1. Integration of family planning with basic health care makes it acceptable to initiate discussion of the topic of child spacing at the village level, and family planning can then be associated with the much appreciated health services.

2. Although the leadership of the University College Hospital was invaluable in initiating the project, supervision by government facility personnel was more effective when the university role in administration was reduced and the local roles in training and management were expanded. The successful transfer of the pilot project to the government was the result of a carefully planned "apprenticeship." State personnel first observed the functioning of the pilot program, then participated in a training-of-trainers program, then

observed and assisted university staff in the initial steps of the expanded project, and gradually took over the training and other local program functions.

3. The community-based approach changed the MCH program emphasis from the provision of services for those attending a fixed facility to the provision of services for all people living within a particular area.

4. The nonprofessional MCH personnel effectively assisted in implementing the community-based program, especially in supervision of the field workers and in family planning education.

5. A major value of the TBAs and voluntary health workers was to link the people in the rural areas to the facilities and services provided by the government, especially through information on the services and referrals (workers frequently accompany clients to the facility).

6. Individual monetary incentives were not necessary to motivate the volunteers. Once incentives have been given, however, the system is hard to change. (The incentives were the most costly item in the budget of the pilot project, and when the government took over it could not accept this expense.)

7. Small service fees can be an acceptable part of the community-based program, but they are not likely to be adequate for complete support of the program.

8. Illiterate field workers can properly treat malaria and other common illnesses, and they can keep reasonably accurate records using pictograph forms.

9. Open communication about family planning is very difficult, and it is important to have both male and female community agents to introduce and promote modern contraceptives in the rural areas.

10. Controlled quasi-experimental trials are extremely difficult to carry out in some rural settings, such as this part of Nigeria. It is more fruitful to study the naturally occurring variations in the program, basing analysis on service statistics, records, and field interviews.

(References: Weiss 1984; Ladipo and others 1981.)

Case 4: Le Programme d'Education Familiale

Type, Time, and Place. The program involved integrated community-based distribution from 1980 to the present in the region of Bas, Zaire.

Population. The project area includes the city of Matadi, with a target population of 133,000, and the neighboring zone of Songololo, with a target population of 25,000 living in fifty-three villages.

Institutions. The project was implemented by the Communauté Baptiste du Zaire Ouest (Baptist Community of West Zaire) in collaboration with Tulane University, with funding from the U.S. Agency for International Development.

Objective. The program aimed to try community-based distribution of contraceptives, specifically household distribution, in a francophone area, among both rural and urban populations having low contraceptive prevalence. It was carried out in combination with the delivery of drugs to combat malaria, intestinal parasites, and dehydration from diarrhea among children below age five.

Interventions. Two alternative strategies were tested for increasing the use of contraceptives and drugs. Both used readily accessible resupply outlets, but one (Treatment A) added home visits to distribute contraceptives and to educate mothers about the products, along with group meetings to increase community awareness and knowledge regarding child health and family planning. The other strategy (Treatment B) had no outreach activities and involved only stocking and resupplying service outlets with contraceptives and drugs for children under five. The urban program was family planning only, whereas in the rural program family planning was integrated with the three interventions for children under five: antimalarial drugs, antihelminthic drugs, and Oralyte. Three household visits were made by the "community-based distributors" (matrones) in rural communities lacking dispensaries. Husbands were encouraged to be present. After discussing benefits of child spacing and explaining the different methods, the matrone offered a free limited supply of one of the methods (pill, foam, vaginal tablet, or condom), with a coupon for resupply for acceptors.

Research Design. The research design included a baseline survey and service statistics and a follow-up survey in the rural area, conducted in July–November 1983. In the urban area, a follow-up survey was begun in January 1984. Service statistics included the volume of sales of contraceptives and drugs distributed through the different service outlets over time. Data were also collected by home visitors during each of the three home visiting rounds.

Results. Service statistics obtained during home visits indicate that only about 43 percent of urban women and 56 percent of rural women were reached during the first visit. Among the eligible women visiting during the first round, 37 percent in urban and 25 percent in rural areas obtained a free supply of contraceptives. The second and third rounds resulted in a substantial number of additional new users in both urban and rural areas.

Information was obtained to assess whether women who accepted contraceptives actually used them. Of the 1,261 urban women who had obtained a contraceptive in the first round and were revisited later, 83 percent indicated that they had used the method (Bertrand and others 1984). Continuation, as measured during the second visit, was not impressive. Overall, 51 percent of first round acceptors reported at the second visit that they were still using the method. The main reason for not using the contraceptive method obtained at the first round was that the woman had become pregnant. The second most frequently reported reason was that women did not know where to get resupplies. Other reasons for discontinuation were fear of side effects, desire for another pregnancy, husband's opposition or absence, and unfavorable attitudes on the part of the woman herself.

In urban areas the most popular methods were vaginal tablets (selected by 39 percent) and the pill (selected by 35 percent). The proportion of pill users increased in the second and third rounds, probably because of a change in project policy, which held that the pill no longer needed to be restricted to nonlactating women. In rural areas vaginal tablets were not available in the first round of home visits and 54 percent chose foam, 23 percent condoms, and 17 percent the pill.

Some of the more important conclusions drawn from this project about the feasibility of the community-based distribution approach in Sub-Saharan Africa are summarized below, drawing on Bertrand and others (1984).

"The household distribution of contraceptives is acceptable in this population, provided that certain cultural norms are respected" (p. 24). Acceptability was enhanced by the following factors: (a) the director of program was a public health physician well known and respected by the rural population. (b) Conventional channels of authority were respected. (c) Special consideration was given to social norms governing male-female relationships. Home visitors distributed contraceptives only if the husband was present or gave his written consent.

"The promotion of family planning services is facilitated if they are integrated with child health services, but this does not seem to be essential in urban areas" (pp. 24–25). It was easier to build rapport with rural women by talking about the health of their children before introducing the subject of family planning. In urban areas where family planning alone was offered,

this was not a problem, perhaps because health services were more accessible there.

"Emphasis in family planning services should be placed on child spacing, not family limitation" (p. 25). There is widespread recognition of the importance of child spacing in traditional societies in Sub-Saharan Africa. The practice of postpartum abstinence is widespread but with modernization it is no longer acceptable to some. Therefore the concept of child spacing is well received. Family limitation, however, is so far an unpopular concept.

"In an area where there is a scarcity of trained health personnel, the use of paraprofessionals to distribute contraceptives is acceptable to community officials and the general population" (p. 25).

"Household distribution of contraceptives achieves levels of awareness and initiation of use that would take much longer to achieve if the methods were simply made available in service outlets" (p. 25).

"Spermicides are more popular in this population than would be expected from experiences in other regions of the developing world" (p. 25). One reason is that lactating women are a prime target group, and they are reluctant to use the pill. Service personnel also are reluctant to prescribe it. Vaginal methods appear to be quite culturally acceptable.

Case 5: The Kenya/Kinga Experiment

Type, Time, and Place. The project involved social marketing, from October 1972 to November 1973 in the Meru district (Kenya) with a total population of about 600,000.

Institution. Population Services, Inc., implemented the project.

Objective. The objective was to discern the implications for Kenya and the donor community of social marketing—the application of commercial marketing techniques to accomplish social objectives—in a national contraceptive program.

Research Design. Besides the experimental area, Kirinyaga district was used as a control area.

Intervention. The name, color, and sales symbol of lubricated condoms were selected on the basis of an initial marketing survey. An advertising and sales promotion campaign was then launched using all available media (radio, cinema, and displays). Condoms were sold through village stores, and the price was subsidized. Ongoing market research was used to ascertain and monitor the reactions to the promotion.

Results. In the experimental area the current use of condoms among survey respondents increased from 4 percent before the program to 15 percent twelve months after its initiation; current use of any method increased from 21 percent prior to the campaign to 35 percent after twelve months. There was no change in the level of contraceptive use in the control area.

Remarks. The experiment demonstrated that commercial distribution of subsidized contraceptives through local outlets offers an effective avenue for reaching the rural market. In its early stages the experiment encountered some opposition. An influential physician who operated four private rural family planning clinics alleged that the program was selling to children. This assertion prompted local shopkeepers to become more vocal in their support of the program. Sales were largely unaffected by the controversy, and the issue was eventually resolved. This project ended in 1974 but was immediately followed by another.
(References: Black and Harvey 1976; Population Services International 1972.)

Case 6: International Postpartum Program

Time and Place. The program took place in 1969–73 and onward in three participating hospitals: Korle Bu in Accra, Effia Nkwanta in Sekondi, and Komfo Anokye in Kumasi, Ghana.

Institutions. The above-mentioned hospitals, with assistance from the Population Council and USAID, implemented the program. After 1973, financial assistance came from the Ghana government and USAID.

Objectives. The objective was to test the postpartum approach in hospitals.

Research Design. The program involved an experimental group only. Service statistics provided continuous monitoring.

Intervention. Contraceptive services and information were offered to women delivering at the hospitals and to those returning for the six-week postpartum checkup visit. Services were also available to "indirect acceptors," that is, to individuals who learned of the program by word of mouth and came in or who waited more than three months after birth to seek contraception. Multiple methods were offered, especially the IUD, the pill, and sterilization.

Results. In the three hospitals combined, there were 93,000 obstetric/abortion cases. Some 9,000 of these women became direct acceptors, and there were 11,000 indirect acceptors. Thus the ratio of all acceptors to all cases was about 22 percent. The figure was of course lower in the early years, beginning at 5 percent in 1969 and rising to 11 percent in 1970 and 26 percent by 1973. One reason for the relatively high proportion of indirect acceptors was the limited availability of contraception elsewhere. Some 25 percent of acceptors chose the IUD, 60 percent the pill, 7 percent sterilization, and the rest other methods, a mix that produced an average of three couple years of protection per acceptor. The estimated cost per acceptor was US$3.60 in contrast with an estimated US$23 in Ghana's small national program in the same year (1972).

Remarks. The ratio of all acceptors (both direct and indirect) to the obstetric/abortion caseload was 25–26 percent after a few years of operation, at a very low cost per acceptor. The method mix was favorable, and the steady improvement in the response to the program was encouraging. On the basis of this evidence, the postpartum concept clearly deserves a place among program options. As tested in this experiment, it pertains only to urban hospitals, but equal attention should go to extensions into rural areas, using institutions and personnel in contact with women at the time of pregnancy and delivery. In some areas, the custom of postpartum abstinence and breastfeeding may make the suggestion of contraception somewhat irrelevant at the time of birth, but the question remains how large the subgroup is in each area that observes neither of these and actively desires contraceptive protection.

Case 7: The Commodity Experiment

Type, Time, and Place. The program involved incentives over a five-week period in 1970 in urban areas of Accra, Ghana.

Institutions. The program was implemented by the Planned Parenthood Association of Ghana with the support of the International Planned Parenthood Federation.

Objective. The objective was to evaluate the effectiveness of a simple commodity incentive in increasing the proportion of women who, having been referred, actually came to the clinic for service. Powdered milk was chosen as a commodity that had both real and symbolic value.

Research Design. The research design provided for a time series, alternating experimental and control phases.

Intervention. During the first and third weeks, field workers distributed numbered gift coupons to all women they were referring for family planning. The coupons informed the woman that if she came within ten days she would receive a free two-pound tin of powdered milk for herself and her baby. During the second and fourth weeks, workers distributed only the regular numbered referral slip and did not mention the free milk offer. During the fifth week, free milk coupons were again offered, and the workers were also offered an incentive. (The worker with the most points received six tins of milk, the equivalent of one week's wages.) A registration fee of US$1 was charged as a way of ensuring that the woman had serious intentions of practicing and was not coming merely to receive the milk.

Results. During the control weeks, 11 percent of referred women accepted family planning; during the incentive weeks, more than 20 percent did so. During the fifth week (client and worker incentives), acceptance was three times greater than the control weeks and 1.6 times greater than with client incentives only.

Remarks. The experiment demonstrated the attractiveness of a nonmonetary commodity incentive for both clients and workers. The presence of an incentive also shortened the interval between referral and acceptance. The cost of the commodity incentive was more than offset by the increase in the number of acceptors. During the fifth week the cost was approximately US$3.47 for each acceptor.

(References: Cuca and Pierce 1977; Perkin 1970.)

References

Altman, D. L., and P. T. Piotrow. 1980. "Social Marketing: Does It Work?" *Population Reports*, ser. J-21, 8(1).

Barnett, P. G. 1984. *Incentives for Family Planning?* Washington, D.C.: Population Crisis Committee. Revised 1987.

Berelson, Bernard. 1977. "Where Are We Going? An Outline." Working Paper. Center for Policy Studies, Population Council.

Bertrand, Jane T., and Nlandu Mangani. 1983. "Operations Research Project Experience: The Zaire Family Planning Project." In I. Sirageldin, D. Salkever, and R. Osborn, eds., *Evaluating Population Programs.* New York: St. Martin's Press.

Bertrand, Jane T., Nlandu Mangani, and Matondo Mansilu. 1984. "The Acceptability of Household Distribution of Contraceptives in Zaire." *International Family Planning Perspectives* 10(1): 21–26.

Bertrand, Jane T., and others. 1983. *The Dynamics of Fertility Control in Bas Zaire.* New Orleans: Tulane University.

Black, T. R., and P. D. Harvey. 1976. "A Report on a Contraceptive Social Marketing Experiment in Rural Kenya." *Studies in Family Planning* 7(4): 101–7.

Boohene, Esther, and T. E. Dow. 1987. "Contraceptive Prevalence and Family Planning Program Effort in Zimbabwe." *Studies in Family Planning Perspectives* 13(1): 1–7.

Castadot, R. G., I. Sivin, P. Reyes, J. O. Alers, M. Chapple, and J. Russell. 1975. "The International Postpartum Family Planning Program: Eight Years of Experience." *Reports on Population/Family Planning*, no. 18.

Cuca, R., and C. S. Pierce. 1977. *Experiments in Family Planning: Lessons from the Developing World.* Baltimore, Md.: Johns Hopkins University Press for the World Bank.

Dow, T., J. Chombo, L. Ndhlovu, P. Shumba, and B. Dhlodhlo. 1986. "Characteristics of New Contraceptive Acceptors in Zimbabwe." *Studies in Family Planning* 17(2): 107–13.

Family Planning International Assistance (FPIA). 1984. "Project Summary: Health for the Family." New York.

Financioglu, Nuray. 1982. "Carrots and Sticks." *People* 9(4): 3–8.

Heaver, Richard. 1984. *Adapting the Training and Visit System for Family Planning, Health, and Nutrition Programs.* Staff Working Paper No. 662. Washington, D.C.: World Bank.

Jacobsen, Judith. 1983. "Promoting Population Stabilization: Incentives for Small Families." *Worldwatch Paper*, no. 54 (June): 1–46.

Kols, A. J., and M. J. Wawer. 1982. "Community-Based Health and Family Planning." *Population Reports*, ser. L-3, 10(6): L77–L111.

Ladipo, O. A., E. M. Weiss, G. E. Delano, and J. Revson. 1981. *Community-Based Delivery of Low-Cost Family Planning and Maternal and Child Health Services in Rural Nigeria.* New York: Center for Population and Family Health; processed.

Liskin, Laurie, Richard Blackburn, and Rula Ghani. 1987. "Hormonal Contraception: New Long-Acting Methods." *Population Reports*, ser. K, no. 3: K57–K87.

Liskin, Laurie, and A. H. Rutledge. 1984. "After Contraception: Dispelling Rumors about Later Childbearing." *Population Reports*, ser. J. no. 28: J697–J731.

Mangani, Nlandu, and others. 1982. *Results of the PRODEF/Tulane Survey in Bas Zaire.* Pt. 1. *Population Characteristics, Reproductive Ideals, and Fertility Control.* Processed.

———. 1983. *Results of the PRODEF/Tulane Survey in Bas Zaire.* Pt. 2. *Indicators of Morbidity and Nutritional Status in Preschool Aged Children.* Processed.

Perkin, G. W. 1970. "Nonmonetary Commodity Incentives in Family Planning Programs: A Preliminary Trial." *Studies in Family Planning* 1(57): 12–15.

Population Services International. 1972. *A Preliminary Examination of Contraceptive Social Marketing Program in Kenya.* New York.

Rosenfield, A. 1984. "The Integration of Family Planning and Primary Health Care: Lessons Learned from Operational Research Studies." In D. Kluge, ed., *Selected Papers of the 1984 Annual Conference of the National Council for International Health, Arlington, Va., June 11–13, 1984.*

Washington, D.C.: National Council for International Health; Phoenix, Ariz.: Samaritan Medical Foundation.

Simpson-Hebert, Mayling, P. T. Piotrow, L. J. Christie, and Janelle Streich. 1980. "Traditional Midwives and Family Planning." *Population Reports*, ser. J-22, 8(3): J437–J488.

Sirageldin, I., D. Salkever, and R. Osborn. 1983. *Evaluating Population Programs*. New York: St. Martin's Press.

United Nations. 1986. *Demographic Yearbook 1984*. New York.

Weiss, E. A. 1984. *Lessons Learned in the Oyo State Community Health and Family Planning Project*. Processed.

Zimbabwe National Family Planning Council. 1984. *Zimbabwe Reproductive Health Survey*. Final Report.

————. 1988. "The Zimbabwe CBD Program." Harare, Zimbabwe.

Contributors

George T. F. Acsadi
Acsadi Associates, New York, and consultant in demography and statistics

Douglas F. Barnes
Industry and Energy Department, World Bank

John Bongaarts
Population Council, New York

Edward K. Brown
Sahelian Department, World Bank

Rodolfo A. Bulatao
Population and Human Resources Department, World Bank

John C. Caldwell
Australian National University, Canberra

Pat Caldwell
Australian National University, Canberra

Susan H. Cochrane
Population and Human Resources Department, World Bank

Virginia DeLancey
University of South Carolina, Columbia, and American University in Cairo, Arab Republic of Egypt

Abdul-Aziz Farah
United Nations Population Fund, San'a, Yemen Arab Republic

Samir M. Farid
Technical director, Gulf Child Health Survey, London, England

Odile Frank
World Health Organization, Geneva

Stein Hansen
Consultant, Environment Department, World Bank

Althea Hill
Africa Technical Department, World Bank

Teresa J. Ho
Sahelian Department, World Bank

Gwendolyn Johnson-Acsadi
Acsadi Associates, New York, and International Planned Parenthood Federation, London, England

Ron Lesthaeghe
Vrije Universiteit, Brussels, Belgium

Regina McNamara
Columbia University, New York

Deborah Maine
Columbia University, New York

Mark R. Montgomery
State University of New York, Stony Brook

Janet Nassim
Consultant, Population and Human Resources Department, World Bank

John A. Ross
Population Council, New York

Fred T. Sai
Population and Human Resources Department, World Bank

Marilyn Wallace
Columbia University, New York

Joe Wray
Columbia University, New York

15 14 97

151497